INTERNATIONAL FINANCIAL ACCOUNTING AND REPORTING

SECOND EDITION

INTERNATIONAL FINANCIAL ACCOUNTING AND REPORTING

SECOND EDITION

Ciaran Connolly

Chartered
Accountants
Ireland

Published in 2009 by
Chartered Accountants Ireland
Chartered Accountants House
47-47 Pearse Street
Dublin 2

ISBN 978-0-903854-72-6

This publication is designed to provide accurate and authoritative information in regard to the subject matter covered. It is provided on the understanding that the ICAI is not engaged in rendering professional services. If professional advice or other expert assistance is required, the services of a competent professional should be sought.

Typeset by Hurix Systems

Printed by Colour Books, Dublin, Ireland

CONTENTS

Section Four   Disclosures

Section Five   Accounting for Business Combinations

Section Six   Further Issues

INTRODUCTION

This Second Edition of International Financial Accounting and Reporting is designed to meet the continued and growing demand for coverage of International Accounting Standards (IASs) and International Financial Reporting Standards (IFRSs). It is particularly suitable for the intermediate and advanced levels of undergraduate accounting degree programmes, together with postgraduate and professional accounting courses. This edition has been fully revised and incorporates, for example, the recent revisions to IAS 1 *Presentation of Financial Statements*, IAS 27 *Consolidated and Separate Financial Statements*, IAS 32 *Financial Instruments: Presentation*, IAS 39 *Financial Instruments: Recognition and Measurement*, IFRS 3 *Business Combinations* and IFRS 7 *Financial Instruments: Disclosures*.

The text is designed to assist students to gain the knowledge and skills required to enable them to apply current IFRSs and critically appraise the underlying concepts and financial reporting methods. Each chapter, which is supported by numerous worked examples, concludes with self test questions, review questions and challenging questions. The broad structure of the text is as follows:

- Section One addresses the theoretical underpinnings of financial reporting and also illustrates the presentation of financial statements;
- Section Two and Section Three focus on the core IFRSs associated with the preparation of a statement of comprehensive income and statement of financial position, together with a statement of cash flows, for individual companies;
- Section Four concentrates on disclosure-related issues including earnings per share and financial instruments;
- Section Five deals in depth with the preparation of group accounts, including subsidiaries, associates and joint ventures. It also covers foreign operations and the group statement of cash flows; and
- Section Six, together with completing the coverage of extant IFRSs, concludes the text by dealing with the analysis and interpretation of financial information.

The term 'IFRS' has both a narrow and a broad meaning: narrowly, IFRS refers to the new numbered series of pronouncements issued by the International Accounting Standards Board, as distinct from the IASs issued by its predecessor, the International Accounting Standards Committee (IASC); and more broadly, IFRSs refer to the entire body of pronouncements, including standards and interpretations approved by the IASB and IASs and SIC interpretations approved by the IASC. The broader definition is applied throughout this text. In addition, while IASs and IFRSs have international application, the examples, and questions included in this text are denominated in the 'Euro'/'€' for convenience.

On 6 September 2007, the IASB issued a revised IAS 1 (see Chapter 2). While the amendments are relatively minor, the titles of financial statements have been changed and all existing IASs/IFRSs are being amended to reflect the new terminology (although entities are *not* required to use the new titles in their financial statements). The key changes in terminology are:

- a statement of financial position (previously balance sheet);
- a statement of comprehensive income (previously income statement); and
- a statement of cash flows (previously cash flow statement); and

With the exception of Chapter 36, this new terminology is applied throughout this text.

In addition to the *Framework for the Preparation and Presentation of Financial Statements* and the *Preface to International Financial Reporting Standards*, extant IASs and IFRSs as at 30 June 2009 are:

IFRS 1 *First-time Adoption of International Financial Reporting Standards*
IFRS 2 *Share-based Payment*
IFRS 3 *Business Combinations*
IFRS 4 *Insurance Contracts*
IFRS 5 *Non-current Assets Held for Sale and Discontinued Operations*
IFRS 6 *Exploration for and Evaluation of Mineral Assets*
IFRS 7 *Financial Instruments: Disclosures*
IFRS 8 *Operating Segments* (IFRS 8 replaces IAS 14 *Segment Reporting*, effective for annual periods beginning 1 January 2009.)

IAS 1 *Presentation of Financial Statements*
IAS 2 *Inventories*
IAS 7 *Statement of Cash Flows*
IAS 8 *Accounting Policies, Changes in Accounting Estimates and Errors*
IAS 10 *Events After the Reporting Period*
IAS 11 *Construction Contracts*
IAS 12 *Income Taxes*
IAS 14 *Segment Reporting* (IAS 14 is replaced by IFRS 8 *Operating Segments*, effective for annual periods beginning 1 January 2009.)
IAS 16 *Property, Plant and Equipment*
IAS 17 *Leases*
IAS 18 *Revenue*
IAS 19 *Employee Benefits*
IAS 20 *Accounting for Government Grants and Disclosure of Government Assistance*
IAS 21 *The Effects of Changes in Foreign Exchange Rates*
IAS 23 *Borrowing Costs*
IAS 24 *Related Party Disclosures*
IAS 26 *Accounting and Reporting by Retirement Benefit Plans*
IAS 27 *Consolidated and Separate Financial Statements*
IAS 28 *Investments in Associates*

IAS 29 *Financial Reporting in Hyperinflationary Economies*
IAS 31 *Interests in Joint Ventures*
IAS 32 *Financial Instruments: Presentation* (Disclosure provisions superseded by IFRS 7, effective for annual periods beginning 1 January 2007.)
IAS 33 *Earnings per Share*
IAS 34 *Interim Financial Reporting*
IAS 36 *Impairment of Assets*
IAS 37 *Provisions, Contingent Liabilities and Contingent Assets*
IAS 38 *Intangible Assets*
IAS 39 *Financial Instruments: Recognition and Measurement*
IAS 40 *Investment Property*
IAS 41 *Agriculture*

SECTION ONE

ACCOUNTING FRAMEWORK

CHAPTER 1

FRAMEWORK FOR THE PREPARATION AND PRESENTATION OF FINANCIAL STATEMENTS

INTRODUCTION

The purpose of this chapter is to explain the framework that governs the preparation and presentation of financial statements that are prepared in accordance with International Accounting Standards (IASs) and International Financial Reporting Standards (IFRSs). The chapter begins by examining what is meant by the term 'financial reporting', together with its objectives, desirable characteristics and the content of financial reports. This is followed by a review of the regulatory framework within which financial statements are prepared, including consideration of why there is a need for regulation and the principal forms that it takes. The chapter concludes by defining and outlining the main features of a conceptual framework for financial accounting and reporting.

After having studied this chapter on the framework for the preparation and presentation of financial statements, you should be able to describe the following:

- The objectives of financial reporting;
- The desirable characteristics of financial reports;
- The regulatory framework;
- What is meant by a conceptual framework and the need for such a framework; and
- The *Framework for the Preparation and Presentation of Financial Statements*.

FINANCIAL REPORTING

What is Financial Reporting?

Financial reporting is the reporting of financial information; it is an information system. Traditional financial statements are generally recognised as key documents in the discharge of financial accountability to external users. A company's directors are responsible for the preparation of the annual report and financial statements, which, together, are perceived as central to the discharge of accountability to external users. Indeed, *The Corporate Report* (Accounting Standards Steering Committee (ASSC), 1975, p.16) states that 'such information packages are the primary means by which the management of an entity is able to fulfil its reporting responsibility'.

What is the Objective of Financial Reporting?

The Corporate Report (ASSC, 1975) was the first major initiative in Britain and Ireland to examine the objective of financial reporting, with the conclusion being that the fundamental objective of corporate reports is to communicate economic measurements of, and information about, the resources and performance of the reporting entity useful to those having reasonable rights to such information. The ASSC's terms of reference were to:

> re-examine the scope and aims of published financial reports in the light of modern needs and conditions, and its basic philosophy was that reports should seek to satisfy the information needs of users, that is, they should be useful (p.2).

The Corporate Report was concerned with the types of organisations that should be expected to publish regular financial information, the users of such information, and the form of report that should be produced.

With respect to the types of organisations, the ASSC (1975) believed that there was an implied responsibility for every economic entity whose size made it significant to report publicly. By 'economic entity' the ASSC meant every type of organisation in modern economic society, that is: central government departments, local authorities, co-operatives, limited companies, unincorporated firms and non-profit-making entities such as trade unions and charities. *The Corporate Report* identified seven user groups as being entitled to receive accounting information and whose information needs should be satisfied by a financial report. These groups, together with their information requirements, were:

- **existing and potential equity investors** – who need information to help make a decision about buying or selling shares; about the level of dividend, past, present and future and any changes in share price; as to whether the management has been running the company efficiently, about the liquidity position of the company, the company's future prospects and how the company's shares compare with those of its competitors;
- **existing and potential loan creditors** – who need information to help them decide whether to lend to a company. They will also need to check that the value of any security remains adequate, that the interest repayments are secure, that the cash is available for redemption at the appropriate time and that any financial restrictions (such as maximum debt/equity ratios) have not been breached;
- **existing, potential and past employees** – who need information about the employment security and future job prospects in the company, and to help with collective pay bargaining;
- **analysts/advisers** including financial analysts, financial journalists, economists, statisticians, researchers, trade unions, stockbrokers and others such as credit rating agencies – who need information to pass on to clients;
- **the business contact group** (customers, trade creditors, suppliers, competitors, business rivals, parties interested in mergers and takeovers) – for example, suppliers need to know

whether the company will be a good customer and pay its debts; customers need to know whether the company will be able to continue producing and supplying goods; competitors will be interested in information about the company; and in merger/acquisition situations, all parties will want information about each other;

- **the government** (the tax authorities, regulatory departments and local authorities) – their interest in a company may be one of creditor or customer, as well as being specifically concerned with compliance with tax and company law, ability to pay tax and the general contribution of the company to the economy; and

- **the public** (taxpayers, ratepayers, consumers and community groups and special interest groups, for example, consumer and environmental groups) – need to have information for all the reasons mentioned above.

The Corporate Report (ASSC, 1975) was a comprehensive treatise that reviewed users, purposes and measurement bases for financial reporting. Unfortunately, its immediate impact was not great because many felt that it went too far in the identification of the user groups beyond the shareholders and creditors; too far in the demand for additional statements; and too far in wishing to discard historic cost as the measurement base. However, as time has progressed, the report has been seen to be a seminal document.

In a similar vein, the International Accounting Standards Committee (IASC) published a *Framework for the Presentation and Preparation of Financial Statements* (IASC, 1988), and its impact can be traced to *The Statement of Principles* (Accounting Standards Board (ASB), 1999). For example, the IASC views on the objective of financial statements and the qualitative characteristics that determine the usefulness of information in financial statements are largely incorporated into Chapters One and Two of *The Statement of Principles*. With regards to the former, the IASC suggest that financial statements should provide information about the financial position, performance and changes in financial position of an enterprise. The IASC document also addresses the definition, recognition and measurement of elements from which financial statements are constructed and the concepts of capital, capital maintenance and profit.

Both the ASB and IASC have adopted ASSC's (1975) list of users, except for the omission of any reference to analysts/advisers, presumably on the basis that analysts/advisers will be acting as agents for one of the other user groups. *The Statement of Principles* identifies the investor group as the primary group for whom the financial statements are being prepared, arguing that investors need information to help them decide whether to hold, buy or sell shares, to assess ability to pay dividends, and to assess the performance of the management. Furthermore, it states that awarding primacy to investors does not imply that other users are to be ignored, just that the information prepared for investors is useful as a frame of reference for other users, against which they can evaluate more specific information that they may obtain in their dealings with the enterprise.

However, although the ASB (1999) refers to the financial statements being directed toward the common information needs of a wide range of users, the focus is on providing information that is relevant to the investor group. This seems to indicate that the needs of other groups that are not also needs of the investor group will not be met by the financial statements. It is important for all of the other users to be aware that this is one of the principles since, if they require specific disclosures that might be relevant to them, they will need to take their own steps to obtain it, particularly where there is a conflict of interest.

Desirable Characteristics of Financial Reports

In broad terms, the above publications argue that annual reports should provide information to satisfy the information needs of users, and that accounting information should possess qualities such as relevance, objectivity, comparability, understandability, reliability and timeliness. However, because users are a disparate group and therefore some of these characteristics may pull in opposite directions, trade-offs and judgements will be required:

- **Relevance** – the information provided should be that which is required to satisfy the needs of users of reports. Such needs will vary as between user groups and over time.
- **Objectivity** – this will be enhanced by the application of standards, which are neutral as between competing interests.
- **Comparability** – this involves consistency in the application of accounting concepts and policies.
- **Understandability** – too much detail is as much a defect as too little.
- **Reliability** – this will be enhanced in the case of reports which are independently verified.
- **Timeliness** – the usefulness of information is diminished the later it is produced after the time to which it relates, and also if the intervals at which it is produced are unreasonably long.
- **Completeness** – reports should present a rounded picture of the economic activities of the reporting entity.

Content of Financial Reports

Guidance on the form and content of annual reports states that:

> the fundamental objective of corporate reporting is to communicate economic measurement of and information about the resources and performance of the reporting entity useful to those having reasonable rights to such information (ASSC, 1975, p.28).

> Financial or corporate reports consist of the financial statements (a statement of financial position; a statement of comprehensive income; a statement of changes in equity; a statement of cash flows; and notes, comprising a summary of significant accounting policies and other explanatory notes) of a company, as well as such narrative information as a chairman's report, i.e. the corporate report consists of the published accounts plus other (often non-statutory) material.

REGULATORY FRAMEWORK

What is the Regulatory Framework?

It is a framework set up to regulate the format and content of financial reports.

Why is There a Need for Regulation?

Financial statements and reports prepared for shareholders and other users are based on principles and rules that can vary widely from country to country. Multinational organisations may have to prepare reports on activities on several bases for use in different countries, and this can cause unnecessary financial costs. Furthermore, preparation of accounts based on different principles makes it difficult for investors and analysts to interpret financial information. This lack of comparability in financial reporting can affect the creditability of a company's reporting and the analysts' reports, and can have a detrimental effect on financial investment. The increasing levels of cross-border financing transactions, securities trading and direct foreign investment has resulted in the need for a single set of rules by which assets, liabilities and income are recognised and measured. Thus, regulation can help to:

- protect the users of financial reports;
- ensure consistency in financial reporting;
- ensure comparability between the financial reports of different companies; and
- ensure that financial reports give a true and fair view of a company's financial performance and position.

Accounting disclosure is regulated through a combination of company law, the Stock Exchange and accounting standards.

Company Law

On 7 June 2002, the EU Council of Ministers adopted a regulation passed by the European Parliament requiring all EU *listed* companies to prepare their *consolidated financial statements* in accordance with international standards by 1 January 2005 at the latest. Consequently, the legal framework under which companies prepare their financial statements changed significantly in 2004–05, with EU Member States being required to use local legislation to implement their options under the EU IAS Regulation 1606/2002. The statutory instruments giving effect to the options available in the Republic of Ireland and Northern Ireland are as follows:

Republic of Ireland

- European Communities (International Financial Reporting Standards and Miscellaneous Amendments) Regulations 2005, SI No. 116 of 2005;
- European Communities (Fair Value Accounting) Regulations 2004, SI No. 765 of 2004; and
- European Communities (Adjustment of Non-Comparable Amounts in Accounts and Distributions by Certain Investment Companies) Regulations 2005, SI No. 840 of 2005.

Northern Ireland

- The Companies (1986 Order) (International Accounting Standards and Other Accounting Amendments) Regulations (Northern Ireland) 2004 – 9 December 2004.

EU IAS Regulation 1606/2002 made it mandatory for all *listed* entities in the EU to prepare their *consolidated financial statements* in accordance with IASs/IFRSs for all accounting periods beginning on or after 1 January 2005. Companies and groups that are not directly impacted by the EU IAS Regulations have a choice as to the financial reporting framework that they apply in preparing their individual and group accounts. As a result, two financial reporting frameworks are available for accounting periods beginning on or after 1 January 2005. These are:

- company law-based financial statements prepared in accordance with the formats and accounting rules of (Republic of Ireland and Northern Ireland) company law and accounting standards. The applicable accounting standards are the Financial Reporting Standards issued by the Accounting Standards Board in the UK; and
- financial statements prepared in accordance with IASs/IFRSs adopted/issued by the International Accounting Standards Board (IASB) and certain mandatory disclosures carried forward from company law.

Generally speaking, the move from company law-based financial statements to IAS/IFRS-based financial statements is a one-way street and only with 'relevant changes in circumstances' can a company revert to preparing company law-based financial statements. It should be noted that the parts of company law that do not deal with the preparation of financial statements still continue to apply to all Republic of Ireland and Northern Ireland companies regardless of which financial reporting framework they adopt. Therefore, current requirements regarding the filing and signing of accounts, the rules regarding redemption and purchase of own shares or financial assistance for purchase of own shares, and the rules regarding distributions still continue to apply to IAS/IFRS-based financial statements.

The Stock Exchange

The securing of a Stock Exchange listing binds a company to the requirements of the Stock Exchange Regulations contained in the Listing Rules or 'Yellow Book' issued by the London Stock Exchange (2009). This requires a company to observe certain rules and procedures regarding its status as a listed company. Some of these concern its behaviour; while others concern the disclosure of accounting information, which is more extensive than the disclosure requirements of companies' legislation. The reason for the additional disclosure requirements for listed companies is that their shares are freely available in the open market and the Stock Exchange wants to ensure that all potential investors have access to all available information about the company.

Many requirements of the Yellow Book do not have the backing of law, but the ultimate sanction which can be imposed on a listed company which fails to abide by them is the withdrawal of its securities from the Stock Exchange list, i.e. the company's shares would no longer be traded on the market.

The US Securities and Exchange Commission recommended in May 2000 that international standards should be accepted for cross-border listings without reconciliation to US GAAP (Generally Accepted Accounting Principles).

Accounting Standards

An accounting standard is a rule or set of rules that prescribes the method by which accounts should be prepared and presented. They are issued by a national or international body of the accountancy profession, and they are intended to apply to all financial accounts which are intended to give a true and fair view of the financial position and profit/loss. Standards are detailed working regulations within the framework of government legislation and they cover areas in which the law is silent.

IASs were issued by the IASC from 1973 to 2000. The IASB replaced the IASC in 2001. Since then, the IASB has amended some IASs, has proposed to amend other IASs, has proposed to replace some IASs with new IFRSs, and has adopted or proposed certain new IFRSs on topics for which there was no previous IAS. The formal objectives of the IASB are to:

- develop, in the public interest, a single set of high quality, understandable and enforceable global accounting standards that require high quality, transparent and comparable information in the financial statements and other financial reporting to help participants in the world's capital markets, and other users who make economic decisions; and
- promote the use and rigorous application of those standards; and bring about convergence of national accounting standards and international accounting standards to high quality solutions.

The process for the development of a standard involves the following steps:

- During the early stages of a project, IASB may establish an Advisory Committee to advise on the issues arising in the project. Consultation with this committee and the Standards Advisory Council occurs throughout the project.
- IASB may develop and publish discussion documents for public comment.
- Following receipt and review of comments, IASB develops and publishes an Exposure Draft for public comment.
- Following the receipt and review of comments, IASB issues a final IFRS.

The term 'IFRS' has both a narrow and a broad meaning: narrowly, IFRS refers to the new numbered series of pronouncements that the IASB is issuing, as distinct from the IASs issued by its predecessor. More broadly, IFRSs refers to the entire body of IASB pronouncements, including standards and interpretations approved by the IASB, and IASs and SIC interpretations approved by the predecessor IASC. The principles underlying both the narrow and broad definitions are embraced in the *Preface to International Financial Reporting Standards*, which sets out the IASB's objectives, the scope of IFRSs, due process and policies on effective dates, format and language for IFRSs. When the IASB publishes a standard it also publishes a Basis of Conclusions to explain publicly how it reached its conclusions and to promote background information that may help users apply the standard in practice.

Through committees, the IASB (and previously the IASC) also publishes a series of Interpretations of International Accounting Standards (Standing Interpretations

Committee (SIC)) developed by the International Financial Reporting Interpretations Committee (IFRIC) and approved by the IASB. The role of IFRIC is to both:

- interpret existing IASs/IFRSs in light of the *Framework for the Preparation and Presentation of Financial Statements* document in order to prevent confusion; and additionally
- provide authoritative guidance on issues that would otherwise be developed by other parties leading to differing practices. Financial statements may not be described as complying with IASs/IFRSs unless they comply with all of the requirements of each applicable standard and each applicable interpretation.

While not a standard, the *Framework for the Preparation and Presentation of Financial Statements* serves as a guide to resolving accounting issues that are not addressed directly in a standard. Moreover, in the absence of a standard or an interpretation that specifically applies to a transaction, IAS 8 *Accounting Policies, Changes in Accounting Estimates and Errors* requires that an entity must use its judgement in developing and applying an accounting policy that results in information that is relevant and reliable. In making that judgement, IAS 8 requires management to consider the definitions, recognition criteria and measurement concepts for assets, liabilities, income and expenses in the *Framework*.

In addition to the *Framework for the Preparation and Presentation of Financial Statements* and the *Preface to International Financial Reporting Standards*, extant IASs and IFRSs as at 30 June 2009 are:

IFRS 1 *First-time Adoption of International Financial Reporting Standards*
IFRS 2 *Share-based Payment*
IFRS 3 *Business Combinations*
IFRS 4 *Insurance Contracts*
IFRS 5 *Non-current Assets Held for Sale and Discontinued Operations*
IFRS 6 *Exploration for and Evaluation of Mineral Assets*
IFRS 7 *Financial Instruments: Disclosures*
IFRS 8 *Operating Segments* (IFRS 8 replaces IAS 14 *Segment Reporting*, effective for annual periods beginning 1 January 2009.)
IAS 1 *Presentation of Financial Statements*
IAS 2 *Inventories*
IAS 7 *Statement of Cash Flows*
IAS 8 *Accounting Policies, Changes in Accounting Estimates and Errors*
IAS 10 *Events After the Reporting Period*
IAS 11 *Construction Contracts*
IAS 12 *Income Taxes*
IAS 14 *Segment Reporting* (IAS 14 is replaced by IFRS 8 *Operating Segments*, effective for annual periods beginning 1 January 2009.)
IAS 16 *Property, Plant and Equipment*
IAS 17 *Leases*
IAS 18 *Revenue*
IAS 19 *Employee Benefits*

IAS 20 *Accounting for Government Grants and Disclosure of Government Assistance*
IAS 21 *The Effects of Changes in Foreign Exchange Rates*
IAS 23 *Borrowing Costs*
IAS 24 *Related Party Disclosures*
IAS 26 *Accounting and Reporting by Retirement Benefit Plans*
IAS 27 *Consolidated and Separate Financial Statements*
IAS 28 *Investments in Associates*
IAS 29 *Financial Reporting in Hyperinflationary Economies*
IAS 31 *Interests in Joint Ventures*
IAS 32 *Financial Instruments: Presentation* (Disclosure provisions superseded by IFRS 7, effective for annual periods beginning 1 January 2007.)
IAS 33 *Earnings per Share*
IAS 34 *Interim Financial Reporting*
IAS 36 *Impairment of Assets*
IAS 37 *Provisions, Contingent Liabilities and Contingent Assets*
IAS 38 *Intangible Assets*
IAS 39 *Financial Instruments: Recognition and Measurement*
IAS 40 *Investment Property*
IAS 41 *Agriculture*

CONCEPTUAL FRAMEWORK OF ACCOUNTING

Definition of a Conceptual Framework

A conceptual framework has been defined as a coherent system of interrelated objectives and fundamentals that can lead to consistent standards that prescribe the nature, functions and limits of financial accounting and financial statements. It is a statement of generally accepted theoretical principles which form the frame of reference for financial reporting. These theoretical principles provide the basis for the development of new accounting standards and the evaluation of those already in existence.

The Need for a Conceptual Framework

One of the major challenges for those communicating financial information is the number and variety of users of that information. It is difficult to assess its ultimate usefulness when you are unsure how the information is being used and by whom. It would be almost impossible to address all technical issues in a business context that would meet the needs of every user. It is therefore important that all users appreciate the general principles of financial reporting, i.e. the theory of how things should be treated. A conceptual framework goes some way to providing this. It gives guidance on the broad principles on how items should be recorded and how they should be presented.

Where there are no standards specifically covering an issue, a conceptual framework provides a point of reference for preparers of financial information. The framework can provide guidance on how like items are treated and give definitions and criteria that can be used in deciding the recognition and measurement of the item.

Accounting standards deal with a variety of specific technical issues. The existence of a conceptual framework can remove the need to address the underlying issues over and over again. For example, the framework gives definitions of assets and liabilities. These definitions must be met for items to be included in financial statements. This is an underlying principle, and as the accounting standards are based on the principles within the framework they need not be dealt with fully in each of the standards.

The process of creating a new accounting standard can be a long one, but where conceptual frameworks exist the issue can be dealt with temporarily by providing a short term solution until a specific standard is developed.

The Framework for the Preparation and Presentation of Financial Statements

The *Framework* is a conceptual accounting framework that sets out the concepts that underlie the preparation and presentation of financial statements for external users. It was approved in 1989 by the IASB's predecessor, the IASC, and adopted by the IASB in April 2001. The *Framework* assists the IASB in:

- the development of future IFRSs and in its review of existing accounting standards; and
- promoting the harmonisation of regulations, financial reporting standards and procedures relating to the presentation of financial statements by providing a basis for reducing the number of alternative accounting treatments permitted by IASs/IFRSs.

In addition, the *Framework* may assist:

- national standard-setting bodies in developing national standards;
- preparers of financial statements in applying IASs/IFRSs and in dealing with topics that have yet to form the subject of an IFRS;
- auditors in forming an opinion as to whether financial statements conform with IASs/IFRSs;
- users of financial statements in interpreting the information contained in financial statements prepared in conformity with IASs/IFRSs; and
- those who are interested in the work of the IASB, providing them with information about its approach to the formulation of IASs/IFRSs.

The *Framework* is not an accounting standard and does not define standards for any particular measurement or disclosure issue. In a limited number of cases there may be a conflict between the *Framework* and the requirement of an IAS/IFRS. In those cases where there is a conflict, the requirements of the IAS/IFRS prevail over those of the *Framework*.

Scope

The *Framework* applies to the general-purpose financial statements of both private and public enterprises. A full set of financial statements prepared using IASs/IFRSs will normally include a statement of: financial position; comprehensive income; changes in equity; cash flows; and any notes which form an integral part of the financial statements. Supplementary information e.g. segment reports are also included but not the directors' report, discussion and analysis statement or chairman's report. The *Framework* identifies the following users of financial statements, together with their information needs:

- **Investors** – concerned about risk and return provided by their investments. Need information to determine buy, hold or sell decisions and to assess ability to pay dividends;
- **Employees** – concerned about stability and profitability of their employers and to assess the ability to provide remuneration, retirement benefits etc,. to employees;
- **Lenders** – concerned about whether their loans and interest can be repaid;
- **Suppliers and other trade creditors** – concerned whether or not they will be paid when due;
- **Customers** – concerned about the continuance of the business especially if long-term involvement with the entity;
- **Governments and their agencies** – interested in the allocation of resources and information on taxation policies, national statistics etc; and
- **The public** – can provide information about local economy, numbers employed, environmental issues etc.

The *Framework* acknowledges that not all the needs of these users can be met and does not indicate that the needs of one set of users are more important than any other. The *Framework* does point out, however, that financial statements that meet the needs of investors will generally also meet the needs of other users. Information for management purposes is specialised although published statements may be used by them in assessing financial performance, position and changes in financial position of the entity.

Contents

The Framework has seven chapters:

1. The Objective of Financial Statements   The *Framework* states that the objective of financial statements is to provide information about the financial position, performance and changes in financial position of an enterprise that is useful to a wide range of users in making economic decisions. Information about:

- the *financial position* is primarily provided in the *statement of financial position (balance sheet)*. The resources the enterprise controls, its financial structure, liquidity and solvency all affect the financial position;
- *performance* is primarily found in the *statement of comprehensive income*. Performance measures, particularly profitability, are required to help assess the enterprise's ability to

generate future cash flows from trading and other activities. It also helps users evaluate how effective the enterprise is at using its resources; and

- *changes in financial position* is held primarily in a *statement of cash flows*. This is a useful illustration of the enterprise's investing, financing and operational activities and how these activities have affected the financial position over the reporting period.

The *Framework* asserts that financial statements prepared for this purpose should meet the common needs of most users, and should also show the results of steward-ship and accountability of management. However, financial statements do not provide all the information that users may need to make economic decisions as they illustrate the financial effects of past transactions. Users are expected to use this reliable his-toric information to help them evaluate future performance and make their economic decisions.

Users make better economic decisions if they are provided with information that focuses on the ability of an entity to generate cash and to meet its cash repayments. That will require details about the current financial position, the performance for the period and changes in its financial position. The latter, in particular, can help entities predict their ability in the future to generate cash and information about the financial structure is useful in predicting future borrowing needs and how profits and cash flows will be distrib-uted. Information on liquidity and solvency is useful in predicting the ability of the entity to meet its financial commitments as they fall due. The former covers the short-term and the latter the long-term availability of cash to meet financial commitments. Profitability information and its variability are important in assessing potential changes in economic resources. Information on the financial position is useful in assessing its investing, financ-ing and operating activities during the reporting period. The latter is usually provided via a statement of financial position and information on performance via a statement of comprehensive income.

The component parts of the financial statements interrelate because they reflect different aspects of the same transactions. Each depends on the other. A statement of comprehensive income, for example, provides an incomplete picture unless it is used in conjunction with the statement of financial position and the statement of changes in equity.

2. Underlying Assumptions   There are two underlying assumptions outlined in the Framework.

(a) Going concern   Financial statements are normally prepared on the assumption that an enterprise is a going concern and will continue in operation for the foreseeable future. Any intention to liquidate or significantly reduce the scale of its operations would require the accounts to be prepared on a different basis and this basis would have to be disclosed.

(b) Accruals basis of accounting   Financial statements are prepared on the accruals basis of accounting where the effects of transactions are recognised when they occur and are recorded and reported in the accounting periods to which they relate, irrespective of cash flows arising from these transactions.

3. The Qualitative Characteristics of Financial Information Qualitative characteristics are the attributes that make the information useful to users. The five principal characteristics are:

(a) Understandability An essential quality of financial information is that it is readily understandable by users. For this purpose, users are assumed to have a reasonable knowledge of business and economic activities and accounting and a willingness to study the information with reasonable diligence. Information on complex issues should be included if relevant and should not be excluded on the grounds that it is too difficult for the average user to understand.

(b) Relevance To be useful, information must be relevant to the decision-making needs of users. Information is relevant when it influences the economic decisions of users by helping them to evaluate past, present or future economic events or confirming or correcting their past evaluations. Financial statements do not normally contain information about future activities; however, historical information can be used as the basis for predicting future financial position and performance. The users will then use their predictions as the basis for their decision making. An example of this could be where the financial statements show the profitability of a division that has been sold during the year. The users then know to eliminate that division's resources and profitability in evaluating performance of the total enterprise for the following year.

(c) Materiality Information that helps users assess the future performance and financial position of an enterprise is likely to be relevant. An item is likely to be relevant by virtue of its nature and materiality. Information is material if its omission or misstatement could influence the decision making of users. Information can be relevant because of its nature irrespective of materiality. For example, if an enterprise has commenced operating activities in a country with an unstable economy, this could change the users' assessment of the overall risk that the enterprise is exposed to and as a result change the users' assessment of the enterprise's future results. Irrespective of the materiality of that segment's results, the information may be disclosed. Information should be released on a timely basis to be relevant to users.

(d) Reliability To be useful, information must also be reliable. Information is reliable when it is free from material error and bias and can be considered by users to be a faithful representation of the underlying transactions and events. This implies:

- **Faithful representation** – to be reliable, the information must faithfully represent the transactions it is intended to represent;
- **Substance over form** – to show a faithful representation, the transactions must be accounted for and presented on the basis of their commercial reality rather than their legal form. Only by applying substance over form will users see the effects of the economic reality of the transactions;
- **Neutrality** – to be reliable, the information must be neutral, that is, free from bias;
- **Prudence** – to be reliable, the information must be prudent. Many estimates are made in the preparation of financial statements, e.g. inventory valuation, estimated useful lives of assets, recoverability of debts. Being cautious when exercising judgement in arriving at these estimates is known as prudence. This is a generally accepted concept

in accounts' preparation. The concept does not, however, extend to including excess provisions, overstating liabilities or understating income or assets. This would bias the information and make it unreliable to users; and

- **Completeness** – to be reliable the information must be complete. An omission can cause information to be false or misleading and therefore unreliable.

However, there are constraints on information being relevant and reliable. For example:

- **Timeliness** – undue delay in reporting loses relevance but information on a timely basis is less reliable. In achieving a balance between relevance and reliability, the over-riding consideration is how best to satisfy the decision making needs of users;
- **Benefit and cost** – the benefits derived from providing information should exceed the cost of providing it. The process of evaluating benefits and costs, however, is judgmental; and
- **Qualitative characteristics** – in practice a trade-off between qualitative characteristics must take place and the aim is to achieve an appropriate balance across them. The relative importance of the characteristics will be a matter of judgement.

(e) Comparability   Comparability of financial information is vital to users in their decision making. The ability to identify trends in performance and financial position and compare those both from year to year and against other enterprises assists users in their assessments and decision making. It is important that users are able to understand the application of accounting policies in order to compare financial information. To achieve comparability users must be able to identify where an enterprise has changed its policy from one year to the next and where other enterprises have used different accounting policies for like transactions. The requirement of IASs/IFRSs to disclose accounting policies adopted and the inclusion of prior periods' comparative figures helps promote comparability.

4. The Elements of Financial Statements   The *Framework* provides definitions of the elements of financial statements. These definitions, applied together with the recognition criteria, provide guidance as to how and when the financial effect of transactions or events should be recognised in the financial statements:

- **Asset** – a resource controlled by the enterprise as a result of past events and from which future economic benefits are expected to flow to the enterprise. Future economic benefits represent the potential to contribute to the cash flow of the entity. Future economic benefits embodied in an asset may flow to the entity in a variety of ways: asset is used singly or in combination with others to produce goods/services to be sold by the entity; asset may be exchanged for other assets; asset may be used to settle a liability; or asset may be distributed to the owners of the entity. Many assets have a physical form, e.g. plant, but others do not, e.g. patents. Many assets are associated with legal rights, e.g. receivables, but others are not, e.g. finance leases, know-how. Past transactions are normally signified by the purchase or production of assets but not necessarily, e.g. government grant receipts. Intentions to purchase or produce assets are not assets – they are merely future intentions. Expenditure is normally required to receive an asset but it is not necessary, e.g. donated assets;

- **Liability** – a present obligation of the enterprise arising from past events, the settlement of which is expected to result in an outflow of resources from the enterprise. A liability can be legally enforceable, e.g. binding contract but can also arise from normal business practice or custom, e.g. company policy to rectify faults even after warranty has expired. A distinction must be made between a present obligation and a future commitment. A management decision, by itself, is not sufficient. It requires the asset to be delivered or the entity to be put into a position of having very little discretion to avoid an outflow of resources. A settlement usually involves the entity giving up resources to satisfy the claim of the other party. Settlement may occur in a number of ways: payment of cash; transfer of other assets; provision of services; replacement of an obligation by another obligation; or conversion of the obligation into equity. It could also be extinguished by other means e.g. creditor waiving or forfeiting its rights. They must be the result of past transactions, e.g. delivery of goods, receipt of bank loan. Some require considerable estimation – described as provisions. It is therefore broader than a legal obligation;

- **Equity** – the residual interest in the assets of the enterprise after deducting all its liabilities. It may be sub-classified e.g. retained earnings, capital maintenance adjustments etc. These may reflect differing rights or showing restrictions on the ability of the entity to distribute certain reserves. The creation of reserves is sometimes required by statute or law to protect creditors from losses. The existence and size of these is important information for users as well as transfers during the period. The equity value will not correspond with the market value of the shares in the entity or the sum that could be raised by disposing the assets either on a piecemeal or going concern basis. There are different types of entity, e.g. sole traders, partnerships, limited companies regulated in different ways, but the definition of equity is appropriate for all such enterprises. In assessing whether an item meets the definition of an asset, liability or equity, attention should be paid to the substance and economic reality and not merely legal form, e.g. finance leases as assets in the lessee's books;

- **Income** – increases in economic benefits during the accounting period in the form of inflows or enhancements of assets or decreases of liabilities that result in increases in equity, other than those relating to combinations from equity participants. Income includes both revenues and gains. The former arises in the ordinary course of business e.g. sales, royalties, rents, fees and interest. Gains represent other items of income which may not normally arise in the ordinary course of business, e.g. gain on disposal of non-current assets. Both types of income, however, are treated the same for accounting purposes. Income also includes unrealised gains, e.g. revaluation of marketable securities and long term assets. Gains are often reported net of related expenses; and

- **Expenses** – decreases in economic benefits during the accounting period in the form of outflows or depletions of assets that result in decreases in equity, other than those relating to distributions to equity participants. This includes losses as well as ordinary expenses such as wages, depreciation and cost of sales. Usually result in an outflow or depletion of assets. Other items representing decreases in economic benefits are also included, e.g. fire and flood losses and losses on disposal of non-current assets. They include unrealised losses in foreign currency. They are often reported net of related income. Income and expenses are presented in the statement of comprehensive income in different ways so as to provide relevant information for making economic decisions, e.g. ordinary/unusual items. Distinguishing between items of income and expense and combining them in different ways also permits several measures of performance to be displayed, e.g. gross margin, profit before taxation, profit after taxation and net profit.

5. Recognition of the Elements of Financial Statements   To be recognised the item must meet the definition of an element (see above). The *Framework* then has a further two criteria which must be met for an item to be recognised:

- it is probable that any future economic benefit associated with the item will flow to or from the enterprise; and
- the item has a cost or value that can be measured with reliability.

In the *first criterion*, the idea of *probability* is used regularly in the preparation of financial statements, for example the probability that your credit customers will pay in order that you can reliably include receivables in the statement of financial position. The assessment of the degree of uncertainty that an event will take place must be completed using the evidence available when the financial statements are prepared. Where economic benefits are to arise over time, any related expenses should be systematically recognised over the same periods and matched with the income. Where no future benefits are anticipated, expenses should be recognised immediately.

The *second criterion* requires that a *monetary value* be attached to the item. For some transactions this is straightforward but often the value we attach to items has to be estimated. This is acceptable, provided that it is a reasonable estimate and does not undermine reliability (a qualitative characteristic noted above). Where information is relevant to users it should not be excluded from the financial statements because it fails to meet the recognition criteria. For example, where a contingent liability exists at the end of the reporting period but cannot be measured with any degree of certainty, it fails the second recognition criterion; however, due to its nature and existence it should be disclosed to users on the grounds that it is relevant. An item that initially fails the reliability test may qualify later as a result of subsequent events.

Materiality must always be considered when assessing these criteria and it must be remembered that the recognition of an asset will affect another element (e.g. an increase in a liability or creation of income) as they are all interrelated:

- **Recognition of assets** – should be recognised in the statement of financial position when it is probable that future economic benefits will flow to the entity and the asset has a cost or value that can be reliably measured. If expenditure incurred is seen to be improbable in terms of future benefits, it should be expensed. The intention may still be to improve future benefits but the uncertainty means an asset may not be recorded;
- **Recognition of liabilities** – should be recognised in the statement of financial position when it is probable that an outflow of resources will result from the settlement of a

present obligation and the amount can be measured reliably. Orders for inventory may be liabilities if the recognition criteria are met despite the fact that the contracts are unperformed. However, generally these would not pass the recognition criteria;

- **Recognition of income** – occurs simultaneously with the recognition of assets and liabilities. Income recognition is restricted to those items that can both be measured reliably and provided with a sufficient degree of certainty; and
- **Recognition of expenses** – occurs simultaneously with the recognition of an increase in liabilities or a decrease in assets.

Where benefits are expected to arise over several accounting periods and the link between income and expenses can only be loosely determined expenses should be recognised in the statement of comprehensive income on the basis of systematic and rational allocation procedures, e.g. depreciation, amortisation.

An expense should be recognised immediately in the statement of comprehensive income when no future economic benefit exists or the item ceases to qualify for recognition as an asset. An expense is also recognised in the statement of comprehensive income when a liability is incurred, e.g. warranty arises.

6. Measurement of the Elements of Financial Statements   Once it is decided that an item is to be recognised in the financial statements it is then necessary to decide on what basis it is to be measured. To be included in the financial statements the item must have a monetary value attached to it. The Framework refers to four measurement bases that are often used in reporting, being historic cost, current cost, realisable value and present value. It highlights that historic cost is the most commonly adopted although often within a combination of bases, for example valuing inventories using the lower of cost and net realisable value.

(a) Historic cost   Assets are recorded at cash paid at date of acquisition. Liabilities are recorded at the amount of proceeds received in exchange for the obligation or the amount of cash expected to be paid to satisfy the liability, e.g. taxation.

(b) Current cost   Assets are recorded at cash that would have to be paid to acquire the same or equivalent asset. Liabilities are carried at the undiscounted amount of cash required to settle the obligation.

(c) Realisable value   Assets are recorded at cash that would be obtained by selling the asset in an orderly disposal. Liabilities are carried at their settlement values, i.e. the undiscounted amounts of cash expected to be paid to satisfy the liabilities in the normal course of business.

(d) Present value   Assets are recorded at the present discounted value of future net cash inflows that the item is expected to generate in the normal course of business. Liabilities are carried at the present discounted value of the future net cash outflows that are expected to be required to settle the liabilities in the normal course of business.

The most popular basis is historic cost but it is usually combined with other bases, e.g. inventories at lower of cost and net realisable value, marketable securities at market value and pension liabilities at present value. Some entities adopt current cost accounting to cope with the inability of historic cost accounting to deal with the effects of changing prices.

7. Concepts of Capital and Capital Maintenance

(a) Concepts of capital The *Framework* refers to two concepts of capital: financial concept of capital and physical concept of capital. Most enterprises adopt the financial concept of capital which deals with the net assets or equity of the enterprise. If, instead of being primarily concerned with the invested capital of the enterprise, the users are concerned with, for example, the operating capability of the enterprise, then the physical concept of capital should be used. The selection of the most appropriate basis to adopt should be based on user needs.

(b) Determining profit Under the financial concept of capital a profit is earned if the financial amount of the net assets at the end of the period is greater than that at the beginning of the period, after deducting any distributions to and contributions from owners. Financial capital maintenance is measured in either nominal monetary units or units of constant purchasing power.

Under the physical concept of capital a profit is earned if the physical productive capacity (or operating capacity) of the enterprise (or the resources or funds needed to achieve that capacity) at the end of the period is greater than that at the beginning of the period, after deducting any distributions to and contributions from owners. Physical capital maintenance requires the adoption of the current cost basis of measurement i.e. an appreciation of what it would cost to replace assets at current prices.

The main difference between the two types of capital maintenance is on the effects of changes in the prices of assets and liabilities of the entity. Generally capital is maintained if an entity has as much capital at the end of the period as at the start. Any amount over and above that is profit. Under financial capital maintenance, where capital is defined in nominal terms, profit is the increase in nominal money capital over the period. Holding gains are therefore included in profit, but only disposed of. Under the current purchasing power approach, profit represents the increase in purchasing power over the period. Thus only that part of the increase in prices of assets that exceeds the increase in the general level of prices is regarded as profit. The rest is a capital maintenance adjustment and therefore part of equity. Under physical capital maintenance, where capital is defined in terms of productive capacity, profit represents the increase in that capital over the period. All price changes are viewed as changes in the measurement of the physical productive capacity of the entity, and thus are treated as capital maintenance adjustments that are part of equity.

(c) Capital maintenance In general terms, an enterprise has maintained its capital if it has as much capital at the end of the period as it had at the beginning of the period. The key in capital maintenance is deciding which concept is being adopted, because this then defines the basis on which profit is calculated. The choice of model will depend on the different degrees of relevance and reliability available and management must seek an appropriate bal-

ance between the two. The *Framework* is applicable to a range of accounting models and provides guidance on preparing and presenting the financial statements constructed under the chosen model. At present, the IASB does not prescribe a particular model, except in exceptional circumstances, e.g. hyperinflationary economies (IAS 29 *Financial Reporting in Hyperinflationary Economies* (see Chapter 31)).

In October 2004, the IASB and the US Financial Accounting Standards Board (FASB) agreed to develop a common conceptual framework based upon their respective conceptual framework documents that both would then use as a basis for their accounting standards. The IASB and FASB decided that the joint project should:

- initially focus on concepts applicable to business entities in the private sector. Later, the applicability of those concepts to other sectors, beginning with not-for-profit entities, would be considered;
- be divided into phases, with the initial focus being on achieving the convergence of the frameworks and improving particular aspects of the frameworks dealing with objectives, qualitative characteristics, elements, recognition, and measurement; and
- be in the form of a single document.

The joint project is being conducted in eight phases: Phase A – objectives and qualitative characteristics; Phase B – elements and recognition; Phase C – measurement; Phase D – reporting entity; Phase E – presentation and disclosure; Phase F – purpose and status; Phase G – application to not-for-profit entities; and Phase H – remaining issues. Phases A, B, C and D of the project are currently active (as at 30 June 2009).

CONCLUSION

The main purpose of accounting is to reduce or eliminate variations in accounting practices and to introduce a degree of uniformity into financial reporting.

The IASB's *Framework* presents a set of definitions and fundamental principles which underpin financial accounting and reporting. One of its main purposes is to assist in the review and development of accounting standards. The objective of financial statements is to provide users with relevant, reliable, comparable and understandable information about an entity's financial position, performance and changes in financial position.

The regulatory framework within which company financial statements are prepared consists of a combination of legislation, stock exchange regulations (if applicable) and accounting standards. Company legislation typically sets out broad rules with which companies must comply when preparing their financial statements, while the stock exchange regulations offer more detailed guidance for public limited companies. Accounting standards provide rules and policies to assist with the accounting treatment of transactions and balances.

QUESTIONS

Self-test Questions

1. What is relevance?
2. What is objectivity?
3. What is a conceptual framework?
4. List the contents which make up the IASB's framework for the preparation and presentation of financial statements

Review Questions

(See APPENDIX ONE for Suggested Solutions to Review Questions.)

Question 1

(a) Who were considered to be the potential users of financial reports in *The Corporate Report?*
(b) What do you consider to be their information needs?
(c) How would you expect a consideration of user needs to influence financial reporting?

Question 2

The Technical Committee of the International Organisation of Securities Commissions (IOSCO) and the IASC agree that there is a compelling need for high-quality, comprehensive international accounting standards.

Requirement   Discuss briefly why the development of international accounting standards is considered to be important.

Question 3

The *Framework for the Preparation and Presentation of Financial Statements* has a number of purposes, including assisting:

- the IASB in the development of future accounting standards and in its review of existing IASs/IFRSs;
- the IASB in promoting harmonisation of regulations, accounting standards and procedures relating to the presentation of financial statements by providing a basis for reducing the number of alternative treatments permitted by IASs/IFRSs; and
- preparers of financial statements in applying IASs/IFRSs and in dealing with topics that have yet to be covered in an accounting standard.

Requirement   Discuss how a conceptual framework could help the IASC achieve these objectives.

Challenging Questions

Question 1

The *Framework* includes the following definition:

> 'An asset is a resource controlled by the enterprise as a result of past events and from which future economic benefits are expected to flow to the enterprise.'

Requirement   Explain this definition, using the example of a trade receivable.

Question 2

Relevance and reliability are two of the five main qualitative characteristics of financial information, as set out in the *Framework*.

Requirement
(a) Briefly discuss what is meant by these terms; and
(b) Give an example of when these two attributes could come into conflict and what the outcome is likely to be.

Question 3

In 1989, the IASC issued the *Framework for the Preparation and Presentation of Financial Statements*. It is intended to establish a broad set of accounting principles on which standards and accounting rules will be based.

Requirement   Evaluate the relationship between the *Framework* and the standard-setting process.

REFERENCES

Accounting Standards Board (ASB) (1999), *Statement of Principles for Financial Reporting*, London: ASB.
Accounting Standards Steering Committee (ASSC) (1975), *The Corporate Report*, London, ASSC.
International Accounting Standards Committee (IASC) (1988), *Framework for the Presentation and Preparation of Financial Statements*, London: IASC.
London Stock Exchange (2009), *Rules of the London Stock Exchange*, March, London: London Stock Exchange.

CHAPTER 2

PRESENTATION OF FINANCIAL STATEMENTS

INTRODUCTION

This chapter follows on from the previous chapter which explained the framework that governs the preparation and presentation of financial statements that are prepared in accordance with International Accounting Standards (IASs) and International Financial Reporting Standards (IFRSs). Focusing on the requirements of IAS 1 *Presentation of Financial Statements*, the objective of this chapter is to describe the basis for the presentation of general purpose financial statements. In order to place this in context, the chapter begins by briefly reviewing the principles of financial reporting before concentrating upon the structure and content of financial statements.

After having studied this chapter, you should be able to:

- identify the components of a set of financial statements;
- describe the structure and content of each component;
- explain the detailed disclosure requirements of IAS 1; and
- prepare financial statements in accordance with the requirements of IAS 1.

PRINCIPLES OF FINANCIAL REPORTING

IAS 1 sets out a number of principles that govern the presentation of financial statements, many of which are driven by the *Framework for the Preparation and Presentation of Financial Statements* (see Chapter 1). The main principles addressed in IAS 1 are discussed below.

Fair Presentation and Compliance with IASs/IFRSs

Financial statements should present fairly the financial position, financial performance and cash flows of an enterprise. Financial statements that comply with all relevant IASs/IFRSs almost always achieve this objective of fair presentation. Fair presentation requires faithful representation of the effects of transactions, events and conditions in accordance with the definitions and recognition criteria for assets, liabilities, income and expenses set out in the *Framework* document. The application of IASs/IFRSs (i.e. Standards and

Interpretations), with additional disclosure when necessary, is presumed to result in financial statements that achieve a fair presentation. An entity must make an explicit and unreserved statement of compliance with IASs/IFRSs in the notes to the financial statements, and such a statement should only be made on compliance with *all* of the requirements of IASs/IFRSs. This compliance statement is often included in the accounting policies and is usually the first stated policy.

In the (unlikely) event that the management decides that compliance with a particular requirement would result in misleading information they can depart from that requirement in order to achieve fair presentation. In this event the enterprise should disclose:

- that management has concluded that the financial statements are a fair presentation of the enterprise's financial position, performance and cash flows;
- that it has complied with all relevant IASs/IFRSs and has departed from a standard to achieve fair presentation;
- the IAS/IFRS that it has departed from and details of why the departure was necessary and the treatment that has been adopted; and
- the financial impact of the departure.

A departure from IASs/IFRSs is acceptable only in the extremely rare circumstances in which compliance with IASs/IFRSs conflicts with providing information useful to users in making economic decisions. IAS 1 specifies the disclosures required when an entity departs from a requirement of an IAS/IFRS.

Going Concern

Financial Statements should be prepared on a going concern basis, unless there are plans to liquidate or cease trading. When financial statements are not prepared on a going concern basis, that fact must be disclosed, together with the basis on which the financial statements are prepared and the reason why the entity is not regarded as a going concern.

Accruals Basis of Accounting

Financial statements should be prepared under the accruals basis of accounting, with the exceptions of cash flow.

Consistency of Presentation

Financial statements should retain a consistent approach to presentation and classification of items year on year unless:

- it is apparent, following a significant change in the nature of the entity's operations or a review of its financial statements that another presentation or classification would be more appropriate having regard to the criteria for the selection and application of

accounting policies in IAS 8 *Accounting Policies, Changes in Accounting Estimates and Errors*; or
- a standard requires a change in presentation.

Materiality and Aggregation

Each material class of similar items should be presented separately in the financial statements. Items of a dissimilar nature or function should be presented separately unless they are immaterial. Omissions or misstatements are material if they could influence the economic decisions of users.

Offsetting

Assets and liabilities, and income and expenses, should not be offset, unless required or permitted by a standard.

Comparative Information

Comparative information should be disclosed for the previous period for all numerical information. Where presentation or classification of an item has changed, the comparative figures should be restated using the new treatment if possible. When comparative figures can be restated, the entity should disclose the:
- nature of the reclassification;
- amount of each item or class of items that is reclassified; and
- reason for the reclassification.

If it is impracticable to reclassify comparative figures, the entity should state the:

- reason for not reclassifying the amounts; and
- nature of the adjustments that would have been made if the amounts had been reclassified.

STRUCTURE AND CONTENT OF FINANCIAL STATEMENTS

The form and content of financial statements is addressed in IAS 1, the objective of which is to prescribe the basis for presentation of general purpose financial statements, ensure comparability both with the entity's financial statements of previous periods and with the financial statements of other entities. To achieve this objective, IAS 1 sets out overall requirements for the presentation of financial statements, guidelines for their structure and minimum requirements for their content. IAS 1 applies to all general purpose financial statements prepared and presented in accordance with IASs/IFRSs; it does not apply to interim financial statements prepared in accordance with IAS 34 *Interim Financial Reporting* (see Chapter 34).

Financial statements are a structured representation of the financial position and financial performance of an entity. Their objective is to provide information about the financial position, financial performance and cash flows of an entity that is useful to a wide range of users in making economic decisions. To meet this objective, financial statements provide information about an entity's: assets; liabilities; equity; income and expenses, including gains and assets; other changes in equity; and cash flows. This information, along with other information in the notes, assists users of financial statements in predicting the entity's future cash flows and, in particular, their timing and certainty. Financial statements, which also show the results of management's stewardship of the resources entrusted to it, should be presented at least annually and issued on a timely basis to be useful to users.

On 6 September 2007, the International Accounting Standards Board (IASB) issued a revised IAS 1, which is effective for annual periods beginning on or after 1 January 2009 (early adoption is permitted). While the changes are relatively minor, they represent the first step in the IASB's comprehensive project on reporting financial information. The revised IAS 1 changes the titles of financial statements and all existing IASs/IFRSs are being amended to reflect the new terminology; although entities are *not* required to use the new titles in their financial statements. A complete set of financial statements includes:

- a statement of financial position;
- a statement of comprehensive income;
- a statement of changes in equity;
- a statement of cash flows; and
- accounting policies and explanatory notes.

With the exception of Chapter 36, the new terminology is applied throughout this text.

Statement of Financial Position

IAS 1 does not prescribe the format of the statement of financial position. Assets can be presented current then non-current, or vice versa. Similarly, liabilities can be presented current then non-current then equity, or vice versa. A net asset presentation (assets less liabilities) is allowed, as is a long-term financing approach (non-current assets plus current assets less current liabilities). A suggested format for the statement of financial position is presented in **Figure 2.1**.

All assets should be classified as either non-current or current on the face of the statement of financial position. All liabilities should be classified under either current or non-current. An exception to the above is when a presentation based on liquidity provides information that is reliable and more relevant. In this case all assets and liabilities are

Figure 2.1: X Limited – Statement of Financial Position as at 31 December 2009

	€	€
ASSETS		
Non-current Assets		
Property, plant and equipment	x	
Goodwill	x	
Other intangible assets	x	
Investments in associates	x	
Available-for-sale-investments	x	x
Current Assets		
Inventories	x	
Trade receivables	x	
Other current assets	x	
Cash and cash equivalents	x	x
Total Assets		x
EQUITY AND LIABILITIES		
Equity attributable to owners of the parent		
Issued share capital	x	
Retained earnings	x	
Other companents of equity	x	x
Non-controlling interests		x
Total Equity		x
Non-current Liabilities		
Long-term borrowings	x	
Deferred tax	x	
Long-term provisions	x	x
Current Liabilities		
Overdraft	x	
Trade and other payables	x	
Short-term borrowings	x	
Current portion of long-term borrowings	x	
Tax payable	x	x
Total Equity and Liabilities		X

presented broadly in order of liquidity. IAS 1 requires that, as a minimum, the following line items appear on the face of the statement of financial position (where there are amounts to be classified within these categories):

(a) Property, plant and equipment;
(b) Investment property;
(c) Intangible assets;
(d) Financial assets (non-current);
(e) Investments accounted for using equity accounting*;
(f) Biological assets;
(g) Inventories;
(h) Trade and other receivables;
(i) Cash and cash equivalents;
(j) Trade and other payables;
(k) Provisions;
(l) Financial liabilities;
(m) Current tax assets/liabilities;
(n) Deferred tax assets/liabilities**;
(o) Non-controlling interests*;
(p) Issued capital and reserves;
(q) Total of assets 'held for sale' under IFRS 5 *Non-current Assets Held for Sale and Discontinued Operations*; and
(r) Liabilities held 'for sale'.

*   These items relate to group accounts.
** Deferred tax assets/liabilities must not be classified as current (IAS 12 *Income Taxes*).

Additional line items, headings and subtotals should be shown on the face of the statement of financial position if another IAS/IFRS requires it or where it is necessary to show a fair presentation of the financial position. In deciding whether additional items should be separately presented, management should consider:

- the nature and liquidity of assets and their materiality (for example, the separate disclosure of monetary and non-monetary amounts and current and non-current assets);
- their function within the enterprise (for example, the separate disclosure of operating assets and financial assets, inventories and cash); and
- the amounts, navture and timing of liabilities (for example, the separate disclosure and interest bearing and non-interest bearing liabilities and provisions and current and non-current liabilities).

Assets and liabilities that have a different nature or function within an enterprise are sometimes subject to different measurement bases, for example plant and equipment may be carried out at cost or held at a revalued amount (in accordance with IAS 16 *Property, Plant and Equipment*). The use of these different measurement bases for different classes of items suggests separate presentation is necessary for users to fully understand the accounts.

Further sub-classifications of the line items should be presented either on the face of the statement of financial position or in the notes. The size, nature and function of the amounts involved, or the requirements of another IAS/IFRS will normally determine whether the disclosure is on the face of the statement of financial position or in the notes. The disclosures will vary with each item, but IAS 1 gives the following examples:

1. Tangible assets are analysed by class, e.g. property, plant and equipment;
2. Receivables are analysed between:
   - amounts receivable from trade customers,
   - amounts receivable from other members of the group,
   - receivables from related parties,
   - prepayments,
   - other amounts;
3. Inventories are sub-classified into classifications like merchandise, production supplies, materials, work in progress and finished goods;
4. Provisions are analysed showing provisions for employee benefit cost separate from any other provisions; and
5. Equity capital and reserves are analysed showing separately the various classes of paid-up share capital, share premium and reserves.

IAS 1 also requires that the following information on share capital and reserves be made either on the face of the statement of financial position or in the notes:

(a) for each class of share capital:
   (i) the number of shares authorised;
   (ii) the number of shares issued and fully paid; and issued but not fully paid;
   (iii) par value per share, or that the shares have no par value;
   (iv) a reconciliation of the number of shares outstanding at the beginning and at the end of the year;
   (v) the rights, preferences and restrictions attaching to that class, including restrictions on the distribution of dividends and the repayment of capital;
   (vi) shares in the enterprise held by the enterprise itself or by subsidiaries or associates of the enterprise; and
   (vii) shares reserved for issuance under options and sales contracts, including the terms and amounts.
(b) A description of the nature and purpose of each reserve within owners' equity; and
(c) The amount of dividends that was proposed or declared after the end of the reporting period but before the financial statements were authorised for issue; and
(d) The amount of any cumulative preference dividends not recognised.

Each enterprise should determine, based on the nature of its operations, whether or not to present current and non-current assets and current and non-current liabilities as separate classifications on the face of the statement of financial position. Where an enterprise chooses not to make this classification, assets and liabilities should be presented broadly in order of their liquidity. Whichever method of presentation is adopted, an enterprise should disclose, for each asset and liability, the amount that is expected to be recovered or settled after more than twelve months.

Most enterprises will show both current and non-current liabilities on the face of the statement of financial position. However, say, for example, an enterprise does not normally have non-current trade liabilities but as a result of one particular transaction had a payable due 20 months after the end of the reporting period. The enterprise may, in this case, classify the entire amount as a trade payable under current liabilities and then show separately a one-off amount that is due in 20 months' time (that is, in more than 12 months from the end of the reporting period).

In judging the most suitable presentation, management should consider the usefulness of the information they are providing. Information about the financial position of an enterprise is often used to predict the expected future cash flows and the timing of those cash flows. Information about the expected date of recovery and settlement of items is likely to be useful and therefore worth disclosing.

An asset should be classified as a current asset when it is:

- expected to be realised in the normal course of business (trade receivable), or is held for sale in the normal course of business (inventories);
- held primarily for trading purposes or for the short term and expected to be realised within the 12 months of the end of the reporting period (short-term investment); or
- cash or cash equivalent (see IAS 7 Statement of Cash Flows).

All other assets should be classified as non-current assets. IAS 1 uses the term 'non-current' to include tangible and intangible and financial assets of a long-term nature.

Current liabilities are those which satisfy any one of four criteria:

(i)   expected to be settled in the normal operating cycle;
(ii) held primarily for the purpose of being traded;
(iii) due to be settled within 12 months after the end of the reporting period; or
(iv) the entity does not have the right to defer settlement for at least 12 months after the end of the reporting period.

All other liabilities should be classified as non-current liabilities. An overdraft with the ability to be rolled over can be presented as non-current.

Statement of Comprehensive Income

IAS 1 (revised) requires that all items of income and expense (including those accounted for directly in equity) be presented in either:

(a) a single statement of comprehensive income (see **Figure 2.2** and **Figure 2.3**). This is the IASB's preferred approach and effectively means combining the income statement with the statement of recognised income and expense; or
(b) two statements comprising of:
    - an income statement which presents income and expenses recognised in the calculation of profit or loss; and
    - a statement of comprehensive income which begins with profit or loss from the income statement and then lists other items of income and expense that are not recognised in profit or loss as required or permitted by other IASs/IFRSs to show

total comprehensive income. These non-owner changes in equity include gains and losses arising from revaluations, translating the financial statements of a foreign operation and re-measuring available-for-sale financial assets. Such items can *no longer* be presented as separate items in the statement of changes in equity so as to clearly segregate changes in equity arising from transactions with owners in their capacity as owners from non-owner changes in equity.

If an item of expense or income is material, then its nature and amount should be disclosed separately either on the face of the statement of comprehensive income or in the notes. Examples include:

- write downs of inventories to net realisable value;
- write downs of property, plant and equipment to recoverable amount;
- restructuring costs;
- disposals of plant, property and equipment; and
- disposals of investments.

IAS 1 permits the preparation of a statement of comprehensive income on either the 'function of expenditure' (cost of sales method) or the 'nature of expenditure' method. The choice between the two being made according to which most fairly presents the elements of the enterprise's performance. A significant feature of the standard, which aids financial analysts with inter-firm comparisons, is the requirement that 'enterprises classifying expenses by function should disclose additional information on the nature of expenses including depreciation and staff costs'. This enables analysts to determine value-added ratios from the financial statements. A pro forma for each of the formats is shown below in **Figure 2.2** and **Figure 2.3**.

'By Function' Format

An analysis based on the function of the event (or cost of sales method) classifies expenses according to their function as part of cost of sales, distribution or administrative activities. While this presentation can provide more relevant information to users, the allocation of costs to functions can often be arbitrary. **Figure 2.2** illustrates this form of presentation.

Figure 2.2: X Limited – Statement of Comprehensive Income for the Year Ended 31 December 2009

	€
Revenue	x
Cost of sales	(x)
Gross profit	x
Other operating income	x
Distribution costs	(x)
Administrative expenses	(x)
Other expenses	(x)
Finance costs	(x)
Share of profit/(loss) of associates	x
Profit/(loss) before tax	x
Income tax expense	(x)
Profit/(loss) for the year	x
Other comprehensive income:	
Exchange differences on translating foreign operations	x
Gain/(loss) on property revaluation	x
Gain/(loss) on available-for-sale investments	x
Other comprehensive income for the year	x
Total comprehensive income for the year	x
Profit/(loss) attributable to:	
Owners of the parent	x
Non-controlling interests	x
	x
Total comprehensive income/(loss) attributable to:	
Owners of the parent	x
Non-controlling interests	x
	x

Enterprises choosing to classify expenses by function should disclose additional information on the nature of expenses, including depreciation and staff costs. The enterprise should choose the analysis that provides the fairest presentation of the business activities.

'By Nature' Format

An analysis based on the nature of expenses would, for example, result in classifications for depreciation, purchases, wages and salaries, marketing costs, etc. The expenses would be presented in total for each type of expense. This format is normally adopted for manufacturing enterprises and is illustrated in **Figure 2.3**.

Figure 2.3: X Limited – Statement of Comprehensive Income for the Year Ended 31 December 2009

	€	€
Revenue		x
Other operating income		x
Changes in inventories of finished goods and work in progress	(x)	
Work performed by the enterprise and capitalised	x	
Raw materials and consumables used	(x)	
Staff costs	(x)	
Depreciation and amortisation expense	(x)	
Impairment of property, plant and equipment	(x)	
Other operating expenses	(x)	
Finance costs	(x)	
Share of profit/loss of associates	x̲	x̲
Profit/(loss) before tax		x
Income tax expense		(x̲)
Profit/(loss) for the year		x̲
Other comprehensive income:		
Exchange differences on translating foreign operations		x
Gain/(loss) on property revaluation		x
Gain/(loss) on available-for-sale investments		x̲
Other comprehensive income for the year		x̲
Total comprehensive income for the year		x̲

	€	€
Profit/(loss) attributable to:		
Owners of the parent		x
Non-controlling interests		x
		x
Total comprehensive income/(loss) attributable to:		
Owners of the parent		x
Non-controlling interests		x
		x

The first item of expense in this format can be slightly confusing i.e. changes in inventories of finished goods and work in progress. The change represents an adjustment to production expenses to reflect that fact, either:

- production has increased inventory levels; or
- sales exceeds production activity resulting in a reduction in inventory levels.

Note that changes in raw materials inventories are not included here. The change in raw materials inventories is in the next expense line and is calculated as follows:

Figure 2.4: Raw Materials and Consumables Used

	€
Opening inventory of raw materials	x
Plus: purchase of raw materials	x
	x
Less: closing inventory of raw materials	(x)
Raw materials and consumables used	x

IAS 1 requires that certain minimum information is presented on the face of the statement of comprehensive income:

(a) revenue;
(b) finance costs;
(c) share of the profit or loss of associates and joint ventures accounted for using the equity method;

(d) tax expense;
(e) a single amount comprising the total of:
    (i) the post-tax profit or loss of discontinued operations, and
    (ii) the post-tax gain or loss recognised on the measurement to fair value less costs to sell or on the disposal of the assets or disposal group(s) constituting the discontinued operation;
(f) profit or loss;
(g) each component of other comprehensive income classified by nature (excluding amounts in (h));
(h) share of the other comprehensive income of associates and joint ventures accounted for using the equity method; and
(i) total comprehensive income.

The following must also be shown on the face of the statement of comprehensive income as allocations for the period:

(a) profit or loss for the period attributable to:
    (i) non-controlling interests, and
    (ii) owners of the parent.
(b) total comprehensive income for the period attributable to:
    (i) non-controlling interests, and
    (ii) owners of the parent.

Additional line items, headings and subtotals should be shown on the face of the statement of comprehensive income if another IAS/IFRS requires it or where it is necessary to show a fair presentation of the financial position. Materiality, the nature and function of the item are likely to be the main considerations when deciding whether to include an additional line item on the face of the statement of comprehensive income.

An enterprise should present an analysis of expenses using a classification based on either the nature of expenses or their function within the enterprise. This analysis can be on the face of the statement of comprehensive income (which is encouraged) or in the notes.

Example

An extract of balances in the financial statements of X Limited at 31 December 2009 is provided below to illustrate the two different formats for the statement of comprehensive income:

	€m
	10.1
Cost of sales	4.6
Distribution costs	1.3
Loan note interest	1.4
Administrative expenses	2.1

An analysis of the costs other than interest, i.e. €8.0m (€4.6m + €1.3m + €2.1m) showed the following:

	€m
Raw materials and consumables	3.1
Increase in inventories finished goods and work in progress	(0.2)
Depreciation	1.8
Staff costs	2.9
Other operating expenses	0.4
	8.0

A provision for income tax expense has been agreed at €0.2 million. From this information we can now produce a statement of comprehensive income under both formats.

'By Function' Format:

X Limited
Statement of Comprehensive Income for the Year Ended 31 December 2009

	€m	€m
Revenue		10.1
Cost of sales		(4.6)
Gross profit		5.5
Distribution costs	1.3	
Administration expenses	2.1	(3.4)
Profit from operations		2.1
Interest payable		(1.4)
Profit before tax		0.7
Income tax expense		(0.2)
Profit for the year		0.5

'By Nature' Format:

X Limited
Statement of Comprehensive Income for the Year Ended 31 December 2009

	€m	€m
Revenue		10.1
Increase in inventories of finished goods and work in progress		0.2
		10.3

Raw materials and consumables	3.1	
Staff costs	2.9	
Depreciation	1.8	
Other operating expenses	0.4	(8.2)
Profit from operations		2.1
Interest payable		(1.4)
Profit before tax		0.7
Income tax expense		(0.2)
Profit for the year		0.5

Value added is defined as sales revenue less the cost of all bought out materials and services, and a ratio of value added per € of employee costs can be easily determined from the 'by nature' format statement.

Example

Using the information from the previous example:

	€m	€m
Revenue		10.1
Less:		
Raw materials and consumables	3.1	
Other operating expenses	0.4	3.5
		6.6
Add back increase in inventories of finished goods and work in progress		0.2
Value added		6.8
Value added per € of employee costs (€6.8m/€2.9m)		2.35

The definition and disclosure of discontinued operations is dealt with in IFRS 5, which states that discontinued operations should be disclosed at the foot of the statement of comprehensive income. This is illustrated in **Figure 2.5**.

Figure 2.5: X Limited – Statement of Comprehensive Income for the Year Ended 31 December 2009 (including discontinued operations)

	€m
Continuing Operations	
Revenue	x
Cost of sales	(x)
Gross profit	x
Other operating income	x
Distribution costs	(x)
Administrative expenses	(x)
Other expenses	(x)
Finance costs	(x)
Share of profit/(loss) of associates	x
Profit/(loss) before tax	x
Income tax expense	(x)
Profit/(loss) for the period for continuing operations	x
Discontinued Operations	
Profit/(loss) for the year for discontinued operations*	x
Profit/(loss) for the year	x
Other comprehensive income:	
Exchange differences on translating foreign operations	x
Gain/(loss) on property revaluation	x
Gain/(loss) on available-for-sale investments	x
Other comprehensive income for the year	x
Total comprehensive income for the year	x
Profit/(loss) attributable to:	x
Owners of the parent	x
Non-controlling interests	x
Total comprehensive income/(loss) attributable to:	
Owners of the parent	x
Non-controlling interests	x
	x

*Earnings per share (in currency units i.e. cents)

Alternatively, profit from discontinued operations could be analysed in a separate column on the face of the statement of comprehensive income.
Other Points:

- Proposed dividends are not accrued until approved by shareholders at the Annual General Meeting (see IAS 10 *Events After the Reporting Period*);
- Extraordinary items are banned and it is a decision for the company to highlight/separately disclose 'exceptional' items. IAS 1 makes no reference to 'super exceptional' items; and
- Comparative information is disclosed for all amounts reported in the financial statements, unless an IAS/IFRS requires or permits otherwise.

Statement of Changes in Equity

This is the third component of a set of financial statements, and it is based upon the principle that changes in an enterprise's equity between two reporting dates reflect the increase or decrease in its net assets or wealth during the period. This information is useful to users as such changes, excluding changes resulting from transactions with shareholders (e.g. capital injections and dividends), represent the total gains and losses generated by the enterprise in that period.

As noted above with respect to the statement of comprehensive income, under the revised IAS 1, the components that make up an entity's comprehensive income must not be shown in the statement of changes in equity. While this statement includes the total amount of comprehensive income, its main purpose is to show the amounts of transactions with owners (e.g. share issues and dividends) and to provide a reconciliation of the opening and closing balance of each class of equity and reserve. An example is presented in **Figure 2.6**.

Figure 2.6: X Limited – Statement of Changes in Equity for the Year Ended 31 December 2008

	Share capital €m	Other reserves €m	Retained earnings €m	Total €m
Opening balance	x	x	x	x
Changes in accounting policy	–	–	x	x
Restated balance	x	x	x	x
Changes in equity for the year				
Dividends			(x)	(x)
Total comprehensive income		x	x	x
Issue of share capital	x	–	–	x
Total changes in equity	x	x	x	x
Closing balance	x	x	x	x

Statement of Cash Flows

This is the fourth component of financial statements and its form and content is governed by IAS 7 *Statement of Cash Flows* (see Chapters 19 and 33).

Notes to the Financial Statements

Notes to the financial statements normally include narrative descriptions or more detailed analysis of items on the face of the financial statements, as well as additional information such as contingent liabilities and commitments. IAS 1 also provides guidance on the structure of the accompanying notes to financial statements, the accounting policies and other required disclosures. The notes to the financial statements of an enterprise should:

- present information about the basis of preparation of the financial statements and the specific accounting policies adopted for significant transactions;
- disclose the information required by other IASs/IFRSs that is not presented elsewhere in the financial statements; and
- provide additional information which is not presented on the face of the financial statements but that is necessary for a fair presentation.

Notes to the financial statements should be presented in a systematic manner and any item on the financial statements should be cross-referenced to any related information in the notes. Notes are normally provided in the following order in order to assist users in understanding the financial statements and compare them with those of other enterprises:

- Statement of compliance with IASs/IFRSs;
- Statement of the measurement bases (e.g. historic cost) and accounting policies applied;
- Supporting information for items presented on the face of each financial statement in the order in which each line item and each financial statement is presented; and
- Other disclosures, including contingencies, commitments and other financial disclosures, and non-financial disclosures.

The accounting policies section of the notes to the financial statements should describe:

- the measurement basis (or bases) used in preparing the financial statements; and
- each specific accounting policy that is necessary for a proper understanding of the financial statements.

Other Disclosures

The following disclosures should be provided if not covered elsewhere in the financial statements:

- the domicile and legal form of the enterprise, its country of incorporation and the address of the registered office (or principal place of business, if different from the above);

- a description of the nature of the enterprises' operation and its principal activities;
- the name of the parent enterprise and the ultimate parent enterprise of the group; and
- either the number of the employees at the end of the period or the average for the period.

Financial Review

Enterprises are encouraged to present, outside the financial statements, a financial review by management which describes and explains the:

- main features of the financial performance and financial position; and
- principal uncertainties facing the business.

OTHER ISSUES

Service Concession Arrangements

These arrangements are related to IAS 1 and guidance on how to deal with them is contained in SIC 29 *Disclosure – Service Concession Arrangements*.

Issue

A service concession arrangement exists when an entity (the Concession Operator) enters into an arrangement with another entity (the Concession Provider) to provide services that give the public access to major economic and social facilities. A Concession Operator both receives a right and incurs an obligation to provide public services. Examples of service concession arrangements include water treatment and supply facilities, motorways, car parks, tunnels, bridges, airports and telecommunication networks. The outsourcing of internal services is not a service concession arrangement. SIC 29 considers what information should be disclosed in the notes to the financial statements of a Concession Operator and a Concession Provider about a service concession arrangement.

Consensus

A Concession Operator and a Concession Provider should disclose the following information for each service concession arrangement (or each class of such arrangements of a similar nature) in each period:

- a description of the arrangement;
- significant terms of the arrangement that may affect the amount, timing and certainty of future cash flows (e.g. the period of the concession, re-pricing dates and the basis upon which re-pricing or re-negotiation is determined);
- the nature and extent (e.g. quantity, time period or amount as appropriate) of:
  - rights to use specified assets,
  - obligations to provide or rights to expect provision of services,

  - obligations to acquire or build items of property, plant and equipment,
  - obligations to deliver or rights to receive specified assets at the end of the concession period,
  - renewal and termination options,
  - other rights and obligations (e.g. major overhauls); and
- changes in the arrangement occurring during the period.

CONCLUSION

The revised version of IAS 1 is effective for annual periods beginning on or after 1 January 2009 (early adoption is permitted). While the changes are relatively minor, the most significant change is to the titles of financial statements as they will be used in IASs/IFRSs; although entities are *not* required to use the new titles in their financial statements. IAS 1 states that a complete set of financial statements comprises of:

- a statement of financial position;
- a statement of comprehensive income;
- a statement of changes in equity showing either: all changes in equity; or changes in equity other than those arising from transactions with equity holders acting in their capacity as equity holders;
- a statement of cash flows; and
- accounting policies and explanatory notes.

Financial statements should be prepared on a going concern and accruals basis, and the effects of transactions and other items should be faithfully represented in the financial statements. Compliance with IASs/IFRSs should normally ensure that this is the case.

QUESTIONS

Self-test Questions

1. What are the components of a complete set of financial statements?
2. What criteria determine whether assets should be classified as current?
3. What criteria determine whether liabilities should be classified as current?
4. What minimum information should be presented on the face of the statement of comprehensive income?
5. Distinguish between the nature of expense method and the function of expense method of classifying expenses in the statement of comprehensive income.

Review Questions

(See APPENDIX ONE for Suggested Solutions to Review Questions.)

Question 1

The following information relates to V Limited, a manufacturing company.

V Limited – Trial Balance as at 30 September 20X1

	Notes	€'000	€'000
Sales revenue			430
Inventory as at 1 October 20X0	(a)	10	
Purchases		102	
Advertising		15	
Administration salaries		14	
Manufacturing wages		60	
Interest paid		14	
Dividends received	(e)		12
Audit fees		7	
Bad debts		10	
Taxation	(d)	10	
Dividends paid	(e)	120	
Grant received	(c)		30
Premises (cost)	(b)	450	
Plant (cost)	(c)	280	
Premises (depreciation)			40
Plant (depreciation)			160
Investments (long term)		100	
Receivables		23	
Bank		157	
Payables			7
Deferred taxation	(f)		62
Loan notes			140
Share capital			100
Accumulated profit at 1 October 20X0			391
		1372	1372

Additional Information

(a) Inventory was worth €13,000 on 30 September 20X1.
(b) Premises consist of land costing €250,000 and buildings costing €200,000. The buildings have an expected useful life of 50 years.
(c) Plant includes an item purchased during the year at a cost of €70,000. A government grant of €30,000 was received in respect of this purchase. These were the only transactions involving non-current assets during the year. Depreciation of plant is to be charged at 10 per cent per annum on a straight-line basis.
(d) The balance on the tax account is an under-provision for tax brought forward from the year ended 30 September 20X0.
(e) The company paid €48,000 on 27 November 20X0 as a final dividend for the year ended 30th September 20X0. A dividend of €12,000 was received on 13 January 20X1 (record the €12,000 received with no adjustment). The 20X1 interim dividend of €72,000 was paid on the 15th April 20X1.
(f) The provision for deferred tax is to be reduced by €17,000.
(g) The directors have estimated that tax of €57,000 will be due on the profits for this year.
(h) The directors have proposed a final dividend for the year of €50,000.
(i) It is company policy to charge depreciation to cost of sales.

Requirement Prepare a statement of comprehensive income for V Limited for the year ended 30th September 20X1 and a statement of financial position at that date. These should be in a form suitable for presentation to the shareholders and be accompanied by notes to the accounts in so far as is possible from the information provided.

Question 2

Extracts from the statement of financial position of Rose Limited as at 31 December 2007 are as follows:

€1 ordinary shares	€300,000
Share premium account	€50,000
Revaluation reserve	€80,000
Retained earnings	€1,280,000

The following information is relevant with respect to the year ended 31 December 2008.

- 1 April 2008 – company made a bonus issue of 1 for 10 from the share premium account.
- 1 June 2008 – company made a rights issue of 1 for 11 @ €1.50 per share.
- 1 July 2008 – a firm of Chartered Surveyors carried out a valuation of the company's properties which showed surpluses as follows:

Land	€20,000
Buildings	€50,000

- The company had two financial assets, X and Y, classified as available-for-sale as at 31 December 2007:
  - o X – after classification as available for sale the fair value of this asset increased by €30,000. This was recognised through equity in the year ended 31 December 2007. The asset was sold during the year under review; and
  - o Y – this asset was classified as available for sale during the year ended 31 December 2007 and valued at fair value less cost to sell. During the year under review the fair value increased by €10,000.
- Profit after tax for year ended 31 December 2008 amounted to €120,000.
- Proposed (and approved by shareholders prior to end of reporting period) dividends for year ended 31 December 2008 amounted to €25,000.
- During 2008, Rose Limited changed its accounting policy for the treatment of borrowing costs that are directly attributable to the acquisition of property, plant and equipment. In previous periods, Rose Limited had capitalised such costs. The company now treats these costs as an expense. Management judges that the new policy is preferable because it results in a more transparent treatment of finance costs and is consistent with local industry practice, making Rose Limited's financial statements more comparable. The company had capitalised €35,000 borrowing costs to 31 December 2007.

Requirement   Prepare the statement of changes in equity for the year ended 31 December 2008 for Rose Limited.

Challenging Questions

Question 1 (Based on ICAI, P3 Summer 2006, Question 6)

ZIPCO Limited (ZIPCO), a company which was incorporated on 23 January 1986, is involved in the production and distribution of electronic games. Prior to 1 January 2005, ZIPCO had issued 100,000 € ordinary shares as follows:

- 90,000 €1 ordinary shares were issued for €2 per share cash on 23 January 1986;
- 5,000 €1 ordinary shares were exchanged on 3 September 1990 for a patent that had a fair value at the date of exchange of €50,000; and
- 5,000 €1 ordinary shares were issued on 14 July 2004 for €20 per share cash.

At 1 January 2005, ZIPCO had a balance in its retained earnings of €500,000, while the general reserve and the revaluation reserve had credit balances of €200,000 and €300,000 respectively. The purpose of the general reserve is to reflect ZIPCO's need to regularly replace certain computer equipment because of technological advances.

During the year ended 31 December 2005, the following transactions occurred:

23 January   ZIPCO paid a €20,000 dividend that had been declared and approved by shareholders in November 2004;

11 April	10,000 € ordinary shares at €25 per share were offered to the public. The shares were fully subscribed and issued on 14th June 2005. On the same date, a further 10,000 € ordinary shares were placed with major investors at €25 per share;
12 July	ZIPCO paid an interim dividend of €20,000;
2 August	ZIPCO revalued land by €100,000 (ignore any deferred tax implications);
4 August	ZIPCO adopted a new international financial reporting standard early. The transitional liability on initial adoption was €100,000 more than the liability recognised under the previous accounting standard, and under the transitional arrangement should be recognised as a movement in retained earnings in 2005;
1 October	ZIPCO declared a one for eight bonus issue to existing shareholders, using the general reserve to create the bonus issue;
1 December	ZIPCO repurchased 1,000 €1 ordinary shares on the open market for €20 per share. The repurchase was accounted for by writing down share capital/share premium and retained earnings by an equal amount; and
31 December	ZIPCO calculated that its profit after tax for the year ended 31 December 2005 was €400,000. The directors proposed a final dividend of €25,000 and transferred €100,000 to the general reserve from retained earnings.

Requirement:
(a) If a company announces a final dividend at the end of its financial period, discuss whether the dividend payable should be recognised.
(b) Prepare the statement of changes in equity for ZIPCO for the year ended 31 December 2005.

CHAPTER 3

FIRST-TIME ADOPTION OF INTERNATIONAL FINANCIAL REPORTING STANDARDS

INTRODUCTION

This is the third and final chapter in Section One, which deals with the Accounting Framework. The first two chapters focused upon the general principles that apply when preparing and presenting general purpose financial statements. This chapter concentrates upon the issues facing an entity adopting International Accounting Standards (IASs) and International Financial Reporting Standards (IFRSs) for the first time. After having studied this chapter, you should be familiar with:

- the language of IASs/IFRSs; and
- an entity's reporting obligations when it adopts IASs/IFRSs for the first time.

THE LANGUAGE OF INTERNATIONAL STANDARDS

IASs/IFRSs are now firmly embedded in the accounting syllabi of most professional accounting bodies, and the differences between IASs/IFRSs and national accounting standards have diminished greatly in recent years. However, in Britain and Ireland, IASs/IFRSs only apply to listed companies and the vast majority of companies (and practitioners) continue to use Statements of Standard Accounting Practice and Financial Reporting Standards (notwithstanding the minimal technical accounting differences). Arguably one of the main issues still to be overcome is the different terminology. Some of the more common differences are outlined in **Table 3.1**.

Table 3.1: Different Accounting Terminology

Britain and Ireland	International
Profit and loss account	Statement of comprehensive income (Income statement)
Balance sheet	Statement of financial position
Cash flow statement	Statement of cash flows
Reconciliation of movements in shareholders' funds	Statement of changes in equity
Turnover or sales	Revenue
Taxation	Income tax
Fixed assets	Non-current assets
Tangible fixed assets	Property, plant and equipment
Debtors	Receivables
Creditors	Payables
Stock	Inventory
Shareholders' funds } Capital and reserves }	Equity
Acquisition accounting	Purchase accounting

FIRST-TIME ADOPTION OF INTERNATIONAL ACCOUNTING STANDARDS

Introduction

Following its initial publication in June 2003, IFRS 1 had been amended a number of times and had become increasingly complex. Consequently, on 27 November 2008, the International Accounting Standards Board (IASB) issued a revised version of IFRS 1 *First-time Adoption of International Financial Reporting Standards*. The objective of the revision was to improve the structure of the IFRS 1, with no new or revised technical material being introduced.

The revised IFRS 1 moves most of the Standard's numerous exceptions and exemptions to appendices as follows:

- exceptions to the retrospective application of other IASs/IFRSs (Appendix B);
- exemptions for business combinations (Appendix C); and
- exemptions from other IASs/IFRSs (Appendix D).

The revised IFRS 1 reflects:

- the May 2008 amendments to IFRS 1 regarding investments in subsidiaries, jointly controlled entities and associates; and
- consequential amendments to IFRS 1 (including updated transitional provisions) arising from other recent developments – notably IAS 1 *Presentation of Financial Statements* (2007), improvements to IFRSs issued in May 2008 and IFRS 3 *Business Combinations* (2008).

The revised IFRS 1 originally required application where an entity's first IFRS financial statements are for a period beginning on or after 1 January 2009, with earlier application permitted. However, at its December 2008 meeting, the IASB decided to change the effective date to 1 July 2009, correcting a potential technical problem arising from the interaction of IFRS 1 and other Standards.

Scope

IFRS 1 applies when an entity adopts the complete package of IFRSs for the first time, that is, it includes an 'explicit and unreserved statement of compliance with IFRSs'. IFRS 1 sets out how an entity should make the transition to IFRSs from another accounting basis. The IASB has sought 'to address the demand of investors to have transparent information that is comparable over all periods presented, while giving reporting entities a suitable starting point for their accounting under IFRSs'. IFRS 1 also applies to each interim financial report, if any, that the entity presents under IAS 34 *Interim Financial Reporting* for part of the period covered by its first IFRS financial statements.

Key Points

IFRS 1 requires that the same accounting policies are used in all periods presented. IFRSs effective for an entity's first IFRS period should be applied to all periods reported regardless of whether an earlier version of the standard existed. One year of comparative IFRS information is required. If historical summaries are presented these do not have to be restated from previous Generally Accepted Accounting Principles (GAAP). However, clear labelling is essential and disclosure of the nature of the main differences is required.

IFRS 1 grants limited exemptions from these requirements in specified areas where the cost of complying would be likely to exceed the benefits to users of financial statements. IFRS 1 requires disclosures that explain how the transition from previous GAAP to IFRSs affected the entity's reported financial position, financial performance and cash flows. The transition provisions in other IFRSs do not apply to a first-time adopter's transition to IFRSs.

Key Questions and Answers

Who is a first-time adopter?

A first-time adopter is an entity that, for the first time, makes an explicit and unreserved statement that its general-purpose financial statements comply with IFRS.

Can an entity be a first-time adopter if, in the preceding year, it has prepared IFRS financial statements for internal management use?

Yes, as long as those IFRS financial statements were not given to owners or external parties such as investors or creditors. If a set of IFRS statements was, for any reason, given to an external party in the preceding year, then the entity will already be considered to be on IFRS and IFRS 1 does not apply.

What if, last year, an entity said it complied with selected, but not all, IFRS, or it included in its previous GAAP financial statements a reconciliation of selected figures to IFRS figures?

It can still qualify as a first-time adopter.

When an entity adopts IFRS for the first time in its annual financial statements, what is it required to do?

1. The reporting entity must make an explicit and unreserved statement of compliance. For example:

   The financial statements have been prepared in accordance with International Financial Reporting Standards issued by the International Accounting Standards Board.

2. A reporting entity must use the same accounting policies in its opening IFRS statement of financial position and in all periods presented in the first IFRS financial statements. Typically, the periods involved will be the first reporting period and one comparative period which will begin with the opening IFRS statement of financial position. The opening statement of financial position should:

   - recognise all assets and liabilities required by IFRS (and only those). Some reclassification may be necessary to change from previous GAAP to IFRS's; and
   - apply IFRS's in measuring the reported assets and liabilities.

   Preparation of the opening IFRS statement of financial position may involve adjustments to amounts reported at the same date under previous GAAP, so disclosure must be given of the effects of those adjustments on the reporting entity's results, financial position and cash flows. All adjustments should be recognised in retained profits or other category of equity and not in the statement of comprehensive income.

What adjustments are required to move from previous GAAP to IFRS?

1. Derecognition of some old assets and liabilities   The entity should eliminate previous-GAAP assets and liabilities from the opening statement of financial position if they do not qualify for recognition under IFRS. For example:

(a) IAS 38 Intangible Assets does not permit recognising expenditure on any of the following as an intangible asset: research; startup, pre-operating, and pre-opening costs; training;

advertising and promotion; and moving and relocation. If previous GAAP recognised these as assets, they should be eliminated in the opening IFRS statement of financial position;

(b) If previous GAAP allowed accrual of liabilities for 'general reserves', restructurings, future operating losses, or major overhauls that do not meet the conditions for recognition as a provision under IAS 37 Provisions, Contingent Liabilities and Contingent Assets, these are eliminated in the opening IFRS statement of financial position; and

(c) If previous GAAP had allowed recognition of reimbursements or contingent assets that are not virtually certain, these are eliminated in the opening IFRS statement of financial position.

2. Recognition of some new assets and liabilities   Conversely, the entity should recognise all assets and liabilities required to be recognised by IFRS even if they were never recognised under previous GAAP. For example:

(a) IAS 39 Financial Instruments: Recognition and Measurement requires recognition of all derivative financial assets and liabilities, including embedded derivatives. These were not recognised under many local GAAPs;

(b) IAS 19 Employee Benefits requires an employer to recognise its liabilities under defined benefit plans. These are not just pension liabilities but also obligations for medical and life insurance, vacations, termination benefits, and deferred compensation. In the case of 'over-funded' plans, this would be a defined benefit asset;

(c) IAS 37 requires recognition of provisions as liabilities. Examples could include obligations for onerous contracts, restructurings, decommissioning, site restoration, warranties, guarantees, and litigation; and

(d) Deferred tax assets and liabilities would be recognised in conformity with IAS 12 Income Taxes.

3. Reclassification   Reclassify previous-GAAP opening statement of financial position items into the appropriate IFRS classification. For example:

IFRS 7 *Financial Instruments: Presentation* has principles for classifying items as financial liabilities or equity. Thus, mandatorily redeemable preferred shares and puttable shares that may have been classified as equity under previous GAAP would be reclassified as liabilities in the opening IFRS statement of financial position. The scope of consolidation might change depending on the consistency of the previous GAAP requirements with those in IAS 27 *Consolidated and Separate Financial Statement.*

4. Measurement   The general principle is to apply IFRS in measuring all recognised assets and liabilities; although there are several significant exceptions (see below).

What are the exceptions to the basic measurement principle in IFRS 1?

1. Optional exceptions   There are some important exceptions to the general restatement and measurement principles. For example:

(a) For business combinations that occurred before the start of the reporting period, an entity may keep the original previous GAAP accounting, i.e. not restate previous mergers or goodwill written-off from reserves, the carrying amounts of assets and liabilities recognised at the date of acquisition or merger and how goodwill was initially determined. However, in all cases, the entity must make an initial IAS 36 *Impairment of Assets* test of any remaining goodwill in the opening IFRS statement of financial position, after reclassifying, as appropriate, previous GAAP intangibles to goodwill.

(b) Property, plant, and equipment, intangible assets, and investment property carried under the cost model:

- These assets may be measured at their fair value at the start of the IFRS reporting period (this option applies to intangible assets only if an active market exists). Fair value becomes the 'deemed cost' going forward under the IFRS cost model. 'Deemed cost' is a surrogate for an actual cost measurement;
- If, before the date of its first IFRS statement of financial position, the entity had revalued any of these assets under its previous GAAP either to fair value or to a price-index-adjusted cost, that previous GAAP revalued amount at the date of the revaluation can become the deemed cost of the asset under IFRS; and
- If, before the date of its first IFRS statement of financial position, the entity had made a one-time revaluation of assets or liabilities to fair value because of a privatisation or initial public offering, and the revalued amount became deemed cost under the previous GAAP, that amount (adjusted for any subsequent depreciation, amortisation, and impairment) would continue to be deemed cost after the initial adoption of IFRS.

The above rules are also applicable to investment properties, if an entity wishes to use the cost model under IAS 40 *Investment property*, as well as to intangible assets that meet the revaluation criteria as set out in IAS 38.

(c) An entity may elect to recognise all cumulative actuarial gains and losses for all defined benefit plans at the start of the IFRS reporting period (that is, reset any corridor recognised under previous GAAP to zero), even if it elects to use the IAS 19 corridor approach for actuarial gains and losses that arise after first-time adoption of IFRS. If an entity does not elect to apply this exemption, it must restate all defined benefit plans under IAS 19 since the inception of those plans.

(d) An entity may elect to recognise all translation adjustments arising on the translation of the financial statements of foreign entities in accumulated profits or losses at the start of the IFRS reporting period (that is, reset the translation reserve included in equity under previous GAAP to zero). If the entity elects to apply this exemption, the gain or loss on subsequent disposal of the foreign entity will be adjusted only by those accumulated translation adjustments arising after the start of the IFRS reporting period. If the entity does not elect to apply this exemption, it must restate the translation reserve for all foreign entities since they were acquired or created (IAS 21 *The Effects of Changes in Foreign Exchange Rates*).

2. Mandatory exceptions   There are important exceptions to the general restatement and measurement principles set out above that are mandatory. These are:

(a) A first-time adopter is not permitted to recognise financial assets or financial liabilities that had been derecognised under its previous GAAP (IAS 39 *Financial Instruments: Recognition and Measurement*). However, if a special purpose entity (SPE) was used to effect the derecognition of financial instruments and the SPE is controlled at the start of the IFRS reporting period, the SPE must be consolidated;

(b) The conditions in IAS 39 for a hedging relationship that qualifies for hedge accounting should be applied as of the start of the IFRS reporting period. The hedge accounting practices, if any, that were used in periods prior to the opening IFRS statement of financial position may not be retrospectively changed; and

(c) In preparing IFRS estimates retrospectively, the entity must use the inputs and assumptions that had been used to determine previous GAAP estimates in prior periods, provided that those inputs and assumptions are consistent with IFRS. The entity is not permitted to use information that became available only after the previous GAAP estimates were made except to correct an error.

How will the change to IFRS affect an entity's ongoing disclosures?

For many entities, new areas of disclosure will be added that were not requirements under the previous GAAP (perhaps segment information, earnings per share, discontinuing operations, contingencies, and fair values of all financial instruments) and disclosures that had been required under previous GAAP will be broadened (perhaps related party disclosures).

IAS 1 only requires one year of full comparative financial statements. If a first-time adopter wants to disclose selected financial information for periods before the date of the opening IFRS statement of financial position, is it required to conform that information to IFRS as well?

No, conforming that earlier selected financial information to IFRS is optional. If the entity elects to present the earlier selected financial information based on its previous GAAP rather than IFRS, it must prominently label that earlier information as not complying with IFRS and, further, it must disclose the nature of the main adjustments that would make that information comply with IFRS. This latter disclosure is narrative and not necessarily quantified.

Of course, if the entity elects to present more than one year of full comparative prior-period financial statements at the time of its transition to IFRS, that will change the date of the opening IFRS statement of financial position.

What disclosures are a first-time adopter required to make when switching to IFRS?

IFRS 1 requires disclosures that explain how the transition from previous GAAP to IFRS affected the entity's reported financial position, financial performance and cash flows. This includes:

1. Reconciliations of equity reported under previous GAAP to equity under IFRS both (a) at the date of the opening IFRS statement of financial position and (b) at the end of the last annual period reported under the previous GAAP. For an entity adopting IFRS for the first time in its 31 December 2005 financial statements, the reconciliations would be as of 1 January 2004 and 31 December 2004;
2. Reconciliations of profit or loss for the last annual period reported under the previous GAAP to profit or loss under IFRS for the same period;
3. Explanation of material adjustments (including error corrections and impairment losses) that were made, in adopting IFRS for the first time, to the statement of financial position, statement of comprehensive income and statement of cash flows; and
4. Appropriate explanations if the entity has availed itself of any of the specific recognition and measurement exemptions permitted under IFRS 1 – for instance, if it used fair values as deemed cost.

Example

Tom Limited first adopts IFRS's in 2008. The date of transition to IFRS's is 1 January 2007. Its last financial statements under previous GAAP were for the year ended 31 December 2007.

The company must include the reconciliations of equity at two dates, i.e. 1 January 2007 and 31 December 2008. Furthermore, the adjustments to the financial statements under previous GAAP should be explained in the notes.

Example

Reconciliation of Equity at 1 January 2007 (Date of transition to IFRS's):

Note		Previous GAAP €	Effect of Transition to IFRS's €	IFRS's €
	ASSETS			
	Non-current Assets			
1	Property, plant and equipment	8,299	100	8,399

2	Financial assets	3,471	420	3,891
		11,770	520	12,290
	Current Assets			
	Trade receivables	3,710	0	3,710
3	Inventories	2,962	400	3,362
4	Other receivables	333	431	764
	Cash and cash equivalents	748	0	748
		7,753	831	8,584
	Total Assets	19,523	1,351	20,874
	EQUITY AND LIABILITIES			
	Capital and Reserves			
	Issued capital	1,500	0	1,500
2	Revaluation reserve	0	294	294
4	Hedging reserve	0	302	302
6	Retained earnings	3,882	500	4,382
		5,382	1,096	6,478
	Non-current Liabilities			
	Interest-bearing loans	9,396	0	9,396
5	Deferred tax liability	579	255	834
	Current Liabilities			
	Trade and other payables	4,124	0	4,124
	Current tax liability	42	0	42
		19,523	1,351	20,874

Notes to the Reconciliation of Equity at 1 January 2007:

1. Depreciation was influenced by tax requirements under previous GAAP but under IFRS's reflects the useful lives of the assets. The cumulative adjustment increases the carrying amount of property, plant and equipment by €100.

2. Financial assets are all classified as available for sale under IFRSs and are carried at their fair value of € 3,891. They were carried at cost under previous GAAP. The resulting gain of €294 (€420 less deferred tax €126) is included in the revaluation reserve.
3. Inventories include fixed and variable production overheads of €400 under IFRSs, but this overhead was excluded under previous GAAP.
4. Unrealised gains of €431 on unmatured forward foreign exchange contracts are recognised under IFRSs, but were not recognised under previous GAAP. The resulting gains of €302 (€431 less related deferred tax €129) are included in the hedging reserve.
5. The above adjustments increased the deferred tax liability as follows:

	€
Financial assets (Note 2)	126
Forward foreign exchange contracts (Note 4)	129
	255

6. The adjustments to retained earnings are as follows:

	€
Depreciation (Note 1)	100
Inventories (Note 3)	400
	500

Example

A reconciliation of the profit or loss reported under previous GAAP for the latest period in the entity's most recent annual financial statements to its profit or loss under IFRSs for the same period could be presented as follows:

Reconciliation of profit or loss for the year ended 31 December 2008:

Notes		Effect of Previous GAAP	Transition to IFRS's	IFRS's
		€	€	€
	Revenue	20,910	0	20,910
1, 2	Cost of sales	(15,283)	(97)	(15,380)
	Gross profit	5,627	(97)	5,530

1	Distribution costs	(1,907)	(30)	(1,937)
1	Administrative expenses	(2,842)	(50)	(2,892)
	Financial income	1,446	0	1,446
	Finance costs	(1,902)	0	(1,902)
	Profit before tax	422	(177)	245
3	Tax expense	(158)	53	(105)
	Net profit (loss)	264	(124)	140

Notes to the reconciliation of profit or loss for 2008:

1. A pension liability is recognised under IFRSs, but was not recognised under previous GAAP. The pension liability increased by €130 during 2008, which caused increases in cost of sales (€50), distribution costs (€30) and administrative expenses (€50).
2. Cost of sales is higher by €47 under IFRSs because inventories include fixed and variable production overheads under IFRSs but not under previous GAAP.
3. Adjustments 1 and 2 led to a reduction of €53 in the tax expense.

If an entity is going to adopt IFRS for the first time in its annual financial statements for the year ended 31 December 2008, is any disclosure required in its financial statements prior to the 31 December 2008 statements?

Yes, but only if the entity presents an interim financial report that complies with IAS 34. Explanatory information and a reconciliation are required in the interim report that immediately precedes the first set of IFRS annual financial statements. The information includes changes in accounting policies compared to those under previous local GAAP.

A parent or investor may become a first-time adopter earlier than or later than its subsidiary, associate, or joint venture investee. In these cases, how is IFRS 1 applied?

1. If the subsidiary has adopted IFRS in its entity-only financial statements before the group to which it belongs adopts IFRS for the consolidated financial statements, then the subsidiary's first-time adoption date is still the date at which it adopted IFRS for the first time, not that of the group. However, the group must use the IFRS measurements of the subsidiary's assets and liabilities for its first IFRS financial statements except for adjustments relating to the business combinations exemption and to conform group accounting policies.
2. If the group adopts IFRS before the subsidiary adopts IFRS in its entity-only financial statements, then the subsidiary has an option either to:

    (a) elect that the group date of IFRS adoption is its transition date; or
    (b) first-time adopt in its entity-only financial statements.

3. If the group adopts IFRS before the parent adopts IFRS in its entity-only financial statements, then the parent's first-time adoption date is the date at which the group adopted IFRS for the first time.

4. If the group adopts IFRS before its associate or joint venture adopts IFRS in its entity-only financial statements, then the associate or joint venture should have the option to elect that either the group date of IFRS adoption is its transition date or to first-time adopt in its entity-only financial statements.

CONCLUSION

The globalisation of capital markets requires a single set of global accounting, reporting and disclosure standards. Due to the high volume of cross-border capital flows and the growing number of foreign direct investments via mergers and acquisitions, the need for the harmonisation of different accounting practices and the acceptance of worldwide standards has arisen. It is likely that many of those organisations, in both the private and public sectors, that have so far avoided the need to adopt IASs/IFRSs will be required to make the transition in the near future. Consequently an entity's reporting obligations when it adopts IFRSs for the first time, the focus of this chapter, should have growing relevance.

QUESTIONS

Self-test Questions

1. Explain the main requirements of IFRS 1 which must be satisfied when a company adopts IASs/IFRSs for the first time.
2. Identify the reconciliations which a company must include in its financial statements when it adopts IASs/IFRSs for the first time.

Review Questions

(See APPENDIX ONE for Suggested Solutions to Review Questions.)

Question 1

'There can be few who work for multinational companies, with some involvement with their financial reporting systems, who have not thought how good it would be to have one accounting language throughout the world. At present, accounting is far from that objective. Accountants inhabit a kind of Tower of Babel, where we not only speak different languages but also give different interpretations of the same events and transactions.' *Sir Bryan Carsberg, Secretary-General of the International Accounting Standards Committee, 1995.*

Requirement Discuss:

(a) The advantages of harmonising accounting standards;
(b) The reasons why global harmonisation has not yet been achieved.

Challenging Questions

Question 1 (Based on ICAI, P3 Summer 2005, Question 6)

The directors of EMERALD plc (EMERALD), an Irish listed company, have decided to adopt International Financial Reporting Standards (IFRSs) for the first time in the company's financial statements for the year ended 31 December 2008.

Requirement   With respect to the financial statements for the year ended 31 December 2008, prepare a *memorandum* addressed to the directors of EMERALD explaining:

(a) What EMERALD will be required to do when it adopts IFRSs for the first time;
(b) In general terms, explain the type of accounting adjustments that EMERALD is likely to have to make when moving from Irish/UK Generally Accepted Accounting Practice to IFRSs; and
(c) Outline the disclosures that EMERALD is likely to have to make as a first-time adopter of IFRSs.

SECTION TWO

PREPARATION OF STATEMENT OF COMPREHENSIVE INCOME AND STATEMENT OF FINANCIAL POSITION

CHAPTER 4

REVENUE RECOGNITION

INTRODUCTION

As explained in Chapter 1, income is defined in the Framework for the Preparation and Presentation of Financial Statements as increases in economic benefits during the accounting period in the form of inflows or enhancements of assets or decreases of liabilities that result in increases in equity, other than those relating to contributions from equity participants. Income encompasses both revenue and gains. Revenue is income that arises in the course of ordinary activities of an entity and is referred to by a variety of different names including sales, fees, interest, dividends and royalties. Revenue is often discussed in terms of inflows of assets to an organisation that occur as a result of outflows of goods and services from that organisation. Consequently, the concept of revenue recognition has traditionally been associated with specific accounting procedures that are primarily directed towards determining the timing and measurement of revenue. Accordingly, the revenue recognition debate has taken place in the context of the historical cost double entry system, with accounting principles focusing on determining when transactions should be recognised in the financial statements, what amounts are involved in each transaction, how these amounts should be classified and how they should be allocated between accounting periods.

Historical cost accounting in its pure form avoids having to take a valuation approach to financial reporting by virtue of the fact that it is transaction based, i.e. it relies on transactions to determine recognition and measurement of assets, liabilities, revenues and expenses. Over an organisation's life, its total income will be represented by net cash flows generated. However, because of the requirement to prepare periodic financial statements, it is necessary to break up an organisation's operating cycle into artificial periods. Therefore, at each reporting date, an organisation will have entered into a number of incomplete transactions, e.g. a product has been delivered or service rendered for which payment has not yet been received. As a result, the important questions to be answered with respect to revenue recognition revolve around how to allocate the effects of incomplete transactions between the periods for reporting purposes, rather than simply letting them fall into the periods in which cash is received or paid.

After having studied this chapter on revenue recognition you should understand the following key points:

- The term 'revenue' can apply to the supply of goods, the provision of services, rent from the hire of equipment or property, interest or dividends received on a trade investment;
- Revenue should be measured at the fair value of the consideration received or receivable;
- The conditions that must be met before the revenue from the sale of goods can be recognised in the statement of comprehensive income;
- The conditions that must be met before revenue from services may be recognised;
- When you can recognise revenue from interest, royalties and dividends in the statement of comprehensive income; and
- The disclosure requirements.

APPROACHES TO REVENUE RECOGNITION

The critical event in the operating cycle of a business is the point at which most or all of the uncertainty surrounding a transaction is removed. This is usually when the goods or services are delivered, and is (normally) the point at which revenue is recognised. However the critical event could occur at other times in the operating cycle, depending on the circumstances. Different points in the operating cycle are explained in **Table 4.1**.

Table 4.1: The Revenue Operating Cycle

Timing of Recognition	Criteria	Examples of Practical Application
Placing of an order by a customer, prior to manufacture.	As there is likely to be uncertainty regarding the final outcome of such contracts it would not be prudent to recognise profit at this point.	Long-term contracts.
During production.	Revenues accrue over time, and no significant uncertainty exists as to measurability or collectability.	Accrual of interest, dividends and royalties.
	A contract of sale has been entered into and future costs can be estimated with reasonable certainty.	Accounting for long-term contracts using the percentage of completion method.

Timing of Recognition	Criteria	Examples of Practical Application
At the completion of production, i.e. from goods in inventory.	This is nearing the point where most of the uncertainties are resolved; however recognition is usually delayed until delivery. There should exist a ready market for the commodity, together with a determinable and stable market price. There should be insignificant marketing costs involved.	Certain precious metals and commodities.
At the time of sale (but before delivery).	The goods must have already been acquired or manufactured, and be capable of immediate delivery. The selling price should be established and all material related expenses, including delivery, ascertained. No significant uncertainties remain, e.g. ultimate cash collection or returns.	Certain sales of goods, e.g. bill and hold sales. Property sales where there is an irrevocable contract.
On delivery.	Criteria for recognition before delivery were not met and no significant uncertainties remain. In the vast majority of cases this is the point at which revenue is recognised.	Most sales of goods and services. Property sales where there is doubt that the sale will be completed.
Subsequent to delivery.	Significant uncertainty regarding collectability at the time of delivery. At the time of sale it was not possible to value the consideration with sufficient accuracy.	Sales where right of return exist. Goods shipped subject to conditions, e.g. installation, inspection or maintenance.
On an apportionment basis (revenue allocation approach).	Where the revenue represents the supply of initial and subsequent goods/services.	Franchise fees. Sales of goods with after sales services.

In Ireland and Britain, attempts have been made to address revenue recognition in, for example, SSAP 2 *Disclosure of Accounting Policies*, which has been replaced by FRS 18 *Accounting Policies*, Chapter Five of the *Statement of Principles for Financial Reporting* and FRS 5 *Reporting the Substance of Transactions*.

The *Statement of Principles for Financial Reporting* adopts a 'balance sheet' approach, defining gains and losses in terms of changes in assets and liabilities, rather than in terms of matching transactions with accounting periods. The *Statement of Principles for Financial Reporting* establishes three recognition criteria:

- An item must meet the definition of an element within the statement;
- There must be evidence that a change in the inherent asset or liability has occurred; and
- The item can be measured in monetary terms and with sufficient reliability.

The revenue recognition process starts with the effect the transaction has on the reporting organisation's assets and liabilities:

- If net assets increase, a gain is recognised; and
- A loss is recognised if, and to the extent that, previously recognised assets are reduced or eliminated.

FRS 5 stipulates that the seller needs to have performed its contractual obligations by transferring the principal benefits and risks of the goods to the customer:

- If the substance of the transaction is that the goods represent an asset of the customer, then the seller has a right to be paid and the seller should recognise the related changes in the assets or liabilities and turnover. The amount recognised should be adjusted for the time value of money where significant and risk (in particular, returns risk where applicable); or
- If the substance of the transaction is that the goods represent an asset of the seller, it should be retained in the seller's statement of financial position (balance sheet). Any amounts received from the customer should be included within creditors. The inventory should be removed from the seller's statement of financial position and part or all of any related creditor balance released to turnover on the earlier of the point at which the criteria for recognition of the bill and hold arrangement as a sale have been met, even if the goods remain in the hands of the seller, or the goods are delivered to the customer.

In November 2003, the Accounting Standards Board (ASB) issued an Application Note 'G' to FRS 5, which sets out the basic principles of revenue recognition and specifically addresses five types of arrangement that give rise to turnover and have been subject to differing interpretations in practice:

- Long-term contractual performance;
- Separation and linking of contractual arrangements;
- Bill and hold arrangements;
- Sales with right of return; and
- Presentation of turnover as principal or as agent.

The Application Note also provides guidance on the measurement of turnover where there are deferred payment terms or where there is a significant risk about the customer's ability to pay. Introducing the Application Note, Mary Keegan, ASB Chairman, said 'Many investors focus on revenue growth as an important indicator of a company's performance. Recent reports of questionable practice have highlighted the need for us to set out best practice. Our consultation, earlier this year, and our subsequent research have emphasised the need for this new standard'. She added 'The standard will also assist those faced with making the transition to International Financial Reporting Standards in 2005, as both its principles and its specific requirements are consistent with the international standard, IAS 18'.

However, the various sources of guidance referred to above arguably offer limited assistance, and thus reliance has to be placed on international pronouncements, such as, IAS 18 *Revenue*.

IAS 18 *REVENUE*

The objective of IAS 18 is to prescribe the accounting treatment for revenue arising from certain types of transactions and events, namely the:

- sale of goods;
- rendering of services; and
- use by others of organisation assets yielding interest, royalties and dividends.

It does not deal with revenue arising from transactions covered by other Standards (e.g. revenue arising from lease agreements is dealt with in IAS 17 *Leases*).

IAS 18 defines revenue as 'the gross inflow of economic benefits (cash, receivables, other assets) arising from the ordinary operating activities of an organisation such as sales of goods, sales of services, interest, royalties, and dividends' [IAS 18.7]. Revenue should be measured at the fair value of the consideration receivable [IAS 18.9]. The consideration is usually cash. If the inflow of cash is significantly deferred, and there is no interest or a below-market rate of interest, the fair value of the consideration is determined by discounting expected future receipts. This would occur, for instance, if the seller is providing interest-free credit to the buyer or is charging a below-market rate of interest. Interest must be imputed based on market rates [IAS 18.11]. If dissimilar goods or services are exchanged (as in barter transactions), revenue is the fair value of the goods or services received or, if this is not reliably measurable, the fair value of the goods or services given up.

Sale of Goods

Revenue arising from the sale of goods should be recognised when all of the following criteria have been satisfied [IAS 18.14]:

- the seller has transferred to the buyer the significant risks and rewards of ownership;
- the seller retains neither continuing managerial involvement to the degree usually associated with ownership nor effective control over the goods sold;
- the amount of revenue can be measured reliably;
- it is probable that the economic benefits associated with the transaction will flow to the seller; and
- the costs incurred or to be incurred in respect of the transaction can be measured reliably.

However, if it is unreasonable to expect ultimate collection then it should be postponed. In most cases the transfer of legal title coincides with the transfer of risks but in other cases they may occur at different times. Each transaction must be examined separately. In certain specific industries, e.g. harvesting of crops, extraction of mineral ores, performance may be substantially complete prior to the execution of the transaction generating revenue.

Rendering of Services

For revenue arising from the rendering of services, provided that all of the following criteria are met, revenue should be recognised by reference to the stage of completion of the transaction at the reporting date (the percentage-of-completion method) [IAS 18.20]:

- the amount of revenue can be measured reliably;
- it is probable that economic benefits will flow to the service provider;
- the stage of completion of the transaction can be measured reliably; and
- the costs of the transaction (including future costs) can be measured reliably.

When the above criteria are not met, revenue arising from the rendering of services should be recognised only to the extent of the expenses recognised that are recoverable (the 'cost-recovery approach') [IAS 18.26].

Interest, Royalties and Dividends

For interest, royalties and dividends, provided that it is probable that the economic benefits will flow to the organisation and the amount of revenue can be measured reliably, revenue should be recognised as follows [IAS 18.29-30]:

- Interest – on a time proportion basis that takes into account the effective yield;
- Royalties – on an accruals basis in accordance with the substance of the relevant agreement; and
- Dividends – when the shareholder's right to receive payment is established.

In foreign countries revenue recognition may need to be postponed if exchange permission is required and a delay in remittance is expected. Where the ability to assess the ultimate collection with reasonable certainty is lacking, revenue recognition should be postponed. In such cases, it may be appropriate to recognise revenue only when cash is collected. If the uncertainty relates to collectability, it is more appropriate to make a separate provision for bad debts.

Disclosure Requirements

1. The accounting policies adopted for the recognition of revenue; and
2. The amount of each significant category of revenue recognised (i.e. figures for sale of goods, rendering of services, interest, royalties and dividends, if material).

Example

The following extract gives an illustration of how this requirement may be adopted in practice:

Extract from the consolidated financial statements of the Bayer group for the year ended 31 December 2000.

Notes to the statement of financial position:

Income and expenses for the year are recognised on an accruals basis. Income from the sale of products, merchandise and services is recognised when delivery has taken place, transfer of risk has been completed and the amount of future returns can be reasonably estimated.

Product returns are accepted as a matter of contract or as a matter of practice. In the reported periods, product returns were insignificant. Sales rebates and discounts as well as amounts collected on behalf of third parties such as sales taxes and goods and services taxes are excluded from net sales. Costs for research and development are charged to expenses as incurred.

OTHER RELATED GUIDANCE

SIC 31 *Revenue – Barter Transactions Involving Advertising Services* is effective on 31 December 2001 and relates to IAS 18 *Revenue*.

Issue

An entity (seller) may enter into a barter transaction to provide advertising services in exchange for receiving advertising services from its customer. According to IAS 18 Revenue, a seller recognises revenue from barter transactions when, amongst other criteria, the services exchanged are dissimilar and the amount of the revenue can be measured reliably. SIC 31 does not apply to an exchange of similar advertising services, as such transactions do not generate revenue under IAS 18 *Revenue*. Under what circumstances does a seller reliably measure revenue at the fair value of advertising services received or provided in a barter transaction?

Consensus

Revenue from a barter transaction involving advertising cannot be measured reliably at the fair value of advertising services received. However, a seller can reliably measure revenue at the fair value of the advertising services it provides in a barter transaction by reference to non-barter transactions that meet certain criteria specified in SIC 31.

CONCLUSION

This chapter considers when revenue should be recognised in the financial statements. It begins by outlining different sources of guidance with respect to revenue recognition before focusing on the requirements of IAS 18 *Revenue*. The growing complexity and diversity of business activity has resulted in a variety of forms of revenue-earning transactions that were never considered when the 'point of sale' was established as the general rule for revenue recognition. As we move further towards a 'balance sheet' based fair-value approach to revenue recognition, long established principles centred on accruals and prudence may no longer be appropriate. In addition, with the prospect of a single statement of financial performance, there is the possibility that traditional concepts of revenue resulting from success, or otherwise, of selling goods and services may become meshed with newer concepts of holding gains and losses.

QUESTIONS

Self-test Questions

1. At what value should revenue be measured?
2. What conditions must be met before revenue from the sale of goods may be recognised?
3. What conditions must be met before revenue from the delivery of services may be recognised?

Review Questions

(See APPENDIX ONE for Suggested Solutions to Review Questions)

Question 1 (Based on ICAI, P3 Summer 2006, Question 4)

Issue 1

ANTRIM Limited (ANTRIM) owes CORK Limited (CORK) €250,000, due on 31 July 2009. CORK owes ANTRIM €200,000, due on 30 June 2009. A legal right of set-off between the two companies is documented in writing, and both companies have indicated their intent to settle amounts on a net basis whenever possible.

ANTRIM also owes DOWN Limited (DOWN) €250,000, due on 30 June 2009. ANTRIM has a building with a fair value of €250,000 that it has pledged to DOWN as collateral for the debt.

Requirement With respect to each of the above situations, explain whether the financial asset and the financial liability may be offset in the financial statements of ANTRIM as at 31 December 2008.

Issue 2

On 3 September 2008, MASTERTICKETS Limited (MASTERTICKETS), a concert ticket agency, made a number of concert reservations for customers, receiving €5,000 from them. The customers collected the concert tickets from the agency on the same day. MASTERTICKETS remitted €4,500 to the concert promoter on 4 September 2008, retaining €500 as commission. MASTERTICKETS acts purely as an agent for the concert promoter and has no responsibility for the concert, which is taking place in July 2009.

Requirement How should MASTERTICKETS reflect this transaction in its financial statements for the year ended 31 December 2008?

Issue 3

LAGAN Limited (LAGAN) operates an internet site from which it sells the products of various manufacturers. Customers, using the internet site, select the products that they wish to purchase, provide their credit card details and the address to which the goods are to be delivered. Once the credit card authorisation is received, LAGAN passes the order details immediately to the relevant manufacturer. The manufacturer is responsible for delivering the goods directly to the customer, and is also responsible for any disputed credit card charges, product returns or warranty claims. LAGAN charges each manufacturer a fee of 8% of the product's selling price. During the year ended 31 December 2008, total product sales through the internet site amounted to €500,000, earning LAGAN commission of €40,000.

Requirement How should LAGAN reflect this transaction in its financial statements for the year ended 31 December 2008?

Issue 4

PURPLE Limited (PURPLE) provides mobile telephone services. Customers subscribing to PURPLE initially pay a non-refundable activation fee followed by a quarterly call usage charge. Only nominal costs are incurred by PURPLE to activate the telephone service, and the quarterly call usage charge is more than adequate to cover operating costs.

Requirement How should PURPLE reflect this transaction in its financial statements for the year ended 31 December 2008?

Issue 5

NECTAR Limited (NECTAR), on 1 February 2008, entered into a €15,000,000 contract to build a multi-storey car park, with a completion date of 30 June 2009. NECTAR has not yet accounted for the contract in its financial statements for the year ended

31 December 2008. It is company policy to adjust cost of sales by the amount of attributable profit or loss to be recognised in the period to arrive at contract revenue. Further details in relation to the contract at 31 December 2008 are as follows:

	€'000		€'000
Amount invoiced	9,500	Costs incurred	9,250
Amount received	9,000	Costs certified	8,500
		Costs to complete	4,000

Requirement   How should NECTAR reflect the contract in its financial statements for the year ended 31 December 2008?

Challenging Questions

Question 1

You are the Financial Accountant of Incara plc, a company that operates from a number of retail outlets throughout Ireland, selling vehicle entertainment and navigation systems. Incara plc prepares its financial statements to the 31 December each year. Incara plc received and accepted an order for car CD changers from a regular customer, CCE Limited, on 21 December 2007 for an agreed price of €50,000. However, due to the Christmas holidays, the goods were not despatched until 4 January 2008. CCE Limited received the goods on the same day, and paid for them on 13 January 2008. The goods are included in Incara plc's inventory at 31 December 2007 at their cost price of €40,000.

During the year ended 31 December 2007, Incara plc began selling a particular model of satellite navigation system with a three-year warranty at no extra cost to the customer. Incara plc sells the navigation systems for €500 and, during the year ended 31 December 2007, 200 of these navigation systems were sold and included in revenue for the year ended 31 December 2007 at €500 each. One of Incara plc's competitors sells an identical navigation system without a warranty for €475, while an unrelated insurer offers an equivalent warranty for €75. The experience of other retailers suggests that the navigation systems have an equal probability of breaking down in each of the three years covered by the warranty.

Requirement   Prepare a memorandum addressed to the board of directors of Incara plc which explains:

(a) how the order from CCE Limited and the income from the sale of the navigation systems, together with the related warranties, have been accounted for in the financial statements of Incara plc for the year ended 31 December 2007; and

(b) the principles underlying revenue recognition and their application to different industries.

CHAPTER 5

INVESTMENT PROPERTY

INTRODUCTION

IAS 16 *Property, Plant and Equipment* requires all companies to depreciate their non-current assets (see Chapter 6). Investment properties are land and/or buildings held to earn rentals or for capital appreciation or both. Consequently, investment properties are not considered to be like most non-current assets since they are not acquired for 'use' in the organisation's operations in the traditional sense. Consequently, IAS 16 was considered inappropriate and a separate accounting standard was needed to account for investment properties. IAS 40 *Investment Property* prescribes the accounting treatment for investment properties, together with the related disclosure requirements.

After having studied this chapter, you should understand the following key points:

- The definition of investment properties;
- How to account for investment properties initially;
- The two allowable methods of measuring investment property subsequent to recognition;
- How to account for gains/losses using the fair value model;
- How to account for gains/losses on disposal of investment property; and
- The disclosure requirements of IAS 40.

IAS 40 *INVESTMENT PROPERTY*

Objective

The objective of IAS 40 is to prescribe the accounting treatment for investment property and related disclosure requirements.

Definitions and Examples

An investment property is property (land or a building – or part of a building – or both) held (by the owner or by the lessee under a finance lease) to earn rentals or for capital appreciation or both, rather than for:

- use in the production or supply of goods or services or for administrative purposes; or
- sale in the ordinary course of business.

The following are examples of items that *are* investment property:

(a) Land held for long-term capital appreciation rather than for short-term sale in the ordinary course of business;
(b) Land held for a currently undetermined future use (if any entity has not determined that it will use the land as owner occupied property, or for short-term sale in the ordinary course of business, the land is regarded as held for capital appreciation);
(c) A building owned by the entity (or held by the entity under a finance lease) and leased out under one or more operating leases;
(d) A building that is vacant but is held to be leased out under one or more operating leases; and
(e) Property that is being constructed or developed for future use as investment property.

The following are examples of items that *are not* investment property:

(a) Property intended for sale in the ordinary course of business or in the process of construction or development for such sale (IAS 2 *Inventories*);
(b) Property being constructed or developed on behalf of third parties (IAS 11 *Construction Contracts*);
(c) Owner occupied property (IAS 16); and
(d) Property that is leased to another entity under a finance lease.

Recognition and Initial Measurement

An investment property should be recognised as an asset when and only when:

(a) it is probable that the future economic benefits that are associated with the investment property will flow to the entity; and
(b) the cost of the investment property can be measured reliably i.e. the normal requirements for the recognition of assets.

Investment property should initially be measured at cost. Cost includes purchase price and any directly attributable expenditure such as professional fees for legal services, property transfer taxes and other transaction costs for self-constructed investment properties. Cost is the cost at the date when the construction or development is complete.

Subsequent expenditure is only recognised when it is probable that future economic benefits in excess of the originally assessed standard of performance will flow to the enterprise (all other subsequent expenditure is recognised as an expense in the period incurred).

Measurement after Recognition

An entity should choose as its accounting policy either the fair value model or the cost model and should apply that policy to *all* of its investment properties. When a property interest held under an operating lease is classified as an investment property there is no choice of accounting policy – the fair value model *must* be applied.

Fair Value Model

The fair value model measures all of its investment properties at fair value, on an annual basis. The fair value of investment property is the price at which property could be exchanged between knowledgeable, willing parties in an arm's length transaction. A gain or loss arising from a change in the fair value of investment property should be recognised in profit or loss for the period in which it arises.

Note

Fair value will normally be obtainable by reference to current prices on an active market for similar properties in the same location and conditions as the property under review. In the absence of such an active market, information from a variety of sources may have to be considered, including:

- current prices on an active market for properties of a different nature, condition or location adjusted to reflect those differences;
- recent prices on less active markets; and
- discounted cash flow projections based on reliable estimates of future cash flows.

When fair value cannot be reliably determined on a continuing basis (exceptional cases), the cost model should be used and retained until the property is disposed of.

Note

The fair value model under IAS 40 is not the same as the revaluation model under IAS 16 (the alternative accounting treatment of IAS 16). In the fair value model, all changes in fair value are recognised in the statement of comprehensive income for the period. In the revaluation model, increases in carrying amount are credited to a revaluation reserve.

The International Accounting Standards Board (IASB) believes that the fair value model is appropriate for investment properties, since this is consistent with the accounting for financial assets held as investments required by IAS 39 *Financial Instruments: Recognition and Measurement.*

Cost Model

An entity that chooses the cost model should measure all of its investment properties in accordance with IAS 16's requirements for that model (i.e. cost less accumulated depreciation and impairment losses). The exception to this rule is those properties that meet the criteria to be classified as held for sale (or are included in a disposal group that is classified as held for sale) in accordance with IFRS 5 *Non-Current Assets Held for Sale and Discontinued Operations*. These properties should be measured in accordance with IFRS 5.

Note
- IAS 8 *Accounting Policies, Changes in Accounting Estimates and Errors* states that a voluntary change in accounting policy should be made only if the change will result in a more appropriate presentation of transactions, other events or conditions in the entity's financial statements.
- IAS 40 requires all entities to determine the fair value of investment property for the purpose of either measurement (if the entity uses the fair value model) or disclosure (if it uses the cost model). An entity is encouraged, but not required, to determine the fair value of investment property on the basis of a valuation by an independent valuer who holds a recognised and relevant professional qualification and has recent experience in the location and category of the investment property being valued.

Example

ABC, a manufacturing company, purchases a property for €1,000,000 on 1 January 200X for its investment potential. The land element of the cost is believed to be €400,000 and the buildings element is expected to have a useful life of 50 years. At 31 December 200X, local property indices suggest that the fair value of the property has risen to €1,100,000

Requirement Show how the property would be presented in the financial statements as at 31 December 200X if ABC adopts a:

(a) cost-based policy; and
(b) fair value policy.

Solution

(a) Depreciation in the year is €600,000/50 = €12,000

   Therefore:
   - In the statement of comprehensive income, there will be a depreciation charge of €12,000; and
   - In the statement of financial position, the property will be shown at a net book value of €1,000,000 − €12,000 = €988,000.

(b) In the statement of financial position, the property will be shown at its fair value of €1,100,000. In the statement of comprehensive income, there will be a gain of €100,000 representing the fair value adjustment.

Transfers

Transfers to or from investment property should be made when and only when there is a change in use. For example:

- **Transfers from investment property** e.g. from investment property to owner occupied property the deemed cost for subsequent accounting is the fair value at the date of change in use;
- **Transfers to investment property** e.g. end of construction or development. The property would cease to be accounted for under IAS 16 and changed to IAS 40. Any difference between the carrying amount at the date of change and the fair value should be treated as a revaluation under IAS 16.

Table 5.1: Investment Property Transfers

Type	Treatment of Gain or Loss on Transfer
(a) Commencement of owner-occupation (investment property →owner-occupied)	Cost is fair value at date of transfer
(b) Commencement of development with a view to sale (investment property → inventories)	Cost is fair value at date of transfer
(c) End of owner-occupation (owner-occupied property →investment property)	IAS 16 applies till date of transfer; any difference is revaluation under IAS 16
(d) Commencement of an operating lease to another party (inventories →investment property)	Any difference is gain/loss in profit/loss for period
(e) End of construction or development (assets under course of construction (IAS 16) →investment property)	Any difference to fair value is recognised in profit/loss for period.

Disposals

Gains or losses arising from the retirement or disposal of investment property is the difference between the net disposal proceeds and the carrying amount of the asset and should be recognised in the profit or loss in the period of the retirement or disposal.

Disclosure Requirements

Disclosure requirements applicable to both cost based and fair value based investment properties

(a) Whether the cost model or the fair value model has been applied.
(b) Amounts included in the statement of comprehensive income for rental income for the period and operating expenses for the period.

(c) Details of any restrictions on the reliability of investment property or the remittance of income and proceeds of disposal.
(d) Contractual obligations to purchase, construct or develop investment properties.

Disclosure requirements for fair value based investment properties

(a) Methods and assumptions applied in determining the fair value of investment properties.
(b) The extent to which the fair value of investment property has been based on valuations by a qualified independent valuer.
(c) Additions and disposals during the period.
(d) Net gains or losses from fair value adjustments.
(e) Transfers (see above).

Disclosure requirements for cost based investment properties

(a) Depreciation methods used.
(b) Useful lives or depreciation rates used.
(c) Gross carrying amount and accumulated depreciation (including impairment losses) at the beginning and end of the period.
(d) A reconciliation of the carrying amount at the beginning and end of the period showing additions, disposals, depreciation, impairment losses recognised or reversed and transfers (see above).
(e) The fair value of the investment property or, if that fair value cannot be determined reliably, a description of the property, an explanation of why fair value cannot be determined reliably and, if possible, the range of estimates within which fair value is likely to be. Disclosures (a) and (b) above with respect to fair value based investment properties are required in connection with this disclosure by note of the fair value of cost based investment properties.

CONCLUSION

This chapter explains how to account for investment properties and illustrates the disclosure requirements for investment properties in accordance with IAS 40. Investment properties have the distinguishing feature that they earn cash flows largely independently of an enterprise's other assets, whereas owner-occupied properties earn revenues in combination with other assets normally in the production or supply process. The IASB believes this difference justifies a different accounting treatment for investment properties. Investment properties are held mainly to earn rental income or for capital appreciation (or both). They include properties that are owned and properties that are held on a finance lease by an enterprise. However, investment properties that are under construction or development are treated under IAS 16 *Property, Plant and Equipment* (see Chapter 6) until they are completed. The principle of recognition (i.e. meeting the definition of an asset), initial measurement (at cost) and subsequent expenditure on investment properties is similar to other assets (IAS 16 – see Chapter 6).

QUESTIONS

Self-test Questions

1. What is meant by an investment property?
2. How do you account for investment property?
3. How do you account for gains/losses on disposals of investment property?
4. Do you depreciate investment property?
5. What are the main disclosure requirements of IAS 40?

Review Questions

(See APPENDIX ONE for Suggested Solutions to Review Questions.)

Question 1

HELIX Limited (HELIX) purchased three identical properties (RIGHT, LEFT and UP), and leased a fourth (DOWN), during the year ended 31 December 2008.

*   RIGHT is used as HELIX's head office;
*   LEFT is let to, and occupied by, a subsidiary of HELIX;
*   UP is let to, and occupied by, an associate of HELIX; and,
*   DOWN is let to, and occupied by, a company outside the HELIX Group. The unexpired term on the lease is 12 years.

Requirement

Explain how each of the four properties should be treated in the financial statements of HELIX for the year ended 31 December 2008.

Challenging Questions

Question 1

United Limited, a company which manufactures sporting equipment and accessories, owns a number of properties which are listed below.

1. Trafford Lane: a freehold factory and office block used entirely by United Limited for its own manufacturing and administration.

2. Stretford Road: a freehold office block, let at commercial rates to a large insurance company.
3. Red Way: a property held by United Limited under a finance lease and leased out to City Limited under an operating lease.
4. Numbers 2, 4, 6 and 8 Black Street: four freehold cottages which were originally purchased to provide assistance to employees but are now let commercially to tenants who have no other connection with the company.

United Limited had all the above properties valued by an independent professional valuer on 31 May 2007. The following is a summary of the valuations and original costs of the properties:

	Cost		Valuation	
	Land	Buildings	Land	Buildings
Freehold Properties:	€	€	€	€
(1) Trafford Lane	10,000	24,000	40,000	90,000
(2) Stretford Road	25,000	60,000	30,000	80,000
(4) Black Street	4,000	8,000	16,000	24,000

Each of the above properties is estimated to have a further useful life of 40 years.

	Cost	Valuation
Leasehold Properties:	€	€
(3) Red Way	72,000	120,000

United Limited adopts a straight-line depreciation policy.

Requirement   Prepare the necessary journal entries to incorporate the above revaluations in the books of United Limited as at 31 December 2007.

CHAPTER 6

PROPERTY, PLANT AND EQUIPMENT

INTRODUCTION

The main purpose of this chapter is to explain the accounting treatment of property, plant and equipment in accordance with IAS 16 *Property, Plant and Equipment* so that users of financial statements can assess an entity's investment in such assets, together with any changes. Property, plant and equipment consist of tangible non-current assets that are held for use in the production or supply of goods or services, or for rental to others or for administrative purposes. It is important to clearly distinguish between properties that fall under IAS 16 and properties that fall under IAS 40 *Investment Property* (see Chapter 5).

After having studied this chapter on property, plant and equipment you should understand the following key points:

- non-current assets should be initially recognised as cost;
- the definition of cost;
- subsequent expenditure should be expensed but may be capitalised in certain circumstances;
- non-current assets may be revalued if the company adopts such a policy;
- the treatment of revaluation gains and losses;
- the definition of depreciation;
- how to account for a change in depreciation method; and
- the IAS 16 disclosure requirements.

IAS 16 *PROPERTY, PLANT AND EQUIPMENT*

Objective

The objective of IAS 16 is to prescribe the accounting treatment for property, plant and equipment, primarily dealing with the timing of recognition of the assets, their carrying amounts and associated depreciation.

Scope

IAS 16 prescribes the accounting treatment for property, plant and equipment, unless another standard requires or permits a different accounting treatment. For example:

- property, plant and equipment classified as held for sale in accordance with IFRS 5 *Non-current Assets Held for Sale and Discontinued Operations* (see Chapter 20);
- IAS 17 *Leases* (see Chapter 8); and
- IAS 40 *Investment property* (see Chapter 5).

Key Definitions

It is important to understand and be familiar with the following definitions.

1. **Carrying amount** – the amount at which an asset is recognised after deducting any accumulated depreciation and accumulated impairment losses.
2. **Cost** – the amount of cash or cash equivalents paid or the fair value of the other consideration given to acquire an asset at the time of its acquisition or construction or, where applicable, the amount attributed to that asset when initially recognised in accordance with the specific requirements of other IFRSs, e.g. IFRS 2 *Share-based Payment* (see Chapter 34).
3. **Depreciable amount** – the cost of an asset, or other amount substituted for cost, less its residual value.
4. **Depreciation** – the systematic allocation of the depreciable amount of an asset over its useful life.
5. **Entity-specific value** – the present value of the cash flows an entity expects to arise from the continuing use of an asset and from its disposal at the end of its useful life or expects to incur when settling a liability.
6. **Fair value** – the amount for which an asset could be exchanged between knowledgeable, willing parties in an arm's length transaction.
7. **Impairment loss** – the amount by which the carrying amount of an asset exceeds its recoverable amount. Impairment should be recognised in accordance with IAS 36 *Impairment of Assets* (see Chapter 10).
8. **Property, plant and equipment are tangible items that:**
   (a) are held for use in the production or supply of goods or services, for rental to others, or for administrative purposes; and
   (b) are expected to be used during more than one period.
9. **Recoverable amount** – the higher of an asset's net selling price and its value in use.
10. **Residual value of an asset** – the estimated amount that an entity would currently obtain from disposal of the asset, after deducting the estimated costs of disposal, if the asset were already of the age and in the condition expected at the end of its useful life.
11. **Useful life** is the:
    (a) period over which an asset is expected to be available for use by an entity; or
    (b) number of production or similar units expected to be obtained from the asset by an entity.

Recognition

The cost of an item of property, plant and equipment should be recognised as an asset if, and only if:

(a) it is probable that future economic benefits associated with the item will flow to the entity; and
(b) the cost of the item can be measured reliably.

An entity should *not* recognise in the carrying amount of an asset the costs of its day-to-day servicing – they should be expensed to the statement of comprehensive income as incurred.

Measurement at Recognition

All items of property, plant and equipment are initially recognised at cost, which includes:

- purchase price, including import duties and non-refundable purchase taxes, after deducting trade discounts and rebates; and
- any costs directly attributable to bringing the asset to the location and condition necessary for it to be capable of operating in the manner intended by management.

Examples of directly attributable costs are:

- costs of site preparation;
- initial delivery and handling costs;
- installation and handling costs;
- costs of testing whether the asset is functioning properly, after deducting the net proceeds from selling and items produced while bringing the asset to that location and condition (such as samples produced when testing equipment);
- professional fees; and
- the initial estimate of the costs of dismantling and removing the item and restoring the site on which it is located, the obligation for which an entity incurs either when the item is acquired or as a consequence of having used the item during a particular period for purposes other than to produce inventories during the period.

Example

A manufacturing company commissioned the building of a new factory. The costs associated were as follows:

	€
Site selection	30,000
Site purchase	1,000,000
Architect's fees	50,000
Engineer's fees	150,000
Legal fees	50,000
Construction costs	1,500,000
Testing and checking of machinery (Note 1)	250,000
Administration Costs	500,000

The plant was available for use on 31 March 200X and reached normal production levels by 31 October 200X.

Note 1

Included in testing and checking of machinery costs was €50,000 in connection with a six-monthly diagnostic check of machinery.

Requirement   Calculate the cost to be capitalised.

Solution

	€
Site cost	1,000,000
Construction cost	1,500,000
Architect's fees	50,000
Legal fees	50,000
Engineer's fees	150,000
Testing costs	200,000
Total cost	2,950,000

Note 1

€50,000 relating to the six-monthly diagnostic check is not included as it is a direct cost and neither was it a cost relating to the start-up period.

Note 2

Site selection and administration overheads are not direct costs.

Note 3

Subsequent expenditure on property, plant and equipment is only recognised as an asset when the expenditure *improves* the asset beyond its originally assessed standard of performance. For example:

- Modification extending useful life of plant; and
- Upgrading a machine.

Example

An aircraft is repainted. How should this expenditure be treated?

Solution

It should be written off to the statement of comprehensive income. This expenditure is too regular an occurrence to be seen as a separate 'component'.

Example

Manders Limited installs a new production process in its factory at a cost of €50,000. This enables a reduction in operating costs (as assessed when the original plant was installed) of €10,000 per year for at least the next fifteen years.

How should the expenditure be treated?

Solution

It should be capitalised and added to the original cost of the plant as it results in enhancement of economic benefits.

Measurement after Recognition

An entity should choose either the cost model or the revaluation model for each class of non-current assets.

Cost Model

Property, plant and equipment should be carried at cost less accumulated depreciation.

Revaluation Model

Property, plant and equipment should be carried at a revalued amount, being its fair value at the date of the revaluation less any subsequent accumulated depreciation and subsequent accumulated impairment losses. Fair value of land and buildings is usually market value determined by professionally qualifyied valuers. Fair value of plant and equipment is usually their market value determined by appraisal. In the rare case where there is no recognised market (e.g. because items are rarely sold) items are valued at their depreciated replacement cost.

Where an item of property, plant and equipment is revalued, **all** other assets in the same class should also be revalued. Revaluations should be made with sufficient regularity such that the carrying amount does not differ materially from that which would be determined using fair value at the reporting date. When an item of property, plant and equipment is revalued, the entire class of assets to which the item belongs must be revalued. Examples of separate classes include: land; land and buildings; machinery; motor vehicles; fixtures and fittings; and office equipment.

Accounting Treatment of Revaluations

If an asset's carrying amount is decreased as a result of a revaluation, the decrease should be recognised as an expense in the statement of comprehensive income in arriving at profit/loss for the year.

If an asset's carrying amount is increased as a result of a revaluation, the increase should be credited directly to 'equity' through 'other comprehensive income' (e.g. under the heading of gain on property revaluation) (see note below).

However, the increase should be recognised in the statement of comprehensive income in arriving at profit/loss for the year to the extent that it reverses a revaluation decrease of the same asset previously recognised in the statement of comprehensive income in arriving at profit/loss for the year (see note below).

Note

As a consequence of the revisions to IAS 1 *Presentation of Financial Statements* (effective for accounting periods beginning on or after 1 January 2009) (see Chapter 2), revaluation gains and losses which would previously have been shown in the statement of changes in equity are now included in the 'other comprehensive income' section of the statement of comprehensive income.

Example

X Limited had buildings with a book value of €142,000 at 31 December 200W (its year end). On 1 January 200X the property was professionally valued at €250,000.

Solution

Accounting entry:	DR	CR
DR Buildings	€108,0000	
CR Other comprehensive income – revaluation gain		€108,000

Example

Ben Limited purchased a tangible non-current asset for €200,000 on 1 April 200T. Depreciation is charged at 10% straight line. Net book value at 31 March 200V is €160,000. A revaluation in April 200V showed a valuation of €130,000.

Solution

Accounting entry:	DR	CR
DR Statement of comprehensive income – expenses	€30,000	
CR Tangible non-current assets		€30,000

Depreciation per annum for the year ending 31 March 200W and 200X:
= €130,000/8 = €16,250

Net Book Value 31 March 200X:
€130,000 – (2 x €16,250) = €97,500

Year ended 31 March 200Y:
On 1 April 200Y, the asset is revalued to €120,000.

Accounting entry:	DR	CR
DR Non-current asset	€22,500	
CR Statement of comprehensive income (in arriving at profit/loss for year)		€22,500

While the normal treatment for a revaluation deficit is to recognise it as an expense in the statement of comprehensive income, it can be debited to equity to the extent of any previous reserve in respect of the same asset.

Example

Ross Limited purchased a property for €1 million on 1 August 200T. The property has a useful life of 20 years and no residual value. Depreciation is charged on a straight line basis, and property is revalued annually. Depreciation is calculated on the opening book value. The property was valued as follows:

- 31 July 200U   €1,064,000; and
- 31 July 200V   €700,000.

Solution

	31.7.200U €	31.7.200V €
Cash/opening book value	1,000,000	1,064,000
Depreciation	50,000[1]	56,000[2]
Book value	950,000	1,008,000
Revaluation gain/(loss)	114,000	308,000
Recognised in 'other comprehensive income	114,000	(114,000)
Recognised in arriving at profit/loss	0	(194,000)
Closing book value	1,064,000	700,000

1. €1,000,000 ÷ 20 years
2. €1,064,000 ÷ 19 years

Depreciation

Key Points

1. The depreciable amount of an asset should be allocated on a systematic basis over its useful life. The charge for each year must be recognised in the statement of comprehensive income unless it is included in the carrying amount of another asset.
2. Each part of an item of property, plant and equipment with a cost that is significant in relation to the total cost of the item must be depreciated separately e.g. the airframe and engines of an aircraft.
3. The method of depreciation used must reflect the pattern in which the asset's future economic benefits are expected to be consumed.
4. The useful life of an asset and its residual value should be reviewed at each year end and adjusted as a change in accounting estimate (IAS 8 *Accounting Policies, Changes in Accounting Estimates and Errors*).

5. The method of depreciation should be reviewed at each year end and changed if there is a change in the expected pattern of consumption of future economic benefits – this is a change in an accounting estimate.
6. In general land has an unlimited useful life and is not depreciated.
7. An asset should not be depreciated when it becomes classified or held for sale under IFRS 5 or when it becomes derecognised (sold or no future economic benefits).

Depreciable Amount and Depreciation Period

The depreciable amount of an asset (cost/revalued amount less residual value) is allocated on a systematic basis over its useful life.

The residual value and the useful life of an asset should be reviewed at least at each financial year end, if expectations differ from previous estimates, the change should be accounted for as a change in accounting estimate in accordance with IAS 8.

If a useful economic life is revised, the carrying amount of the asset at the date of revision should be depreciated over the revised remaining useful economic life. There is no retrospective application. Frequently the date of revision is the first day of the year of change.

Example

Team Limited purchased a machine for €800,000 in June 200T. It is company policy to depreciate machinery over 10 years on a straight line basis, charging a full year in the year of purchase and none in the year of sale. During the year ended 31 March 200W the useful life of this machine was revised to 6 years in total because of technological advances.

Calculate the net book value of the asset at the date of revision – in this case the start of the year of change, i.e. 1 April 200V.

Solution

NBV at 1 April 200V: €800,000 × 80% = €640,000

Write off this amount over the remaining revised useful life: €640,000/4 = €160,000 p.a. i.e. no retrospective application

Depreciation Method

The depreciation method used should reflect the pattern in which the asset's future economic benefits are expected to be consumed by the entity.

Straight Line Method

This method requires three items of information:

1. Original cost of asset (C);
2. Estimated useful life of asset in years (N); and
3. Estimated scrap or realisable value at end of useful life (S).

Annual depreciation charge (D) is given by:

$$D = \frac{(C - S)}{N}$$

Example

Original cost of asset	€4,200
Estimated useful life	4 years
Estimated scrap value	€200

Solution

Annual depreciation charge:

$$= \frac{€4,200 - €200}{4} = €1,000 \text{ p.a.}$$

Reducing Balance

The depreciation charge is calculated by applying a fixed percentage to the net book amount (or written down value) of the asset. In the year in which the asset is acquired, the percentage is applied to the original or historical cost. In successive periods, the percentage is applied to the asset's written down value. The aim of this method is to reduce the net book amount to its scrap value at the end of the estimated useful life of the asset.

The depreciation method applied to an asset should be reviewed at least at *each* financial year end and, if there has been a significant change in the expected pattern of

Example

An asset cost €1,000. It has an expected nil scrap value and the business depreciates at the rate of 50% reducing balance.

Solution

	Depreciation Charge €	
Year 1	500	(€1000 × 50%)
Year 2	250	(€500 × 50%)
Year 3	125	(€250 × 50%)
Year 4	62	(€125 × 50%)
	937	

Note

Depreciation in the last year could be increased by (€1000 – €937) i.e. €63 to €125. One particular feature of the reducing balance method is that the net book value never equals zero.

consumption of the future economic benefits embodied in the asset, the method *should be* changed to reflect the changed pattern. Such a change should be accounted for as a change in an accounting estimate in accordance with IAS 8.

Example

An item of plant cost €600,000 in March 200T and was depreciated at 12½% reducing balance. During the year ended 31 December 200V, the directors changed the method to 20% straight line in order to give a fairer reflection of consumption of benefits. It is company policy to charge a full year's depreciation in the year of acquisition and none in the year of disposal.

Solution

1. Calculate the net book value at the start of the year of change.
   €600,000 × 87½% × 87½% = €459,375. i.e. to calculate net book value at 31 December 200V
2. Write off the NBV over the remaining life using the new method.
   Annual depreciation year ended 31 December 200V onwards = €459,375/3* = €153,125.
   *change to 20% −5 years, less 200T and 200V results in 3 years remanining.

Depreciation of Revalued Assets

The depreciation charge on a revalued asset should be calculated on the carrying amount of the asset (i.e. based on the revalued amount) and all charged to the statement of comprehensive income. The revaluation surplus included in equity in respect of an item of property, plant and equipment that has been revalued may be transferred directly to retained earnings when the asset is derecognised. This may involve transferring the whole of the surplus when the asset is retired or disposed of. Transfers from revaluation surplus to retained earnings are not made through profit or loss. However, some of the surplus may be transferred from the revaluation reserve as the asset is used by an entity to offset the additional depreciation. In such a case, the amount of the surplus transferred would be the difference between depreciation based on the revalued carrying amount of the asset and depreciation based on the asset's original cost. (See second example in section below dealing with 'Derecognition'.)

Other Issues

1. Separate Components

Some items of property, plant and equipment comprise separate components with different useful lives. For example, an aeroplane might itself have a life of 30 years while the seats and fabric in the interior only have a life of 5 years. In such situations the separate components should be capitalised as separate assets and each depreciated over their useful lives.

2. Major Inspection or Overhaul Costs

Normally all inspection and overhaul costs are expensed as they are incurred. However, to the extent that they satisfy the IAS 16 rules for separate components, such costs should be capitalised separately as a non-current asset and depreciated over their useful lives. The seats and fabric in the aeroplane in the above example show this rule in action. Every five years the cost of overhauling the interior of the plane should be capitalised as a non-current asset and depreciated over the five-year period before the next overhaul is carried out.

3. Treatment of Accumulated Depreciation at Date of Revaluation

When an item of property, plant and equipment is revalued any accumulated depreciation at the date of revaluation is treated in either of the following ways:

Method 1   The accumulated depreciation is restated proportionately with the gross carrying amount so that the carrying amount after revaluation equals the revalued amount.

Method 2   The accumulated depreciation is eliminated against the gross carrying amount and the net amount restated to the revalued amount of the asset.

Example

Top Limited has a building with the following carrying value at 1 January 200X:

	€
Cost	500,000
Cumulative depreciation	100,000
Carrying value	400,000

The building is revalued on 1 January 200X to €800,000.

Method 1:

	Before Revaluation	After Revaluation
	€	€
Cost/revalued amount	500,000	1,000,000
Cumulative depreciation	100,000	200,000
	400,000	800,000

Accounting Entry

DR	Buildings	€500,000	
CR	Cumulative depreciation		€100,000
CR	Revaluation reserve		€400,000

Buildings

	€		€
Balance b/d	500,000		
Revaluation reserve	500,000	Balance c/d	1,000,000
	1,000,000		1,000,000

Accumulative Depreciation

	€		€
Balance c/d	200,000	Balance c/d	100,000
		Revaluation reserve	100,000
	200,000		200,000

Method 2

	Before Revaluation	After Revaluation
	€	€
Cost/revalued amount	500,000	800,000
Cumulative depreciation	100,000	-
Carrying amount	400,000	800,000

Accounting Entries

DR		Cumulative depreciation	€100,000	
	CR	Buildings		€100,000
DR		Buildings	€400,000	
	CR	Revaluation reserve		€400,000

Buildings

	€		€
Balance b/d	500,000	Accumulated depreciation	100,000
Revaluation reserve	400,000	Balance c/d	800,000
	900,000		900,000

Accumulated Depreciation

	€		€
Buildings	100,000	Balance b/d	100,000
	100,000		100,000

Derecognition

The carrying amount of an item of property, plant and equipment should be derecognised:

(a) on disposal; or
(b) when no future economic benefits are expected from its use or disposal.

The gain or loss arising from derecognition of an item of property, plant and equipment should be included in profit or loss when the item is derecognised. Gains should not be classified as revenue
    The gain or loss arising from the derecognition of an item of property, plant and equipment should be determined as the difference between the net disposal proceeds, if any, and the carrying amount of the item.

Example

FIXIT Limited is preparing its financial statements for the year ended 31 December 2008. A van, which had cost €5,000 and had a net book value of €2,813 at 1 January 2008, was traded in on 1 March 2008 as a part exchange for the purchase of a new van which cost €7,800. A cheque for €5,800 was paid by the company to complete the purchase. Depreciation is charged on vans at 25% per annum on a straight line basis. A full year's depreciation is to be charged in the year of purchase and none in the year of sale.

Prepare the journal entries necessary to record the above in the company's financial statements for the year ended 31 December 2008.

Solution

	Dr €	Cr €
(1)		
Van – Cost of Additions	5,800	
Bank		5,800
Cheque payment for acquisition of new van		
Van – Cost of Additions	2,000	
Profit/loss on sale		2,000
Accumulated depreciation – Vans	2,187	
Cost of disposals – Vans		5,000
Profit/loss on sale	2,813	
Depreciation charge – Vans	1,950	
Accumulated depreciation – Van		1,950

Example

A company revalues its property every 2 years. Company policy is to charge a full year's depreciation in the year of acquisition and none in the year of disposal. Before the change on 31 December 2006 (see below), property was depreciated at 20% pa using the reducing balance method.

- 1 January 2005: Property purchased at a cost of €390,000.
- 31 December 2006: Property revalued to €275,000, with remaining useful economic life revised to 4 years and depreciation method being changed to straight line.
- 31 December 2008: Property revalued to €112,500, with decline believed to be permanent.
- 30 September 2009: Property sold for €125,000.

How would the property be reflected in the company's financial statements in each of the years ending 31 December 2005 to 2009?

Solution

		€
Cost		390,000
Deprecition @ 20% (RB)	(SCI)	(78,000)
NBV at 31/12/05		312,000
2006:		
Deprecition @ 20% (RB)	(SCI)	(62,400)
		249,600
Revlued at 31/12/06	(RR & SCE)	25,400
NBV at 31/12/06		275,000
2007:		
Depreciation @ 25% (SL)	(W1)	(68,750)
NBV at 31/12/07		206,250
2008:		
Depreciation @ 25%	(SL)	(68,750)
NBV at 31/12/08		137,500
Revaluation loss	(Transfer RR balance €19,050 to RE)	(25,000)
		112,500

2009:

30/9/09 proceeds	(125,000)
Profit on disposal	12,500
W1	€
Depreciation based on HC (€249,600/4 years)	62,400
Depreciation based on valuation	(68,750)
Transfer from revaluation reserve	6,350

RR balance €19,050 (€25,400 – €6,350). The transfer cannot be reported in the SCI as the gain reported in SCE in 2006.

Disclosure Requirements

IAS 16 has extensive disclosure requirements. These include:

(a) Measurement bases used (e.g. cost or valuation);
(b) Depreciation methods used;
(c) Useful lives or depreciation rates used;
(d) Gross carrying amount and accumulated depreciation, at the beginning and end of the period;
(e) Reconciliation of opening and closing figures with details of additions, disposals and depreciation;
(f) Details of any pledging of items of property, plant and equipment as security for liabilities;
(g) Commitments for future capital expenditure;
(h) If the asset has been revalued:
  (i) basis of valuation;
  (ii) date of valuation;
  (iii) whether an independent valuer was used;
  (iv) the carrying value of the assets if no revaluation had taken place; and
  (v) the revaluation surplus.

CONCLUSION

The accounting treatment prescribed in IAS 16 applies to most property, plant and equipment unless another IAS/IFRS requires or permits an alternative accounting treatment: for example, IFRS 5 *Non-current Assets Held for Sale and Discontinued Operations* (see Chapter 20) and IAS 40 *Investment Property* (see Chapter 5).

Property, plant and equipment is vital to business operations, but often cannot be easily liquidated. Depending on the nature of a company's business, the total value of property, plant and equipment can range from very low to extremely high compared to total assets. An example of a business with a high amount of property, plant and equipment might be a shipping company, because most of its assets will be tied into its fleet of ships and administrative buildings. On the other hand, an accounting firm is likely to have less property, plant and equipment because it is likely to need only computer equipment and an office in a building to provide its services. Property, plant and equipment is disclosed separately in financial statements because it is treated differently. This is because improvements, replacements and betterments can pose accounting issues depending on how the costs are recorded.

QUESTIONS

Self-test Questions

1. What elements of expenditure are included in the production cost of a non-current asset?
2. What disclosures are required when a non-current asset is revalued?
3. In what circumstances may an amount be transferred from the revaluation reserve to a credit on the statement of comprehensive income?
4. What is depreciation?
5. What accounting treatment is required if the estimated useful life of a fixed asset is revised?

Review Questions

(See APPENDIX ONE for Suggested Solutions to Review Questions.)

Question 1

You have just been given the fixed assets section from the audit file of WELLER Limited (WELLER) in relation to the financial statements for the year ended 31 December 2008 with a note from the partner-in-charge asking you to clear the outstanding review points.

Review point 1   WELLER owns two freehold properties, one in Derry and the other in Cork. The company uses both as regional administrative offices. The properties had an expected useful life of 50 years on their date of acquisition, and the directors believe that this assumption is still appropriate at 31 December 2008. It is company policy to depreciate the properties on a straight-line basis over their estimated useful economic life.

	Derry property	Cork property
Date of acquisition	1 January 1999	1 January 1999
Original cost	€5,000,000	€5,000,000
Net book value at 31 December 2008	€4,000,000	€4,000,000
Market value at 31 December 2008	€3,000,000	€7,000,000

In the financial statements for the year ended 31 December 2008, the directors of WELLER are proposing to show the Cork property at market value and the Derry property at its depreciated historic cost. The directors believe the fall in the market value of the Derry property is only temporary and property values in the Derry area will rise in the next one to two years.

Is the policy put forward by the directors of WELLER acceptable?

Review point 2   On 1 January 2008, WELLER entered into a contract with a building company to build a new manufacturing facility for the company at a cost of €10,000,000. In order to finance the cost of the contract, WELLER entered into a short-term loan agreement with its bankers to borrow €10,000,000 at an interest rate of 6% per annum for the year that the manufacturing facility would take to build. The manufacturing facility was completed on 31 December 2008 and the loan was repaid on the same date. As WELLER's profits for the year ended 31 December 2008 are lower than expected, the directors of WELLER wish to capitalise the loan interest paid.

Is the policy put forward by the directors of WELLER acceptable?

Review point 3   On 1 July 2008, WELLER signed, as tenant, an operating lease of a warehouse which it intends to use as a distribution depot. However the warehouse needed to be fitted out before it could be used. The monthly rental for the warehouse is €10,000, commencing on 1 July 2008. The fitting was completed on 1 December 2008 and the warehouse became operational on this date.

The directors of WELLER wish to capitalise the rent paid during the five month fitting out period together with the cost of the fixtures and fittings.

Is the policy put forward by the directors of WELLER acceptable?

Review point 4   TAYLOR Limited (TAYLOR) is also an audit client of your firm. The company operates in the same business as WELLER and is similar in size. Both companies purchased identical equipment from the same supplier on 1 January 2007 at a cost of €6,000,000. Shown below are extracts from the fixed assets notes of both companies in respect of this equipment.

	WELLER	TAYLOR
	€	€
Plant and equipment – cost	6,000,000	6,000,000
Plant and equipment – accumulated depreciation	(2,400,000)	(1,500,000)
Net book value at 31 December 2008	3,600,000	4,500,000

What are the possible reasons for the difference in the net book value of the equipment held by the two companies at 31 December 2008 and what problems might this present when reading and comparing financial statements?

Review point 5   In 1996, WELLER purchased freehold land that it carries in its financial statements at its original cost of €1,000,000 without charging depreciation.

Are there valid reasons for the policy of non-depreciation of freehold land?

Requirement   Prepare a memorandum addressed to the partner-in-charge of the audit of WELLER addressing the issues raised in each of the review points.

Challenging Questions

Question 1

Seamus plc manufactures and operates a fleet of small aircraft. It draws up its financial statements to 31 March each year.

Seamus plc also owns a small chain of hotels (carrying value of €16 million), which are used in the sale of holidays to the public. It is the policy of the company not to provide depreciation on the hotels as they are maintained to a high standard and the economic lives of the hotels are long (20 years remaining life). The hotels are periodically revalued and on 31 March 2006, their existing use value was determined to be €20 million, the replacement cost of the hotels was €16 million and the open market value was €19 million. One of the hotels included above is surplus to the company's requirements as at 31 March 2006. This hotel had an existing use value of €3 million, a replacement cost of €2 million and an open market value of €2.5 million, before expected estate agent's and solicitor's fees of €200,000. The company wishes to revalue the hotels as at 31 March 2006. There is no indication of any impairment in the value of the hotels.

The company has recently finished manufacturing a fleet of five aircraft to a new design. These aircraft are intended for use in its own fleet for domestic carriage purposes. The company commenced construction of the assets on 1 April 2004 and wishes to recognise them as fixed assets as at 31 March 2006 when they were first utilised. The aircraft were completed on 1 January 2006 but their exterior painting was delayed until 31 March 2006.

The costs (excluding finance costs) of manufacturing the aircraft amounted to €28 million and the company has adopted a policy of capitalising the finance costs of manufacturing the aircraft. Seamus plc had taken out a three-year loan of €20 million to finance the aircraft on 1 April 2004. Interest is payable at 10% per annum but is to be rolled over and paid at the end of the three-year period together with the capital outstanding. Corporation tax is 30%.

During the construction of the aircraft, certain computerised components used in the manufacture fell dramatically in price. The company estimated that at 31 March 2006 the net realisable value of the aircraft was €30 million and their value in use was €29 million.

The engines used in the aircraft have a three-year life and the body parts have an eight-year life; Seamus plc has decided to depreciate the engines and the body parts over their different useful lives on the straight line basis from 1 April 2006. The cost of replacing the engines on 31 March 2009 is estimated to be €15 million. The engine costs represent thirty per cent of the total cost of manufacture.

The company has decided to revalue the aircraft annually on the basis of their market value. On 31 March 2007, the aircraft have a value in use of €28 million, a market value of €27 million and a net realisable value of €26 million. On 31 March 2008 the aircraft have a value in use of €17 million, a market value of €18 million and a net realisable value of €18.5 million. There is no consumption of economic benefits in 2008 other than the depreciation charge. Revaluation surpluses or deficits are apportioned between the engines and the body parts on the basis of their year end carrying values before the revaluation.

Requirement

(a) Explain how the hotels should be valued in the financial statements of Seamus plc on 31 March 2006 and explain whether the current depreciation policy relating to the hotels is acceptable under IAS 16 *Property, Plant and Equipment*.
(b) Show the accounting treatment of the aircraft fleet in the financial statements on the basis of the above scenario for the financial years ending on:
   (i) 31 March 2006;
   (ii) 31 March 2007 and 2008;
   (iii) 31 March 2009 before revaluation.
(c) Discuss the economic consequences of asset revaluations.

CHAPTER 7

BORROWING COSTS

INTRODUCTION

Borrowings costs are 'traditionally' recognised as an expense when incurred. Indeed, the previous version of IAS 23 *Borrowing Costs* (which was in force until 1 January 2009) required that borrowing costs be normally recognised as an expense in the period incurred (benchmark treatment). As an alternative, the previous IAS 23 allowed borrowing costs that were directly attributable to the acquisition, construction or production of a qualifying asset (i.e. an asset that takes a substantial period of time to get ready for its intended use or sale) to be capitalised as part of the cost of that asset. In contrast, the revised IAS 23 (effective for accounting periods beginning on or after 1 January 2009) requires that qualifying borrowing costs *must be* capitalised. This is a significant change and is likely to involve increased compliance costs for those organisations that previously expensed borrowing costs. The International Accounting Standards Board (IASB) believes that these increased compliance costs will be offset by the improved comparability of financial statements.

After having studied this chapter on borrowing costs, you should understand the following key points:

- IAS 23 regulates the extent to which enterprises are allowed to capitalise borrowing costs incurred on money borrowed to finance the acquisition of certain assets;
- Qualifying borrowing costs *must be* capitalised as part of the cost of an asset if that asset is one which necessarily takes a substantial time to get ready for its intended use or sale; and
- IAS 23 disclosure requirements.

IAS 23 *BORROWING COSTS*

The objective of IAS 23 is to prescribe the accounting treatment for borrowing costs. This standard now requires the capitalisation of borrowing costs that are directly attributable to the acquisitions, construction or production of a qualifying asset.

Definitions

- **Borrowing costs** – interest and other costs incurred by an entity in connection with the borrowing of funds. Examples of borrowing costs include:
  - interest on bank overdrafts and other short-term and long-term borrowings;
  - amortisation of discounts and premiums on borrowings;
  - finance charges in respect of finance leases (IAS 17 *Leases*); and
  - exchange differences arising from foreign currency borrowings when they cause adjustments to interest costs.
- **Qualifying asset** – an asset that necessarily takes a substantial period of time to get ready for its intended use or sale.

Accounting Treatment

Borrowing costs *must be* capitalised as part of the cost of an asset when:

1. it is probable that the costs will result in future economic benefits and the costs can be reliably measured; and
2. they are directly attributable and they would have been avoided if the asset was not bought, constructed or produced.

Where borrowings specifically relate to expenditure on an asset, the amount of borrowing costs which should be capitalised is the actual costs less any investment income received from the temporary reinvestment of unutilised borrowings (i.e. barrowings drawn down but not yet spent and therefore available for investment until required). When funds are borrowed generally and used to obtain a qualifying asset, the amount to be capitalised is calculated as follows: asset cost x capitalisation rate (weighted average). The total cost of a qualifying asset to be recognised cannot exceed its recoverable amount, and the amount of borrowing costs capitalised in a period cannot exceed the amount incurred in that period. IAS 23 allows exchange differences arising from foreign currency borrowings to be capitalised as borrowing costs to the extent that they are regarded as an adjustment to interest costs. From a practical aspect, this involves determining how much of the exchange difference can be capitalised. This would be to the extent that the exchange difference represents an adjustment to the interest cost of the borrowings. This could involve identifying another local currency loan which could have been taken at the same time for the same purpose and based on that calculating how much of the borrowing cost can be capitalised.

Period of Capitalisation

Capitalisation should commence when expenditure on the asset and borrowing costs are being incurred.

Capitalisation of borrowing costs should be suspended during extended periods in which active development is interrupted.

Capitalisation should cease when substantially all the activities necessary to prepare the relevant asset for its intended use have been completed.

Example

On 1 January 200Y, X began to construct a supermarket. It purchased a leasehold interest in the site for €25 million. The construction of the building cost €9 million and the fixtures and fittings cost €6 million. The construction of the supermarket was completed on 30 September 200Y and it was brought into use on 1 January 200Z.

X borrowed €40 million in order to finance this project. The loan carried interest at 10% per annum. It was repaid on 30 June 200Z.

Requirement   Calculate the total amount to be included in property, plant and equipment in respect of the development at 31 December 200Y.

Solution

The total amount to be included in property, plant and equipment at 31 December 200Y is:

	€m
Lease	25
Building	9
Fittings	6
Interest capitalised (40 x 10% x 9/12)	3
Carrying value	43

Only nine months interest can be capitalised, because IAS 23 activities states that capitalisation of borrowing costs must cease when substantially all the activates necessary to prepare the assets for its intended use or sale are complete. The interest incurred from the date the construction was completed to the date when the loan is repaid is charged to the statement of comprehensive income. No depreciation is charged in 200Y, because the supermarket is not brought into use until 1 January 200Z.

Disclosure Requirements

The financial statements must disclose the:
(a) amount of borrowing costs capitalised during the period; and
(b) capitalisation rate used to determine the amount of borrowing costs eligible for capitalisation.

CONCLUSION

The amendments to IAS 23 eliminate the option available under the previous version of the IAS to recognise all borrowing costs immediately as an expense. To the extent that borrowing costs relate to the acquisition, construction or production of a qualifying asset, the revised IAS 23 requires that they be capitalised as part of the cost of that asset. All other borrowing costs should be expensed as incurred. The amendments were made as part of the IASB's ongoing convergence project with US Generally Accepted Accounting Principles (US GAAP). They eliminate the main difference in the fundamental accounting recognition principle between IASs/IFRSs and US GAAP (FAS 34 *Capitalization of Interest Cost*) in this area, although significant measurement differences remain. However, other differences also remain; in particular regarding the definition of borrowing costs that are eligible for capitalisation, the definition of a qualifying asset and the detailed calculation of the amount to be capitalised. Therefore, even after the amendments to IAS 23 have been adopted, in many cases the amount capitalised under IAS 23 will not be the same as the amount that would be capitalised under US GAAP

QUESTIONS

Self-test Questions

1. What are the arguments for and against the capitalisation of borrowing costs?
2. What is the accounting treatment for qualifying borrowing costs?
3. When may capitalisation of borrowing costs begin and when must it end?

Review Questions

(See APPENDIX ONE for Suggested Solutions to Review Questions.)
Question 1

On 1 January 2009, ROBINSON plc (ROBINSON) entered into a contract with a building company to build a new administrative and visitors' facility for the company at a cost of €10,000,000. In order to finance the cost of the contract, ROBINSON entered into a short-term loan agreement with its bankers to borrow €10,000,000 at an interest rate of 6% per annum for the year that it would take to build the facility. The construction of the facility is expected to be completed on 31 December 2009 and the company intends to repay the loan on the same date. As ROBINSON's profits for the year ended 31 December 2009 are likely to be lower than expected, the directors wish to capitalise the loan interest paid.

Requirement   Is the policy put forward by the directors of ROBINSON acceptable?

Challenging Questions

Question 1

YELLOW Limited (YELLOW), a company that prepares its financial statements to 31 December each year, is involved in the manufacture of made-to-order customised sports cars. The company commenced trading in January 2002 and has gained an excellent reputation within this specialised industry.

In January 2006, YELLOW commenced a programme to extend and modernise the company's manufacturing facilities. The programme cost €1,000,000 and YELLOW financed the work through a mixture of general and specific debt. The directors estimate that 50% of the programme was financed by general debt and 50% by specific debt. YELLOW's current general borrowing rate is 10% per annum, while the specific debt carries an interest rate of general 15% per annum. The programme was completed on 31 December 2006.

Requirement   Explain how YELLOW should account for the borrowing costs in the financial statements for the year ended 31 December 2006.

CHAPTER 8

LEASES

INTRODUCTION

A lease is an agreement whereby the lessor conveys to the lessee, in return for a payment or series of payments, the right to use an asset for an agreed period of time. A finance lease is one that transfers substantially all of the risks and rewards of ownership to the lessee, while an operating lease is one that does not. This chapter addresses the accounting treatment of, and disclosure requirements for, finance leases and operating leases in the books of lessees and lessors in accordance with current recommended practice. IAS 17 *Leases* prescribes, for lessees and lessors, the accounting policies and disclosures that apply to leases. Exceptions to IAS 17 are:

(a) property accounted for as an investment property (IAS 40 *Investment Property*); and
(b) biological assets held by lessees under finance leases or held by lessors under operating leases.

After having studied this chapter, you should understand the following key points:

- The distinction between a finance and an operating lease;
- How to account for an operating lease;
- How to account for a finance lease from the lessee point of view; and
- The disclosure requirements for both operating leases and finances leases (lessee only).

KEY DEFINITIONS

Operating Lease

This type of lease does not transfer all the risks and rewards incidental to ownership. The lessor retains most of the risks and rewards of ownership of an asset in the case of an operating lease. At the inception of the lease, the present value of minimum lease payments *does not* amount to substantially all of the fair value of the leased asset. Other indicators are that the lease term is significantly less than the useful life of the asset, e.g. leasing a car for

2 years. An operating lease involves the lessee paying a rental for the hire of an asset for a period of time which is normally substantially less than its useful economic life.

Finance Lease

A finance lease is a lease that transfers substantially all the risks and rewards incidental to the ownership of an asset (to the lessee). Title may or may not be eventually transferred. The substance of the transaction dictates rather than the form of the contract. A finance lease usually involves payment by a lessee to a lessor at the full cost of the asset together with a return on the finance provided by the lessor. IAS 17 identifies five situations which would normally lead to a lease being classified as a finance lease:

1. The lease transfers ownership of the asset to the lessee at the end of the lease term;
2. The lessee has the option to purchase the asset at a price sufficiently below fair value at exercise date and it is reasonably certain the option will be exercised;
3. The lease term is for a major part of the asset's economic life even if title is not transferred;
4. The present value of minimum lease payments amounts to substantially all of the asset's value at inception; and
5. The leased asset is so specialised that it could only be used by the lessee without major modifications being made.

Other indicators include:

(a) when the lessee can cancel the agreement and any losses are borne by the lessee; or
(b) when the lessee has the right to continue the lease for a secondary period at a rent which is much lower than market rent;

Lease Term

The lease term is the non-cancellable period for which the lessee has contracted to lease the asset together with any further terms for which the lessee has the option to continue to lease the asset, with or without further payment, which option at the inception of the lease it is reasonably certain that the lessee will exercise.

Minimum Lease Payments

The minimum lease payments are the payments over the lease term that the lessee is, or can be, required to make, excluding contingent rent, costs for services and taxes to be paid by and reimbursed to the lessor, together with any amounts guaranteed by the lessee or related party.

Fair Value

Fair value is the amount for which an asset could be exchanged or a liability settled, between knowledgeable willing parties in an arm's length transaction.

Interest Rate Implicit in the Lease

This is the discount rate that, at the inception of a lease, causes the aggregate present value of the minimum lease payments and the unguaranteed residual value to be equal to the fair value of the leased asset.

Land and Buildings

When classifying a lease of land and buildings, the elements of the land and the buildings should be treated separately. Land would normally be classified as an operating lease, unless title passes at the end of the lease term. The buildings' element should be classified in accordance with the criteria in IAS 17.

ACCOUNTING FOR OPERATING LEASES

Operating Leases in the Financial Statements of Lessors

The asset is capitalised and depreciated in the normal way. The depreciation policy should be consistent with the lessor's normal depreciation policy for similar assets and accounted for under IAS 16 *Property, Plant and Equipment*.

Lease income should be recognised in the statement of comprehensive income on a straight line basis over the lease term unless another systematic basis gives a better representation of the time pattern in which use benefit from the asset is diminished.

Operating Leases in the Financial Statements of Lessees

Operating leases do not really pose an accounting problem. Payments by the lessee are charged to the lessee's statement of comprehensive income. The rentals should be charged/credited to the statement of comprehensive income on a straight line basis over the lease term. (Consequently, an accrual or prepayment will be necessary if the rental payments are uneven.)

The standard requires the use of the straight line method unless a more systematic and more rational basis is appropriate, e.g. where the time pattern of the benefits received would be better represented by other than a straight line method.

The notes to the financial statements of the lessee must disclose the minimum lease payments for each of the following periods:

1. not later than one year;
2. later than one year but not later than five years; and
3. later than five years.

Example

Ben Limited leased a car for its Managing Director with the following terms:

Cost of car	€24,000	Term	2 years
Rental	€1,040 per month	Implied rate of interest	18%

Solution

The rental should be written off to the statement of comprehensive income on a straight line basis over two years.

Operating Lease Rentals:

Cash   €12,480   Statement of comprehensive income €12,480

ACCOUNTING FOR FINANCE LEASES

Finance Leases in the Financial Statements of Lessors

- Lessors should recognise assets held under a finance lease in their statement of financial position as a receivable at an amount equal to the net investment in the lease.
- Each rental received should be split between interest receivable and a reduction in the asset, i.e. investment in finance leases.
- The recognition of finance income (interest) should be based on a pattern reflecting a constant periodic rate of return on the lessor's net investment in the lease – use the actuarial method as in the lessee's books.
- There is no non-current asset in the statement of financial position.
- There is no depreciation charge.

Example

CROSSBOW Limited, a manufacturer of machinery, leased out two machines during the year ended 31 December 2008 as follows:

	Machine A	Machine B
Annual rental	€8,000	€10,000
Cost of production	€25,000	€30,000

Expected useful life	8 years	8 years
Lease term	2 years	8 years
Normal sales value	€40,000	€45,000

Requirement

In accordance with IAS 17 Leases, calculate the selling profit in respect of machines A and B that should be recognised in the statement of comprehensive income of CROSSBOW Limited for the year ended 31 December 2008.

Solution

Machine A is an operating lease and therefore no selling profit should be recognised. Machine B is a finance lease and the selling profit is restricted to the excess of the normal sales value over cost, i.e. €15,000 (€45,000 - €30,000).

Finance Leases in the Financial Statements of Lessees

IAS 17 requires that a finance lease be capitalised (i.e. shown as a tangible non-current asset under the subheading 'leased assets') in the lessee's accounts, despite the fact that the lessee is not the legal owner of the asset. This treatment recognises that, on occasions, the substance of a transaction should take precedence over its 'legal form', to ensure that the financial statements show as fair a picture as possible for the user. The explanatory note to the standard argues that it is not the asset itself, but the lessee's 'rights in the asset' which are being capitalised. Note that, in addition to capitalising the asset, the obligation of the lessee to make future payments will be shown as a liability. Rentals payable should be apportioned between the finance charge and a reduction of the outstanding obligation for future amounts payable. The finance charge is then apportioned to accounting periods so as to produce a constant periodic rate of charge on the remaining balance of the obligation for each accounting period.

Statement of Financial Position

The finance lease should be included in the statement of financial position of the lessee by recording an asset (e.g. leased plant) and a liability (obligation under finance lease) at the fair value of the asset or the present value of the minimum lease payment if lower. The discount rate used to calculate the present value is the interest rate implicit in the lease.

DR   Asset
CR   Obligation under finance lease

The amount to be recorded in this way is the capital cost or fair value of the asset. This may be taken as the amount which the lessee might expect to pay for it in a cash transaction. The amount shown as a liability will be reduced each year by the capital element of payments made each year.

Depreciation for non-current assets held under finance leases must be consistent with that for similar assets which are owned. If there is no reasonable certainty that the lessee will obtain ownership at the end of the lease, the asset should be depreciated over the shorter of the lease term or the life of the asset.

Apportionment of Rental Payments

When the lessee makes a rental payment it will comprise of two elements:

1. An interest charge on the finance provided by the lessor. The total finance charge is allocated to each period over the lease term so as to produce a constant periodic rate of interest on the remaining balance of the obligation. This proportion of each payment is interest payable in the statement of comprehensive income; and
2. A repayment of part of the capital cost of the asset. In the lessee's books this proportion of each rental payment must be debited to the lessor's account to reduce the outstanding liability.

The accounting problem is to decide what proportion of each instalment paid by the lessee represents interest, and what proportion represents a repayment of the capital advanced by the lessor. There are three ways in which you may do this:

*   The level spread method;
*   The actuarial method; or
*   The sum-of-the-digits method

Contingent rents must be charged as expenses in the year in which incurred.

The Level Spread Method

The level spread method is based on the assumption that finance charges accrue evenly over the term of the lease agreement.

For example, if an asset with a fair value of €3,000 is being 'acquired' on a finance lease for five payments of €700 each, the total interest is €(3,500 – 3,000) = €500. This is assumed to accrue evenly and therefore €100 interest is structured into each rental payment, the €600 balance of each instalment being the capital repayment.

The level spread method is quite unscientific and takes no account of the commercial realities of the transaction.

Actuarial Method

This method is the best and most scientific method. It derives from the assumption that the interest charged by the lessor company will equal the rate of return desired by the company, multiplied by the amount of capital it has invested.

Therefore

(a) At the beginning of the lease the capital invested is equal to the fair value of the asset (less any initial deposit paid by the lessee).
(b) This amount reduces as each instalment is paid. It follows that the interest accruing is greatest in the early part of the lease term, and gradually reduces as capital is repaid.

Example

(Payment of rentals in arrears)

On 1 January 200W DEF Limited, a wine merchant, buys a small bottling machine from BAS Limited on hire purchase terms. The cash price of the machine was €7,710 while the total lease price was €10,000. The lease agreement required the immediate payment of a €2,000 deposit with the balance being settled in four equal annual instalments commencing on 31 December 200W. The lease charge of €2,290 represents interest of 15% per annum, calculated on the remaining balance of the liability during each accounting period. Depreciation on the plant is to be provided for at the rate of 20% per annum on a straight-line basis assuming a residual value of nil.

Requirement   Show the breakdown of each instalment between interest and capital using the actuarial method.

Solution

Interest is calculated as 15% of the outstanding capital balance at the beginning of each year. The outstanding capital balance reduces each year by the capital element in each instalment. The outstanding capital balance at 1 January 200W is €5,710 (€7,710 fair value less €2,000 deposit).

	Total	Capital	Interest
	€	€	€
Capital balance at 1 January 200W		5,710	
1st Instalment	2,000	1,144	856
(Interest €5,710 x 15%)			
Capital balance at 1 January 200X		4,566	
2nd instalment	2,000	1,315	685

(Interest €4,566 x 15%)			
Capital balance at 1 January 200Y		3,251	
3rd Instalment	2,000	1,512	488
(Interest €3,251 x 15%)			
Capital balance 1 January 200Z		1,739	
4th Instalment	2,000	1,739	261
(Interest €1,739 x 15%)			
	8,000	-	2,290

Example

(Payment of rentals in advance)

The terms of a finance lease are as follows:

Cost of asset – €25,000;
Estimated useful life – 5 years;
Lease terms for 5 years at €6,500 per annum in advance; and
Implied rate of interest – 15.2%

Solution

Finance Charge – the total finance charge is the total payment less the cost of the asset.

	€
Total payments (€6,500 x 5)	32,500
Cost of asset	(25,000)
Total finance charge	7,500

Calculation of finance charge element and capital element:

Year	Opening Capital Balance	Rental	Capital	Accrued Finance Charge 15.2%	Closing Capital Balance
	€	€	€	€	€
1	25,000	6,500	6,500	2,812(a)	18,500

2	18,500	6,500	3,688	2,251(b)	14,812
3	14,812	6,500	4,249	1,606	10,563
4	10,563	6,500	4,894	862	5,669
5	5,669	6,500	5,638	—	—
			24,969		

(€25,000 – €6,500) x 15.2%
(€18,500 – €3,688) x 15.2%

Assumptions

The first payment is in advance and it is deemed to be all capital. Therefore, as the payment in year one was deemed to be a 'capital' advance, an accrual of €2,812 must be made in respect of the finance charge for year one in accordance with the matching concept.

Note
It is arguably equally valid to assume that the first payment (in advance) includes the repayment of both interest and capital for year one. While there would still be an interest expense in the statement of comprehensive income in year one, there would be no interest accrual in the statement of financial position at the end of year one. This assumption would therefore result in a different Current Liability/Non-Current Liability (CL/NCL) split.

The payment on the first day of year two will first go towards clearing this finance charge accrual. The balance is available to reduce the capital outstanding to €14,812 for year two.

Statement of Comprehensive Income:

Year	Finance Charge	Depreciation Charge	Total Charge
	€	€	€
1	2,812	5,000	7,812
2	2,251	5,000	7,251
3	1,606	5,000	6,606
4	(862 - 31)	5,000	5,831
5	—	5,000	5,000

There is no finance charge in year five because the full liability is paid off on the first day of the year and so no interest is chargeable.

Statement of Financial Position (Extract)

	Year 1 €	Year 2 €	Year 3 €	Year 4 €	Year 5 €
Tangible assets held under finance leases:					
Cost	25,000	25,000	25,000	25,000	25,000
Accumulated depreciation	5,000	10,000	15,000	20,000	25,000
Net book value	20,000	15,000	10,000	5,000	-
Non-current liabilities					
Net obligations under finance leases:	14,812	10,563	5,669	-	-
Current Liabilities					
Net obligation under finance lease	3,688	4,249	4,894	5,638	-
Accruals (finance charges due)	2,812	2,251	1,606	831	-
	6,500	6,500	6,500	6,500	Nil

Leased Asset

	Year 1 (€)		Year 1 (€)
Obligation under finance			
Lease (fair value)	25,000	Balance c/d	25,000

Obligation under Finance Lease

	Year 1 (€)		Year 1 (€)
Cash (rental)	6,500		25,000
Balance c/d net obligation	18,500	Leased asset	25,000
Interest	2,812	SCI (interest)	2,812
	27,812		27,812

Depreciation - Leased Asset

	Year 1 (€)		Year 1 (€)
Balance c/d	5,000	SCI	5,000

Sum-of-the-Digits Method

IAS 17 states that in practice when allocating the finance charge to periods during the term a lessee may use some form of approximation to simplify the calculation. The rule of 78 (sum of digits) is an acceptable approximation. When the payment is in advance use the sum of the digits of the term minus 1.

This method approximates to the actuarial method, splitting the total interest in such a way that the greater proportion falls in the earlier years. The procedure is as follows:

(a) Assign a digit to each instalment. The digit 1 should be assigned to the final instalment, 2 to the penultimate instalment and so on;
(b) Add the digits. If there are twelve instalments, then the sum of the digits will be 78 etc.

Example

Using the information from the above example (Payment of rentals in arrears), show the breakdown of each instalment between interest and capital using the sum-of-the-digits method.

Solution

Each instalment is allocated a digit as follows:

Instalment	Digit
1st (200W)	4
2nd (200X)	3
3rd (200Y)	2
4th (200Z)	1
	10

The €2,290 interest charges can then be apportioned:

		€
1st Instalment	€2,290 × 4/10	916
2nd Instalment	€2,290 × 3/10	687
3rd Instalment	€2,290 × 2/10	458
4th Instalment	€2,290 × 1/10	229
		2290

	1st Instalment	2nd Instalment	3rd Instalment	4th Instalment
	€	€	€	€
Interest	916	687	229	458
Capital (bal)	1,084	1,313	1,542	1,771
	2,000	2,000	2,000	2,000

Example

Using the information from the above example (Payment of rentals in advance) shown for the actuarial method:

Number of payments (excluding advance) = 4 sum of digits = 4 + 3 + 2 + 1 = 10.

The split of rentals between capital and finance charge would be as follows:

Year	Finance Charge		Rental	Capital Repayment
	€	€	€	€
1	4/10 × 7,500	3,000	6,500	6,500
2	3/10 × 7,500	2,250	6,500	3,500
3	2/10 × 7,500	1,500	6,500	4,250
4	1/10 × 7,500	750	6,500	5,000
5	–	–	–	5,750
		7,500	26,000	18,500

The accountancy treatment will be as before, only the split between the finance charge and capital repayments has changed, giving a higher finance charge in earlier periods and a lower charge towards the end of the lease.

Note
As before, it could have been assumed that the first payment (in advance) included the repayment of both interest and capital for year one.

Comparison of Finance Charges:

Year	Actuarial		Rule of 78		Straight Line	
	€	%	€	%	€	%
1	2,812	38	3,000	40	1,875	25
2	2,251	30	2,250	30	1,875	25
3	1,606	21	1,500	20	1,875	25
4	831	11	750	10	1,875	25
	7,500	100	7,500	100	7,500	100

The smaller the lease in relation to the size of the lessee, the less material will be the difference between the straight line method and more accurate methods; the higher the rate of interest, then the greater the difference between the 'rule of 78' and the actuarial method.

Example

(Payments of Rentals in Arrears)

X Limited leased an asset under the following terms:

Fair value of asset – €10,000;
Rentals 4 years – €3,000 p.a. in arrears;
Implied rate of interest – 7.72%; and
Useful life of asset – 4 years

Solution

Year	Opening Balance	Rental	Interest	Capital	Closing Balance
	€	€	€	€	€
1	10,000	3,000	772 (1)	2,228	7,772
2	7,772	3,000	600 (2)	2,400	5,372
3	5,372	3,000	415	2,585	2,787
4	2,787	3,000	215	2,787	-

(1) €10,000 × 7.72%
(2) €7,772 × 7.72%

Opening Entry:

DR		Leased assets		€10,000	
	CR	Obligation under finance lease			€10,000

Obligation under finance lease:	€		€
Cash	3,000	Leased assets	10,000
Bal c/d	7,772	SCI	772
	10,772		10,772
Cash	3,000	Bal b/d	7,772
Bal c/d	5,372	SCI	600
	8,372		8,372

Extracts from Financial Statements

Statement of comprehensive income:

Year	1	2	3	4
	€	€	€	€
Depreciation	2,500	2,500	2,500	2,500
Finance charge	772	600	415	215

Statement of financial position:

Non-current assets

Leased assets at NBV	7,500	5,000	2,500	-

Non-current liabilities

Obligations under finance lease	5,372	2,787	-	-

Current liabilities

Obligations under finance lease	2,400	2,585	2,787	-

Year 1 – note to accounts

Obligations under finance lease	€
Payable next year	2,400

Payable 2 – 5 years   5,372

                                        7,772

Statement of comprehensive income:

As illustrated above, the statement of comprehensive income of the lessee will show the finance charge relating to the lease and the depreciation charge of the asset.

Note

It is standard practice that, unless the implicit interest rate is provided, the sum of digits should be used. These two methods are preferred to the straight line method (which admittedly may often provide a close approximation).

SALE AND LEASEBACK TRANSACTIONS

1. Where the sale and leaseback results in a finance lease, any excess of sales proceeds over the carrying amount cannot be immediately recognised as income by the seller/lessee – it must be deferred and amortised over the lease term.
2. When a sale and leaseback results in an operating lease:
   (a) Any profit or loss on sale can be recognised immediately as long as the transaction is at fair value;
   (b) If the sale price is above fair value, the excess must be amortised over the period for which the asset will be used;
   (c) If the sale price is below fair value any profit/loss should be recognised immediately except when a loss is compensated by future lease payments at below fair value, when the loss should be deferred and amortised over the period for which the asset will be used.

DISCLOSURE REQUIREMENTS

Operating Leases (Lessees)

(a) The total of operating lease rentals charged as an expense in the statement of comprehensive income should be disclosed.
(b) Disclosure should be made of payments to which the lessee is committed under operating leases, analysed between those in which the commitment expires:

   (i) Within a year from the statement of financial position date;
   (ii) In the second to fifth years inclusive; and
   (iii) Later than five years from the statement of financial position date.

(c) The lessee should also provide a description of the lessee's significant arrangements and a note on how these have been dealt with in the financial statements.

Finance Leases (Lessees)

IAS 17 requires lessees to disclose the following information:

(a) For each class of asset, the net carrying amount at the statement of financial position date;

(b) Reconciliation between the total of minimum lease payments at the statement of financial position date and their present value. In addition, an enterprise should disclose the total of minimum lease payments at the statement of financial position date and their present value for each of the following periods:

    (i) not later than one year;
    (ii) later than one year and not later than five years; and
    (iii) later than five years.

(c) Although not specifically required by IAS 17 companies also tend to disclose the following in the notes to the statement of comprehensive income:

    (i) the finance charge on finance assets; and
    (ii) depreciation on assets held under finance leases.

(d) Any contingent rents charged during the period.

OTHER GUIDANCE

SIC 15 *Operating Leases – Incentives*

Issue

How are incentives in an operating lease recognised in the financial statements of both the lessor and the lessee?

Consensus

Lease incentives (such as rent-free periods or contributions by the lessor to the lessee's relocation costs) are recognised as an integral part of the net consideration for the use of the leased asset.

    The lessor recognises the aggregate cost of the incentives as a reduction of rental income over the lease term, in line with the recognition of the rental income (usually on a straight-line basis in accordance with IAS 17).

The lessee recognises the aggregate benefit of the incentives as a reduction of rental expense over the lease term, in line with the recognition of the rental expense (usually on a straight-line basis in accordance with IAS 17).

The costs incurred by the lessee, including costs in connection with a pre-existing lease, are accounted for in accordance with the applicable standards. For example, relocation costs are recognised as an expense when incurred. The accounting for such costs does not depend on whether or not they are reimbursed through an incentive arrangement.

SIC 27 *Evaluating the Substance of Transactions Involving the Legal Form of a Lease*

Issue

When an arrangement involves the legal form of a lease:

- When is a series of transactions regarded as linked, and accounted for as one transaction?
- Does the arrangement meet the definition of a lease under IAS 17 and, if not, does a separate investment account and lease payment obligations represent assets and liabilities of the entity?
- How does the entity account for other obligations resulting from the arrangement?
- How does the entity account for a fee it might receive from an investor?

Consensus

A series of transactions that involves the legal form of a lease is linked and is accounted for as one transaction when the overall economic effect cannot be understood without reference to the series of transactions as a whole.

Accounting for an arrangement reflects the substance of the arrangement. All aspects of an arrangement are evaluated to determine its substance, with weight given to those aspects and implications that have an economic effect. SIC 27 includes a list of indicators that individually demonstrate that an arrangement may not, in substance, involve a lease under IAS 17.

If an arrangement does not meet the definition of a lease, SIC 27 specifies indicators that collectively demonstrate that, in substance, a separate investment account and lease payment obligations do not meet the definitions of an asset and a liability and are not recognised by the entity.

Other obligations of an arrangement, including any guarantees provided and obligations incurred upon early termination, are accounted for under IAS 37 *Provisions, Contingent Liabilities and Contingent Assets*, IAS 39 *Financial Instruments: Recognition and Measurement* or IFRS 4 *Insurance Contracts*, depending on the terms.

An entity applies the criteria in IAS 18 *Revenue* (para. 20) to the facts and circumstances of each arrangement in determining when to recognise as income a fee that it might receive.

SIC 27 specifies the disclosures to be made about the arrangement.

CONCLUSION

A finance lease is one that transfers substantially all of the risks and rewards of ownership to the lessee, while an operating lease is one that does not. As explained above IAS 17 (at present) distinguishes between finance leases and operating leases and prescribes a different accounting treatment for each. However, this may change in the future.

In March 2009, the International Accounting Standards Board (IASB) and the US Financial Accounting Standards Board (FASB) launched a public discussion on lease accounting by publishing a joint discussion paper, *Leases: Preliminary Views*, in response to concerns raised by investors and other users of financial statements regarding the accounting treatment of lease contracts. Many lease contracts do not appear in an entity's statement of financial position because (as explained above) IAS 17 and US Generally Accepted Accounting Principles (GAAP) classify leases into two categories, finance leases (capital leases under US GAAP) and operating leases, and only the assets and liabilities arising from finance leases are recognised in the statement of financial position. For an operating lease the lessee simply recognises lease payments as an expense over the lease term.

The different accounting treatment of finance and operating leases has given rise to various problems, in particular:

- many users of financial statements believe that all lease contracts give rise to assets and liabilities that should be recognised in the financial statements of lessees. Therefore these users routinely adjust the recognised amounts in the statement of financial position in an attempt to assess the effect of the assets and liabilities resulting from operating lease contracts;
- the split between finance leases and operating leases can result in similar transactions being accounted for very differently, reducing comparability for users of financial statements; and
- the difference in the accounting treatment of finance leases and operating leases also provides opportunities to structure transactions so as to achieve a particular lease classification.

In the discussion paper the IASB and the FASB discuss a possible new approach to lease accounting whereby all leases give rise to liabilities for future rental payments and assets (the right to use the leased asset) that should be recognised in an entity's statement of financial position. This approach is aimed at ensuring that leases are accounted for consistently across sectors and industries. Both boards have decided to defer consideration of lessor accounting in order to resolve the problems associated with lessee accounting as quickly as possible. Consequently, the discussion paper deals mainly with lessee accounting.

QUESTIONS

Self-test Questions

1. What is the difference between a finance and an operating lease?
2. With respect to a finance lease, what should you show in the statement of financial position of the lessee?
3. With respect to a finance lease, how do you account for the rental payments from the lessee's point of view?
4. What is the preferred method of apportioning the rental repayments between the interest and capital element?
5. List the disclosure requirements for both operating and finance leases.

Review Questions

(See APPENDIX ONE for Suggested Solutions to Review Questions.)

Question 1

You are the Finance Director of a medium-sized manufacturing company. The Managing Director has taken a recent interest in the financial statements of the company and requests information regarding the treatment of leases.

Requirement   Write an explanatory memorandum which should set out:

(a) The definition of finance and operating leases;
(b) The treatment of both types of leases in the books of the lessee;
(c) The disclosure requirements attaching to both operating and finance leases in the company accounts.

Question 2

On 1 January 2008, ARIES Limited acquired a machine under a finance lease which could have been purchased outright for €64,000. The lease provided for four annual payments of €20,000 in arrears commencing on 31 December 2008. The implicit rate of interest was 10% and the machine is expected to have no residual value at the end of the lease term. ARIES Limited calculates depreciation on a straight-line basis.

Requirement   Applying the provisions of IAS 17 Leases, calculate the effect of the above lease on the financial statements of ARIES Limited for the year ended 31 December 2008.

Question 3

The Managing Director of LEES Limited is considering a proposal to acquire a new, fully automatic machine to increase production capacity and efficiency. The machine would cost €150,000 to purchase outright but, because the company has insufficient resources, a lease contract has been proposed with the following terms:

1. Primary period – four years at an annual rental of €45,690 payable annually in advance. The implicit rate of interest is 15% per annum;
2. Secondary period – unlimited and at an annual rental of €1; and
3. Cancellation – the lease may not be cancelled by LEES Limited during the primary period, but may be terminated at any time during the secondary period.

The Managing Director has been advised that the machine will have an effective useful life of six years after which time its value would be negligible. The company depreciates all machinery on a straight-line basis over their effective useful lives, commencing from the date of acquisition.

It is proposed to acquire the machine and enter into the lease on 30 November 200W, and to make the first rental payment on that date.

Requirement   You are required to prepare a schedule for the Managing Director showing, in columnar form:

(a) The effect of the lease on the projected profits for each of the three years ending 31 May 200X, 200Y and 200Z; and
(b) Extracts from the projected statement of financial position as at 31 May 200X, 200Y and 200Z, showing how LEES Limited would be required to reflect the lease and the machine.

Note: Calculations should be made to the nearest month and nearest €.

Question 4

Sam Limited has entered into a finance lease in respect of a crane. The terms of the lease are:

1. Three-year primary period with a quarterly rent payable in advance of €2,500, i.e. total payment of €30,000; and
2. Ten-year secondary period at a nominal rent (which can be ignored for the purposes of this question).

The cost of a new crane, if purchased outright, would be €25,000. Its estimated useful life is six years with a nil scrap value. Sam Limited uses the straight-line basis of depreciation for plant.

It is not reasonably certain that ownership of the asset will transfer to Sam Limited.

Requirement

(a) Compute the charge in the statement of comprehensive income, assuming the lease is an operating lease.

(b) Compute the charge in the statement of comprehensive income, assuming the leasing commitment is capitalised using the:

  (i) sum-of-the-digits approach, spreading the interest charge over 12 quarters;
  (ii) actuarial approach.

(c) Show the relevant entries in the statement of financial position for the first year, using the actuarial method.

Note: The implicit rate of interest in each lease payment is 3.5%.

Challenging Questions

Question 1

(Based on ICAI, P3 Summer 2002, Question 6)
    JAZZ Limited (JAZZ) is currently preparing its financial statements for the year ended 31 December 2004. A number of issues need to be resolved before the financial statements for the year ended 31 December 2004 can be finalised.

Issue 1   On 1 January 2004, JAZZ leased drilling equipment to SOUL Limited (SOUL). The finance lease, which runs for a period of five years, requires SOUL to make five annual payments of €150,000 with the first payment due on 1 January 2004. The present value of the minimum lease payments is €625,500 and the implicit rate of interest in the lease is 10%. The equipment originally cost JAZZ €500,000.

Issue 2   On 1 April 2004, JAZZ entered into two non-cancellable operating leases. One of the leases relates to equipment and runs for a period of two years with monthly payments of €10,000, while the other lease is in respect of property rental and extends for three years with quarterly payments of €25,000.

Issue 3   On 1 January 2004, JAZZ sold excavation machinery with a remaining useful life of four years to RAP Limited (RAP). Although the book value of the machinery at the date of disposal was €25,000,000, the machinery was sold for its fair market value of €38,000,000. Immediately after the sale, JAZZ leased back the machinery from RAP for a period of four years on a non-cancellable lease. Rental payments under the lease amount to €10,875,000 per annum for four years, payable in advance. At the end of the four-year term, JAZZ may purchase the machinery from RAP for €1. During the term of the lease, JAZZ is responsible for the upkeep and maintenance of the machinery. Prior to the sale, the machinery was depreciated on a straight-line basis. The implicit rate of interest in the lease is 10% per annum.

Requirement   Show how each of the issues should be reflected in the financial statements of JAZZ for the year ended 31 December 2004.

CHAPTER 9

INTANGIBLE ASSETS

INTRODUCTION

Intangible assets are defined as identifiable non-monetary assets that cannot be seen, touched or physically measured, which are created through time and/or effort and that are identifiable as a separate asset. There are two primary forms of intangibles: (1) legal intangibles (such as trade secrets (e.g. customer lists), copyrights, patents, trademarks, and goodwill); and (2) competitive intangibles (such as knowledge activities (know-how, knowledge), collaboration activities, leverage activities, and structural activities). Legal intangibles are known under the generic term intellectual property and generate legal property rights defensible in a court of law. Competitive intangibles, whilst legally non-ownable, directly impact effectiveness, productivity, wastage, and opportunity costs within an organisation and consequently costs, revenues, customer service, satisfaction, market value, and share price. Human capital is the primary source of competitive intangibles for organisations today. Competitive intangibles are the source from which competitive advantage flows, or is destroyed

Entities frequently expend resources, or incur liabilities, on the acquisition, development, maintenance or enhancement of intangible resources such as scientific or technical knowledge, design and implementation of new processes or systems, licences, intellectual property, market knowledge and trademarks. IAS 38 *Intangible Assets* was introduced in order to give guidance on how to account for intangible assets, including research and development activities.

After having studied this chapter, you should be familiar with the following key points:

- The definition of an intangible asset;
- When expenditure on an intangible asset can be capitalised;
- How such expenditure should be recognised and initially measured;
- How to account for internally generated goodwill;
- How to account for internally generated intangible assets, including research and development expenditure;
- How to measure intangible assets after initial recognition; and
- The main disclosure requirements.

IAS 38 *INTANGIBLE ASSETS*

Objective and Scope

The objective of IAS 38 is to prescribe the accounting treatment for intangible assets that are *not* dealt with specifically in another standard. This standard requires an entity to recognise an intangible asset if, and only if, specified criteria are met. The standard also specifies how to measure the carrying amount of intangible assets and requires specified disclosures about intangible assets.

IAS 38 prescribes the accounting treatment for intangible assets, except for:

- intangible assets covered by another standard, e.g. those for sale in the ordinary course of business, deferred tax assets, leases under IAS 17 *Leases,* employee benefits under IAS 19 *Employee Benefits* and goodwill;
- financial assets as defined per IAS 32 *Financial Instruments: Presentation* and IAS 39 *Financial Instruments: Recognition and Measurement* and IFRS 7 *Financial Instruments: Disclosures*;
- mineral rights and expenditure on the exploration for, or development and extraction of, minerals, oil, natural gas and similar non-regenerative resources; and
- insurance contracts with policyholders.

Some intangibles may be contained in a physical asset, e.g. compact disc. Judgement is required to decide if IAS 16 *Property, Plant and Equipment* or IAS 38 should be applied. Where software is not an integral part of related hardware, it is an intangible asset. There is no separate international standard on research and development. IAS 38 deals with all intangible assets, excluding goodwill, which is addressed in IFRS 3 *Business Combinations.* Licensing agreements, patents, copyrights etc., are excluded from IAS 17 and fall within the scope of IAS 38.

Key Terms

Intangible Asset

An intangible asset is an identifiable non-monetary asset without physical substance.

Research

This is an original and planned investigation undertaken with the prospect of gaining new scientific or technical knowledge and understanding.

Development

The application of research findings or other knowledge to plan or design the production of new or substantially improved materials, devices, products, processes, systems or services prior to the commencement of commercial production or use.

Amortisation

The systematic allocation of the depreciable amount of an intangible asset over its useful life.

Cost

The amount of cash and cash equivalents paid or the fair value or other consideration given to acquire an asset at the time of its acquisition or construction, except if an asset is received as consideration for equity instruments of the entity in a share-based payment transaction.

Residual Value of an Intangible Asset

This represents the estimated amount that the entity would currently expect to obtain from disposal of the asset, after deducting the estimated costs of disposal, if the asset were of the age and in the condition expected at the end of its estimated useful life.

Entity Specific Value

The present value of the cash flows an entity expects to arise from the continuing use of an asset, including the proceeds from disposal at the end of its useful life.

Monetary Assets

Money held and assets to be received in fixed or determinable amounts of money, e.g. cash, trade receivables.

Carrying Amount

This is the amount at which an asset is recognised in the statement of financial position after deducting any accumulated amortisation and any accumulated impairment losses.

Capitalising Intangible Assets

Examples of intangible assets include computer software, patents, copyrights, motion picture films, customer lists, mortgage servicing rights, fishing licences, import quotas, franchises, customer or supplier relationships, customer loyalty, market share and marketing rights.

In order for expenditure on such items to be capitalised it must meet the definition of an intangible asset. This includes: identifiability; control over a resource; and existence of future economic benefits. If it fails, then expenditure should be expensed unless it is part of a business combination and would therefore be treated as part of goodwill.

Identifiability

Goodwill, in a business combination, represents a payment in anticipation of future economic benefits from assets that are not capable of being individually identified and separately recognised. An intangible asset meets the identifiability criterion asset when it:

(a) is separable, i.e. capable of being separated or divided from the entity and sold, transferred, licensed, rented or exchanged, either individually or together with a related contract, asset or liability; or
(b) arises from contractual or other legal rights, regardless of whether those rights are transferable or separable from the entity or from other rights and obligations.

Control

An entity controls an intangible asset if it has the power to obtain future economic benefits and restrict the access of others to those benefits. Capacity to control is usually via legal rights but that is not a necessary condition. Market and technical knowledge may give rise to future economic benefits if protected by legal rights such as copyrights, a restraint of trade agreement or by a legal duty on employees to maintain confidentiality. Skilled staff, specific management or technical talent are unlikely to meet the definition of an intangible asset unless protected by legal rights and capable of satisfying the other criteria in the definition. An entity has not sufficient control over customer loyalty and customer relationships and thus is unlikely to meet the definition.

Future Economic Benefits

This can include revenue from the sale of products or services, cost savings or other benefits resulting from the use of the asset e.g. use of intellectual property may reduce future production costs rather than increase future revenues.

Recognition and Initial Measurement of an Intangible Asset

Recognition of an intangible asset requires an entity to demonstrate that the item meets the:

(a) definition of an intangible asset; and
(b) recognition criteria set out in IAS 38.

An intangible asset should be recognised if, and only if:

(a) it is probable that the future economic benefits attributable to the asset will flow to the entity; and
(b) the cost of the asset can be measured reliably.

An entity should assess the probability of future economic benefits using reasonable and supportable assumptions that represent management's best estimate of the economic conditions that will exist over the asset's useful life. Greater weight will be put on external evidence when using judgement as to the degree of certainty attached to future flows.

An intangible asset should be measured initially at cost.

Separate Acquisition

The price an entity pays to acquire separately an intangible asset normally reflects expectations about the probability that the future economic benefits embodied in the asset will flow to the entity. Probability is already reflected in the cost of the acquired asset. In addition, the cost of a separately acquired intangible asset can usually be measured reliably. That is specially the case if paid out in cash. The cost of a separately acquired intangible asset comprises of:

(a) its purchase price, including import duties but after deducting trade discounts and rebates; and
(b) any directly attributable expenditure on preparing the asset for its intended use, e.g. costs of employee benefits as per IAS 19, professional fees.

Costs incurred in using or redeploying intangible assets are excluded from the cost of those assets, e.g. costs incurred while the asset is capable of operating in the manner intended by management and initial operating losses. Incidental operations are not necessary to bring an asset to normal working condition thus they should be recognised in the statement of comprehensive income.

Acquisition as Part of a Business Combination

In accordance with IFRS 3, if an intangible asset is acquired in a business combination, the cost of the asset is *its fair value at acquisition date*. Under IFRS 3, the fair value of an intangible asset reflects market expectations about the probability that future economic benefits will flow to the entity. Probability is already reflected in the fair value measurement and thus the probability criterion is always satisfied for acquired intangible assets.

IAS 38 requires, at acquisition date, that an acquirer recognises all of the acquiree's intangible assets (excluding assembled workforces) separately from goodwill if their fair value can be measured reliably, irrespective of whether those assets had been recognised in the acquiree's financial statements before the business combination. Research and development projects that meet the definition should be recognised separately. If an intangible asset acquired in a business combination can be deemed to be separable, but only together with a related asset (e.g. a trademark for natural spring water might relate to a particular spring and therefore could not be sold separately from the spring), the acquirer should recognise the group of assets as a single asset.

A non-monetary asset without physical substance must be identifiable to meet the definition of an intangible asset, i.e. when the asset is separable or arises from contractual or other legal rights. Sufficient evidence must exist to reliably measure a fair value that is separable from the entity. It is unlikely that a workforce and its related intellectual capital would be measured with sufficient reliability to be separately recognised.

Measuring the Fair Value of an Intangible Asset Acquired in a Business Combination:

Quoted market prices are the most reliable estimates of fair values of intangible assets. That is usually the current bid price or, if not available, the price of the most recent similar transaction provided no significant change in the economic circumstances between the transaction date and the date of fair value.

If no active market, fair value is the amount that an entity would have paid for the asset, at acquisition date, in an arm's length transaction. Recent transactions should help in this. Certain entities that are regularly involved in the purchase and sale of unique intangible assets have developed techniques for estimating their fair values indirectly. These techniques may be used to calculate initial measurement of an intangible asset if their objective is to estimate fair value for that purpose.

Acquisition by way of a Government Grant

Intangible assets could be acquired for free or for a nominal consideration, e.g. landing rights, import licences, licences to operate radio stations etc. Under IAS 20, an entity may choose to recognise both the asset and the grant at fair value initially. If it chooses not to do that, the entity recognises the asset initially at a nominal amount plus any expenditure that is directly attributable to preparing the asset for its intended use.

Exchanges of Assets

The cost of such an asset is measured at the fair value of the asset given up, adjusted by the amount of any cash or cash equivalents transferred. The fair value of the asset received is used to measure its cost if it is more clearly evident than the fair value of the asset given up. The cost of an intangible asset acquired in exchange for a similar asset is measured at the carrying amount of the asset given up when the fair value of neither of the assets exchanged can be determined reliably.

Internally Generated Goodwill

Some expenditure may be incurred with the aim of generating future revenues but does not result in an intangible asset being recognised in the accounts. For example, money spent on developing customer relationships may help generate future revenues but won't result in an identifiable asset that could be sold separately from the business activities. This expenditure is often referred to as contributing to internally generated goodwill.

Internally generated goodwill should *not* be recognised as an asset. It is not an identifiable resource (i.e. not separable nor does it arise from contractual or other legal rights) controlled by the entity that can be measured reliably at cost.

Differences between the market value of an entity and the carrying amount of its identifiable net assets may capture a range of factors that affect the value of the entity. Such differences cannot be considered to represent the cost of intangible assets controlled by the entity.

Internally Generated Intangible Assets

The main internally generated asset considered in IAS 38 is development costs. This expenditure can be classified between the research and development phases. If the enterprise is unable to distinguish between the research and development phases, then the entire expenditure must be recorded as research phase expense.

Internally generated brands, mastheads, publishing titles, customer lists and similar items are *not* recognised as assets as they cannot be distinguished from the cost of developing the business as a whole. Expenditure on research is recognised as an expense. There is no recognition of an intangible asset arising from research.

An intangible asset arising from development is recognised only if specified criteria are met. Under IAS 38 if expenditure passes the 'development' test, it must be capitalised. The choice has been removed.

Research Phase

It is often difficult to assess whether or not an identifiable internal intangible asset exists or not. Thus, in addition, to ensure that there are probable economic benefits flowing to the entity and measuring cost reliably, an entity must classify the generation of the asset into its research and development phases. If it is not possible to separate one from the other, then it must be classified as research.

No intangible asset can arise from the research phase and must be written off as an expense. No demonstration of probable future economic benefits exists. Examples include:

- activities aimed at obtaining new knowledge;
- the search for, evaluation and final selection of, applications of research findings;
- the search for alternatives for materials, devices, products, processes, systems or services; and
- the formulation, design, evaluation and final selection of possible alternatives for new or improved materials, products, devices, processes, systems or devices.

Expenditure on research should be recognised as an expense in the statement of comprehensive income when it is incurred.

Development Phase

This expenditure should be recognised in the statement of financial position if, and only if, an entity can demonstrate all of the following:

1. The technical feasibility of completing the intangible asset so that it will be available for use or sale;
2. Its intention to complete the intangible asset and use or sell it;
3. Its ability to use or sell the intangible asset;

4. How the intangible asset will generate probable future economic benefits. It should demonstrate the existence of a market for the output of the intangible asset or, if used internally, its usefulness;
5. The availability of adequate technical, financial and other resources to complete the development and to use or sell the intangible asset; and
6. Its ability to measure the expenditure attributable to the intangible asset during its development reliably.

These could be verified by an internal business plan or by lenders to provide external finance for the project. Internal costing systems can often measure reliably the cost of generating an intangible asset internally such as salary and other expenditure in securing copyrights or licences or developing computer software. Examples of development activities are the:

- design, construction and testing of pre-production or pre-use prototypes and models;
- design of tools, jigs, moulds and dies involving new technology;
- design, construction and operation of a pilot plant that is not of a scale economically feasible for commercial production; and
- design, construction and testing of a chosen alternative for new or improved materials, devices, products, processes, systems or services.

Cost of an Internally Generated Intangible Asset

The cost of an internally generated intangible asset comprises all expenditure that can be directly attributable and is necessary to creating, producing and preparing the asset so that it is capable of operating in the manner intended by management. The cost includes, if applicable:

- expenditure on materials and services used or consumed in generating the intangible asset;
- the salaries, wages and other employment-related costs of personnel directly engaged in generating the asset; and
- any expenditure directly attributable to generating the asset, such as fees to register a legal right and the amortisation of patents and licences.

The following are not included:

- selling, administration and other general overheads unless directly attributable to the asset;
- clearly identified inefficiencies and initial operating losses; and
- expenditure on training staff to operate the asset.

Expenditure initially expensed in previous years may not be reinstated as part of an asset at a later date.

Example

An entity is developing a new production process. During 200X, expenditure incurred was €1,000, of which €900 was incurred before 1 December 200X and €100 was incurred in December 200X. At 1 December 200X, the production process met the criteria for recognition as an intangible asset.

At the end of 200X an intangible asset of €100 should be recorded with €900 being expensed (pre-criteria).

During 200Y expenditure incurred is €2,000. At the end of 200Y the recoverable amount of know-how is estimated to be €1,900.

At the end of 200Y, the cost of the production process is €2,100 (€100 + €2,000). An impairment loss of €200 needs to be recorded which may be reversed in a subsequent period if requirements in IAS 36 are met.

Example

The draft statement of comprehensive income of TAG Limited for the year ended 31 December 200Y showed a retained profit for the year of €250,000. The draft statement of financial position at 31 December 200Y included the following:

	200Y	200X
Intangible asset – development expenditure	€180,000	€275,000

For many years the company has followed a policy of capitalising development expenditure wherever possible, but the directors have now decided to revise the draft accounts to give effect to a policy of writing off all development expenditure as it is incurred. The actual expenditure incurred during the year ended 31 December 200Y was €310,000.

Requirement Calculate the revised retained profit for the year ended 31 December 200Y to be included in the statement of comprehensive income for TAG Limited for the year ended 31 December 200Y.

Solution

Profit for the year ended 31 December 200Y would be €345,000 since the €95,000 written off the intangible asset balance during 200Y would have been written off in previous years.

Subsequent Expenditure

Subsequent expenditure should be expensed when incurred unless:

(a) it is probable that the expenditure will increase future economic benefits beyond that originally assessed prior to the expenditure taking place; and
(b) the expenditure can be attributed to the asset and be reliably measured.

If both conditions are met the subsequent expenditure should be added to the cost of the intangible asset. Normally the nature of such assets is that it is not possible to determine whether or not the subsequent expenditure is likely to enhance or maintain the future economic benefits. Only rarely will they pass (a) and (b) above.

Subsequent expenditure on brands, mastheads, customer lists, publishing titles should always be expensed to avoid the recognition of internally generated goodwill. Research and development expenditure that:

- relates to an in-process research or development project acquired separately or in a business combination and recognised as an intangible asset; and
- is incurred after the acquisition of that project;

should be accounted for in accordance with research and development expenditure referred to above. Effectively that means that subsequent expenditure should be expensed if it is in the nature of research expenditure, expensed if development, but fails to satisfy the criteria as an intangible asset, and added to the asset if it satisfies the recognition criteria.

Measurement after Initial Recognition

Benchmark Treatment

The intangible asset should be carried at cost less accumulated amortisation and impairment losses.

Allowed Alternative Treatment

The intangible asset should be carried at a revalued amount, being its fair value at the date of the revaluation less any subsequent accumulated amortisation and impairment losses. Fair value should refer to an active market. Revaluations should be carried out with sufficient regularity so that the carrying values are not materially different from the fair value at the statement of financial position date. The frequency of revaluations depends on the volatility of the fair values and, if they are significant, an annual valuation may be necessary.

If an intangible asset is revalued, any accumulated amortisation at the date of revaluation is either:

- restated proportionately with change in the gross carrying amount of the asset so that the carrying amount of the asset after revaluation equals its revalued amount; or

- eliminated against the gross carrying amount of the asset and the net amount restated to the revalued amount of the asset.

If an intangible asset is revalued, all the other assets in that class should also be revalued unless there is no active market for those assets. That is to prevent selective revaluation and reporting of a mixture of costs and values as at different dates.

The cumulative revaluation surplus included in equity may be transferred directly to retained earnings when the surplus is realised, i.e. on retirement or disposal of the asset. It is uncommon to find an active market in intangible assets but they can occur, e.g. taxi licences, fishing licences, production quotas etc. However, it cannot exist for brands, newspaper mastheads, music and film publishing rights, patents or trademarks because each asset is unique and transactions are infrequent. If there is no active market then the class of asset must be carried at cost less accumulated amortisation and impairment losses. Also if the fair value can no longer be determined by reference to an active market, the carrying amount of the asset should be its revalued amount at the date of the last revaluation less accumulated amortisation and impairment losses. The fact that there is no active market should also trigger off an impairment review.

Increases in Fair Value

If the carrying amount of an intangible asset is increased as a result of a revaluation, the increase should be credited directly to 'equity' (and shown in 'other comprehensive income') *unless* it reverses a revaluation decrease (of the same asset) previously recognised in arriving at profit/loss in which case the increase should also be recognised in arriving at profit/loss. This is the same accounting treatment as used for property, plant and equipment (IAS 16).

Decreases in Fair Value

The normal treatment for a decrease in the carrying amount as a result of a revaluation is to recognise it in profit/loss *except* to the extent that it reverses a surplus on the same asset in which case it should be debited directly to 'equity' (and shown in 'other comprehensive income') to the extent of a previous surplus on the same asset. This is the same accounting treatment as used for property, plant and equipment (IAS 16) (see Chapter 6).

Note   As a consequence of the revisions to IAS 1 *Presentation of Financial Statements* (effective for accounting periods beginning on or after 1 January 2009) (see Chapter 2), revaluation gains and losses which would previously have been shown in the statement of changes in equity are now included in the 'other comprehensive income' section of the statement of comprehensive income.

Useful Life

An entity should assess whether its useful life of an intangible asset is infinite or finite. An indefinite life is one where there is no foreseeable limit to the period over which the asset is expected to generate net cash inflows for the entity. An intangible asset with a finite life should be amortised but not an intangible asset having an indefinite life. Many factors must be considered in determining the useful life including:

- the expected usage of the asset and whether it can be managed efficiently;
- typical product life cycles;
- technical, technological, commercial or other types of obsolescence;
- the stability of the industry in which the asset operates and changes in market demand;
- expected actions by competitors;
- the level of maintenance expenditure required to obtain future benefits;
- the period of control over the asset;
- whether the useful life is dependent on the useful life of other assets in the entity.

The term indefinite does not mean infinite. A conclusion that the useful life is indefinite should not depend on planned future expenditure in excess of that required to maintain the asset at that standard of performance.

Computer software is susceptible to changes in technology and should be written off over a short useful life. The useful life may be very long but uncertainty justifies estimating the useful life on a prudent basis although it does not justify an unrealistically short life.

The useful life of an intangible asset that arises from contractual or other legal rights should not exceed the period of the legal or contractual rights but may be shorter. The useful life may include a renewal period but only if there is evidence to support renewal by the entity without significant cost. If there are both legal and economic factors influencing the useful life of an intangible asset then economic factors determine the period over which benefits will be received but legal factors may restrict the period over which the entity controls access to those benefits. The useful life is the shorter of the periods determined by these factors.

Examples Illustrating the Determination of Useful Life

1. An Acquired Customer List A direct mail company acquires a customer list and expects to derive benefit for at least 1 year but not more than three years. The customer list would be amortised over best estimate of useful life, say 18 months. Even the intention to add customer names to the list must be ignored as the asset relates only to the list of customers that existed at the date it was acquired. It should also be reviewed for impairment under IAS 36 Impairment of Assets.

2. An Acquired Patent that Expires in 15 Years   The patent is protected for 15 years. There is a commitment to sell the patent after five years to a third party for 60% of the fair value of the patent at the date it was acquired. The patent should be amortised over five years with a residual value of 60% of the present value of the patent's fair value at the date it was acquired. It should also be reviewed for impairment under IAS 36.

3. An Acquired Copyright that has a Remaining Legal Life of 50 Years   Assume an analysis of consumer habits provides evidence that there are only 30 years left of future benefits. The asset must now be amortised over the new expected remaining estimated useful life of 30 years as well as reviewing the asset for impairment.

4. An Acquired Broadcast Licence that Expires in Five Years   The licence is renewable every 10 years but can be renewed indefinitely at little cost and the entity intends to renew the licence. The technology is not expected to be replaced in the foreseeable future. The licence would be treated as having an indefinite useful life thus the licence would not be amortised until its useful life is determined to be finite. The licence would be tested for impairment at the end of each annual reporting period and whenever there is an indication of impairment.

5. The Broadcast Licence is Revoked   Assume the licensing authority will no longer renew licences but decides to auction them. There are three years before the licence expires. The useful life is no longer infinite and must be amortised over the remaining useful life of three years as well as being tested for impairment.

6. An Acquired Airline Route Authority between Two Major Cities Expires in Three Years   The route authority must be renewed every five years and this is routinely granted at minimal cost and, historically, this route authority has been renewed. The acquiring entity expects to service the route indefinitely and cash flow analysis supports that view. The intangible asset therefore has an indefinite life and should not be amortised until its useful life is determined to be finite. It must, however, be tested annually for impairment and whenever there is an indication of an impairment.

7. An Acquired Trademark Used to Identify and Distinguish a Leading Consumer Product that has been a Market Leader for the Past Eight Years   A trademark has a legal life of five years but is renewable every 10 years at little cost and the entity intends to renew. This asset has an indefinite life and should not be amortised until its useful life is determined to be definite. It should also be tested for impairment annually or when there is an indication of impairment.

8. A Trademark Acquired 10 Years Ago that Distinguishes a Leading Consumer Product   Unexpected competition has emerged which will reduce future sales by 20% but management expects that the 80% will continue indefinitely. An impairment must be recognised immediately to the reduce the trademark to the recoverable amount. It would continue to be subject to annual impairment although not amortised.

9. A Trademark for a Line of Products Acquired Several Years Ago in a Business Combination   This is a well-established product, on the market for 35 years. There is an expectation that there was no limit to the period of time it would contribute to cash flows, thus it has not been amortised. Management has recently decided that the product line will be discontinued over the next four years. It must now be tested for impairment and subsequently amortised over the next four years.

Intangible Assets with Finite Useful Lives

Amortisation Period and Amortisation Method

The depreciable amount of an intangible asset should be allocated over its useful life. As with tangible assets, the most difficult decision for management is determining the useful life of the asset. The useful life of an intangible asset should take account of such things as the: expected usage of the asset; possible obsolescence and expected actions of competitors; stability of the industry; and market demand for the products and services that the asset is generating.

Amortisation should be allocated on a systematic basis over its useful life from the day it is available for use. It should reflect the pattern of economic benefits being consumed but straight line should be adopted if it cannot be determined reliably. The standard requires it to be expensed unless permitted by another standard to be capitalised, e.g. IAS 2 *Inventory*. The method should be applied consistently but it would be rare for persuasive evidence to support a method that would result in lower amortisation than that achieved by straight line.

Residual Value

The residual value should be assumed to be *zero* unless there is:

(a) a commitment by a third party to purchase the asset at the end of its useful life; or
(b) an active market for the asset and:
    (i) residual value can be determined by reference to the market; and
    (ii) it is probable that such a market will exist at the end of the asset's useful life.

The depreciable amount is determined after deducting residual value but the latter is based on prices prevailing at the date of the estimate and is reviewed at each statement of financial position date. Any change in that value is treated as an adjustment to future amortisation.

Review of Amortisation Period and Amortisation Method

The amortisation period and method should be reviewed at the end of each annual reporting period. If the expected useful life is different from previous estimates, the amortisation period should be changed. If there is a change in the expected pattern of consumption of future benefits the amortisation period should be accounted for as a change in accounting estimates as per IAS 8 *Accounting Policies, Changes in Accounting Estimates and Errors*, e.g. it may become apparent that the diminishing balance method is more appropriate than straight line.

Intangible Assets with Indefinite Useful Lives

An intangible asset with an indefinite useful life should not be amortised. However it is required to be tested annually for impairment and whenever there is an indication of an impairment.

Review of Useful Life Assessment

Useful life should be reviewed each period to determine whether events and circumstances support an indefinite useful life. If not, the change should be treated as a change in accounting estimate by amortising the asset over its remaining useful life in accordance with IAS 8. A reassessment of useful life is a sign that the asset should be tested for impairment. Any excess of the carrying amount over the recoverable amount should be treated as an impairment loss.

Derecognition, Retirement and Disposal

An intangible asset should be derecognised when:

(a) it is disposed of; or
(b) there are no future economic benefits expected from its use or disposal.

Gains or losses should be calculated as the difference between the net disposal proceeds and the carrying amount of the asset and should be recognised as income/expenses in the period in which the retirement or disposal occurs. The date of disposal should be determined by applying IAS 18 and the consideration should be valued initially at fair value. If the latter is deferred then it should be recognised at the cash price equivalent. The difference between the nominal amount of the consideration and the cash price equivalent is recognised as interest revenue under IAS 18 according to the effective yield on the receivable.

Amortisation should not cease on temporary idleness unless already fully depreciated.

DISCLOSURE

General

The following should be disclosed for each class of intangible assets, analysed between internally generated and other intangible assets:

- whether the useful lives are indefinite or finite and, if the latter, their useful lives or amortisation rates used;
- the amortisation methods adopted;
- the gross carrying amount and accumulated amortisation at the start and end of the period;
- the line item of the statement of comprehensive income in which the amortisation charge is included;
- a reconciliation of the carrying amount at the start and end of the period showing: additions, split between internal, acquired and via business combinations;
  - retirements and disposals;
  - revaluations;
  - impairment losses;
  - impairment losses reversed;
  - amortisation during the period;
  - net exchange differences; and
  - other changes in carrying amount.

A class of intangible assets may include:

- brand names;
- mastheads and publishing rights;
- computer software;
- licences and franchises;
- copyrights, patents and other industrial property rights;
- recipes, formulae, models, designs and prototypes; and
- intangible assets under development.

Further disaggregation may be required if it involves providing more relevant information. The financial statements should also disclose:

(a) if an intangible asset has an indefinite useful life, the carrying amount and the reasons supporting the assessment of that life. The significant factors should be described;
(b) a description, the carrying amount and remaining amortisation period of any individual intangible asset that is material to the entity as a whole;
(c) for acquired intangibles via grant – the initial fair value, their carrying amount and whether carried under the benchmark or allowed alternative treatment for subsequent measurement;
(d) the existence and carrying amounts of intangibles whose title is restricted or pledged for security; and
(e) the amount of contractual commitments for acquisition of intangibles.

Intangible Assets Carried under the Allowed Alternative Treatment

The following should be disclosed:

(a) by class of intangible assets:

    (i)   the effective date of the revaluation;

    (ii) the carrying amount; and

    (iii) the carrying amount had the benchmark treatment been adopted (historic cost);

(b) the amount of the revaluation surplus at the start and end of the period indicating any changes and any restrictions on distribution; and

(c) the methods and significant assumptions applied in estimating the asset fair values.

Research and Development Expenditure

The aggregate amount of research and development expenditure expensed during the period.

Other Information

An entity is encouraged to disclose the following:

(a) a description of any fully amortised intangible asset that is still in use; and

(b) a brief decription of significant intangible assets controlled by the entity but not recognised as assets as they failed to meet the recognition criteria in IAS 38 or were generated prior to IAS 38 being made effective.

OTHER GUIDANCE

SIC 32 *Intangible Assets – Web Site Costs*

When accounting for internal expenditure on the development and operation of an entity's own web site for internal or external access, important issues include:

- Is the web site an internally generated intangible asset that is subject to the requirements of IAS 38 *Intangible Assets*; and
- How is such expenditure accounted for?

Consensus

An entity's own website that arises from development and is for internal or external access is an internally developed intangible asset that is subject to the requirements of IAS 38. A website arising from development is recognised as an intangible asset if it meets the criteria in IAS 38.21 and IAS 38.57. Any internal expenditure on the development and operation of an entity's own website is accounted for in accordance with IAS 38. The nature of each activity for which expenditure is incurred and the website's stage of development or post-development is evaluated to determine the appropriate accounting treatment. SIC 32 specifies examples of the accounting treatment for costs incurred in the different stages of a website's development.

All expenditure on developing a website solely or primarily for promoting and advertising an entity's own products and services is recognised as an expense when incurred.

CONCLUSION

This chapter addresses the following areas:

1. The accounting treatment for intangible assets that are *not* specifically covered by other standards;
2. The criteria necessary for the recognition of intangible assets;
3. How to measure the carrying amount of intangible assets; and
4. The disclosure requirements for intangible assets.

IAS 38 is an important accounting standard that impacts upon, and is impacted by, a number of issues in financial reporting, including accounting for business combinations (see Section Five) and impairment (see Chapter 10). Consequently, it is important to have a clear understanding of the definition of an intangible asset and how such expenditure should be recognised and initially measured, in particular research and development expenditure.

QUESTIONS

Self-test Questions

1. Under IAS 38, what are the categories of internally generated intangible assets which may never be recognised?
2. What conditions must be satisfied before development expenditure may be capitalised?
3. If all the conditions in the previous question are met, is it a requirement that development costs must be capitalised?

Review Questions

(See APPENDIX ONE for Suggested Solutions to Review Questions.)

Question 1

Sea Pharmaceuticals plc has negotiated a special government grant to provide 40% of the research costs of finding a suitable drug for the treatment of the virus disease which has seriously affected the seal population. The grant will also extend to a similar proportion of the costs of developing the drug for the treatment of infected seals. Payment of the grant will be made every quarter on production of an audited statement of costs. The grant will be available for a minimum period of two years.

Requirement Draft a letter to the Managing Director of Sea Pharmaceuticals plc advising him of the accounting treatment you recommend in relation to the above project in accordance with IAS 38 *Intangible Assets* and IAS 20 *Accounting for Government Grants and Disclosure of Government Assistance* (see Chapter 16).

Question 2

The following information has been extracted from the original draft accounts of THIMBLE Limited for the year ended 31 December 200Y:

	200Y	200X
	€'000	€'000
Profit for the year	200	100
Intangible asset – development expenditure account balance	300	400
Actual development expenditure incurred during the year	500	800

The company has always adopted a policy of capitalising all development expenditure to the maximum amount permitted. After preparation of the above draft accounts for the year ended 31 December 200Y, the company decided to change this policy and write off all development expenditure as it arises.

Requirement Calculate the amount disclosed as profit for the year ended 31 December 200Y in the revised statement of comprehensive income of THIMBLE Limited.

Challenging Questions

Question 1

Nov Laboratories Limited has been involved in pharmaceuticals research projects for 15 years. The Managing Director has expressed concern that the variability in the level of research and development expenditure has distorted the reported profits for the company over the past 5 years.

The following information is available:
1. Research and development expenditure over the past 5 years has been analysed as follows:

Year ended 31 December	Property Plant & Equipment Acquired	Research Costs	Development Costs
	€	€	€
200V	50,000	445,000	125,000
200W	150,000	77,000	150,000
200X	210,000	40,000	215,000

200Y	–	125,000	160,000
200Z	–	88,000	145,000

2. The company depreciates all property, plant and equipment on the straight line basis over 10 years, but writes off all other expenditure as incurred. The only non-current asset acquired prior to 200V was plant, costing €200,000 and purchased in 200S.
3. The company is planning to acquire €300,000 of new property, plant and equipment in connection with its research and development activities over the next 2 years. In addition, it is anticipated that research and development expenditure will average €400,000 p.a. over the next 5 years. Approximately 70% of this expenditure will be classified as development expenditure.

Requirement As financial director of Nov Laboratories Limited, prepare a memorandum addressed to the managing director on the current accounting policy of the company, any possible changes that could be implemented and their impact on the company's reported results. (Assume any development costs which are to be capitalised are amortised over 5 years.)

Question 2

Grotto Limited makes up its accounts to 31 December each year. Its research and development expenditure for the years ending 31 December is as follows:

	Research	Development	Total
	€	€	€
Year ending 31 December 200V	34,000	56,000	90,000
Year ending 31 December 200W	37,000	54,000	91,000
Year ending 31 December 200X	48,000	77,000	125,000
Year ending 31 December 200Y	53,000	82,000	135,000
Year ending 31 December 200Z	66,000	97,000	163,000

The development expenditure has been incurred as follows:

	200V	200W	200X	200Y	200Z
	€	€	€	€	€
Product C	56,000	19,000			
Product D		35,000	18,000	7,000	
Product E			44,000	26,000	
Product F			15,000	49,000	21,000
Product G					76,000

The accounting policy for research and development expenditure has been in accordance with the requirements of IAS 38 *Intangible Assets*. Development expenditure is recognised as an intangible asset when the conditions of IAS 38 are met. In applying this policy, the directors write off the development expenditure in relation to estimated sales of the product (in units). Arising from this policy, in the accounts for the four years to 31 December 200Y, research expenditure in the amount of €172,000 has been written off. Development expenditure has been written off as follows:

- Product C: €50,000 has been written off. Sales of this product are at a standstill and are not expected to recover.
- Product D: All the development expenditure on this product has been written off because it was a failure. Sales of only 20,000 units were made in 200Y and prospects of further sales appeared slight. However, it now appears that sales of this product are picking up, sales of 45,000 units being expected for 200Z and further sales of approximately 250,000 units being anticipated in later years.
- Product E: In 200Y 48,000 units of product E were sold. It was then estimated that approximately 200,000 further units would be sold over the next four years and that the sales would occur fairly evenly over that period. Arising from this, €14,000 of the expenditure was written off in 200Y. Sales in 200Z should amount to approximately 30,000 units. Estimated further sales in the next two years are expected to total 70,000 units approximately. No further sales are expected in the years after this.
- Product F: It is considered that approximately 600,000 units of this product will be sold in total of which approximately 80,000 units will be sold in 200Z.
- Product G: This product is still in the course of development. However since there have been consumer association objections to a similar product in the USA, certain revisions are being considered to this product. It is not yet known how successful or how costly these revisions will prove to be.

Requirement
(a) Outline the accounting concepts you would have considered in accounting for research and development expenditure before any accounting standard was issued on the topic.
(b) Estimate the charge for research and development expenditure in the accounts of Grotto Limited for the year ended 31 December 200Z and illustrate the disclosure of that expenditure in accordance with IAS 38 *Intangible Assets*.

Chapter 10

IMPAIRMENT

INTRODUCTION

This chapter addresses the procedures that an entity should apply in order to ensure that its assets are carried at no more than their recoverable amount. After having studied this chapter, you should be able to:

- define the term 'impairment loss';
- calculate whether an impairment has occurred; and
- allocate an impairment loss amongst the assets of a cash generating unit.

Impairment is a sudden diminution in the value of a non-current asset over and above the normal wear and tear or reduction in value recognised by depreciation. Impairment occurs because something happens to the non-current asset itself or to the economic environment in which the non-current asset operates.

But how do you measure if impairment has occurred?

→ Compare the carrying amount of the asset with the recoverable amount.

Where

Recoverable amount = the higher of the fair value less costs to sell and the value in use.

If the carrying amount exceeds the recoverable amount, the asset is impaired and should be written down to the recoverable amount. **Figure 10.1** illustrates how to assess if an asset has been impaired.

Figure 10.1:   The Impairment Decision

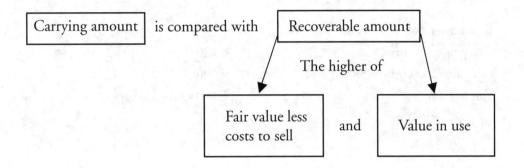

Where carrying amount < recoverable amount – no impairment has occurred;
But
Where carrying amount > recoverable amount – there has been impairment.

Example

Take an asset at 31 December 200X:

Carrying amount   €10,000
Fair value less costs to sell   €12,000
Value in use   €13,000 - take higher

No impairment because carrying amount < recoverable amount.

Example

Take an asset at 31 December 200X:

Carrying amount   €10,000
Fair value less costs to sell   €8,000
Value in use   €9,000 - take higher

Impairment = carrying amount - recoverable amount = €10,000 - €9,000 = €1,000

Example

Take an asset at 31 December 200X:

Carrying amount	€120
Fair value less costs to sell	€100
Value in use	€110 - take higher

Impairment is €10

Now, after having outlined the basic principles, it is important to examine in detail the requirements of IAS 36 *Impairment of Assets*.

IAS 36 *IMPAIRMENT OF ASSETS*

IAS 36 prescribes the procedures that an entity applies to ensure that its assets are carried at no more than their recoverable amount. If the asset value is above its future use or sale value it is said to be impaired and an impairment loss should be recognised immediately. IAS 36 also covers situations when an impairment should be reversed as well as disclosures. IAS 36 applies to accounting for impairment of all assets other than:

- inventories (IAS 2 *Inventories*);
- assets arising from construction contracts (IAS 11 *Construction Contracts*);
- deferred tax assets (IAS 12 *Income Taxes*);
- assets arising from employee benefits (IAS 19 *Employee Benefits*);
- financial assets within the scope of IAS 39 *Financial Instruments: Recognition and Measurement*;
- investment property measured at fair value (IAS 40 *Investment Property*);
- biological assets related to agricultural activity that are measured at fair value less estimated point-of-sale costs (IAS 41 *Agriculture*);
- deferred acquisition costs and intangible assets, arising from insurance contracts within the scope of IFRS 4 *Insurance Contracts*; and
- non-current assets (or disposal groups) classified as held for sale in accordance with IFRS 5 *Non-current Assets Held for Sale and Discontinued Operations*.

However, it does apply to subsidiaries as defined in IAS 27 *Consolidated and Separate Financial Statements*, associates as defined in IAS 28 *Investments in Associates* and joint ventures as defined in IAS 31 *Interests in Joint Ventures*. It also applies to revalued assets governed by IAS 31 *Interests in Joint Ventures*. In the latter case, if the fair value is its market value, the only difference is the direct incremental costs of disposal and if these are negligible then no impairment has occurred. If the disposal costs are substantial then IAS 36 applies. If the asset is valued at other than market value then IAS 16 only should be applied after the revaluation adjustments have been applied to determine whether or not it has been impaired.

Key Definitions

1. **Carrying Amount** – Carrying amount is the amount at which an asset is recognised (in the statement of financial position) after deducting accumulated depreciation (amortisation) and any accumulated impairment losses.
2. **Cash Generating Unit (CGU)** – This is the smallest identifiable group of assets that generates cash flows that are largely independent of cash inflows from other assets or groups of assets.
3. **Costs of Disposal** – Costs of disposal are incremental costs directly attributable to the disposal of an asset but excluding finance costs and income tax.
4. **Fair Value Less Cost to Sell** – This is the amount obtainable from the sale of an asset or CGU in an arms length transaction less costs of disposal. It is also referred to as the net selling price.
5. **Impairment Loss** – Impairment loss is the amount by which the carrying amount of an asset or CGU exceeds its recoverable amount.
6. **Recoverable Amount** – Recoverable amount is the higher of an asset's fair value less costss to sell and its value in use.
7. **Value in Use** – Value in use is present value of future cash flows expected to be derived from the asset or cash CGU.

Identifying an Asset that may be Impaired

An asset is impaired when the carrying amount of an asset exceeds its recoverable amount. Except for intangible assets with indefinite lives and goodwill a formal estimate of recoverable amount does not occur annually unless there is an indication of a potential impairment loss. At the end of each reporting period, however, an entity should assess whether or not there are indications of impairment losses. In making an assessment of whether or not there are indications of impairment an entity, as a minimum, should consider the following:

External sources

*   A significant decline in an asset's market value.
*   Significant changes with an adverse effect on the entity that have taken place during the period or are set to take place in the near future – in the technological, economic or legal environments.
*   Market interest rates have increased during the period which have affected the discount rate.
*   The carrying amount of the net assets in the entity is more than its market capitalisation.

Internal sources

*   Evidence of obsolescence or physical damage.
*   Plans to discontinue or restructure the operation to which the asset belongs or plans to dispose of the asset or reassessing its useful life.
*   Evidence that economic performance is worse than expected.

The list is not intended to be exhaustive and there may be other indications that are equally important.

Evidence from internal reporting of impairment includes the existence of:

- cash flows for operating and maintaining the asset that are considerably higher than budgeted;
- actual cash flows that are worse than budgeted;
- a significant decline in budgeted cash flows or operating profit; or
- operating losses.

Intangible assets with infinite lives or not yet in use, as well as goodwill, should be tested for impairment on an annual basis. Materiality, however, applies and, if interest rates have increased during the period, an asset's recoverable amount need not be formally estimated if the discount rate is unlikely to be affected or if previous sensitivity analysis makes it unlikely that a material decrease has occurred or result in a material impairment loss.

If an asset is impaired depreciation should also be reviewed and adjusted as the remaining useful life may be considerably shorter.

Timing of Impairment Tests

The test may be carried out at any time during the year provided it is at the same time every year. Different CGUs may be tested for impairment at different times. However, if some of the goodwill was acquired in a business combination during the year that CGU should be tested for impairment before the end of the current reporting period. If other assets or smaller CGUs are tested at the same time as the larger unit they should be tested for impairment before the larger unit.

The most recent detailed calculation made in a proceeding reporting period may be adopted for the test provided all of the following criteria are met:

- The assets and liabilities have not changed significantly since the most recent recoverable amount calculation;
- The most recent recoverable amount calculation resulted in an amount substantially in excess of the CGU's carrying amount; and
- Based on an analysis of events and changed circumstances the likelihood that a current recoverable amount determinable would be less than the current carrying amount of the CGU is remote.

If the carrying amount of a CGU exceeds its recoverable amount but the entity has not completed its determination of whether goodwill is impaired or not it may use its best estimate of any probable impairment loss. Any adjustment should be recognised in the succeeding reporting period.

Measuring Recoverable Amount

Recoverable amount is the higher of the fair value less costs to sell and value in use. Both need not necessarily be determined if either exceeds the carrying amount (i.e. Net Book Value (NBV)) then the asset is not impaired. If it is not possible to determine the fair value less costs to sell as there is no reliable estimate then value in use should be adopted instead. Also if there is no reason to believe that an asset's value in use is materially different from exceeding its fair value less costs to sell then the asset's recoverable amount will be its fair value less costs to sell.

Recoverable amount is determined for individual assets unless the asset does not generate cash flows that are largely independent of those from a group of assets. If the latter then recoverable amount is determined for the CGU to which the asset belongs unless either:

- the assets fair value less costs to sell is higher than its NBV; or
- the assets value in use can be determined to be close to its fair value less costs to sell.

In some cases averages may provide a reasonable approximation of the detailed computations.

Fair Value Less Costs to Sell

Best evidence is a binding sale agreement at arms length, adjusted for incremental costs directly attributable to disposal of the asset. If there is no binding sale agreement but it is traded on an active market, fair value less costs to sell is the asset's market price less costs of disposal. The price should be the current bid price or the price of the most recent transaction. If none exists, it should be based on the best information available to reflect what would be received between willing parties at arms length but it should not be based on a forced sale. Costs of disposal include legal costs, stamp duty and other direct incremental costs but not reorganisation or termination benefits.

Value in Use

The following elements should be reflected in the calculation of value in use:

- an estimate of future cash flows to be derived from the asset;
- expectations about possible variations in the amount or timing of such flows;
- the time value of money;
- the price for bearing the uncertainty inherent in the asset; and
- other factors, including illiquidity, that market participants would reflect in pricing expected future cash flows.

This requires estimating future cash flows to be derived from continuing use of the asset and from ultimate disposal as well as applying the appropriate discount rate to those flows. Either cash flows or the discount rate can be adjusted to reflect the elements above.

Basis for Estimates of Future Cash Flows   Cash flows should be based on reasonable and supportable assumptions that represent management's best estimate of a range of economic conditions that exist over the life of the asset and take into account past ability of management to accurately forecast cash flows. Greater weight should be given to external evidence and cash flows should be based on the most recent financial forecasts approved by management covering a normal maximum period of five years. If a longer period is justified budgets/forecasts should be extrapolated using a steady or declining growth rate that should not exceed the long-term average growth rate for the products, industries or countries in which the entity operates, unless a higher rate is justified. If appropriate, the growth rate should be zero or negative.

Composition of Estimates of Future Cash Flows   These should include:

(a) projections of cash inflows from continuing use of the asset;
(b) projections of cash outflows necessarily incurred to generate the cash inflows and can be directly attributed to the asset; and
(c) net cash flows to be received for the disposal of the asset at the end of its useful life.

Estimates should reflect consistent assumptions about price increases due to general inflation and should include future overheads that can be directly attributed or allocated to the asset. If the asset is not in use yet, all expected future costs to get it ready should be included within future cash outflows. Future cash flows should be estimated for the asset in its current condition and should not include cash inflows from restructuring (under IAS 37 *Provisions Contingent Liabilities and Contingent Assets*) or from future capital expenditure that will enhance or improve the asset's performance.

Cash flows do not include either cash inflows from assets that generate cash inflows largely independent of the cash inflows from the asset nor cash outflows related to obligations already recognised as liabilities. Furthermore, in order to avoid double counting of the interest cost and ensure that the discount rate is determined on a pre-tax rate basis, the estimates of future cash flows should not include:

• cash inflows from financing activities; or
• income tax receipts or payments.

Estimates of net cash flows to be received from disposal are those expected to be obtained on an arms length basis after deducting disposal costs, and should be based on prices prevailing at the date of the estimate for assets operating under similar conditions and should reflect the effect of both future price increases (general and specific).

Foreign Currency Future Cash Flows   These are estimated in the currency in which they are generated and then discounted using an appropriate rate for that currency.

Discount Rate   This should be a pre-tax rate that reflects both the time value of money and the specific risks attached to the asset. The latter is the return that investors would require if they were to choose an investment that would generate cash flows equivalent to those expected to be derived from the asset. Where an asset specific rate is not directly available then surrogates may be adopted.

Measuring the Recoverable Amount of an Intangible Asset with an Indefinite Useful Life

This must be measured at the end of each reporting period but a previous detailed calculation in a preceding period may be adopted provided all of the following criteria are met:

(a) The intangible asset does not generate cash inflows largely independent from other assets and is therefore tested as part of a CGU whose assets and liabilities have largely remain unchanged since the last calculation;
(b) The most recent recoverable amount resulted in an amount that exceeded the assets NBV by a considerable amount; and
(c) Based on an analysis of events since the last valuation, the likelihood that a current recoverable amount would be less than the asset's NBV is remote.

Recognising an Impairment Loss

Assets other than Goodwill

The asset should be reduced to its recoverable amount *only if* the recoverable amount is less than its NBV (i.e. also known as carrying amount). This reduction is known as an impairment loss and should be expensed in the statement of comprehensive income in arriving at profit/loss for the year unless the asset is carried at valuation. A revaluation decrease should be charged as an expense in the statement of comprehensive income in arriving at profit/loss for the year to the extent that the impairment exceeds the amount held in the revaluation reserve for the same asset (otherwise decrease/loss would be included under 'other comprehensive income' in the statement of comprehensive income).

Where the impairment loss is greater than the NBV a liability should be recognised only if required by another standard. After recognition of the impairment loss, depreciation should be adjusted in future periods to allocate the asset's revised book value over the asset's remaining useful life. Any related deferred tax assets or liabilities are determined under IAS 12 by comparing the revised NBV of the asset with its tax base.

Note As a consequence of the revisions to IAS 1 *Presentation of Financial Statements* (effective for accounting periods beginning on or after 1 January 2009) (see Chapter 2), revaluation gains and losses which would previously have been shown in the statement of changes in equity are now included in the 'other comprehensive income' section of the statement of comprehensive income.

Cash Generating Units

If there is any indication that an asset may be impaired, the recoverable amount should be estimated for that individual asset. If it is not possible to estimate the recoverable amount of the individual asset then the entity should determine the recoverable amount of the CGU to which the asset belongs. This occurs when an asset's value in use cannot be estimated to be close to its fair value less costs to sell and the asset does not generate cash inflows from continuing use that are largely independent of those from other assets.

In such cases the value in use and thus recoverable amount must be determined only for the asset's CGU.

Example

A mine owns a private railway to support its mining activities. It could only be sold for scrap and does not generate independent cash flows from those of the mine. The CGU, in this case, is therefore the mine as a whole, including the railway as the railway's value in use cannot be independently determined and would be very different from its scrap value.

Identification of an asset's CGU involves judgement and should be the lowest aggregation of assets that generate largely independent cash inflows from continuing use.

Example

A bus company has a contract to provide a minimum service on five separate routes. Cash flows can be separately identified for each route. Even if one route is operating at a loss the entity has no option to curtail any one route and the lowest independent level is the group of five routes together. The CGU is the bus company itself.

Cash inflows should be from outside parties only and should consider various factors including how management monitors the entity's operations. If an active market exists for the asset's or group of assets output then they should be identified as a CGU, even if some of the output is used internally. If this is the case, management's best estimate of future market prices should be used in determining the value in use of:

- the CGU when estimating the future cash inflows relating to internal use; and
- other CGUs of the entity, when estimating future cash outflows that relate to internal use of the output.

CGUs should be identified consistently from period to period unless a change is justified. IAS 36 provides a number of examples to illustrate the identification of CGUs.

Example

Retail Store Chain

Store X belongs to retail chain M. X makes all purchases through M and pricing, marketing, advertising and human resources policies are decided by M which also owns five other stores in the same city as X and 20 other stores in other cities. All are managed in the same way as X and X was purchased with four other stores five years ago.

As X generates independent cash inflows and the stores are in different neighbourhoods, it appears X is a CGU.

Plant for an intermediate step in a production process

A significant raw material used for Y's final production is an intermediate product bought from X. X sells to Y at a transfer price that passes all margins to X. 80% of X's output is sold to Y and 20% to outside customers.

Case 1 – X could sell to Y in active market. Internal prices are higher than market prices.
Case 2 – There is no active market for the products X sells to Y.

Case 1: It is likely that X is a separate CGU and Y is also. However, internal transfer prices do not reflect the market price for X's output. Thus, in determining value in use for both X and Y, the entity should adjust financial forecasts/budgets to reflect management's best estimate of future market prices for those of X's products.

Case 2: It is likely that the recoverable amount of each plant cannot be assessed independently as the majority of X's production is used internally and could not be sold in an active market and the two plants are managed together. X and Y is the smallest group of assets that are largely independent.

Single Product Entity

Entity M produces a single product and owns plants A, B and C in different continents. A produces a component that is assembled in either B or C. The combined capacity of B and C is not fully utilised. M's products are sold worldwide from either B or C and utilisation levels depend on the allocation of sales between the two sites.

Case 1 – There is an active market for A's products.
Case 2 – There is no active market for A's products.

Case 1: It is likely that A is a separate CGU but B and C cannot be determined individually thus A + B is the smallest identifiable group of assets that are largely independent. M must adjust its financial budgets/forecasts to reflect its best estimate of future market prices for A's products.

Case 2: There are no independent CGUs as there is no active market for A's products. B and C are not independent as the cash flows for B and C depend on the allocation of production across the two sites. A, B and C represent the smallest identifiable CGU.

Magazine Titles

A publisher owns 150 titles (70 purchased and 80 self-created). Purchased titles are intangible assets and the costs of creating titles are expensed. Cash inflows are identifiable for each title and these are managed by customer segments. Old titles are abandoned for new titles in the same customer segments.

A CGU would be individual titles as cash inflows are largely independent.

Building Half Rented to Others and Half Occupied for Own Use

M is a manufacturing company. It owns a headquarters building that used to be fully occupied for internal use. After downsizing 50% of the building is now used internally and 50% rented to third parties on a five year lease. It is primarily a corporate asset thus the building cannot be considered to generate cash inflows that are largely independent of the cash inflows of the entity as a whole.

The CGU is therefore M as a whole.

Recoverable Amount and Carrying Amount of a CGU

The recoverable amount of a CGU is the higher of its fair value less costs to sell and value in use. The carrying amount should be determined consistently with the way the recoverable amount is determined.

The carrying amount of a CGU includes the carrying amount of only those assets that can be attributed directly or allocated on a reasonable and consistent basis to the CGU and does not include the carrying amount of any recognised liability unless the recoverable amount of the CGU cannot be determined without its consideration.

The CGU should exclude cash flows relating to assets that are not part of a CGU. However, all assets that generate cash flows for the CGU should be included. In some cases, e.g. goodwill and head office assets, future cash flows cannot be allocated to the CGU on a reasonable and consistent basis. This is covered later. Also certain liabilities may have to be considered, e.g. on disposal of a CGU, if a buyer is forced to take over a liability. In that case the liability must be included as illustrated in the example below:

Example

A company must restore a mine by law, and it has provided €500 for the cost of restoration which is equal to the present value of restoration costs. The CGU is the mine as a whole. Offers of €800 have been received to buy the mine and disposal costs are negligible. The value in use is €1,200 excluding restoration costs and the carrying amount €1,000.

Fair value less costs to sell	€800	
Value in use	€700	(€1,200 less €500)
Carrying amount of CGU	€500	(€1,000 less €500)

The recoverable amount of €800 exceeds its carrying amount of €500 by €300 and there is no impairment.

Allocating Goodwill to CGUs

Goodwill should be allocated to one or more CGUs and the CGUs should represent the smallest CGU to which a portion of the carrying amount of goodwill can be allocated on a reasonable and consistent basis. It is capable of being allocated only when a CGU represents the lowest level at which management monitors the return on investment in assets that include the goodwill. The CGU should not be larger than a *segment* based on IAS 14 Segment *Reporting*/IFRS 8 *Operating Segments* (IFRS 8 replaces IAS 14 for annual periods beginning 1 January 2009).

Goodwill does not generate cash flows independently, the benefits are not capable of being individually identified and separately recognised and they often contribute to multiple CGUs. If the initial allocation of goodwill cannot be completed before the end of the first annual reporting period in which the business combination occurs it must be completed before the end of the first annual reporting date beginning after the acquisition date.

If provisional values are adopted the acquirer must initially adopt those provisional figures and then adjust within 12 months to final. Additional information must be disclosed regarding the adjustments.

If a CGU is disposed, which includes goodwill previously allocated, the goodwill associated with the disposal should be:

- included in the NBV of the operation when determining gain or loss on disposal; and
- measured on the basis of relative values of the operation disposed of and the portion of the CGU retained.

Example

An entity sells for €100 an operation that was part of a CGU to which goodwill was allocated. The goodwill allocated to the unit cannot be identified or associated with an asset group at a level lower than that unit, except arbitially. The recoverable amount of the portion of the CGU retained is €300. Because the goodwill allocated to the CGU cannot be 10% arbitrarily identified, it is measured on the basis of the relative values disposed of and retained. Therefore, of the goodwill allocated, 25% is included in the NBV of operation that is sold.

If an entity reorganises so that there are changes in the composition of one or more CGUs (to which goodwill has been allocated) the goodwill should be reallocated to units affected by adopting a relative value approach similar to that used when an entity disposes of an operation within a CGU.

Example

Goodwill was previously allocated to CGU A. The goodwill allocated to A cannot be identified with an asset group at a level lower than A, except arbitiarily. A is to be divided and integrated into three other CGUs, B, C and D. Therefore the goodwill allocated to A is reallocated to B, C and D based on the relative values of the three portions of A before those portions are integrated with B, C and D. If A is to be allocated 20:30:50 to B, C and D respectively then the goodwill previously allocated to A would be allocated to B, C and D in these proportions.

Non-controlling Interests

Note   The revisions to IAS 27 *Consolidated and Separate Financial Statements* and IFRS 3 *Business Combinations* (both effective for accounting periods beginning on or after 1 July 2009), including the calculation of non-controlling interests (NCI) (previously minority interest), are addressed in detail in Section Five.

Any CGU containing goodwill should be tested for impairment annually. However, the way entities choose to measure the goodwill and NCI affects the impairment test and the amount of impairment loss recognised. Under the proportionate share method, a notional gross-up of the entity's goodwill balance is required to ensure the carrying value of the CGU includes the goodwill attributable to the NCI. This grossed up amount is compared to the recoverable amount of the CGU, which includes the entire cash flows or fair value attributable to the CGU as well as the cash flows attributable to the controlling interest (CI).

This is not a new requirement as entities were previously required to gross up goodwill from partial business combinations in impairment tests. Application of the fair value method means that gross up is not required but does introduce other complexities. Management needs to consider the impact on impairment tests when choosing the method to use.

Example

	Proportionate method	Fair value method
	€	€
Identifiable net assets	1,000	1,000
Goodwill	400	450
Gross-up (€400 × 20%/80%)	100	–
Total carrying amount of CGU	1,500	1,450
Less recoverable amount	(1,100)	(1,100)
Impairment	400	350
Impairment included in statement of comprehensive income	320	350[1]

[1] The allocation of the impairment loss between CI and NCI is discussed below.

Under the proportionate share method, only the CI's share of the impairment loss is recognised in the statement of comprehensive income because only the CI's share of goodwill is recognised. Under the fair value method, the impairment loss is recognised in full in the statement of comprehensive income. The headline loss is therefore higher for the entity that elects to adopt the fair value method.

There are new requirements for allocating goodwill impairment losses between the CI and the NCI. The accounting is usually straightforward if the subsidiary with the NCI represents a CGU or group of CGUs for goodwill impairment-testing purposes, i.e. the allocation is done on the same basis as the allocation of profit.

Based upon the example above, if profit is allocated on the basis of ownership interests, 20% of the impairment loss is allocated to the NCI. Therefore, under the proportionate share method, €80 of the €400 impairment loss is allocated to the NCI; however, it is not accounted for in the statement of comprehensive income because only the CI's share of goodwill is recognised. The full impairment loss of €350 is recognised when the goodwill has been recognised on the fair value method, but €70 (20%) is allocated to the NCI.

The allocation of impairment losses between the CI and the NCI becomes more complex if the subsidiary is part of a larger CGU or group of CGUs for goodwill impairment-testing purposes.

Corporate Assets

This includes headquarters buildings, research centres etc. Their key characteristics are that they do not generate independent cash flows thus their recoverable amount cannot be determined. Thus if there is an indication that a corporate asset may be impaired, recoverable amount is determined for the CGU to which the corporate asset belongs compared with the carrying amount of this CGU and any impairment loss recognised.

If a portion of the carrying amount of a corporate asset:

1. can be allocated on a reasonable and consistent basis then the entity should compare the carrying amount of the CGU (including corporate asset) with its recoverable amount and recognise any losses;
2. cannot be allocated on a reasonable and consistent basis then the entity should:
   (a) compare the carrying amount of the CGU, excluding the corporate asset, with its recoverable amount and recognise any impairment loss,
   (b) identify the smallest CGU to which a portion of the corporate asset can be allocated on a reasonable and consistent basis, and
   (c) compare the carrying amount of the larger CGU, including a portion of the corporate asset, with its recoverable amount and recognise any impairment loss.

Example

Background

Entity M has three CGUs – A, B and C. They do not include goodwill. At the end of 20X0 the carrying amounts are €100, €150 and €200. Corporate assets have a carrying amount of €200 (building €150, research centre €50). The remaining useful life of CGU A is 10 years and CGUs B and C 20 years each. The entity adopts a straight-line basis for depreciation. There is no basis to calculate the fair value less costs to sell for each CGU thus recoverable value is based on value in use using a 15% pre-tax discount rate.

Identification of corporate assets

The carrying amount of headquarter buildings can be allocated on a reasonable and consistent basis. The research centre cannot be allocated in such a manner.

Allocation of corporate assets:

End of 20X0	A	B	C	Total
Carrying amount	€100	€150	€200	€450
Useful life	10 years	20 years	20 years	
Weighting based on useful life	1	2	2	
Carrying amt after weighting	€100	€300	€400	€800
Pro rata allocation of building (1:3:4)	12.5%	37.5%	50%	100%
Alloc. carrying amt of blding (€150)	€19	€56	€75	€150
Carrying amt after allocation	€119	€206	€275	€600

Determination of recoverable amount and calculation of impairment losses

The recoverable amount of each individual CGU must be compared with its carrying amount, including the portion of the headquarters, and any impairment loss recognised. IAS 36 then requires the recoverable amount of M as a whole to be compared with its carrying amount, including the headquarters and the research centre.

Calculation of A, B, C and M's value in use at the end of 20X0 (see W1):
A - Future cash flows for 10 years discounted at 15% = €199
B - Future cash flows for 20 years discounted at 15% = €164
C - Future cash flows for 20 years discounted at 15% = €271, and
M - Future cash flows for 20 years discounted at 15% = €720

Impairment testing A, B and C

End of 20X0	A	B	C
	€	€	€
Carrying amount after allocation of building	119	206	275
Recoverable amount	199	164	271
Impairment loss	0	(42)	(4)

Allocation of Impairment losses for CGUs B and C

	B	C
	€	€
To headquarters building	(42 x 56/206) (12)	(1) (4x75/275)
To assets in CGU	(42 x 150/206) (30)	(3) (4x200/275)
	(42)	(4)

Because the research centre could not be allocated on a reasonable and consistent basis to A, B and C's CGUs, M compares the carrying amount of the smallest CGU to which the carrying amount of the research centre can be allocated (i.e. M as a whole) to its recoverable amount.

Impairment testing the 'larger' CGU (i.e. M as a whole)

End of 20X0	A	B	C	Building	Research Centre	M
	€	€	€	€	€	€
Carrying amt after alloc of bldg	100	150	200	150	50	650
Impairment loss (first step)	-	(30)	(3)	(13)	-	(46)
Carrying amount (after first step)	100	120	197	137	50	(604)
Recoverable amount						720
Impairment loss for the larger CGU						0

Thus, no additional impairment loss results from the application of the impairment test to the 'larger' CGU. Only €46 uncovered in step one is recognised.

W1 Year	A Future cash flows	A Discount at 15%	B Future cash flows	B Discount at 15%	C Future cash flows	C Discount at 15%	M Future cash flows	M Discount at 15%
	CU	CU	CU	CU	CU	CU	CU	CU
1	18	16	9	8	10	9	39	34
2	31	23	16	12	20	15	72	54
3	37	24	24	16	34	22	105	69
4	42	24	29	17	44	25	128	73
5	47	24	32	16	51	25	143	71
6	52	22	33	14	56	24	155	67
7	55	21	34	13	60	22	162	61
8	55	18	35	11	63	21	166	54
9	53	15	35	10	65	18	167	48
10	48	12	35	9	66	16	169	42
11			36	8	66	14	132	28
12			35	7	66	12	131	25
13			35	6	66	11	131	21
14			33	5	65	9	128	18
15			30	4	62	8	122	15
16			26	3	60	6	115	12
17			22	2	57	5	108	10
18			18	1	51	4	97	8
19			14	1	43	3	85	6
20			10	1	35	2	71	4
VIU		199		164		271		720

Impairment Losses and CGUs

An impairment loss should be recognised only if its recoverable amount is less than its carrying amount. The impairment is allocated to reduce the carrying amount of the assets:

- First against goodwill to its implied value; and
- Then to other assets on a pro rata basis based on the carrying amount of each asset in the unit.

These are treated as impairment losses on individual assets. In allocating the loss an asset should not be reduced below the highest of:

(a) its fair value less costs to sell (if determinable);
(b) its value in use (if determinable); and
(c) zero.

The amount of the loss that would otherwise have been allocated to the asset should be allocated to the other assets on a pro rata basis.

If the recoverable amount of each individual asset in a CGU cannot be estimated without undue cost or effort, IAS 36 requires an arbitrary allocation between assets of the CGU other than goodwill. If the recoverable amount of an individual asset cannot be determined:

- An impairment loss is recognised for the asset if its carrying value is greater than the higher of its fair value less costs to sell and the results of procedures described above;
- No impairment loss is recognised if the related CGU is not impaired even if its fair value less costs to sell is less than its carrying amount.

Example

A machine has suffered physical damage but is still working, although not as well as before it was damaged. The machine's fair value less costs to sell is less than its carrying amount. The machine does not generate independent cash inflows. The smallest identifiable group of assets that includes the machine and generates cash inflows that are largely independent of the cash inflows from other assets is the production line to which the machine belongs. The recoverable amount of the production line shows that the production line taken as a whole is not impaired.

Assumption 1: Budgets/forecasts approved by management reflect no commitment of management to replace the machine.

The recoverable amount of the machine alone cannot be estimated because the machine's value in use:

(a) may differ from its fair value less costs to sell; and
(b) can be determined only for the CGU to which the machine belongs (the production line).

The production line is not impaired. Therefore, no impairment loss is recognised for the machine. Nevertheless, the entity may need to reassess the depreciation period or the depreciation method for the machine. Perhaps a shorter depreciation period or a faster depreciation method is required to reflect the expected remaining useful life of the machine or the pattern in which economic benefits are expected to be consumed by the entity.

Assumption 2: Budgets/forecasts approved by management reflect a commitment of management to replace the machine and sell it in the near future. Cash flows from continuing use of the machine until its disposal are estimated to be negligible.

> The machine's value in use can be estimated to be close to its fair value less costs to sell. Therefore, the recoverable amount of the machine can be determined and no consideration is given to the cash-generating unit to which the machine belongs (i.e. the production line). Because the machine's fair value less costs to sell is less than its carrying amount, an impairment loss is recognised for the machine.

Reversal of an Impairment Loss

An entity should assess at the end of each reporting period whether there is any indication that an impairment loss recognised in prior periods, other than goodwill, may no longer exist. If such exists the entity should estimate the recoverable amount of that asset. In assessing whether or not there is a reversal, the entity should consider the following indications, as a minimum:

External Sources of Information

(a) The asset's market value has increased significantly during the period;
(b) Significant changes with a favourable impact in the technological, market, economic or legal environment in which the entity operates;
(c) Market interest rates have decreased and are likely to affect the discount rate and the recoverable amount;

Internal Sources of Information

(a) Significant changes with a favourable effect during the period or in the near future. It includes capital expenditure that enhances an asset's standard of performance; and
(b) Evidence indicates that economic performance is better than expected.

An impairment loss in prior periods, for assets other than goodwill, should be reversed only if there is a change in estimate used to determine the asset's recoverable amount since the loss was recognised. Examples of changes in estimate include:

- A change in the basis for recoverable amount;
- If recoverable amount was based on value in use – a change in amount or timing of cash flows or in the discount rate; and
- If recoverable amount was based on fair value less costs to sell – a change in components of fair value less costs to sell

An impairment loss, however, is not reversed just because of the passage of time.

Reversal of an Impairment Loss for an Individual Asset

The increased carrying value of an asset, other than goodwill, due to a reversal should not exceed the carrying amount that would have existed had the asset not been impaired in prior years. Any increase in the carrying amount above the carrying amount had no impairment taken place would have been a revaluation.

A reversal should be recognised immediately in the statement of comprehensive income unless the asset is carried at a revalued amount under another standard. Any reversal of an impairment loss on a revalued asset should be treated as a revaluation reserve increase and credited directly to equity. However, to the extent a loss was previously recognised as an expense in the statement of comprehensive income, a reversal is also recognised in the statement of comprehensive income.

After a reversal, the depreciation charge should be adjusted in future periods to allocate its revised carrying amount over its remaining useful life:

$$\frac{\text{Revised carrying amount} - \text{residual value}}{\text{Remaining useful life}}$$

Reversal of an Impairment Loss for a CGU

A reversal of an impairment loss for a CGU should be allocated to the assets in the unit, except for goodwill, on a pro-rata basis with the carrying amount of those assets. In allocating a reversal for a CGU, the carrying amount of an asset should not be increased above the lower of:

(a) its recoverable amount (if determinable);
(b) the carrying amount that would be determined had no impairment taken place.

The amount of the reversal of the impairment loss that would otherwise have been allocated to the asset should be allocated on a pro-rata basis to the other assets of the CGU, except for goodwill.

Reversal of an Impairment Loss for Goodwill

An impairment loss recognised for goodwill should *not* be reversed in subsequent periods as IAS 38 expressly forbids the creation of internally generated goodwill.

DISCLOSURE

An entity should disclose the following for each class of assets:

- The amount of impairment losses recognised in profit or loss during the period;
- The amount of reversals of impairment losses recognised in the statement of comprehensive income during the period;
- The amount of impairment losses recognised directly in equity during the period; and
- The amount of reversals of impairment losses recognised directly in equity during the period.

This information may be included in a reconciliation of the carrying amount of property, plant and equipment as required by IAS 16. Under IAS 14/IFRS 7, the following should be disclosed for each reportable segment based on the entity's primary reporting format:

- The amount of impairment losses recognised in profit or loss and in equity; and
- The amount of reversals of impairment losses recognised in profit or loss and in equity.

The following should be disclosed for each material impairment loss recognised or reversed during the period for an individual asset, including goodwill, or a CGU:

(a) The events and circumstances that led to the recognition or reversal of the impairment;

(b) The amount of the impairment loss recognised or reversed;

(c) For an individual asset
   (i) the nature of the asset,
   (ii) the reportable segment to which the asset belongs, if applicable;

(d) For a CGU
   (i) a description of the CGU,
   (ii) the amount of the impairment loss recognised or reversed by class of asset and, if applicable, by reportable segment under IAS 14/IFRS 7,
   (iii) If the aggregation of assets for identifying the CGU has changed since the previous estimate of the CGU's recoverable amount, a description of the current and former way of aggregating assets and the reasons for changing the way the CGU is identified;

(e) Whether the recoverable amount of the asset is its fair value less costs to sell or its value in use;

(f) If recoverable amount is fair value less costs to sell, the basis used to determine fair value less costs to sell; and

(g) If recoverable amount is value in use, the discount rate used in the current and previous estimates of value in use.

An entity should disclose the following information for the aggregate impairment losses and the aggregate reversals of impairment losses recognised during the period for which no information is disclosed above:

(a) The main classes of assets affected by impairment losses and the main classes of assets affected by reversals of impairment losses; and

(b) The main events and circumstances that led to the recognition of these impairment losses and reversals of impairment losses.

An entity is encouraged to disclose key assumptions used to determine the recoverable amount of assets (CGUs) during the period but required to do so when goodwill or intangible assets with indefinite useful lives are included in a CGU. If goodwill has not been allocated to a CGU, the amount should be disclosed together with reasons for non-allocation. If an entity recognises the best estimate of a probable impairment loss for goodwill the following should be disclosed:

(a) the fact that the impairment loss recognised for goodwill is an estimate, not yet finalised; and

(b) the reasons why the impairment loss has not been finalised.

In the immediate succeeding period, the nature and amount of any adjustments should be disclosed.

CONCLUSION

Impairment testing must be carried out annually at the same time of the year for goodwill and intangible assets with an indefinite useful life. Other assets should be tested if there are indications of impairment. An impairment loss occurs when the carrying value of an asset or CGU is greater than its recoverable amount

i.e. impairment loss = carrying amount − recoverable amount.

The recoverable amount is the higher of its fair value less costs to sell and its value in use. Value in use is calculated by discounting the future cash flows which the asset or CGU is expected to generate.

Impairment losses are usually recognised as an expense in the statement of comprehensive income. However, if an asset is carried at a revalued amount, impairment losses are treated in the same way as revaluation losses.

QUESTIONS

Self-test Questions

1. Define the term 'impairment loss'.
2. Define the term 'cash generating unit'.
3. List the factors which suggest that an asset may have been impaired.
4. Explain how the recoverable amount of an asset is determined.

Review Questions

(See APPENDIX ONE for Suggested Solutions to Review Questions.)

Question 1

Keano Limited has identified an impairment loss of €60 million in one of its cash generating units (CGUs). The CGU showed a carrying amount of €160 million and a recoverable amount of €100 million at 31 December 200X.

Details of the carrying amount	€m
Goodwill	20
Property	60
Machinery	40
Motor vehicles	20
Other assets	20
	160

The fair value less costs to sell of the CGU's assets is less than their carrying values except for the property which had a market value of €70 million at 31 December 200X.

Requirement   Allocate the impairment loss arising in accordance with IAS 36 Impairment of Assets.

Question 2

(Based on ICAI, P3 Summer 2003, Question 4)
BLUES Limited (BLUES) prepares its financial statements to 31 December each year. The company manufactures paint, and its operations are divided into two income-generating units, domestic and commercial. The following issue needs to be resolved before the financial statements for the year ended 31 December 2008 can be finalised.

The following information is available in relation to the two income-generating units.

	Domestic	Commercial
	€'000	€'000
Goodwill	-	1,200
Other intangible assets	1,500	300
Property, plant and equipment	2,400	6,400
Inventory	3.300	1,400
Historic cost based carrying value	7,200	9,300
Net realisable value	7,500	4,200
Future net cash inflows:		
2009	1,200	1,200
2010	900	1,300
2011	2,700	1,600
2012	1,500	1,500
2013	1,600	900
2014	1,800	1,800
Discount rate appropriate to activities of income generating units	10%	12%

Requirement
(a) Calculate whether an impairment loss arises for either of the two income-generating units, domestic and commercial.
(b) Allocate any impairment loss arising in accordance with IAS 36 Impairment of Assets.

Present value factors:

Rate/Period	1	2	3	4	5	6
10%	0.909	0.826	0.751	0.683	0.620	0.564
12%	0.893	0.797	0.712	0.636	0.567	0.507

Challenging Questions

Question 1

You are the financial controller of VERTIGO Limited (VERTIGO), an Irish company that prepares its financial statements to 31 December each year. The following issue needs to be resolved before the financial statements for the year ended 31 December 2006 can be finalised.

On 1 January 2006, VERTIGO purchased all the shares of SAN JUAN Limited (SAN JUAN) for €12,000,000. The fair value of the identifiable net assets of SAN JUAN at that date was €10,800,000. During the year ended 31 December 2006, SAN JUAN traded at a loss and the fair value of its net assets at 31 December 2006 was as follows:

	€'000
Non-current assets – property, plant and equipment	7,800
Non-current assets – capitalised development costs	1,200
Net current assets	1,500
	10,500

An impairment review at 31 December 2006 indicated that the value in use of SAN JUAN at that date was €9,000,000 and that its net realisable value was €8,500,000.

Requirement
(a) Calculate the impairment loss that would arise in the consolidated financial statements of the VERTIGO Group for the year ended 31 December 2006 as a result of the impairment review of SAN JUAN.
(b) Assuming the capitalised development expenditure has no ascertainable market value, show how the impairment loss calculated in (a) would affect the carrying values of the various net assets in the consolidated statement of financial position of the VERTIGO Group as at 31 December 2006.

CHAPTER 11

INVENTORIES

INTRODUCTION

The term 'inventory' refers to raw materials, work in progress (WIP), finished goods produced and goods purchased and held for resale by a business. While there are many reasons why a business may hold inventory, the three basic reasons are:

1. **time** – time lags present in the supply chain, from supplier to user at every stage, usually require that it is essential to maintain a certain level of inventory to use in this 'lead time';
2. **uncertainty** – inventory may be held as a buffer to meet uncertainties in demand, supply and movements of goods; and
3. **economies of scale** – the notion of 'one unit at a time at a place where the user needs it when he needs it' is unrealistic and would incur significant costs in terms of logistics. Therefore bulk buying, movement and storing can bring economies of scale.

These reasons are applicable at any stage of the production process. While, from an overall business perspective, there are a myriad of issues surrounding inventory, this chapter focuses on the accounting treatment of inventory and, in particular, the amount of cost to be recognised as an asset in accordance with IAS 2 *Inventories* and carried forward until the related revenues are recognised.

After having studied this chapter, you should be able to:

- define the term 'inventory';
- measure the value of inventory in accordance with IAS 2; and
- apply cost formulae such as FIFO and weighted average.

IAS 2 *INVENTORIES*

IAS 2 prescribes the accounting treatment for inventories, except:

- WIP arising under construction contracts (IAS 11 *Construction Contracts*) (see Chapter 12);

- Financial instruments (IAS 39 *Financial Instruments*) (see Chapter 25); and
- Biological assets related to agricultural activity and agricultural produce at the point of harvest (IAS 41 *Agriculture*) (see Chapter 34).

Measurement of Inventories

Under IAS 2, inventory should be measured at the lower of cost and net realisable value (NRV). The cost of inventories consists of:

- cost of purchase;
- cost of conversion; and
- any other costs incurred in bringing the inventories to their present location and condition.

Cost of Purchase

This is the total of:

- purchase price less trade discounts and rebates;
- import duties and other taxes not recoverable; and
- transport and handling costs.

Cost of Conversion

This comprises of:

- costs directly related to the units of production, e.g. direct materials, direct labour and direct expenses; and
- allocated fixed and variable production overheads.

Fixed Production Overheads   These remain relatively constant regardless of the volume of production, e.g. depreciation and maintenance of factory buildings and equipment, the cost of factory management and administration.

Example

DEF plc manufactures mechanical parrots which trade under the name Parker. In the year ended 31 December Year 4, 10,000 Parkers are manufactured and the related costs were:

	€
Materials	3,000
Labour	4,000

Depreciation of machinery	2,000
Factory rates	1,000
Sundry factory expenses	2,000
Warehouse expenses	1,000
Selling expenses	2,000
Expenses at head office	4,000
	19,000

Requirement At the year end there were 1,000 Parkers in inventory and, assuming that these have a resale value of €4 each, what value should be placed on the closing inventory?

Solution

		€
Cost:	Materials	3,000
	Labour	4,000
	Depreciation of machinery	2,000
	Factory rates	1,000
	Sundry factory expenses	2,000
	Warehouse expenses	1,000
		13,000

No. of Parkers produced	10,000
Therefore cost per item	€1.30
Number in inventory at year end	1,000
Therefore cost of closing inventory	€1,300
Net realisable value = 1,000 x €4	€4,000

Therefore inventory should be valued in the statement of financial position at €1,300.

Note Examples of costs excluded from the cost of inventories and recognised as expenses in the period in which they are incurred are:

• abnormal amounts of wasted materials, labour or other production costs;
• storage costs, unless those costs are necessary in the production process before a further production stage;

- administrative overheads that do not contribute to bringing inventories to their present location and condition; and
- selling costs.

Note   Fixed production overheads must be allocated to items of inventory on the basis of normal capacity of the production facilities:

- Normal capacity is the expected achievable production based on the average over several periods. This includes capacity lost through planned maintenance;
- Low production or idle plant will not result in a higher fixed overhead allocation to each unit;
- Unallocated overheads must be written off as an expense in the year in which they are incurred; and
- When production is abnormally high, the fixed production overhead allocated to each unit is decreased so that inventories are not valued above cost.

Example

The following information related to Unipoly plc, a manufacturer of can openers, for the year ended 31 December 200X

	€
Direct materials cost of can opener per unit	1
Direct labour cost of can opener per unit	1
Direct expenses cost of can opener per unit	1
Production overheads per year	600,000
Administration overheads per year	200,000
Selling overheads per year	300,000
Interest payments per year	100,000

There was no finished goods inventory at the start of the year and no work in progress. There were 250,000 units in finished goods at the year end. The normal annual level of production is 750,000 can openers. However, in the year ended 31 December 200X, only 450,000 were produced because of a labour dispute.

Requirement   Calculate the cost of finished goods at 31 December 200X in accordance with IAS 2 Inventories.

Solution

Cost per unit:		€
	Material	1.00
	Labour	1.00

Other expenses	1.00
Production overheads	0.80
(€600,000/€750,000)	3.80
Valuation of finished goods inventory	
250,000 units x €3.80 =	950,000

Variable Production Overheads   Those indirect costs of production that vary directly or nearly directly with the volume of production, e.g. indirect material and indirect labour. Variable production overheads are allocated to each unit of production on the basis of the actual use of the production facilities.

Other Costs   These can only be included in the cost of inventories if they are incurred in bringing them to their present location and condition, e.g. the cost of designing products for specific customers. The following costs *cannot* be included in the cost of inventories – they must be written off as expenses immediately:

- abnormal amounts of wasted materials;
- storage costs – except where they are necessary in the production process before a further stage of production;
- administrative overheads that do not contribute to bringing products to their present location; and
- selling costs.

Techniques for the Measurement of Cost

IAS 2 deals with two methods:

1. **Standard Cost** – This takes into account normal levels of materials and supplies, labour, efficiency and capacity utilisation. Standard costs *must* be reviewed regularly and revised if necessary.
2. **The Retail Method** – i.e. sales value *less* percentage gross margin. This method is used in the retail industry for valuing inventories of large numbers of rapidly changing items with similar margins where other costing methods are impractical.

Cost Formulae

These are only used when inventories consist of a large number of interchangeable (i.e. identical or very similar) items. In these circumstances specific identification of costs is not appropriate and costs should be assigned using either:

- First In First Out (FIFO); or
- weighted average cost.

Weighted average can be calculated on a periodic basis or as each additional purchase is made.

Example

A toy shop buys two batches of dolls during its accounting period:

Batch 1 purchased in month 1: 5 @ €10 each; and
Batch 2 purchased in month 2: 5 @ €12 each.

During month 3, 3 dolls were sold @ €25 each.

Requirement   Calculate the value of closing inventory at the end of month 3 using both FIFO and the weighted average methods.

Solution

Valuation of Closing Inventory (FIFO):

		€
2 @ €10 =		20
5 @ €12 =		60
		80

Valuation of closing inventory (weighted average):

		€
5 @ €10 =		50
5 @ €12 =		60
10 @ €11 =		110
Closing inventory 7 @ €11		77

IAS 2 *Inventories* eliminates the option of using the Last In First Out (LIFO) method of measuring the cost of inventory.

Net Realisable Value

Net realisable value (NRV) is the estimated selling price in the ordinary course of business less the estimated costs of completion and *less* the estimated costs necessary to make the sale. Where the cost of inventories may not be recoverable (e.g. damaged, obsolete, selling prices declined) they should not be carried in excess of the amounts expected to be realised from their sale, i.e. they must be valued at NRV.

Comparison of cost and NRV:

- Ideally – item by item;
- In some circumstances – by groups, i.e. items in same product line; and
- Not appropriate – general classification, e.g. finished goods.

Example

Finished goods of dissimilar items at 31 December 200X

Item	Cost	NRV
	€	€
1	1,000	1,400
2	800	700
3	2,500	2,800
4	1,800	1,700
5	200	300
6	300	250
	6,600	7,150

Inventory should be recorded in the financial statements at 31 December 200X at:

Item	€
1	1,000
2	700
3	2,500
4	1,700
5	200
6	250
	6,350

The assessment of NRV should take place *at the same time* as estimates are made of selling price. A new assessment of NRV should be made in each subsequent accounting period. If the circumstances that previously caused inventories to be written down below cost no longer exist or if there is clear evidence of an increase in NRV because of changed economic circumstances, the amount of the write down should be reversed (i.e. the reversal is limited to the amount of the original write down) so that the new carrying amount is the lower of the cost and the NRV. This might occur, for example, when an item of inventory that is carried at NRV, because its selling price has declined, is still on hand in a subsequent period and its selling price has increased.

Recognition as an Expense

- When inventories are sold, they should be expended in the period when the revenue is recognised;
- Any write downs or reversals should be recorded in the period they occur; and
- If any inventories are used in the construction of property, plant etc., they should be capitalised and expended over the useful life of the (tangible) non-current asset created.

Disclosure

- The accounting policy adopted in measuring inventories, including cost formulas;
- The total carrying amount of inventories analysed under major headings, e.g. raw materials, WIP and finished goods
- The carrying amount of inventories at fair value less costs to sell;
- The amount expended in the period;
- The amount of any write downs of inventories;
- The amount of any reversal of write downs;
- The cause of write downs; and
- The carrying amount of inventories pledged as security for liabilities.

CONCLUSION

Inventories are measured at the lower of cost and NRV, which is the estimated selling price in the ordinary course of business less the estimated costs of completion and the estimated costs necessary to make the sale. Cost includes all costs of purchase, costs of conversion and other costs incurred in bringing the inventories to their present location and condition. The cost of inventories, other than those for which specific identification of costs are appropriate, is assigned by using the FIFO or weighted average cost formula.

When inventories are sold, the carrying amount of those inventories is recognised as an expense in the same period as the revenue.

The amount of any write-down of inventories to NRV is recognised as an expense in the period the write-down or loss occurs. The amount of any reversal of a write-down of inventories is recognised as a reduction in the amount of inventories recognised as an expense in the period in which the reversal occurs.

QUESTIONS

Self-test Questions

1. How should inventory be measured in accordance with IAS 2?
2. What does the cost of inventory comprise?
3. Name and describe two methods identified in IAS 2 for the measurement of cost.

Review Questions

(See APPENDIX ONE for Suggested Solutions to Review Questions.)

Question 1

You are the accounting consultant to a public holding company which has four trading subsidiaries: Screws Limited, Brackets Limited, Frames Limited and Concrete Blocks Limited. All the subsidiaries tend to be of roughly equal value. The accounts of the company are made up annually to 31 December.

Two weeks before the year-end the Group Chief Accountant brings the following matters to your attention:

(a) The Group Chief Accountant has suggested to the management of Screws Limited, a manufacturing company, that their finished goods inventory must be accurately costed this year. However, the management of Screws Limited insist that their usual basis of selling price less 20% is convenient and also consistent since the same percentage is used each year.

(b) Brackets Limited, which manufactures a range of brass sockets, is currently facing a price war with its main competitor. It is anticipated that the company's trading results for the last quarter of the year will be as follows:

	Units (Tonnes)	€'000
Sales	700	300
Brass consumed	700	(200)
Conversion costs		(120)
Selling costs		(30)
Loss		(50)

On 31 December, inventories consist only of 200 tonnes of completed brass sockets. The last consignment was purchased on 1 December at €500 per tonne and the published market price on 31 December is expected to be €520 per tonne. The Group Chief Accountant is uncertain how the brass inventory should be valued. The note on the group accounts will read: 'Inventories are valued at cost (in the case of finished goods, factory cost) or net realisable value if lower'.

(c) Frames Limited imported a shipment of windows from America on 15th November and the cost at the rate of exchange on that date was €100,000. The goods were not paid for until 10th December and the payment amounted to €120,000 due to an appreciation in the value of the US dollar during the three-week period. It is thought that only 5% of the consignment will have been sold by 31 December and the management of Frames Limited wish to value the windows on that date at €114,000.

(d) Concrete Blocks Limited have hitherto included fixed costs and variable costs (in particular fixed factory overheads) when valuing their inventory of finished goods. They now wish to move over to a variable-cost-only basis of valuation which they claim will give a truer picture of their performance.

Requirement   Prepare a memorandum for the attention of the Group Chief Accountant that addresses each of the points above.

Question 2

Techniques for the measurement of the cost of inventories such as the 'retail method' may be used for convenience if the results approximate cost. The cost of the inventory is determined by reducing the sales value by the appropriate percentage gross margin.

Requirement
(a) Discuss when might it be appropriate to use the method referred to above.
(b) If a company traditionally applied a policy of calculating actual cost by item but changed to the above method, would a prior year adjustment (as defined by IAS 8 *Accounting Policies, Changes in Accounting Estimates and Errors*) be required?
(c) You are the audit senior of a company which uses the above method of inventory valuation. What factors would you consider in the audit of inventory?

Challenging Questions

Question 1

Details of inventories of five separate products are as follows:

Product:	A	B	C	D	E
	€	€	€	€	€
Materials	1,000	2,000	1,500	6,000	1,200
Labour	500	500	600	600	600
Production overheads	400	400	500	500	500
Marketing overheads (yet to be incurred)	350	350	400	400	300

Selling overheads (yet to be incurred)	200	200	200	200	200
Administration costs	150	300	100	900	110
	2,600	3,750	3,300	8,600	2,910
Selling Price	2,800	3,700	3,000	7,200	2,900

Requirement Assuming that none of the above items have been sold at the year end, value the inventory on the basis of IAS 2 *Inventories*.

Question 2

Micro Limited processes and sells a single product. Purchases of raw materials during the year were made at a regular rate of 1,000 tonnes at the beginning of each week. The price was €200 per tonne on 1 January 200X and was increased to €300 per tonne on 1 July 200X and remained constant from then on until the end of the year, 31 December 200X. In addition to this price a customs duty of €20 per tonne was paid throughout the year and transport from the docks to the factory cost €40 per tonne.

Variable costs of processing were €50 per tonne. There was capacity to process 1,000 tonnes per week and the fixed production costs for all levels of activity up to this capacity level were €60,000 per week. One tonne of raw materials is processed into one tonne of finished products and sold, at a delivery price of €480 per tonne, by a sales force whose cost was fixed at €6,000 per week. Average delivery costs to customers were €15 per tonne.

At the beginning of the year there was no inventory and at the end of the year there were 5,000 tonnes of raw material and 2,000 tonnes of finished product. It is expected that the costs and prices current at 31 December 200X will continue during 200Y.

Requirement Draft the accounting policy on inventory for the company to include in its financial accounts.

(a) Calculate the value of inventory at 31 December 200X on a basis acceptable under IAS 2 *Inventories.*
(b) Comment upon the relative merits of FIFO and any other basis recognised under IAS 2 for valuing inventory.

Note You should assume that inventories of raw material can only be used to produce finished goods and cannot be re-sold as raw material at a realistic price.

Note Assume a 52-week productive year with production and sales spread evenly throughout the year.

CHAPTER 12

CONSTRUCTION CONTRACTS

INTRODUCTION

A construction contract is a contract for the construction of a single asset or a combination of assets that are related. Contracts can often span more than one accounting period and this creates some unusual accounting problems:

- How much revenue should be included in the statement of comprehensive income?
- How much should be charged for related costs?
- How much profit should be recognised in the period in respect of this contract?

Normally revenues and profits are only recognised in the statement of comprehensive income once they are realised. However, the nature of construction contracts can mean that the contract is only invoiced and revenues realised on completion of the contract. The statement of comprehensive income must show a fair representation of the activities of the enterprise for the period. Consequently, the prudence and the accruals/matching concept are head to head, with the accruals/matching concept winning. In order for the financial statements to show a fair presentation of the activities of the enterprise and provide useful and relevant information to users, an appropriate part of revenue and profits of the contract in the period in which the activity has taken place is included.

This chapter focuses on the accounting treatment of revenue and costs associated with construction contracts in accordance with IAS 11 *Construction Contracts*, and after having studied this chapter you should ensure that you understand the following key points:

- Profit on construction contracts can be recognised once the outcome of the contract can be estimated reliably as profitable;
- If the expected outcome is a profit, revenue and expenses will be recognised according to the stage of completion of the contract;
- If the expected outcome is a loss, the whole loss to completion should be recognised immediately; and
- The disclosure requirements.

IAS 11 *CONSTRUCTION CONTRACTS*

IAS 11 applies to the accounting treatment of construction contracts in the financial statements of contractors. As noted above, due to the nature of the activity undertaken in construction contracts, the date at which the contract activity is entered into and the date when the activity is completed usually fall into different periods. Therefore the primary issue in accounting for construction contracts is the allocations of contract revenue and contract costs to the accounting periods in which construction work is performed.

Important Definitions and Concepts

Construction Contract

This is a contract specifically negotiated for the construction of an asset or a combination of assets that are closely interrelated or interdependent in terms of their design, technology and function or their ultimate purpose or use.

Contract Revenue

This comprises of:

(a) the initial amount of revenue agreed in the contract; and
(b) variations in contract work, claims and incentive payments to the extent that it is probable that they will result in revenue and they are capable of being reliably measured.

The revenue is measured at the fair value received or receivable. Uncertainties which may affect the measurement of contract revenue include:

- agreed variations between contractor and customer in a subsequent period;
- cost escalation clauses in a fixed price contract; and
- penalties imposed on the contractor because of delays.

A variation is included in contract revenue when:

- it is probable that the customer will approve the variation; and
- the revenue can be measured reliably.

Contract Costs

These comprises of:

- costs that relate directly to the specific contract;
- costs that are attributable to contract activity in general and can be allocated to the
- contract; and
- such other costs as are specifically chargeable to the customer under the terms of the contract.

Costs that relate directly to a specific contract include:

- site labour costs, including site supervision;
- cost of materials used in construction;
- depreciation of plant and equipment used on the contract;
- costs of moving plant, equipment and materials to and from the contract site;
- costs of hiring plant and equipment;
- cost of design and technical assistance that is directly related to the contract;
- the estimated costs of rectification and guarantee work, including expected warranty cost; and
- claims from third parties.

Costs that may be attributable to contract activity in general that can be allocated to specific contracts include:

- insurance;
- costs of design and technical assistance that are not directly related to a specific contract; and
- construction overheads.

ACCOUNTING FOR CONSTRUCTION CONTRACTS

Each contract must be accounted for separately and then the totals aggregated and included in the financial statements. There are three important categories in IAS 11:

Category 1

When the outcome of a profitable construction contract can be estimated reliably, contract revenue and contract costs associated with the construction contract should be recognised as revenue and expenses respectively by reference to the stage of completion of the contract activity at the end of the reporting period.

Category 2

When a contract's outcome cannot be estimated reliably:

- recognise revenue to the extent of contract costs incurred which are expected to be recoverable; and
- recognise contract costs as an expense in the period in which incurred.

This situation arises during the early stages of a contract when it is difficult to reliably estimate the outcome, but likely that costs will be recovered.

Category 3

When it is probable that total contract costs will exceed total contract revenue, the expected loss should be recognised as an expense immediately. The whole loss to completion should be recognised. The amount of such a loss is determined irrespective of whether work has commenced on the contract and the stage of completion of contract activity.

Example – *Category 1*

Contract X at 31 December 200W

Commencement date	1 January 200W
Completion date	31 December 200X
Contract price	€3,000,000
Cost to date	€1,000,000
Cost to complete	€1,000,000

Suggested Approach

Step 1: Calculate the outcome for the contract

	€	€
Price		3,000,000
Costs		
To date	1,000,000	
To complete	1,000,000	
Total cost		(2,000,000)
Profit		1,000,000

Step 2: Determine the stage of completion

Cost to Date / Total Cost
€1,000,000 / €2,000,000 = 50%

Step 3: Statement of Comprehensive Income

	€
Revenue (€3m x 50%)	1,500,000
Cost of Sales (€2m x 50%)	(1,000,000)
Profit	500,000

Example – *Category 2*

Contract Y at 31 December 200W

Commencement date	1 November 200W
Completion date	31 March 200Y
Contract price	€5,000,000
Cost to date	€400,000
Cost to complete	€3,600,000

The stage of completion is to be determined by reference to cost to date and total costs.

Suggested Approach

Step 1:   Calculate the outcome for the contract

	€	€
Price		5,000,000
Costs		
To date	400,000	
To complete	3,600,000	
Total cost		(4,000,000)
Profit		1,000,000

Step 2:   Determine the stage of completion

Cost to Date / Total Cost
€4,000,000 / €4,000,000 = 10%
→ Too early to recognise any profit.

Step 3:   Statement of Comprehensive Income

	€
Revenue	400,000
Cost of Sales (€4m x 10%)	(1,000,000)
Profit	0

The amount taken to revenue is the same as the cost of sales.

Example – *Category 3*

Contract Z at 31 December 200W

Commencement date	1 September 200W
Completion date	30 April 200Y
Cost to date	€440,000
Cost to complete	€1,760,000
Contract price	€2,000,000
% completion	20

The stage of completion is to be determined by reference to cost to date and total costs.

Suggested Approach

Step 1:   Calculate the outcome for the contract

	€	€
Price		2,000,000
Costs		
To date	440,000	
To complete	1,760,000	
Total cost		(2,200,000)
Profit		(200,000)

Step 2:   Determine the stage of completion

Cost to Date / Total Cost
€4,400,000 / €2,200,000 = 20%

Step 3:   Statement of Comprehensive Income

	€
Revenue (€2m x 20%)	400,000
Cost of Sales (€2.2m x 10%)	(440,000)
Profit	40,000
Provision for foreseeable loss (160,000)	(160,000)
	200,000

When a contract is loss making irrespective of the stage of completion the full amount of the contract loss must be recognised.

Different aspects of the three categories will now be considered in more detail.

When Can the Outcome be Estimated Reliably?

Fixed Price Contract

When all four of the following conditions are satisfied:

1. Total revenue can be measured reliably;
2. It is probable that the economic benefits associated with the contract will flow into the entity;
3. Both the contract costs to complete and the stage of completion at the end of the reporting period can be measured reliably;
4. The contract costs attributable to the contract can be clearly identified and measured.

Cost Plus Contract

When two conditions are met:

1. It is probable that the economic benefits associated with the contract will flow to the entity; and
2. The contract costs attributable to the contract can be identified and measured.

Stage of Completion

The stage of completion is usually calculated using ONE of these formulae:

$$\frac{\text{Costs incurred to date}}{\text{Estimated total costs}}$$

or

$$\frac{\text{Value of Work Certified}}{\text{Contract price}}$$

Sales Revenue

In order to estimate an appropriate part of contract revenue to be included in the statement of comprehensive income, we must first establish the stage of completion of each contract. There is no set rule on how to determine turnover, but the two main methods in practice are:

- By reference to the proportion of work done, established either by certification of work by the surveyor, or by comparing the costs incurred to date to the total contract costs anticipated to give an estimate of work completed so far; and
- By identifying specific points in the contract where the work completed has separately ascertainable sales values. For example, a contract for residential property development could have a sales value for the building of the house, and separate values for the construction of the garage, swimming pool, stables etc.

Sales revenue should be recognised based on the activity on the contract in the period, regardless of the profit that is likely. Items that are included in the statement of comprehensive income are recorded only once. Therefore for a contract that spans, say, four years, any contract revenues recognised in previous years must be deducted. For example:

- Year 1 – (Total contract revenue × % stage of completion) = sales revenue for year 1;
- Year 2 – (Total contract revenue × % stage of completion) less revenue recognised in year 1 = sales revenue for year 2;
- Year 3 – (Total contract revenue × % stage of completion) less revenue recognised in year 1 and 2 = sales revenue for year 3.

Example

Moby Limited has the following contract details for a contract that started in 200W:

	200W	200X	200Y
Total contract sales value	€10m	€11m	€11.5m
Estimated % completion	40%	75%	100%

Note   As the total contract value has changed over the duration of the contract, this can only be included in the revenue calculation if these amendments have been agreed with the customer. This is a common occurrence as the costs associated with labour and materials during the course of the contract may change, an unforeseen obstacle may occur which is beyond the control of the contractor, or the customer specifications may change.

The revenue to be recognised is as follows:

	200W	200X	200Y
Revenues recognisable to date:	€m	€m	€m
200W: 40% x €10m	4.00		
200X: 75% x €11m		8.25	
200Y: 100% x €11.5m			11.50
Less revenues recognised in prior periods		(4.00)	(8.25)
Revenue for the period	4.00	4.25	3.25

Recognisable Contract Profits

The recognition of contract profit is again usually based on the percentage of work completed on the contract. Usually the amount of revenue and profit to be included will be decided based on work done, and the cost of sales figure will be the balancing figure. This is different from the normal statement of comprehensive income recognition, which is transaction-led (make a sale, match the costs, the profit is the result).

Example

ABC Limited commenced Contract A in 200W and has the following details for the year ended 31 December 200X:

Total contract value	€80m
Costs incurred to date	€50m
Estimated costs to complete	€7m
Completion	80%
Profit recognized in 200W	€11m

The first step is to calculate the total estimated profit on the contract:

	€m	€m
Total sales value of the contract		80
Less contract costs incurred to date	(50)	
Less estimated costs to completion	(7)	
Total estimated contract costs		(57)
Total estimated contract profit		23

The second step is to establish the stage of completion of the contract and calculate the profit recognisable to date:

Total estimated contract profit x % completion of the contract = recognisable profit to date €23m x 80% completion = €18.4m.

The third step is to calculate the profit reportable for this accounting period:

	€m
Recognisable profit to date	18.4
Less cumulative profit recognised in prior periods	(11.0)
Profit recognisable in this period	7.4

In this case it is the €7.4m that will appear within the profit in the statement of comprehensive income for the period.

Expected Contract Losses

Whenever an overall contract loss is expected, the loss must be recognised as soon as it is anticipated. The first step, calculating the overall profit or loss on the contract, would still be performed. However, if the overall contract is loss-making the full amount of the loss will be recognised immediately.

Example

ABC Limited commenced Contract B during 200X and will complete it in 200Y. It has the following details for the year ended 31 December 200X:

Total contract value	€70m
Costs incurred to date	€40m
Estimated costs to complete	€39m
Completion	50%

The first step is to calculate the overall outcome for this contract:

	€m	€m
Total sales value of the contract		70
Less contract costs incurred to date	(40)	
Less estimated costs to completion	(39)	
Total estimated contract costs		(79)
Total estimated contract loss		(9)

Contract B is 50% complete and revenue recognised must reflect this activity in the period, so the fact that the contract is loss-making does not remove the need to recognise sales revenue. However, what it does mean is that cost of sales must be charged with an amount that results in the full-time contract loss of €9m being recognised immediately.

Year 1 Statement of comprehensive income (extract)	€m
Sales revenue (50% x €70)	35
Cost of sales	(44)
Loss on contract	(9)

Cost of sales must be charged with €44m to ensure that the full contract loss of €9m is recognised in the first year (i.e. as soon as it is anticipated).

In this case, the cost of sales charge is made up of two elements:

1. 50% of total contract costs of €79m = €39.5m; and
2. the remaining amount of the loss that is expected to occur next year, which is €4.5m.

The revenues and costs will occur as follows (50% of revenue and 50% of costs, resulting in 50% of loss in the period. This would leave the same again to be recognised next year).

Statement of comprehensive income (Extract)

	200X	200Y
	€m	€m
Sales revenue (50% in each of the two years)	35.0	35.0
Cost of sales	(39.5)	(39.5)
Loss on contract	(4.5)	(4.5)

IAS 11 and prudence require that we recognise the whole of the loss as soon as it is anticipated and so the €4.5m loss expected to occur in 200Y is pulled back and charged to 200X's statement of comprehensive income through cost of sales. The statement of comprehensive income extract now shows:

Statement of comprehensive income (Extract)

	200X	200Y
	€m	€m
Sales revenue (50% in each of the two years)	35	35
Cost of sales (€39.5 + €4.5)	(44)	(35)
Profit/Loss on contract	(9)	–

Uncertain Outcome

If the outcome of the contract cannot be estimated with reasonable certainty then no profit should be recognised. However, the statement of comprehensive income must still reflect the activity in the period and so an appropriate part of revenue must still be recognised.

Example

ABC Limited commenced Contract C in 200Y and has the following details for the year ended 31 December 200Y.

	€m
Total contract value	40
Costs incurred to date	3
Estimated costs to complete	30
Completion	10%

ABC Limited has only just commenced work on this contract and cannot be certain of its outcome at the year-end date. The overall contract is expected to be profit-making. However, the contract has only just started (10% complete) and so the outcome cannot be measured with reasonable certainty. In this case, prudence dictates that no profit should be recognised in the year ended 31 December 200Y.

Revenue would normally include 10% of revenue and cost of sales would be made to match the revenue to create a nil profit:

Statement of comprehensive income (Extract)

	€m
Sales revenue (10% x €40m)	4
Costs of sales	(4)
Profit/loss on contract	–

However, in this case we cannot transfer €4m to cost of sales as we have only incurred costs of €3m to date. Where costs to date are less than the required costs of sales charge, we instead restrict the revenue figure to the level of costs incurred to date. The statement of comprehensive income for 200Y would therefore include the following for contract C:

Statement of comprehensive income (Extract)

	€m
Sales revenue	3
Costs of sales	(3)
Profit/loss on contract	–

Inventories

Any contract costs incurred but not yet transferred to cost of sales should be included within contract costs under the heading 'inventories' in the statement of financial position. Remember that each contract is accounted for separately so some contracts may have inventories, some may not. Each contract is calculated and then the total from each contract is aggregated in the statement of financial position.

Example

Using ABC Limited's Contract A again.

ABC Limited commenced Contract A in 200W and has the following details for the year ended 31 December 200X:

Total contract value	€80m
Costs incurred to date	€50m
Estimated costs to complete	€7m
Completion	80%
Profit recognised in 200W	€11m

Solution

Costs incurred to date total €50m:	€m	€m
DR Contract Costs	50	
CR Bank/Payables		50

The amount we will have charged to cost of sales to date (200W and 200X) is based on the percentage completion x the total contract cost (80% x €57m) = €45.6m. Over the two years of the contract we will have recorded:

Transfer to cost sales:	€m	€m
DR Cost of sales	45.6	
CR Contract costs		45.6

There is therefore a balance remaining on contract costs at 31 December 200X of €50m – €45.6m = €4.4m. This amount represents contract costs incurred that relate to a future activity and is therefore recognised as an asset and will be included in inventories in the statement of financial position.

Receivables

Using the above example, the impact on receivables in the statement of financial position can be examined. Where sales revenue recognised to date exceeds the progress payments received, the balance should be included as a separate item within receivables, and referred to as 'unbilled contract revenue'.

The progress payments received to date at 31 December 200X for Contract A totalled €60m:

			€m	€m
DR		Bank	60	
	CR	Progress payments		60

The total sales revenue recognised to date at 31 December 200X is €64m (80% x €80m).

			€m	€m
DR		Progress payments	64	
	CR	Sales revenue		64

This results in €4m receivable in respect of this contract. We have calculated (based on percentage completion) that sales and therefore amounts due from customers to date total €64m and the customer has paid €60m to date. The remaining €4m is therefore a receivable and is referred to as 'unbilled contract revenue'.

Payables

Where sales revenue recognised to date is less than the progress payments received the balance should be included as a separate item within payables, and referred to as 'progress payments received'.

Assume that for Contract A the progress payments received at 31 December 200X totalled €70m.

			€m	€m
DR		Bank	70	
	CR	Progress payments		70

The total sales revenue recognised to date at 31 December 200X is €64m (80% × €80m).

			€m	€m
DR		Progress payments	64	
	CR	Sales revenue		64

In this case we have calculated that €64m is due on this contract and the customer has already paid €70m. We have received customer monies that have not yet been earned and so the balance of €6m is included within payables as 'progress payments received' (included as a liability until the money has been earned through next year's activity on the contract).

Provisions for Foreseeable Losses

Whenever a loss is provided for it is charged to the statement of comprehensive income and the corresponding credit entry is made in the statement of financial position. IAS 11 permits foreseeable losses to first be offset against any related (from the same contract) balance on contract costs, with any remaining balance being included in provisions in the statement of financial position. Foreseeable losses charged to cost of sales are therefore recorded as:

DR Cost of sales
  CR Contract costs/provision

Offset Against Remaining Contract Costs

Where there are remaining contract costs on a contract after transferring amounts to cost of sales, the balance can be used as an offset, firstly against foreseeable losses and then against excess progress payments received from the same contract.

Example

ABC Limited commenced Contract D in 200W and has the following details for the year ended 31 December 200X:

Total contract value	€70m
Costs incurred to date	€60m
Estimated costs to complete	€15m
Completion	60%
Progress payments received	€50m

	€m
The overall contract is loss making:	
Total contract value	70
Less total contract costs (€60m + €15m)	(75)
Overall anticipated contract loss	(5)

An amount of this loss will be included in the cost of sales charge for this year as the 60% completion is applied to total contract costs, 60% x €75m = €45m. Sales revenue is 60% x €70m = €42m, resulting in a loss of €3m. However, the full loss of €5m must be recognised in the period, so an additional €2m must be charged in addition to cost of sales. This additional €2m loss can be deducted from any related balance on contract costs. If there are insufficient contract costs to absorb this €2m then the balance will be included in provisions in the statement of financial position.

There is also excess progress payments received in the period. Sales revenue recognised to date is €42m (60% x €70m) and progress payments received total €50m. The excess amounts received of €8m can also be offset against any related contract cost balance, but only after the deduction of any foreseeable loss.

The calculation for inventory for contract D is as follows:

	€m
Costs incurred to date	60
Transferred to cost of sales (60% x total contract costs €75m)	(45)
Remaining contract balance	15
Less foreseeable loss not charged through cost of sales	(2)
Remaining contract costs	13
Less excess progress payments received	(8)
Inventories – contract costs	5

Example

Crave Limited has three contracts in progress during the year and the following details are available for the year ended 31 December 200X:

Contract	Alpha	Beta	Gamma
Commenced	June 200W	January 200X	November 200X
Total contract value	€90m	€60m	€100m
Costs incurred to date	€70m	€45m	€15m
Estimated costs to complete	€10m	€23m	€70m
Completion	80%	60%	10%
Progress payments received	€65m	€32m	€20m

Additional Information

1. Contract Alpha commenced during 200W and at 31 December 200W was 50% complete; accordingly, appropriate amounts for revenue and profit were included in the 200W statement of comprehensive income.

2. Crave Limited has a policy of recognizing profit on contracts once the contracts have reached a minimum of 30% completion, to ensure that their outcome can be assessed with reasonable certainty.

Requirement   How should Crave Limited reflect the contracts in its financial statements for the year ended 31 December 200X?

Solution

Sales Revenue:

	Alpha	Beta	Gamma
	€m	€m	€m
Revenues recognisable to date:			
Alpha (80% x €90m)	72		
Beta (60% x €60m)		36	
Gamma (10% x €100m)			10
Revenues previously recognised:			
Alpha (50% x €90m)	(45)		
Revenues recognisable in the period	27	36	10

Total sales revenue that is recognisable and will be included in the statement of comprehensive income for the year ended 31 December 200X is €73m (27 + 36 + 10).

Contract Profits and Losses:

	Alpha	Beta	Gamma
	€m	€m	€m
Overall contract position:			
Total contract value	90	60	100
Total contract costs (incurred to date plus cost to complete)	(80)	(68)	(85)
Contract profit/(loss)	10	(8)	15
Profits/(loss) recognisable to date			
Alpha (80% x €10m)	8		
Beta (100% x (loss of €8m))		(8)	
Gamma (nil – only 10% complete)			-

Amounts previously recognised:

Alpha (50% x €10m)	(5)	—	—
Profits/(losses) in the period	3	(8)	—

Using the revenues and profits calculated above we can now draft the statement of comprehensive income extract for Crave Limited for the year ended 31 December 200X:

	Alpha €m	Beta €m	Gamma €m	Total €m
Sales revenue	27	36	10	73
Cost of sales	(24)	(44)	(10)	78
Contract profits/(losses)	3	(8)	-	(5)

Note

Alpha – We must remember to deduct the revenues and therefore profits previously recognised;

Beta – the overall contract is expected to make a loss of €8m and therefore the entire loss must be recognised immediately. The cost of sales figure therefore, includes cost of sales for 200X of €40.8m (60% x total contract costs of €45m incurred and €23m to complete) plus anticipated loss for 200Y of 3.2m (40% x €8m);

Gamma – the contract is only 10% complete and so 10% of revenue can be recognised but no profit must be recognised as the contract outcome cannot be assessed with reasonable certainty. Cost of sales is therefore charged with an amount to match revenue (provided that there is sufficient in contract costs for this contract to transfer to cost of sales).

Inventories:

	Alpha €m	Beta €m	Gamma €m	Total €m
Contract costs incurred to date	70	45	15	73
Transferred to cost of sales to date	(64)	(44)	(10)	—
Balance to be included in inventories	6	1	5	12

Alpha is 80% complete to date and has therefore transferred 80% of total contract costs to cost of sales over 200W and 200X.

Receivables and Payables:

	Alpha	Beta	Gamma	Total
	€m	€m	€m	€m
Progress payments received	65	32	20	
Sales revenue recognised to date	72	36	10	
Receivables – unbilled contract revenue	7	4	-	11
Payables – progress payments received			10	10

IAS 11 ILLUSTRATIONS

IAS 11 also contains illustrations showing the procedure. They are given below and you should work through them once you have fully understood the procedure described above.

Illustration 1

A contractor has a fixed-price contract for €9 million to build a bridge. The initial amount of revenue agreed in the contract is €9 million. The contractor's initial estimate of contract costs is €8 million. It will take three years to build the bridge. By the end of year 1, the contractor's estimate of contract costs has increased to €8,050. In year 2, the customer approves a variation resulting in an increase in contract revenue of €200,000 and estimated additional contract costs of €2150 million. At the end of year 2, costs incurred include €100,000 for standard materials stored at the site to be used in year 3 to complete the project.

The contractor determines the stage of completion of the contract by comparing the proportion of contract costs incurred for work performed to date with the latest estimated total contract costs. In this company policy to recognise profit on construction contracts when the stage of completion is greater than 20%. A summary of the financial data during the construction period is as follows:

	Year 1	Year 2	Year 3
	€'000	€'000	€'000
Initial amount of revenue agreed in contract	9,000	9,000	9,000
Variation	–	200	200
Total contract revenue	9,000	9,200	9,200

Contract costs incurred to date	2,093	6,168	8,200
Contract costs to complete	5,957	2,030	–
Total estimated contract costs	8,050	8,200	8,200
Estimated profit	950	1,000	1,000
Stage of completion	26%	74%	100%

The stage of completion for year 2 (74%) is determined by excluding from contract costs incurred for work performed to date the €100,000 of standard materials stored for use in year 3.

The amounts of revenue, expenses and profit recognised in the statement of comprehensive income in the three years are as follows:

		To date	Recognised in prior year	Recognised in current year
	€'000	€'000	€'000	€'000
Year 1	Revenue (9,000 × .26)	2,340		2,340
	Expenses (8,050 × .26)	2,093		2,093
	Profit	247		247
Year 2	Revenue (9,200 × .74)	6,808	2,340	4,468
	Expenses (8,200 × .74)	6,068	2,093	3,975
	Profit	740	247	493
Year 3	Revenue (9,200 × 1.00)	9,200	6,808	2,392
	Expenses	8,200	6,068	2,132
	Profit	1,000	740	260

Illustration 2

A contractor has reached the end of its first year of operation. All its contract costs incurred have been paid for in cash and all its progress billings and advances have been received in cash. Contract costs incurred for contracts B, C and E include the costs of materials that have been purchased for the contract but which have not been used in contract performance to date. For contracts B, C and E the customers have made advances to the contractor for work not yet performed. The status of its five contracts in progress at the end of year 1 is as follows:

Contract	A	B	C	D	E	Total
	€'000	€'000	€'000	€'000	€'000	€'000
Contract revenue recognised	145	520	80	200	55	1,300
Contract expenses recognised	110	450	350	250	55	1,215
Expected losses recognised	–	–	–	40	30	70
Recognised profits less recognised losses	35	70	30	(90)	(30)	15
Contract costs incurred in the period	110	510	450	250	100	1,420
Contract costs incurred recognised as contract expenses	110	450	350	250	55	1,215
Contract costs that relate to future activity recognised as an asset	–	60	100	–	45	205
Contract revenue (see above)	145	520	380	200	55	1,300
Progress billings	100	520	380	180	55	1,235
Unbilled contract revenue	45	–	–	20	–	65
Advances	–	80	20	–	25	125

The amounts to be disclosed in accordance with the standard are as follows:

	€'000
Contract revenue recognised as revenue in the period	1,300
Contract costs incurred and recognised profits (less recognised losses) to date	1,435
Advances received	125
Gross amount due from customers for contract work – presented as an asset	220
Gross amount due to customers for contract work – presented as a liability	(20)

The amounts to be disclosed are calculated as follows:

Contract	A	B	C	D	E	Total
	€'000	€'000	€'000	€'000	€'000	€'000
Contract costs incurred	110	510	450	250	100	1,420
Recognised profits less recognised losses	35	70	30	(90)	(30)	15

	145	580	480	160	70	1,435
Progress billings	100	520	380	180	55	1,235
Due from customers	45	60	100		15	220
Due to customers				(20)		(20)

APPLYING DOUBLE ENTRY

In general terms, the double entry for construction contracts is as follows:

(a) DR Work in progress
CR Bank
With cost incurred to date

(b) DR Statement of comprehensive income
CR Work in progress
With portion of cost to date being treated as 'cost of sales'

(c) DR Receivables – amounts recoverable on contracts
CR Revenue (turnover)
With portion of contract price being recorded as revenue

(d) DR Trade receivables
CR Receivables – amounts recoverable on contracts
With progress billings

(e) DR Bank
CR Trade receivables
With advances received

DISCLOSURE REQUIREMENTS

An enterprise should disclose the following for construction contracts:
1. The amount recognised as revenue in the period;
2. The method used to determine the revenue recognised;
3. The method used to determine stage of completion;
4. For each contract in progress
    (a) cost incurred to date and recognised profits (less losses),
    (b) the amount of advances received (i.e. payments from customers before the related work is performed),
    (c) the amount of retentions (i.e. progress buildings not paid until satisfaction of conditions in contract or until defects are rectified);

5. The gross amount due from customers for contract work where 5 (a) > (b). This is shown as follows:
   (a) cost incurred plus recognised profits, less
   (b) the total of recognised losses and progress billings.
6. The gross amount due to customers, i.e. where 5 (a) < 5 (b).

CONCLUSION

When the outcome of a construction contract can be estimated reliably, contract revenue and contract costs are recognised as revenue and expenses respectively by reference to the stage of completion of the contract activity (percentage of completion method). The outcome can be estimated reliably when the contract revenue, contract costs to date and to completion, and the stage of completion can be measured reliably.

When the outcome of a construction contract cannot be estimated reliably, revenue is recognised only to the extent where it is probable that contract costs incurred are recoverable. Contract costs are recognised as expenses when incurred. If the outcome of the contract subsequently can be estimated reliably, the percentage of completion method is used for recognition of revenue and expenses.

Any expected loss on a construction contract is recognised as an expense immediately.

QUESTIONS

Self-test Questions

1. How would you define a construction contract?
2. When may profits and losses on construction contracts first be recognised?
3. How does the recognition of a profit on a construction contract differ from the recognition of a loss?

Review Questions

(See APPENDIX ONE for Suggested Solutions to Review Questions.)

Question 1

During the course of examining the draft accounts of BRIGADE plc for the year ended 31 December 200X, you have noted the following matter:

At 31 December 200X, the company was engaged in a long-term contract with CONTOUR Limited which had commenced in February 200X, and was expected to take a further two years to complete. The following data was used at 31 December 200X, in order to prepare the draft accounts in accordance with IAS 11 *Construction Contracts*.

	€'000
Fixed contract price	3,000
Total costs incurred to date	1,420
Estimated further costs to completion	1,350
Progress payments received to date	1,200

Profits are taken to arise evenly over the life of the contract which, at 31 December 200X, was estimated to be 45% complete.

On 1 April 200Y, due to technical difficulties, it was found that the estimated further costs to complete the contract had increased by which existed at 31 December 200X an additional €500,000. None of these additional costs can be passed on to the customer or claimed from any third party.

Requirement   Set out in journal form (narratives are not required) any adjustments to the draft accounts which are required as a result of the additional costs of completing the CONTOUR Limited contract.

Question 2

Builders Limited, a medium-sized firm of building contractors, was engaged in the construction of a shopping centre in Bray. Details of the contract which extended over three accounting periods are:

	31 July 20X8 €'000	31 July 20X9 €'000	31 July 20Y0 €'000
Contract price	950	1,000	1,100
Cost to date	230	520	820
Estimated total cost (updated)	750	780	820
Cost to billings invoiced (cumulative)	270	680	1,100
Progress billings received (cumulative)	250	500	1,100
% completion	30	65	100

Note: Assume that Attributable profit = % completion x estimated total profit.

Requirement
(a) Show the accounting entries for each of the three years ending 31 July 20Y0;
(b) Show the extracts from the financial statements of Builders Limited for the year ending 31 July 20X9.

Question 3

Bull Limited is currently engaged in three long-term contracts, details of which are set out below:

Contract	20D	21D	22D
Contract commencement date	1 August 200W	1 November 200W	1 January 200X
	€	€	€
Contract value	500,000	300,000	400,000
Direct costs to date	180,000	150,000	120,000
Indirect costs to date	27,000	22,500	18,000
Estimated direct costs to complete	220,000	160,000	330,000
Estimated indirect costs to complete	33,000	24,000	49,500
Cash received to date	200,000	100,000	40,000
Progress billings to date	220,000	100,000	70,000
Estimated date of completion	31 July 200Y	30 June 200Y	30 September 200Y

The company includes all expenses directly incurred by specific contracts under direct costs. Indirect costs are charged against each contract at 15% of direct costs.

Note: Assume that degree of completion = $\dfrac{\text{Costs to date}}{\text{Total estimated costs}}$

Requirement Show the information which would appear in the statement of comprehensive income and statement of financial position in the accounts for the year ended 30 June 200X.

Challenging Questions

Question 1

You are the Financial Controller of DRY Limited a firm of building contractors. The following details relate to three incomplete contracts in the company's books at 30 June 20X2:

	Contract No. 1 €'000	Contract No. 2 €'000	Contract No. 3 €'000
Cost of work to 30 June 20X2 as certified (note 2)	205	385	150
Value of work to 30 June 20X2 as certified	241	425	140
Progress billings invoiced to 30 June 20X2	200	400	125
Progress billings received by 30 June 20X2	190	380	120
Estimated costs to completion	135	470	700
Fixed contract price	400	935	850
Starting date	1 July 20X1	1 July 20X1	1 October X1
Agreed completion date	31 December X2	30 June X3	30 June X3

Additional Information

1. The cost of work to 30 June 20X2 has been determined after crediting unused materials and the written down value of plant in use.
2. Each contract provides for penalty payments for delays in completion at the following weekly rates:

Contract	€
No. 1	5,000
No. 2	10,000
No. 3	10,000

3. Due to an unofficial strike of bricklayers at the Contract No. 3 site, it is estimated that the completion date of this contract will be four weeks later than anticipated.
4. It has been decided that attributable profit is to be recognised on a basis of costs incurred to date as a proportion of total estimated costs.

Requirement   You are required to show the information which would appear in the statement of comprehensive income and statement of financial position in the accounts for the year ended 30 June 20X2.

Question 2

Expert Builders Limited is involved in three different construction contracts at 31 December 200W:

Contracts	1	2	3
Contract price	€4,000,000	€2,000,000	€900,000
Cost incurred to date	€2,560,000	€450,000	€100,000
Estimated cost to complete	€640,000	€1,350,000	€850,000
Value of work certified	€2,400,000	€200,000	€90,000
Progress billings to 31 December 200W	€2,200,000	€200,000	€80,000
Cash receipts to 31 December 200W	€2,000,000	€180,000	€70,000

This company determines stage of completion by reference to value of work certified as a proportion of total contract revenue.

Requirement   Show how the above contracts would be included in the financial statements and notes of Expert Builders Limited for the year ended 31 December 200W.

CHAPTER 13

INCOME TAXES

INTRODUCTION

This chapter addresses the accounting treatment of both current tax and deferred tax in accordance with IAS 12 *Income Taxes*. It is important to appreciate that IAS 12 deals with the *accounting treatment* and not the actual calculation of tax liabilities. Moreover, despite its title, IAS 12 deals with any taxes payable on company profits regardless of what they are called (for example, corporation tax). Given the different national tax systems, this chapter assumes that the tax calculations have been completed and the issue is therefore how to account for the taxation in the financial statements.

After having read this chapter, you should be able to:

- define the terms 'current tax', 'deferred tax' and 'temporary differences'; and
- calculate the deferred tax asset/liability.

CURRENT TAX

Current tax is the amount of income taxes payable (recoverable) in respect of taxable profit (tax loss) for the period. IAS 12 states that current tax for the current and prior periods should be recognised as a liability to the extent that it has not yet been settled, and as an asset to the extent that the amounts already paid exceed the amount due. The benefit of a tax loss which can be carried back to recover current tax of a prior period should be recognised as an asset. Current tax assets and liabilities should be measured at the amount expected to be paid to (recovered from) taxation authorities, using the rates/laws that have been enacted or substantially enacted by the reporting date. Current tax assets and liabilities should only be offset if there is a legally enforceable right to set off the amounts concerned and the entity intends to do so. Any adjustments necessary to reflect under/over-estimates of current tax in previous periods should be included in the tax charge/credit for the current period.

Example

Aquaria Limited prepares its financial statements to 31 December each year. The following information is relevant for the year ended 31 December 20X8:

- The current tax due is €1,000,000. This figure takes into account proposed new tax rates announced in September 20X8 which are expected to be enacted in 20X9. If the old rates are applied, the amount due would be €900,000;
- During 20X8, payments on account amounted to €450,000 in respect of 20X8 current tax; and
- Current tax for 20X7 was underestimated by €75,000.

Requirement   Calculate the current tax expense which should be shown in Aquaria Limited's statement of comprehensive income for the year ended 31 December 20X8 and the current tax balance which should be included in the statement of financial position as at that date.

Solution

As the new tax rates can be treated as 'substantially enacted', the current tax for 20X8 is €1,000,000. In addition, the 20X7 underestimate must also be taken into account, resulting in a 20X8 tax charge of €1,075,000.
The current tax liability at 31 December 20X8 is €550,000 (€1,000,000 – POA €450,000).

Tax Consequences of Dividends

In some jurisdictions, income taxes are payable at a higher or lower rate if part or all of the net profit or retained earnings is paid out as a dividend. In other jurisdictions, income taxes may be refundable if part or all of the net profit or retained earnings is paid out as a dividend. Possible future dividend distributions or tax refunds should not be anticipated in measuring deferred tax assets and liabilities.

IAS 10 *Events after the Reporting Period* requires disclosure, and prohibits accrual, of a dividend that is proposed or declared after the end of the reporting period but before the financial statements were authorised for issue. IAS 12 requires disclosure of the tax consequences of such dividends as well as disclosure of the nature and amounts of the potential income tax consequences of dividends.

DEFERRED TAX

The amount of current tax due for a reporting period depends upon the taxable profit for that period. However, it is likely that the taxable profit will be different from the reported accounting profit because of:

Permanent Differences

Some income and expenses may not be chargeable/deductable for tax and consequently there will be a permanent difference (i.e. one that will not reverse in the future) between the accounting and taxable profit; and

Temporary Differences

Some income and expenses included in the financial statements in one accounting period may be dealt with for tax purposes in a different accounting period. While permanent differences cause no accounting problems and can be ignored, temporary differences can distort the reported figure for profit after tax. IAS 12 assumes that each asset and liability has a value for tax purposes and this is called a tax base. Deferred tax relates to differences between the carrying amount of assets and liabilities in the statement of financial position, and the tax base of assets and liabilities. The differences between the carrying amount of an asset and liability and its tax base are temporary differences. There are two kinds of temporary differences:

A Taxable Temporary Difference

A taxable temporary difference results in the payment of tax when the carrying amount of the asset or liability is settled. This means that a deferred tax liability will arise when the carrying value of the asset is greater than its tax base, or the carrying value of the liability is less than its tax base.

A Deductible Temporary Difference

A deductible temporary difference results in amounts being deductible in determining taxable profit or loss in future periods when the carrying value of the asset or liability is recovered or settled. When the carrying value of the liability is greater than its tax base or the carrying value of the asset is less than its tax base, then a deferred tax asset may arise.

The principle utilised in IAS 12 is that an entity will settle its liabilities and recover its assets eventually over time and, at that point, the tax consequences will crystallise. A deferred tax asset or liability arises if recovery (settlement) of assets (liabilities) affects the amount of future tax payments. IAS 12 requires deferred tax to be provided on temporary differences rather than timing differences and, subject to the exceptions noted below, IAS 12 requires the entity to recognise a deferred tax liability in full.

Recognition of Deferred Tax Liabilities

The general principle in IAS 12 is that deferred tax liabilities should be recognised for all taxable temporary differences. It is important to note that deferred tax is required on all revaluation gains (rather than only when there is an agreement to sell a revalued asset) and on the unremitted earnings of associates (rather than only to the extent that distribution of earnings has been agreed).

Example

An entity has the following assets and liabilities recorded in its statement of financial position at 31 December 20X8:

	Carrying Value € million	Tax Base € million
Property	20	14
Plant and equipment	10	8
Inventory	8	12
Trade receivables	6	8
Trade payables	12	12
Cash	4	4

The entity had made a provision for inventory obsolescence of €4,000,000 that is not allowable for tax purposes until the inventory is sold, and an impairment charge against trade receivables of €2,000,000 that will not be allowed in the current year for tax purposes but will be in the future. The tax rate is 30%.

Requirement Calculate the deferred tax provision at 31 December 20X8.

Solution

	Carrying Value € million	Tax Base € million	Temporary Difference € million
Property	20	14	6
Plant and equipment	10	8	2
Inventory	8	12	(4)
Trade receivables	6	8	(2)
Trade payables	12	12	-
Cash	4	4	-

The deferred tax provision should be €2,000,000 × 30% = €600,000. The provision against inventory and the impairment charge for trade receivables will cause the tax base to be higher than the carrying value by the respective amounts.

Every asset or liability is assumed to have a tax base. Normally this will be the amount that is allowed for tax purposes. However, some items of income and expenditure may not be taxable or tax deductible and they will never enter into the computation of taxable profit, i.e. permanent differences. Generally speaking, these items will have the same tax base as their carrying amount and no temporary difference will arise. For example, if an entity has in its statement of financial position interest receivable of €2,000,000, which is not taxable then its tax base will be the same as its carrying value, i.e. €2,000,000. There is no temporary difference in this case and, therefore, no deferred taxation will arise.

There are some temporary differences that are not recognised for deferred tax purposes. The three exceptions to the requirement to recognise a deferred tax liability are liabilities arising from:

- goodwill for which amortisation is not deductible for tax purposes. IAS 12 does not allow a deferred tax liability for goodwill on initial recognition or where any reduction in the value of goodwill is not allowed for tax purposes. Because goodwill is the residual amount after recognising assets and liabilities at fair value, recognising a deferred tax liability in respect of goodwill would simply increase the value of goodwill and, therefore, the recognition of a deferred tax liability in this regard is not allowed;
- the initial recognition of an asset/liability other than in a business combination which, at the time of the transaction, does not affect either the accounting or the taxable profit; and
- undistributed profits from investments where the enterprise is able to control the timing of the reversal of the difference and it is probable that the reversal will not occur in the foreseeable future.

Group Financial Statements

Temporary differences can also arise from adjustments on consolidation. The tax base of an item is often determined by the value in the entity accounts – that is, for example, the financial statements of a subsidiary. Deferred tax is determined on the basis of the consolidated financial statements and not the individual entity accounts. Therefore, the carrying value of an item in the consolidated accounts can be different from that in the individual entity accounts, thus giving rise to a temporary difference. An example of this is the consolidation adjustment that is required to eliminate unrealised profits and losses on the inter group transfer of inventory. Such an adjustment will give rise to a temporary difference which will reverse when the inventory is sold outside the group.

IAS 12 does not specifically address how inter-group profits and losses should be measured for tax purposes, simply stating that the expected manner of recovery or settlement of tax should be taken into account. This would generally mean that the receiving company's tax rate should be used when calculating the provision for deferred tax, as the receiving company would be taxed when the asset or liability is realised.

Example

A 100% subsidiary sold goods costing €30,000,000 to its holding company for €33,000,000 and all of these goods are still held in inventory at the year end. The unrealised profit of €3,000,000 will have to be eliminated from the consolidated statement of comprehensive income and from the consolidated statement of financial position in group inventory. The sale of the inventory is a taxable event and it causes a change in the tax base of the inventory. The carrying amount in the consolidated financial statements of the inventory will be €30,000,000 but the tax base is €33,000,000. This gives rise to a deferred tax asset of €3,000,000 at the tax rate of 30%, which is €900,000 (this is assuming that both the holding company and subsidiary are resident in the same tax jurisdiction).

Recognition of Deferred Tax Assets

Deductible temporary differences give rise to deferred tax assets. A deferred tax asset should be recognised only to the extent that it is probable that a tax benefit will be realised in the future. Examples include tax losses carried forward or temporary differences arising on provisions that are not allowable for taxation until the future. Notwithstanding that the existence of current tax losses is probably evidence that future taxable profit will not be available, deferred tax assets can be recognised if it is probable that the deferred tax asset will be realised. Its realisation will depend on whether or not there are sufficient taxable profits available in the future. Sufficient taxable profits can arise from three different sources:

1. Existing taxable temporary differences: in principle these differences should reverse in the same accounting period as the reversal of the deductible temporary difference, or in the period in which a tax loss is expected to be used;
2. If there are insufficient taxable temporary differences, the entity may recognise the deferred tax asset where it feels that there will be future taxable profits, other than that arising from taxable temporary differences. These profits should relate to the same taxable authority and entity;
3. The entity may be able to prove that it can create tax planning opportunities whereby the deductible temporary differences can be utilised. Wherever tax planning opportunities are considered, management must have the capability and ability to implement them.

A deferred tax asset should be recognised for deductible temporary differences, unused tax losses and unused tax credits to the extent that it is probable that taxable profit will be available against which the deductible temporary differences can be utilised in the future, unless the deferred tax asset arises from:

- negative goodwill which was treated as deferred income under IAS 22 *Business Combinations*; or
- the initial recognition of an asset/liability other than in a business combination which, at the time of the transaction, does not affect the accounting or the taxable profit.

Deferred tax assets for deductible temporary differences arising from investments in subsidiaries, associates, branches and joint ventures should be recognised to the extent that it is probable that the temporary difference will reverse in the foreseeable future and that taxable profit will be available against which the temporary difference will be utilised.

The carrying amount of deferred tax assets should be reviewed at the end of each reporting period and reduced to the extent that it is no longer probable that sufficient taxable profit will be available to allow the benefit of part, or all, of the deferred tax asset to be utilised. Any such reduction should be subsequently reversed to the extent that it becomes probable that sufficient taxable profit will be available.

Measurement of Deferred Tax Assets and Liabilities

Deferred tax assets and liabilities should be measured at the tax rates that are expected to apply to the period when the asset is realised or the liability is settled (liability method), based on tax rates/laws that have been enacted or substantially enacted by the end of the reporting period. The measurement should reflect the entity's expectations, at the reporting date, as to the manner in which the carrying amount of its assets and liabilities will be recovered or settled. Deferred tax assets and liabilities should not be discounted (because it is difficult to accurately predict the timing of the reversal of each temporary difference).

In summary, the process of accounting for deferred tax is as follows:

- determine the tax base of the assets and liabilities in the statement of financial position;
- compare the carrying amounts in the statement of financial position with the tax base. Any differences will normally affect the deferred taxation calculation;
- identify the temporary differences that have not been recognised due to exceptions in IAS 12;
- apply the tax rates to the temporary differences;
- determine the movement between opening and closing deferred tax balances;
- decide whether the offset of deferred tax assets and liabilities between different companies is acceptable in the consolidated financial statements;
- recognise the net change in deferred taxation.

In broad terms, if temporary differences cause:

- taxable profit to be lower than accounting profit then the tax charge in the statement of comprehensive income should be increased (credit deferred tax account in the statement of financial position); or
- taxable profit to be higher than accounting profit then the tax charge in the statement of comprehensive income should be reduced (debit deferred tax account in the statement of financial position).

IAS 1 *Presentation of Financial Statements* requires that the balance on the deferred tax account should be shown as a non-current liability (or asset) in the statement of financial position.

RECOGNITION OF TAX EXPENSE OR INCOME

The tax consequences of transactions and events should be recognised in the same financial statement as the transaction or event. This means that current and deferred taxes are:

- recognised in equity if the items to which they relate are credited/charged to equity;
- recognised as identifiable assets or liabilities at the acquisition date if they arise as part of a business combination in accordance with IFRS 3 *Business Combinations*; and
- otherwise recognised as tax income or expense. There will usually be a single tax figure made up of both current and (where applicable) deferred tax.

PRESENTATION AND DISCLOSURE

Current tax assets and current tax liabilities should be offset on the statement of financial position only if the enterprise has the legal right and the intention to settle on a net basis.

Deferred tax assets and deferred tax liabilities should be offset on the statement of financial position only if the enterprise has the legal right to settle on a net basis and they are levied by the same taxing authority on the same entity or different entities that intend to realise the asset and settle the liability at the same time.

IAS 1 requires:

- disclosure of tax expense (tax income) on the face of the statement of comprehensive income; and
- disclosures on the face of the statement of financial position about current tax assets, current tax liabilities, deferred tax assets, and deferred tax liabilities.

In addition to the disclosures required by IAS 1, IAS 12 requires disclosure of the:

- tax expense (tax income) relating to ordinary activities on the face of the statement of comprehensive income;
- major components of tax expense (tax income) including:
  - current tax expense (income),
  - any adjustments of taxes of prior periods,
  - amount of deferred tax expense (income) relating to the origination and reversal of temporary differences,
  - amount of deferred tax expense (income) relating to changes in tax rates or the imposition of new taxes,
  - amount of the benefit arising from a previously unrecognised tax loss, tax credit or temporary difference of a prior period,
  - write down, or reversal of a previous write down, of a deferred tax asset, and
  - amount of tax expense (income) relating to changes in accounting policies and corrections of errors;

- aggregate current and deferred tax relating to items reported directly in equity;
- tax relating to each component of other comprehensive income;
- relationship between tax expense (income) and the tax that would be expected by applying the current tax rate to accounting profit or loss (this can be presented as a reconciliation of amounts of tax or a reconciliation of the rate of tax);
- changes in tax rates;
- amounts and other details of deductible temporary differences, unused tax losses, and unused tax credits;
- temporary differences associated with investments in subsidiaries, associates, branches, and joint ventures;
- amount of deferred tax assets or liabilities recognised in the statement of financial position and the amount of deferred tax income or expense recognised in the statement of comprehensive income for each type of temporary difference and unused tax loss and credit;
- tax relating to discontinued operations;
- tax consequences of dividends declared after the end of the reporting period;
- details of deferred tax assets; and
- tax consequences of future dividend payments.

OTHER RELATED GUIDANCE

SIC 21 *Income Taxes – Recovery of Revalued Non-Depreciable Assets*

Issue

IAS 12.20 notes that the revaluation of an asset does not always affect taxable profit (tax loss) in the period of the revaluation and that the tax base of the asset may not be adjusted as a result of the revaluation. If the future recovery of the carrying amount is taxable, any difference between the carrying amount of the revalued asset and its tax base is a temporary difference and gives rise to a deferred tax liability or asset. But how is the term 'recovery' interpreted in relation to an asset that is not depreciated and is revalued in accordance with IAS 16 *Property, Plant and Equipment*? (SIC 21 also applies to investment properties that are revalued under IAS 40 *Investment Property* but would be considered non-depreciable if IAS 16 were applied (e.g. land).)

Consensus

The deferred tax liability or asset that arises from the revaluation of a non-depreciable asset under IAS 16 *Property, Plant and Equipment* or under IAS 40 *Investment Property* is measured on the basis of the tax consequences that would follow from recovery of the carrying amount of that asset through sale. Because the asset is not depreciated, no part of its carrying amount is expected to be recovered through use.

SIC 27 *Evaluating the Substance of Transactions Involving the Legal Form of a Lease*

Issue

How does an entity account for the tax consequences of a change in its tax status or that of its shareholders?

Consensus

A change in the tax status of an entity or its shareholders does not give rise to increases or decreases in amounts recognised directly in equity. The current and deferred tax consequences of a change in tax status are included in profit or loss for the period. However, where the tax consequences relate to transactions and events that result in a direct credit or charge to the recognised amount of equity, they are charged or credited directly to equity.

CONCLUSION

As the accounting recognition criteria are different from those which are normally set out in tax law, certain income and expenditure in financial statements will not be allowed for taxation purposes, thus causing temporary differences. IAS 12 accounts for the temporary differences between the accounting and tax bases of assets and liabilities rather than accounting for the timing differences between the accounting and tax consequences of revenue and expenses. IAS 12 uses a liability method and adopts a statement of financial position approach to accounting for taxation. It adopts a full provision statement of financial position approach to accounting for tax, assuming that the recovery of all assets and the settlement of all liabilities have tax consequences and that these consequences can be estimated reliably and cannot be avoided.

QUESTIONS

Self-test Questions

1. Explain the difference between current tax and deferred tax.
2. Explain the difference between permanent differences and temporary differences
3. Explain the concept of the tax base of an asset or liability, and how this concept helps to identify situations in which deferred tax adjustments are required.
4. Explain how temporary differences between accounting profits and taxable profits would affect the tax expense unless deferred tax was taken into account.

Review Questions

(See APPENDIX ONE for Suggested Solutions to Review Questions.)

Question 1 (Based on ICAI, P3 Summer 2005, Question 4)

GATEWAY Limited (GATEWAY), a company that prepares its financial statements to 31 December each year, has been trading at a loss for the last 3-4 years. However, the directors expect the company to return to profitability in the near future. GATEWAY pays corporation tax at 25%, and the following information has been extracted from GATEWAY's books and records in respect of the year ended 31 December 20X5:

1. Depreciation charged in the statement of comprehensive income amounted to €3,250,000, while capital allowances of €4,750,000 were included in the tax computation;
2. The estimated tax loss for the year ended 31 December 20X5 is €250,000 and, because prior year losses have been fully utilised, the tax loss for the year ended 31 December 20X5 will have to be carried forward to future years;
3. The net book value of non-current assets qualifying for capital allowances at 31 December 20X4 was €13,000,000 against a tax written down value of €12,000,000. This gave rise to a deferred tax provision at 31 December 20X4 of €250,000. No other timing differences existed at 31 December 20X4; and
4. Although €500,000 was charged to the statement of comprehensive income in the year ended 31 December 20X5 in respect of royalties, the amount actually paid was €550,000.

Requirement
(a) Calculate the deferred tax charge to be included in the statement of comprehensive income of GATEWAY for the year ended 31 December 20X5, and the deferred tax provision required as at that date, in accordance with IAS 12 Income Taxes.
(b) Included in GATEWAY's non-current assets at 31 December 20X5 is property recorded at €1,400,000. The property cost €2,000,000 when purchased, and depreciation totalling €600,000 has been charged up to 31 December 20X5. GATEWAY has claimed total tax allowances of €800,000 on the property up to 31 December 20X5, and is considering recording the property at its valuation of €1,800,000 in the financial statements for the year ended 31 December 20X5. GATEWAY does not intend to sell the property.

Requirement   Explain whether:
(a) GATEWAY is permitted to record the property at valuation in the financial statements for the year ended 31 December 20X5;
(b) Recording the property at its valuation of €1,800,000 will create an unavoidable incremental tax liability; and
(c) GATEWAY is permitted to discount any deferred tax asset or liability that may arise.

Challenging Questions

Question 1 (Based on ICAI, P3 Summer 2008, Question 6)

BRUCE plc (BRUCE), an Irish listed company that prepares its financial statements to 31 December each year, sells products to those involved in magic and illusion.

BRUCE
Statement of Financial Position as at 31 December 2007

	Notes	Book Value €'000	Tax Value €'000
ASSETS			
Non-current Assets			
Property	(1)	40,000	10,000
Plant and equipment	(1)	20,000	8,000
Development costs	(2)	4,000	-
		64,000	18,000
Current Assets			
Inventory		8,000	8,000
Trade receivables		6,000	6,000
Bank and cash		2,000	2,000
		80,000	34,000
EQUITY AND LIABILITIES			
Capital and Reserves			
€1 ordinary shares		10,000	10,000
Retained earnings		41,000	1,000
		51,000	11,000
Non-current Liabilities			
Loan	(3)	8,000	9,000
Deferred income	(4)	4,000	-
Employee retirement benefit scheme	(5)	2,000	-
Deferred taxation	(6)	10,000	10,000

Current Liabilities

Trade payables		4,000	4,000
Deferred income	(4)	1,000	-
		80,000	34,000

Additional Information

1. The directors of BRUCE have decided to record the company's property, plant and equipment at fair value rather than depreciated historic cost. The fair value of the property at 31 December 2007 is deemed to be €50,000,000, while the fair value of plant and equipment on the same date is €25,000,000.
2. Development costs are capitalised and amortised over future periods in determining accounting profit but deducted in determining taxable profit in the period in which they are incurred.
3. During the year ended 31 December 2007, BRUCE negotiated a new loan with repayments commencing in 2009. For accounting purposes, the loan has been recorded net of the associated transaction costs paid in 2007. These costs are allowable for tax in the year in which they are paid.
4. The deferred income relates to a non-taxable government grant received by BRUCE.
5. Employee retirement benefit costs are deducted in determining accounting profit when the service is provided by the employees, but deducted in determining taxable profit when contributions or retirement benefits are paid by BRUCE.
6. This represents the deferred taxation liability at 31 December 2006. During the year ended 31 December 2007, the taxation rate changed from 25% to 20%.
7. BRUCE's employee retirement benefit scheme is managed by the same investment bank that negotiated the new loan raised during 2007 (see note 3). Furthermore, one of the investment managers in the investment bank is also a non-executive director of BRUCE. During the year ended 31 December 2007, BRUCE paid €7,000,000 into the employee retirement benefit scheme and paid fees amounting to €300,000 to the investment bank in relation to the administration of the employee retirement benefit scheme. In addition, during 2007, the investment manager received €20,000 from BRUCE for his services as a non-executive director. This fee was paid to all non-executive directors.

Requirement

(a) Calculate the deferred taxation expense to be included in the statement of comprehensive income of BRUCE for the year ended 31 December 2007 and the deferred taxation liability as at that date.
(b) Discuss whether BRUCE's relationship and transactions with the investment bank should be disclosed in the financial statements for the year ended 31 December 2007.

CHAPTER 14

PROVISIONS, CONTINGENT LIABILITIES AND CONTINGENT ASSETS

INTRODUCTION

A number of problems have arisen in the past with respect to provisions. For example:

- There has been no consistency in accounting treatment. Some provisions are very popular, e.g. restructuring and warranties whereas others are rarely adopted in practice, e.g. environmental.
- Companies have deliberately manipulated their statement of comprehensive income to smooth out earnings by the adoption of 'big bath' accounting provisions which have no real substance.
- Some provisions have been created which will never occur in practice. They are mere intentions rather than firm obligations of the reporting entity.
- There has been a lack of detailed disclosure about provisions in general.

IAS 37 *Provisions, Contingent Liabilities and Contingent Assets* sets out the principles of accounting for provisions and contingencies. Its objective is to ensure that appropriate criteria and measurement bases are applied to these aspects of accounting and that sufficient information is disclosed in the notes to the financial statements so as to enable the reader to understand their nature, timing and amounts recorded.

IAS 37 does not apply to provisions, contingent liabilities and contingent assets, which are:

- as a result of executory contracts, except where the contract is onerous; and
- covered by another Standard, including:
  - contingent liabilities assumed in business combinations (IFRS 3 *Business Combinations*);
  - provisions with regard to construction contracts (IAS 11 *Construction Contracts*); income taxes (IAS 12 *Income Taxes*); leases (IAS 17 *Leases*); employee benefits (IAS 19 *Employee Benefits*); and insurance contracts (IFRS 4 *Insurance Contracts*).

IAS 37 also does not apply to financial instruments (including guarantees) within the scope of IAS 39 *Financial Instruments: Recognition and Measurement*.

After having read this chapter you should be able to explain:

- the terms 'provision', 'contingent liability' and 'contingent asset';
- when a provision should be recognised and how it should be measured; and
- the accounting treatment for contingent liabilities and contingent assets.

Important Definitions

1. **Provision** – this is a liability of uncertain timing or amount.
2. **Liability** – this is a present obligation of a reporting entity arising from past events the settlement of which is expected to result in an outflow from the entity of economic benefits.
3. **Obligating Event** – this is an event that creates a legal or constructive obligation where an entity has no realistic alternative but to settle that obligation.
4. **Legal Obligation** – this is an obligation that derives from a contract, legislation or other operation of law.
5. **Constructive Obligation** – this is an obligation which derives from the reporting entity's actions where:
   (a) past practice, published policies or current statement indicate that the entity will accept certain responsibilities; and
   (b) the entity has created a valid expectation that it will discharge those responsibilities.
6. **Contingent Liability** – this is a:
   (a) possible obligation arising from past events whose existence will only be confirmed by the occurrence, or non-occurrence, of one or more uncertain future events not wholly within the entity's control; or
   (b) present obligation arising from past events but is not recognised because it is not probable that a transfer of economic benefits will be required to settle the obligation, or the amount of the obligation cannot be measured with sufficient reliability.
7. **Contingent Gain/Asset** – this is a possible asset arising from past events whose existence will be confirmed only by the occurrence or non-occurrence of one or more uncertain future events not wholly within the entity's control.
8. **Restructuring** – the following are examples of events that may fall under the definition of restructuring: sale or termination of a line of business; closure of business locations in a country or region or the relocation of business activities from one country or region to another; changes in management structure, for example, eliminating a layer of management; and fundamental reorganisations that have a material effect on the nature and focus of the entity's operations.

RELATIONSHIP BETWEEN PROVISIONS AND CONTINGENT LIABILITIES

Provisions

They are recognised as liabilities (if reliably measured) because they are present obligations where it is probable that a transfer of economic benefits will be required to settle the obligation.

Contingent Liabilities

These are not recognised as liabilities because either they are only possible or they are present obligations that do not meet the recognition criteria as they are either not probably likely to be settled or a sufficiently reliable estimate cannot be made of the obligation. Contingent liabilities can be ignored if they are likely to be remote.

RECOGNITION

Provisions

These should be recognised when there is a PRESENT OBLIGATION (legal or constructive) as a result of a PAST EVENT and it is PROBABLE that a TRANSFER OF ECONOMIC BENEFITS will occur and it can be RELIABLY MEASURED

Present Obligation

If it is not clear that a present obligation exists, a past event is deemed to lead to a present obligation if, taking into account all evidence, it is more likely than not that a present obligation exists at the reporting date.

Past Event

Must be no realistic alternative to settling the obligation, i.e. legal or constructive (i.e. creates valid expectations in other parties that entities will discharge the obligation). An event may not lead immediately to an obligation but may do so at a later date due to a change in legislation or because of a specific public statement. If a new law has yet to be finalised, an obligation can only arise when the legislation is virtually certain.

Probable Transfer of Economic Benefits

A transfer is only probable if an outflow is more likely than not to occur. If there are a number of similar obligations, e.g. warranties, the probability should be determined by considering the class as a whole, e.g. expected value technique.

Reliable Estimate of Obligation

This can usually be determined by examining the range of possible outcomes and making an estimate of obligation which is sufficiently reliable to use. If no reliable estimate can be made, a liability cannot be recognised and therefore it should be treated as a contingent liability.

Example

In which of the following circumstances might a provision be recognised?

(a) On 13 December 20X9 the board of an entity decided to close down a division. The accounting date of the company is 31 December. Before 31 December 20X9, the decision was not communicated to any of those affected and no other steps were taken to implement the decision.
(b) The board agreed a detailed closure plan on 20 December 20X9 and details were given to customers and employees.
(c) A company is obliged to incur clean up costs for environmental damage (that has already been caused).
(d) A company intends to carry out future expenditure to operate in a particular way in the future.

Solution

(a) No provision would be recognised as the decision has not been communicated.
(b) A provision would be made in the 20X9 financial statements.
(c) A provision for such costs is appropriate.
(d) No present obligation exists and under IAS 37 no provision would be appropriate. This is because the entity could avoid the future expenditure by its future actions, maybe by changing its method of operation.

Contingent Liability

A contingent liability should not be recognised but should be disclosed unless the transfer of economic benefits is likely to be remote. If there is joint and several liability, then the entity should only provide for its own share and disclose the other parties' shares as contingent liabilities. These need to be monitored regularly and if they become probable then they will need to be disclosed as provisions in the year they became probable.

Contingent Asset

An entity should not recognise a contingent asset as it would probably include an unrealised profit. If realisation, however, is certain it should be recorded as an asset. A contingent asset, if probable, should be disclosed. It should be continually assessed and if it becomes certain then an asset should be recognised in the year that it occurs.

Note

A number of examples dealing with the issue of recognition are included of the end of this chapter.

MEASUREMENT

The key factors to be considered are:

Best Estimate

The amount recognised should be the best estimate (on a pre-tax basis) of the expenditure required to settle the present obligation at the reporting date.

Risks and Uncertainties

These should be taken into account in reaching the best estimate but care must be taken not to avoid an overstatement of the provision.

Present Value

If the time value of money is material, a provision should be discounted on a pre tax basis and on a current market assessment of the specific risks attached to the liability.

Future Events

These should only be included in the measurement process if there is objective evidence that they will occur, e.g. new legislation is virtually certain.

Expected Disposal of Assets

Any gains on the expected disposal of assets should be ignored when measuring a provision.

Example

Parker plc sells goods with a warranty under which customers are covered for the cost of repairs of any manufacturing defect that becomes apparent within the first six months of purchase. The company's past experience and future expectations indicate the following pattern of likely repairs.

Percentage of Goods Sold	Defects	Cost of Repairs € million
75%	None	-
20%	Minor	1.0
5%	Major	4.0

Requirement   Calculate the expected cost of repairs.

Solution

The cost is found using 'expected values' (75% x €nil) + (20% x €1.0m) + (5% x €4.0m) = €400,000.

REIMBURSEMENT

Where a provision is likely to be reimbursed by a third party, the reimbursement should only be recognised if it is virtually certain that it will be received. The reimbursement should be treated as a separate asset. However, it must not be recorded at a value higher than the amount of the provision.

In the statement of comprehensive income any expenses relating to the provision may be presented net of any amounts recognised for reimbursement.

CHANGES IN PROVISIONS

Provisions should be reviewed at the end of each reporting date and adjusted to reflect the current best estimate. If it is no longer probable that a transfer of economic benefits will occur, the provision must be reversed.

Where discounting is adopted, the subsequent unwinding of that discount should be treated as an interest expense, but separately disclosed.

A provision should only be used for the expenditures for which it was originally recognised.

ONEROUS CONTRACTS

An onerous contract is one in which the unavoidable costs of meeting the contracts' obligations exceed the economic benefits expected to be received. In such circumstances, the present obligation under the contract should be recognised and provided for.

DISCLOSURES

1. Provisions (For each class)
   - Opening balance;
   - Additional or adjustment to provisions;
   - Amounts used;
   - Amounts reversed; and
   - Change in discounted amount, e.g. unwinding or change in discount rate.

   In addition, a brief description of the nature of the provision should be provided together with expected timing of outflows. An indication of the uncertainties re the amount and timing of outflows and the amount of any reimbursement and associate asset recognised.

2. Contingent Liability

   Unless remote, for each class of contingent liability, the following:

   - Brief description of the nature of the contingency;
   - An estimate of its financial effect and an indication of the uncertainties; and
   - The possibility of any reimbursement.

3. Contingent Asset

   If probable, a brief description of their nature and financial effect, if practicable.

CONCLUSION

Appendix A accompanies, but is not part of, IAS 37. Its purpose is to summarise the main requirements of IAS 37. These are:

Provisions and Contingent Liabilities

Where, as a result of past events, there may be an outflow of resources embodying future economic benefits in settlement of: (a) a present obligation; or (b) a possible obligation whose existence will be confirmed only by the occurrence or non-occurrence of one or more uncertain future events not wholly within the control of the entity.		
There is a present obligation that probably requires an outflow of resources.	There is a possible obligation or a present obligation that may, but probably will not, require an outflow of resources.	There is a possible obligation or a present obligation where the likelihood of an outflow of resources is remote.
A provision is recognised.	No provision is recognised.	No provision is recognised.
Disclosures are required for the provision.	Disclosures are required for the contingent liability.	No disclosure is required.

A contingent liability also arises in the extremely rare case where there is a liability that cannot be recognised because it cannot be measured reliably. Disclosures are required for the contingent liability.

Contingent Assets

Where, as a result of past events, there is a possible asset whose existence will be confirmed only by the occurrence or non-occurrence of one or more uncertain future events not wholly within the control of the entity.		
The inflow of economic benefits is virtually certain.	The inflow of economic benefits is probable, but not virtually certain.	The inflow is not probable.
The asset is not contingent.	No asset is recognised.	No asset is recognised.
	Disclosures are required.	No disclosure is required.

Reimbursements

Some or all of the expenditure required to settle a provision is expected to be reimbursed by another party.		
The entity has no obligation for the part of the expenditure to be reimbursed by the other party.	The obligation for the amount expected to be reimbursed remains with the entity and it is virtually certain that reimbursement will be received if the entity settles the provision.	The obligation for the amount expected to be reimbursed remains with the entity and the reimbursement is not virtually certain if the entity settles the provision.
The entity has no liability for the amount to be reimbursed.	The reimbursement is recognised as a separate asset in the statement of financial position and may be offset against the expense in the statement of comprehensive income.	The expected reimbursement is not recognised as an asset.
	The amount recognised for the expected reimbursement does not exceed the liability.	
No disclosure is required.	The reimbursement is disclosed together with the amount recognised for the reimbursement.	The expected reimbursement is disclosed.

RECOGNITION EXAMPLES

Appendix C accompanies, but is not part of, IAS 37. All of the entities in the examples have 31 December year-ends. In all cases, it is assumed that a reliable estimate can be made of any outflows expected. In some examples, the circumstances described may have resulted in impairment of the assets – this aspect is not dealt with in the examples. References to 'best estimate' are to the present value amount, where the effect of the time value of money is material.

Example – *Warranties*

A manufacturer gives warranties at the time of sale to purchasers of its product. Under the terms of the contract for sale the manufacturer undertakes to make good, by repair or replacement, manufacturing defects that become apparent within three years from the date of sale. On past experience, it is probable (i.e. more likely than not) that there will be some claims under the warranties.

Present obligation as a result of a past obligating event – the obligating event is the sale of the product with a warranty which gives rise to a legal obligation.

An outflow of resources embodying economic benefits in settlement – probable for the warranties as a whole.

Conclusion

A provision is recognised for the best estimate of the costs of making good, under the warranty products sold before the reporting date.

Example – *Contaminated Land (legislation virtually certain to be enacted)*

An entity in the oil industry causes contamination but cleans up only when required to do so under the laws of the particular country in which it operates. One country in which it operates has had no legislation requiring cleaning up and the entity has been contaminating land in that country for several years. At 31 December 2000, it is virtually certain that a draft law requiring a clean-up of land already contaminated will be enacted shortly after the year end.

Present obligation as a result of a past obligating event – the obligating event is the contamination of the land because of the virtual certainty of legislation requiring cleaning up.

An outflow of resources embodying economic benefits in settlement – probable.

Conclusion

A provision is recognised for the best estimate of the costs of the clean-up.

Example – *Contaminated Land and Constructive Obligation*

An entity in the oil industry causes contamination and operates in a country where there is no environmental legislation. However, the entity has a widely published environmental policy in which it undertakes to dean up all contamination that it causes. The entity has a record of honouring this published policy.

Present obligation as a result of a past obligating event – the obligating event is the contamination of the land, which gives rise to a constructive obligation because the conduct of the entity has created a valid expectation on the part of those affected by it that the entity will clean up contamination.

An outflow of resources embodying economic benefits in settlement – probable.

Conclusion

A provision is recognised for the best estimate of the costs of clean-up.

Example – *Offshore Oilfield*

An entity operates an offshore oilfield where its licensing agreement requires it to remove the oil rig at the end of production and restore the seabed. Ninety per cent of the eventual costs relate to the removal of the oil rig and restoration of damage caused by building it, and 10% arise through the extraction of oil. At the reporting date, the rig has been constructed but no oil has been extracted.

Present obligation as a result of a past obligating event – the construction of the oil rig creates a legal obligation under the terms of the licence to remove the rig and restore the seabed and is thus an obligating event. At the reporting date, however, there is no obligation to rectify the damage that will be caused by extraction of the oil.

An outflow of resources embodying economic benefits in settlement – probable.

Conclusion

A provision is recognised for the best estimate of 90% of the eventual costs that relate to the removal of the oil rig and restoration of damage caused by building it. These costs are included as part of the cost of the oil rig. The 10% of costs that arise through the extraction of oil are recognised as a liability when the oil is extracted.

Example – *Refunds Policy*

A retail store has a policy of refunding purchases by dissatisfied customers, even though it is under no legal obligation to do so. Its policy of making refunds is generally known.

Present obligation as a result of a past obligating event – the obligating event is the sale of the product which gives rise to a constructive obligation because the conduct of the store has created a valid expectation on the part of its customers that the store will refund purchases.

An outflow of resources embodying economic benefits in settlement – probable that a proportion of goods are returned for refund.

Conclusion

A provision is recognised for the best estimate of the costs of refunds.

Example – *Closure of a Division (no implementation before reporting date)*

On 12 December 20X0 the board of an entity decided to close down a division. Before the reporting date (31 December 20X0) the decision was not communicated to any of those affected and no other steps were taken to implement the decision.

Present obligation as a result of a past obligating event – there has been no obligating event and so there is no obligation.

Conclusion

No provision is recognised.

Example – *Closure of a Division (communication/implementation before end of reporting date)*

On 12 December 20X0, the board of an entity decided to close down a division making a particular product. On 20 December 20X0 a detailed plan for closing down the division was agreed by the board. Letters were sent to customers warning them to seek an alternative source of supply and redundancy notices were sent to the staff of the division.

Present obligation as a result of a past obligating event – the obligating event is the communication of the decision to the customers and employees, which gives rise to a constructive obligation from that date because it creates a valid expectation that the division will be closed.

An outflow of resources embodying economic benefits in settlement – probable.

Conclusion

A provision is recognised at 31 December 20X0 for the best estimate of the costs of closing the division.

Example – *Legal Requirement to Fit Smoke Filters*

Under new legislation, an entity is required to fit smoke filters to its factories by 30 June 20X0. The entity has not fitted the smoke filters.

(a) At the reporting date of 31 December 19X9
Present obligation as a result of a past obligating event – There is no obligation because there is no obligating event either for the costs of fitting smoke filters or for fines under the legislation.

Conclusion

No provision is recognised for the cost of fitting the smoke filters.

(b) At the reporting date of 31 December 20X0
Present obligation as a result of a past obligating event – there is still no obligation for the costs of fitting smoke filters because no obligating event has occurred (the fitting of the filters). However, an obligation might arise to pay fines or penalties under the legislation because the obligating event has occurred (the non-compliant operation of the factory).

An outflow of resources embodying economic benefits in settlement – assessment of probability of incurring fines and penalties by non-compliant operation depends on the details of the legislation and the stringency of the enforcement regime.

Conclusion

No provision is recognised for the costs of fitting smoke filters. However, a provision is recognised for the best estimate of any fines and penalties that are more likely than not to be imposed.

Example – *Staff Retraining as a Result of Changes in the Income Tax System*

The government introduces a number of changes to the income tax system. As a result of these changes, an entity in the financial services sector will need to retrain a large proportion of its administrative and sales workforce in order to ensure continued compliance with financial services regulation. At the reporting date, no retraining of staff has taken place.

Present obligation as a result of a past obligating event – there is no obligation because no obligating event (retraining) has taken place.

Conclusion

No provision is recognised.

Example – *An Onerous Contract*

An entity operates profitably from a factory that it has leased under an operating lease. During December 20X0 the entity relocates its operations to a new factory. The lease on the old factory continues for the next four years, it cannot be cancelled and the factory cannot be re-let to another user.

Present obligation as a result of a past obligating event – the obligating event is the signing of the lease contract, which gives rise to a legal obligation.

An outflow of resources embodying economic benefits in settlement – when the lease becomes onerous, an outflow of resources embodying economic benefits is probable. (Until the lease becomes onerous, the entity accounts for the lease under IAS 17 *Leases*.)

Conclusion

A provision is recognised for the best estimate of the unavoidable lease payments.

Example – *A Single Guarantee*

On 31 December 19X9, Entity A gives a guarantee of certain borrowings of Entity B, whose financial condition at that time is sound. During 2000, the financial condition of Entity B deteriorates and at 30 June 20X0 Entity B files for protection from its creditors.

(a) At 31 December 19X9

Present obligation as a result of a past obligating event – the obligating event is the giving of the guarantee, which gives rise to a legal obligation.

An outflow of resources embodying economic benefits in settlement – no outflow of benefits is probable at 31 December 19X9.

Conclusion

The guarantee is recognised at fair value.

(b) At 31 December 20X0

Present obligation as a result of a past obligating event – the obligating event is the giving of the guarantee, which gives rise to a legal obligation.

An outflow of resources embodying economic benefits in settlement – at 31 December 20X0, it is probable that an outflow of resources embodying economic benefits will be required to settle the obligation.

Conclusion

The guarantee is subsequently measured at the higher of (a) the best estimate of the obligation, and (b) the amount initially recognised less, when appropriate, cumulative amortisation in accordance with IAS 18 Revenue.

Note: Where an entity gives guarantees in exchange for a fee, revenue is recognised under IAS 18 *Revenue*.

Example – *A Court Case*

After a wedding in 20X0, ten people died, possibly as a result of food poisoning from products sold by the entity. Legal proceedings are started seeking damages from the entity but it disputes liability. Up to the date for issue of authorisation of the financial statements for the year to 31 December 20X0 for issue, the entity's lawyers advise that it is probable that the entity will not be found liable. However, when the entity prepares the financial statements for the year to 31 December 20X1, its lawyers advise that, owing to developments in the case, it is probable that the entity will be found liable.

(a) At 31 December 20X0

Present obligation as a result of a past obligating event – on the basis of the evidence available when the financial statements were approved, there is no obligation as a result of past events.

Conclusion

No provision is recognised. The matter is disclosed as a contingent liability unless the probability of any outflow is regarded as remote.

(b) At 31 December 20X1
Present obligation as a result of a past obligating event – on the basis of the evidence available, there is a present obligation.
   An outflow of resources embodying economic benefits in settlement – probable.

Conclusion

A provision is recognised for the best estimate of the amount to settle the obligation.

Example – *Refurbishment Costs (no legislative requirement)*

A furnace has a lining that needs to be replaced every five years for technical reasons. At the reporting date, the lining has been in use for three years.

Present obligation as a result of a past obligating event – there is no present obligation.

Conclusion

No provision is recognised. The cost of replacing the lining is not recognised because, at the reporting date, no obligation to replace the lining exists independently of the company's future actions – even the intention to incur the expenditure depends on the company deciding to continue operating the furnace or to replace the lining. Instead of a provision being recognised, the depreciation of the lining takes account of its consumption, i.e. it is depreciated over five years. The re-lining costs then incurred are capitalised with the consumption of each new lining shown by depreciation over the subsequent five years.

Example – *Refurbishment Costs (legislative requirement)*

An airline is required by law to overhaul its aircraft once every three years.

Present obligation as a result of a past obligating event – there is no present obligation.

Conclusion

No provision is recognised. The costs of overhauling aircraft are not recognised as a provision for the same reasons as the cost of replacing the lining is not recognised as a provision in the previous example. Even a legal requirement to overhaul does not make the costs of overhaul a liability, because no obligation exists to overhaul the aircraft independently of the entity's future actions. The entity could avoid the future expenditure by its future actions, for example by selling the aircraft. Instead of a provision being recognised, the depreciation of the aircraft takes account of the future incidence of maintenance costs, i.e. an amount equivalent to the expected maintenance costs is depreciated over three years.

Example – *Self Insurance*

An entity expects to pay €100,000 in damages based on previous experience. As there is no obligating event until an accident occurs, no provision is recognised.

QUESTIONS

Self-test Questions

1. How does IAS 37 define a provision?
2. According to IAS 37, when, and only when, can a provision be recognised?
3. Can a provision ever be made for future operating losses?
4. How does IAS 37 define a contingent liability?
5. When should a contingent liability be recognised?

Review Questions

(See APPENDIX ONE for Suggested Solutions to Review Questions.)

Question 1

During 20X9, Bad Limited gives a guarantee of certain borrowings of Girls Limited whose financial condition at that time is sound. During 20Y0, the financial condition of Girls Limited deteriorates and at 30 June 20Y0 Girls Limited files for protection from its creditors.

Requirement What accounting treatment is required at:
(a) 31 December 20X9; and
(b) 31 December 20Y0?

Question 2

King Limited gives warranties at the time of sale to purchasers of its products. Under the terms of the warranty the manufacturer undertakes to make good, by repair or replacement, manufacturing defects that become apparent within a period of three years from the date of the sale.

Requirement   Explain whether a provision should be recognised.

Question 3

After a wedding in the year 200W ten people died, possibly as a result of food poisoning from products sold by Crippen Limited. Legal proceedings are initiated seeking damages from Crippen but it disputes liability. Up to the date of approval of the financial statements for the year to 31 December 200W, Crippen's lawyers advise that it is probable that it will not be found liable. However, when Crippen prepares the financial statements for the year to 31 December 200X its lawyers advise that, owing to developments in the case, it is probable that it will be found liable.

Requirement   What is the required accounting treatment at:
(a) 31 December 200W; and
(b) 31 December 200X?.

Question 4

RUÁ Limited (RUÁ), a company which prepares its financial statements to 31 December each year, is involved in mining and exploration. Before the financial statements for the year ended 31 December 2003 can be finalised, a number of outstanding issues need to be resolved.

Issue 1   On 1 January 2003, RUÁ was granted a licence to commence mining for silver. As a condition of being granted the licence, RUÁ is obliged to restore the mountainside to its original state when the mining licence expires in six years' time. The directors of RUÁ estimate that the total cost of restoration will be €120,000,000 of which 80% will be incurred when mining ceases and the remainder during mining. Mining commenced on 1 January 2003. RUÁ's cost of capital is 10% and the risk-free rate is 4%. The directors of RUÁ are proposing to provide for the restoration costs over the next six years based upon projected production at the mine.

Issue 2   RUÁ purchased a private jet on 1 January 2003 at a cost of €24,000,000. The jet is to be used for transporting company executives to and from the various locations where the company is conducting mining and exploration work. Air regulations require the jet to be overhauled every three years, and it is estimated that each overhaul will cost €1,500,000. RUÁ is proposing to charge depreciation on a straight-line basis over the jet's useful economic life of 12 years. Furthermore, it is proposed to create an annual provision of €500,000 to meet the overhaul costs every three years.

Issue 3   In 2001, RUÁ incurred development expenditure amounting to €5,000,000. This expenditure was expensed in the statement of comprehensive income for the year ended 31 December 2001 as the conditions for capitalisation had not been met. However the uncertainties that led to write-off were resolved during the year ended 31 December 2003 and the directors of RUÁ are proposing to reverse the original write-off and capitalise the expenditure in the financial statements for the year ended 31 December 2003.

Issue 4   RUÁ carried out a joint contract with COLUMBUS Limited (COLUMBUS). Under the terms of the contract, RUÁ is liable for penalties if certain restoration work is not completed satisfactorily. RUÁ has a separate agreement with COLUMBUS that enables the company to recover 50% of any penalties incurred from COLUMBUS. At 31 December 2003 the directors of RUÁ estimate that penalties of €5,000,000 will become payable but are uncertain how this should be reflected in the financial statements for the year ended 31 December 2003.

Issue 5   In February 2004, a customer commenced legal action against RUÁ alleging that drilling work completed in September 2003 had not been carried out in accordance with the terms of the contract. The directors of RUÁ intend to defend the allegations vigorously and RUÁ's legal advisors estimate that the company has a 75% chance of successfully defending the claim. If the customer is successful, penalties and legal fees are expected to amount to €1,000,000. If RUÁ wins the case, non-recoverable legal fees of €25,000 will have been incurred. The directors of RUÁ are proposing to omit reference to the legal action in the financial statements for the year ended 31 December 2003 as the writ was not issued until February 2004.

Issue 6   In order to provide funds for exploration work, bills receivable amounting to €4,000,000 were discounted on 1 December 2003. These are due for maturity on 1 November 2004. The directors of RUÁ are uncertain whether it is necessary to disclose this in the financial statements for the year ended 31 December 2003.

Requirement   Prepare a memorandum addressed to the finance director of RUÁ explaining how each of the issues should be treated in the financial statements for the year ended 31 December 2003.

NB

Present value factors:

Years	4%	10%
1	0.962	0.909
2	0.925	0.826
3	0.889	0.751
4	0.855	0.683
5	0.822	0.621
6	0.790	0.564

Challenging Questions

Question 1 (Based on ICAI, P2 Autumn 1997, Question 1)

Pelican Limited advised its solicitors to commence an action against its major supplier claiming damages of €500,000 in respect of losses sustained as a result of the supply of faulty goods. According to legal advice, Pelican Limited stands a very good chance of winning its case.

Requirement   Indicate how this situation should be dealt with in order to comply with standard accounting practice. (Assume a financial year end of 31 December 1996 and that the issue is material.)

Question 2 (Based on ICAI, P2 Summer 1996, Question 1)

Highgrove plc is a manufacturing and distribution company. You are acting as auditor to Highgrove plc and you have been asked by the Board of Directors of the company to explain how the following items should be treated in the published accounts of the company for the year ended 31 December 1995.

In June 1995, Highgrove plc engaged a firm of building contractors to build an extension to the factory. In December 1995, just as the building was due to be completed, the structure collapsed and destroyed the canteen which was directly underneath.

The company is suing the builder for compensation. Highgrove plc is claiming €150,000. The insurers of the building contractor have offered an out of court settlement of €80,000. Highgrove plc's lawyer believes that the offer made by the building contractor is unreasonable and, when the case comes to court in March 1996, Highgrove plc stands a very good chance of winning the full €150,000.

Requirement   Prepare a memorandum to the Board of Directors of Highgrove plc in which you state how the above should be reflected in the company's published financial statements for the year ended 31 December 1995. (Assume all transactions are material, and ignore taxation.)

Question 3 (Based on ICAI, P2 Summer 2000, Question 4)

(a) In accordance with IAS 37 *Provisions, Contingent Liabilities and Contingent Assets*, define a provision and explain briefly when a provision should be recognised in financial statements.
(b) JEANS AND JUMPERS plc is a well-known, high street retail outlet with branches all over Ireland. The year end of the company is 31 December 1999. The following information is available:

  (i) As part of its customer service, the company has a policy of refunding purchases to dissatisfied customers, even though there is no legal obligation to do so. In the past, approximately 10% of goods sold were returned and refunds given.

(ii) During November 1999, a decision was taken in principle to close the company's Cork branch. However, no formalised plan in connection with the closure had been devised, the decision had not been communicated to the employees of the company at the date of the statement of financial position and no other steps had been taken to implement this decision at that date.

(iii) The company is famous for its in-store 'tea rooms', where tired shoppers can avail of light refreshments. During the year ended 31 December 1999, 200 people became ill after eating the JEANS AND JUMPERS plc 'special super deluxe gateau'. Ten of these people died. Legal proceedings have been started against the company for compensation. However, the company denies liability, stating that, at the time of the food poisoning outbreak, the local council was working on the water mains fixing burst pipes and it firmly believes that the water became contaminated during the repair process. The company's lawyers indicated, up to the date of approval of the financial statements, that the company would probably be found not liable.

(iv) The company had a lease on an old warehouse in Galway. As part of a centralisation programme, all merchandise is now being stored in Dublin warehouses. JEANS AND JUMPERS plc has tried to cancel the Galway lease which still has 3 years to run. However, due to the terms of the lease contract, it has been unable to do so.

Requirement In respect of the financial statements of JEANS AND JUMPERS plc for the year ended 31 December 1999, outline each of the following in accordance with IAS 37 *Provisions, Contingent Liabilities and Contingent Assets*:

(a) The accounting treatment for each of the above items; and
(b) Where appropriate, the disclosure requirements for each of the items.
(Assume materiality exists in all cases.)

Question 4

BLUES Limited (BLUES) prepares its financial statements to 31 December each year. The company manufactures paint, and its operations are divided into two income-generating units, domestic and commercial. The following issue needs to be resolved before the financial statements for the year ended 31 December 2008 can be finalised.

In December 2008, BLUES announced publicly its intention to reduce the level of additives in all of the company's domestic and commercial paints. This will involve modifying the company's plant and equipment at an estimated cost of €12,000,000, payable in equal annual instalments over the next six years, commencing in December 2009. Plant and equipment at 31 December 2008 had an average remaining useful economic life of six years. The changes were prompted by market pressures and evaluated using discounted cash flow techniques. The discount rate used was 10%.

Requirement   Explain how this should be accounted for, and show the amounts to be included in the financial statements for the year ended 31 December 2008.

Present value factors:

Rate/Period	1	2	3	4	5	6
10%	0.909	0.826	0.751	0.683	0.620	0.564
12%	0.893	0.797	0.712	0.636	0.567	0.507

EVENTS AFTER THE REPORTING PERIOD

INTRODUCTION

It is a fundamental principle of accounting that regard must be given to all available information when preparing financial statements. This must include relevant events occurring after the date of the statement of financial position and up to the date on which the financial statements are authorised for issue. The purpose of IAS 10 *Events After the Reporting Period* is to define the extent to which different types of events after the end of the reporting period are reflected in the financial statements.

After having studied this chapter, you should be able to give an account of the following key points:

- The definition of events after the end of the reporting period;
- The distinction between an adjusting and a non-adjusting event;
- The accounting treatment for an adjusting and non-adjusting event;
- The IAS 10 requirements regarding proposed dividends; and
- The circumstances when a non-adjusting event may become an adjusting event, i.e. going concern.

ACCOUNTING TREATMENT

An 'event after the reporting period' is an event, which could be favourable or unfavourable, that occurs between the end of the reporting period and the date that the financial statements are authorised for issue. IAS 10 differentiates between an adjusting event and a non-adjusting event after the reporting period.

Adjusting Event after the Reporting Period

This is an event after the reporting period that provides further evidence of conditions that existed at the end of the reporting period, including an event that indicates that the going concern assumption in relation to the whole or part of the enterprise is not appropriate. Examples include the:

- subsequent determination of the purchase price or of sale proceeds of assets purchased or sold before the year end;
- valuation of a property which provides evidence of a permanent diminution in value;
- receipt of information after the date of the statement of financial position which indicates that an asset was impaired at the date of the statement of financial position or that a previously recognised impairment was not adequate;
- sale of inventories after the date of the statement of financial position which gives evidence about their net realisable value at the date of the statement of financial position;
- renegotiation of amounts owing by debtors or the insolvency of a debtor;
- bankruptcy of a debtor after the date of the statement of financial position that confirms that a loss existed at the date of the statement of financial position on trade receivables;
- amounts received or receivable in respect of insurance claims which were in the course of negotiation at the date of the statement of financial position; and
- discovery of errors or frauds which show the financial statements were incorrect.

IAS 10 states that where there is an adjusting event, the financial statements must be changed to reflect this event.

Non-adjusting Event after the Reporting Period

This is an event after the reporting period that is indicative of a condition that arose after the end of the reporting period. Examples include:

- closing a significant part of the trading activities if not anticipated at the year end;
- the acquisition or disposal of a subsidiary after the date of the statement of financial position;
- major purchases and disposals of assets after the end of the reporting period;
- a fire after the end of the reporting period which results in the destruction of a major production plant;
- a decline in the value of property and investments held as non-current assets, if it can be demonstrated that the decline occurred after the year end;
- a decline in market value of investments between the date of the statement of financial position and the date when the financial statements are authorised for issue;
- announcing a plan to discontinue an operation; and
- commencing major litigation arising solely out of events that occurred after the date of the statement of financial position.

Non-adjusting events after the balance date do not result in changes in the amounts in financial statements. They may, however, be of such materiality that their disclosure is required by way of a note to ensure that the financial statements are not misleading. For material non-adjusting events after the end of the reporting period the following disclosure is required:

- the nature of the event;
- an estimate of the financial effect, or a statement that it is not practicable to make such an estimate; and
- the estimate of the financial effect should be disclosed before taking account of taxation; and the taxation implications should be explained where necessary for a proper understanding of the financial position.

Note   The date on which the financial statements are approved by the board of directors should be disclosed in the financial statements.

Going Concern Issues Arising after the End of the Reporting Period

An entity should not prepare its financial statements on a going concern basis if management determines after the end of the reporting period either that it intends to liquidate the entity or to cease trading, or that it has no realistic alternative but to do so.

Proposed Dividends

Proposed dividends should not be recognised as a liability until approved by shareholders at the AGM.

DISCLOSURE

As indicated above, non-adjusting events should be disclosed if they are of such importance that non-disclosure would affect the ability of users to make proper evaluations and decisions. The required disclosure is (a) the nature of the event and (b) an estimate of its financial effect or a statement that a reasonable estimate of the effect cannot be made.

A company should update disclosures that relate to conditions that existed at the end of the reporting period to reflect any new information that it receives after the reporting period about those conditions.

Companies must disclose the date when the financial statements were authorised for issue and who gave that authorisation. If the enterprise's owners or others have the power to amend the financial statements after issuance, the enterprise must disclose that fact.

CONCLUSION

In summary, the key aspects of IAS 10 are:

- Adjust the financial statements for adjusting events, i.e. events after the reporting period that provide further evidence of conditions that existed at the end of the reporting period, including events that indicate that the going concern assumption in relation to the whole or part of the enterprise is not appropriate;

- do not adjust for non-adjusting events, i.e. events or conditions that arose after the end of the reporting period; and
- if an entity declares dividends after the reporting period, the entity should not recognise those dividends as a liability at the end of the reporting period. That is a non-adjusting event.

QUESTIONS

Self-test Questions

1. What is an event after the end of the reporting period?
2. What is an adjusting event?
3. Give three examples of an adjusting event.
4. Give three examples of a non-adjusting event.
5. In what circumstances will a non-adjusting event require changes in the amounts to be disclosed in the financial statements?

Review Questions

(See APPENDIX ONE for Suggested Solutions to Review Questions). (Assume all transactions are material and ignore taxation.)

Question 1

The following events which are considered to be material occurred after the date of the statement of financial position of Bellamy Limited but before the completion of its financial statements.

(a) Cronser Limited, owing €20,000 to Bellamy Limited at the date of the statement of financial position, went into liquidation and available information suggests that there is little prospect of a dividend for unsecured creditors. The debt had increased to €30,000 at the date of the winding-up order;

(b) The liquidator of Bogmore Limited announced his intention to pay a dividend of 50 cents in the € to unsecured creditors. Three years previously, Bellamy Limited had provided for the full debt owing by Bogmore Limited at that time.

(c) A fire in one of Bellamy Limited's warehouses caused €50,000 worth of damage to inventory which had cost €80,000. This damage had not been covered by insurance. Of the damaged inventory, approximately 75% was in inventory at the date of the statement of financial position, the remaining 25% having been purchased after the date of the statement of financial position.

Requirement   Indicate to what extent the foregoing events should affect the accounts of Bellamy Limited. State the reasons that support your conclusions.

Question 2

Fabricators Limited, an engineering company, makes up its financial statements to 31 March in each year. The financial statements for the year ended 31 March 20X1 showed a turnover of €3,000,000 and trading profit of €400,000. Before approval of the financial statements by the board of directors on 30 June 20X1 the following events took place.

(a) The financial statements of Patchup Limited for the year ended 28 February 20X1 were received which indicated a permanent decline in that company's financial position. Fabricators Limited had bought shares in Patchup Limited some years ago and this purchase was included in unquoted investments at its cost of €100,000. The financial statements received indicated that the investment was now worth only €50,000.

(b) There was a fire at the company's warehouse on 30 April 20X1 when inventory to the value of €500,000 was destroyed. It transpired that the inventory in the warehouse was under-insured by some 50%.

(c) On 31 March 20X1 a provision had been made of €60,000 in respect of any remedial work required on plant supplied and installed at a customer's premises on 26 March 20X1. No remedial work had been carried out and on 1 May 20X1 the customer had confirmed acceptance of the plant. Accordingly, no further liability would be involved.

Requirement Explain, giving reasons as to how the above events should be dealt with in the company's financial statements for the year ended 31 March 20X1.

Challenging Questions

(Assume all transactions are material and ignore taxation.)

Question 1

(Based on ICAI, P2 Summer 1997, Question 1)

Blade Limited is a furniture manufacturing company. The company was informed on 1 February 19X7 that one of its major customers, Greenwood Limited, had gone into liquidation. The liquidator indicated that no payments would be made to unsecured creditors. The amount owed by Greenwood Limited on 1 February 19X7 amounted to €55,000, of which €30,000 related to goods invoiced on 10 December 19X6 and €25,000 to goods invoiced on 15 January 19X7.

Requirement Prepare a memorandum for the Board of Directors in which you, acting as auditor, should explain how the above item should be dealt with in the financial statements of Blade Limited for the year ended 31 December 19X6.

Question 2

(Based on ICAI, P2 Autumn 1997, Question 1)

Sword Limited had inventory amounting to €120,000 in its statement of financial position at 31 December 19X6. On 3 January 19X7, a fire in the company's warehouse severely damaged this inventory. The inventory will now realise only €50,000.

Requirement   Indicate how this situation should be dealt with in order to comply with standard accounting practice. (Assume a financial year end of 31 December 19X6.)

Question 3 (Based on ICAI, P2 Summer 1996, Question 1)

Highgrove plc is a manufacturing and distribution company. You are acting as auditor to Highgrove plc and you have been asked by the Board of Directors of the company to explain how the following items should be treated in the published accounts of the company for the year ended 31 December 19X5:

(a) On 11 February 19X6 Highgrove plc raised additional share capital of €100,000 by way of an issue of shares at full market price. This action had been planned and approved in October 19X5; and

(b) On 19 December 19X5 Highgrove plc sold an old warehouse which was surplus to requirements. The profit on sale was recorded in the accounts at €100,000. On 20 January 19X6 the purchaser discovered that the roof of the warehouse was defective. Under the terms of the sale agreement, Highgrove plc was responsible for rectifying the problem. On 3 March Highgrove plc received a bill for €30,000 in connection with this rectification work.

Requirement   You are required to prepare a memorandum to the Board of Directors of Highgrove plc in which you state how each of the above items should be reflected in the company's published financial statements for the year ended 31 December 19X5.

Question 4 (Based on ICAI, P2 Autumn 1998, Question 1)

TOFFEE plc ('TOFFEE') is a manufacturer and distributor of confectionery goods. The company's year end is 31 December. The directors of TOFFEE are due to sign the company's financial statements for the year ended 31 December 1997 on 5 March 1998. The company accountant collapsed in early January 1998, leaving the assistant accountant to prepare the year-end financial statements. Due to lack of experience, the assistant accountant was unsure of the accounting treatment of the following items and thus ignored them when drafting the year-end accounts:

(a) On 13 February 1998, TOFFEE terminated a contract with CRISP Inc., a US company based in Dallas, Texas. The contract had been in place for a number of years. In early January 1998, CRISP Inc. had been the subject of a federal investigation carried out by the public health agency. Under the terms of the contract, TOFFEE is obliged to pay €500,000 for early termination of the contract.

(b) Caramel used in the production of chocolate bars was included in year-end inventory at its cost of €120,000. Audit work carried out in February 1998 indicated that the caramel could have been purchased for €80,000 in January 1998, due to a fall in world commodity prices.

(c) During 1997, there had been industrial unrest amongst TOFFEE production workers following the automation of one of the manufacturing processes. Management had sought to make 20% of the workforce redundant. In February 1998, following protracted negotiations, it was agreed that 15% of the workforce would be made redundant at a cost of €400,000.

(d) On 31 January 1998, €250,000 was paid to Tony Raisin as compensation for his removal as Marketing Director. Mr Raisin had been dismissed by the Chairman at the December 1997 Board meeting as a result of a serious disagreement over marketing strategy for 1998.

Requirement

(a) Define an event after the end of the reporting period and distinguish between an adjusting event after the end of the reporting period and a non-adjusting event after the end of the reporting period.

(b) Explain briefly how each of the above transactions should be treated in the financial statements of TOFFEE for the year ended 31 December 1997, in accordance with the relevant accounting standard.

Question 5 *(Based on ICAI, P2 Summer 1999, Question 1)*

TOBACCO Limited ('TOBACCO') manufactures cigars. The following information is available for the company for the year ended 31 December 1998. The financial statements are due to be signed by the directors at the forthcoming board meeting in May 1999.

(a) TOBACCO's revenue for the financial year ended 31 December 1998 includes €300,000 relating to the sale, in October 1998, of a consignment of special cigars to the Moravian Government to celebrate the Silver Jubilee of its ruler. Following a coup in December 1998, the ruler was deposed and the Silver Jubilee celebrations were cancelled. TOBACCO does not now expect to receive payment of this debt.

(b) In January 1999, one of TOBACCO's French subsidiaries, LUM-METTE Limited, declared a dividend of €80,000 for the year ended 31 December 1998. TOBACCO holds a 75% interest in LUM-METTE Limited.

(c) At the December 1998 Board meeting of TOBACCO, a decision was taken in principle to dispose of SMOKE Limited, a subsidiary company based in Cork. This investment was valued in the statement of financial position of TOBACCO, at 31 December 1998, at €1,300,000. On 20 January 1999, the management of SMOKE Limited decided to buy the company for €2,000,000.

(d) TOBACCO Limited owned 60% of PIPE Limited which it had acquired 2 years earlier at a cost of €1,500,000. The financial statements of PIPE Limited for the year ended 31 December 1998 were received by TOBACCO on 10 January 1999 and they showed a permanent decline in the company's financial position. The cost of

PIPE Limited (€1,500,000) was included under unquoted investments in the statement of financial position of TOBACCO. A review of the financial statements of PIPE Limited indicated that the investment was now worth only €700,000.

Requirement   Indicate how each of the above items should be dealt with in the financial statements of TOBACCO Limited for the year ended 31 December 1998.

CHAPTER 16

ACCOUNTING FOR GOVERNMENT GRANTS AND DISCLOSURE OF GOVERNMENT ASSISTANCE

INTRODUCTION

This chapter addresses the accounting treatment and disclosure of government grants. Government grants include all forms of assistance from governments and government agencies, be they local or international. Most grants are to assist in the purchase of non-current assets but some relate to income. Such grants can take the form of cash or asset transfer and can be given in return for past, present or future compliance with the conditions of receiving them.

IAS 20 *Accounting for Government Grants and Disclosure of Government Assistance* prescribes the accounting treatment for, and disclosure of, government grants and the disclosure of other forms of government assistance. IAS 20 does not deal with:

- Government assistance that is provided in the form of benefits that are available in determining taxable income;
- Government participation in the ownership of an entity; and
- Government grants covered by IAS 41 *Agriculture*.

After having studied this chapter, you should be able to explain the following key points:

- The distinction between grants related to income and grants related to assets;
- The accounting treatment of grants related to income;
- The two allowable methods of accounting for grants related to assets;
- When grants become repayable; and
- The disclosure requirements relating to government grants.

Important Definitions

- **Government** includes central government, government agencies and similar bodies whether local, national or international.

- **Government Assistance** refers to action by government designed to provide an economic benefit specific to an entity or range of entities qualifying under certain criteria.
- **Government Grants** incorporates all assistance by government in the form of transfer of resources to an entity in return for past or future compliance with certain conditions relating to the operating activities of the entity.
- **Forgivable Loans** are loans where the lender would waive repayment under certain conditions.

ACCOUNTING TREATMENT

Grants should not be recognised in the statement of comprehensive income until the conditions for receipt have been complied with and there is reasonable assurance that the grant will be received (prudence). Subject to this condition, the general principle is that all grants should be recognised in the statement of comprehensive income to correspond with the expenditure to which they contribute once any conditions for the receipt of the grant have been met. Grants must not be credited directly to shareholders interests (equity).

Grants Related to Income

These grants cover the costs of certain categories of revenue expenditure, e.g. training costs. IAS 20 allows two possible treatments:

1. Presented as a credit in the statement of comprehensive income, either separately or under a general heading, such as 'other income', by debiting bank and crediting income; or
2. Deducted from the related expense, by debiting bank and crediting the expense.

Whichever method is chosen, disclosure of the grant may be necessary for a proper understanding of the financial statements.

Example

In 20X1, a company incurred training expenses of €500,000 and received a grant towards 10% of this cost.

Requirement   How should the grant be accounted for under the two methods allowed in IAS 20 *Accounting for Government Grants and Disclosure of Government Assistance?*

Solution

Method 1

	€
Gross Profit	X
plus: Other Income	50,000
	X
Less: Expenses	
Training Expenses	(500,000)
Net Profit	X

Method 2

	€
Gross Profit	X
Less: Expenses	
Training Expenses	
(€500,000–€50,000)	450,000
Net Profit	X

Grants Related to Assets

These grants cover the costs of certain categories of capital expenditure, e.g. property, plant and equipment, fixtures and fittings etc. The accounting treatment is to credit the amount of the grant to revenue in the statement of comprehensive income over the useful life of the asset to which it relates by:

1. reducing the cost of the asset by the amount of the grant and depreciating the 'net' cost; or
2. treating the amount of the grant as a deferred credit in the statement of financial position, a portion of which is transferred to revenue in the statement of comprehensive income annually over the life of the asset.

Example

Company A purchases a machine for €120,000. It received a grant towards 20% of the cost of the machine. The machine has an expected life of three years with an expected nil residual value. Profit for each year is €100,000 (before depreciation).

Requirement   Account for the capital grant under the two methods allowed in IAS 20.

Solution

Method 1 – Reducing Cost of Asset:

Statement of comprehensive income	Year 1	Year 2	Year 3
	€	€	€
Profit before depreciation	100,000	100,000	100,000
Depreciation	*(32,000)	(32,000)	(32,000)
Profit	68,000	68,000	68,000

*(€120,000 – €24,000) ÷ 3

Statement of financial position	Year 1	Year 2	Year 3
	€	€	€
Non-current Asset at Cost	96,000	96,000	96,000
Accumulated Depreciation	32,000	64,000	96,000
Net Book Value	64,000	32,000	–

Method 2 – Treating the Grant as a Deferred Credit:

Statement of comprehensive income	Year 1	Year 2	Year 3
	€	€	€
Profit before grant & depreciation	100,000	100,000	100,000
Depreciation	(40,000)	(40,000)	(40,000)
Grant	8,000	8,000	8,000
Profit	68,000	68,000	68,000

Statement of financial position	Year 1	Year 2	Year 3
	€	€	€
Non-current asset (cost)	120,000	120,000	120,000
Accumulated depreciation	40,000	80,000	120,000
Net book value	80,000	40,000	–

	€	€	€
Non-current liabilities			
Deferred income – govt grants	8,000	0	0
Current liabilities			
Deferred income – govt grants	8,000	8,000	Nil
Closing balance	16,000	8,000	–

The main argument in favour of the first alternative is its simplicity. By crediting the grant to the cost of the asset, the resulting depreciation charge automatically credits the amount of the grant to revenue over the life of the asset.

The arguments in favour of the second alternative are:

- it shows non-current assets at their true cost value;
- depreciation charge is more 'correct';
- netting off is in principle bad accountancy; and
- it leads to better comparability from year to year and between companies.

IAS 20 permits the use of either method.

Repayment of Grants

A grant that becomes repayable should be treated as a revision of an accounting estimate. If the grant (relating to an expense item) has been fully credited to income, the repayment would normally be charged against profits in the year.

If the grant (relating to an expense item) has not been fully amortised, the repayment should firstly be offset against the unamortised balance, with any excess being charged as an expense.

The repayment of a grant relating to an asset should be accounted for by either increasing the carrying amount of the asset or reducing the deferred income balance. The cumulative additional depreciation that would have been recognised to date (in the absence of the grant) should be charged immediately as an expense.

Government Assistance

Government assistance, such as the provision of free technical or marketing advice, does not need to be reflected in the financial statements but disclosure of the nature of the assistance may be necessary so that the financial statements are not misleading.

DISCLOSURE

- The accounting policy adopted, including the methods of presentation adopted in the financial statements;
- The nature and extent of government grants recognised in the financial statements and an indication of other forms of government assistance from which the entity has directly benefited; and
- Unfulfilled conditions and other contingencies attaching to government assistance that has been recognised.

OTHER GUIDANCE

SIC 10 *Government Assistance – No Specific Relation to Operating Activities*

Issue

In some countries government assistance to entities can be aimed at encouragement or long-term support of business activities either in certain regions or industry sectors. Conditions to receive such assistance may not be specifically related to the operating activities of the entity.

Is such government assistance a government grant within the scope of IAS 20 *Accounting for Government Grants and Disclosure of Government Assistance* and therefore is it accounted for in accordance with this Standard?

Consensus

Government assistance to entities meets the definition of government grants in IAS 20, even if there are no conditions specifically relating to the operating activities of the entity other than the requirement to operate in certain regions or industry sectors. Such grants are therefore not credited directly to equity.

CONCLUSION

A government grant is not recognised until there is reasonable assurance that:

- the entity will comply with the conditions attached to it; and
- the grant will be received.

A government grant is recognised as income on a systematic basis over the periods necessary to match the grant income with the related costs that it is intended to compensate. If the related costs have already been incurred, the grant is recognised as income in the period in which it becomes receivable. A government grant is not credited directly to equity, with those related to assets being presented in the statement of financial position either as deferred income or as a deduction in determining the carrying amount of the asset.

A government grant that becomes repayable is accounted for as a revision to an accounting estimate *(IAS 8 Accounting Policies, Changes in Accounting Estimates and Errors)*.

QUESTIONS

Self-test Questions

1. How should grants related to income be accounted for?
2. What are the two allowable methods of accounting for grants related to assets?
3. What are the disclosure requirements listed in IAS 20?
4. When and how should potential liabilities to repay grants be accounted for?

Review Questions

(See APPENDIX ONE for Suggested Solutions to Review Questions)

Question 1

Electronic Manufacturers Limited is installing a new production plant at a cost of €1 million, in respect of which government grants have been approved as follows:

  Capital costs -   40%
  Training costs -   100%

The company depreciated its plant and equipment on the basis of 20% on original cost. The directors are aware that the accounting treatment for grants is dealt with in IAS 20 *Accounting for Government Grants and Disclosure of Government Assistance*, and they have asked you to advise them on the accounting options available and the effect which they would have on the company's financial statements.

Requirement   You are required to draft a report to the directors which:
(a) outlines the accounting treatment of the foregoing grants under IAS 20;
(b) recommends (with reasons) the treatment which you believe would be the most suitable in the case of Electronic Manufacturers Limited; and
(c) indicates the form of accounting policy or other notes which should be included in the annual financial statements of the company.

Question 2

An item of plant and equipment was purchased for €25,000 on 1 May 20X0. It is expected that its useful life will be 4 years and that its residual value will be €1,000 at the end of its life. A government grant of €6,000 was received to assist with the cost of purchase, and a further grant of €500 was received to subsidise the wages of the skilled employees who will operate the plant and equipment during the first year of its use.

Requirement   The Chief Accountant wishes to have your opinion as to how this should be reflected in the company's published financial statements for the year ended 30 April 20X1. Your answer should include reference to appropriate International Accounting Standards.

Challenging Questions

Question 1 (Based on ICAI, P2 Summer 1997, Question 1)

Blade Limited is a furniture manufacturing company. You are acting as auditor to the company and have been asked by the Board of Directors to indicate how the following item should be dealt with in the financial statements for the year ended 31 December 1996. During 1996, Blade Limited received a grant from the European Union of €500,000 towards the cost of a new machine which would be used in the production of wooden cabinets. The equipment has a useful economic life of 5 years.

Requirement   Prepare a memorandum for the Board of Directors in which you explain how each of the above should be dealt with in the financial statements of Blade Limited for the year ended 31 December 1996.

Question 2 (Based on ICAI, P2 Summer 2001, Question 4)

ABC NEWSPAPER Limited has received a grant for €120,000 over 4 years in respect of providing employment in a deprived area.

Requirement   Explain briefly the treatment of this grant in the company's financial statements.

Question 3 (Based on ICAI, P2 Summer 2002, Question 2)

CAMCON Limited ('CAMCON') operates a successful light engineering business with workshops in Belfast, Dublin and Galway. CAMCON is to prepare accounts for the year ended 31 December 2001, and these have yet to be finalised and signed off. You have been provided with the following information regarding the company:

Sale of Belfast Workshop   The Belfast workshop was sold to ECLIPSE plc on 1 November 2001 for €500,000, and the sale agreement stated that a further €80,000 relating to the sale of the Belfast workshop would be receivable by CAMCON if a major new contract with BLACKWELL Bakery was to be secured. Negotiations for this new contract with BLACKWELL Bakery had commenced in late October 2001 but were still ongoing at 31 December 2001. At that time the directors of CAMCON stated that the negotiations appeared to be going well and that it was probable that the contract would be signed within three months, but that it was still too early to suggest that the final outcome was virtually certain. In early February 2002, negotiations with BLACKWELL Bakery concluded successfully and a contract was subsequently agreed and signed on 12 February 2002. CAMCON then received the extra €80,000 from the sale of the Belfast workshop from ECLIPSE plc on 20 February 2002.

Bad Debts   On 11 January 2002, a major customer, MACBETH & DUNCAN, went into liquidation. In April 2002, CAMCON received only 30% of the balance owing from MACBETH & DUNCAN as at 31 December 2001. No further monies are expected to be received from MACBETH & DUNCAN.

Fire at Galway Workshop   A fire in the storeroom of the Galway workshop on 19 January 2002 destroyed €18,000 of inventory.

Government Grants   During the year ended 31 December 2001, a package of government grant assistance was negotiated in respect of the Dublin and Galway workshops, the terms of which are as follows:

Grant Available	€
	Qualifying Expenditure
Graphic design for marketing brochure	1,000
Purchase of plant and machinery	5,000
Total	6,000

Scrutiny of the accounting records revealed the following:

(a) A marketing brochure was designed in November 2001 and final copies were printed and distributed in December 2001 at a cost of €10,000. The printer's invoice was received in November 2001. Due to a dispute over the colours used in the brochure, CAMCOM paid 75% of the printer's invoice in December 2001. The balance was paid in January 2002.

(b) New plant and machinery costing €20,000 was ordered from a German manufacturer in November 2001, but was only delivered, installed and paid for in February 2002. There have been no other additions to non-current assets since 1 January 2001.

(c) The company submitted a claim form in respect of these grants in March 2002 and lodged the resultant cheque for €6,000 in April 2002.

(d) The company's accounting policy is to depreciate plant and machinery over 5 years on a straight-line basis, charging a full year's depreciation in the year of purchase.

Requirement   Write a letter to the Financial Controller of CAMCON, outlining how each of the above matters should be treated in the company's accounts for the year ended 31 December 2001 detailing, if appropriate, their financial effect and specific disclosure requirements.

CHAPTER 17

EMPLOYEE BENEFITS

INTRODUCTION

Most entities have both permanent and temporary employees, and employee costs constitute a significant portion of their business costs. While accounting for wages, salaries and other short-term benefits is for the most part relatively straightforward, post-employment benefits can be more troublesome. All benefits provided to employees, both short- and long-term, should be accounted for so as to ensure that an entity's financial statements reflect a liability when employees have worked in exchange for future benefits. The following are examples of employee benefits as defined by IAS 19 *Employee Benefits*:

- **Short-term benefits** – wages, salaries, holiday pay, sick leave, bonuses payable within 12 months of the reporting period and social security contributions payable in respect of employee benefits;
- **Long-term benefits** – long-term incentive plans, long-service awards and bonuses payable more than 12 months after the reporting period;
- **Termination benefits** – redundancy payments; and
- **Post-employment benefits** – retirement benefits, pensions and post-retirement medical insurance.

After having read this chapter, you should be able to:

- define each of the main categories of employee benefits identified in IAS 19, and explain the required accounting treatment for each;
- distinguish between benefit contribution and defined benefit pension plans; and
- outline the main disclosures that should be made in respect of employee benefits in accordance with IAS 19.

OBJECTIVE OF IAS 19

IAS 19 *Employee Benefits* prescribes the accounting for, and disclosure of, employee benefits by employers (that is, all forms of consideration given by an enterprise in exchange for service rendered by employees), except those to which IFRS 2 *Share-based Payment applies*. IAS 19 does not deal with reporting by employee benefit plans (IAS 26 *Accounting and Reporting by Retirement Benefit Plans*). The principle underlying IAS 19 is that the cost of providing employee benefits should be recognised in the period in which the benefit is earned by the employee, rather than when it is paid or payable. In addition to the benefits noted above, IAS 19 also applies (among other kinds of employee benefits) to profit sharing plans; medical and life insurance benefits during employment; housing benefits; free or subsidised goods or services given to employees; post-employment life insurance benefits; long-service or sabbatical leave; 'jubilee' benefits; and deferred compensation programmes.

ACCOUNTING TREATMENT

Short-term Employee Benefits

For short-term employee benefits (those payable within 12 months after service is rendered, such as wages, paid vacation and sick leave, bonuses, and non-monetary benefits such as medical care and housing), the undiscounted amount of the benefits expected to be paid in respect of service rendered by employees in a period should be recognised in that period. The expected cost of short-term compensated absences should be recognised as the employees render service that increases their entitlement or, in the case of non-accumulating absences, when the absences occur.

Profit-sharing and Bonus Payments

The enterprise should recognise the expected cost of profit-sharing and bonus payments when, and only when, it has a legal or constructive obligation to make such payments as a result of past events and a reliable estimate of the expected cost can be made.

Post-employment Benefit Plans

The most common type of post-employment benefit is a pension. As IAS 19 requires the cost of providing employee benefits to be recognised in the period in which the benefits are earned, the accounting treatment for a post-employment benefit plan will be determined according to whether the plan is a defined contribution or a defined benefit plan.

Defined Contribution

Under defined contribution pension plans, the level of benefits depend on the value of contributions paid in by each member and the investment performance achieved on those contributions. Therefore, the employer's liability is limited to the contributions it has agreed to pay and it has no legal or constructive obligation to pay further contributions if the fund does not have sufficient assets to pay employee benefits relating to employee service in the current and prior periods. For defined contribution plans (including multi-employer plans, state plans and insured schemes where the obligations of the employer are similar to those arising in relation to defined contribution plans), the cost to be recognised in the period is the contribution payable in exchange for service rendered by employees during the period. For defined contribution plans the contribution payable to the fund is expensed and the pension liability equals the unpaid contributions for past service. If contributions to a defined contribution plan do not fall due within 12 months after the end of the period in which the employee renders the service, they should be discounted to their present value.

Actuarial and investment risks of defined contribution plans are assumed either by the employee or the third party. Plans not defined as contribution plans are classed as defined benefit plans. If an employer is unable to show that all actuarial and investment risk has been transferred to another party, and its obligations are limited to contributions made during the period, a plan is defined benefit.

Defined Benefit

A defined benefit plan is a post-employment benefit plan other than a defined contribution plan. These include both formal plans and those informal practices that create a constructive obligation to the enterprise's employees. For defined benefit pension plans the rules specify the benefits to be paid and they are financed accordingly. The benefits are typically based on such factors as age, length of service and compensation. The employer retains the actuarial and investment risks of the plan. For example, under the terms of a particular pension plan, a company contributes 6% of an employee's salary. The employee is guaranteed a return of the contributions plus interest of 4% a year. The plan would be classified as a defined benefit plan as the employer has guaranteed a fixed rate of return and as a result carries the investment risk.

Plan Assets and Liabilities   IAS 19 approaches accounting for defined benefit plans from a statement of financial position perspective by describing how a defined benefit liability should be recognised and measured. To achieve this, the plan liabilities are measured at each reporting date. The plan liabilities are measured on an actuarial basis and discounted to present value. The amount recognised in the statement of financial position, which could be either an asset or a liability, will be:

- the present value of the defined benefit obligation, plus
- any actuarial gains less losses not yet recognised, minus
- any past service cost not yet recognised, and minus
- the fair value of the plan assets.

If the result of the above is a positive amount then a liability has occurred and it is recorded in full in the statement of financial position. Any negative amount is an asset, and IAS 19 restricts the amount that can be shown as a defined benefit asset. The asset may not exceed the aggregate of:

- any cumulative, unrecognised net actuarial losses and past service costs; and
- the present value of any refunds from the plan or reductions in future contributions.

Over the life of the plan, changes in benefits under the plan will result in increases or decreases in the enterprise's obligation. Plan assets and plan liabilities from the different plans are normally presented separately in the statement of financial position.

Measurement   The defined benefit obligation will include both legal obligations and any constructive obligation arising from the employer's usual business practices such as an established pattern of past practice. IAS 19 encourages the involvement of a qualified actuary in measuring defined benefit obligations, and while IAS 19 does not require an annual actuarial valuation of the defined benefit obligation, the employer is required to determine the present value of the defined benefit obligation and the fair value of the plan assets. IAS 19 states that the Projected Unit Credit Method should be used to determine the present value of the defined benefit obligation, the related current service cost and past service cost. The Projected Unit Credit Method looks at each period of service, which gives rise to additional units of benefit and measures each unit separately to build up the final obligation. The whole of the post-employment benefit obligation is then discounted.

Current service cost is the increase in the present value of the defined benefit obligation which occurs as a result of employee service in the current period. In simple terms, this is the amount of pension entitlement that employees have earned in the accounting period. Therefore, it will increase the pension liability in the statement of financial position and be expensed in the statement of comprehensive income.

Past service cost is the term used to describe the change in the obligation for employee service in prior periods, arising as a result of changes to plan arrangements in the current period. Past service cost may be either positive (where benefits are introduced or improved) or negative (where existing benefits are reduced). The pension liability in the statement of financial position will increase or decrease and the statement of comprehensive income will be affected accordingly. Past service cost should be recognised immediately to the extent that it relates to former employees or to active employees already vested. Otherwise, it should be amortised on a straight-line basis over the average period until the amended benefits become vested.

Plan assets are measured at fair value, which is normally market value. Fair value can be estimated by discounting expected future cash flows. The rate used to discount estimated cash flows should be determined by reference to market yields at the reporting date on high-quality corporate bonds. IAS 19 is not specific on what it considers to be a high-quality bond and therefore this can lead to variation in the discount rates used.

Valuations should be carried out with sufficient regularity so that the amounts recognised in the financial statements do not differ materially from those that would be determined at the reporting date. A volatile economic environment will require frequent valuations at least annually. The assumptions used for the purposes of such valuations should be unbiased and mutually compatible, and will include demographic assumptions such as mortality, turnover and retirement age, and financial assumptions such as discount rates, salary and benefit levels.

Actuarial Gains and Losses   On an ongoing basis, actuarial gains and losses arise that comprise of experience adjustments (the effects of differences between the previous actuarial assumptions and what has actually occurred) and the effects of changes in actuarial assumptions. In the long-term, actuarial gains and losses may offset one another and, as a result, the enterprise is not required to recognise all such gains and losses immediately. IAS 19 states that a company should recognise its actuarial gains and losses under one of three methods:

1. The 'corridor' approach: actuarial net gains and losses are recognised as income or expenditure if cumulative, unrecognised, actuarial gains and losses at the end of the previous reporting period (i.e. at the beginning of the current financial year) exceed the greater of:
   - 10% of the present value of the defined benefit obligation at the beginning of the year; and
   - 10% of the fair value of the plan assets at the same date.

   These limits should be calculated and applied separately for each defined plan. The excess determined by the above method is then divided by the expected average remaining working lives of the employees in the plan in order to give the income or expense to be recorded in the statement of comprehensive income.

2. Recognised in full as they occur in the statement of recognised income and expense.
3. Any other systematic method that results in a faster recognition of actuarial gains and losses in the statement of comprehensive income, provided that the same basis is applied to both gains and losses and that the basis is applied consistently from period to period.

Delays in the recognition of gains and losses can give rise to misleading figures in the statement of financial position. Also, multiple options for recognising gains and losses can lead to poor comparability.

Example

A plc:	1 January 2008 €m	31 December 2008 €m
Fair value plan assets	100	110
Present value-defined benefit obligation	90	96
Unrecognised actuarial gain	16	26
Average working life of employees	10 years	10 years

A plc has decided to use the corridor approach in recognising actuarial gains and losses. It must recognise the portion of the net actuarial gain or loss in excess of 10% of the greater of defined benefit obligation or the fair value of the plan assets at the beginning of the year. Unrecognised actuarial gain at the beginning of the year was €16 million. The limit of the corridor is 10% of €100 million (value of plan assets) i.e. €10 million, as this is greater than the present value of the obligation. The difference is €6 million, which divided by 10 years is €600,000.

Statement of Comprehensive Income   The charge to income recognised in a period in respect of a defined benefit plan will be made up of the following components:

- current service cost;
- interest cost[1];
- expected return on plan assets[2];
- actuarial gains and losses, to the extent recognised;
- past service cost, to the extent recognised; and
- the effect of any plan curtailments or settlements[3].

1. Interest cost is the increase in the period in the present value of the defined benefit obligation which arises because the benefits payable are one year closer to the settlement of the scheme. It represents the unwinding of the discount on the plan's liabilities. It is calculated by multiplying the discount rate at the beginning of the period by the present value of the defined benefit obligation throughout the period. This, in theory, means that a form of averaging should take place to calculate the 'average' present value of the obligation in the period. For exam purposes, the approach taken by the example in IAS 19 is usually adopted. That is, the interest cost will be calculated on the basis of the opening obligation. The interest cost will increase the obligation and will be charged to the statement of comprehensive income.

2. The return on plan assets is interest, dividends and other revenue derived from the plan assets, together with realised and unrealised gains or losses on the plan assets, less any costs of administering the plan (other than those included in the actuarial assumptions used to measure the defined benefit obligation) and less any tax payable by the plan itself. The difference between the expected return and actual return on plan assets is an actuarial gain or loss. The expected return on plan assets is based on the market's expectations of the return expected from the pension scheme's assets. It is calculated using the expected long-term rate of return on the plan assets at the beginning of the period. The amount so calculated is added to the scheme's assets and credited to the statement of comprehensive income. This return is a very subjective assumption and an increase in the return can create income at the expense of actuarial losses, which may not be recognised when entities use the corridor approach.

3. Gains or losses resulting from plan curtailments or settlements of a plan are recognised when the curtailment or settlement occurs. A curtailment occurs where a company either reduces the number of employees covered by the plan or amends

the terms of a defined benefit plan. An amendment would normally be such that a material element of future service by current employees will no longer qualify for benefits or will qualify for a reduction in benefits. Curtailments can have a material impact on the entity's financial statements and are often linked to restructuring or reorganisation. A company settles its obligations where it enters into a transaction that eliminates future legal and constructive obligation for part or all of the benefits provided under a defined benefit plan. Settlements are usually lump sum cash payments made to, or on behalf of, the plan participants in exchange for the extinguishment of the right to receive future benefits. Where a curtailment relates only to some employees covered by the plan, the obligation is only partly settled. Any gain or loss calculated should include a proportionate share of the previously unrecognised past service cost and actuarial gains and losses. Before determining the effect of a curtailment, the company has to re-measure the obligation and plan assets using current actuarial assumptions.

Example – *Dealing with defined benefit plans in the financial statements*

	Scheme assets	Scheme liabilities	Statement of comprehensive income
	€m	€m	€m
Opening balance 1 January 2XX1	1,000	2,000	
Interest cost (5% of €2,000 million)		100	(100)
Expected return on plan assets (7% of €1,000 million)	70		70
Current service cost		40	(40)
Past service cost		20	(20)
Benefits paid	(30)	(30)	
Contributions	20		
Gain on plan assets (difference)	140		
Loss on obligation (difference)		170	
Net amount charged			(90)
Closing balance 31 December 2XX1	1,200	2,300	

(This example does not deal with the recognition of actuarial gains and losses arising out of the scheme. It is assumed there are no actuarial gains and losses arising at 1 January 2XX1.)

The total amount charged in the statement of comprehensive income is €90 million. The gain on the plan assets and the loss on the obligation are just the balancing figures and amount to a net loss of €30 million (€140 million – €170 million) and this has not been recognised anywhere in the financial statements.

As a result, the liability in the statement of financial position will be €1,070 million (€2,300 million – €1,200 million – €30 million). Another way of showing this amount is:

	€m
Opening net liability (€1,000 million - €2,000 million)	1,000
Net amount charged in statement of comprehensive income	90
Contributions	(20)
	1,070

As can be seen, the liability is either calculated by taking the opening balances and adjusting for the charge in the statement of comprehensive income and contributions to the scheme, or by taking the closing balances and deducting the unrecognised loss. Either way should obviously produce the same result.

In summary, as explained above, the amount recognised in the statement of financial position will be as follows:

- the present value of the defined benefit obligation, plus
- any actuarial gains less losses not yet recognised, minus
- any past service cost not yet recognised, and minus
- the fair value of the plan assets.

If the result of the above is a positive amount then a liability occurs and it is recorded in full in the statement of financial position. Any negative amount is an asset, which is subject to a recoverability test. As outlined above, the pension expense is the net of the following items: current service cost; interest cost; expected return of any plan assets; actuarial gains and losses to the extent recognised; past service cost; and the effect of any curtailments or settlements.

Other Long-term Benefits

IAS 19 requires a simplified application of the model described above for other long-term employee benefits. This method differs from the accounting required for post-employment benefits in that:

- actuarial gains and losses are recognised immediately and no 'corridor' (as discussed above for post-employment benefits) is applied; and
- all past service cost is recognised immediately.

Termination Benefits

For termination benefits, IAS 19 specifies that amounts payable should be recognised when, and only when, the enterprise is demonstrably committed to either:

- terminating the employment of an employee or group of employees before the normal retirement date; or
- providing termination benefits as a result of an offer made in order to encourage voluntary redundancy.

The enterprise will be demonstrably committed to a termination when, and only when, it has a detailed formal plan for the termination and is without realistic possibility of withdrawal. Where termination benefits fall due after more than 12 months after the reporting date, they should be discounted.

OTHER ISSUES

'Asset Ceiling'

The International Accounting Standards Board (IASB) published the final 'asset ceiling' amendment to IAS 19 on 31 May 2002. The amendment prevents the recognition of gains solely as a result of deferral of actuarial losses or past service cost, and prohibits the recognition of losses solely as a result of deferral of actuarial gains. This can happen if an entity has a surplus in a defined benefit plan and cannot, based on the current terms of the plan, recover that surplus fully through refunds or reductions in future contributions. In such cases, deferral of past service cost and actuarial losses that arise in the period will increase the cumulative unrecognised net actuarial losses and past service cost. If that increase does not result in a refund to the entity or a reduction in future contributions to the pension fund, a gain would have been recognised under IAS 19 prior to this amendment. This amendment, however, prohibits recognising a gain in these circumstances. The opposite effect arises with deferred actuarial gains that arise in the period. This amendment prohibits recognising a loss in these circumstances.

Reporting Actuarial Gains and Losses

In December 2004, the IASB finalised an amendment to IAS 19 to allow the option of recognising actuarial gains and losses in full in the period in which they occur, outside profit or loss, in a statement of recognised income and expense. The amendment also provides guidance on allocating the cost of a group defined benefit plan to the entities in the group.

CONCLUSION

Accounting for post-employment benefits is an important financial reporting issue. IAS 19 may not only have a significant impact on the statement of financial position and statement of comprehensive income, but may also require an increased effort in terms of valuing pension deficits or surpluses together with external specialists such as actuaries. It has been suggested that many users of financial statements do not fully understand the information that entities provide about post-employment benefits. Both users and preparers of financial statements have criticised the accounting requirements for failing to provide high-quality, transparent information about post-employment benefits.

QUESTIONS

Self-test Questions

1. List, and briefly explain, the four main categories of employee benefits identified by IAS 19.
2. Define the following key terms:
   (a) Defined contribution pension plan;
   (b) Defined benefit pension plan;
   (c) Current service cost;
   (d) Past service cost;
   (e) Interest cost; and
   (f) Expected return on plan assets.

Review Questions

(See APPENDIX ONE for Suggested Solutions to Review Questions)

Question 1

The following information is available in relation to a company's pension plan:

- The fair value of the plan assets is €130 million;
- The present value of the defined benefit obligation is €105 million;
- There are cumulative unrecognised actuarial losses of €4 million; and
- The present value of refunds from the plan, and reductions in future contributions, is €23 million.

Requirement Calculate the amount that can be recognised as a defined benefit asset.

Question 2

A company has a defined benefit pension plan. At 1 January 20X1 the following values relate to the plan:

- The fair value of the plan assets is €30 million;
- The present value of the defined benefit obligation is €25 million;
- There are cumulative unrecognised actuarial gains of €4 million; and
- The average remaining working lives of employees is 10 years.

At the end of the period, at 31 December 20X1, the following values relate to the pension scheme:

- The fair value of the plan assets has risen to €35 million;
- The present value of the defined benefit obligation has risen to €28 million;
- The actuarial gain is €5 million; and
- The average remaining working lives of employees is 10 years.

Requirement   Show the ways in which actuarial gain could be treated for the period ending 31 December 20X1. (Ignore the asset ceiling test.)

Question 3

A company closes down its subsidiary, and the employees of that subsidiary no longer earn further pension benefits. The company has a defined benefit obligation with a net present value of €60 million. The plan assets have a fair value of €48 million. There are net cumulative and actuarial unrecognised gains of €4 million. The curtailment reduces the net present value of the obligation by €6 million.

Requirement   Calculate the curtailment gain and the net liability recognised in the statement of financial position after the curtailment.

Challenging Questions

Question 1

APF plc prepares its financial statements to 31 December each year. The company has a defined benefit pension plan. On 31 December 2XX7, present value of the defined benefit obligation was €22,500,000 and the fair value of the plan's assets was €21,900,000. The following information is available in relation to the year ended 31 December 2XX8:

(a) While the expected returns on plan assets were €2,300,000, actual returns were €2,700,000;
(b) APF plc made contributions of €3,800,000 into the plan, with employees contributing a further €1,500,000;
(c) The plan paid out benefits of €1,900,000 to past employees;

(d) The present value of the current service cost for the year ended 31 December 2XX8, before deducting employee contributions, was €3,700,000; and
(e) At 31 December 2XX8, the present value of the defined benefit obligation was €27,400,000 and the fair value of plan assets was €28,200,000.

A discount rate of 8% is considered appropriate for calculating the interest cost.

Requirement   With respect to the financial statements for the year ended 31 December 2XX8, calculate the:

(a) defined benefit expense
(b) defined benefit liability or asset; and
(c) reconcile the expense to the employer contributions.

CHAPTER 18

DISTRIBUTION OF PROFITS AND ASSETS

INTRODUCTION

Perhaps the question that most regularly arises, with respect to the move to International Financial Reporting Standards (IFRS) based financial statements, is the impact on profits available for distribution. The rules regarding distribution set out in company legislation are unchanged by the new legislation. However, the 'relevant accounts' referred to in that section may now be IFRS accounts and not company legislation accounts. The company law accounting rules generally state that only 'realised' profits may be included in the statement of comprehensive income of company legislation accounts; but IFRS permit many unrealised gains to be included in the statement of comprehensive income of IFRS accounts.

However, profits available for distribution will still comprise only realised profits less losses. The meaning of 'realised' has not been changed and in essence an item is only realised when it has passed out of a company's control and the company has received cash or cash equivalents in return for it. Consequently, it will be important in future for companies to track the extent to which profits recognised in their IFRS accounts (or company legislation accounts) are in fact realised.

After having studied this chapter on the distribution of profits and assets, you should be able to describe the following:

- The general rule governing the distribution of profits;
- The distinction between public and private companies as regards distributable profits;
- The distinction between realised and unrealised profits; and
- How to deal with revaluation surpluses and deficits.

DISTRIBUTABLE PROFITS

A distribution is defined as every description of distribution of a company's assets to members (shareholders) of the company whether in cash or otherwise, with the exception of:

- an issue of bonus shares;
- the redemption or purchase of the company's own shares out of capital (including the proceeds of a new issue) or out of unrealised profits;

- the reduction of share capital by:
  reducing the liability on shares in respect of share capital not fully paid up;
  paying off paid-up share capital; and
- a distribution of assets to shareholders in a winding up of the company.

All companies are prohibited from paying dividends except out of profits available for that purpose. The general principle is 'distributable profits consist of accumulated realised profits less accumulated realised losses'.

Note This definition permits the distribution as dividend of a capital profit, i.e. a surplus over book value realised on the sale of a non-current asset. But the words are:

- **accumulated** – which means that the balance of profit or loss from previous years must be brought into account in the current period; and
- **realised** – this prohibits the inclusion of unrealised profits arising from, e.g., the revaluation of non-current assets retained by the company.

There is a further requirement for public limited companies that the total of the net assets of a public limited company must be equal to or more than the aggregate of the called up share capital plus undistributable reserves both at the date of and immediately after the distribution. Undistributable reserves of a public limited company are defined as:

- the share premium account;
- the capital redemption reserve fund;
- the excess of accumulated unrealised profits, not previously capitalised, over accumulated unrealised losses not previously written off by a reduction or reorganisation of capital; and
- any other reserve that the company is prohibited from distributing by any enactment, or by its Memorandum of Articles.

Example

Calculate the distributable profits of both Companies A and B assuming that each is a:

(a) private company; and
(b) public company.

	A		B	
	€'000		€'000	
Share capital		1,000		1,000
Unrealised profits	200		200	
Unrealised losses	-	200	(300)	(100)
Realised profits	300		800	
Realised losses	-	300	(200)	600
Share capital & reserves		1,500		1,500

Solution

A Limited:

(a) Private Company
Realised Profits – Realised Losses = €300,000

(b) Public Company
Net Realised Profits less Net Unrealised Losses = €300,000

B Limited:

(a) Private Company
   €800,000 – €200,000 = €600,000

(b) Public Company
   €600,000 - €100,000 = €500,000

Any excess depreciation on a revalued non-current asset above the amount of depreciation that would have been charged on its historical cost can be treated as a realised profit for the purpose of distributions. This is to avoid penalising companies that make an unrealised profit on the revaluation of an asset, and then charge depreciation on the revalued amount.

Example

Assume a company buys an asset for €20,000, which has a life of four years and a nil residual value. If it is immediately revalued to €30,000, an unrealised profit of €10,000 would be credited to the revaluation reserve. Annual depreciation must be based on the revalued amount, in this case, 25% of €30,000 or €7,500. This exceeds depreciation, which would have been charged on the asset's cost (€5,000 p.a.) by €2,500 per annum. This €2,500 can be treated as a distributable profit.

REALISED AND UNREALISED PROFITS AND LOSSES

Company legislation typically does not define realised profits or unrealised profits; but rather deals with specific problems. Any determination of whether a profit or loss is realised must be made in light of best accounting practice. The following are the rules contained in company legislation:

- A provision made in the accounts is a realised loss;
- A revaluation surplus is an unrealised profit;
- When a surplus arises on the revaluation of a non-current asset and this is shown in the accounts, a higher depreciation charge will arise. The difference between the depreciation charge based on the revalued amount and the depreciation charge based on the book cost should be regarded as a realised profit;
- On the disposal of a revalued asset, any unrealised surplus or loss on valuation immediately becomes realised;
- If there is no available record of the original cost of an asset, its cost may be taken as the value put on it in the earliest available record; and
- If it is impossible to establish whether a profit or loss brought forward was realised or unrealised, any such profit may be treated as realised and any such loss as unrealised.

REVALUATION DEFICITS

A provision made in the accounts is a realised loss. Therefore a revaluation deficit is a realised loss. If a revaluation deficit arises on a revaluation of all non-current assets (or on a revaluation of all non-current assets other than goodwill) the revaluation deficit is an unrealised loss. Consequently, where a company undertakes a partial revaluation of non-current assets, a deficit on one asset is a realised loss and cannot therefore be offset against a surplus on another asset (an unrealised profit) for the purposes of arriving at distributable profits. A partial remedy to this problem is contained in company legislation.

Deficits arising on an asset where there has been a partial revaluation of the assets are to be treated as unrealised losses provided that:

1. the directors have 'considered' the aggregate value of the non-current assets which have not been revalued at the date of the partial revaluation;
2. the directors are satisfied that the aggregate value is not less than their aggregate book value; and
3. a note to the accounts states the above two facts.

Example

X Limited has the following statement of financial position:

	€'000
Net Assets	300

Share capital	100
Share premium	50
Revaluation reserve	70
Retained earnings	80
	300

Two of the company's assets were revalued during the year, one giving rise to a surplus of €100,000, the other a deficit of €30,000.

Requirement What are the profits available for distribution and how would the figure differ if all the company's assets had been revalued?

Solution

Profits available for distribution:

	€'000
Net realised profits (SCI)	80
Less realised losses – revalued deficit	(30)
	50

If all the company's assets had been revalued (or the directors had 'considered' the value of the assets not revalued), the revalued deficit would be unrealised and therefore the profits available for distribution would be €80,000.

REVALUATION SURPLUSES

Revaluation surpluses are unrealised profits in the accounting period in which the revaluation takes place. The only exception to this rule is where the same asset was:

- previously revalued giving rise to a deficit; and
- the deficit was treated as a realised loss.

In such a case, the revaluation surplus will be a realised profit to the extent that it makes good the realised loss. It should also be remembered that revaluation surpluses can eventually become realised profits when the asset is either depreciated or sold.

DEVELOPMENT EXPENDITURE

Deferred development expenditure is treated as an unrealised loss if the expenditure is carried forward under the provision of IAS 38 *Intangible Assets*. A note to the accounts is required stating this fact. It should also be noted that, if the expenditure is not treated as a realised loss in the year of expenditure, it will be a realised loss when written off in future years.

CONCLUSION

Accountants (and company directors) over the years have faced the problem of:

- What is meant by distributable profits?
- Can unrealised gains be distributed (i.e. paid out as dividend)?
- Must account be taken of unrealised losses before a distribution is paid? and
- What is meant by 'realised'?

While company legislation has attempted to rationalise the whole area of what constitutes distributable profits, like many areas of accounting, there remains areas of debate and judgement.

QUESTIONS

Self-test Questions

1. What is the general rule as to which profits are available for distribution?
2. With a public company how is this general rule amended?
3. Is there a strict legal definition of what is meant by 'realised profits'?
4. Is the profit attributable to construction contracts a realised or unrealised profit?

Review Questions

(See APPENDIX ONE for Suggested Solutions to Review Questions.)

Question 1

John Sykes is an ordinary shareholder in Prosperous plc and has recently received the consolidated accounts of the Prosperous Group for the year ended 31 December 20X0. He has been discussing the accounts with his accountants, Know Most & Co., and mentioned that he was not clear as to the amount of distributable reserves available for the payment of dividends.

Requirement

(a) Define profits available for distribution for a public company and the disclosure requirements for the company and the group.

(b) Explain the implications of the following items to profits available for distribution:
  (i) Research and development activities;
  (ii) Net deficit on revaluation reserve arising from an overall deficit on the revaluation of non-current assets; and
  (iii) Excess depreciation.

Question 2

Below are extracts from the statements of financial position of three companies as at 31 December Year 6:

	Hay plc €'000	Bee plc €'000	Sea Limited €'000
ASSETS			
Tangible Non-current Assets	800	700	300
Current Assets	600	400	300
	1,400	1,100	600
EQUITY AND LIABILITIES			
Capital and Reserves			
Issued share capital	300	300	300
Reserves:			
Revaluation	(200)	200	100
Profit on sale of non-current assets	200	100	–
Retained earnings start of year	600	(200)	(200)
Statement of comprehensive income for year	300	600	300
	1,200	1,000	500
Current Liabilities	200	100	100
	1,400	1,100	600

Bee's tangible non-current assets were revalued on 1 January Year 6 from a cost price of €300,000 to a revalued amount of €500,000. All of Bee's tangible non-current assets have been purchased since Year 1. They are depreciated over 10 years, using the straight-line method.

Sea's tangible non-current assets were revalued on 31 December Year 6 from a cost price of €200,000 to a revalued amount of €300,000. However, in Sea's statement of comprehensive income for Year 6 the depreciation charge was based on the cost price figure.

Requirement   Calculate the maximum distribution which Hay, Bee and Sea can each make.

Question 3

(a) What is the general rule for determining distributable profits?
(b) State whether each of the following are realised or unrealised profits or losses. Briefly explain the reason for your answer.

(i) A charge to the statement of comprehensive income as a provision for bad debts;
(ii) The final dividend receivable from a subsidiary in respect of an accounting period ending before the end of the parent company's financial year; and
(iii) Surpluses arising on revaluation of assets (before sale).

(c) The summarised statement of financial position at 30 September 20X6 of Global Sports Limited is set out below:

	€'000
Authorised Share Capital	
250,000 ordinary shares of €1 each	250
Called Up Share Capital	
200,000 ordinary shares of €1 each	200
Share Premium Account	175
Revaluation Reserve (net deficit)	(175)
Other Reserves	
Capital Redemption Reserve Fund	125
General Reserve	100
Retained Earnings	200
	625
Non-current Assets	400
Net Current Assets	225
	625

The deficit on the revaluation reserve arose as a result of a revaluation of all the non-current assets, and the articles of association state that the general reserve is non-distributable.

Requirement:

(a) What are the legally distributable profits of Global Sports if:
   - it is a private company?
   - it is a public company?

(b) What difference, if any, would it make to your answers in (a) if the deficit on the revaluation reserve had arisen on the revaluation of an individual asset?

Challenging Questions

Question 1

(Based on ICAI, P2 Summer 1997, Question 1)
The following information is available for Halogen Limited:

Draft Statement of comprehensive income (Extract) for the Year Ended 31 December 1996

	€'000
Profit before taxation	500
Taxation	(50)
Profit after taxation	450

Draft Statement of Changes in Equity (Extract) for the Year Ended 31 December 1996

	Note	€'000
Profit for the financial year (as per draft above)		450
Unrealised surplus on revaluation of Property X	(1)	60
Unrealised loss on trade investments		(270)
Total recognised gains and losses since last annual report		240

Additional Information

1. Property X was revalued for the first time in 1996.
2. The company is entirely equity financed as follows:

	€'000
Share capital (€1 ordinary shares)	200
Share premium	50
Capital redemption reserve fund	40

3. Retained profits were €90,000 at 1 January 1996.

4. Just before the year end, the company sold some land at a profit of €70,000. This profit was not reflected in the draft profit figure above. The tax charge associated with this profit is €30,000 and this has not been included in the draft taxation charge shown above.
5. A fire in part of the company's warehouse just before the year end destroyed inventory worth €50,000. No adjustment has been made to reflect this fact in the draft profit figure.
6. Taxation is at a rate of 10%.

Requirement:
(a) What profits are statutorily available for distribution? What additional restrictions are placed on public limited companies?
(b) What is the maximum distribution that Halogen Limited, as a private limited company, can make?
(c) If Halogen Limited was a public limited company, what would be the maximum distribution it could make?

Question 2 (Based on ICAI, P2 Autumn 1995, Question 1)

Demo Limited is a private company with a 31 December year-end. The following is the summarised statement of financial position for Demo Limited as at 31 December 1994:

Summarised Draft Statement of financial position as at 31 December 1994

	€'000	€'000
Net assets		400
Share capital		350
Share premium		40
Unrealised losses on asset revaluations		(20)
Realised profits	60	
Realised losses	(30)	30
		400

Requirement
(a) As a private company, what is the maximum distribution of profits that Demo Limited can make?
(b) If Demo Limited were a public limited company, what would be the maximum distribution of profits the company could make?

Question 3 (Based on ICAI, P2 Autumn 1999, Question 2)

(a) Outline what profits are available for distribution by each of the following:
   (i) A private limited company; and
   (ii) A public limited company.
(b) You are given the following extracts from the draft statement of comprehensive income of MORGAN ENTERPRISES for the year ended 31 December 1998:

Draft Statement of comprehensive income Extracts for the Year Ended 31 December 1998

	€'000
Profit before taxation	1,000
Taxation	(200)
Profit after taxation	800

The following additional information is also available:

1. During 1998 two of the company's assets were revalued as follows:

   Property A –   surplus of €200,000; and

   Land –   deficit of €110,000.

2. With respect to Property A, the depreciation charge for 1998 had been based on the revalued amount of the asset. The depreciation charge for 1998 was €30,000 more than would have been charged on a historical cost basis.
3. A flood occurred in the main warehouse of MORGAN ENTERPRISES just before the year end and inventory worth €70,000 was destroyed. No adjustment has been made for this in the draft statement of comprehensive income.
4. Just before the year end, 2 employees were made redundant at a total cost of €20,000. No adjustment has been made for this in the draft statement of comprehensive income.
5. Deferred development expenditure in the statement of financial position of MORGAN ENTERPRISES at 31 December 1998 amounted to €1,000,000.
6. An increase in trade investments before the year end, amounting to €150,000, had not been reflected in the financial statements.
7. A portion of the company car park was sold before the year end, yielding an after-tax profit of €900,000. No adjustment has been made for this in the draft profit and loss account.
8. The company is financed by equity capital as follows:

	€'000
Share capital - ordinary shares €1 each fully paid	2,000
Share premium	400

9. Retained profits at 1 January 1998 were €2,800,000.
10. The tax rate is 20%

Requirement
(a) Assuming that MORGAN ENTERPRISES is a private limited company, show what profits are available for distribution.
(b) Assuming that MORGAN ENTERPRISES is a public limited company, show what profits are available for distribution.
(c) Would your answers in (a) and (b) above have been any different if all of the company's non-current assets had been revalued during the year?

SECTION THREE

PREPARATION OF STATEMENT OF CASH FLOWS

Chapter 19:   Statement of Cash Flows – Single Company

CHAPTER 19

STATEMENT OF CASH FLOWS – SINGLE COMPANY

INTRODUCTION

As explained in Chapter 1, the International Accounting Standards Board issued a revised IAS 1 *Presentation of Financial Statements* on 6 September 2007, with the changes being effective for annual periods beginning on or after 1 January 2009 (early adoption is permitted). The revised IAS 1 changes the titles of financial statements as they will be used in International Accounting Standards (IASs) and International Financial Reporting Standards (IFRSs); although entities are *not* required to use the new titles in their financial statements. All existing IASs/IFRSs are being amended to reflect the new terminology. As a result a 'cash flow statement' is now referred to as a 'statement of cash flows'.

The fundamental purpose of being in business is to generate profit, and it is profit that increases the owners' wealth. However, profitability is arguably a long-term objective. In the short term, business viability is determined by its ability to generate cash. Ultimately profit, particularly profit determined under the broad variations possible under Generally Accepted Accounting Principles, is of little value if it cannot be translated into cash. Even profitable companies will collapse if they do not have access to sufficient cash resources when it becomes necessary to settle a bill. Very few businesses could survive a prolonged outflow of cash. Information about cash flows is therefore needed in order to help users form an opinion on a company's liquidity, viability, and financial adaptability. The statement of financial position provides information about the entity's financial position at a particular point in time including assets, liabilities and equity and their relationship with each other at the reporting period date. The statement of financial position is often used to obtain information on liquidity, but the information is incomplete for this purpose as the balance is drawn up at a particular point in time. Consequently, the statement of cash flows, together with the statement of financial position and statement of comprehensive income, can provide information about past cash flows and should therefore assist users in assessing future cash flows. The statement of cash flows is one of the primary financial statements and it provides users with information to enable them to assess the entity's liquidity, solvency and the quality of its earnings. The statement is intended to answer questions such as:

- Did the company's profits generate sufficient funds for its continued operations? For example, profits are calculated on an accruals basis (not cash). Therefore, revenue shown in the statement of comprehensive income may not yet have been received, and indeed (in the extreme) may never be received if the customer defaults or goes bankrupt.
- Is the company capable of generating funds, as opposed to profit from its trading activities?
- Why has the bank overdraft increased, despite the company having had a profitable year? For example, a company may deliberately build up its inventory at the end of the reporting period; however, while the inventory will have to be paid for there will be no impact on profit until the inventory is sold.
- How has the company financed its increased non-current assets? Did it finance them from long-term sources or from operating activities? For example, while the purchase of non-current assets has an immediate cash impact if purchased for cash, the impact on the statement of comprehensive income will be gradual in the form of depreciation charges.
- What was done with the loan that was taken out during the year?
- How did the company meet its dividend and interest payments? Was it from operating activities, from increased borrowing or from sales of non-current assets?

This chapter focuses on the preparation of a statement of cash flows for a single entity in accordance with IAS 7 *Statement of Cash Flows*. Issues relating specifically to the preparation of a consolidated statement of cash flows are dealt with in Section Five, Chapter 33. Having studied this chapter on IAS 7 *Statement of Cash Flows*, you should understand the following key points:

- The scope of IAS 7 *Statement of Cash Flows*;
- The advantages of cash flow reporting; and
- How to prepare a statement of cash flows for a single entity in accordance with the requirements of IAS 7.

IAS 7 *STATEMENT OF CASH FLOWS*

A statement of cash flows should be presented as part of an entity's financial statements. As all types of entity can provide useful information about cash flows, whatever the nature of their revenue-producing activities, all entities are required to prepare a statement of cash flows. The objective of IAS 7 *Statement of Cash Flows* is to provide information to users of financial statements about the cash flows of an entity and its ability to generate cash and cash equivalents, together with indicating the cash needs of the entity.

Important Definitions

1. **Cash** refers to cash in hand and deposits repayable on demand.
2. **Cash equivalents** are short-term highly liquid investments that are readily convertible to known amounts of cash and which are subject to an insignificant risk of changes in value. Cash equivalents are not held for investment or other long-term purposes, but rather to meet short-term cash commitments. Therefore the investment's maturity date should normally be three months from its acquisition date. Loans and other borrowings are 'investing' activities, bank overdrafts, since repayable on demand, are included under cash and cash equivalents.
3. **Cash flow** refers to inflows and outflows of cash and cash equivalents.
4. **Operating activities** are the principal revenue-producing activities of the entity, and other activities that are not investing or financing.
5. **Investing Activities** Investing activities relate to the acquisition and disposal of non-current assets and other investments not included in cash equivalents.
6. **Financing Activities** Financing activities are activities that result in changes in the size and composition of the equity capital and borrowings of the entity.

Format of Statement of Cash Flows

IAS 7 requires the cash flows to be classified into three separate sections: operating; investing; and financing. For example:

	€'000
Cash flows from operating activities	X
Cash flows from investing activities	X
Cash flow from financing activities	X
Net increase/(decrease) in cash and cash equivalents during period	X
Cash and cash equivalents at the beginning of period	X
Cash and cash equivalents at end of period	X

Each of these three sections is now dealt with in more detail.

Cash Flows from Operating Activities

It is recognised that, although an enterprise may have generated a profit during the year and increased its assets, it may not necessarily have readily accessible cash as the money could be tied up in inventory, receivables etc. Also, in arriving at profit a number of non-cash deductions and additions have been included, e.g. depreciation. These need to be taken into account when calculating the actual cash generated. Cash flows from operating activities are in general the cash effects of transactions and other events relating to operating or trading activities normally shown in the statement of comprehensive income in arriving at operating profit. This section of the statement of cash flows indicates whether, and to what extent, companies can generate cash from their operations.

Examples of cash flows from operating activities are:

- cash receipts from the sale of goods and the rendering of services;
- cash receipts from royalties, fees, commissions and other revenue;
- cash payments to suppliers for goods and services;
- cash payments to and on behalf of employees;
- cash receipts and cash payments of an insurance entity for premiums and claims, annuities and other policy benefits;
- cash payments or refunds of income taxes unless they can be specifically identified with financing and investing activities; and
- cash receipts and payments from contracts held for dealing or trading purposes.

IAS 7 permits two methods of calculating operating cash flows – the direct method and the indirect method. Both methods lead to the same figure.

1. **Direct Method**   The direct method shows operating cash receipts and payments, e.g., cash paid to suppliers and employees and cash received from customers. This is useful to users as it shows the actual sources and uses of cash. For example:

	€'000
Cash received from customers	X
– Cash payments to suppliers	(X)
– Cash paid to and on behalf of employees	(X)
– Other cash payments	(X)
+ Interest received	X
– Interest paid	(X)
– Tax paid	(X)
– Dividends paid	(X)
= Net cash inflow from operating activities	X

The use of the direct method is encouraged where the necessary information is not too costly to obtain, as it discloses information not available elsewhere in the financial statements. However, many enterprises will not generate this information as a matter of course so it may prove expensive to produce. IAS 7 does not require the direct method to be used and actually favours the indirect method. In practice, the direct method will rarely be used.

2. **Indirect Method**   The indirect method requires the profit to be reconciled to the cash flow being generated by operations. The indirect method starts with operating profit (as stated in the statement of comprehensive income) and adjusts

for non-cash charges and credits to arrive at the net cash flow from operating activities. For example:

	€'000
Operating Profit	X
Depreciation charges	X
– Profit on disposal of equipment	(X)
– Increase in inventories	(X)
– Increase in receivables	(X)
+ Increase in payables	X
= cash generated from operations	X
+ Interest received	X
– Interest paid	(X)
– Tax paid	(X)
– Dividends paid	(X)
= Net cash inflow from operating activities	X

The principal advantage claimed for this method is that it highlights the differences between operating profit and net cash flow from operating activities. As some investors and creditors assess future cash flows by estimating future income and then allowing for accruals adjustments, knowledge of past accruals adjustments may be useful for this purpose.

Cash flows from interest and dividends received/paid should be disclosed separately. Each should be classified consistently from period to period as operating, investing or financing; however, IAS 7 is not prescriptive about where they are disclosed. If dividends paid are included as part of cash flows from operating activities, users can assess the entity's ability to pay dividends out of cash flows; if included as part of cash flows from financing activities, then it indicates the cost of obtaining financial resources.

Tax cash flows should be separately disclosed and classified as operating activities, unless specifically identified with financing or investing activities.

Example

The following financial information relates to ABC Limited for the year ended 31 December 20X1.

Statement of Comprehensive Income for the Year Ended 31 December 20X1

	€'000
Revenue	222
Operating expenses	(156)

Profit from operations	66
Finance costs	(9)
Profit before tax	57
Income tax expense	(21)
Profit for year	36

The following operating expenses were incurred in the year:

	€'000
Wages	(36)
Auditor's remuneration	(6)
Depreciation	(42)
Cost of material used	(111)
Gain on sale of non-current assets	30
Rental income	9
	(156)

The following information is also available:

	31 December 20X1	31 December 20X0
	€'000	€'000
Inventories	21	12
Trade receivable	24	21
Trade payables	(15)	(9)

Requirement Calculate the net cash flow from operating activities using the indirect method.

Solution

	€'000	€'000
Operating Profit		66
Adjustment for non-cash items:		
Depreciation	42	
Gain on sale of non-current assets	(30)	12
Movements in working capital:		
Increase in receivables	(3)	
Increase in payables	6	

Increase in inventories	(9)	(6)
Net cash inflow from operations		72

Cash Flows from Investing Activities

Under this heading purchases and sales of long-term assets and the purchase and sales of investments not qualifying as cash equivalents are included. Interest and dividends received may be classified under this heading but they may also be included under operating activities or financing. The specimen provided in IAS 7 includes them as investing. Only one figure for cash should be provided for subsidiaries acquired or disposed, with disclosure by note of the assets and liabilities acquired/disposed. The separate disclosure of cash flows arising from investing activities is important because the cash flows represent the extent to which expenditures have been made for resources intended to generate future income and cash flows.

Examples of cash flows arising from investing activities are:

- cash payments to acquire property, plant and equipment, intangibles and other long-term assets;
- cash receipts from sales of property, plant and equipment, intangibles and other long-term assets;
- cash payments to acquire equity or debt instruments of other activities and interests in joint ventures;
- cash advances and loans made to other parties;
- cash receipts from sales of equity or debt instruments of other entities and interests in joint ventures;
- cash receipts from the repayment of advances and loans made to other parties;
- cash payments for future contracts, forward contracts, option contracts and swap contracts except when the contracts are held for dealing or trading purposes, or the payments are classified as financing activities; and
- cash receipts from futures contracts, forward contracts, option contracts and swap contracts except when the contracts are held for dealing or trading purposes or the receipts are classified as financial activities.

Example

	€'000
Cash paid to acquire property, plant and equipment	(X)
Cash receipts from the sales of property, plant and equipment	X
Cash paid/received for shares and debentures in other entities	(X)

Loans received/repaid	X
Dividends received	X
Interest received	X
Net cash unflows from investing activities	X

Cash Flows from Financing Activities

The separate disclosure of cash flows arising from financing activities is important because it is useful in predicting claims on future cash flows by providers of capital to the equity.
Examples of cash flows arising from financing activities:

- cash proceeds from issuing shares or other equity instruments;
- cash payments to owners to acquire or redeem the equity's shares;
- cash proceeds from issuing debentures, loans, notes, bonds, mortgages and other short or long-term borrowings;
- cash repayments of amounts borrowed; and
- cash payments by a lessee for the reduction of the outstanding liability relating to a finance lease.

Example

	€'000
Proceeds from share issue	X
Cash paid to acquire/redeem own shares	(X)
Cash proceeds from issuing debentures and loans	X
Capital repayments of finance leases	(X)
Dividends paid	(X)
Net cash unflows from financing activities	X

€'000

The statement of cash flows is completed as follows:

Sum of operating investing and financing sections represents the net increase/
decrease in cash equivalents   X

+ cash and cash equivalents at the start of the year   X

= cash and cash equivalents at the end of the year   X

Example of Notes to the Statement of Cash Flows

1. **Property, Plant and Equipment**   During the period, the group acquired property, plant and equipment with an aggregate cost of €1,250 of which €900 was acquired by means of finance leases. Cash payments of €350 were made to purchase property, plant and equipment.
2. **Cash and Cash Equivalents**   Cash and cash equivalents consist of cash on hand and balances with banks and investments in money market instruments. Cash and cash equivalents included in the statement of cash flows comprise the following statement of financial position amounts:

	€'000	€'000
Cash on hand and balances with banks	40	25
Short-term investments	370	135
Cash and cash equivalents as previously reported	410	160
Effect of exchange rate changes	–	(40)
Cash and cash equivalents as restated	410	120

Cash and cash equivalents at the end of the period include deposits with banks of €100,000 held by a subsidiary that are not freely remittable to the holding company because of currency exchange restrictions. The group has undrawn borrowing facilities of €2,000,000 of which €700,000 may be used only for future expansion.

3. **Segment Information**

	Segment A	Segment B	Total
Cash flows from:	€m	€m	€m
Operating activities	1,700	(140)	1,560
Investing activities	(640)	160	(480)
Financing activities	(570)	(220)	(790)
	490	(200)	290

Exceptional Items, Discontinued Activities and Non-Cash Transactions

1. **Exceptional Items in the Statement of Comprehensive Income**   Where cash flows relate to items that are classified as exceptional in the statement of comprehensive income, they should be shown under the appropriate standard headings, according to the nature of each item. The cash flows relating to exceptional items should be identified in the statement of cash flows or a note to it and the relationship between the cash flows and the originating exceptional item should be explained.
2. **Exceptional Cash Flows**   Where cash flows are exceptional because of their size and incidence but are not related to items that are treated as exceptional in the statement of comprehensive income, sufficient disclosure should be given to explain their cause and nature. For a cash flow to be exceptional on the grounds of its size alone, it must be exceptional in relation to cash flows of a similar nature.
3. **Discontinued Activities**   Cash flows relating to discontinued activities should be shown separately, either on the face of the statement of cash flows or by note.
4. **Major Non-cash Transactions**   Material transactions not resulting in movements of cash of the reporting entity should be disclosed in the notes to the statement of cash flows if disclosure is necessary for an understanding of the underlying transactions. Consideration for transactions may be in a form other than cash. The purpose of a statement of cash flows is to report cash flow; non-cash transactions should, therefore, not be reported in a statement of cash flows. However, to obtain a full picture of the alterations in financial position caused by the transactions for the period, separate disclosure of material non-cash transactions is also necessary. Examples of non-cash transactions are finance leases and the conversion of debt to equity.

Finance Leases

Finance leases are accounted for by the lessee capitalising the fair value of the related asset, or the present values of the minimum lease payments if lower. A liability and a corresponding asset are produced which do not reflect cash flows in the accounting period. The statement of cash flows records the cash flow, i.e. the rentals paid, with the reduction in liability shown under financing.

Foreign Currency Cash Flows

(a) The Individual Company Cash flows arising from transactions in a foreign currency should be recorded in the entity's functional currency at the exchange rate at the date of the cash flow.
(b) Foreign Subsidiaries The cash flows of a foreign subsidiary must be translated at the exchange rates between the functional currency and the foreign currency at the dates of the cash flows – a weighted average rate for the period can be used. For further information on foreign subsidiaries and the preparation of a consolidated statement of cash flows, see Section Five, Chapter 33.

ILLUSTRATIVE EXAMPLE

This illustration is based on the example in the Appendix to IAS 7. It uses the illustrative layout from IAS 7 and shows both the indirect and direct methods of calculating operating cash flows. As the purpose of this example is primarily to illustrate the preparation of a single company statement of cash flows, the draft financial statements provided do not strictly comply with IAS 1 (revised).

The draft financial statements of CCE Limited for the year ended 31 December 20X2 are as follows:

Statement of Comprehensive Income for the Year Ended 31 December 20X2

	€
Sales revenue	30,650
Cost of sales	(26,000)
Gross profit	4,650
Depreciation	(450)
Administrative and selling expenses	(950)
Interest expense	(400)
Investment income	500
Profit before tax	3,350
Income tax expense	(120)
Profit for the year	3,230

Statement of Financial Position as at 31 December 20X2

	20X2 €	20X2 €	20X1 €	20X1 €
ASSETS				
Property, plant and equipment at cost	3,730		1,910	
Accumulated depreciation	(1,450	2,280	(1,060)	850
Long-term investments		2,500		2,500
Inventory		1,000		1,950
Accounts receivable		1,900		1,200
Cash and cash equivalents (see note below)		410		160
Total assets		8,090		6,660

EQUITY AND LIABILITIES

Capital and Reserves

Share capital	1,500	1,250
Retained earnings	3,410	1,380
Total shareholders' equity	4,910	2,630

Liabilities

Trade payables	250	1,890
Interest payable	230	100
Income taxes payable	400	1,000
Long-term debt (including finance leases)	2,300	1,040
Total liabilities	3,180	4,030
Total equity and liabilities	8,090	6,660

Cash and cash equivalents at 31 December are made up as follows:

	31 December	
	20X2	20X1
	€	€
Cash	40	25
Short-term investments	370	135
	410	160

The following additional information is also available.

1. Interest expense was €400 of which €170 was paid during the period. €100 relating to interest expense of the prior period was also paid during the period. €200 of interest was received during the period.
2. Dividends paid were €1,200.
3. The liability for tax at the beginning and end of the period was €1,000 and €400 respectively.
4. During the period, a further €20 tax was provided for. Withholding tax on dividends rece-ived amounted to €100, thus leading to the total tax expense of €20 + €100 = €120.
5. During the period, the group acquired property, plant and equipment with an aggregate cost of €1,900 of which €900 was acquired by means of finance leases. Cash payments of €1,000 were made to purchase property, plant and equipment.

6. €90 of capital repayment was paid under the finance leases.
7. Plant with an original cost of €80 and accumulated depreciation of €60 was sold for €20.
8. Accounts receivable as at the end of 20X2 include €100 of interest receivable.
9. €250 was raised from the issue of share capital and a further €450 was raised from long-term borrowings.

Requirement

(a) Prepare a statement of cash flows for the year ended 31 December 20X2 using the indirect method in accordance with the illustrative format in IAS 7 *Statement of Cash Flows*; and
(b) Show the calculation of operating cash flow using the direct method.

Suggested Approach

Figures for the statement of cash flows are derived from the differences between the opening and closing balances sheet figures, using the information in the notes and in the statement of comprehensive income to make necessary calculations. One approach to developing the answer is to adopt a standard procedure. Here is a suggested procedure for the indirect method (the more usual exam requirement).

Step 1

Set up the statement in outline (main headings only). Leave plenty of space to insert detail. A whole page will be needed.

Step 2

Study the additional information and mark with a cross those items affecting statement of financial position amounts.

Step 3

Begin the statement of cash flows by using the statement of comprehensive income to work down to operating profit before working capital changes.

Step 4

Proceed line by line through the statements of financial position. If an item is not marked with a cross, the difference may be entered direct to the statement; if it is marked, a working is required. Use working ledger accounts to calculate missing figures. Insert the opening and closing balances from the statements of financial position into the working accounts, and then add information from the notes to complete the ledger account. Balancing figures on the working accounts are then transferred to the statement of cash flows.

(a) Statement of Cash Flows for the Year Ended 31 December 20X2

	Workings	€	€
Cash flows from operating activities			
Net profit before tax		3,350	
Adjustments for:			
Depreciation		450	
Investment Income		(500)	
Interest expense		400	
Operating profit from working capital changes		3,700	
Interest in trade receivables	1	(600)	
Decrease in inventories		950	
Decrease in trade payables		(1,640)	
Cash generated from operations		2,410	
Interest paid	3	(270)	
Income taxes paid	4	(720)	
Net cash from operating activities			1,420
Cash flows from investing activities			
Purchases of property, plant and equipment	5	(1,000)	
Proceeds of sale of equipment	7	20	
Interest received	2	200	
Dividends received	2	200	
Net cash used in investing activities			(580)
Cash flows from financing activities			
Proceeds from issue of shares		250	
Proceeds from long-term borrowings		450	
Payment of finance lease liabilities		(90)	
Dividends paid		(1,200)	
Net cash used in financing activities			(590)
Net increase in cash and cash equivalents			250
Cash and cash equivalents at beginning of period			160
Cash and cash equivalents at end of period			410

Analysis of Cash and Cash Equivalents at 31 December

	20X2	20X1
	€	€
Cash on hand and balances with banks	40	25
Short-term investments	370	135
Cash and cash equivalents	410	160

Workings:

(W1) Trade Receivables

	€		€
Opening balances	1,200	Closing balance	1,800
Movement (bal fig)	600	(€1,900 – €100*)	
	1,800		1,800

* €100 relates to interest and is not a trade receivable. Interest receivable included in W3

(W2) Interest and dividends receivable

	€		€
SCI	500	Interest receivable c/f	100
		Dividend received (bal fig)	200
		Interest received	200
	500		500

(W3) Interest paid

	€		€
Cash (bal fig)	270	Opening balance	100
Closing balance	230	SCI	400
	500		500

(W4) Income taxes

	€		€
Cash (bal fig)	720	Opening balance	1,000
Closing balance	400	SCI (€20 + €100)	120
	1,120		1,120

(W5) Property, plant and equipment - cost

	€		€
Opening balance	1,910	Transfer disposal	80
Leases	900	Closing balance	3,730
Cash – additions (bal fig)	1,000		
	3,810		3,810

(W6) Property, plant and equipment - depreciation

	€		€
Transfer disposal	60	Opening balance	1,060
Closing balances	1,450	SCI	450
	1,510		1,510

(W7) Property, plant and equipment – disposal

	€		€
Cost	80	Depreciation	60
		Cash	20
	80		80

(W8) Long-term debt (to reconcile balances)

	€		€
Payments under finance leases	90	Opening balance	1,040
Closing balances	2,300	Finance leases	900
		Long-term borrowing	450
	2,390		2,390

(W9) Retained earnings (to reconcile balances)

	€		€
Dividend paid	1,200	Opening balance	1,380
Closing balance	3,410	SCI	3,230
	4,610		4,610

(b) Operating cash flow – direct method

	Workings	€
Cash receipts from customers	1	30,050
Cash paid to suppliers and employees	2	(27,640)
Cash generated from operations (as in (a))		2,410
Interest paid		(270)
Income taxes paid		(720)
Net cash from operating activities (as in (a))		1,420

Workings:

(W1) Cash receipts from customers

	€
Opening trade receivables	1,200
Sales	30,650
	31,850
Less: closing trade receivables (€1,900 – €100)	1,800
	30,050

(W2) Cash paid to suppliers and employees

	€
Opening trade payables	1,890
Purchases (€26,000 – €1,950 + €1,000)	25,050
	26,940
Less: closing trade payables	250
	26,690
Administrative and selling expenses	950
	27,640

CONCLUSION

This chapter focuses on the preparation of a statement of cash flows for a single entity in accordance with IAS 7 *Statement of Cash Flows*. Issues relating specifically to the preparation of a consolidated statement of cash flows are dealt with in Section Five, Chapter 33.

Accounting profit is unlikely to be a reliable indicator of a company's cash position. A statement of cash flows can provide valuable information on cash inflows and outflows during the accounting period and can be used to assess a company's ability to generate cash from its operations. Analysts and other users of financial information often, formally and informally, develop models to assess and compare the present value of the future cash flow of entities. Historical cash flow information could be useful to check the accuracy of past assessments. It should be stressed, however, that a historical statement of cash flows does not provide complete information for assessing future cash flows. Statements of cash flows should normally be used in conjunction with statements of comprehensive income and statements of financial position when making an assessment of future cash flows.

QUESTIONS

Self-test Questions

1. What are the standard headings under which IAS 7 requires cash flows to be classified?
2. How does IAS 7 define cash and cash equivalents?
3. What does the direct method of reporting net cash flows from operating activities show?
4. What are the advantages of a statement of cash flows?

Review Questions

Question 1

BEN LIMITED
Statement of Comprehensive Income for the Year Ended 31 December 200X

	€'000
Revenue	2,553
Cost of sales	(1,814)
Gross profit	739
Distribution costs	(125)
Administrative expenses	(264)
Operating profit	350
Interest received	25
Interest paid	(75)
Profit on ordinary activities before taxation	300
Taxation	(140)
Profit for year	160

BEN LIMITED
Statement of Financial Position as at 31 December

	200X €'000	200W €'000
ASSETS		
Non-current assets		
Tangible assets	380	305
Intangible assets	250	200
Investments	–	25
Current assets		
Inventories	150	102
Receivables	390	315
Short-term investments	50	–
Cash in hand	2	1
Total assets	1,222	948
EQUITY AND LIABILITIES		
Equity		
Share capital (€1 ordinary shares)	200	150
Share premium account	160	150
Revaluation reserve	100	91
Retained earnings	160	100
	620	491
Non-current liabilities		
Long-term loan	170	50
Current liabilities		
Trade payables	127	119
Bank overdraft	85	98
Taxation	120	110
Dividends proposed	100	80
	432	407
Total equity and liabilities	1,222	948

Additional Information

(a) The proceeds of the sale of non-current asset investments amounted to €30,000.
(b) Fixtures and fittings, with an original cost of €85,000 and a net book value of €45,000 were sold for €32,000 during the year.
(c) The following information relates to tangible non-current assets.

	31 December 200X	31 December 200W
	€'000	€'000
Cost	720	595
Accumulated depreciation	340	290
Net book value	380	305

(d) 50,000 €1 ordinary shares were issued during the year at a premium of 20c per share.
(e) Wages charged in the statement of comprehensive income amounted to €90,000 of which €5,000 was unpaid at the year end.
(f) During the year ended 31 December 200X, dividends amounting to €100,000 were debited to equity. Dividends proposed, which are included in current liabilities, were approved by the shareholders prior to the relevant reporting period date.

Requirement   Prepare a statement of cash flows for the year ended 31 December 200X for Ben Limited using both direct and indirect methods in accordance with IAS 7 *Statement of Cash Flows*.

Question 2

The statement of comprehensive income of HANSOL plc for the year ended 31 December 2003, and the statement of financial position as at that date, are shown below.

HANSOL plc
Statement of Comprehensive Income for the Year Ended 31 December 2003

	€'000
Revenue – continuing operations	37,182
Cost of sales	(28,340)
Gross profit	8,842
Operating expenses	(4,453)
Operating profit – continuing operations	4,389
Gain on sale of property, plant and equipment in continuing operations	194

Interest receivable and similar income	308
Interest payable and similar charges	(224)
Profit on ordinary activities before taxation	4,667
Tax on profit on ordinary activities	(1,540)
Profit for the year	3,127

HANSOL plc

Statement of Financial Position as at 31 December 2003

	Note	2003 €'000	2002 €'000
ASSETS			
Non-current Assets			
Property, plant and equipment			
Intangible assets	2	10,877	9,970
	1	162	270
		11,039	10,240
Current Assets			
Inventory		2,080	886
Trade receivables		6,006	4,542
Cash in hand and at bank		3,070	1,840
		11,156	7,268
Total assets		22,195	17,508
EQUITY AND LIABILITIES			
Capital and Reserves			
Called up share capital	5	1,300	1,200
Share premium account	5	2,950	2,800
Other reserves		300	300
Retained earnings		5,848	4,921
		10,398	9,221
Non-current Liabilities	4	1,964	358
Provisions for liabilities and charges – deferred taxation		2,740	1,650

Current Liabilities	3	7,093	6,279

Total equity and liabilities		22,195	17,508

During the year ended 31 December 2003, dividends amounting to €2,200,000 were debited to equity.

Additional Information

1. Intangible assets represent patents held by the company. These are amortised over the shorter of the anticipated period of profitable exploitation and the period to the expiry of the right. The company registered no new patents during 2003.

2. Property, plant and equipment

	Land & property	Plant & equipment	Total
Cost or valuation:	€'000	€'000	€'000
At 1 January 2003	3,242	11,223	14,465
Additions	900	1,689	2,589
Disposals	–	(546)	(546)
	4,142	12,366	16,508
Accumulated depreciation:			
At 1 January 2003	1,291	3,204	4,495
Charge for year	410	1,116	1,526
On disposal	–	(390)	(390)
	1,701	3,930	5,631
Net book value:			
At 31 December 2003	2,441	8,436	10,877
At 31 December 2002	1,951	8,019	9,970

3. Current liabilities

Bank overdraft	52	–
Trade payables	4,108	3,520
Fixed asset payable	1,196	1,178
Finance lease creditor	70	101
Corporation tax	1,258	1,178
Dividends	382	296
Accruals and deferred income	27	6
	7,093	6,279

Accruals and deferred income comprise interest payable on:

– Finance leases	3	3
– Bank overdraft	24	3
	27	6

4. Non-current liabilities

Medium-term bank loans	1,726	–
Finance lease obligations	238	358
	1,964	358

5 Called up share capital and share premium account

	€1 Ordinary shares	Share premium
	€'000	€'000
At 1 January 2003	1,200	2,800
Shares issued on acquisition	100	200
Expenses connected with share issue	–	(50)
At 31 December 2003	1,300	2,950

Requirement   In accordance with IAS 7 *Statement of Cash Flows*, prepare each of the following for HANSOL plc in respect of the year ended 31 December 2003:

(a) A statement of cash flows;
(b) A reconciliation of operating profit to net cash flows from operating activities.

Challenging Questions

Question 1 (Based on ICAI, P3 Autumn 1998, Question 6)

The following information is provided for SAPIENT Limited in respect of the year ended 31 December 2003:

SAPIENT Limited
Statement of Comprehensive Income for the Year Ended 31 December 2003

	€'000	€'000
Revenue		4,020
Cost of sales		(2,060)
Gross profit		1,960
Distribution costs		(816)

Administrative expenses		(294)
Operating profit		850
Profit on sale of plant	100	
Loss on sale of equipment	(20)	80
Interest receivable and similar income		108
Interest payable and similar charges		(128)
Profit on ordinary activities before taxation		910
Tax on profit on ordinary activities		(70)
Profit for year		840

SAPIENT Limited
Statement of Financial Position as at 31 December 2003

	2003		2002	
	€'000	€'000	€'000	€'000
ASSETS				
Non-current Assets				
Plant at cost	2,860		2,060	
Accumulated depreciation	(860)	2,000	(660)	1,400
Equipment at cost	1,260		1,140	
Accumulated depreciation	(660)	600	(620)	520
		2,600		1,920
Current Assets				
Inventory	370		410	
Trade receivables	590		290	
Investments	1,000		–	
Bank and cash	610	2,570	300	1,000
		5,170		2,920
EQUITY AND LIABILITIES				
Capital and Reserves				
Called up share capital		2,300		2,000
Share premium account		100		–
Retained earnings		1,250		450
		3,650		2,450

Non-current Liabilities

12% debentures		1,200		–
Current Liabilities				
Bank overdraft	–		100	
Trade payables	205		305	
Taxation	85		55	
Dividends	30	320	10	470
		5,170		2,920

Additional Information:

1. Depreciation of non-current assets has been charged to distribution costs.
2. Included in administration expenses is €30,000 paid in connection with the share issue.
3. Plant with a net book value of €600,000, which had originally cost €1,000,000, was sold during the year.
4. Equipment with a net book value of €60,000, which had originally cost €200,000, was sold during the year.
5. All non-current asset additions during the year were paid for in cash.
6. Investments included within current assets relate to a nine-month term deposit that matures on 1 February 2004. If the deposit is withdrawn before the maturity date, all rights to interest in the month of withdrawal are forfeited.
7. Dividends of €40,000 were debited to equity during the year ended 31 December 2003.

Requirement   Using both the direct and indirect methods, prepare a statement of cash flows for SAPIENT Ltd. for the year ended 31 December 2003 in accordance with IAS 7 *Statement of Cash Flows*.

Question 2 (Based on ICAI, P3 Summer 2005, Question 5)

The statement of comprehensive income for the year ended 31 December 2005 of CLINIC Limited (CLINIC) and a statement of financial position as at that date, together with comparative figures, are as follows.

Statement of Comprehensive Income for the Year Ended 31 December

	2005	2004
	€'000	€'000
Revenue	11,250	9,900
Cost of sales	(7,890)	(6,750)
Gross profit	3,360	3,150
Other operating expenses	(2,670)	(2,610)

Operating profit	690	540
Interest payable and similar charges	(540)	(270)
Profit on ordinary activities before taxation	150	270
Income tax expense	(30)	(60)
Profit on ordinary activities after taxation	120	210

Statement of Financial Position as at 31 December

	2005	2004
	€'000	€'000
ASSETS		
Non-current Assets	1,440	1,320
Current Assets		
Inventory	1,890	1,530
Trade receivables	2,850	2,130
Bank and cash	30	30
	6,210	5,010
EQUITY AND LIABILITIES		
Share Capital and Reserves		
€1 ordinary shares	300	270
€1 10% preference shares	300	300
Share premium account	30	–
Retained earnings	210	180
	840	750
Non-current Liabilities		
Bank loans	2,190	1,800
10% debentures	1,140	900
	3,330	2,700
Current Liabilities		
Bank overdraft	30	–
Current instalments due on loans	540	540
10% debentures	300	–
Trade payables	1,080	870
Taxation	30	90
Equity dividends	60	60
	2,040	1,560
	6,210	5,010

Additional Information:

1. On 1 July 2005, CLINIC issued 60,000 €1 ordinary shares at €2 per share. Additionally, CLINIC purchased and cancelled 30,000 of its own €1 ordinary shares on 1 October 2005 at €2 per share.

2. During the year ended 31 December 2005, CLINIC sold non-current assets with a net book value of €90,000, which had originally cost €750,000, for cash. Included in trade payables at 31 December 2005 is an amount of €450,000 in respect of non-current assets purchased during the year ended 31 December 2005.

3. Depreciation of €600,000 was charged during the year ended 31 December 2005. This amount is included in 'other operating expenses', together with a profit on disposal on non-current assets of €60,000. Also included in other operating expenses is €30,000 paid in connection with the issue and purchase of ordinary shares during the year.

4. During the year ended 31 December 2005, the following dividends were debited to equity:

	2005	2004
	€'000	€'000
Preference dividends	30	30
Ordinary dividends	60	60

Requirement   Prepare a statement of cash flows for CLINIC for the year ended 31 December 2005 in accordance with IAS 7 *Statement of Cash Flows*.

Note   You are not required to prepare notes to the statement of cash flows.

SECTION FOUR

DISCLOSURES

CHAPTER 20

NON-CURRENT ASSETS HELD FOR SALE AND DISCONTINUED OPERATIONS

INTRODUCTION

Non-current assets, which typically include property, plant and equipment, are normally held for use in the day-to-day operations of the business rather than for sale. The 'cost' of using such assets is usually reflected in the financial statements through depreciation and, notwithstanding issues of impairment, the net realisable value (NRV) of these assets is generally of little interest to users of the financial statements. However, if non-current assets are held for sale rather than for use, then concepts of useful economic life and depreciation are no longer relevant and NRV becomes more important. As a result many of the accounting principles contained in IAS 16 *Property, Plant and Equipment* are largely inappropriate. Moreover, as non-current assets that are held for sale were often used in operations that have been discontinued, it is logical that one accounting standard should address these (often) related issues.

Having studied this chapter on non-current assets held for sale and discontinued operations, you should be able to:

- identify, measure and disclose non-current assets held for sale;
- explain the concept of a disposal group;
- define a discontinued operation;
- account for a discontinued operation in the statement of comprehensive income; and
- outline the disclosure requirements relating to non-current assets held for sale and discontinued operations.

IFRS 5 *NON-CURRENT ASSETS HELD FOR SALE AND DISCONTINUED OPERATIONS*

A disposal group could be a group of cash generating units (CGUs) or part of a CGU. It is really the disposal of a group of assets and liabilities as part of a single transaction.

The objective of IFRS 5 is to improve the information about assets and disposal groups that are about to be disposed of and discontinued operations. It does this by specifying the:

- requirements for the classification, measurement and presentation of non-current assets held for sale, in particular requiring that such assets should be presented separately on the face of the statement of financial position; and
- rules for the presentation of discontinued operations, in particular requiring that the results of discontinued operations should be presented separately in the statement of comprehensive income.

Scope

The measurement provisions of IFRS 5 apply to all non-current assets and disposal groups, except for:

- deferred tax assets (IAS 12 *Income Taxes*);
- assets arising from employee benefits (IAS 19 *Employee Benefits*);
- financial assets within the scope of IAS 39 *Financial Instruments: Recognition and Measurement;*
- non-current assets that are accounted for in accordance with the fair value model in IAS 40 *Investment Property;*
- non-current assets that are measured at fair value less estimated point-of-sale costs in accordance with IAS 41 *Agriculture;* and
- contractual rights under insurance contracts as defined in IFRS 4 Insurance Contracts.

Important Definitions

(a) **Cash Generating Unit** – the smallest identifiable group of assets that generate cash inflows that are largely independent of the cash inflows from other assets or groups of assets.
(b) **Costs to Sell** – the incremental costs directly attributable to the disposal of an asset or disposal group excluding finance costs and tax expense.
(c) **Discontinued Operation** – a component of an entity that either has been disposed of or is classified as 'held for sale' and: represents a separate major line of business or geographical area of operations; is part of a single co-ordinated plan to dispose of a separate major line of business or geographical area of operations; or is a subsidiary acquired exclusively with a view to resale.
(d) **Disposal Group** – a group of assets to be disposed of, by sale or otherwise, together as a group in a single transaction, and liabilities directly associated with those assets that will be transferred in the transaction.
(e) **Fair value** – the amount for which an asset could be exchanged or liability settled in an arms length transaction.

(f) **Firm purchase commitment** – an agreement with an unrelated party binding on both parties and legally enforceable that: (i) specifies all significant terms; and (ii) includes a disincentive for non-performance that is likely to make performance highly probable.

NON-CURRENT ASSETS HELD FOR SALE

Classification and Measurement

The key points are:

- An entity must classify a non-current asset (or disposal group) as held for sale if its carrying amount will be recovered principally through a sale transaction rather than through continuing use. This means that the asset or disposal group must be available for *immediate sale* in its present condition and the sale must be highly probable, i.e. management must be committed to the disposal. The period to complete the sale may extend beyond one year due to circumstances outside the entity's control – this does not preclude the asset or disposal group from being treated in accordance with the standard;
- An entity must measure a non-current asset (or disposal group) held for resale at the lower of the carrying amount and fair value, less costs to sell. When the sale is expected to occur after one year, costs to sell must be measured at their present value;
- An entity should not depreciate or amortise a non-current asset while it is classified as held for resale. However, expenses and interest that relate to liabilities in a disposal group should be recognised;
- If a newly acquired asset meets the criteria as 'held for sale' it should be measured initially at fair value less costs to sell; and
- An entity must recognise an impairment loss for any initial or subsequent write down of an asset (or disposal group) from carrying amount to fair value less costs to sell.

Changes to a Plan of Sale

If an entity has classified an asset (or group) as 'held for sale' in its statement of financial position, but the criteria no longer apply, it must reclassify it at the lower of:

- the carrying value at the date it was classified as 'held for sale' adjusted by relevant depreciation; *and*
- the recoverable amount at the date of the decision not to sell.

The entity should include, in income from continuing operations, any required adjustments to the carrying value of a non-current asset that ceases to be classified as held for sale.

Non-current Assets to be Abandoned

These are not included as 'held for sale', as their carrying amount will be recovered through use. However, if the disposal group to be abandoned is a component of an entity, the entity should present the results and cash flows of the disposal group as discontinued on the date it ceases to be used. A non-current asset that has been temporarily taken out of use as if abandoned should not be accounted for.

Example

An entity ceases to use a manufacturing plant because demand has declined. However, the plant is maintained in workable condition and it is expected to be brought back into use if demand picks up.

It is not, therefore, abandoned.

Example

In October 2008 an entity decides to abandon all of its cotton mills (major line of business). All work stops during 2009.

For 2008 the results and cash flows should be treated as continuing operations but in 2009 the entity discloses the information for discontinued operations including a restatement of any comparative figures.

Classification of a Non-current Asset or Disposal Group as held for Sale

An entity should classify a non-current asset (or disposal group) as held for sale in the reporting period in which all of the following criteria are met:

1. Management are committed and have the authority to approve the action to sell;
2. The asset or disposal group is available for immediate sale in its present condition subject to usual terms;
3. An active programme to locate a buyer is initiated;
4. The sale is highly probable and is expected to qualify for recognition as a completed sale within one year from the date of classification as 'held for sale';
5. The asset or disposal group is being actively marketed for sale at a reasonable price in relation to its fair value; and
6. Actions required to complete the plan indicate that it is unlikely that significant changes to the plan will be made or the plan withdrawn.

Example

An entity is committed to a plan to sell its HQ and has initiated action to find a buyer.

Situation 1

The entity intends to transfer the building to a buyer after it vacates the building. The time to vacate is normal. The criterion is met at the plan commitment date

Situation 2

The entity will continue to use the building until a new HQ is built. The building will not be transferred until construction is completed. The delay demonstrates that the building is not available for immediate sale and thus the criterion is not met even if a firm purchase commitment is obtained earlier.

Example

An entity is committed to a plan to sell a manufacturing facility and has initiated action to locate a buyer but there is a backlog of customer orders.

Situation 1

If the entity intends to sell the manufacturing facility with its operations, any uncompleted orders will transfer to the buyer. The criterion will be met at plan commitment date.

Situation 2

If the entity intends to sell the manufacturing facility but without its operations, and it does not intend to transfer it until it eliminates the backlog of orders, the delay means that the facility is not available for immediate sale and thus the criterion is not met until the operations cease even if a firm purchase commitment were obtained earlier.

Example

An entity acquires a property via foreclosure comprising land and buildings that it intends to sell.

- If the entity does not intend to sell until it completes renovations, the delay means the property is not available for immediate sale until the renovations are completed.
- If after renovations are completed and the property classified as held for sale, the entity becomes aware of environmental damage, the property cannot be sold until remediation takes place. The property is thus not available for immediate sale and the criterion would not be met. It would have to be reclassified.

Example

To qualify as 'held for sale', the sale of a non-current asset must be highly probable and be expected to qualify as a sale within one year. The criterion would not be met if, for example:

- an entity that is a commercial leasing company is holding for sale or lease equipment that has recently ceased to be leased and the ultimate form of a future transaction has not yet been determined; or
- an entity is committed to sell a property that is in use and the transfer will be accounted for as a sale and leaseback.

Example

An entity in the power generation industry is committed to plan to sell a disposal group that represents a significant portion of its regulated operations. The sale requires regulatory approval that could extend beyond one year. Actions to obtain approval cannot be initiated until a buyer is located and firm purchase commitment obtained. However the commitment is highly probable and thus may be classified as 'held for sale' even though it extends beyond one year.

Example

An entity is committed to sell a manufacturing facility but, after a firm purchase commitment is obtained, the buyer's inspection identifies environmental damage that must be made good and this will extend beyond one year. However, the entity has initiated remediation and rectification is highly probable thus it can be classified as 'held for resale'.

Example

An entity is committed to sell a non-current asset and classifies the asset as held for sale at that date.

Situation 1

If during the initial one-year period: (i) market conditions deteriorate; (ii) the asset is not sold; (iii) no reasonable offers received; and (iv) the asset continues to be actively marketed. Then at the end of the first year the asset would continue to be classified as 'held for sale'.

Situation 2

If during the following year: (i) market conditions deteriorate further; (ii) the asset is not sold; and (iii) the sale price has not been reduced. As a result, in the absence of a price reduction, the asset is not available for immediate sale and therefore the criterion is not met. The asset will need to be reclassified.

Events may extend the period to complete the sale beyond one year. Extension does not preclude an asset or disposal group from being classified as held for sale if the delay is caused by events beyond the entity's control and there is sufficient evidence that the entity remains committed to its plan to sell the asset. As a result an exception to the one-year requirement should therefore apply in the following situations:

(a) at the date an entity commits itself to a plan to sell, it reasonably expects that others will impose conditions on the transfer of the asset that will extend the period beyond one year and:

   (i) actions cannot be initiated until after a firm purchase commitment is obtained, and
   (ii) a firm purchase commitment is highly probable within one year;

(b) an entity obtains a firm purchase commitment and a buyer unexpectedly imposes conditions to extend the period beyond one year and:

   (i) timely actions necessary to respond have been taken, and
   (ii) a favourable resolution of the delaying factors is expected;

(c) during the initial one year period, circumstances arise which were previously considered unlikely and;

   (i) during the initial one year the entity took action to respond to the change in circumstances,
   (ii) the non-current asset is being actively marketed given the change in circumstances, and
   (iii) the criteria in 1 to 6 above are met.

When an entity acquires a non-current asset exclusively with a view to subsequent disposal, it should classify the non-current asset as held for sale at the acquisition date only if the one year is met and it is highly probable that any other criteria that are not met will be met within a short period following the acquisition.

If the criteria are met after the statement of financial position date, but before they are authorised, an entity should not classify a non-current asset as held for sale. However, the entity should disclose the information in the notes.

Impairment Losses and Subsequent Increases in Fair Values less Costs to Sell of Assets that were Previously Revalued

Any asset carried at a revalued amount under another IFRS should be revalued under that IFRS immediately before it is classified as held for sale under this IFRS. Any impairment loss that arises on reclassification of the asset should be recognised in the statement of comprehensive income.

Subsequent Impairment Losses

Any subsequent increases in costs to sell should be recorded in income. Any decreases in fair value should be treated as revaluation decreases in accordance with the IFRS under which the assets were revalued before their classification as held for sale.

Subsequent Gains

Any subsequent decreases in costs to sell should be recognised in income. For individual assets that were revalued prior to classification under another IFRS, any subsequent increase should be treated as a revaluation increase. For disposal groups, any subsequent increases in fair value should be recognised to the extent that the carrying value of the non-current assets in the group after the increase has been allocated does not exceed their fair value less costs to sell. The increase should be treated as a revaluation increase in accordance with the IFRS under which the assets were revalued.

Gains or Losses Relating to Continuing Operations

Any gain/loss on remeasurement of a non-current asset that does not meet the definition of a component should be included in the profit/loss from continuing operations.

Presentation and Disclosure

Information should be presented to enable users to evaluate the financial effects of discontinued operations and disposals of non-current assets.

Presentation of a Non-current Asset or Disposal Group Classified as Held for Sale

These should be separately disclosed from other assets. The liabilities of a disposal group classified as 'held for sale' should be presented separately from other liabilities. These assets and liabilities should not be offset but separately disclosed on the face of the statement of financial position.

Example

At the end of 20X5 an entity decides to dispose of part of its assets and directly associated liabilities. This disposal, which meets the criteria as held for sale, takes the form of two disposal groups as follows:

	NBV after classification as held for sale	
	Disposal group 1	Disposal group 2
	€	€
Property, plant and equipment	4,900	1,700
Asset for sale financial asset	1,400*	-
Liabilities	(2,400)	(900)
NBV of disposal group	3,900	800

* An amount of €400 relating to these assets has been recognised directly in equity.

The presentation in the entity's statement of financial position of the disposal groups classified as held for sale can be shown as follows:

	20X5	20X4
	€	€
Assets		
Non-current assets		
AAA	X	X
BBB	X	X
CCC	X	X
	X	X
Current assets		
DDD	X	X
EEE	X	X
	X	X

Non-current assets classified as held for sale (€4,900 + €1,400 + €1,700)	8,000	–
	X	X
Total assets	X	X
Equity and Liabilities		
Equity attributable to equity holders of the parent FFF	X	X
GGG	X	X
Amounts recognised directly in equity relating to non-current assets held for sale	400	=
	X	X
Non-controlling interests	X	X
Total equity	X	X
Non-current liabilities		
HHH	X	X
III	X	X
JJJ	X	X
	X	X
Current liabilities		
KKK	X	X
LLL	X	X
MMM	X	X
Liabilities directly associated with non-current assets classified as held for sale (€2,400 + €900)	3,300	=
	X	X
Total liabilities	X	X
Total equity and liabilities	X	X

Example

Measuring and Presenting Subsidiaries Acquired with a View to Sale and Classified as Held for Sale:

Entity A acquires H (holding company + two subsidiaries). Subsidiary 2 (S2) was acquired exclusively with a view to sale and meets the criteria as held for sale. S2 is a discontinued operation. The estimated fair value less costs to sell of S2 is €135m. S2 is accounted for as follows:

- Initially, A measures the identifiable liabilities of S2 at fair value – say €40m;
- Initially, A measures the acquired assets of S2 at NRV of €135m + €40m = €175m;
- At the reporting date, A remeasures the disposal group at lower of cost and NRV of €130m. Liabilities are remeasured at €35m. Total assets are €130m + €35m = €165m;
- At the reporting date, A presents assets and liabilities separately from other assets and liabilities as per last example; and
- In the statement of comprehensive income, A presents the total of the post-tax profit or loss of S2 and the post-tax gain or loss recognised on the subsequent remeasurement of S2 which equals the remeasurement of the disposal group from €135m to €130m.

Further analysis is not required.

Additional Disclosures

The following should be disclosed in the notes:

- a description of the non-current asset (or disposal group);
- a description of the facts and circumstances leading to the expected disposal and manner and timing of that disposal;
- the gain or loss on impairment or subsequent increase in fair value for assets previously not revalued; and
- if applicable, the segment in which the non-current asset is presented under IAS 14 *Segment Reporting*/IFRS 8 *Operating Segments* (IFRS 8 replaces IAS 14 *Segment Reporting*, effective for annual periods beginning 1 January 2009).

Any changes to a plan should be described and the facts and circumstances leading to the decision to change the plan provided.

DISCONTINUED OPERATIONS

A discontinued operation may be a subsidiary, or a major line of business or geographical area. It will have been a cash-generating unit (or group of cash-generating units) as defined in IAS 36 *Impairment of Assets*. A component of an entity comprises operations and cash flows that can clearly be distinguished from the rest of the entity. A discontinued operation is a component of an entity that has either been disposed of or is classified as 'held for sale' and:

- represents a separate major line of business or geographical area of operations; or
- is part of a single co-ordinated plan to dispose of a separate major line of business or geographical area of operations; or
- is a subsidiary acquired exclusively with a view to resale.

Presentation and Disclosure

An entity should disclose for all periods presented:

(a) As a single amount on the face of the statement of comprehensive income comprising
   (i) Post-tax profit/loss of discontinued operations, and
   (ii) Post-tax gains/losses on measurement to fair value or on disposal of discontinued operations;
(b) Analysis of (a) into
   (i) revenue, expenses and pre-tax profits/losses of discontinued operations,
   (ii) related tax expense,
   (iii) gains/losses on measurement to fair value or on disposal of discontinued operations, and
   (iv) related tax expense.
(c) The net cash flows attributable to the operating, investing and financing activities of discontinued operations.

The disclosures required by (a) must be on the face of the statement of comprehensive income but the others may be presented in the notes or on the face of the statement of comprehensive income. Prior periods for disclosures (a) to (c) are also required. Adjustments to previous discontinued operations of prior periods should be classified separately, e.g. resolution of uncertainties.

An example of how discontinued operations might be presented using the 'By Function' format (see Chapter 2) is:

	€m
Continuing Operations	
Revenue	x
Cost of sales	(x)
Gross profit	x
Other operating income	x
Distribution costs	(x)
Administrative expenses	(x)
Other expenses	(x)
Finance costs	(x)
Share of profit of associates	x
Profit before tax	x
Income tax expense	(x)
Profit for period for continuing operations	x
Discontinued Operations	
Net profit for period for discontinued operations*	x
Net profit for period	x
Attributable to:	
Equity holders of the parent	x
Non-controlling interest	x

Example

* The required analysis would be given in the notes. Alternatively, profit from discontinued operations could be analysed in a separate column on the face of the statement of comprehensive income.

Presentation in the Statement of Cash Flows

An enterprise must disclose, either in the notes or on the face of the statement of cash flows, the net cash flows attributable to the operating, investing and financing activities of discontinued operations

CONCLUSION

This chapter explains how an entity should account for, and disclose, non-current assets held for sale and discontinued operations in accordance with IFRS 5 *Non-current Assets Held for Sale and Discontinued Operations*. If a non-current asset is 'held for sale', the economic benefit of that asset is obtained through the asset's sale rather than through its continuous use in the business (future economic benefit). Such assets cease to be depreciated as they are no longer being consumed by the business. Moreover, an asset held for sale is valued at the lower of either the asset's carrying cost or the asset's fair value less the cost of selling this asset. For a non-current asset to be classified as 'held for sale', *all* of the following conditions must be satisfied:

- the asset must be available for immediate sale in its present condition and location;
- the asset's sale is expected to be completed within 12 months of classification as 'held for sale';
- there must be no expectation that the plan for selling the asset will be withdrawn or changed significantly; and
- the successful sale of the asset must be highly probable, signified by both:
  - the management's commitment to the asset-selling plan; and
  - existence of active marketing to support the sale of the asset.

A discontinued operation is a component of an enterprise that has either been disposed of, or is classified as 'held for sale', and:

- represents a separate major line of business or geographical area of operations; and
- is part of a single, co-ordinated plan to dispose of this separate major line of business or geographical area of operations; or
- is a subsidiary acquired exclusively with a view to resale.

QUESTIONS

Self-test Questions

1. What is a discontinued operation?
2. What information must be disclosed in the financial statements for discontinued operations?

Review Questions

(See APPENDIX ONE for Suggested Solutions to Review Questions)

Question 1

APF Limited is a divisionalised Irish company which trades from a number of retail outlets throughout Ireland. The company, which commenced trading approximately five years ago, prepares its financial statements to 31 December each year. During the last quarter of 2007, and the first half of 2008, APF Limited experienced severe trading difficulties and liquidity problems for the first time. Consequently, following a review of the business by the directors, it was decided to run down the non-core activities and focus upon the 'premium' end of the company's market.

Issue 1   During 2008, APF Limited sold, for €1,000,000 cash, a division of the company. The sale proceeds represent the profit on the sale of the business and the directors wish to classify the proceeds as an extraordinary item in the company's statement of comprehensive income for the year ended 31 December 2008. The directors believe that, while withdrawal from this market will have a material effect on the nature and focus of the company's operations, the company will benefit in the long-term because this market was too specialised and the division's customer base was entirely different from that of the company's core business. Up to the point of sale, this division had contributed the following:

	€'000
Revenue	2,500
Cost of sales	1,500
Administrative expenses	500

Issue 2   In December 2008, the directors of APF Limited decided to close all of the company's retail outlets that sell less expensive, less exclusive items. The directors estimate that it will take nine months to wind down these operations and that the net loss from these retail operations during this period will be €800,000. No provision has yet been made in the draft 2007 financial statements for this loss. The directors believe that any assets relating to these retail outlets are stated at their recoverable amount at 31 December 2008.

Requirement   Explain how each of the above issues should be reflected in APF Limited's financial statements for the year ended 31 December 2008.

Challenging Questions

Question 1 (Based on ICAI, P3 Autumn 2007, Question 4)

IT Global Limited (GLOBAL), a divisional company that prepares its financial statements to 31 December each year, is involved in the assembly of bespoke PC systems for home use (Assembly division), together with the retailing of computer hardware, software and related accessories (Retail division). Due to the deteriorating performance of the Assembly division as a result of strong price competition and changes in customer buying patterns, the directors of GLOBAL decided to significantly change the nature of the company's business focus.

Consequently, the directors approved the closure of the Assembly division, despite it typically generating approximately 25% of the company's revenue. Although details of the closure plan were announced publicly on 1 November 2006, including the cessation of advertising and promotion and the notification of suppliers, the Assembly division did not formally close until 31 March 2007.

GLOBAL
Draft Trial Balance as at 31 December 2006

	DR €'000	CR €'000
Revenue – Assembly division		2,500
Revenue – Retail division		7,500
Purchases – Assembly division	1,500	
Purchases – Retail division	4,500	
Administrative expenses – Assembly division	300	
Administrative expenses – Retail division	1,200	
Selling and distribution costs – Assembly division	150	
Selling and distribution costs – Retail division	850	
Finance costs – Retail division	200	
Income tax expense – Assembly division	50	
Income tax expense – Retail division	150	
Property – cost	20,000	
Property – accumulated depreciation at 31 December 2006		4,000
Plant and equipment – cost	11,000	
Plant and equipment – accumulated depreciation at 31 December 2006		3,000
Inventory – Assembly division at 1 January 2006	500	
Inventory – Retail division at 1 January 2006	2,000	
Trade receivables/Trade payables	2,500	2,400
Other receivables/Other payables	500	400
Bank and cash	800	
€1 ordinary shares		1,000
Retained earnings at 1 January 2006		25,400
	46,200	46,200

Additional Information

1. Property, plant and equipment shown in the trial balance above have been depreciated in accordance with company policy and relevant accounting standards in respect of the year ended 31 December 2006, with the depreciation charge being included in the appropriate expense category.

2. Inventory at 31 December 2006 consists of:

	€'000
Assembly division	200
Retail division	1,900
	2,100

Included in the inventory of the Retail division at 31 December 2006 are items that originally cost €240,500. However, the items, which were not insured, were accidentally damaged while being moved in GLOBAL's warehouse and it will cost €90,000 to repair them. The normal selling price of the items is €375,000. GLOBAL has arranged to sell the items as refurbished goods through an agent once the repair work has been completed at a discount of 25% on the normal selling price. The agent will receive a commission of 12% of the reduced selling price.

3. The directors of GLOBAL would like to make a provision of €2,000,000 at 31 December 2006 for the costs of closing the Assembly division. This amount is net of €1,500,000 for the estimated profit on the disposal of property belonging to the division. During November and December 2006, GLOBAL pursued an active policy to locate a buyer for the property which has a carrying value at 31 December 2006 of €2,500,000 and a fair value of €4,000,000. The contract for the sale of the property was signed on 17 March 2007 and completed on 11 April 2007 for €4,250,000.

4. The plant and equipment shown in the trial balance includes items relating to the Assembly division which are being carried at a value of €1,000,000 at 31 December 2006. The directors anticipate that the plant and equipment will generate cash flows of €700,000 in the three months to 31 March 2007 and that its net selling price at 31 December 2006 was €800,000. The plant and equipment was sold on 31 March 2007 for €600,000.

5. It is anticipated that during the period 1 January 2007 to 31 March 2007 the Assembly division will incur operating losses of €250,000 before it closes. Furthermore, it is estimated that the company will incur retraining costs of €150,000 during this period.

Requirement   Prepare the statement of comprehensive income of GLOBAL for the year ended 31 December 2006 and the statement of financial position as at that date.

(Notes to the financial statements are not required, and the tax effects of any adjustments can be ignored.)

CHAPTER 21

ACCOUNTING POLICIES, CHANGES IN ACCOUNTING ESTIMATES AND ERRORS

INTRODUCTION

IAS 1 *Presentation of Financial Statements* (see Section One, Chapter 2) deals with many matters connected with the presentation of financial statements. After IAS 1, the accounting standard that has most direct relevance to the presentation of financial statements is IAS 8 *Accounting Policies, Changes in Accounting Estimates and Errors*. After having studied this chapter you should be familiar with the:

- criteria for selecting and changing accounting policies; and
- accounting treatment and disclosure requirements for changes in accounting policies, changes in accounting estimates and corrections of errors.

IAS 8 *ACCOUNTING POLICIES, CHANGES IN ACCOUNTING ESTIMATES AND ERRORS*

The objective of IAS 8 is to prescribe the criteria for selecting and changing accounting policies, together with the accounting treatment and disclosure of changes in accounting policies, changes in accounting estimates and correction of errors.

Accounting Policies

These are the specific principles, bases, conventions, rules and practices applied by an entity in preparing and presenting financial statements.

The key principles when selecting and applying accounting policies are:

- accounting policies should comply with International Accounting Standards (IASs)/ International Financial Reporting Standards (IFRSs);
- where there is no specific IAS/IFRS, management should develop policies to ensure that the financial statements provide information that is
  - relevant,
  - reliable,
  - reflects the substance of transactions,
  - neutral, i.e. free from bias,
  - are prudent, and
  - complete in all material respects; and
- accounting policies should be selected and applied consistently for similar transactions.

Accounting policies are normally kept the same from period to period to ensure comparability of financial statements over time. However, there are three important situations:

1. A change in accounting policy which results from the initial application of an IAS/ IFRS (or Interpretation) should be accounted for using the specific transitional provisions of that standard if any;
2. When a change in accounting policy results from the initial application of an IAS/IFRS (or Interpretation) which does not contain specific transitional provisions, the effect of the change in policy must be applied retrospectively (i.e. prior period adjustment); and
3. IAS 8 requires retrospective application of voluntary changes in accounting policies unless it is impracticable to determine the cumulative effect of the change. In such cases prospective application is allowed.

Retrospective Changes in Accounting Policies

The reporting entity must adjust the opening balance of each affected component of equity for the earliest prior period presented and any other relevant comparative amounts as if the new accounting policy had always been applied. This means that there will be a prior period adjustment to the balance of retained earnings brought forward in the statement of changes in equity. The total prior period adjustment is the cumulative effect on opening reserves as if the new policy had always been applied.

Comparative information should be restated unless it is impracticable to do so. If the adjustment to opening retained earnings cannot be reasonably determined, the change should be adjusted prospectively, i.e. included in the current period's statement of comprehensive income.

When a change in accounting policy has a material effect on the current period or any prior period presented, or may have a material effect in subsequent periods the following disclosures should be made:

- The reasons for the change;
- The amount of the adjustment recognised in the current period; and
- The amount of the adjustment included in each period prior to those included in the financial statements.

Accounting Estimates

As a result of the uncertainties inherent in business activities, many items in financial statements cannot be measured with precision but can only be estimated. Estimation involves judgements based on the latest available, reliable information. For example, estimates may be required of:

- bad debts;
- warranty obligations;
- inventory obsolescence; and
- useful lives of depreciable assets.

Changes in Accounting Estimates

An estimate may need revision if changes occur in the circumstances on which the estimate was based or as a result of new information or more experience. By its nature, the revision of an estimate does *not* relate to prior periods and is not the correction of an error. A change in the measurement basis applied is a change in accounting policy and is not a change in accounting estimate.

The effect of a change in an accounting estimate should be recognised prospectively by including it in profit or loss in:

- the period of the change, if the change affects that period only (e.g. bad debts estimate); or
- the period of the change and future periods, if the change affects both (e.g. revising the useful life of a non-current asset).

To the extent that a change in an accounting estimate gives rise to changes in assets and liabilities, or relates to an item of equity, it should be recognised by adjusting the carrying amount of the related asset, liability or equity item in the period of the change.
If the effect of the change is material, its nature and amount must be disclosed.

Prior Period Errors

These are omissions from, and misstatements in, the entity's financial statements for one or more prior periods arising from a failure to use, or misuse of, reliable information that:

(a) was available when financial statements for those periods were authorised for issue; and
(b) could reasonably be expected to have been obtained and taken into account in the preparation and presentation of those financial statements.

Such errors include the effects of mathematical mistakes, mistakes in applying accounting policies, oversights or misinterpretations of facts and fraud.

While current period errors can be corrected before the financial statements are authorised for issue, sometimes material errors are not discovered until a later period and these should be corrected retrospectively in the first set of financial statements authorised for issue after the discovery. The total prior period adjustment is the cumulative error to the start of the period when the error is discovered net of any attributable tax.

An entity should correct material prior period errors retrospectively in the first set of financial statements authorised for issue after their discovery by:

- restating the opening balance of assets, liabilities and equity as if the error had never occurred, and presenting the necessary adjustment, to the opening balance of accumulated profits in the statement of changes in equity; and
- restating the comparative figures presented, as if the error had never occurred.

In applying these rules, the enterprise should disclose in the notes:

- the nature of the prior period error;
- the amount of the correction to each financial statement line item presented for the prior periods; and
- the amount of the correction at the beginning of the earliest prior period presented.

Note   Only when it is impracticable to determine the cumulative effect of an error on prior periods can an entity correct an error prospectively.

Example

Angel plc has a retained profit of €32,781 for the year ended 30 June Year 4 and its balance on its retained earnings stood at €709,311 on 1 July Year 3.

It has been discovered, whilst producing the year 4 accounts, that the closing inventory figure as at 30 June Year 3 was overstated by €48,099, thus overstating the profit for the year ended 30 June Year 3 by €48,099 (the retained profit figure for the year ended 30 June Year 4 has been determined by using the correct inventory figure as at 1 July Year 3).

The retained profit for the year ended 30 June Year 3 was originally stated at €90,342, using the incorrect closing inventory figure.

In the notes to the accounts under movements on reserves this adjustment would be shown as follows:

Angel plc Movement on Reserves

Balance at 30 June 20X3	€
As previously reported	709,311
Prior period adjustment (note x)	(48,099)
Restated	661,212

Retained profit for year	<u>32,781</u>
Balance at 30 June 20X4	<u>693,993</u>

Note: The prior period adjustment represents an overstatement of the closing inventory figure as at 30 June Year 3.

Example

Wick Limited was established on 1 January 20X0. In the first three years' accounts deferred development expenditure was carried forward as an asset in the statement of financial position. During 20X3 the directors decided that, for the current and future years, all development expenditure should be written off as it is incurred. This decision has not resulted from any change in the expected outcome of development projects on hand, but rather from a desire to favour the prudence concept. The following information is available:

(a) Movements on the Deferred Development Account

Year	Deferred development expenditure incurred during year	Transfer from deferred development expenditure account to Statement of Comprehensive Income
	€'000	€'000
20X0	525	–
20X1	780	215
20X2	995	360

(b) The 20X2 accounts showed the following:

	€'000
Retained reserves b/f	2,955
Retained profit for the year	<u>1,825</u>
Retained profits carried forward	<u>4,780</u>

(c) The retained profit for 20X3 after charging the actual development expenditure for the year was €2,030,000.

Requirement   Show how the change in accounting policy should be reflected in the statement of reserves in the company's 20X3 accounts. (Ignore taxation.)

Solution

If a new accounting policy had been adopted since the company's incorporation, additional charges to the statement of comprehensive income would have been:

	€'000
20X0	525
20X1 (€780 – €215)	565
	1,090
20X2 (€995 – €360)	635
	1,725

Statement of Reserves

	20X3	20X2
	€	€
Retained profits at beginning of year		
As previously reported	4,780	2,955
PYA	(1,725)	(1,090)
Restated	3,055	1,865
Retained profit for year	2,030	(€1,825 – €635) 1,190
Retained profit at y/e	5,085	3,055

Disclosure Requirements

1. Changes in Accounting Policies
   (a) reason for change;
   (b) amount of the adjustment on the current period and for each period presented; and
   (c) the fact that comparative figures have been restated or that it was not practicable to do so.

2. Correction of Errors
   (a) the nature of the prior period error;
   (b) the amount of the correction for each period presented;
   (c) the amount of the correction at the start of the earlier prior period presented; and
   (d) if retrospective correction is not practicable, a description of how and when the error was corrected.

3. Changes in Accounting Estimates
   (a) the nature of the change;
   (b) the effect on the current periods financial statements; and
   (c) the effect in future periods if this is practicable.

CONCLUSION

When an IAS/IFRS specifically applies to a transaction, event or condition, the accounting policy applied to that item is determined by applying the IAS/IFRS and considering any relevant Implementation Guidance for the IAS/IFRS. Accounting policies need not be applied when the effect of applying them is immaterial, as defined in IAS 1 *Presentation of Financial Statements*. In the absence of an IAS/IFRS that specifically applies to a transaction, event or condition, management should use its judgement in selecting and applying an accounting policy that results in relevant and reliable financial information. IAS 8 specifies the following hierarchy of guidance which management uses when selecting accounting policies in such circumstances:

- requirements of IASs/IFRSs and Interpretations dealing with similar matters;
- the definitions, recognition criteria and measurement concepts for assets, liabilities, income and expenses in the *Framework for the Preparation and Presentation of Financial Statements*; and
- the most recent pronouncements of other standard-setting bodies that use a similar conceptual framework, other accounting literature and accepted industry practices, to the extent that these do not conflict with IASs/IFRSs and the *Framework*.

An entity should apply its accounting policies consistently for similar transactions, other events and conditions, unless an IAS/IFRS specifically requires or permits categorisation of items for which different policies may be appropriate. An entity should only change an accounting policy if the change is required by an IAS/IFRS, or results in the financial statements providing more relevant and reliable information about the entity's financial position, financial performance or cash flows. A change in accounting policy, resulting from the initial application of an IAS/IFRS, is accounted for in accordance with any specific transitional provisions of that IAS/IFRS. Otherwise a change in accounting policy is applied retrospectively to all periods presented in the financial statements as if the new accounting policy had always been applied.

The effect of a change in an accounting estimate is recognised prospectively in profit or loss in the period of the change, and also in profit or loss in future periods if the change affects both periods. Any corresponding changes in assets and liabilities, or to an item of equity, are recognised by adjusting the carrying amount of the asset, liability or equity item in the period of the change.

IAS 8 eliminates the distinction between fundamental errors and other material errors. All material errors should be corrected by restating the financial statements as if the error had never occurred. IAS 8 specifies the accounting treatment when it is impracticable to account for a change in accounting policy or a correction of a prior period error using retrospective restatement in accordance with the Standard. IAS 8 also specifies disclosures about accounting policies, changes in accounting estimates and errors.

QUESTIONS

Self-test Questions

1. On what basis should accounting policies be selected?
2. In what circumstances may an entity change one of its accounting policies?
3. How are changes in accounting estimates accounted for?
4. How are prior period errors accounted for?
5. What are the disclosures if an accounting policy is changed?

Review Questions

(See APPENDIX ONE for Suggested Solutions to Review Questions.)

Question 1

Keano Limited adopted an accounting policy of capitalising development expenditure and amortising it to the Statement of Comprehensive Income over 4 years. During 2004 the Directors decided that for 2004 and future years all development expenditure should be written off as incurred. This decision has not resulted from any change in the expected outcome of projects on hand, but rather from a desire to give a fairer presentation of results and financial position.

Movements on Development Expenditure Account:

Year	Expenditure Incurred €'000	Amortised to Statement of Comprehensive Income €'000
2001	400	100
2002	600	250
2003	300	325
2004	500	500

The 2003 financial statements showed:

	€'000
Retained earnings 1 January 2003	2,860
Retained earnings for the year	1,580
Retained earnings 31 December 2003	4,440

The retained earnings for the year ended 31 December 2004 were €1,820. This was arrived at after charging development expenditure of €500.

Requirement   Show how the change in accounting policy would be reflected in the financial statements of Keano Limited.

Question 2

The following are the draft summarised statements of comprehensive income of Top Limited for the year ended 31 May 2005:

	2005	2004
	€	€
Profit before tax	820,000	640,000
Income tax expenses	(328,000)	(256,000)
Profit after tax	492,000	384,000
Retained profit brought forward	1,174,000	890,000
Retained profit carried forward	1,666,000	1,274,000

During the audit of the financial statements for the year ended 31 May 2005, it was discovered that advertising expenditure was omitted from financial statements as follows:

	€
31 May 2005	110,000
31 May 2004	80,000
31 May 2003	60,000

The correction of these errors is not included in the above draft statements of comprehensive income. The company's profits are taxable at 40%.

Requirement   Re-draft the statement of comprehensive income of Top Limited for the year ended 31 May 2005.

Challenging Questions

Question 1

(Based on ICAI, P3 Autumn 2005, Question 4)
Following the retirement of her father, the new Chief Executive of GOLD is proposing to change how certain items have been accounted for in GOLD's draft financial statements for the year ended 31 December 2005.

Proposal 1   Inventory, which is currently considered in aggregate on a FIFO basis, will be measured on a weighted average basis so that all items of inventory are measured on a similar basis.

Proposal 2   Plant and machinery, which is currently depreciated using the reducing balance method at 20% per annum, will be depreciated straight-line over five years and the depreciation will be charged to net operating expenses rather than cost of sales as is currently the case.

Proposal 3   Interest incurred in connection with the construction of plant and machinery, which was previously written off to the statement of comprehensive income, will be added to the cost of the plant and machinery.

Proposal 4   Following a discussion with an art dealer in December 2005, the new Chief Executive of GOLD discovered a painting that had hung in her father's office for many years could fetch at least €1,000,000 at auction. It is intended to sell the painting at auction as soon as possible and recognise the €1,000,000 gain in the financial statements for the year ended 31 December 2005.

Proposal 5   GOLD received a letter in January 2006 from BLING Limited (BLING), a company that had used GOLD's precious metals in the manufacture of jewellery during 2005. However, the innovative design of the jewellery has not proved popular and sales have been poor. BLING has threatened to sue GOLD for loss of earnings of €1,000,000 on the grounds that the precious metals are 'useless'. The Chief Executive of GOLD proposes to net the gain on the sale of the painting against the threatened claim for loss of earnings.

Requirement   Prepare a memorandum to the new Chief Executive of GOLD explaining the accounting implications of each of the proposals.

Chapter 22

RELATED PARTY DISCLOSURES

INTRODUCTION

In the absence of information to the contrary, it is assumed that a reporting entity has independent discretionary power over its transactions and resources and pursues its activities independently of the interests of its owners and management. The organisation's transactions are presumed to have been undertaken at arm's length. However, these assumptions may not be justified when related party relationships exist.

After having studied this chapter, you should be able to:

- explain the term 'related party';
- identify an entity's related party relationships; and
- describe the disclosures required when a related party relationship exists.

WHAT IS A RELATED PARTY?

A party is related to an entity if it:

- directly or indirectly controls, is controlled by, or is under common control with, the entity;
- has significant influence over the entity;
- has joint control over the entity;
- is a close member of the family of any individual who controls, or has significant influence or joint control over, the entity;
- is an associate of the entity;
- is a joint venture in which the entity is a venturer;
- is a member of the key management personnel of the entity or its parent;

- is a close member of the family of any of the aforementioned key management personnel;
- is an entity that is controlled, jointly controlled or significantly influenced by, or for which significant voting power in such entity resides with, any of the key management personnel or their close family members; and
- is a post-employment benefit plan for the benefit of employees of the entity, or of any of its related parties.

IAS 24 emphasises that the following are *not necessarily* related parties:

- two organisations simply because they have a common director or common key management personnel;
- two venturers simply because they share joint control over a joint venture;
- providers of finance, trade unions and government departments simply by virtue of their normal dealings with an entity (even though they may affect the freedom of action of the entity); and
- a customer, supplier, distributor with whom an entity transacts a significant volume of business.

WHY ARE RELATED PARTY DISCLOSURES NECESSARY?

Reasons include:

- knowledge of related party transactions may affect a user's assessment of the reporting entity's operations, or risks and opportunities facing the entity;
- a related party relationship could have an effect on the reporting entity's results; and
- transaction between related parties may not be made at arm's length.

However, it should be noted that while such relationships are a normal feature of business IAS 24 requires certain information to be disclosed for the benefit of users of financial statements.

POTENTIAL RELATED PARTY INDICATORS

While IAS 24 defines what is meant by the term related party and also provides examples of related party transactions, the identification of related parties is fraught with difficulty in practice. Naturally, auditors should be alert to indicators of potential related party issues that may require special attention when performing the audit. Through the use of examples, this section considers some related party relationships and issues that, if present, suggest the possible existence of material related party relationships or transactions. Difficult economic times increase the possibility that the economic substance of certain transactions may be other than their legal form, or that transactions may lack economic substance.

Example   *Agreements under which one party pays expenses on behalf of another party*

A related party is to pay certain expenses on behalf of a company and then recharge the expenses back to that company. Under this type of arrangement, the recharge and expense recognition by the company may never occur, resulting in understated expenses on the company's financial statements, particularly when the company is struggling financially.

Example   *Circular arrangements between related parties*

Sales arrangements in which the seller of goods or services has concurrent obligations to the buyer to purchase goods or services or provide other benefits should be examined closely. In addition, collectability and liquidity should be closely examined in cases in which a party's ability to repay a loan is dependent on continued cash funding or sales from a related party.

Example   *Engaging in business deals (such as leases) at more or less than market value*

A company may enter into a lease agreement with another party owned in part by a member of an officer's family at less than market rates. This relationship and the related transactions should be appropriately disclosed in the company's financial statements.

Example   *Identification of an unidentified related party*

When an undisclosed related party has been identified, it may be necessary to assess whether management's failure to disclose was merely an oversight or a deliberate attempt to hide the relationship. If the latter, the auditor may have to reassess the overall audit scope and the ability to rely on management's representations in other areas. If the auditor believes management can no longer be trusted, the best course of action, after seeking legal advice, might be to withdraw from the engagement.

Example *Inadequate disclosures*

A common observation regarding related parties is that companies fail to satisfactorily describe the nature of related party relationships and transactions and disclose the terms and monetary amounts of related party transactions and amounts due to or from related parties as required by IAS 24.

Example *Payments for services at inflated prices*

An officer, director or management representative of a company may be also employed by another organisation (e.g. consulting) utilised by the company. This could lead to the organisation charging inflated fees for services rendered.

Example *Revenue recognition*

Revenue recognition is not appropriate when a substantive exchange is not present. Sales transactions should stem from express or implied contracts and represent exchanges between independent parties at arm's length prices and terms. Arm's length transactions may be difficult to achieve between related parties as well as in situations in which a seller can exercise substantial control over a buyer or vice-versa. Fictitious sales and sales to related parties lacking economic substance may be more prevalent where management representatives are anxious to meet sales quotas and earnings performance goals.

Example *Sale of land with arranged financing*

If a principal owner of a company sold land at fair market value and obtained financing for the buyer who was a marginal credit risk, the transaction would require related party disclosure by the company if the financing were obtained from a lender who agreed to the transaction primarily to preserve a significant business relationship with the company.

Example   *Sale of securities*

The sale of marketable securities, by a principal owner of a company, at a significant discount from quoted market prices to a large customer of the company, would be a related party transaction. As the transaction has no apparent business purpose, the facts may require disclosure of the transaction to reflect a fair presentation of financial position and results of operations of the company. However, it should be noted that, if the owner had sold the securities to the same party at fair market value, there would be no presumption of a related party transaction.

Example   *Sales without substance*

Funds transferred to the company from a related party for goods or services that were never rendered.

Example   *Services or goods purchased from a party at little or no cost*

An arrangement like this should be investigated for related party relationships and, if they exist, disclosed accordingly.

Example   *Unusual material transactions, particularly close to quarter or year-end*

A company may recognise revenue on large, unusual transactions with another party conducted close to the end of the reporting period. Consideration should be given to whether or not the two parties might be related in some way. These transactions may not always be individually significant, but rather may involve several small sales transactions that in total are material. Repetitive period end transactions with the same party should also be investigated for potential related party relationships.

> **Example**   *Utilisation of related party to mitigate market risks*
>
> A company may create a 'shell' company to help mitigate market risks on various equity transactions; but circumstances may change over time, requiring the company to consolidate the shell company. Earnings may be affected if the company failed to consolidate. The existence of complex legal structures may be an indication of related party relationships.

DISCLOSURE REQUIREMENTS

1. If there have been transactions between the reporting entity and related parties the following disclosing must be mode:
   (a) the nature of the relationship;
   (b) the amount of the transactions (but items of a similar nature may be disclosed in aggregate);
   (c) outstanding balances including details of any securities or guarantees;
   (d) provisions for doubtful debts on outstanding balances; and
   (e) any bad debts written off during a period on amounts due from related parties.
2. Key management compensation (all benefits) must be disclosed in total and for each of the following categories:
   (a) Short-term employee benefits, e.g. wages and salaries;
   (b) Post-employment benefits, e.g. pensions;
   (c) Other long-term benefits, e.g. long-service leave;
   (d) Termination benefits; and
   (e) Share-based payments.
3. In the separate financial statements of an entity that is part of a consolidated group, it is necessary to disclose inter-group transactions and comply with other requirements of IAS 24.
4. Relationships between parent and subsidiaries:
   (a) these must be disclosed irrespective of whether there have been transactions between those related parties; and
   (b) an entity must disclose the name of its parent or its ultimate controlling party.

Examples of Transactions which require Disclosure if with a Related Party

- Purchases/sales of goods;
- Purchases/sales of non-current tangible assets;
- Rendering/receiving services;
- Leases; and
- Provisions of guarantees.

CONCLUSION

This chapter describes the disclosures required by IAS 24 *Related Party Disclosures* to draw attention to the possibility that the financial position and profit or loss of an entity may have been affected by the existence of related parties and by transactions and outstanding balances with such parties. IAS 24 should be applied when:

- identifying related party relationships;
- identifying related party transactions;
- identifying outstanding balances between an entity and its related parties;
- identifying the circumstances when disclosures are necessary; and
- determining the disclosures when required.

QUESTIONS

Self-test Questions

1. In the context of IAS 24, what are the main parties to which a company may be related?
2. What are the disclosures required by IAS 24 with respect to related parties?

Review Questions

(See APPENDIX ONE for Suggested Solutions to Review Questions.)

1. Groups of companies are considered to be related parties:

   (a) Sometimes
   (b) Never.
   (c) Always.

2. Intragroup transactions and balances appear in:

   (a) Consolidated financial statements.
   (b) Financial statements of individual statements.
   (c) Neither.

3. A parent company can control or influence its subsidiary's:

   (a) Financial policies.
   (b) Operating policies.
   (c) Both.

4. If no transactions occur between the related parties, can the profits and financial position of either party be affected by the other?

   (a) Yes.
   (b) No.

5. What is the likely response of users of financial statements to the knowledge of related parties, their transactions and balances?

   (a) Ignore them.
   (b) Adjust their assessments of the risks and opportunities facing the undertaking.
   (c) Refuse to deal with the undertaking on principle.

6. Which of the following are related parties?

   (a) Major shareholders.
   (b) Group companies.
   (c) Key managers.
   (d) Pension funds.
   (e) All suppliers.
   (f) All government departments.
   (g) Relatives of any member of staff.

7. A major shareholder can avoid the consequences of related party transactions by transacting other business through his wife, or her husband, when the undertaking in which he, or she, has invested is involved.

   (a) True.
   (b) False.
   (c) Sometimes.

8. If services are provided without charge between group companies, does this qualify as a related party transaction?

   (a) Yes.
   (b) No.

9. Close family members of a related party: does a brother of the related party qualify as a related party in his own right?

   (a) Never.
   (b) Always.
   (c) Only if he is expected to influence, or be influenced by, the first related party in dealings with the undertaking.

10. Close family members are included as related parties to:

   (a) Avoid related parties disguising their activities.
   (b) Help related parties disguise their activities.

11. Classify each of the following transactions as either:

   (a) Short-term employment benefits.
   (b) Post-employment benefits.
   (c) Long-term employment benefits.
   (d) Equity compensation benefits.

Transactions:

  (i)   Share option schemes
 (ii)   Pensions
(iii)   Paid sick leave
(iv)   Sabbatical leave
 (v)   Subsidised goods or services provided to employees

12. Compensation relating to a director that is paid to the director's firm, rather than to the director directly:

  (a) Can be ignored.
  (b) Should be reported without mentioning the director's firm.
  (c) Should be reported with a note detailing to whom it is paid.

13. Significant influence in an undertaking is:

  (a) Control of an undertaking.
  (b) Power to participate in the financial and operating policy decisions.
  (c) Holding 10% of the shares, without board representation.

14. In considering any related party relationship, attention should be directed primarily to the:

  (a) Legal form of the relationship.
  (b) Substance of the relationship.
  (c) Neither of these.

15. Two venturers who share a joint venture are:

  (a) Always related parties.
  (b) Never related parties.
  (c) Not necessarily related parties.

16. Related party relationships need not be disclosed, if no transactions have taken place.

  (a) True.
  (b) False.

Challenging Questions

Question 1

A bank is financing a construction company with a loan that provides 90% of the construction company's capital requirements. The construction company is owned by a friend of the Chief Executive Officer of the bank. The loan is secured on the assets of the construction company.

Requirement   Is the construction company a related party?

Question 2

Company T trades with Company K. They are not in the same group of companies, but both of their parent companies have the same person as majority shareholder.

Requirement   Are Company T and Company K related parties?

Question 3

Company M bought a franchise to run a Mexican food restaurant in Dublin.

Requirement   Is Company M a related party to the company that sold it the franchise?

CHAPTER 23

EARNINGS PER SHARE

INTRODUCTION

Earnings are the profits of a company, and typically refer to profit after interest and tax. Ultimately, a business's earnings are the main determinant of its share price because earnings, and the circumstances relating to them, can indicate whether the business will be profitable and successful in the long run. Investors and analysts look to earnings to determine the attractiveness of a particular share. Companies with poor earnings prospects will typically have lower share prices than those with good prospects since a company's ability to generate profit in the future plays a very important role in determining a share's price. A business's quarterly and annual earnings are typically compared to analyst estimates and guidance provided by the business itself. In most situations, when earnings do not meet either of those estimates, a business's share price will tend to drop. On the other hand, when actual earnings beat estimates by a significant amount, the share price will likely surge.

After having studied this chapter, you should understand the:

- definition of earnings quality
- concept of pro forma earnings
- notion of earnings management
- principles for the determination and presentation of basic and diluted earnings per share (EPS) in an entity's financial statements in accordance with IAS 33 *Earnings per Share*.

EARNINGS: QUALITY MEANS EVERYTHING

There is no debating that shares with high-quality earnings are more likely than others to beat the market. High-quality earnings can be characterised as repeatable, controllable and bankable. So how do you know quality when you see it?

Quantity versus Quality

Earnings quantity (not quality) tends to get the lion's share of attention during quarterly reporting seasons. Investors focus on actual EPS delivered, resulting either in share prices going up when companies beat earnings estimates, or falling when numbers come in below projection. At first glance at least, when it comes to earnings, size matters most to investors. Savvy investors, however, take time to look at the quality of those earnings. The quality rather than quantity of corporate earnings is a much better gauge of future earnings performance. Firms with high-quality earnings typically generate above-average Price-Earnings multiples. They also tend to outperform the market for a longer time. More reliable than a other earnings, high-quality earnings give investors a good reason to pay more for them.

Defining Quality

When analysing quarterly reports, investors should ask themselves three simple questions: Are the company's earnings repeatable? Are they controllable? And, finally, are the earnings bankable?

Repeatable Earnings

Consider a company that posts earnings well ahead of stock market expectations, especially against the background of a slowing economy. This would be expected to result in a rise in share price. However, if for example the increased earnings come by way of job cuts and/or the sale of investments, it is likely that the share price will drop as the market realises that earnings quality is questionable: the sale of assets is never repeatable. Once sold, assets cannot be sold again to produce more earnings. Sales growth and cost cutting are the best routes to high-quality earnings. Both are repeatable. Sales growth in one quarter is normally (albeit not all the time) followed by sales growth in the next quarter. Similarly, costs, once cut, typically stay that way. Repeatable and fairly predictable earnings that come from sales and cost reductions are what investors prefer.

Controllable Earnings

There are many factors affecting earnings that companies cannot control. Consider the effects of exchange rates. For example, if a US company must convert its European profits back into the US dollar, a dollar that is falling against the euro will boost the company's earnings. But, management has nothing to do with those extra earnings or with repeating them in the future. On the other hand, if the dollar moves upwards, earnings growth could come in lower.

There are other uncontrollable factors that can raise earnings. Inflation, for instance, can give companies a brief profits boost when products in inventory are sold at prices increased by inflation. The price of inputs is another uncontrollable factor: falling jet fuel prices, for example, can improve airline industry profits. Even changes in the weather can boost earnings growth. Think of the extra profits from electrical utilities when temperatures are unusually hot or cold.

In reality, the highest-quality earnings go straight to the bank. Indeed, cash sales – which the company does control – are the source of the highest-quality earnings; investors should seek firms with earnings figures that closely resemble cash that is left after expenses are subtracted from revenues.

Bankable Earnings

Most companies, however, must wait before they can deposit revenues in the bank. Cash payments often arrive later than receivables, so most companies, at times, enter sales as revenues even though no money has exchanged hands. The fact that customers can cancel or refuse to pay creates large uncertainties, which lower earnings quality. At the same time, generally accepted accounting principles give room for choices about what counts as reliable revenues and earnings. Smart investors should see surges in accounts receivable as a warning sign, a good reason to take the time to examine earnings quality in detail.

Conclusion

High earnings are not as important as high-quality earnings: those that are repeatable, controllable and bankable. Earnings that experience a surge because of a one-time, uncontrollable event are not earnings that are inherent to the activities of the business. These earnings are the result of luck, which is never a reason to invest. Those businesses that generate revenue but not cash are not engaging in profitable activities. Quality earnings are taken to the bank.

PRO-FORMA EARNINGS

Pro-forma earnings describe a financial statement which has hypothetical amounts, or estimates, built into the data to give a 'picture' of a company's profits if certain non-recurring items were excluded. Pro-forma earnings are not computed using standard Generally Accepted Accounting Principles (GAAP), and usually leave out one-time expenses which are not part of normal company operations, such as restructuring costs following a merger. Essentially, a pro-forma financial statement can exclude anything a company believes obscures the accuracy of its financial outlook, and can be a useful piece of information to help assess a company's future prospects. While investors should stress GAAP net income, a look at pro-forma earnings can also be an informative exercise.

For example, net income doesn't tell the whole story when a company has one-time charges that are irrelevant to future profitability. Some companies therefore strip out certain costs that get in the way. This kind of earnings information can be very useful to investors who want an accurate view of a company's normal earnings outlook but, by omitting items that reduce reported earnings, this process can make a company appear profitable even when it is losing money.

Pro-forma earnings are designed to give investors a clearer view of a company's operations, and by their nature exclude unique expenses and charges. The problem, however, is that there isn't nearly as much regulation of pro-forma earnings as there is of financial statements falling under GAAP rules, so sometimes companies abuse the rules to make earnings appear better than they really are. Because traders and brokers focus so closely on whether or not the company beats or meets analyst expectations, the headlines that follow their earnings announcements can mean everything. And, if a company missed non-pro-forma expectations but stated that it beat the pro-forma expectations, its share price will not suffer as badly, and it might even go up – at least in the short term.

Problems with Pro-Forma Earnings

Companies all too often release positive earnings reports that exclude things like share-based compensation and acquisition-related expenses. Such companies, however, are expecting people to forget that these expenses are real and need to be included. Sometimes companies even take unsold inventory off their statements of financial position when reporting pro-forma earnings. But does producing that inventory cost money? Of course it does, so why should the company simply be able to write it off? It is bad management to produce goods that can't be sold, and a company's poor decisions shouldn't be erased from the financial statements.

This isn't to say companies are always dishonest with pro-forma earnings – pro forma doesn't mean the numbers are automatically being manipulated. To evaluate the legitimacy of pro-forma earnings, it is important to consider what the excluded costs are and decide whether or not these costs are real. Intangibles like depreciation and goodwill are okay to write down occasionally but, if the company is doing it every quarter, the reasons for doing so might be less than honourable.

Benefits of Pro-Forma Analysis

Pro-forma figures are supposed to give investors a clearer view of company operations. For some companies, pro-forma earnings provide a much more accurate view of their financial performance and outlook because of the nature of their businesses. Companies in certain industries tend to utilise pro-forma reporting more than others, as the impetus to report pro-forma numbers is usually a result of industry characteristics. For example, some cable and telephone companies almost never make a net operating profit because they are constantly writing down big depreciation costs. In cases where pro-forma earnings do not include non-cash charges, investors can see what the actual cash profit is.

When a company undergoes substantial restructuring or completes a merger, significant one-time charges can occur as a result. These types of expenses do not compose part of the ongoing cost structure of the business, and therefore can unfairly weigh on short-term profit numbers.

Pro-forma financial statements are also prepared and used by corporate managers and investment banks to assess the operating prospects for their own businesses in the future and to assist in the valuation of potential takeover targets. They are useful tools to help identify a company's core value drivers and analyse changing trends within company operations.

Conclusion

Pro-forma earnings are informative when official earnings are blurred by large amounts of asset depreciation and goodwill. But it is important to question why a company is treating its earnings as such. Moreover, it is important to remember that pro-forma figures have not undergone the same level of scrutiny as GAAP earnings and are not subject to the same level of regulation.

EARNINGS MANAGEMENT

Earnings management is a strategy used by the management of a company to deliberately manipulate the company's earnings so that the figures match a pre-determined target. This practice is carried out for the purpose of income smoothing. Thus, rather than having years of exceptionally good or bad earnings, companies will try to keep the figures relatively stable by adding and removing cash from reserve accounts (known colloquially as 'cookie jar' accounts) whereby a company uses generous reserves from good years against losses that might be incurred in bad years. This gives the sense of 'income smoothing', because earnings are understated in good years and overstated in bad years.

Abusive earnings management is deemed by the Securities and Exchange Commission (SEC) to be 'a material and intentional misrepresentation of results'. When income smoothing becomes excessive, the SEC may issue fines. Unfortunately, there's not much individual investors can do. Accounting laws for large corporations are extremely complex, which makes it very difficult for regular investors to pick up on accounting scandals before they happen. Although the different methods used by managers to smooth earnings can be very complex and confusing, the important thing to remember is that the driving force behind managing earnings is to meet a pre-specified target (often an analyst's consensus on earnings). However, as Warren Buffett stated, 'managers that always promise to "make the numbers" will at some point be tempted to make up the numbers'.

According to Healy and Wahlen (1999), earnings management occurs when managers use judgement in financial reporting and in structuring transactions to alter financial reports to either mislead some stakeholders about the underlying economic performance of a company or to influence contractual outcomes that depend on reported accounting numbers. Earnings management usually involves the artificial increase (or decrease) of revenues, profits, or EPS figures through aggressive accounting tactics. Aggressive earnings management is a form of fraud and differs from reporting error.

Management wishing to show a certain level of earnings or following a certain pattern seek loopholes in financial reporting standards that allow them to adjust the numbers as far as is practicable to achieve their desired aim or to satisfy projections by financial analysts. These adjustments amount to fraudulent financial reporting when they fall outside the bounds of acceptable accounting practice. Drivers for such behaviour include market expectations, personal realisation of a bonus, and maintenance of position within a market sector. In most cases conformance to acceptable accounting practices is a matter of personal integrity. Aggressive earnings management becomes more probable when a company is affected by a downturn in business.

Earnings management is seen as a pressing issue in current accounting practice. Part of the difficulty lies in the accepted recognition that there is no such thing as a single 'right' earnings figure and that it is possible for legitimate business practices to develop into unacceptable financial reporting. It is relatively easy for an auditor to detect error but earnings management can involve sophisticated fraud that is covert. The requirement for management to assert that the accounts have been prepared properly offers no protection where those managers have already entered into conscious deceit and fraud. Auditors need to distinguish fraud from error by identifying the presence of intention.

The main forms of earnings management are as follows:

- unsuitable revenue recognition;
- inappropriate accruals and estimates of liabilities;
- excessive provisions and generous reserve accounting; and
- intentional minor breaches of financial reporting requirements that aggregate to a material breach.

IAS 33 *EARNINGS PER SHARE*

The remainder of this chapter addresses the principles for the determination and presentation of EPS in an entity's financial statements in accordance with IAS 33. EPS is widely used by investors as a measure of a company's performance and are of particular importance in:

(a) comparing the results of a company over a period of time; and
(b) comparing the performance of one company's equity shares against the performance of another company's equity, and also against the returns obtainable from loan stock and other forms of investment.

The purpose of any earnings yardstick is to achieve as far as possible clarity of meaning, comparability between one company and another, one year and another, and attribution of profits to the equity shares. IAS 33 goes some way to ensuring that all these aims are achieved. IAS 33 prescribes principles for the determination and presentation of EPS, so as to improve performance comparisons between different reporting organisations in the same reporting period and between different reporting periods for the same entity.

IAS 33 applies to organisations whose ordinary shares or potential ordinary shares are publicly traded and by organisations that are in the process of issuing ordinary shares or potential ordinary shares in public markets. EPS need only be presented on the basis of consolidated data. If an entity is not publicly traded but wishes voluntarily to disclose EPS, then it should be prepared on the same basis as IAS 33. The focus is primarily on ensuring consistency in the calculation of the denominator.

Important Definitions

(a) **An Ordinary Share** – an equity instrument that is subordinate to all other classes of equity instruments;
(b) **A Potential Ordinary Share** – a financial instrument or other contract that may entitle its holder to ordinary shares;
(c) **Dilution** – a reduction in EPS or an increase in loss per share resulting from the assumption that convertible instruments are converted, that options or warrants are exercised, or that ordinary shares are issued upon the satisfaction of specified conditions;

(d) **Antidilution** – an increase in EPS or a reduction in loss per share resulting from the assumption that convertible instruments are converted, that options or warrants are exercised, or that ordinary shares are issued upon the satisfaction of specified conditions;

(e) **Contingently issuable ordinary shares** – ordinary shares issuable for little or no cash or other consideration upon the satisfaction of specified conditions in a contingent share agreement;

(f) **Put options on ordinary shares** – contracts that give the holder the right to sell ordinary shares at a specified price for a given period; and

(g) **Options and warrants** – financial instruments that give the holder the right to purchase ordinary shares.

BASIC EARNINGS PER SHARE

Definition

An entity must calculate basic EPS for profit or loss attributable to ordinary equity holders and if presented profit or loss from continuing operations attributable to their equity holders.

EPS is profit in cents attributable to each equity share. The basic EPS calculation is:

$$\frac{\text{Profit/Loss attributable to Ordinary Shareholders (Earnings)}}{\text{Weighted average number of ordinary shares outstanding during the period}}$$

An ordinary share is an equity instrument that is subordinate to all other classes of equity instrument.

Example

A company has profits (or earnings) for the year of €100,000 and has 200,000 ordinary shares.

$$\text{EPS} = \frac{€100,000}{200,000} \times 100 = 50 \text{ cent per share}$$

The problem is defining what is meant by 'earnings' and what is meant by 'number of ordinary shares':

- Earnings are the net profits after tax, interest, minority interest (in the case of a group) and dividends on other classes of shares (i.e. preference dividends); and
- Issued ordinary shares are all ordinary shares in circulation during the year. The weighted average approach is taken to calculate this amount.

Dealing with Preference Dividends

The following should be deducted in arriving at the figure for earnings:

(a) any dividend on non-cumulative preference shares declared for the period; and
(b) only dividend on cumulative preference shares whether declared or not.

Example

A company has the following issued share capital throughout the year:

- 200,000 ordinary shares of €1; and
- 50,000 10% preference shares of €1.

Extracts from the company's financial statements for the year ending 31 December Year 8 of the company's profit showed:

	€	€
Net profit before taxation		60,000
Taxation		20,000
Net profit after taxation		40,000
Preference dividend	5,000	
Ordinary dividend	9,000	(14,000)
Retained profit for the year		26,000

Requirement   Calculate EPS for Year 8.

(*Note* – dividends paid are an appropriation and therefore should be taken through reserves. Proposed dividends are not accrued until approved by shareholders at the AGM.)

Solution

$$EPS = \frac{\text{Net Profit x 100}}{\text{Number of Ordinary Shares}}$$

$$EPS = \frac{€35,000 \times 100}{200,000} = 17.5 \text{ cent}$$

Example

BEANO plc
Statement of comprehensive income for the year ended 31 December 2004

	€	€
Revenue		6,400,000
Cost of sales		(4,480,000)
Gross profit		1,920,000
Other income		60,000
Distribution costs		(168,000)
Administrative expenses		(280,000)
Other expenses		(112,000)
Finance costs		(197,000)
Profit before tax		1,223,000
Tax		(366,900)
Profit after tax		856,100
Dividends:		
Preference	100,000	
Ordinary	200,000	(300,000)
		556,100

Additional Information

1. At 1 January 2004 and 31 December 2004 the company had in issue:
   - 2,000,000 ordinary shares of 50 cent each; and
   - 1,000,000 10% cumulative preference shares of €1 each.

2. During the year ended 31 December 2004, BEANO Plc paid the following dividends:

	€
Preference	100,000
Ordinary	200,000
	300,000

Requirement   Calculate BEANO Plc's EPS for the year ended 31 December 2004.

Solution

Calculation of Earnings:

	€
Profit before tax	1,223,000
Income Tax expense	(366,900)
Preference dividend	(100,000)
Profit attributable to ordinary shareholders	756,100

Calculation of Number of Ordinary Shares:

The general principle is that the number of ordinary shares is the weighted average number outstanding during the reporting period. If there are no ordinary shares issued during a reporting period, the number of shares for the basic EPS calculation is the number of shares in issue at the reporting period date. Therefore, the number of shares (denominator) for BEANO plc is 2,000,000.

BEANO plc's EPS is : $\dfrac{€756,100}{2,000,000}$ = 37.81 cent

Note : If ordinary shares are issued during a period, the weighted average number outstanding during the period must be calculated.

Losses

If the earnings figure is a negative figure then the EPS should be calculated in the normal way but shown as a loss per share.

Changes in Ordinary Share Capital and its Effect on Basic EPS

If new shares are issued, the denominator in the calculation of basic EPS will have to be changed. There are four ways in which the capital structure may change which will affect the calculation of EPS:

1. Issue at full market price;
2. Bonus issue, share split and share consolidation;
3. Rights issues; and
4. Shares issued as part of the purchase consideration for a business combination.

Note   If the number of ordinary shares outstanding increases as a result of a capitalisation, bonus issue or share split or decreases as a result of a share consolidation, the calculation of basic EPS for all periods presented (as comparatives) should be adjusted.

Issue at Full Market Price

1. Where new ordinary shares have been issued either for cash at full market price or as consideration for the acquisition of an asset, the earnings should be apportioned over the average number of shares ranking for dividend during the period *weighted on a time basis*. There is no retrospective effect.

Example

At 31 December 20X8 the issued ordinary share capital of Top plc was 4 million shares of 50 cent each. On 1 October 20X9 the company issued 1 million shares at market value €1.50. Earnings were:

- y/e 31 December 20X8 – €400,000; and
- y/e 31 December 20X9 – €500,000.

Solution

20X9:
No of Shares
(4,000,000 x 9/12) + (5,000,000 x 3/12) = 4,250,000 shares

$$\frac{€500,000}{4,250,000} = 11.8 \text{ cent}$$

Do not adjust comparative figure for 20X9 accounts.

$$\frac{€400,000}{4,000,000} = 10 \text{ cent}$$

Example

RP plc prepares its financial statements to 31 December each year and has a capital structure consisting of:

- 100,000 10% preference shares €1; and
- 100,000 €1 ordinary shares.

In Year 1, RP plc had profits after tax of €50,000.
In Year 2, RP plc had profits after tax of €60,000.

On 30 September Year 2, RP plc made an issue at full market price of 50,000 €1 ordinary shares.

Requirement   Calculate the EPS for Year 2 and the corresponding figure for Year 1.

Solution

	Year 2	Year 1
	€	€
Profit after Taxation	60,000	50,000
Less: Preference Dividend	(10,000)	(10,000)
	50,000	40,000

Shares at 1 January	100,000	100,000
Issue at full market price:		
Before the year end (50,000 x 3/12)	12,500	---------
	112,500	100,000
EPS:		
€50,000 112,500	44 cent	
€40,000 100,000		40 cent

Bonus Issue, Share Split and Share Consolidation

Bonus Issue   A bonus issue is a capitalisation of reserves and will have no effect on the earning capacity of the company. There is no inflow of funds. Where new equity shares have been issued by way of a bonus issue during the period, the earnings should be apportioned over the number of shares ranking for dividend after the capitalisation. Therefore the corresponding figures for all earlier periods should be adjusted accordingly

Example

Background information as RP plc example for weighted average number of shares. On 30 September Year 2, bonus issue of 100,000 ordinary shares was made by RP Plc.

Requirement   Calculate the EPS for Year 2 and the corresponding figure for Year 1.

Solution

	Year 2	Year 1
	€	€
Profit after Taxation	60,000	50,000
Less: Preference Dividend	(10,000)	(10,000)
	50,000	40,000
Shares at 1 January	100,000	100,000
Bonus Issue	100,000	100,000
	200,000	200,000
EPS	25 cent	20 cent

Example

At 31 December 20X8, Ben plc had 4 million ordinary 25 cent shares in issue and 500,000 10% cumulative preference shares of €1 each. On 1 October 20X9, the company made a one for four bonus issue out of reserves. The profit after tax for the year ended 31 December 20X9 was €550,000, and for the year ended 31 December 20X8 was €450,000.

EPS 31 December 20X9:

Earnings	€
Profit after tax	550,000
Preference dividend	50,000
	500,000

EPS $\dfrac{€500,000}{5m}$ 10 cent

Comparative figure on 20X9 financial statements must be adjusted:

Either: $\dfrac{€\ 400,000}{5m}$ = 8 cent

Or:

$\dfrac{400,000}{4m}$ x 4/5 = 8 cent

Share Splits and Share Consolidations   Similar considerations apply where equity shares are split into shares of smaller nominal value, i.e. a share of €1 nominal value is divided into 4 shares of 20 cent each or consolidated into shares of a higher nominal value, i.e. 4 shares of 25 cent each are consolidated into one share of €1. In both cases the number of shares outstanding before the event is adjusted for the proportionate change. The comparative figure must be adjusted.

Example

Oak Plc has 100,000 €1 ordinary shares in issue on 1st January 20X9. On the 1st October 20X9, the company divides its shares into 400,000 ordinary shares of 25 cent each. When calculating the EPS for 31st December 20X9 divide by 400,000 shares.

Rights Issues

A rights issue is an issue of shares for cash to existing shareholders at a price (usually) below the current market price. It is equivalent to a cash issue at full market price combined with a subsequent bonus issue. When a company makes a rights issue at less than full market price, this will result in there being a new market price (after the rights issue), which will be less than that which existed when the rights issue took place. The new market price is known as the *theoretical ex rights price*.

To arrive at figures for EPS when a rights issue is made, we need firstly to calculate the theoretical ex rights price.

Example

ABC has the following capital structure:

- 200,000 10% preference shares €1; and
- 200,000 ordinary shares €1.

On 1 October 20X6, ABC plc made a one for five rights issue at a price of €1.20. The market value on the last day of quotation cum rights was €1.50. The calculation of the theoretical ex rights price can be made in several ways – here we will make the calculation of the new market price from the point of view of the shareholder who, before the rights issue, has 5 ordinary shares and €1.20 in cash.

	€
Wealth of Shareholder with 5 ordinary shares prior to rights issue:	
5 x 1.50	7.50
Cost of taking up the right to buy one ordinary share:	
1 x 1.20	1.20
	8.70
No of shares in issue:	6
Therefore theoretical ex rights price (€8.70/6):	€1.45

The procedure for calculating the EPS for the current year and the corresponding figure for the previous year is then as follows:

1. The EPS for the corresponding previous period should be multiplied by the fraction:

$$\frac{\text{Theoretical Ex Rights Price}}{\text{Market price on last day of quotation (cum rights)}}$$

2. To obtain the EPS for the current year, you should:

(a) multiply the number of shares before the rights issue by the fraction of the year before the date of issue and by the fraction;

$$\frac{\text{Market price on the last day of quotation (cum rights)}}{\text{Theoretical Ex Rights Price}}$$

(b) multiply the number of shares after the rights issue by the fraction of the year after the date of issue and add to the figure arrived at in (a).

Example

	20X7	20X8	20X9
Net profit as at 31 December	€24,000	€30,400	€36,000
Shares before the rights issue	100,000		

The rights issue is to be one share for every five currently held (giving 20,000 new shares). Exercise price €1.00. The last date to exercise rights is 1 April 20X8.

The fair value of an ordinary share before the issue is €2.20.

Requirement   Calculate the EPS for 20X7, 20X8 and 20X9.

Solution

20X7:

$$\text{EPS} = \frac{€24,000}{100,000} = 24 \text{ cent}$$

20X8:

Rights issue takes place.

(a) Calculate the theoretical ex rights price

5 shares at €2.20	=	11.00
1 share at €1.00	=	1.00
6 shares	=	12.00
Therefore T.E.R.P	=	€2.00

(b) Adjust EPS for 20X7

$$\frac{24c \times €2.00}{€2.20} = \qquad 21.82 \text{ cent}$$

(c) EPS for 20X8

a) $100,000 \times 3/12 \times €2.20/€2.00$	=	27,500
b) $120,000 \times 9/12$		90,000
Number of shares to be used		117,500

$$\text{EPS} = \frac{€30,400}{117,500} \qquad = \qquad 25.87 \text{ cent}$$

20X9

$$\text{EPS} = \frac{€36,000}{120,000} \qquad = \qquad 30 \text{ cent}$$

Shares Issued as Part of the Purchase Consideration for a Business Combination

The shares issued are included in the weighted average number of shares as at the date of acquisition. Why? The results of the new subsidiary are included in the consolidated accounts from that date only.

Example

Pete plc has 1 million shares in issue on 1 January 20X9. On 1 July 20X9, Pete plc acquired 80% of the ordinary shares of Sue plc. As part of the consideration, Pete plc issued 400,000 ordinary shares at a market value of €2.50.

Year ending 31 December 20X9 – shares for EPS calculation:

(1 million x 6/12) + (1.4 million x 6/12) = 1.2 million

Alternative EPS Figures

While IAS 33 aims to ensure that the EPS is calculated in a uniform, consistent and comparable manner, readers ought to be cautious in interpreting the results. Quoted companies are simply too complex to make it possible to sum up a whole year's performance in a single statistic. Companies may attempt to help readers in this regard by disclosing alternative versions of EPS.

IAS 33 permits the disclosure of additional EPS figures, calculated on another level of earnings. This additional EPS data should, however, be calculated using the same weighted average number of ordinary shares as for the basic EPS calculated according to IAS 33.

Disclosure Requirements for Basic EPS

- A reporting entity is required to present on the face of the statement of comprehensive income the basic EPS for profit/loss from continuing operations attributable to the ordinary equity holders, including comparative figures.
- Disclosure is still required when the basic EPS is negative, i.e. a loss per share.
- The amount used as the numerator in calculating the basic EPS must be disclosed (in the notes) and a reconciliation of that amount to the net profit/loss for the period.
- The weighted average number of ordinary shares used in the calculation must also be disclosed.

DILUTED EPS

At the end of an accounting period a company may have securities which do not have a claim to equity earnings, but they may do in the future. These include:

(a) Separate classes of equity share not yet entitled to a share of equity earnings, but becoming so at a future date;
(b) Convertible loan stock or convertible preference shares which enable their holders to exchange their securities at a later date for ordinary shares at a predetermined rate;
(c) Options or warrants – these securities have the potential effect of increasing the number of equity shares ranking for dividend and so diluting or 'watering down' the EPS. These securities may be dilutive potential ordinary shares;
(d) Rights granted under employee of other share purchase plan; and
(e) Contingently issuable shares.

Note   A dilutive potential ordinary share is one which decreases net profit, or increases net loss per share.

The diluted EPS gives users of the accounts a view on the potential ordinary shares of the entity. There is the potential to forecast the future EPS from the amounts given.

The calculation of diluted EPS is consistent with that for basic whilst giving effect to all dilutive potential ordinary shares. For the purpose of calculating diluted EPS, an entity should adjust profit or loss attributable to ordinary equity holders of the entity, as calculated by the after tax effects of:

(a) any dividends or other items related to dilutive potential ordinary shares deducted in arriving at profit or loss attributable to ordinary equity holders of the entity;
(b) any interest recognised in the period related to dilutive potential ordinary shares; and
(c) any other changes in income or expense that would result from the conversion of the dilutive potential ordinary shares.

Note   When calculating Diluted EPS (DEPS) always begin with both the earnings and number of shares used in the basic EPS.

The following are the simple pro forma calculations for the three main sets of securities.

(a) Shares not yet ranking for dividend

(i) Earnings	€
Earnings per basic EPS	$\underline{\underline{X}}$
(ii) Number of shares	
	No
Shares per basic EPS	X
Add shares that will rank in future periods	X
Diluted number	$\underline{\underline{\overline{X}}}$

(b) Convertible loan stock or preference shares

(i) Earnings	€
Earnings per basic EPS	X
Add back loan stock interest net of CT	
(or preference dividends) 'saved'	X
Diluted earnings	$\underline{\underline{\overline{X}}}$
(ii) Number of shares	
	No
Shares per basic EPS	X
Add additional shares on conversion	
(using terms giving maximum dilution	
available after the year end)	X
Diluted number	$\underline{\overline{X}}$

(c) Options or warrants

(i) Earnings	€
Earnings per basic EPS	$\underline{\underline{X}}$
(ii) Numbers of shares	
	No
Shares per basic EPS	X
Add additional shares issued at nil consideration	X
Diluted number	$\underline{\underline{\overline{X}}}$

Share Options

A share option allows the purchase of shares at a favourable amount, which is less than the fair value of existing shares. The assumed proceeds are deemed to be a mixture of:

(a) an issue at fair (market) value; and
(b) an issue for no consideration.

The calculation of diluted EPS includes those shares deemed as issued for no consideration as the issue at market value are deemed to be non-dilutive. For this purpose, the following calculation is used:

$$\frac{\text{Shares under option x exercise price}}{\text{Fair value of ordinary shares}}$$

This gives the number of shares that are to be excluded from the EPS calculation. This will become clearer in the following example.

Example

Net profit for 20X9		€1,000,000
Weighted average number of ordinary shares for 20X9		10 Million
Average fair value of one ordinary share		€2.40
Weighted average number of shares under option during 20X9		3 million
Exercise price for shares under option in 20X9		€2.00

Solution

	Shares	Net profit	EPS
Net profit for 20X9		€1,000,000	
Weighted average shares for 20X9	10m		
Basic EPS			10 cent
Number of shares on option	3m		
Number of shares that would have been issued at fair value: $\frac{\text{3m x €2}}{\text{€2.40}}$	(2.5m)		
Issued at no consideration	0.5m		
Diluted EPS	10.5m	€1,000,000	9.5 cent

Note that the net profit has not been increased. This is because the calculation only includes shares deemed to be issued for no consideration.

Employee Share Option Schemes

Employee share option schemes have become increasingly popular as an incentive scheme in organisations. Many schemes relate to performance criteria which mean that they are contingent on certain conditions being met. The section on contingently issuable shares (see below) explains how these schemes should be treated when calculating diluted EPS.

Certain schemes do not have performance measures. As with the share option approach, only those shares deemed as issued for no consideration are included. The following example shows how these schemes should be treated.

Example

Share Option Scheme (Not Performance Related)

A company runs a share option scheme based on the employee's period of service with the company. As at 31 December 20X7 the provisions of the scheme were:

Date of grant	1 January 20X7
Market price at grant date	€2.24
Exercise price of option	€1.80
Date of vesting	31 December 20X9
Number of shares under option	3 million
Net profit for the year 20X7	€1,000,000
Weighted average number of ordinary shares	10 million
Average fair value of an ordinary share	€2.70

Solution

	Shares	Net profit	EPS
Net profit for 20X7		€1,000,000	
Weighted average shares for 20X7	10m		
Basic EPS			10 cent
Number of shares on option	3m		
Number of shares that would have been issued at fair value: (3m x €1.80)/€2.70	(2.0m)		
Issued for no consideration	1.0m		
Diluted EPS	11.0m	€1,000,000	9.1 cent

Contingently Issuable Shares

These are shares issued after certain criteria have been met. For the purposes of the diluted EPS calculation these shares are included in full.

The following example gives two contingent events arising after the acquisition of a business. Most contingent events will be based on target sales or profit. The example includes the opening of new branches. This is also a measure of the entity's successful expansion. Note that many employee share option schemes operate in this manner.

Example

A company has 500,000 ordinary shares in issue at 1 January 20X7. A recent business acquisition has given rise to the following contingently issuable shares:

- 10,000 ordinary shares for every new branch opened in the three years 20X7 – 20X9; and
- 1,000 ordinary shares for every €2,000 of net profit in excess of €900,000 over the three years ended 31 December 20X9 (shares will be issued on 1 January following the period in which a condition is met).

A new branch was opened on 1 July 20X7, another on 31 March 20X8 and another on 1 October 20X9.

Reported net profits over the three years were €350,000, €400,000 and €600,000 respectively.

Solution

Basic EPS

	20X7 €		20X8 €		20X9 €	
Numerator	350,000		400,000		600,000	
Denominator						
Ordinary shares	500,000		510,000		520,000	
Branch contingency	5,000	(i)	7,500	(i)	2,500	(i)
Earnings contingency	-	(ii)	-	(ii)	-	(ii)
Total shares	505,000		517,500		522,500	
Basic EPS	69.3 cent		77.3 cent		114.8 cent	

Diluted EPS

	20X7 €		20X8 €		20X9 €	
Numerator per basic EPS	350,000		400,000		600,000	
Denominator						
Ordinary shares in basic EPS	505,000		517,500		522,500	
Additional shares:						
Branch contingency	5,000	(iii)	2,500	(iii)	7,500	(iii)
Earnings contingency	-		-		225,000	(iv)
Total shares	510,000		520,000		755,000	
Diluted EPS	68.6 cent		76.9 cent		79.5 cent	

(i) This figure is simply the shares due for opening a branch pro-rated over the year.
(ii) It is not certain the net profit condition has been satisfied until after the three-year period.
(iii) The contingently issuable shares are included from the start of the period in which they arise so these figures are increasing the denominator by the full 10,000 shares.
(iv) This is (€1,350,000 – €900,000)/€2,000 x 1,000. This figure will be included in the basic EPS figure in the following year 20X0. Note that the €900,000 criterion was not exceeded in the prior year.

Convertible Bonds

In cases where the issue of shares will affect earnings, the numerator should be adjusted accordingly. This occurs when bonds are converted. Interest is paid out on the bond. When conversion takes place this interest is no longer payable.

Example

Net profit	€500
Ordinary shares in issue	1,000
Basic EPS	50 cent
Convertible 15% bonds	200

Each block of five bonds is convertible to eight ordinary shares. The tax rate (including any deferred tax) is 40%.

Solution

Basic EPS = 500/1000 = 50 cent

Diluted EPS	€
Earnings per basic EPS	500
Add interest saved net of tax 200 x 15% x 60%	18
	518
Shares per basic EPS	1,000
Add maximum shares on conversion 200 x 8/5	320
	1,320

DEPS = 518/1320 = 39.2 cent

Earnings should be adjusted for savings or expenses occurring as a result of conversion.

Other examples are:

(a) preference dividends saved when preference shares are converted; and
(b) additional liability on a profit-sharing scheme as a result of higher profits (i.e. if conversion of bonds increases profit, a higher amount will be payable to members of a profit-related pay scheme).

Ranking Dilutive Securities

The approach prescribed by IAS 33 involves including only dilutive potential ordinary shares. Antidilutive shares are not to be included. This is a prudent approach which recognises potential reduction of earnings but not increases.

The following examples show how dilutive potential ordinary shares are identified and included in the calculation of EPS. The standard also states that the dilutive shares should be ranked and taken into account from the most dilutive down to the least dilutive. Potential ordinary shares likely to have a dilutive effect on EPS include options, convertible bonds and convertible preference shares.

Example

Ranking Dilutive Securities for the Calculation of Weighted Average Number of Shares

Net profit attributable to ordinary shareholders	€20 million
Net profit from discontinued activities	€5 million
Ordinary shares outstanding	50 million
Average fair value of one ordinary share	€5.00

Potential ordinary shares:

Convertible preference shares – 500,000 entitled to a cumulative dividend of €5. Each is convertible to 3 shares.

3% convertible bond – nominal amount €50 million. Each €1,000 bond is convertible to 50 shares. There is no amortisation of premium or discounting affecting the interest expense.

Options – 10 million with exercise price of €4.

Tax rate - 30%

Solution

The effect on earnings on conversion of potential ordinary shares:

	Increase in Earnings	Increase in ordinary shares	Effect on earnings per incremental share
	€	Number	€

Convertible preference shares

Increase in net profit (€5 x 500,000) 2,500,000 (i)

Incremental shares (3 x 500,000)   1,500,000   1.67

3% convertible bonds

Increase in net profit

50,000,000 x 0.03 x 70%   1,050,000

Incremental shares (50,000 x 50)   2,500,000   0.42

Options

Increase in earnings: nil

Incremental shares 10 million x (€5 – €4)/€5   2,000,000 (W1)   nil

Therefore options are the most dilutive as the increase in shares does not lead to any increase in EPS; this is followed by the 3% convertible bonds and finally the convertible preference shares in terms of their dilutive potential.

(W1)

Number of shares that would be issued at market value = 10m x 4/5 = 8m

Number of shares at no consideration   2m

Identifying the dilutive shares to include in the diluted EPS:

	Net profit from continuing Operations	Ordinary shares	Per Share	
	€	Number	€	
Reported	15,000,000	50,000,000	0.30	
Options	-	2,000,000		
	15,000,000	52,000,000	0.29	Dilutive
3% convertible bonds	1,050,000	2,500,000		
	16,050,000	54,500,000	0.29	Antidilutive
Convertible preference shares	2,500,000	1,500,000		
	18,550,000	56,000,000	0.33	Antidilutive

To maximise the dilution of basic EPS each issue of potential ordinary shares is considered in sequence from the most dilutive to the least dilutive i.e. dilutive potential ordinary shares with the lowest 'Earnings per Incremental Share' are included in the DEPS calculation before those with the higher 'Earnings per Incremental Share'.

Note

- The potential share issues are considered from the most dilutive to the least dilutive.
- Remember, potential ordinary shares should be treated as dilutive only when their conversion to ordinary shares would decrease net profit or increase net loss per share from continuing operations.
- The diluted EPS is increased by both the bonds and the preference shares. These are therefore ignored in the diluted EPS calculation.

Basic EPS including discontinued operations

Net profit	€20 million
Weighted average number of shares	50 million
Basic EPS	40 cent

Diluted EPS

Net profit (remains at)	€20 million
Weighted average number of shares	52 million
Diluted EPS	38.5 cent

- The cumulative dividend on the preference shares is not taken into consideration. Only the dividend for the year is included in the increase in earnings.
- It is important to remember the tax element in the bond interest.

It should be noted that the numerator, for the purposes of ranking the dilutive shares, is net profit from continuing operations only. This is net profit after preference share dividends but excluding discontinued operations and extraordinary items. The EPS calculation includes the full amount of net profit attributable to ordinary shareholders.

The following question is based on the previous example but with dilutive convertible bonds.

Example

Details as above except that the convertible bonds are 1.5% bonds.

Solution

Effect on earnings on conversion of potential ordinary shares:

	Increase in earnings €	Increase in ordinary shares Number	Earnings per share €
1.5% Convertible bonds			
Increase in net profit (50,000,000 x 0.015 x (1 – 0.3)	525,000		
Incremental shares (50,000 x 50)		2,500,000	0.21

Identifying the dilutive shares to include in the diluted EPS:

	Net profit from continuing operations €	Ordinary shares Number	Per share €
Reported	15,000,000	50,000,000	0.30
Options	-	2,000,000	
	15,000,000	52,000,000	0.29 Dilutive
1.5% convertible bonds	525,000	2,500,000	
	15,525,000	54,500,000	0.28 Dilutive

The convertible preference shares will remain antidilutive and basic EPS will remain at 40 cent.

Diluted EPS:

Net profit (€20,000,000 + €525,000) bond interest	€20,525,000
Weighted average number of shares	54.5 million
Diluted EPS	37.7 cent

Disclosure Requirements

- IAS 33 requires that the diluted EPS is disclosed on the face of the statement of comprehensive income, even if the amounts are negative. Comparative figures are also required.
- The amounts used as numerators in calculating the diluted EPS, reconciled to actual net profit (loss) for the period.

Conclusion

EPS is an important, and often confusing, topic. The key issues are summarised below.

An entity should present on the face of the statement of comprehensive income its basic and diluted EPS for each class of ordinary shares that has a different right to share in profit for the period. An entity should calculate basic and diluted EPS for profit or loss from continuing operations attributable to the ordinary equity holders of the parent entity. If an entity reports a discontinued operation, it also discloses basic and diluted EPS for the discontinued operation.

Basic Earnings per Share

Basic EPS is calculated by dividing profit or loss attributable to ordinary equity holders of the parent entity (the numerator) by the weighted average number of ordinary shares outstanding (the denominator) during the period.

The profit or loss attributable to the parent entity is adjusted for the after-tax amounts of preference dividends, differences arising on the settlement of preference shares, and other similar effects of preference shares classified as equity.

The weighted average number of ordinary shares outstanding during the period and for all periods presented is adjusted for events, other than the conversion of potential ordinary shares that have changed the number of ordinary shares outstanding without a corresponding change in resources (e.g. a bonus issue, a share split).

Diluted Earnings per Share

Diluted EPS is calculated by adjusting the profit or loss attributable to ordinary equity holders of the parent entity, and the weighted average number of ordinary shares outstanding, for the effects of all dilutive potential ordinary shares.

The profit or loss attributable to ordinary equity holders of the parent entity, as calculated for basic EPS, is adjusted for the after-tax effects of:

- any dividends or other items related to dilutive potential ordinary shares deducted in arriving at profit or loss attributable to ordinary equity holders;
- any interest recognised in the period related to dilutive potential ordinary shares; and
- any other changes in income or expense that would result from the conversion of the dilutive potential ordinary shares.

The number of ordinary shares is the weighted average number of ordinary shares outstanding, as calculated for basic EPS, plus the weighted average number of ordinary shares that would be issued on the conversion of all the dilutive potential ordinary shares into ordinary shares. Potential ordinary shares are treated as dilutive when their conversion to ordinary shares would decrease EPS or increase loss per share from continuing operations (e.g. options and warrants, convertible instruments, contingently issuable shares).

IAS 33 requires that basic and diluted EPS be disclosed on the face of the profit and loss account both for net profit or loss for the period and also for profit or loss from continuing operations. Basic and diluted EPS for discontinued operations (if reported) may be reported either on the face of the statement or in a note. Additional per share amounts can only be disclosed by way of note.

QUESTIONS

Self-test Questions

1. To what companies does EPS apply?
2. Define basic and diluted EPS.
3. Following a rights issue what is the fraction by which the EPS for the corresponding previous period should be multiplied?
4. Summarise the disclosure requirements of IAS 33.

Review Questions

(See APPENDIX ONE for Suggested Solutions to Review Questions.)

Question 1

The draft financial statements of Plum Plc for year ended 31 December 20X4 include the following:

	€	€
Profit before tax		2,323,000
Less Taxation		
Corporation Tax	1,035,000	
Under provision for 20X3	23,000	
		(1,058,000)
Profit after tax		1,265,000
Transfer to reserves	115,000	
Dividends:		
Paid preference interim dividend	138,000	
Paid ordinary interim dividend	184,000	
Proposed preference final dividend	138,000	
Proposed ordinary final dividend	230,000	
		(805,000)
Retained profit		460,000

On 1 January 20X4 the issued share capital of Plum Plc was 4,600,000 6% preference shares of €1 each and 4,140,000 ordinary shares of €1 each. The proposed dividends were approved by the shareholders during the year ended 31 December 20X4.

Requirement Calculate the EPS (on basic and fully diluted basis) in respect of the year ended 31 December 20X4 for each of the following circumstances. (Each of the four circumstances (a) to (d) is to be dealt with separately.)

(a) On the basis that there was no change in the issued share capital of the company during the year ended 31 December 20X4.
(b) On the basis that the company made a bonus issue on 1 October 20X4 of one ordinary share for every four shares in issue at 30 September 20X4.
(c) On the basis that the company made a rights issue of €1 ordinary shares on 1 October 20X4 in the proportion of 1 for every 5 shares held, at a price of €1.20.

The middle market price for the shares on the last day of quotation cum rights was €1.80 per share.

(d) On the basis that the company made no new issue of shares during the year ended 31 December 20X4 but on that date it had in issue €1,150,000 10% convertible loan stock 20X8 – 20Y1.

This loan stock will be convertible into ordinary €1 shares as follows:
20X8 90 €1 shares for €100 nominal value loan stock
20X9 85 €1 shares for €100 nominal value loan stock
20Y0 80 €1 shares for €100 nominal value loan stock
20Y1 75 €1 shares for €100 nominal value loan stock

Assume tax at 50%.

Question 2

The following are the results of Earno Limited, a public company, for the year ended 31 December.

	20X1	20X0
	€'000	€'000
Revenue	2,000	1,600
Profit before tax	800	600
Taxation	(300)	(200)
Profit after taxation	500	400
Dividends:		
Paid		
14% Non-cumulative Preference	–	(20)
Proposed		
10% Cumulative Preference	(30)	(30)
14% Non-Cumulative Preference	(60)	(40)
Ordinary	(10)	(10)
Transfer to Capital Reserves	(90)	–
Profit for year retained	310	300

The 14% Preference Dividend paid in 20X0 is in respect of previous years. The proposed dividend in 20X0 and 20X1 were approved by shareholders of Earno Limited during the year ended 31 December 20X0 and 20X1 respectively. Earno Limited has issued Ordinary Share Capital of 100,000 @ €1 each.

Requirement

Each of the following questions should be considered independently of one another.

1. Basic EPS

   Calculate the basic EPS for both years

2. Issue at Full Market Price

   Assuming that Earno had issued 5,000 Ordinary Shares on 31 March 20X1 at full market price, calculate the basic EPS for both years.

3. Capitalisation/Bonus/Scrip Issue

   Assuming that on 31 May 20X1 Earno Limited issued one ordinary share for every 5 already held, calculate the basic EPS for both years.

4. Share Exchange

   Assuming that on 30 April 20X1 Earno Limited issued 10,000 Ordinary Shares as consideration for the acquisition of a subsidiary company, calculate the basic EPS for both years

5. Rights issue for less than full market price

   Assuming that on the 30 June 20X1 (Market Price of share €4) Earno Limited invited its shareholders to subscribe to a 1 for 5 rights issue at €2 per share, calculate the basic EPS for both years.

6. Fully Diluted EPS
   (a) Another class of equity ranking for dividend in the future
       Assuming that on 1 January 20X1, Earno Limited had issued 10,000 'A' ordinary shares, which though not ranking for dividend in the current period, would do so subsequently, calculate the fully diluted EPS
   (b) Convertible Securities

   Assume that on 31 March 20X1, Earno Limited issued €5,000 10% Convertible Debentures. These were convertible into Ordinary Shares as follows:

20X1	40 Ordinary Shares for €100 convertible debentures
20X2	30 ' ' ' ' ' '
20X3	20 ' ' ' ' ' '
20X4	15 ' ' ' ' ' '

   None of the debentures had been converted at 31 December 20X1.

   Calculate the fully diluted EPS (assume Corporation Tax @ 50%).

Challenging Questions

Question 1

(Based on ICAI, P3 Summer 2003, Question 6)
CLASSICAL plc (CLASSICAL) had one million ordinary €1 shares in issue on 1 January 2004. On 1 July 2004, CLASSICAL made a rights issue of one ordinary share for every two previously held, at a price of €6 per share. The fair value of one ordinary share was

€9 throughout the year ended 31 December 2004. During the year ended 31 December 2004, the following potential ordinary shares were outstanding:

(a) 3,000,000 share options with an exercise price of €6 per share;
(b) 50,000 convertible preference shares entitled to a dividend of €5 per share. Each preference share is convertible into two ordinary shares; and
(c) 6,000,000 nominal 2% convertible bonds, convertible into 300 shares per each 6,000 bond held.

The reported basic EPS in 2003 was 36 cent. After deducting dividends and other appropriations of profit in respect of non-equity shares, CLASSICAL reported a net profit of €500,000 for the year ended 31 December 2004. CLASSICAL pays corporation tax at 25%.

Requirement

(a) Compute the basic EPS figure, including comparatives, to be reported in the financial statements of CLASSICAL for the year ended 31 December 2004 in accordance with IAS 33 *Earnings per Share*.
(b) Compute the diluted EPS of CLASSICAL for the year ended 31 December 2004 in accordance with IAS 33 *Earnings per Share*. (Comparative figures are not required.)

Question 2 (Based on ICAI, P3 Autumn 2004, Question 4)

The issued ordinary share capital of WELLER plc (WELLER) at 1 January *2002* was 6,000,000 ordinary shares of €0.50 each. On 30 June *2003*, WELLER made a fully subscribed one for three rights issue at €1 per share, when the average price of one ordinary share was €1.50. There were no other changes to WELLER's ordinary share capital in *2002* and *2003*. The average market price of one ordinary share in WELLER during *2002* and *2003* was €1.20 and €1.60 respectively. At 31 December *2002* and *2003*, WELLER had a 5% loan of €1,000,000, which was convertible into 500,000 ordinary shares of €0.50 each. WELLER pays corporation tax at 25%.

The following information is available with respect to the statement of comprehensive income of WELLER for the years ended 31 December *2002* and *2003*.

| | Year ended 31 December | | | |
| | 2003 | | 2002 | |
	€'000	€'000	€'000	€'000
Operating profit		1,900		1,300
Exceptional gain/(loss)		(200)		100
Interest payable		(60)		(50)
Profit before tax		1,640		1,350

Taxation		(410)	(340)
Profit after tax		1,230	1,010
Non-controlling interests		(246)	(202)
		984	808
Preference dividends paid		(102)	(102)
Ordinary dividends paid		(132)	(106)
Retained profit for the year		750	600
Retained profit at start of year as previously stated	1,900		1,300
Prior period adjustment (Note 1)	(100)		–
Retained profit at start of year as restated		1,800	1,300
Retained profit at end of year		2,550	1,900

Note 1 The prior period adjustment relates to the discovery of a fundamental error in **2003**, which would have affected WELLER's operating profit for the year ended 31 December **2002**.

Requirement
(a) Calculate, in accordance with IAS 33 Earnings per Share:
   (i) WELLER's basic EPS for the year ended 31 December **2002**;
   (ii) WELLER's fully diluted EPS for the year ended 31 December **2002**;
   (iii) WELLER's basic EPS for the year ended 31 December **2003**;
   (iv) WELLER's adjusted EPS for the year ended 31 December 2002 to be included as a comparative figure in WELLER's financial statements for the year ended 31 December **2003**.

(b) Outline why it is considered important to measure EPS.

Question 3 (Based on ICAI, P3 Summer 2006, Question 5)

On 1 January 2005, BELLS plc (BELLS) had 1,000,000 €1 ordinary shares and 500,000 6% €1 convertible preference shares in issue. Preference dividends are paid half yearly on 31 March and 30 September each year. BELLS' profit after tax for the year ended 31 December 2005 was:

	€'000
Profit after tax:	
Continuing operations	3,000
Discontinued operations	500
	3,500

On 1 April 2005, BELLS issued a further 500,000 €1 ordinary shares at full market price. Warrants to purchase 450,000 €1 ordinary shares were issued on 31 May 2005 at €3 per share. While the warrants were due to expire on 31 May 2009, all were exercised on 28 February 2006. Convertible loan stock of €800,000 at an interest rate of 6% per annum was issued at par on 30 June 2004. Each €100 of loan stock is convertible into 10 €1 ordinary shares at any time at the option of the holder. Interest is paid half yearly on 31 December and 30 June each year. On 1 July 2005, €300,000 of loan stock was converted when the market price was €4 per share. The preference shares are convertible into ordinary shares at the option of the holder on the basis of one €1 ordinary share for every four convertible preference shares held. Holders of 200,000 preference shares converted them into ordinary shares on 1 October 2005. The average market price of BELLS' ordinary shares during the year ended 31 December 2005 was €5 per share, and the tax rate is 25%.

BELLS' financial statements were approved on 31 March 2006.

Requirement   Calculate the basic and diluted EPS for BELLS for the year ended 31 December 2005 in accordance with IAS 33 *Earnings per share*.

REFERENCES

Healy, P. M. and Wahlen, J. M. (1999). 'A Review of the Earnings Management Literature and its Implications for Standard Setting', *Accounting Horizons*, Vol. 13, No. 4, pp.365–383.

CHAPTER 24

OPERATING SEGMENTS

INTRODUCTION

Many organisations provide a range of products or services and/or operate in different geographical areas. Each product/service or geographical area may be subject to different influences which result in different risks and rewards that may not be obvious when the figures are aggregated in the entity's financial statements. Consequently, organisations are required to separately analyse their results by product/service and geographical area so that users may:

- better understand the organisation's past performance;
- better assess the organisation's risks and returns; and
- make more informed judgements about the organisation as a whole.

This chapter addresses the principles for reporting financial information by segment to help users of financial statements in accordance with IAS 14 *Segment Reporting* and IFRS 8 *Operating Segments*. Both IAS 14 and IFRS 8 apply to organisations whose equity or debt securities are publicly traded and to organisations that are in the process of issuing equity or debt securities in public securities markets. If another organisation chooses to disclose segment information in financial statements that comply with international financial reporting standards, it must comply fully with the requirements of these standards. When both separate and consolidated financial statements are presented in a single financial report, segment information need only be presented by the basis of the consolidated financial statements. IAS 14 is replaced by IFRS 8, which is effective for annual periods beginning on or after 1 January 2009 (with earlier adoption being encouraged).

After having studied this chapter, you should be able to:

- define the terms 'business segment' and 'geographical segment';
- distinguish between primary and secondary segment reports;
- identify an organisation's reportable and operating segments; and
- outline the main disclosure requirements of IAS 14 and IFRS 8.

IAS 14

IAS 14 requires an organisation to identify two sets of segments *(business and geographical)*, and to disclose details of the products and services included in each reported business segment and the composition of each reported geographical segment.

Business Segment

A business segment is a distinguishable component of an entity that is engaged in providing an individual product or service or a group or related products or services and that is subject to risks and rewards that are different from those of other business segments. Some of the factors that should be considered when deciding whether products and services are related include: the nature of the products or services; the nature of the production processes; the type or class of customer; and the distribution methods involved. A single business segment should not include products or services with significantly different risks and rewards.

Geographical Segment

A geographical segment is a distinguishable component of an entity that is engaged in providing products or services within a particular economic environment and that is subject to risks and rewards that are different from those of components operating in other economic environments. Some of the factors that should be considered when identifying geographical segments include: similarity of economic and political conditions; special risks associated with the operations in a particular area; and exchange control regulations and currency risks. A single geographical segment should not include economic environments with significantly different risks and rewards

Having identified its business and geographical segments, an organisation must then determine which one of these should be the *primary reporting format* and which should be the *secondary reporting format*. The source and nature of the organisation's risks and rates of return determine whether the primary reporting format is business segments or geographical segments. This is usually identified by the organisation's internal organisational and management structure and its system of internal financial reporting to senior management. For example, if the organisation's risks and rewards are affected mainly by differences in the products or services (as opposed to different countries or geographical areas) that it supplies, then its primary reporting format will be business segments and its secondary will be geographical

A business or geographical segment is identified as reportable if a majority of its revenue is earned from sales to external customers and:

- its revenue is 10% or more of total revenue, external and internal, of all segments; or
- its result (either profit or loss) is 10% or more of the combined result of all segments in profit or the combined result of all segments in loss, whichever is the greater in absolute amount; or
- its assets are 10% or more of the total assets of all segments.

Any other segment can be designated as a reportable segment. If total external revenue attributable to reportable segments is less than 75% of the total consolidated revenue, additional segments are identified as reportable segments until at least 75% of total revenue is included in reportable segments.

The following should be disclosed for each *primary reportable segment:*

- Revenue, separately disclosing sales to external customers and inter-segment revenue. The basis of inter-segment pricing is also disclosed;
- Result (before interest and taxes) from continuing operations and separately the result from discontinued operations;
- Carrying amount of segment assets;
- Segment liabilities;
- Cost incurred in the period to acquire property, plant and equipment, and intangibles;
- Depreciation and amortisation charges, and other significant non-cash expenses; or cash flows from operating, investing and financing activities in accordance with IAS 7 *Statement of Cash Flows;* and
- Aggregate share of the profit or loss of associates, joint ventures, or other investments accounted for under the equity method.

The following should be disclosed for each *secondary reportable segment:*

- Revenue, separately disclosing sales to external customers and inter-segment revenue;
- Carrying amount of segment assets; and
- Cost incurred in the period to acquire property, plant and equipment, and intangibles.

IFRS 8

IFRS 8's core principle is that an organisation should disclose information to enable users of its financial statements to evaluate the nature and financial effects of the types of business activities in which it engages and the economic environments in which it operates.

Reportable Segments

IFRS 8 requires an organisation to report financial and descriptive information about its *reportable segments.* Reportable segments are operating segments or aggregations of *operating segments* that meet specified criteria:

- its reported revenue, from both external customers and inter-segment sales or transfers, is 10% or more of the combined revenue, internal and external, of all operating segments; or

- the absolute measure of its reported profit or loss is 10% or more of the greater, in absolute amount, of (i) the combined reported profit of all operating segments that did not report a loss and (ii) the combined reported loss of all operating segments that reported a loss; or
- its assets are 10% or more of the combined assets of all operating segments.

If the total external revenue reported by operating segments constitutes less than 75% of the organisation's revenue, additional operating segments must be identified as reportable segments (even if they do not meet the quantitative thresholds set out above) until at least 75% of the organisation's revenue is included in reportable segments. IFRS 8 has detailed guidance about when operating segments may be combined to create a reportable segment. This guidance is generally consistent with the aggregation criteria in IAS 14.

Operating Segments

An operating segment is a component of an organisation:

- that engages in business activities from which it may earn revenues and incur expenses (including revenues and expenses relating to transactions with other components of the same organisation);
- whose operating results are reviewed regularly by the organisation's chief operating
- for which discrete financial information is available.

Not all operations of an organisation will necessarily be an operating segment (nor part of one). For example, the corporate headquarters or some functional departments may not earn revenues or they may earn revenues that are only incidental to the activities of the organisation. These would not be operating segments. In addition, IFRS 8 states specifically that an organisation's post-retirement benefit plans are not operating segments

Example

An organisation has identified the following business components:

Component	Revenue External €'000	Revenue Internal €'000	Profit €'000	Assets €'000
1	80,000	Nil	10,000	50,000
2	Nil	45,000	5,000	30,000
3	10,000	Nil	1,000	4,000
4	8,000	Nil	500	3,000
Total	98,000	45,000	16,500	87,000

Requirement Identify which of the segments should be classified as reportable in accordance with IFRS 8.

Solution

Components 1 and 2 would be separately reportable since they meet all three size criteria.

Components 3 and 4 do not meet any of the size criteria and on the face of it are not separately reportable. The external revenue of component 1 is 82% of the total external revenue so the '75% threshold' is comfortably achieved. However if they had similar economic characteristics then when aggregated they would be over the 10% threshold for revenue and so could be reported as a combined segment.

IFRS 8 requires that current period and comparative segment information be reported consistently. This means that, if a segment is identified as reportable in the current period but was not in the previous period, then equivalent comparative information should be presented unless it would be prohibitively costly to obtain. IFRS 8 gives organisations discretion to report information regarding segments that do not meet the size criteria. Organisations can report on such segments where, in the opinion of management, information about the segments would be useful to users of the financial statements.

What Has Changed?

Identifying Segments

IFRS 8 extends the scope of segment reporting to include organisations that hold assets in a fiduciary capacity for a broad group of outsiders as well as organisations whose equity or debt securities are publicly traded, and organisations that are in the process of issuing equity or debt securities in public securities markets. Upon adoption of IFRS 8, the identification of an organisation's segments may or may not change, depending on how the organisation has applied IAS 14 in the past. IFRS 8 requires operating segments to be identified on the basis of internal reports about components of the organisation that are regularly reviewed by the chief operating decision-maker in order to allocate resources to the segment and to assess its performance. IAS 14 requires an organisation to identify two sets of segments (business and geographical), using a risks and rewards approach, with the organisation's 'system of internal financial reporting to key management personnel' serving only as the starting point for the identification of such segments. One set of segments is regarded as primary and the other as secondary. If under IAS 14 an organisation identified its primary segments on the basis of the reports provided to the person whom IFRS 8 regards as the chief operating decision-maker, those might become the 'operating segments' for the purposes of IFRS 8.

IFRS 8 states that a component of an organisation that sells primarily or exclusively to other operating segments of the organisation will meet the definition of an operating segment if the organisation is managed that way. IAS 14 limits reportable segments to those that earn a majority of their revenue from sales to external parties and did not require the different stages of a vertically-integrated organisation to be identified as separate segments.

Measurement of Segment Information

The IFRS requires the amount reported for each segment item to be the measure reported to the chief operating decision-maker for the purposes of allocating resources to that segment and assessing its performance. IAS 14 requires segment information to be prepared in conformity with the accounting policies adopted for the preparation and presentation of the consolidated financial statements. In contrast to IAS 14, IFRS 8 does not define segment revenue, segment expense, segment result, segment assets or segment liabilities, but does require an explanation of how segment profit or loss, segment assets and segment liabilities are measured for each operating segment. As a consequence, organisations will have more discretion in determining what is included in segment profit or loss under IFRS 8, limited only by their internal reporting practices.

Disclosure

New disclosures include information about the way that the operating segments were determined, the products and services provided by the segments, differences between the measurements used in reporting segment information and those used in the organisation's financial statements, and changes in the measurement of segment amounts from period to period. Interest revenue and interest expense must be reported separately for each reportable segment, if the amounts are included in the measure of segment profit or loss, or are otherwise regularly reported to the chief operating decision-maker, unless the majority of the segment's revenues are from interest and the chief operating decision-maker relies primarily on net interest revenue when making resource allocation decisions and to assess segment performance.

DISCLOSURE

The disclosure principle in IFRS 8 is that an organisation should disclose 'information to enable users of its financial statements to evaluate the nature and financial effects of the types of business activities in which it engages and the economic environments in which it operates'. In meeting this principle, an organisation must disclose:

- general information about how the organisation identified its operating segments and the types of products and services from which each operating segment derives its revenues;
- information about the reported segment profit or loss, including certain specified revenues and expenses included in segment profit or loss, segment assets and segment liabilities and the basis of measurement;

- reconciliations of the totals of segment revenues, reported segment profit or loss, segment assets, segment liabilities and other material items to corresponding items in the organisation's financial statements;
- organisation-wide disclosures even when an organisation has only one reportable segment. These include information about each product and service or groups of products and services;
- an analysis of revenues and certain non-current assets by geographical area are required– with an expanded requirement to disclose revenues/assets by individual foreign country (if material), irrespective of the identification of operating segments. If the information necessary for these analyses is not available, and the cost to develop it would be excessive, that fact must be disclosed; and
- information about transactions with major customers. If revenues from transactions with a single external customer amount to 10% or more of the organisation's revenues, the total amount of revenue from each such customer and the segment or segments in which those revenues are reported must be disclosed. The organisation need not disclose the identity of a major customer, nor the amount of revenues that each segment reports from that customer. For this purpose, a group of organisations known to the reporting organisation to be under common control will be considered a single customer, and a government and organisations known to the reporting organisation to be under the control of that government will be considered to be a single customer.

Amendments to IAS 34 *Interim Financial Reporting*

IFRS 8 expands significantly the requirements for segment information at interim reporting dates.

Amendments to IAS 36 *Impairment of Assets*

IAS 36 requires goodwill to be tested for impairment as part of impairment testing the cash generating unit to which it relates. In identifying the units (or groups of units) to which goodwill is allocated for the purpose of impairment testing, IAS 36 limits the size of such units or groups of units by reference to the organisation's reported segments. As a result of IFRS 8 replacing IAS 14, that maximum limit is now determined by reference to the organisation's operating segments as determined in accordance with IFRS 8 – which may differ from the limit previously arrived at in the context of IAS 14.

CONCLUSION

Segment disclosures are widely regarded as some of the most useful disclosures in financial reports because of the extent to which they disaggregate financial information into meaningful and often revealing groupings. Disaggregation into meaningful and often revealing groupings assists users to understand better the entity's past performance, assess better the entity's risks and returns and make more informed judgements about the entity as a whole. For example, an entity may appear profitable on a consolidated basis but the segment disclosures reveal that one part of the business is performing poorly while another part is performing well. Over time the poorly performing part may affect the entire entity's performance. This affects the entity's share price because analysts frequently look at predicted future cash flows in making their share price determinations.

QUESTIONS

Self-test Questions

1. Explain the objectives of segment reporting and why the users of financial statements may find segmental reporting useful.
2. Define the terms 'business segment' and 'geographical segment' as used in IAS 14.
3. Distinguish between primary and secondary segment reports in the context of IAS 14.
4. Identify an organisation's reportable and operating segments in accordance with IFRS 8.
5. Outline the main disclosure requirements of IAS 14 and IFRS 8.

Review Questions

(See APPENDIX ONE for Suggested Solutions to Review Questions.)

1. Operating segment information should:

   (i)   increase the number of reported segments and provide more information;
   (ii) enable users to see an undertaking through the eyes of management;
   (iii) enable an undertaking to provide timely segment information for external interim reporting with relatively low incremental cost;
   (iv) enhance consistency with the management discussion and analysis or other annual report disclosures;
   (v)   provide various measures of segment performance:
   (vi) reduce staff.

   1. (i)-(ii)
   2. (i)-(iii)
   3. (i)-(iv)
   4. (i)-(v)
   5. (i)-(vi)

2. Segments based on the structure of an undertaking's internal organisation have other significant advantages:

   (i) An ability to see an undertaking 'through the eyes of management' enhances a user's ability to predict actions or reactions of management that can significantly affect the undertaking's prospects for future cash flows.
   (ii) As information about those segments is generated for management's use, the incremental cost of providing information for external reporting should be relatively low.

    (iii) Practice has demonstrated that the term 'industry' is subjective. Segments based on an existing internal structure should be less subjective.

    (iv) Earnings per share calculations can be compared between segments.

1. (i)-(ii)
2. (i)-(iii)
3. (i)-(iv)

3. An operating segment is a component of an undertaking:

    (i) that engages in business activities from which it may earn revenues and incur expenses (including revenues and expenses relating to transactions with other components of the same undertaking);

    (ii) whose operating results are regularly reviewed by the undertaking's chief operating decision-maker to make decisions about resources to be allocated to the segment and assess its performance;

    (iii) for which discrete financial information is available;

    (iv) which is taxed separately from other components.

1. (i)-(ii)
2. (i)-(iii)
3. (i)-(iv)

4. IFRS 8 requires an undertaking to report information about:

    (i) the revenues derived from its products or services (or groups of similar products and services);

    (ii) about the countries in which it earns revenues and holds assets;

    (iii) about major clients;

    (iv) about transactions with governments.

1. (i)-(ii)
2. (i)-(iii)
3. (i)-(iv)

5. IFRS 8 requires an undertaking to give descriptive information about:

    (i) the way the operating segments were determined;

    (ii) the products and services provided by the segments;

    (iii) differences between the measurements used in reporting segment information and those used in the undertaking's financial statements;

    (iv) changes in the measurement of segment amounts from period to period;

    (v) the impact of staff development policies on the segment.

1. (i)-(ii)
2. (i)-(iii)
3. (i)-(iv)
4. (i)-(v)

6. A component of an undertaking that sells primarily or exclusively to other operating segments of the undertaking:

   (i) must be classed as an operating segment.
   (ii) must be excluded from being an operating segment.
   (iii) is included as an operating segment if the undertaking is managed that way.

7. IFRS 8 requires the following information:

   (i) Factors used to identify the undertaking's operating segments, including the basis of organisation (for example, whether management organises the undertaking around differences in products and services, geographical areas, regulatory environments, or a combination of factors and whether segments have been aggregated);
   (ii) Types of products and services from which each reportable segment derives its revenues;
   (iii) The economic environment of each segment;
   (iv) The legal structure of each segment.

   1. (i)-(ii)
   2. (i)-(iii)
   3. (i)-(iv)

8. With respect to 'interest':

   (i) Net interest revenue must be shown.
   (ii) Neither interest revenue nor interest expense is required to be shown.
   (iii) Both interest revenue and interest expense are required to be shown.
   (iv) Both interest revenue and interest expense are required to be shown, unless a majority of the segment's revenues are from interest and the chief operating decision-maker relies primarily on net interest revenue to assess the performance of the segment.

9. IFRS 8 shall apply to:

   (i) listed companies;
   (ii) any company reporting under IFRS that wishes to provide the information;
   (iii) all other companies reporting under IFRS.

   1. (i)-(ii)
   2. (i)-(iii)

10. If information is not presented to the directors in sectors:

   (i) look to the next lower level of internal segmentation that reports information along product and service lines or geographical lines;
   (ii) construct segments solely for external reporting purposes;
   (iii) segment information is not required for published financial statements.

11. If a financial report contains both the consolidated financial statements of a parent, as well as the parent's separate financial statements, segment information is required:

   (i) only in the consolidated financial statements.
   (ii) only in the parent's separate financial statements.
   (iii) both sets of financial statements.

Challenging Questions

1. An operating segment may engage in business activities for which it has yet to earn revenues, for example, start-up operations:

   (i) will be operating segments before earning revenues.
   (ii) may be operating segments before earning revenues.
   (iii) will not be operating segments before earning revenues.

2. Head office expenses:

   (i) can be allocated to segments on a reasonable basis.
   (ii) must not be allocated to segments.
   (iii) must be allocated to segments based on their turnover.

3. An undertaking's pension plans:

   (i) will be operating segments.
   (ii) may be operating segments.
   (iii) will not be operating segments.

4. Two or more operating segments may be aggregated into a single operating segment if aggregation is consistent with the core principle of IFRS 8, the segments have similar economic characteristics and the segments are similar in each of the following respects:

   (i) the nature of the products and services;
   (ii) the nature of the production processes;
   (iii) the type or class of client for their products and services;
   (iv) the methods used to distribute their products or provide their services;
   (v) if applicable, the nature of the regulatory environment, for example, banking, insurance or public utilities;
   (vi) staff numbers.

   1. (i)-(ii)
   2. (i)-(iii)
   3. (i)-(iv)
   4. (i)-(v)

5. As a percentage of sales, profits or assets, a segment should be at least:

(i)   5%
(ii) 7.5%
(iii) 10%
(iv) 15%
(v)   20%

6. The total amount of revenue that should be covered by reportable segments is at least:

(i)   50%
(ii) 60%
(iii) 70%
(iv) 75%
(v)   80%
(vi) 100%

7. Operating segments that do not meet any of the quantitative thresholds:

(i)   may be considered reportable, and separately disclosed.
(ii) must be combined and disclosed in 'all other segments'.
(iii) must be ignored.

8. If an operating segment is identified as a reportable segment in the current period, segment data for a prior period:

(i)   is not required.
(ii) is optional.
(iii) is required unless the necessary information is not available and the cost to develop it would be excessive.

9. IFRS 8 requires reconciliations of segment totals to total undertaking amounts:

(i)   of segment revenues;
(ii) reported segment profit or loss;
(iii) segment assets;
(iv) segment liabilities;
(v)   other material segment items;
(vi) staff numbers.

1. (i)-(ii)
2. (i)-(iii)
3. (i)-(iv)
4. (i)-(v)
5. (i)-(vi)

10. Information about the segments should include:

    (i) revenues from external clients;
    (ii) revenues from transactions with other operating segments of the same undertaking;
    (iii) interest revenue;
    (iv) interest expense;
    (v) depreciation and amortisation;
    (vi) material items of income and expense;
    (vii) the undertaking's interest in the profit or loss of associates and joint ventures accounted for by the equity method;
    (viii) income tax expense or income; and
    (ix) material non-cash items other than depreciation and amortisation.

    1. (i)-(ii)
    2. (i)-(iii)
    3. (i)-(iv)
    4. (i)-(v)
    5. (i)-(vi)
    6. (i)-(vii)
    7. (i)-(viii)
    8. (i)-(ix)

11. An undertaking shall report the following geographical information:

    (i) Revenues from external clients attributed to the undertaking's country of domicile and attributed to all foreign countries in total from which the undertaking derives revenues;
    (ii) Non-current assets other than financial instruments, deferred tax assets, post-employment benefit assets, and rights arising under insurance contracts located in the undertaking's country of domicile and located in all foreign countries in total in which the undertaking holds assets;
    (iii) Non-current liabilities other than financial instruments, deferred tax liabilities, post-employment benefit liabilities, and rights arising under insurance contracts located in the undertaking's country of domicile and located in all foreign countries in total in which the undertaking has liabilities.

    1. (i)-(ii)
    2. (i)-(iii)

CHAPTER 25

FINANCIAL INSTRUMENTS

INTRODUCTION

The issue of financial instruments is arguably one of the most complex subjects in financial accounting and reporting. In a sense, it is a discipline in itself. In general terms, a financial instrument is a means of raising finance and at a very basic level includes 'everyday' loans; in practice, financial instruments are wide ranging, extremely complex financial arrangements. Perhaps the fact that there are separate international accounting standards that deal with how financial instruments should be presented, recognised, measured and disclosed in an entity's statements is indicative of the potential complexity of this topic. The relevant accounting standards are:

- IAS 32 *Financial Instruments: Presentation;*
- IAS 39 *Financial Instruments: Recognition and Measurement; and*
- IFRS 7 *Financial Instruments: Disclosures.*

In general, IAS 32, IAS 39 and IFRS 7 apply to all types of financial instruments except:

- those interests in subsidiaries, associates and joint ventures that are accounted for in accordance with IAS 27 *Consolidated and Separate Financial Statements,* IAS 28 *Investment in Associates* or IAS 31 *Interests in Joint Ventures.* However IAS 32 and 39 apply in cases where under IAS 27, IAS 28, or IAS 31 such interests are to be accounted for under IAS 39 – for example, derivatives on an interest in a subsidiary, associate, or joint venture;
- employers' rights and obligations under employee benefit plans (IAS 19 *Employee Benefits);*
- contracts for contingent consideration in a business combination (IFRS 3 *Business Combinations);*
- rights and obligations under insurance contracts, except IAS 39 does apply to financial instruments that take the form of an insurance (or reinsurance) contract but that principally involve the transfer of financial risks and derivatives embedded in insurance contracts;
- financial instruments that meet the definition of own equity under IAS 32.

In broad terms, financial instruments can be categorised by 'form' depending on whether they are:

1. **Cash instruments** – these are financial instruments whose value is determined directly by markets. They can be divided into securities, which are readily transferable, and other cash instruments such as loans and deposits, where both borrower and lender have to agree on a transfer; or
2. **Derivative instruments** – these are financial instruments which derive their value from the value and characteristics of one or more underlying assets. They can be divided into exchange-traded derivatives and over-the-counter (OTC) derivatives. Examples of derivatives include:
   - *Forwards* – contracts to purchase or sell a specific quantity of a financial instrument, a commodity, or a foreign currency at a specified price determined at the outset, with delivery or settlement at a specified future date. Settlement is at maturity by actual delivery of the item specified in the contract, or by a net cash settlement.
   - *Interest rate swaps and forward rate agreements* – contracts to exchange cash flows as of a specified date or a series of specified dates based on a notional amount and fixed and floating rates.
   - *Futures* – contracts similar to forwards but with the following differences: Futures are generic exchange-traded, whereas forwards are individually tailored. Futures are generally settled through an offsetting (reversing) trade, whereas forwards are generally settled by delivery of the underlying item or cash settlement.
   - *Options* – contracts that give the purchaser the right, but not the obligation, to buy (call option) or sell (put option) a specified quantity of a particular financial instrument, commodity, or foreign currency, at a specified price (strike price), during or at a specified period of time. These can be individually written or exchange-traded. The purchaser of the option pays the seller (writer) of the option a fee (premium) to compensate the seller for the risk of payments under the option.
   - *Caps and floors* – these are contracts sometimes referred to as interest rate options. An interest rate cap will compensate the purchaser of the cap if interest rates rise above a predetermined rate (strike rate) while an interest rate floor will compensate the purchaser if rates fall below a predetermined rate.

Alternatively, financial instruments can be categorised by 'asset class' depending on whether they are:

- **Equity** – these reflect ownership of the issuing entity; or
- **Liability** – these reflect a loan the investor has made to the issuing entity. If it is debt, it can be further categorised into current (less than one year) and non-current (over one year).

Foreign exchange instruments and transactions are neither a liability nor equity and belong in their own category.

In simple terms, examples of each of the above categories are illustrated in **Table 25.1**.

Table 25.1: Categories of Financial Instruments

ASSET CLASS	Cash		FORM Derivatives	
	Securities	Other Cash	Exchange Traded	OTC
Equity	Stock	N/A	Stock options, equity futures	Stock options
Liability: non-current	Bonds	Loans	Bond futures, Options on bond futures	Interest rate caps and floors, Interest rate options
Liability: current	Bills	Deposits	Short-term interest rate futures	Forward rate agreements
Foreign exchange	N/A	Spot foreign exchange	Currency futures	Foreign exchange options, Foreign exchange swaps, Currency swaps

This chapter begins by considering the presentation of financial instruments (IAS 32), before addressing their recognition and measurement (IAS 39) and concluding with how they should be disclosed (IFRS 7). After having studied this chapter, you should be able to:

- define the terms 'financial instrument', 'financial asset', 'financial liability', 'equity instrument' and 'derivative';
- classify financial instruments as either liabilities or equity;
- explain when a financial asset or financial liability should be recognised and calculate the amounts at which they should be measured both initially and subsequently; and
- outline the main disclosures required in respect of financial instruments.

FINANCIAL INSTRUMENTS: PRESENTATION

Objective of *IAS 32*

The objective of IAS 32 is to enhance financial statement users' understanding of the significance of financial instruments to an entity's financial position, performance and cash flows by:

- clarifying the classification of a financial instrument issued by an enterprise as a liability or as equity;

- prescribing the accounting treatment for treasury shares (a company's own repurchased shares);
- prescribing strict conditions under which assets and liabilities may be offset in the statement of financial position; and
- requiring a broad range of disclosures about financial instruments, including information as to their fair values.

IAS 32 applies to those contracts to buy or sell a non-financial item that can be settled net in cash or another financial instrument, except for contracts that were entered into and continue to be held for the purpose of the receipt or delivery of a non-financial item in accordance with the entity's expected purchase, sale, or usage requirements.

Important Definitions

Financial instrument – a contract that gives rise to a financial asset of one entity and a financial liability or equity instrument of another entity.

Financial asset – any asset that is:

- cash;
- an equity instrument of another entity;
- a contractual right:
  - to receive cash or another financial asset from another entity; or
  - to exchange financial assets or financial liabilities with another entity under conditions that are potentially favourable to the entity; or
- a contract that will or may be settled in the entity's own equity instruments and is:
  - a non-derivative for which the entity is or may be obliged to receive a variable number of the entity's own equity instruments; or
  - a derivative that will or may be settled other than by the exchange of a fixed amount of cash or another financial asset for a fixed number of the entity's own equity instruments. For this purpose the entity's own equity instruments do not include instruments that are themselves contracts for the future receipt or delivery of the entity's own equity instruments.

Financial liability – any liability that is:

- a contractual obligation:
  - to deliver cash or another financial asset to another entity; or
  - to exchange financial assets or financial liabilities with another entity under conditions that are potentially unfavourable to the entity; or
- a contract that will or may be settled in the entity's own equity instruments.

Equity instrument – any contract that evidences a residual interest in the assets of an entity after deducting all of its liabilities.
Fair value – the amount for which an asset could be exchanged, or a liability settled, between knowledgeable, willing parties in an arm's length transaction.

Derivative a financial instrument:

- whose value changes in response to the change in an underlying variable such as an interest rate, commodity or security price, or index;
- that requires no initial investment, or one that is smaller than would be required for a contract with similar response to changes in market factors; and
- that is settled at a future date.

Classification as Liability or Equity

The fundamental principle of IAS 32 is that a financial instrument should be classified as either a financial liability or an equity instrument according to the substance of the contract, not its legal form. The enterprise must make the decision at the time the instrument is initially recognised. The classification is not subsequently changed based on changed circumstances.

A financial instrument is an equity instrument only if:

- the instrument includes no contractual obligation to deliver cash or another financial asset to another entity; and
- if the instrument will or may be settled in the issuer's own equity instruments, it is either:
  - a non-derivative that includes no contractual obligation for the issuer to deliver a variable number of its own equity instruments; or
  - a derivative that will be settled only by the issuer exchanging a fixed amount of cash or another financial asset for a fixed number of its own equity instruments.

Example – *preference shares*

If an enterprise issues preference shares that pay a fixed rate of dividend and that have a mandatory redemption feature at a future date, the substance is that they are a contractual obligation to deliver cash and, therefore, should be recognised as a liability. For example:

- X Limited has 200,000 10% €1 preference shares in issue. The shares are redeemable in 5 years at a premium of 25 cent;
- Top Limited entered into a zero coupon loan for €400,000. No interest is payable during the term of the loan but the loan is repayable after 5 years at €440,000.

In contrast, normal preference shares do not have a fixed maturity, and the issuer does not have a contractual obligation to make any payment. Therefore, they are equity.

Example – *issuance of fixed monetary amount of equity instruments*

A contractual right or obligation to receive or deliver a number of its own shares or other equity instruments that varies so that the fair value of the entity's own equity instruments to be received or delivered equals the fixed monetary amount of the contractual right or obligation is a financial liability.

Example – *one party has a choice over how an instrument is settled*

A contractual right or obligation to receive or deliver a number of its own shares or other equity instruments that varies so that the fair value of the entity's own equity instruments to be received or delivered equals the fixed monetary amount of the contractual right or obligation is a financial liability.

Compound Financial Instruments

Compound financial instruments have both a liability and an equity component from the issuer's perspective. IAS 32 requires that the component parts be accounted for and presented separately according to their substance based on the definitions of liability and equity. The split is made at issuance and not revised for subsequent changes in market interest rates, share prices, or other event that changes the likelihood that the conversion option will be exercised.

Example

A convertible bond contains two components. One is a financial liability, namely the issuer's contractual obligation to pay cash, and the other is an equity instrument, namely the holder's option to convert into common shares.

When the initial carrying amount of a compound financial instrument is required to be allocated to its equity and liability components, the equity component is assigned the residual amount after deducting from the fair value of the instrument as a whole the amount separately determined for the liability component.

Interest, dividends, gains, and losses relating to an instrument classified as a liability should be reported in the statement of comprehensive income. This means that dividend payments on preferred shares classified as liabilities are treated as expenses. On the other hand, distributions (such as dividends) to holders of a financial instrument classified as equity should be charged directly against equity, not against earnings.

Example

On 1 January 2008, TILT issued four million €1 bonds at par which are redeemable on 31 December 2016 at €2 per €1 bond. No interest is payable on the bonds during the nine years from 1 January 2008 to 31 December 2016. The implicit rate of interest in the bond is 8%. Bond holders can elect to convert their bond holdings on 31 December 2016 into €1 ordinary shares on the basis of one €1 ordinary share for every one €1 bond held. The market price of each €1 ordinary share in TILT was €1.50 on 1 January 2008 and market analysts expect the share price to increase by approximately 10 cent per annum.

Requirement   Prepare the journal entries to record the issue of the bonds, together with the finance cost, in the financial statements of TILT for the year ended 31 December 2008.

Solution

Bond: The bonds should be regarded as debt instruments on the basis that they are not legally shares and carry an obligation to transfer economic benefits at redemption. Therefore, they should be disclosed in liabilities. The finance cost should be allocated to each accounting period at a constant rate of the amount outstanding.

DR		Bank	€4,000,000	
	CR	Non-current liabilities		€4,000,000

Finance Cost The implicit rate is 8%, therefore the interest charge for y/e 31/12/08 is: 8% x€4,000,000 = €320,000.

DR		SCI – finance costs	€320,000	
	CR	Non-current liabilities		€320,000

Treasury Shares

The cost of an entity's own equity instruments that it has reacquired ('treasury shares') is deducted from equity. The gain or loss is not recognised on the purchase, sale, issue, or cancellation of treasury shares. Treasury shares may be acquired and held by the entity or by other members of the consolidated group. Consideration paid or received is recognised directly in equity.

Offsetting

IAS 32 prescribes rules for the offsetting of financial assets and financial liabilities. It specifies that a financial asset and a financial liability should be offset and the net amount reported when an enterprise:

- has a legally enforceable right to set off the amounts; and
- intends either to settle on a net basis, or to realise the asset and settle the liability simultaneously.

Costs of Issuing or Reacquiring Equity Instruments

Costs of issuing or reacquiring equity instruments (other than in a business combination) are accounted for as a deduction from equity, net of any related income tax benefit.

Example

Explain whether each of the following meet the definition of a financial instrument in accordance with IAS 32:

(a) Issue of ordinary share capital;
(b) Issue of debt;
(c) Sale of goods on credit; and
(d) Purchase of goods on credit.

Solution

(a) Issue of ordinary share capital represents an equity instrument since the share-holders own a financial asset and the company has an equity instrument in the form of new share capital.
(b) Issue of debt creates a contractual obligation between the company and the lender for the debt to be repaid in the future. Therefore the company has a financial liability and the lender has a financial asset.
(c) Sale of goods on credit creates a contractual obligation between the customer and the company. The customer has a financial liability and the company has a financial asset.
(d) Purchase of goods on credit creates a contractual obligation on the part of the company to pay for the goods. Therefore the company has a financial liability and the supplier has a financial asset.

FINANCIAL INSTRUMENTS: RECOGNITION AND MEASUREMENT

Classification as Liability or Equity

Note IAS 39 does not address accounting for equity instruments issued by the reporting enterprise but it does deal with accounting for financial liabilities. Therefore the classification of an instrument as a liability or equity in accordance with IAS 32 is critical.

Classification of Financial Assets

IAS 39 requires financial assets to be classified into one of the following categories which are used to determine how a particular financial asset is recognised and measured in the financial statements.

1. **Financial assets at fair value through profit or loss** This category has two subcategories:
   - *Designated* – this includes any financial asset that is designated on initial recognition as one to be measured at fair value with fair value changes in profit or loss; or
   - *Held for trading* – this includes financial assets that are held for trading. All derivatives (except those designated hedging instruments) and financial assets acquired or held for the purpose of selling in the short term or for which there is a recent pattern of short-term profit taking are held for trading.
2. **Available-for-sale financial assets** (AFS) are any non-derivative financial assets designated on initial recognition as available for sale. AFS assets are measured at fair value in the statement of financial position. Fair value changes on AFS assets are recognised directly in equity, through the statement of changes in equity, except for interest on AFS assets (which is recognised in income on an effective yield basis), impairment losses, and (for interest-bearing AFS debt instruments) foreign exchange gains or losses. The cumulative gain or loss that was recognised in equity is recognised in profit or loss when an available-for-sale financial asset is derecognised.
3. **Loans and receivables** are non-derivative financial assets with fixed or determinable payments, originated or acquired, that are not quoted in an active market, not held for trading, and not designated on initial recognition as assets at fair value through profit or loss or as available-for-sale. Loans and receivables, for which the holder may not recover substantially all of its initial investment, other than because of credit deterioration, should be classified as available-for-sale. Loans and receivables are measured at amortised cost.
4. **Held-to-maturity investments** are non-derivative financial assets with fixed or determinable payments that an entity intends and is able to hold to maturity and that do not meet the definition of loans and receivables and are not designated on initial recognition as assets at fair value through profit or loss or as available for sale. Held-to-maturity investments are measured at amortised cost. If an entity sells a held-to-maturity investment other than in insignificant amounts or as a consequence of a non-recurring, isolated event beyond its control that could not be reasonably anticipated, all of its other held-to-maturity investments must be reclassified as available-for-sale for the current and next two financial reporting years.

Classification of Financial Liabilities

IAS 39 recognises two classes of financial liabilities:

1. **Financial liabilities at fair value through profit or loss**   This category has two subcategories:

    - *Designated* – a financial liability that is designated by the entity as a liability at fair value through profit or loss upon initial recognition; or
    - *Held for trading* – a financial liability classified as held for trading, such as an obligation for securities borrowed in a short sale, which have to be returned in the future.

2. **Other financial liabilities**   measured at amortised cost using the effective interest method.

Initial Recognition

IAS 39 requires recognition of a financial asset or a financial liability when, and only when, the entity becomes a party to the contractual provisions of the instrument, subject to the following provisions in respect of regular way purchases.

A regular way purchase or sale of financial assets is recognised and derecognised using either trade date or settlement date accounting. The method used is to be applied consistently for all purchases and sales of financial assets that belong to the same category of financial asset as defined in IAS 39 (note that for this purpose assets held for trading form a different category from assets designated at fair value through profit or loss). The choice of method is an accounting policy.

IAS 39 requires that all financial assets and all financial liabilities be recognised on the statement of financial position, including all derivatives. Historically, in many parts of the world, derivatives have not been recognised on company statements of financial position. The argument has been that, at the time the derivative contract was entered into, there was no amount of cash or other assets paid. Zero cost justified non-recognition, notwithstanding that as time passes and the value of the underlying variable (rate, price, or index) changes, the derivative has a positive (asset) or negative (liability) value.

Initial Measurement

Initially, financial assets and liabilities should be measured at fair value (including transaction costs, for assets and liabilities not measured at fair value through profit or loss).

Measurement Subsequent to Initial Recognition

Subsequently, financial assets and liabilities (including derivatives) should be measured at fair value, with the following exceptions:

- Loans and receivables, held-to-maturity investments, and non-derivative financial liabilities should be measured at amortised cost using the effective interest method;
- Investments in equity instruments with no reliable fair value measurement (and derivatives indexed to such equity instruments) should be measured at cost;

- Financial assets and liabilities that are designated as a hedged item or hedging instrument are subject to measurement under the hedge accounting requirements of the IAS 39; and
- Financial liabilities that arise when a transfer of a financial asset does not qualify for derecognition, or that are accounted for using the continuing-involvement method, are subject to particular measurement requirements.

Fair value is the amount for which an asset could be exchanged, or a liability settled, between knowledgeable, willing parties in an arm's length transaction. IAS 39 provides a hierarchy to be used in determining the fair value for a financial instrument:

- Quoted market prices in an active market are the best evidence of fair value and should be used, where they exist, to measure the financial instrument;
- If a market for a financial instrument is not active, an entity establishes fair value by using a valuation technique that makes maximum use of market inputs and includes recent arm's length market transactions, reference to the current fair value of another instrument that is substantially the same, discounted cash flow analysis, and option pricing models. An acceptable valuation technique incorporates all factors that market participants would consider in setting a price and is consistent with accepted economic methodologies for pricing financial instruments;
- If there is no active market for an equity instrument and the range of reasonable fair values is significant and these estimates cannot be made reliably, then an entity must measure the equity instrument at cost less impairment.

Amortised cost is calculated using the effective interest method. The effective interest rate is the rate that exactly discounts estimated future cash payments or receipts through the expected life of the financial instrument to the net carrying amount of the financial asset or liability. Financial assets that are not carried at fair value though profit and loss are subject to an impairment test. If expected life cannot be determined reliably, then the contractual life is used.

Note   IAS 39 permits entities to designate, at the time of acquisition or issuance, any financial asset or financial liability to be measured at fair value, with value changes recognised in profit or loss. This option is available even if the financial asset or financial liability would ordinarily, by its nature, be measured at amortised cost – but only if fair value can be reliably measured. Once an instrument is put in the fair-value-through-profit-and-loss category, it cannot be reclassified out.

Note   IAS 39 permits entities to designate, at the time of acquisition, any loan or receivable as available for sale, in which case it is measured at fair value with changes in fair value recognised in equity.

Example

Simple Minds Limited, a company which prepares its financial statements to 31 December each year, issued €750,000 of 3% loan stock on 1 January 2008 at a discount of 5%. Issue costs amounted to €13,175, and interest is payable on 31 December each year. The loan stock is redeemable on 31 December 2011 at a premium of 10%. The effective rate of interest is 7.25%.

Requirement
(a) At what amount should the loan stock be measured on 1 January 2008?
(b) Calculate the amounts at which the loan stock should be recorded in the company's statement of financial position on 31 December 2008, 2009, 2010 and 2011.

Solution

(a)   €

Proceeds   (€750,000 x 95%)   712,500

Issue costs   (13,175)

                                                           699,325

(b)

Year	Balance on 1 January	Interest @ 7.25%	Paid	Balance on 31 December
	€	€	€	€
2008	699,325	50,701	(22,500)	727,526
2009	727,526	52,746	(22,500)	757,772
2010	757,772	54,938	(22,500)	790,210
2011	790,210	57,290	(847,500)	0
		215,675		

Impairment

A financial asset or group of assets is impaired, and impairment losses are recognised, only if there is objective evidence as a result of one or more events that occurred after the initial recognition of the asset. An entity is required to assess at each reporting date whether there is any objective evidence of impairment. If any such evidence exists, the entity is required to do a detailed impairment calculation to determine whether an impairment loss should be recognised. The amount of the loss is measured as the difference between the asset's carrying amount and the present value of estimated cash flows discounted at the financial asset's original effective interest rate.

Assets that are individually assessed and for which no impairment exists are grouped with financial assets with similar credit risk statistics and collectively assessed for impairment.

If, in a subsequent period, the amount of the impairment loss relating to a financial asset carried at amortised cost or a debt instrument carried as available-for-sale decreases due to an event occurring after the impairment was originally recognised, the previously recognised impairment loss is reversed through profit and loss. Impairments relating to investments in available-for-sale equity instruments are not reversed.

Derecognition of a Financial Asset

The basic premise for the derecognition model in IAS 39 is to determine whether the asset under consideration for derecognition is:

- an asset in its entirety;
- specifically identified cash flows from an asset;
- a fully proportionate share of the cash flows from an asset; or
- a fully proportionate share of specifically identified cash flows from a financial asset.

Once the asset under consideration for derecognition has been determined, an assessment is made as to whether the asset has been transferred and, if so, whether the transfer of that asset is subsequently eligible for derecognition. An asset is transferred if either the entity has transferred the contractual rights to receive the cash flows, or the entity has retained the contractual rights to receive the cash flows from the asset, but has assumed a contractual obligation to pass those cash flows on under an arrangement that meets the following three conditions:

- the entity has no obligation to pay amounts to the eventual recipient unless it collects equivalent amounts on the original asset;
- the entity is prohibited from selling or pledging the original asset (other than as security to the eventual recipient); and
- the entity has an obligation to remit those cash flows without material delay.

Once an entity has determined that the asset has been transferred, it then determines whether or not it has transferred substantially all of the risks and rewards of ownership of the asset. If substantially all the risks and rewards have been transferred, the asset is derecognised. If substantially all the risks and rewards have been retained, derecognition of the asset is precluded.

If the entity has neither retained nor transferred substantially all of the risks and rewards of the asset, then the entity must assess whether it has relinquished control of the asset or not. If the entity does not control the asset then derecognition is appropriate; however if the entity has retained control of the asset, then the entity continues to recognise the asset to the extent to which it has a continuing involvement in the asset.

These various derecognition steps are summarised below in **Figure 25.1**.

Figure 25.1:   Derecognition of a Financial Asset

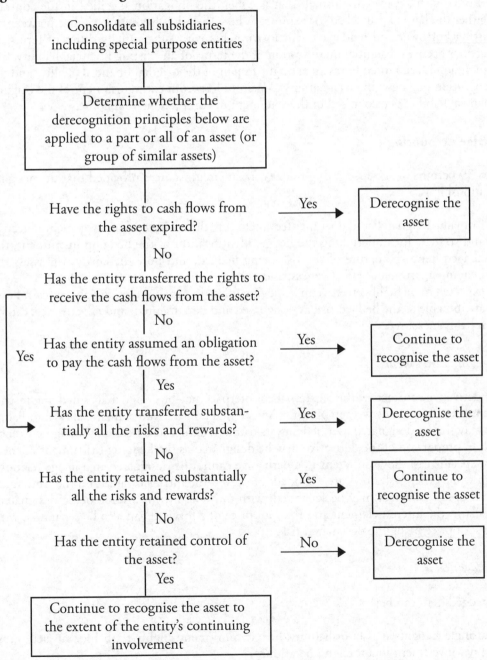

Derecognition of a Financial Liability

A financial liability should be removed from the statement of financial position when, and only when, it is extinguished, that is, when the obligation specified in the contract is either discharged, cancelled, or expired. Where there has been an exchange between an existing borrower and lender of debt instruments with substantially different terms, or there has been a substantial modification of the terms of an existing financial liability, this transaction is accounted for as an extinguishment of the original financial liability and the recognition of a new financial liability. A gain or loss from extinguishment of the original financial liability is recognised in the statement of comprehensive income.

Hedge Accounting

IAS 39 permits hedge accounting under certain circumstances provided that the hedging relationship is:

- formally designated and documented, including the entity's risk management objective and strategy for undertaking the hedge, identification of the hedging instrument, the hedged item, the nature of the risk being hedged, and how the entity will assess the hedging instrument's effectiveness; and
- expected to be highly effective in achieving offsetting changes in fair value or cash flows attributable to the hedged risk as designated and documented, and effectiveness can be reliably measured.

Hedging Instruments

All derivative contracts with an external counterpart may be designated as hedging instruments except for some written options. An external non-derivative financial asset or liability may not be designated as a hedging instrument except as a hedge of foreign currency risk. A proportion of the derivative may be designated as the hedging instrument. Generally, specific cash flows inherent in a derivative cannot be designated in a hedge relationship while other cash flows are excluded. However, the intrinsic value and the time value of an option contract may be separated, with only the intrinsic value being designated. Similarly, the interest element and the spot price of a forward can also be separated, with the spot price being the designated risk.

Hedged Items

A hedged item can be:

- a single recognised asset or liability, firm commitment, highly probable transaction, or a net investment in a foreign operation;
- a group of assets, liabilities, firm commitments, highly probable forecast transactions, or net investments in foreign operations with similar risk characteristics;

- a held-to-maturity investment for foreign currency or credit risk (but not for interest risk or prepayment risk);
- a portion of the cash flows or fair value of a financial asset or financial liability; or
- a non-financial item for foreign currency risk only or the risk of changes in fair value of the entire item.

Effectiveness

IAS 39 requires hedge effectiveness to be assessed both prospectively and retrospectively. To qualify for hedge accounting at the inception of a hedge and, at a minimum, at each reporting date, the changes in the fair value or cash flows of the hedged item attributable to the hedged risk must be expected to be highly effective in offsetting the changes in the fair value or cash flows of the hedging instrument on a prospective basis, and on a retrospective basis where actual results are within a range of 80% to 125%.

All hedge ineffectiveness is recognised immediately in the statement of comprehensive income (including ineffectiveness within the 80% to 125% window).

Main Categories of Hedges

(a) A fair value hedge is a hedge of the exposure to changes in fair value of a recognised asset or liability or a previously unrecognised firm commitment to buy or sell an asset at a fixed price or an identified portion of such an asset, liability or firm commitment, that is attributable to a particular risk and could affect profit or loss. The gain or loss from the change in fair value of the hedging instrument is recognised immediately in profit or loss. At the same time the carrying amount of the hedged item is adjusted for the corresponding gain or loss with respect to the hedged risk, which is also recognised immediately in net profit or loss.

(b) A cash flow hedge is a hedge of the exposure to variability in cash flows that (i) is attributable to a particular risk associated with a recognised asset or liability (such as all or some future interest payments on variable rate debt) or a highly probable forecast transaction and (ii) could affect profit or loss.

The portion of the gain or loss on the hedging instrument that is determined to be an effective hedge is recognised directly in equity and recycled to the statement of comprehensive income when the hedged cash transaction affects profit or loss.

If a hedge of a forecast transaction subsequently results in the recognition of a financial asset or a financial liability, any gain or loss on the hedging instrument that was previously recognised directly in equity is 'recycled' into profit or loss in the same period(s) in which the financial asset or liability affects profit or loss.

If a hedge of a forecast transaction subsequently results in the recognition of a non-financial asset or non-financial liability, then the entity has an accounting policy option that must be applied to all such hedges of forecast transactions:

- **Same accounting as for recognition of a financial asset or financial liability** – any gain or loss on the hedging instrument that was previously recognised directly in equity is 'recycled' into profit or loss in the same period(s) in which the non-financial asset or liability affects profit or loss;

- **'Basis adjustment' of the acquired non-financial asset or liability** – the gain or loss on the hedging instrument that was previously recognised directly in equity is removed from equity and is included in the initial cost or other carrying amount of the acquired non-financial asset or liability.

Discontinuation of Hedge Accounting

Hedge accounting must be discontinued prospectively if:

- the hedging instrument expires or is sold, terminated, or exercised;
- the hedge no longer meets the hedge accounting criteria – for example it is no longer effective;
- for cash flow hedges the forecast transaction is no longer expected to occur; or
- the entity revokes the hedge designation.

For the purpose of measuring the carrying amount of the hedged item when fair value hedge accounting ceases, a revised effective interest rate is calculated.

If hedge accounting ceases for a cash flow hedge relationship because the forecast transaction is no longer expected to occur, gains and losses deferred in equity must be taken to the statement of comprehensive income immediately. If the transaction is still expected to occur and the hedge relationship ceases, the amounts accumulated in equity will be retained in equity until the hedged item affects profit or loss.

If a hedged financial instrument that is measured at amortised cost has been adjusted for the gain or loss attributable to the hedged risk in a fair value hedge, this adjustment is amortised to profit or loss based on a recalculated effective interest rate on this date such that the adjustment is fully amortised by the maturity of the instrument. Amortisation may begin as soon as an adjustment exists and must begin no later than when the hedged item ceases to be adjusted for changes in its fair value attributable to the risks being hedged.

FINANCIAL INSTRUMENTS: DISCLOSURES

IFRS 7 superseded IAS 30 *Disclosures in the Financial Statements of Banks and Similar Financial Institutions* and the disclosure requirements of IAS 32 *Financial Instruments: Presentation* and Disclosure. However the presentation requirements of IAS 32 remain unchanged. In March 2009, the IASB revised IFRS 7 to:

- improve the disclosure requirements regarding fair value measurements; and
- reinforce existing principles for disclosures about the liquidity risk associated with financial instruments.

The amendments formed part of the IASB's response to the financial crisis and sought to address the G20's desire to improve transparency and enhance accounting guidance. The changes also reflected discussions by the IASB's Expert Advisory Panel on measuring and disclosing fair values of financial instruments when markets are no longer active, bringing the disclosure requirements of IFRS 7 more closely into line with US standards. The amendments to IFRS 7 require entities to provide additional disclosures about the relative reliability of fair value measurements and introduce a three-level hierarchy for fair value measurement disclosures:

1. Quoted prices (unadjusted) in active markets for identical assets or liabilities (Level 1);
2. Inputs other than quoted prices included within Level 1 that are observable for the asset or liability, either directly (i.e. as prices) or indirectly (i.e. derived from prices) (Level 2); and
3. Inputs for the asset or liability that are not based on observable market data (unobservable inputs) (Level 3).

In addition, the amendments seek to clarify and enhance the existing requirements for the disclosure of liquidity risk. This is aimed at ensuring that the information disclosed enables users of an entity's financial statements to evaluate the nature and extent of liquidity risk arising from financial instruments and how the entity manages that risk.

The amendments to IFRS 7 apply for annual periods beginning on or after 1 January 2009. However, an entity will not be required to provide comparative disclosures in the first year of application.

Disclosure Requirements of IFRS 7

An entity must group its financial instruments into classes of similar instruments and, when disclosures are required, make disclosures by class. The two main categories of disclosures required by IFRS 7 are information about the:

- significance of financial instruments; and
- nature and extent of risks arising from financial instruments.

Information about the Significance of Financial Instruments

Statement of Financial Position

- Disclosure of the significance of financial instruments for an entity's financial position and performance. This includes disclosures for each of the following categories:
  - Financial assets measured at fair value through profit and loss, showing separately those held for trading and those designated at initial recognition,
  - Held-to-maturity investments,
  - Loans and receivables,
  - Available-for-sale assets,
  - Financial liabilities at fair value through profit and loss, showing separately those held for trading and those designated at initial recognition,
  - Financial liabilities measured at amortised cost;

- Special disclosures about financial assets and financial liabilities designated to be measured at fair value through profit and loss, including disclosures about credit risk and market risk and changes in fair values;
- Reclassifications of financial instruments from fair value to amortised cost or vice versa;
- Disclosures about derecognitions, including transfers of financial assets for which derecogntion accounting is not permitted by IAS 39;
- Information about financial assets pledged as collateral and about financial or non-financial assets held as collateral;
- Reconciliation of the allowance account for credit losses (bad debts);
- Information about compound financial instruments with multiple embedded derivatives; and
- Breaches of terms of loan agreements.

Statement of Comprehensive Income and Equity

- Items of income, expense, gains, and losses, with separate disclosure of gains and losses from:
- Financial assets measured at fair value through profit and loss, showing separately those held for trading and those designated at initial recognition,
  - Held-to-maturity investments,
  - Loans and receivables,
  - Available-for-sale assets,
  - Financial liabilities measured at fair value through profit and loss, showing separately those held for trading and those designated at initial recognition,
  - Financial liabilities measured at amortised cost;
  - Interest income and interest expense for those financial instruments that are not measured at fair value through profit and loss;
- Fee income and expense;
- Amount of impairment losses on financial assets; and
- Interest income on impaired financial assets.

Other Disclosures

- Accounting policies for financial instruments;
- Information about hedge accounting, including:
  - description of each hedge, hedging instrument, and fair values of those instruments, and nature of risks being hedged,
  - for cash flow hedges, the periods in which the cash flows are expected to occur, when they are expected to enter into the determination of profit or loss, and a description of any forecast transaction for which hedge accounting had previously been used but which is no longer expected to occur,

 – if a gain or loss on a hedging instrument in a cash flow hedge has been recognised directly in equity, an entity should disclose the following:
   – the amount that was so recognised in equity during the period,
   – the amount that was removed from equity and included in profit or loss for the period, and
   – the amount that was removed from equity during the period and included in the initial measurement of the acquisition cost or other carrying amount of a non-financial asset or non-financial liability in a hedged highly probable forecast transaction;
 – for fair value hedges, information about the fair value changes of the hedging instrument and the hedged item; and
 – hedge ineffectiveness recognised in profit and loss (separately for cash flow hedges and hedges of a net investment in a foreign operation);
• Information about the fair values of each class of financial asset and financial liability, along with:
   – Comparable carrying amounts,
   – Description of how fair value was determined, and
   – Detailed information if fair value cannot be reliably measured.

Nature and Extent of Exposure to Risks Arising from Financial Instruments

Qualitative Disclosures

These describe:

• Risk exposures for each type of financial instrument;
• Management's objectives, policies, and processes for managing those risks; and
• Changes from the prior period.

Quantitative Disclosures

These provide information about the extent to which the entity is exposed to risk, based on information provided internally to the entity's key management personnel, and include:

• Summary quantitative data about exposure to each risk at the reporting date;
• Disclosures about credit risk, liquidity risk, and market risk as further described below; and
• Concentrations of risk.

Credit Risk   Maximum amount of exposure (before deducting the value of collateral), description of collateral, information about credit quality of financial assets that are neither past due nor impaired, and information about credit quality of financial assets whose terms have been renegotiated;

- For financial assets that are past due or impaired, analytical disclosures are required; and
- Information about collateral or other credit enhancements obtained or called.

Liquidity Risk
- A maturity analysis of financial liabilities; and
- Description of approach to risk management.

Market Risk   This is the risk that the fair value or cash flows of a financial instrument will fluctuate due to changes in market prices. Market risk reflects interest rate risk, currency risk, and other price risks. Disclosures about market risk include:

- A sensitivity analysis of each type of market risk to which the entity is exposed; and
- IFRS 7 provides that if an entity prepares a sensitivity analysis for management purposes that reflects interdependencies of more than one component of market risk (for instance, interest risk and foreign currency risk combined), it may disclose that analysis instead of a separate sensitivity analysis for each type of market risk.

IFRS 7 includes appendices of mandatory and non-mandatory application guidance.

CONCLUSION

The area of financial instruments is an important and complex subject in financial accounting and reporting. A financial instrument is a means of raising finance. While at a very basic level it includes 'everyday' loans, many financial instruments are wide ranging, extremely complicated arrangements. This chapter began by considering the presentation of financial instruments (IAS 32), before addressing their recognition and measurement (IAS 39) and concluding with how they should be disclosed (IFRS 7). After having studied this chapter, you should be able to:

- define the terms 'financial instrument', 'financial asset', 'financial liability', 'equity instrument' and 'derivative';
- calculate the amounts at which a financial asset or financial liability should be measured both initially and subsequently; and
- give an account of the main disclosures required in respect of financial instruments.

QUESTIONS

Self-test Questions

1. Define the terms 'financial instrument', 'financial asset', 'financial liability', 'equity instrument' and 'derivative'.
2. Explain the difference between financial liabilities and equity.

3. Explain how preference shares should be accounted for in accordance with IAS 32.
4. Identify and explain the four categories of financial asset outlined in IAS 39.
5. Explain the terms 'credit risk', 'liquidity risk' and 'market risk' in the context of IFRS 7, and outline the main disclosure required in relation to each of these risks.

Review Questions

(See APPENDIX ONE for Suggested Solutions to Review Questions.)

Question 1

On 1 January 2004, VERTIGO issued 30,000,000 €1 preference shares at par, incurring issue costs of €300,000. The dividend payable on the preference shares was 4% per annum, payable on 31 December each year. The redemption date for the preference shares was 31 December 2008 at a price of €1.35 per share. The effective interest cost of the preference shares is 10%. The statement of financial position of VERTIGO on 30 December 2008, the day prior to the redemption of the preferences shares, was as follows:

	€'000
€1 ordinary share capital	300,000
Redeemable preference shares	40,500
Share premium account	77,000
Retained earnings	182,500
	600,000

Requirement
(a) Calculate the finance cost in respect of the preference shares for EACH of the five years ended 31 December 2004 to 2008.
(b) Assuming the redemption occurred, prepare the capital and reserves section of the statement of financial position of the VERTIGO Group as at 31 December 2008.

Question 2

On 1 January 2008, after discussions with your firm, MIRROR issued 9,000,000 6% debentures of €1 each at an issue price of 95 cent for every €1 debenture. The direct costs associated with the issue amounted to €76,400. MIRROR will redeem the debentures on 31 December 2011 at a premium of 10 cent for every €1 debenture purchased. The effective rate of interest on the debenture issue is 10%.

Requirement   With respect to the debenture issue, calculate the interest to be charged in the statement of comprehensive income of MIRROR for each of the four years ending 31 December 2008 to 2011 and the amount to be shown in the statement of financial position at each of the above reporting dates.

Challenging Questions

Question 1

On 1 January 2008, BEROL Limited (BEROL) raised 500,000 €1 non-equity shares at a premium of €0.10 per share, incurring issue costs of €10,000. The shares have a fixed cumulative dividend of 5% per annum payable half yearly, and are redeemable on 31 December 2012 at a premium of 20%. The implicit rate of interest is 6.544%.

Requirement   Calculate the finance cost to be charged in the statement of comprehensive income of BEROL in each of the five years to 31 December 2012, and the carrying value at the end of each of the five years.

Question 2

You are a trainee chartered accountant with STAND & DELIVER. The Financial Accountant of HOOD Limited (HOOD), an audit client of your firm, has requested your advice on a number of issues prior to the commencement of the audit of the financial statements for the year ended 31 December 2008.

Issue 1   On 1 December 2008, HOOD purchased equipment for $140,000, when the exchange rate was €1 equals $5. At 31 December 2008 the exchange rate was €1 equals $4.8. The account was settled on 28 February 2009 when €1 equals $5.4.

Issue 2   In September 2008, HOOD signed an agreement with TUCK Limited (TUCK), a finance company, to factor its trade receivables. Under the terms of the agreement, TUCK assumes legal title and responsibility for the collection of all HOOD's trade receivables. At the end of each month, HOOD sells 90% of its trade receivables to TUCK, with the remaining 10%, less a deduction for finance and administration costs, being paid to HOOD only when the cash is received. Any trade receivables that do not pay TUCK within ten weeks of the debt being sold are transferred back to HOOD and HOOD refunds the cash advanced by TUCK.

Issue 3   During 2008, one of the directors of HOOD, Mr Sherwood, purchased additional shares in HOOD in the market. Another director, Mr Forest, who was also a partner in a firm of chartered surveyors, was paid €100,000 for property valuation work carried out by the surveying company.

Issue 4   On 1 January 2008, HOOD issued four million €1 bonds at par, redeemable on 31 December 2016 at €2 per €1 bond. No interest is payable during the nine years from 1 January 2008 to 31 December 2016. The implicit rate of interest in the bond is 8%. Bond holders can elect to convert their bond holdings on 31 December 2016 into €1 ordinary shares on the basis of one €1 ordinary share for every one €1 bond held. The market price of each €1 ordinary share in HOOD was €1.50 on 1 January 2008 and the share price is expected to increase by approximately 10 cent per annum.

Requirement   Prepare a memorandum that explains how the above issues should be accounted for in the financial statements of HOOD for the year ended 31 December 2008.

SECTION FIVE

ACCOUNTING FOR BUSINESS COMBINATIONS

CHAPTER 26

BUSINESS COMBINATIONS AND CONSOLIDATED FINANCIAL STATEMENTS

INTRODUCTION

For a variety of legal, tax and other reasons, undertakings often choose to conduct their activities not through a single legal entity but through several undertakings under the ultimate control of the parent undertaking of the group. For this reason, the accounts of an individual parent company by themselves do not present a full picture of its economic activities or financial position. Consolidated financial statements are therefore required in order to reflect the extended business unit that conducts the activities under the control of the parent undertaking. With respect to the preparation of consolidated financial statements, the key accounting standards are:

- IAS 27 *Consolidated and Separate Financial Statements* (see Section Five, Chapter 26);
- IFRS 3 *Business Combinations* (see Section Five, Chapter 26);
- IAS 28 *Investments in Associates* (see Section Five, Chapter 29); and
- IAS 31 *Interests in Joint Ventures* (see Section Five, Chapter 30);

Other relevant accounting standards include:

- IFRS 5 *Non-current Assets Held for Sale and Discontinued Operations* (see Section Four, Chapter 20);
- IAS 7 *Statement of Cash Flows* (see Section Three, Chapter 21 and Section Five, Chapter 33);
- IAS 21 *The Effects of Changes in Foreign Exchange Rates* (see Section Five, Chapter 31);
- IAS 29 *Financial Reporting in Hyperinflationary Economies* (see Section Five, Chapter 31);
- IAS 36 *Impairment of Assets* (see Section Two, Chapter 10); and
- IAS 38 *Intangible Assets* (see Section Two, Chapter 9).

In broad terms, the study of consolidated financial statements involves:

1. The preparation of a consolidated statement of financial position (Chapter 27);
2. The preparation of a consolidated statement of comprehensive income (Chapter 28);
3. Accounting for associates (Chapter 29);
4. Accounting for joint ventures (Chapter 30);
5. Dealing with foreign companies (Chapter 31);
6. The disposal of subsidiaries (Chapter 32); and
7. The preparation of a consolidated statement of cash flows (Chapter 33).

After having studied this chapter, you should understand the key principles that govern the preparation of consolidated financial statements and accounting for business combinations.

TYPES OF INTEREST

The method of preparing group financial statements depends upon how an interest in a company has been defined. As a rough rule of thumb, a company can have four basic types of interest in another company. These are summarised in **Table 26.1.**

Table 26.1: Types of Company Interest

Subsidiary Interest	Associate Interest	Joint Venture	Investment Interest
> 50% ownership	20%-50%	3 broad types	< 20%
IAS 27 and IFRS 3	IAS 28	IAS 31	IAS 39
Full consolidation.	Equity method.	Proportionate consolidation or Equity method.	Initially at fair value.
Imagine that you and a friend are purchasing a car and, for reasons best known to yourselves, your friend buys the tyres and you purchase the rest.	P only owns 30% of the equity shares of another company. It does not have effective control over any more than 30%.	Forms: Jointly controlled operations;	A separate set of consolidated financial statements is not required for such an interest.
If somebody asked you who owned the car, you would probably reply that you do; but, as a quiet aside, you	Then only 30% of the results of an associate company are reflected in P's financial statements.	Jointly controlled assets; and Jointly controlled entities.	

Subsidiary Interest	Associate Interest	Joint Venture	Investment Interest
would mention that your friend owns the tyres.			
Similarly, if P owns (say) 95% of the shares in a company, then we prepare a set of group accounts as if the ownership is actually 100% and deduct an amount in the group accounts to reflect the other 5% that P does not own.			
The reason for this approach is that, while P effectively has full control over the company (subsidiary), it does not have full legal title to 100% of the shares. The 5% shareholders are known as the non-controlling interest.			

This chapter, together with Chapter 27 and Chapter 28, focuses on accounting for subsidiaries, with associates and joint ventures being covered primarily in Chapter 29 and Chapter 30 respectively. Generally speaking, with respect to accounting for subsidiaries, the company owning the shares is referred to as the 'parent' (P) and the 'group' represents the P and any subsidiaries. (Note: For ownership purposes preference shares are not important.)

KEY TERMS

1. **Consolidated financial statements** – the financial statements of a group presented as those of a single economic entity.
2. **Control** – the power to govern the accounting and financial policies so as to obtain benefits from its activities.
3. **Non-controlling interest (NCI)** – the portion of the net results and net assets of a subsidiary attributable to interests not owned directly or indirectly by the parent (previously referred to as minority interest).
4. **Parent** – an entity that has one or more subsidiaries.
5. **Subsidiary** – an entity, including one that is unincorporated, that is controlled by another (the parent).

INTERNATIONAL CONVERGENCE

The International Accounting Standards Board (IASB) announced in July 2001 that it would undertake a project on Business Combinations as part of its initial agenda. The project's objective was to improve the quality of, and seek international convergence on, the accounting for business combinations and for goodwill and intangible assets. The project has a number of phases. The first phase led to the issue of IFRS 3 *Business Combinations* (replacing IAS 22 *Business Combinations*), and revisions to IAS 36 *Impairment of Assets* and IAS 38 *Intangible Assets*, in March 2004.

As part of the second phase, IAS 27 and IFRS 3 were revised in January 2008. This marked the culmination of a joint project with the Financial Accounting Standards Board designed to improve financial reporting and international convergence. The requirements of IFRS 3 (2008) come into effect for those business combinations for which the acquisition date is on or after the beginning of the first annual reporting period beginning on or after 1 July 2009 (early adoption is permitted). Before addressing the requirements of IAS 27 and IFRS 3 in detail, it is useful to highlight the key changes arising out of the 2008 revision of these two standards.

IAS 27(2008) – WHAT HAS CHANGED?

Acquisitions and disposals that do not result in a change of control

Changes in a parent's ownership interest in a subsidiary that do not result in a loss of control are accounted for within shareholders' equity as transactions with owners acting in their capacity as owners. No gain or loss is recognised on such transactions and goodwill is not re-measured. Any difference between the change in the non-controlling interest and the fair value of the consideration paid or received is recognised directly in equity and attributed to the owners of the parent.

Loss of Control

A parent can lose control of a subsidiary through a sale or distribution, or through some other transaction or event in which it takes no part (e.g. expropriation or the subsidiary being placed in administration or bankruptcy). When control is lost, the parent derecognises all assets, liabilities and non-controlling interest at their carrying amount. Any retained interest in the former subsidiary is recognised at its fair value at the date control is lost. A gain or loss arising on the loss of control should be measured as the difference between: (a) the aggregate of the fair value of the proceeds, if any, from the transaction or event that resulted in the loss of control and the fair value of any investment remaining in the former subsidiary at the date control is lost; and (b) the aggregate of the parent's interest in the carrying amount in the consolidated financial statements of the former subsidiary's net assets immediately before control is lost, including the parent's share of gains or losses related to the former subsidiary recognised in consolidated equity. Any such gain or loss is recognised in profit or loss.

Attribution of Profit or Loss to Non-controlling Interests

The revised IAS 27 requires an entity to attribute their share of total comprehensive income to the non-controlling interest even if this results in the non-controlling interest having a deficit balance.

Loss of Significant Influence or Joint Control

Amendments to IAS 28 and IAS 31 extend the treatment required for loss of control to these standards. Thus, when an investor loses significant influence over an associate, it derecognises that associate and recognises in profit or loss the difference between the sum of the proceeds received and any retained interest, and the carrying amount of the investment in the associate at the date significant influence is lost. A similar treatment is required when an investor loses joint control over a jointly controlled entity.

These issues are addressed again below in the main section dealing with IAS 27.

IFRS 3 (2008) – WHAT HAS CHANGED?

Acquisition-related Costs

In what is likely to be an unpopular move with preparers, the IASB has determined that costs incurred in an acquisition are period costs. This means that all acquisition-related costs (e.g. finder's fees; advisory, legal, accounting, valuation, and other professional or consulting fees; and general administrative costs, including the costs of maintaining an internal acquisitions department) are to be recognised as period expenses in accordance with the appropriate IFRS. Costs incurred to issue debt or equity securities will be recognised in accordance with IAS 39 *Financial Instruments: Recognition and Measurement*. Under IFRS 3 (2004) directly related acquisition costs could be included as part of the cost of acquisition.

Step Acquisitions

Changes to IAS 27 and IFRS 3 work together with the effect that a business combination leading to acquisition accounting applies only at the point where control is achieved. This has a number of implications:

- Where the acquirer has a pre-existing equity interest in the entity acquired: that equity interest may be accounted for as a financial instrument in accordance with IAS 39, as an associate or a joint venture using the equity method in accordance with IAS 28 or IAS 31, or as a jointly controlled entity using the proportionate consolidation method in accordance with IAS 31. If the acquirer increases its equity interest sufficiently to achieve control (described in IFRS 3 (2008) as a 'business combination achieved in stages'), it must re-measure its previously-held equity interest in the acquiree at acquisition-date fair value and recognise the resulting gain or loss, if any, in profit or loss.
- Once control is achieved: all other increases and decreases in ownership interests are treated as transactions among equity holders and reported within equity. Goodwill does not arise on any increase, and no gain or loss is recognised on any decrease.

Goodwill

Goodwill is measured as the difference between:

- the aggregate of:
  - the acquisition-date fair value of the consideration transferred;
  - the amount of any non-controlling interest in the entity acquired (see below for two measurement options); and
  - in a business combination achieved in stages, the acquisition-date fair value of the acquirer's previously-held equity interest in the entity acquired; and
- the net of the acquisition-date amounts of the identifiable assets acquired and the liabilities assumed, both measured in accordance with IFRS 3.

If the difference above is positive, the acquirer should recognise the goodwill as an asset. If the difference above is negative, the resulting gain is recognised as a bargain purchase in profit or loss.

Non-controlling Interests (previously referred to as Minority Interests)

IFRS 3 has an explicit option, available on a transaction-by-transaction basis, to measure any non-controlling interest in the entity acquired either at fair value (new method) or at the non-controlling interest's proportionate share of the net identifiable assets of the entity acquired (old method). The latter treatment corresponds to the measurement basis in IFRS 3 (2004). For the purpose of measuring non-controlling interest at fair value, it may be possible to determine the acquisition-date fair value on the basis of market prices for the equity shares not held by the acquirer. When a market price for the equity shares is not available because the shares are not publicly-traded, the acquirer must measure the fair value of the non-controlling interest using other valuation techniques.

It has long been argued (mainly by academics) that the traditional (old) method of calculating goodwill only recognises the goodwill acquired by the parent, and is based on the parent's ownership interest rather than the goodwill controlled by the parent. In other words, any goodwill attributable to the non-controlling interest is not recognised. Consequently, the new method has been introduced. However, the problem with the new method is that goodwill (or what is subsumed within it) is a very complex item. If asked to describe goodwill, traditional aspects such as product reputation, skilled workforce, site location, market share, and so on, all spring to mind. These are perfectly valid, but in an acquisition, goodwill may contain other factors such as a premium to acquire control, and the value of synergies (cost savings or higher profits) when the subsidiary is integrated within the rest of the group. While the non-controlling interest can legitimately lay claim to its share of the more traditional aspects of goodwill, it is unlikely to benefit from the other aspects, as they relate to the ability to control the subsidiary.

Thus, it may not be appropriate to value the non-controlling interest's share of goodwill proportionately with that of the parent. The revised IFRS 3 seeks to resolve this problem (under the new method) by requiring the non-controlling interest to be measured at its 'fair value', rather than at 'its proportionate share of the (fair value of the) acquiree's identifiable net assets'. The difference between these two values is, effectively, the non-controlling interest's share of goodwill which may or may not be proportionate to the parent's share of goodwill. The revised IFRS 3 recognises that there may be many ways of calculating the fair value of the non-controlling interest and does not go into detail on this matter, but it recognises that the market price of the subsidiary's shares prior to the acquisition may be a reasonable basis on which to value the shareholding of the non-controlling interest.

Contingent Consideration

IFRS 3 requires the consideration for the acquisition to be measured at fair value at the acquisition date. This includes the fair value of any contingent consideration payable. IFRS 3 permits very few subsequent changes to this measurement and only as a result of additional information about facts and circumstances that existed at the acquisition date. All other changes (e.g. changes resulting from events after the acquisition date such as the acquiree meeting an earnings target, reaching a specified share price, or meeting a milestone on a research and development project) are recognised in profit or loss. While this fair value approach is consistent with the way other forms of consideration are valued, it is not easy to apply in practice as the definition is largely hypothetical. It is highly unlikely that the acquisition date liability for contingent consideration could be or would be settled by 'willing parties in an arm's length transaction'. In an exam question, the acquisition date fair value (or how to calculate it) of any contingent consideration would be given. The payment of contingent consideration may be in the form of equity or a liability (issuing a debt instrument or cash) and should be recorded as such under the rules of IAS 32, *Financial Instruments: Presentation*, or other applicable standard. The previous version of

IFRS 3 required contingent consideration to be accounted for only if it was *probable* that it would become payable.

Re-acquired Rights

Where the acquirer and acquiree were parties to a pre-existing relationship (e.g. the acquirer had granted the acquiree a right to use its intellectual property), there are two implications for acquisition accounting: firstly, where the terms of any contract are not market terms, a gain or loss is recognised and the purchase consideration adjusted to reflect a payment or receipt for the non-market terms; and, secondly, an intangible asset (being the rights re-acquired) is recognised at fair value and amortised over the contract term.

Reassessments

IFRS 3 clarifies that an entity must classify and designate all contractual arrangements at the acquisition date with two exceptions: (i) leases, and (ii) insurance contracts. In other words, the acquirer applies its accounting policies and makes the choices available to it as if it had acquired those contractual relationships outside of the business combination. The existing treatment applied by the acquiree for classification of leases and insurance is applied by the acquirer and therefore is not reassessed. Reassessing assets and liabilities is particularly relevant when acquiring financial assets and financial liabilities in a business combination. Consideration will be required as to how financial instruments are classified, whether embedded derivatives exist (which the acquiree may not have previously recognised) and whether hedge accounting performed by the acquiree will continue to be highly effective by the acquirer.

These issues are addressed again below in the main section dealing with IFRS 3.

Note   The examples and questions included in this text apply IAS 27 (2008) and IFRS 3 (2008), together with the changes introduced by IAS 1 (revised 2007), regardless of the reporting date.

IAS 27 *CONSOLIDATED AND SEPARATE FINANCIAL STATEMENTS*

As noted above, IAS 27 *Consolidated and Separate Financial Statements* was initially revised in December 2003, and then more recently in January 2008. IAS 27 applies to the preparation and presentation of consolidated financial statements for a group of entities under the control of a parent. It also applies to accounting for investments in subsidiaries, jointly controlled entities and associates in the separate financial statements of a parent. IAS 27 does *not* deal with:

(a) methods of business combinations (see IFRS 3 below);
(b) accounting for investments in associates (see IAS 28, Chapter 29);
(c) accounting for investments in joint ventures (see IAS 31, Chapter 30).

Separate Financial Statements

Where separate financial statements are prepared, investments in subsidiaries should be:

- carried at cost; or
- accounted for as available for sale financial assets as per IAS 39 *Financial Instruments: Recognition and Measurement.*

The same accounting should be applied for each category of investments.

Investments in subsidiaries, jointly controlled entities and associates that are accounted for in accordance with IAS 39 in the consolidated financial statements should be accounted for in the same way in the investor's separate financial statements.

Disclosures

The following disclosures should be made:

(a) The fact that a subsidiary is not consolidated;
(b) Summarised financial information of subsidiaries, either individually or in groups, that are not consolidated, including the amounts of total assets, liabilities, revenues and profit or loss;
(c) The nature of the relationship between the parent and a subsidiary when the parent does not own, directly or indirectly through subsidiaries, more than 50% of the voting power;
(d) The reasons why ownership, directly or indirectly, of more than 50% voting power does not give control;
(e) The reporting date of a subsidiary, if different from the parent, and reason for using it;
(f) The nature and extent of any significant restrictions on the ability of subsidiaries to transfer funds to the parent via cash dividends or to repay loans or advances.

When separate financial statements are prepared for a parent that is permitted not to prepare consolidated financial statements, those separate financial statements should disclose:

(a) the fact that the financial statements are separate; that the exemption from consolidation has been used; the name and country of incorporation or residence of the entity publishing consolidated financial statements in accordance with IFRSs; the address where consolidated financial statements are available;
(b) a list of significant investments in subsidiaries, jointly controlled entities and associates, including the name, country of incorporation or residence, proportion of ownership interest and, if different, proportion of voting power held; and
(c) a description of the method used to account for the investments listed in (a).

When a parent, venturer or investor in associate prepares separate financial statements, those statements must disclose:

(a) the fact that the statements are separate and reasons why prepared, if not by law;
(b) a list of significant investments in subsidiaries, jointly controlled entities and associates, including the name, country of incorporation or residence, proportion of ownership interest and, if different, proportion of voting power held; and
(c) a description of the method used to account for the investments listed under (b).

Consolidated Financial Statements

A parent should present consolidated financial statements in which it consolidates its investment in subsidiaries (those entities that it controls), unless certain conditions are met allowing it not to prepare consolidated financial statements (see below). Control is presumed to exist when the parent owns over 50% of the voting power of an enterprise unless, in exceptional circumstances, it can be clearly demonstrated that such ownership does not constitute control. Control also exists where there is:

(a) power over more than 50% of voting rights via an agreement with other investors;
(b) power to govern the financial and operating policies under statute or agreement;
(c) power to appoint or remove the majority of members of the board;
(d) power to cast the majority of votes at meetings of the board of directors.

In making this judgement, consideration should also be given to the existence and effect of potential voting rights held by another entity, e.g. share warrants, call options, convertible shares/debt etc.

However, a parent need not present consolidated financial statements if and only if:

- the parent itself is a 100% owned subsidiary or is partially owned by another entity whose owners have been informed and do not object to the parent not preparing consolidated financial statements;
- the parent's debt or equity instruments are not traded publicly;
- the parent did not file nor is it in the process of filing its financial statements with a securities commission for the purpose of going on the public market;
- the ultimate or any intermediate parent of the parent publishes consolidated financial statements available for public use that comply with IFR Ss.

A subsidiary should be excluded from consolidation when:

(a) control is only temporary as expected to be disposed in the near future (12 months); and
(b) management is actively seeking a buyer.

Such subsidiaries should be accounted for in accordance with IAS 39 and IFRS 5. A subsidiary is *not* excluded just because its activities are dissimilar from those of the group nor if there are severe restrictions that impair its ability to transfer funds to the parent. Control must be lost for exclusion to occur. Better information is provided by full consolidation, backed up by segment reporting, under IAS 14 *Segment Reporting/IFRS 8 Operating Segments*.

Disclosures

The following disclosures are required in consolidated financial statements:

- The nature of the relationship between the parent and a subsidiary when the parent does not own, directly or indirectly through subsidiaries, more than half of the voting power;
- The reasons why the ownership, directly or indirectly through subsidiaries, of more than half of the voting or potential voting power of an investee does not constitute control;
- The reporting date of the financial statements of a subsidiary when such financial statements are used to prepare consolidated financial statements and are as of a reporting date or for a period that is different from that of the parent, and the reason for using a different reporting date or period; and
- The nature and extent of any significant restrictions on the ability of subsidiaries to transfer funds to the parent in the form of cash dividends or to repay loans or advances.

Consolidation Procedures

In brood terms, the parent and its subsidiaries are combined on a line-by-line basis by adding together like items of assets, liabilities, income and expenses. More common exceptions to this involve equity and inter company balance. The following steps are then taken:

(a) The parent's investment in each subsidiary and the parent's portion of equity of each subsidiary are eliminated;
(b) Non-controlling interests in the net income of subsidiaries are identified and adjusted against group income in order to arrive at the net income attributable to the parent;
(c) Non-controlling interests in the net assets are identified and presented separately from liabilities. Non-controlling interests in net assets consist of the:
  (i) amount at the date of the original combination as per IFRS 3; and
  (ii) non-controlling interest's share of movements in equity since combination.

When potential voting rights exist, the proportions of profit or loss and changes in equity allocated to the parent and non-controlling interests are determined on the basis of present ownership interests and do not reflect the possible exercise or conversion of potential voting rights.

Taxes should be computed in accordance with IAS 12 *Income Taxes*.

Intragroup balances and transactions should be eliminated in full. Unrealised losses should also be eliminated unless cost cannot be recovered. Unrealised profits on inventory and non-current assets should be eliminated in full and any timing differences dealt with in accordance with IAS 12.

The financial statements should be drawn up to the same reporting date for all entities in the group. However, if financial statements are drawn up to different dates, adjustments should be made for the effects of significant transactions that occur between those dates. In any case the difference between reporting dates should be no longer than three months.

Consistency dictates that the length of the reporting periods should be the same from period to period.

Uniform accounting policies must be adopted for like transactions and appropriate adjustments must be made in preparing the consolidated financial statements.

The subsidiary should be included in the consolidated financial statements from the date of acquisition, i.e. the date control is effectively transferred to the buyer, in accordance with IFRS 3. The results of subsidiaries disposed are included in the consolidated statement of comprehensive income until the date of disposal, i.e. date on which control ceases. The difference between the proceeds from disposal and carrying amount should be included in the statement of comprehensive income at the date of disposal. That includes the cumulative amount of any exchange differences that relate to the subsidiary recognised in equity in accordance with IAS 21.

An investment should be accounted for, in accordance with IAS 39, from the date it ceases to fall within the definition of a subsidiary and does not become an associate under IAS 28. The carrying amount is regarded as cost thereafter.

Non-controlling interests must be presented within equity but separate from the parent shareholders' equity. Non-controlling interests in the income should also be separately presented. The losses may exceed the non-controlling interest in the equity and this excess is charged to the majority except to the extent that the minority has a binding obligation and is able to make good the losses. If the subsidiary subsequently reports profits, the majority interest is allocated all such profits until the non controlling interest's share of losses has been recovered.

If the subsidiary has cumulative preference shares held by a non controlling interest and classified as equity the parent computes its share of profits or losses after adjusting for the dividends on such shares, whether or not the dividends are declared.

Partial Disposal of an Investment in a Subsidiary

The accounting treatment depends on whether control is retained or lost:

- Partial disposal of an investment in a subsidiary while control is retained – this is accounted for as an equity transaction with owners, and gain or loss is not recognised;
- Partial disposal of an investment in a subsidiary that results in loss of control – this triggers re-measurement of the residual holding to fair value. Any difference between fair value and carrying amount is a gain or loss on the disposal, recognised in profit or loss. Thereafter, apply IAS 28, IAS 31, or IAS 39, as appropriate, to the remaining holding.

SIC 12 Consolidation – Special Purpose Entities

SIC 12, which relates to IAS 27, focuses upon substance over form.

Issue

An entity may be created to accomplish a narrow and well-defined objective, e.g. to effect a lease, research and development activities or a securitisation. Such a special purpose entity (SPE) may take the form of a corporation, trust, partnership or unincorporated entity. SPEs often include strict limits on their decision-making powers.

The sponsor frequently transfers assets to the SPE, obtains the right to use assets held by the SPE or performs services for the SPE while other parties (capital providers) may provide the funding to the SPE. An entity that engages in transactions with an SPE may in substance control the SPE.

A beneficial interest in an SPE may take the form of a debt instrument, an equity instrument, a participation right, a residual interest or a lease. In most cases the sponsor retains a significant beneficial interest in the SPE's activities, even though it may own little or none of the SPE's equity.

As IAS 27 does not provide explicit guidance on the consolidation of SPEs, the issue is under what circumstances an entity should consolidate an SPE. SIC 12 does not apply to post-employment benefit plans or equity compensation plans.

Consensus

An SPE should be consolidated when the substance of the relationship between an entity and an SPE indicates that the SPE is controlled by that entity. In the context of an SPE, control may arise through the predetermination of the activities of the SPE (autopilot) or otherwise. Control may exist when less than 50% of the voting power rests with the reporting entity. Judgement is required to decide whether or not control exists in the context of all relevant factors.

The following circumstances may indicate a relationship in which an entity controls an SPE and consequently should consolidate the SPE:

(a) In substance, the activities of the SPE are being conducted on behalf of the entity according to the specific business needs so that the entity obtains benefits from the SPE's operation;

(b) In substance, the entity has the decision-making powers to obtain the majority of the benefits of the activities of the SPE or, by setting up an 'autopilot' mechanism, the entity has delegated these decision-making powers;

(c) In substance, the entity has rights to obtain the majority of the benefits of the SPE and therefore may be exposed to risks incident to the activities of the SPE; or

(d) In substance, the entity retains the majority of the residual or ownership risks related to the SPE or its assets in order to obtain benefits from its activities.

Predetermination of the ongoing activities of an SPE by an entity would not represent the type of restrictions referred to in IAS 27.

Indicators of Control over an SPE

The examples (a) to (d) are intended to indicate types of circumstances that should be considered in evaluating a particular arrangement in the light of the substance over form principle.

(a) **Activities** – The activities are, in substance, being conducted on behalf of the reporting entity and include situations where the SPE is principally engaged in providing a source of long-term capital to the entity or it provides a supply of goods and services consistent with the entity's major operations. Economic dependence of an entity on the reporting enterprise does not, by itself, lead to control.

(b) **Decision-making** – The reporting entity, in substance, has the decision-making powers to control or obtain control of the SPE or its assets, including certain decision-making powers coming into existence after the formation of the SPE. Such decision-making powers may have been delegated by establishing an 'autopilot' mechanism. Examples include the power to unilaterally dissolve an SPE, the power of change to the SPE's charter or the power to veto proposed changes of the SPE's charter.

(c) **Benefits** – The reporting entity, in substance, has rights to obtain a majority of the benefits of the SPE's activities through a statute, contract, agreement etc. Such rights may be indicators of control when they are specified in favour of an entity that is engaged in transactions with an SPE and that enterprise stands to gain those benefits from the financial performance of the SPE. Examples are rights to a majority of any economic benefits or rights to majority residual interests such as a liquidation.

(d) **Risks** – Indication of control may be obtained by evaluating the risks of each party engaging in transactions with an SPE. This could be a guarantee to outside investors providing most of the capital to the SPE. Examples are capital providers do not have a significant interest in the underlying net assets of the SPE; capital providers do not have rights to future economic benefits of the SPE; capital providers are not substantively exposed to the inherent risks of the underlying net assets or operations of the SPE or in substance; capital providers receive mainly consideration equivalent to a lender's return through a debt or equity interest.

IFRS 3 *BUSINESS COMBINATIONS*

As noted above, IAS 22 *Business Combinations* was replaced by IFRS 3 (2004).

Reasons for Replacing IAS 22

IAS 22 *Business Combinations* permitted two methods of accounting – the pooling of interests and the acquisition method. Although IAS 22 restricted the use of pooling, analysts indicated that two methods impaired comparability and created incentives for structuring those transactions to achieve a particular accounting result. This combined with the prohibition of pooling by the USA, Canada and Australia prompted the IASB to seek harmonisation. In addition, various jurisdictions dealt differently with goodwill and IAS

22 permitted two methods of applying the acquisition method – benchmark (combination of fair value of acquirer's ownership interest and pre-acquisition carrying amounts for non-controlling interests) or allowed alternative to measure all assets at fair value. The IASB seeks to ensure that similar transactions are not accounted for in dissimilar ways as this impairs their usefulness. Consequently, the publication of IFRS 3 in 2004 was an attempt to improve the quality of and seek international convergence on accounting for business combinations, including the:

- method of accounting for business combinations;
- initial measurement of identifiable net assets acquired;
- recognition of liabilities for terminating the activities of an acquiree;
- treatment of any excess of acquirer's interest in fair values of identifiable net assets acquired; and
- accounting for goodwill and intangible assets.

The 2008 revisions to IFRS 3 result in a high degree of convergence between IASs/IFRSs and US Generally Accepted Accounting Practice (GAAP) in these areas; although some differences do remain. For example, under US GAAP, the full goodwill method is required (rather than permitted). There are also differences in: scope; the definition of control; how fair values, contingencies and employee benefit obligations are measured; and disclosures.

Main Features of IFRS 3 (2008)

IFRS 3 deals with the accounting for business combinations and the ongoing accounting for goodwill acquired in business combinations. A business combination is a transaction or event in which an acquirer obtains control of one or more businesses. A business is defined as an integrated set of activities and assets that is capable of being conducted and managed for the purpose of providing a return directly to investors or other owners, members or participants. In simple terms, a business combination is the bringing together of separate entities into one reporting entity. The agreement may be structured in a number of ways for legal, taxation or other reasons, and may result in the creation of a parent-subsidiary relationship in which the acquirer is the parent and the acquiree the subsidiary. It may result in the purchase of net assets, including goodwill; but not the purchase of the entity itself as this will not result in a parent-subsidiary relationship.

Where a business combination occurs, the acquirer should apply IFRS 3 to its consolidated statements. In its own accounts it records the investment under IAS 27 *Consolidated and Separate Financial Statements* as an investment in a subsidiary. IFRS 3:

(a) requires all business combinations to adopt the acquisition method (previously referred to as the purchase method in IFRS 3 (2004)). The pooling/uniting of interests method is prohibited;

(b) requires an acquirer to be identified for every business combination;

(c) requires an acquirer to measure the cost as the aggregate of fair values of assets given at date of acquisition in exchange for control of acquiree;

(d) requires an acquirer to separately recognise the acquiree's net assets at the date of acquisition and satisfy the following criteria:

  (i) Other than intangibles, assets must have probability of future economic benefits and be measured reliably,
  (ii) For liabilities, must be probable that an outflow of benefits will occur and be measured reliably,
  (iii) For intangible assets, the fair value can be reliably measured, and
  (iv) For contingent liabilities, the fair value can be measured reliably;

(e) requires identifiable net assets to be measured at fair value at acquisition date;
(f) requires goodwill to be recorded as an asset, as excess of cost over acquirer's interest in net fair value of identifiable assets acquired;
(g) prohibits amortisation of goodwill and instead requires annual impairment review or more frequently if circumstances dictate;
(h) requires an acquirer to reassess identifiable assets if net fair value exceeds the cost of business combination. Any excess still remaining after the reassessment must be recognised in the statement of comprehensive income;
(i) requires disclosure of:
  (i) business combinations that occurred in the period,
  (ii) business combinations that occurred after the reporting date but before authorisation, and
  (iii) certain business combinations of previous periods; and
(j) requires disclosure of information that enables users to evaluate changes in the carrying amount of goodwill.

IFRS 3 does not apply to:

• business combinations in which separate entities or businesses are brought together to form a joint venture;
• business combinations involving entities or businesses under common control. These occur where the same party ultimately controls all of the combining entities both before and after the date of business combination. A group of individuals are regarded as controlling an entity if, as a result of contractual arrangements, they collectively have the power to govern its financial and operating policies. These are outside the scope of the IFRS. The extent of non-controlling interests is not relevant to determining whether or not the entity is under common control; and
• business combinations in which separate entities or businesses are brought together to form a reporting entity by contract alone without the obtaining of an ownership interest.

Accounting for Business Combinations

All business combinations should be accounted for under the acquisition method. This method recognises that the acquirer acquires the net assets and that the measurement of the acquirer's own net assets are not affected by the transaction. The following steps should be undertaken in applying the acquisition method: identify the acquirer; determine the acquisition date; recognise and measure the identifiable assets acquired, the liabilities assumed and any non-controlling interest (previously referred to as minority interest); and recognise and measure goodwill or gain from a bargain purchase.

Identify the Acquirer

An acquirer should be identified for all business combinations. The acquirer is the entity that obtains control of the other combining entity. The acquisition method assumes an acquirer. Control is the power to govern the financial and operating policies of an entity in order to obtain benefits. Normally this requires more than 50% of an entity's voting rights. Even if this is not the case the following could result in an acquirer:

(a) Power over more than 50% of voting rights via agreement with other investors; or
(b) Power to govern the financial and operating policies of the other entity under statute or an agreement; or
(c) Power to appoint or remove the majority of the board of directors; or
(d) Power to cast a majority of votes at meetings of the board of directors.

Although it may be difficult to identify an acquirer there are usually indications that one exists. For example:

- If the fair value of one of the combining entities is significantly greater than the other;
- If there is an exchange of voting ordinary shares for cash; and
- If the management of one dominates the selection of the management team of the combined entity.

In a business combination via exchange of equity, the entity that issues the equity shares is usually the acquirer. However, all pertinent facts should be considered in determining which of the combining entities has the power to govern the operating and financial policies of the other entity. In some business combinations, e.g. reverse acquisitions, the acquirer is the entity whose equity interests have been acquired. That occurs when a private operating entity arranges to have itself acquired by a non-operating or dormant public entity as a means of obtaining an inventory exchange listing. Although legally the public entity is the parent the circumstances could indicate that a smaller entity acquires a larger entity.

Determine the Acquisition Date

This is the date on which the acquirer obtains control of the acquiree.

Recognise and Measure the Identifiable Assets Acquired, the Liabilities Assumed and any Non-controlling Interest

The acquirer, at acquisition date, should allocate the cost of a business combination by recognising the acquiree's identifiable net assets at their acquisition-date fair value. Any difference between the cost of the combination and the acquirer's interest in the net fair value of identifiable assets should be accounted for as goodwill. However, non-current assets held for sale and discontinued operations are valued at fair value less costs to sell (as per IFRS 5).

The acquirer should recognise separately the acquiree's identifiable net assets at acquisition date only if they satisfy the following criteria:

(a) For an asset other than an intangible asset, it is probable that any associated future economic benefits will flow to the acquirer and it can be measured reliably;
(b) For a liability other than contingencies, it is probable that an outflow of economic benefits will occur and its fair value can be reliably measured;
(c) For intangible assets, their fair value can be measured reliably; and
(d) For contingent liabilities, its fair value can be reliably measured.

The acquirer's statement of comprehensive income should incorporate the acquiree's post-acquisition profits and losses in the statement of comprehensive income. Expenses should be based on the cost of the business combination, e.g. depreciation should be based on fair values of those depreciable assets at the acquisition date, i.e. based on their cost to the acquirer.

It is not necessary for a transaction to be closed or finalised at law before the acquirer effectively obtains control. All pertinent facts should be considered in assessing when the acquirer has effectively obtained control.

Any non-controlling interest in the acquiree should be stated at their proportion of the net fair values of those items.

Acquiree's Identifiable Assets and Liabilities Only the identifiable net assets that existed at acquisition date and satisfy the recognition criteria in (a) to (d) above may be recognised separately by the acquirer. Thus:

• the acquirer should recognise liabilities for terminating an acquiree only when the acquiree has an existing liability for restructuring recognised via IAS 37 *Provisions, Contingent Liabilities and Contingent Assets*; and
• the acquirer may not recognise liabilities for future losses.

A payment that an entity is contractually required to make, for example, to its employees or suppliers in the event it is acquired in a business combination is a present obligation of the entity that is regarded as a contingent liability until it becomes probable that a business combination will occur. The identifiable net assets might include some never recognised previously, e.g. tax benefit due to acquiree's tax losses when acquirer has adequate future taxable profits against which the losses can be applied.

Acquiree's Intangible Assets An intangible asset of the acquiree may only be recognised if it meets the definition of an intangible asset under IAS 38 and fair value can be measured reliably. A non-monetary asset must be identifiable and be separate from goodwill. Thus this can only happen if it:

• is separable, i.e. capable of being separated and sold, transferred, licensed, rented or exchanged; or
• arises from contractual or other legal rights

Intangible Assets Separate from Goodwill   These must be non-monetary assets without physical substance and be separate from goodwill, i.e. must arise from contractual or other legal rights. The following examples are not intended to be exhaustive.

A. *Marketing Related Intangible Assets*

   (i) Trademarks, trade names, service marks, collective marks and certification marks – these may be protected legally through registration, continuous use in commerce or by other means. A trademark can still be recognised provided it is separable from goodwill.
   (ii) Internet domain name – a unique alphanumeric name used to identify a particular internet address.
   (iii) Trade dress (unique colour, share or package design).
   (iv) Newspaper mastheads.
   (v) Non-competition agreements.

B. *Customer Related Intangible Assets*

   (i) Customer lists – not arising from contractual or other legal rights but they are valuable and are frequently leased or exchanged. These are not a separable asset if there are agreements prohibiting an entity from selling, leasing or exchanging information about its customers.
   (ii) Order or production backlog – must meet the contractual-legal criterion even if these are cancellable.
   (iii) Customer contracts and the related customer relationships – arise if an entity establishes relationships with customers through contractual rights.
   (iv) Non-contractual customer relationships – an intangible asset meets the separability criterion.

C. *Artistic Related Intangible Assets*

   These normally arise from contractual or legal rights such as copyrights. These include:
   (i) Plays, operas and ballets;
   (ii) Books, magazines, newspapers and other literary works;
   (iii) Musical works;
   (iv) Pictures and photographs;
   (v) Video material including films, music videos, television programmes.

D. *Contract Based Intangible Assets*

   (i) Licensing, royalty agreements
   (ii) Advertising contracts
   (iii) Lease agreements
   (iv) Construction permits
   (v) Franchise agreements
   (vi) Operating and broadcasting rights
   (vii) Drilling rights for water, air and minerals
   (viii) Servicing and mortgage service contracts
   (ix) Employment contracts

E. *Technology Based Intangible Assets*

    (i) Patented technology   (iv) Databases
   (ii) Computer software and mask works   (v) Trade secrets, e.g. recipes
 (iii) Unpatented technology

Acquiree's Contingent Liabilities These may only be recognised if their fair values can be measured reliably. If not, they should be disclosed in accordance with IAS 37. After initial recognition the acquirer should measure recognised contingent liabilities at the higher of:

- the amount that would be recognised per IAS 37; and
- the initial amount less cumulative amortisation per IAS 18.

The above does not apply to contracts under IAS 39. However, loan commitments excluded from IAS 39 are accounted for as contingent liabilities, if not, probable outflow will be required to settle the obligation or it cannot be reliably measured.

Non-controlling Interest As explained earlier, IFRS 3 allows an accounting policy choice, available on a transaction by transaction basis, to measure non-controlling interest at either:

- the non-controlling interest's proportionate share of the identifiable net assets of the acquiree (old method);
- fair value (also referred to as the full goodwill method) (new method).

Example (Old Method)

Parent pays €100m for 80% of Subsidiary which has net assets with a fair value of €75m. Goodwill of €40m (€100m − (80% x €75m)) would be recognised, and the non-controlling interests would be €15m (20% x €75m).

		€m
Cost of acquisition		100
Fail value of net assets	€75m	
Group share of net assets	80%	(60)
Goodwill		40

Hypothetically, if we assume that purchasing 100% of Subsidiary would have cost proportionately more, the consideration would have been €125m (€100m/80%) and goodwill would then be €50m (€125m - €75m) and there would be no non-controlling interests. This demonstrates that, where a non-controlling interest exists, the traditional consolidation method only records the parent's share of the goodwill, and the non-controlling interest is carried at its proportionate share of the fair value of the subsidiary's net assets (which excludes any attributable goodwill). The argument goes that as we consolidate the whole of a subsidiary's other assets (and liabilities), why should goodwill be any different? After all, it is an asset!

Example (New Method)

Progressing the above example, assuming that the value of the goodwill of the non-controlling interest is proportionate to that of the parent, consolidated goodwill of €50m would be recognised (this includes both the controlling (€40m) and the non-controlling interest (€10m) in goodwill) and the non-controlling interest would be €25m (€15m + €10m attributed goodwill). In effect, consolidated goodwill and the non-controlling interest are 'grossed up' by the non-controlling interest's share of goodwill (€10m, in this case). Although this may seem new, it is in fact an extension of the methodology in IAS 36 Impairment of Assets when calculating the impairment of goodwill of a cash-generating unit where there is a non-controlling interest (see Chapter 10).

Example (Both Methods)

P pays €800 to purchase 80% of the shares of S. The fair value of 100% of S's identifiable net assets is €600.

If P elects to measure non-controlling interests at their proportionate interest in net assets of S of €120 (20% x €600), the consolidated financial statements show goodwill of €320 (€800 + €120 – €600).

If P elects to measure non-controlling interests at fair value and determines that fair value to be €185, then goodwill of €385 is recognised (€800 + €185 – €600). The fair value of the 20% non-controlling interest in S will not necessarily be proportionate to the price paid by P for its 80%, primarily due to control premium or discount.

Recognise and Measure Goodwill or Gain from a Bargain Purchase

Goodwill is measured as the difference between:

- the aggregate of:
  - the acquisition-date fair value of the consideration transferred;
  - the amount of any non-controlling interest in the entity acquired (see above for two measurement options); and
  - in a business combination achieved in stages, the acquisition-date fair value of the acquirer's previously-held equity interest in the entity acquired; and
- the net of the acquisition-date amounts of the identifiable assets acquired and the liabilities assumed, both measured in accordance with IFRS 3.

If the difference above is positive, the acquirer should recognise the goodwill as an asset.

If the difference above is negative, the resulting gain is recognised as a bargain purchase in profit or loss.

Goodwill represents future economic benefits that are not capable of being individually identified and separately recognised. Goodwill is essentially the residual cost after allocating fair value to identifiable net assets taken over. After initial recognition, the acquirer should measure goodwill at cost less accumulated impairment losses. It should not be amortised but instead tested annually for impairment, or more frequently, if events indicate that it might be impaired, in accordance with IAS 36.

The following arguments are often put forward in support of amortising goodwill:

- Amortisation is a method of allocating the cost of goodwill over the periods it is consumed, and is consistent with the approach taken to other intangible and tangible non-current assets that do not have indefinite useful lives.
- Acquired goodwill is an asset that is consumed over time and replaced with internally generated goodwill. Amortisation therefore ensures that the acquired goodwill is written off and no internally generated goodwill is recognised in its place. This is consistent with the general prohibition on recognising goodwill generated internally by an entity.
- The useful life of acquired goodwill cannot be predicted with a satisfactory level of reliability, nor can the pattern in which that goodwill is consumed be known. Therefore, amortisation over an arbitrary period of time is the only practical solution to an intractable problem.

However, the useful life of acquired goodwill and the pattern in which it diminishes generally are not possible to predict, yet its amortisation depends on such predictions. As a result, the amount amortised in any given period can at best be described as an arbitrary estimate of the consumption of acquired goodwill during that period. In addition, both anecdotal and research evidence supports the view that the amortisation charge for goodwill has little, if any, information value for most users of financial statements, and that an impairment-only model provides users with more useful information. Critics have argued that goodwill may not decline in value and that, even if it does, the arbitrary amounts recorded periodically as goodwill amortisation are unlikely to reflect that decline. In this view, goodwill amortisation simply adds noise to earnings, thereby reducing their usefulness to investors. Accounting standard setters, in contrast, have until recently maintained that goodwill is likely to be a wasting asset in most circumstances and that recording goodwill amortisation makes reported earnings more useful to investors by reflecting its decline in value.

Empirical studies have examined the extent to which variation in inventory prices is explained by earnings before goodwill amortisation and by reported earnings, which includes goodwill amortisation. These studies find evidence consistent with the criticisms of the previous accounting rules for goodwill, i.e. earnings before goodwill amortisation explain more of the variation in share prices than reported earnings and, for each year, the difference in explanatory power is statistically significant. Moreover, the findings strongly suggest that goodwill amortisation merely adds noise to reported earnings. Overall, the results indicate that the recently adopted reporting rules for purchased goodwill are likely to increase the usefulness of earnings as a summary indicator of share value.

Costs of a Business Combination

The acquirer should measure the cost of a business combination as the aggregate of the fair values of assets given, liabilities incurred and equity issued by the acquirer in exchange for control of the acquiree. The published price at the date of exchange of a quoted equity provides the best evidence of the instrument's fair value. Other evidence should only be used in rare circumstances when the published price is unreliable and where that other evidence is a more reliable measure, e.g. thinness of the market. One example would be to use an estimate of their proportional interest in the fair value of the acquirer or by reference to their proportionate interest in the fair value of the acquiree obtained, whichever is more clearly evident. In any event, all aspects of the combination should be considered.

The acquisition date is the date when the acquirer effectively obtains control of the acquiree. When this is achieved through a single transaction the date of exchange coincides with the acquisition date. However if acquired in stages:

(a) The cost is the aggregate of individual transactions; and
(b) The date of exchange is the date of each exchange transaction whereas the acquisition date is the date on which acquirer obtains control.

When settlement of any part of the cost is deferred, the fair value is determined by discounting the amounts payable to their present value at the date of exchange.

The consideration for an acquisition includes the acquisition-date fair value of contingent consideration. If the amount of contingent consideration changes as a result of a post-acquisition event (such as meeting an earnings target), accounting for the change in consideration depends on whether the additional consideration is an equity instrument or cash or other assets paid or owed. If it is equity, the original amount is not re-measured. If the additional consideration is cash or other assets paid or owed, the changed amount is recognised in profit or loss. If the amount of consideration changes because of new information about the fair value of the amount of consideration at acquisition date (rather than because of a post-acquisition event) then retrospective restatement is required. Changes to contingent consideration resulting from events after the acquisition date must be recognised in profit or loss.

The cost of a combination includes liabilities incurred by the acquirer in exchange for control of the acquiree. Future losses should not be included as part of the cost. The costs of issuing debt instruments are accounted for under IAS 39, and costs of issuing equity instruments are accounted for under IAS 32. All other costs associated with the acquisition must be expensed, including reimbursements to the acquiree for bearing some of the acquisition costs. Examples of costs to be expensed include finder's fees; advisory, legal, accounting, valuation, and other professional or consulting fees; and general administrative costs, including the costs of maintaining an internal acquisitions department.

Provisional Accounting

Fair values need to be assigned to the acquiree's identifiable net assets initially. If these can only be determined provisionally at the end of the reporting period then these values may be adopted. However the acquirer should recognise any adjustments, after finalising the initial accounting, to those provisional values within 12 months of the acquisition date. Also any adjustments should be recognised from the acquisition date. Thus:

- Net book value of adjusted net assets fair value at that date;
- Goodwill should be adjusted; and
- Comparatives should be adjusted, e.g. additional depreciation.

Except for contingent consideration or finalisation of any deferred tax assets, adjustments to the initial accounting after initial accounting is complete can only be recognised to correct an error in accordance with IAS 8 *Accounting policies, Changes in Accounting Estimates and Errors*. In that case a prior period adjustment should be recorded.

If the potential benefit of the acquiree's income tax loss carry forwards did not satisfy the criteria for separate recognition on initial accounting, but is subsequently realised, then in addition the acquirer should:

(a) reduce goodwill to amount that would have been recognised if the deferred tax asset had been recognised as an identifiable asset from acquisition date; and
(b) recognise the reduction in the carrying amount of goodwill as an expense.

However, this procedure should not result in the creation of negative goodwill.

Equity Accounted Investments

For equity accounted investments, IFRS 3 applies to:

(a) any goodwill included in the carrying amount of the investment;
(b) any excess included in the carrying amount of the investment of the entity's interest in the net fair value of the investee's net assets over the cost of the investment. That excess should be treated as income.

Investments accounted for by applying the equity method and acquired before the IFRS was issued:

(a) should apply IFRS3 in a prospective basis and therefore should discontinue amortisation of goodwill;
(b) should derecognise any negative goodwill with a corresponding adjustment to retained earnings.

Disclosures

An acquirer should disclose information that enables users to evaluate the nature and financial effect of business combinations that were effected:

(a) during the reporting period;
(b) after the reporting date but before the financial statements are authorised.

To achieve this the following information should be provided for each business combination effected during the reporting period:

(a) The names and descriptions of the combining entities.
(b) The acquisition date.
(c) The percentage of voting equity instruments acquired.
(d) Primary reasons for the business combination.
(e) The cost of the combination and a description of the components of that cost. When equity instruments are issued the following should also be disclosed:
   (i) The number of equity instruments issued; and
  (ii) The fair value of those instruments and the basis for determining that fair value. If no published price or that price has not been used as a reliable indicator, then that fact must be disclosed together with reasons and the method and assumptions actually adopted as well the aggregate amount of the difference between the value attributed to, and the published price of, equity instruments.
(f) Details of operations that the entity has decided to dispose.
(g) The amounts recognised for each class of the acquiree's net assets at acquisition date together with their carrying amounts immediately prior to the combination.
(h) The amount of any excess recognised in profit or loss on creation of negative goodwill.
(i) A description of the factors contributing to the recognition of goodwill.
(j) The amount of the acquiree's profit or loss since the acquisition date included in the acquirer's profit or loss for the period, unless impracticable. If impracticable, fact must be disclosed.

The information above may be disclosed in aggregate for business combinations that are individually immaterial. If the initial accounting was only provisionally determined that fact should also be disclosed together with an explanation of why this is the case.

The following should also be provided unless it would be impracticable:

(a) The revenue of the combined entity for the period as though acquisition date was at the start of the reporting period.

(b) The profit or loss of the combined entity for the period as though the acquisition date was at the start of the reporting period.

If it is impracticable to disclose this information then that fact must be disclosed.

An acquirer should disclose information that enables users to evaluate the financial effects of gains, losses, error corrections and other adjustments recognised in the current period that relate to business combinations that were effected in the current or in previous periods. In that regard the following should be disclosed.

(a) The amount and explanation of any gain/loss recognised in the current reporting period that:
  (i) relates to the identifiable assets acquired or liabilities assumed in a business combination effected in a previous reporting period; and
  (ii) is of such size, nature or incidence that disclosure is relevant to an understanding of the combined entity's financial performance.
(b) If the initial accounting is provisional, the amounts and explanations of adjustments made to provisional values during the reporting period.
(c) Information about error corrections required to be disclosed under IAS 8.

An entity should disclose information that enables users to evaluate changes in the carrying amount of goodwill during the reporting period. That requires a reconciliation of goodwill between the start and end of the reporting period showing separately:

(a) The gross amount and accumulated impairment losses at the start of the period;
(b) Additional goodwill recognised in the period.
(c) Adjustments resulting in the subsequent recognition of deferred tax assets.
(d) Goodwill included in a disposal group (per IFRS 5) and derecognised in the period if not included in a disposal group.
(e) Impairment losses recognised in accordance with IAS 36.
(f) Net exchange differences arising during the period (per IAS 21).
(g) Any other changes in the carrying amount during the period; and
(h) The gross amount and accumulated impairment losses at the end of the period.

Entities should also disclose any additional information as is necessary to meet the objectives of enabling users to properly evaluate the nature and financial effect of business combinations.

CONCLUSION

The 2008 revisions to IAS 27 and IFRS 3 promise significant change, including:

• a greater emphasis on the use of fair value, potentially increasing the judgement and subjectivity around business combination accounting, and requiring greater input by valuation experts;
• focusing on changes in control as a significant economic event, introducing requirements to re-measure interests to fair value at the time when control is achieved or lost and recognising directly in equity the impact of all transactions between controlling and non-controlling shareholders not involving a loss of control; and

- focusing on what is given to the vendor as consideration rather than what is spent to achieve the acquisition. Transaction costs, changes in the value of contingent consideration, settlement of pre-existing contracts, share-based payments and similar items will generally be accounted for separately from business combinations and will generally affect profit or loss.

The revised Standards seek to resolve many of the more contentious aspects of business combination accounting by restricting options or allowable methods. As such, they aim to result in greater consistency in accounting among entities applying IFRSs.

QUESTIONS

Self-test Questions

1. Summarise the main changes to IAS 27 (2008).
2. Outline the main changes to IFRS 3 (2008).
3. Explain how goodwill should be calculated in accordance with IFRS 3 (2008).
4. Describe the two ways in which non-controlling interests may be calculated under IFRS 3 (2008).

Review Questions

(See APPENDIX ONE for Suggested Solutions to Review Questions)

Question 1

Parent owns 80% of Subsidiary. The consolidated statement of financial position contains the following amounts relating to Subsidiary (a CGU) at 31 December 2008:

	€
Identifiable net assets of Subsidiary	500
Consolidated goodwill (Parent share only – old method)	160
	660
NCI (20% x 500)	100

An impairment review of Subsidiary was conducted at 31 December 2008.

Requirement   Calculate the impairment loss and show how it would be allocated if the recoverable amount of Subsidiary at 31 December 2008 was €450.

Challenging Questions

Question 1

Parent owns 80% of Subsidiary. The consolidated statement of financial position contains the following amounts relating to Subsidiary (a CGU) at 31 December 2008:

	€
Identifiable net assets of Subsidiary	500
Consolidated goodwill (Parent share only – old method)	160
	660
NCI (20% x 500)	100

Requirement   Calculate the impairment loss and show how it would be allocated if the recoverable amount of Subsidiary at 31 December 2008 was €550.

CHAPTER 27

CONSOLIDATED STATEMENT OF FINANCIAL POSITION

INTRODUCTION

Companies frequently acquire controlling interests in other companies. In these circumstances, the acquiring (or investing) company reflects the purchase of the subsidiary as an investment in its accounts. However, although the parent company has control over the assets and liabilities of the subsidiary, the members of the parent company are not given any indication of the underlying net assets or earnings attributable to their company's investment, i.e. they do not clearly see the value which the subsidiary is having on the net assets of the group. For this reason, all holding companies are required to submit both a separate company statement of financial position and a consolidated statement of financial position.

By preparing a consolidated statement of financial position, the group is regarded as one business and the consolidated financial statements attempt to show the position and earnings of the group in a manner as near as possible to the way in which such information would have been disclosed if the parent company had acquired the various individual assets and liabilities of the subsidiary (as opposed to acquiring the shares of that subsidiary). This chapter focuses upon the consolidated statement of financial position. After having studied this chapter, you should be able to:

- ascertain the structure of the group;
- calculate goodwill;
- calculate non-controlling interests at both the acquisition and reporting date; and
- prepare a consolidated statement of financial position.

FORMATION OF A GROUP

Throughout this chapter, 'P Limited' refers to the parent company and 'S Limited' to the subsidiary. Before any work is commenced on the consolidation process, the group structure must be established:

1. First identify the parent company (P); then
2. Calculate the percentage holding.

The group structure is determined by the number of ordinary shares held.

Example

P Limited purchased 60,000 shares in S Limited for €20,000. The ordinary share capital of S Limited is 100,000 shares at €1 each.

Requirement   How should S Limited be treated by P Limited? (Consider your answer before reading below.)

Solution
1. P is obviously the parent company.
2. Percentage holding:

	S Limited
Group (60,000/100,000 shares)	60%
Non-controlling Interest	40%
	100%

As P Limited has > 50% of the shareholding of S Limited, S Limited is treated as a subsidiary.

Example

P Limited is a trading company selling widgets. It imports these widgets from European countries for distribution on the Irish market. Its statement of financial position at 31 December 2001 is as follows:

	€
Property, plant and equipment	100,000
Current assets	40,000
	140,000
Ordinary share capital	50,000
Revenue reserves	60,000
Current liabilities	30,000
	140,000

On 31 December 2001, P Limited decides to establish a manufacturing operation and sets up a subsidiary company, S Limited, for this purpose and injects capital of €40,000 financed by way of loan. S Limited purchases property, plant & equipment at a cost of €30,000 on that day. The remaining €10,000 is left in the bank. The statement of financial position of S Limited is now as follows:

	€
Property, plant and equipment	30,000
Current assets (bank)	10,000
	40,000
Ordinary share capital	40,000

Since P Limited has raised a loan of €40,000 to contribute the initial capital of S Limited, the statement of financial position of P Limited reflects the changes as:

(a) an investment of €40,000 in S Limited; and
(b) a loan of €40,000 (which increases its current liabilities).

We can now show the statements of financial position of P Limited and S Limited as at 31 December 2001:

Statements of Financial Position	P Limited	S Limited
	€	€
Property, plant and equipment	100,000	30,000
Investment in S Limited	40,000	-
Current assets	40,000	10,000
	180,000	40,000
Ordinary share capital	50,000	40,000
Revenue reserves	60,000	-
Current liabilities (including loan of €40,000)	70,000	-
	180,000	40,000

When you consider the scenario in group terms, the group has raised a loan of €40,000, it has purchased property, plant & equipment at a cost of €30,000 and now has €10,000 in a bank account as working capital for the new venture.

The group statement of financial position may now be prepared.

P Limited

Consolidated Statement of Financial Position

	P Limited	S Limited	Consolidation Adjustments	Group SFP
	€	€	€	€
Property plant and equipment	100,000	30,000	-	130,000
Investments in S Limited	40,000	-	(40,000)	-
Current assets	40,000	10,000	-	50,000
	180,000	40,000	(40,000)	180,000
Ordinary share capital	50,000	40,000	(40,000)	50,000
Revenue reserves	60,000	-	-	60,000
Current liabilities	70,000	-	-	70,000
	180,000	40,000	(40,000)	180,000

Obviously, it is only the far right column that is published.

Considering the final group statement of financial position, we notice that this statement of financial position shows:

(a) additional property, plant & equipment of €30,000;
(b) additional current assets of €10,000; and
(c) additional current liabilities of €40,000.

This is the exact way the statement of financial position would have looked if S Limited had *not* been formed and if the establishment of the manufacturing venture had simply taken place in P Limited. In this fashion, the consolidated statement of financial position shows the group as one business entity. The net assets of S Limited (€40,000 in this example) have been substituted for the cost of investment in S Limited. The share capital of S Limited is then cancelled out because the net assets of S Limited are included in the consolidated statement of financial position.

From the point of view of the group as a whole, the ordinary share capital of the group is the original €50,000 invested by the members of the holding company. The capital of the subsidiary (€40,000) is cancelled out on consolidation.

In the above example, P Limited founded a subsidiary, S Limited, and held 100% of the share capital of that subsidiary. The same principles apply where a parent company purchases the shares of another company which is already trading (which then becomes a subsidiary).

PREMIUM ON ACQUISITION

An investing company may, in fact, pay more (or less) for a company than the underlying value of its net assets. Where the purchase price *exceeds* the value of the underlying net assets, the difference is known as a 'premium on acquisition', or 'goodwill on consolidation'. It is also referred to as 'purchased goodwill' or 'positive goodwill'. If the purchase price is for less than the underlying value of the net assets negative goodwill will arise. IFRS 3 requires the immediate recognition of negative goodwill as a gain in the statement of comprehensive income. Goodwill is measured as the difference between:

- the aggregate of:
  (i)   the acquisition-date fair value of the consideration transferred;
  (ii) the amount of any non-controlling interest in the entity acquired*; and
  (iii) in a business combination achieved in stages, the acquisition-date fair value of the acquirer's previously-held equity interest in the entity acquired; and
- the net of the acquisition-date amounts of the identifiable assets acquired and the liabilities assumed, both measured in accordance with IFRS 3.

In simple terms, goodwill = consideration paid by parent + non-controlling interest − fair value of the subsidiary's net identifiable assets. If the difference is positive, the acquirer should recognise the goodwill as an asset; whereas if the difference above is negative, the resulting gain is recognised as a bargain purchase in profit or loss.

* Note that the non-controlling interest may be valued at its proportionate share of the subsidiary's net identifiable assets, in which case consolidated goodwill would be that relating to the parent only (the 'old' method). Alternatively, the non-controlling interest may be at its fair value (the 'new' method), in which case the consolidated goodwill represents that of both the parent and the non-controlling interest.

This represents a different approach to the previous, more traditional, method of calculating goodwill which was calculated as the difference between the consideration paid by the parent and its share of the fair value of the subsidiary's net identifiable assets. This method did not refer to the non-controlling interest because it was only intended to recognise the parent's share of goodwill.

It is important to realise that the new 'approach' only applies *at the date of acquisition*. Subsequent to acquisition, both the non-controlling interest and the fair value of the subsidiary's net assets will have changed. IFRS 3 (2008) recognises that there may be many ways of calculating the fair value of the non-controlling interest and does not go into detail on this matter, but it recognises that the market price of the subsidiary's shares prior to the acquisition may be a reasonable basis on which to value the shareholding of the non-controlling interest.

It should be clear that the principle of the cost of investment in S Limited being cancelled against the share capital of S Limited still applies. However, the difference between

Example

P Limited acquired all the shares in S Limited for €50,000 at the date of incorporation of S Limited. At 31 December 2XX2 the statements of financial position were as follows:

	P Limited €	S Limited €
ASSETS		
Sundry net assets	110,000	200,000
Investment in S Limited	50,000	-
	160,000	200,000
EQUITY		
Ordinary share capital	80,000	40,000
Revenue reserves	80,000	160,000
	160,000	200,000

In preparing the consolidated statement of financial position as at 31 December 2XX2, we ascertain that the:

(a) net assets of S Limited at the date of acquisition were represented by share capital of €40,000 and the revenue reserves of €Nil*;
(b) cost of investment was €50,000.

* Note that the reserves at the date of acquisition were €Nil because the shares were purchased at the date of incorporation of S Limited.

Goodwill:

Consideration paid by parent	50,000
+ non-controlling interest (n/a – 100% acquisition)	-
– fair value of the subsidiary's net identifiable assets	(40,000)
Premium on acquisition (positive goodwill)	10,000

The consolidated statement of financial position as at 31 December 2XX2 is as follows:

	P Limited €	S Limited €	Consolidated Adjustments €	Group SFP €
Sundry net assets	110,000	200,000	-	310,000

Investment in S Limited	50,000	-	(50,000)	-
Goodwill	-	-	10,000	10,000
	160,000	200,000	(40,000)	320,000
Ordinary share capital	80,000	40,000	(40,000)	80,000
Revenue reserves	80,000	160,000		240,000
	160,000	200,000	(40,000)	320,000

the two amounts (€10,000 in this example) is represented as goodwill (being premium of cost over net assets acquired). To surmount the difficulty of computing the goodwill or discount on acquisition, a cost of control account is used. In the above example, this account would appear as follows:

Cost of Control Account

	€		€
Cost of investment	50,000	S Limited – share capital	40,000
	-	Balance c/d	10,000
	50,000		50,000
Balance b/d	10,000		

(representing goodwill on consolidation)

The entries in the Cost of Control account are effectively the same as those in the 'Consolidation adjustments' column above.

You should get into the habit of *ALWAYS* preparing a Cost of Control account.

An Alternative Approach: The T A/C Method

Steps

1. Open a T a/c for every heading on the statements of financial position and enter opening balances per the question.
2. Post to T a/c's any journal adjustments necessary – every exam question would involve these.
3. Do consolidation adjustments – all double entry.
4. Close off T a/c's.
5. Produce consolidated statement of financial position.

Sundry Net Assets

	€		€
P	110,000	CSFP	310,000
S	200,000		
	310,000		310,000

Generally the tangible non-current assets, current assets and current liabilities of P Limited. and S Limited. are totalled for the consolidated statement of financial position (subject to any adjustments in question).

Investment in S Limited

	€		€
P	50,000	Cost of control	50,000

All the cost of the investment in S Limited is transferred to cost of control a/c in order to value any goodwill.

Ordinary Shares

	€		€
Cost of control	40,000	P	80,000
(100% x 40k)		S	40,000
CSFP	80,000		
	120,000		120,000

The capital of S Limited must be dealt with in the workings. The capital of P is the capital of the group.

Revenue Reserves

	€		€
Cost of control	Nil	P	80,000
(100% x zero)		S	160,000
CSFP	240,000		
	240,000		240,000

The group's share of the reserves of S Limited at the date of acquisition is transferred to cost of control (to measure goodwill).

Cost of Control

	€		€
Investment in S	50,000	Ordinary shares	40,000
		Revenue reserves	Nil
		CSFP – Goodwill	10,000
	50,000		50,000

Remember, positive goodwill is not amortised; it is tested for impairment annually.

P Limited
Consolidated Statement of Financial Position as at 31 December 2XX2

	€
Assets	
Sundry net assets	310,000
Goodwill	10,000
	320,000
Equity	
Ordinary share capital	80,000
Revenue reserves	240,000
	320,000

If P Limited had paid only €30,000 for the net assets (€40,000) of S Limited at the date of acquisition, negative goodwill of €10,000 would have arisen. IFRS 3 requires the immediate recognition of negative goodwill as a gain in the statement of comprehensive income.

'PRE-ACQUISITION PROFITS'

The illustrations up to now have dealt with a situation where P Limited acquired its interest at the date of incorporation of S Limited and accordingly the net assets of S Limited at the date of acquisition were represented by the share capital of S Limited, as no reserves exist at date of incorporation.

Let us now develop that situation with another example.

Example

P Limited acquired all the shares of S Limited after one year's trading when its reserves were €20,000. The statements of financial position of the two companies at 31 December 2XX2 were as follows:

	P Limited €	S Limited €
Assets		
Sundry net assets	90,000	200,000
Investment in S Limited	70,000	-
	160,000	200,000
Equity		
Ordinary share capital	80,000	40,000
Revenue reserves	80,000	160,000
	160,000	200,000

In this situation, the net assets of S Limited at the date of acquisition were represented by the share capital plus reserves of S Limited at that date. It is both these amounts (i.e. share capital plus reserves at date of acquisition) that are cancelled against the cost of investment in preparing the consolidated statement of financial position.

First, let us calculate the goodwill/discount on acquisition:

Goodwill:	€
Consideration paid by parent	70,000
+ non-controlling interest (n/a – 100% acquisition)	-
– fair value of the subsidiary's net identifiable assets (Share capital + reserves)	(60,000)
Premium on acquisition (positive goodwill)	10,000

Alternatively, this could be calculated as follows:

Cost of Control Account

	€		€
Consideration paid	70,000	Fair value of net assets	60,000
		Goodwill	10,000
	70,000		70,000

Consolidated Statement of Financial Position as at 31 December 2XX2

	P Limited €	S Limited €	Consolidation Adjustments €	Group SFP €
Sundry net assets	90,000	200,000	-	290,000
Investment in S Limited	70,000	-	(70,000)	-
Goodwill	-	-	10,000	10,000
	160,000	200,000	(60,000)	300,000
Ordinary share capital	80,000	40,000	(40,000)	80,000
Revenue reserves	80,000	160,000	(20,000)	220,000
	160,000	200,000	(60,000)	300,000

The effect of P Limited acquiring a controlling interest in S Limited is to freeze and capitalise the pre-acquisition profits. *Therefore, the pre-acquisition profits are not available for distribution by P Limited.*

The Cost of Control Account and the Consolidated Revenue Reserves Account are shown below to aid understanding of the adjustments required.

Note   In the cost of control account you will always credit the account with 'what you got for your purchase price', i.e. the group's share of the capital and all reserves of S Limited at the date of acquisition.

Cost of Control Account

	€		€
Investment in S Limited	70,000	S Limited share capital	40,000
		S Limited - pre-acq. profits	20,000
		Balance c/d	10,000
	70,000		70,000
Balance b/d	10,000		

(representing goodwill on consolidation)

Consolidated Revenue Reserves Account

	€		€
Cost of control	20,000	P Limited	80,000
Balance c/d	220,000	S Limited	160,000
	240,000		240,000
		Balance b/d	220,000

(representing reserves in consolidated statement of financial position)

NON-CONTROLLING INTERESTS

Where the parent company acquires less than a 100% interest in a subsidiary company, the balance of the company is known as the non-controlling interest (previously referred to as minority interest). In preparing the consolidated statement of financial position, the group and non-controlling interest are reflected by showing the combined net assets of the parent and subsidiary companies, and then separately disclosing the non-controlling interest in the net assets of the subsidiary company at the reporting date.

As explained in Chapter 26, IFRS 3 has an explicit option, available on a transaction-by-transaction basis, to measure any non-controlling interest in the entity acquired either at fair value (new method) or at the non-controlling interest's proportionate share of the net identifiable assets of the entity acquired (old method). The latter treatment corresponds to the measurement basis in IFRS 3 (2004). For the purpose of measuring non-controlling interest at fair value, it may be possible to determine the acquisition-date fair value on the basis of market prices for the equity shares not held by the acquirer. When a market price for the equity shares is not available because the shares are not publicly-traded, the acquirer must measure the fair value of the non-controlling interest using other valuation techniques.

As illustrated in Chapter 26, consolidated goodwill is calculated as follows: consideration paid by parent + non-controlling interest − fair value of the subsidiary's net identifiable assets. It is important to remember that the non-controlling interest in the above formula may be valued at its proportionate share of the subsidiary's net identifiable assets, in which case consolidated goodwill would be that relating to the parent only (the 'old' method). Alternatively, the non-controlling interest may be at its fair value (the 'new' method), in which case the consolidated goodwill represents that of both the parent and the non-controlling interest. It is important to realise that the new 'formula' only applies at the date of acquisition. Subsequent to acquisition, both the non-controlling interest and the fair value of the subsidiary's net assets will have changed.

Example

Let us now assume that P Limited acquired 80% of the ordinary share capital of S Limited for €56,000 when S Limited reserves were €20,000. The statements of financial position at 31 December 2XX8 were as follows:

	P Limited €	S Limited €
ASSETS		
Sundry net assets	104,000	200,000
Investment in S Limited	56,000	-
	160,000	200,000

EQUITY

Ordinary share capital	80,000	40,000
Revenue reserves	80,000	160,000
	160,000	200,000

Before any work is commenced on the consolidated financial statements, the group structure must be established.

	S Limited
Group	80%
Non-controlling interest	20%
	100%

As explained above, IFRS 3 has an explicit option, available on a transaction-by-transaction basis, to measure any non-controlling interest in the entity acquired *at the date of acquisition* at either at fair value (new method) or at the non-controlling interest's proportionate share of the net identifiable assets of the entity acquired (old method). For the purposes of this example, it is assumed that the proportionate share method equates to the fair value method:

i.e. 20% of (€40,000 + €20,000) = €12,000 at date of acquisition.

We can now calculate the non-controlling interest in S Limited at 31 December 2XX8:

i.e. 20% of €200,000 = €40,000 at reporting date

We can also ascertain the goodwill/discount on acquisition:

	€
Goodwill:	
Consideration paid by parent	56,000
+ non-controlling interest	12,000
– fair value of the subsidiary's net identifiable assets	(60,000)
Premium on acquisition (positive goodwill)	8,000

Consolidated Statement of Financial Position as at 31 December 2XX8

	P Limited	S Limited	Consolidation Adjustments	Group SFP
	€	€	€	€
Sundry net assets	104,000	200,000	-	304,000
Investment in S Limited	56,000	-	(56,000)	-
Goodwill	-	-	8,000	8,000
	160,000	200,000	(48,000)	312,000
Ordinary share capital	80,000	40,000	(40,000)	80,000
Revenue reserves	80,000	160,000	(48,000)	192,000
Non-controlling interest	-	-	40,000	40,000
	160,000	200,000	(48,000)	312,000

As in previous examples, the cost of investment in S Limited (of €56,000) is cancelled, goodwill (of €8,000) arises on consolidation, and the ordinary share capital of S Limited (€40,000) is cancelled out in preparing the consolidated statement of financial position.

In this example, we also calculated the non-controlling interest in the subsidiary at the reporting date which amounts to 20% of the subsidiary. The final adjustment in preparing the consolidated statement of financial position is to revenue reserves. Consolidated revenue reserves are computed as follows:

	€
Reserves of P Limited	80,000
Reserves of S Limited	160,000
	240,000
Less non-controlling interest in reserves of S Limited (20% x €160,000)	(32,000)
Less holding company share of pre-acquisition reserves (80% x €20,000)	(16,000)
	192,000

Consolidated reserves can therefore be defined as the reserves of the holding company *plus* the group's share of the post-acquisition reserves of the subsidiary company at the reporting date.

The second adjustment above reflects the fact that profits earned by S Limited before being acquired by P Limited will not be distributable by P Limited. This is also taken into account when calculating the goodwill on consolidation.

To provide further explanation of the consolidation adjustments required, the following working accounts are shown:

Cost of Control Account

	€		€
Investment in S Limited	56,000	S Limited share capital	40,000
NCI at acquisition date	12,000	(at date of acquisition)	
		S Limited reserves	20,000
		(at date of acquisition)	
		Goodwill c/d	8,000
	68,000		68,000
Goodwill b/d	8,000		

Consolidated Reserves

	€		€
Non-controlling interest (at reporting date) (€160,000 × 20%)	32,000	P Limited	80,000
		S Limited	160,000
Cost of control a/c (pre-acquisition profits) (€20,000 × 80%)	16,000		
Balance c/d	192,000		
	240,000		240,000
		Balance b/d	192,000

This balance represents:

		€
(a)	100% of P Limited reserves	80,000
(b)	80% of S Limited post-acquisition profits (€160,000 – €20,000) × 80%	112,000
		192,000

Non-controlling Interest Account (at reporting date)

	€		€
Balance c/d	40,000	S Limited share capital	
		(€40,000 x 20%)	8,000

		S Limited reserves	
		(€160,000 x 20%)	32,000
	40,000		40,000
		Balance b/d	40,000

Non-controlling interest have been credited with their share of the capital and reserves of S Limited at the reporting date.

Extra Workings using T a/c Approach in Full

Sundry Net Assets

	€		€
P	104,000	CSFP	304,000
S	200,000		
	304,000		304,000

Investment in S Limited.

	€		€
P	56,000	Cost of control	56,000

Ordinary Shares

	€		€
Cost of control	32,000	P	80,000
(80% x 40k)		S	40,000
Non-controlling interest	8,000		
(20% x 40k)			
CSFP	80,000		
	120,000		120,000

FEATURES OF THE THREE MAJOR WORKING ACCOUNTS

1. Cost of Control Account

This account is used to ascertain the goodwill positive or negative on acquisition of a subsidiary.

2. Consolidated Reserves Account

The reserves of the subsidiary at date of acquisition are represented by a portion of the net assets. Any distribution of these assets would effectively represent a return of

P Limited's investment in S Limited. The effect of P Limited acquiring control of S Limited is to capitalise the subsidiary's reserves at the date of acquisition. These pre-acquisition profits cannot be regarded as distributable by P Limited under company legislation. In this account, the amounts on the reserve accounts per the statements of financial position of P Limited and S Limited are introduced on the credit side. The reserves of S Limited are then allocated as follows:

(i) the non-controlling interest in S Limited get their share of all of S Limited's reserves (at the reporting date) regardless of the date of P Limited's acquisition (this is irrelevant as far as they are concerned); and
(ii) P Limited's interest in the reserves of S Limited at the date of acquisition is transferred to the cost of control account.

Of the reserves of S Limited, all that remains in the consolidated reserves account is P Limited's share of the post-acquisition profits of S Limited. This amount, together with the reserves of P Limited, comprises the balance of consolidated reserves in the consolidated statement of financial position.

3. Non-controlling Interest Account

This account reflects the interest of the non-controlling shareholders (the minority) in the shareholders' funds of S Limited at the reporting date. It is important to remember that, as explained above, IFRS 3 has an explicit option, available on a transaction-by-transaction basis, to measure any non-controlling interest in the entity acquired *at the date of acquisition* at either at fair value (new method) or at the non-controlling interest's proportionate share of the net identifiable assets of the entity acquired (old method).

Note A fair proportion of marks in a consolidated statement of financial position question is normally attributed to the calculation of:

(a) Goodwill;
(b) Consolidated reserves; and
(c) Non-controlling interest.

It is vital that adequate workings are presented to the examiner.

Example

Consolidated Statement of Financial Position as at 31 December 2XX8

	P Limited €	S Limited €
Assets		
Sundry net assets	102,000	74,000
Investment in S Limited	43,000	-
	145,000	74,000

Equity		
Share capital (€1 shares)	100,000	50,000
Revenue reserves	45,000	24,000
	145,000	74,000

P Limited acquired 37,500 shares in S Limited at a cost of €43,000 when S Limited's revenue reserves were €10,000.

Requirement Prepare the consolidated statement of financial position as at 31 December 2XX8.

Solution

Consolidated Statement of Financial Position as at 31 December 2XX8

	P Limited	S Limited	Consolidation Adjustments	Group SFP
	€	€	€	€
Sundry net assets	102,000	74,000	-	176,000
Shares in S Limited	43,000	-	(43,000)	-
	145,000	74,000	(43,000)	176,000
Ordinary share capital	100,000	50,000	(50,000)	100,000
Revenue reserves	45,000	24,000	(11,500)	57,500
Non-controlling interest	-	-	18,500	18,500
	145,000	74,000	(43,000)	176,000

Note The negative goodwill of €2,000 arising on the acquisition of S Limited has been credited to revenue reserves in accordance with IFRS 3.
Workings:

S Limited

Group structure	
Group	75%
MI	25%
	100%

Again, for the purposes of this example, it is assumed that the proportionate share method equates to the fair value method:

Cost of Control Account

	€		€
Cost of shares held	43,000	Share capital – S Limited	50,000
NCI (at acquisition date)	15,000		
Goodwill	2,000	Revenue reserves – S Limited	10,000
	60,000		60,000

Non-controlling Interest Account (at reporting date)

	€		€
Balance c/d	18,500	Share capital – S Limited	12,500
		Revenue reserves – S Limited	
		(25% × €24,000)	6,000
	18,500		18,500

Consolidated Revenue Reserves Account

	€		€
Cost of control account (75% × € 10,000)	7,500	P Limited	45,000
Non-controlling interest	6,000	S Limited	24,000
Balance c/d	57,500	Goodwill	2,000
	71,000		71,000
		Balance b/d	57,500

OTHER POINTS

There are a number of adjustments which frequently arise when dealing with questions on consolidated statements of financial position. The principal ones are as follows:

- Proposed subsidiary dividends
- Dividends out of pre-acquisition profit
- Inter-company balances
- Unrealised profits on the inter-group transfer of assets
- Revaluation of tangible non-current assets

Each of these is now discussed further.

Proposed Dividends

If a subsidiary has proposed or paid a dividend in any given year, this does not affect the profit for the year which is attributable to the parent and non-controlling interests. Furthermore if a dividend has been paid, then the parent and/or non-controlling interests have received their entitlement and no further adjustment is required.

There is no entitlement to ordinary dividends until they are approved at the AGM by the shareholders. Consequently dividends declared after the reporting date should not be recognised as liabilities unless there 'is a legal obligation' to receive the dividend (IAS 10 *Events after the Reporting Date*).

Where S Limited, has 'incorrectly' accrued a proposed dividend in its financial statements and P Limited *has not* taken credit for its share of that dividend, then the appropriate adjustment is:

DR Current liabilities – S
CR Retained earnings – S

Where S Limited has 'incorrectly' accrued a proposed dividend in its financial statements and P Limited *has* taken credit for its share of that dividend, then the appropriate adjustment is:

DR Current liabilities – S
DR Investment income – P
CR Retained earnings – S
CR Receivables – P

However, in the case of proposed dividends that have been 'legitimately' accrued, steps must be made to ensure that the:

(a) proposed dividend of the subsidiary is not included on the group statement of financial position as most of it represents an inter-company liability and the remainder is due to the non-controlling interest;
(b) correct reserves figure of the subsidiary is used for the purposes of calculating the non-controlling interest.

The following is a summary of the adjustments required where the subsidiary has legitimately accrued proposed dividends at the year-end. These depend on whether the parent has taken credit for its share or not.

Where S Limited has legitimately accrued a proposed dividend at the reporting date and P Limited *has* taken credit for its share of that dividend:

Example

P Limited owns 80% of the ordinary shares of S Limited.

Extracts from Statements of Financial Position as at 31 March 2003

	P Limited	S Limited
Current Assets	€	€
Dividends receivable	40,000	
Current Liabilities		
Proposed ordinary dividends	100,000	50,000

The proposed dividends were approved by the shareholders prior to 31 March 2003.

Solution

80% of S Limited's dividend (€40,000) is owed to P Limited and should be eliminated in the workings. The remainder of S Limited's dividend is due to the non-controlling interest (€10,000) and should be disclosed in the consolidated statement of financial position under current liabilities along with the proposed dividend of P Limited.

Journal Adjustment:

		€	€
Jnl 1	DR Proposed dividends	40,000	
	CR Dividends receivable		40,000
	To cancel inter-group dividend		

Using the T a/c Method:

Proposed Dividends

	€		€
Jnl 1	40,000	P	100,000
CSFP P Limited	100,000	S	50,000
Non-controlling interest	10,000		
	150,000		150,000

Dividends Receivable

	€		€
P	40,000	Jnl 1	40,000

Extract from the Consolidated Statement of Financial Position as at 31 March 2003

	€
Current Liabilities	
Proposed dividends	110,000

Example

Where S Limited has legitimately accrued a proposed dividend at the reporting date and P Limited has *not* taken credit for its share of that dividend.

P Limited owns 80% of the ordinary shares of S Limited.

Extracts from Statements of Financial Position as at 31 March 2003		
	P Limited	S Limited
	€	€
Current Liabilities		
Proposed ordinary dividends	100,000	50,000

The proposed dividends were approved by the shareholders prior to 31 March 2003.

Solution

- Bring in the dividend receivable into P Limited's accounts;
- Cancel the inter-group dividend; and
- The remainder of S Limited's dividend is due to the non-controlling interest.

Journal Adjustments:		€	€
Jnl 1	DR Dividends receivable	40,000	
	CR P Limited statement of comprehensive income		40,000
Jnl 2	DR Proposed dividends	40,000	
	CR Dividends receivable		40,000

Using the T a/c Method:

Proposed Dividends

	€		€
Jnl 2	40,000	P	100,000
CSFP P Limited	100,000	S	50,000
Non-controlling interest	10,000		
	150,000		150,000

Dividends Receivable

	€		€
Jnl 1	40,000	Jnl 2	40,000

Extract from the Consolidated Statement of Financial Position as at
31 March 2003

Current Liabilities	€
Proposed dividends	110,000

Note   The two examples have an identical effect on the ultimate consolidated statement of financial position but the adjustments differ. Pay careful attention in questions as to whether P Limited *has* taken credit for its share or P Limited *has not* taken credit.

Dividends out of Pre-acquisition Profits

When a parent company purchases a subsidiary, company law dictates that the reserves of the subsidiary at the date of acquisition are 'frozen'. The effect of this is that, if a dividend is paid by the subsidiary out of pre-acquisition reserves, it cannot be recognised as income in the books of the parent company.

In normal circumstances, when a parent company receives a subsidiary dividend, the following entry is made in the holding company's books:

DR Bank
CR Dividend income

If, however, the dividend was paid out of pre-acquisition reserves, then the amount is treated as a refund of part of the original cost of investment:

DR Bank
CR Cost of investment

A simple example should make it clear why dividends out of pre-acquisition reserves are required to be treated as a refund of the cost of investment, rather than as income in the books of the holding company:

	B Limited	Y Limited
	€	€
Current assets	30,000	30,000
Current liabilities	(10,000)	(10,000)
Ordinary shareholders' funds (Capital and reserves)	20,000	20,000

Both companies B Limited and Y Limited have goodwill, not reflected in the books, valued at €5,000 and are identical in every respect, except that the current liabilities of B Limited are trade payables, while the current liabilities of Y Limited are a proposed ordinary dividend (that has been legitimately accrued).

A Limited, a prospective purchaser of B Limited, is willing to pay €25,000 for 100% of B Limited including goodwill. X Limited, a prospective purchaser of Y Limited, will clearly be willing to pay €35,000 for the acquisition of that company in the knowledge that €10,000 of the cost will immediately be 'refunded' by way of a dividend.

Assume that the two purchases are completed on 31 March 20X4. On 1 April 20X4, B Limited and Y Limited pay off their current liabilities as appropriate. A Limited and X Limited will then own identical investments, each consisting of €20,000 of current assets plus €5,000 of goodwill; and it is clearly appropriate that the cost of investment figures in their own respective statements of financial position should be identical. This will only be the case if X Limited sets off the €10,000 dividend receivable against the €35,000 cost of the acquisition, disclosing the investment in Y Limited at a net cost of €25,000.

The point to grasp is that X Limited cannot credit the dividend to profit because no profit has been made. The correct way of looking at it is to say that X Limited was willing to pay 'over the odds' for its investment on the presumption that a part of its cost would immediately be repaid. When the dividend is paid, this presumption must be pursued to its conclusion by treating the dividend as a reduction of the cost of the investment.

From a consolidation point of view, note that any such reduction in the cost of investment would be a credit to the cost of the control account.

Cost of Control Account

Cost of investment	X	Pre-acquisition dividends	X

A dividend out of pre-acquisition reserves might arise in the following circumstances:

(a) When the subsidiary pays the parent company a dividend and there are inadequate post-acquisition reserves in the books of the subsidiary to cover the full amount of the dividend:

e.g.	S Limited reserves at 1.1.X1	€5,000
	S Limited profit for the year ended 31.12.X1	€1,000

P purchased S Limited on 1.1.X1 and S Limited paid a dividend of €1,500 for the year ended 31.12.X1.

=>   €500 of the dividend would be out of pre-acquisition reserves.

(b) When the subsidiary pays the parent company a dividend in the year of acquisition

e.g.   P Limited purchased S Limited on 30.6.X1

S Limited paid a dividend of €1,500 for the year ended 31.12.X1.

=> by time-apportioning the dividend in the year of acquisition, €750 (6/12) of the dividend would be out of pre-acquisition reserves.

Where a dividend out of pre-acquisition reserves has been paid, the first step is to establish whether or not it has been accounted for correctly in the books of the holding company.

i.e.   Incorrect: DR Bank

CR Dividend income

Correct :   DR Bank

CR Cost of investment

Once established, the following steps should be carried out.

Step 1 – If the dividend has been recognised as income in the books of the parent company, then correct:

DR Consolidated Reserves
CR Cost of investment in S Limited
With the group share of the dividend paid out of pre-acquisition reserves.

Step 2 – Reduce the level of pre-acquisition reserves of S Limited by the total dividend paid out of pre acquisition profits.

Example

Statement of Financial Position as at 31 December 20X5

ASSETS	P Limited	S Limited
Tangible non-current assets	35,000	14,500
Investment in S Limited	25,000	-
	60,000	14,500
Net current assets	27,000	12,500
	87,000	27,000
EQUITY		
Ordinary share capital	50,000	10,000
Revenue reserves	37,000	17,000
	87,000	27,000

P Limited acquired 8,000 of the 10,000 €1 ordinary shares in S Limited on 1 January 20X5 for €25,000. S Limited's current liabilities at 31 December 20X4 included €4,000 in respect of unpaid dividends and retained reserves of €12,000. The dividend was subsequently paid and recognised as income in the books of P Limited. With respect to non-controlling interests, it is assumed that the proportionate share method equates to the fair value method at the acquisition date.

Requirement   Prepare the consolidated statement of financial position as at 31 December 20X5.

Solution

Step 1 – Use the pre-acquisition reserves after the pre-acquisition dividend for the cost of control account:

	€
i.e. Retained reserves 31.12.X4	12,000
	x 80%
Group share of pre-acquisition reserves	9,600

Step 2 – Since the dividend has been recognised as income in P Limited, this must be corrected.

Jnl 1   DR Consolidated Reserves   €3,200

         CR Cost of Investment   €3,200

with the group share of the dividend paid out of pre-acquisition reserves (€4,000 × 80%)

Cost of Control Account

	€		€
Investment	21,800	Ordinary shares	10,000
NCI (€22,000 × 20%)	4,400	Revenue Reserves	12,000
		Goodwill	4,200
	26,200		26,200

Consolidated Reserves

	€		€
Jnl 1	3,200	P	37,000
Revenue Res. (80% × 12,000)	9,600	S	17,000
NCI (20% × 17,000)	3,400		
CSFP	37,800		
	54,000		54,000

Non-controlling Interest (at reporting date)

	€		€
CSFP	5,400	Ordinary shares	2,000
		Revenue Reserves	3,400
	5,400		5,400

Investment in S Limited

	€		€
P Limited	25,000	Jnl 1	3,200
		Cost of control	21,800
	25,400		25,000

P Limited

Consolidated Statement of Financial Position

31 December 20X5

	€
Assets	
Goodwill	4,200
Tangible non-current assets	49,500
Net current assets	39,500
	93,200
Equity	
Ordinary Share Capital	50,000
Consolidated reserves	37,800
	87,800
Non-controlling interest	5,400
	93,200

Inter-company Balances

In preparing consolidated financial statements, one is preparing a form of group accounts that presents the information contained in the separate financial statements of a parent company and its subsidiaries as if they were the financial statements of a single entity. Particular items requiring cancellation are dealt with hereunder.

Loans

In cancelling loans the credit balance of one company is offset against the debit balance of the other company, thus eliminating both balances from the consolidated statement of financial position.

Current Accounts

In situations where the current accounts as between the companies in the group are in agreement, i.e. the creditor company shows the same balance in its books in respect of the indebtedness as the debtor company, the cancellation procedure is exactly the same as with Loans above. However, frequently the current accounts are not in agreement.

This lack of agreement normally stems from cash and/or goods being in transit from one company to the other. Before cancelling inter-company current accounts, they must be brought into agreement. This should be done as follows:

- For items in transit between parent and subsidiary companies, adjustment should be made in the accounts of the parent company regardless of which way the cash or goods are going; and
- For items in transit between fellow subsidiaries the adjustment should be made in the accounts of the company to which goods or cash are in transit.

Example

Current accounts in the books of:

P Limited – with S Limited – €1,490 (debit)
S Limited – with P Limited – €740 (credit)

At year end there were in transit:
Goods – from P Limited to S Limited – €500
Cash – from S Limited to P Limited – €250

Current Account in Books of P Limited

	€		€
Balance b/d	1,490	Goods in transit	500
		Cash in transit	250
		Balance c/d	740
	1,490		1,490

The goods and cash in transit will be incorporated in the consolidated statement of financial position. The current account balance of €740 will be cancelled on consolidation against the equivalent balance in S.

Debentures and Other Loans

For consolidated statement of financial position purposes, the inter-company indebtedness of loans and interest payable and receivable should cancel.

Loans and interest payable to holders outside the group should remain on the consolidated statement of financial position, being disclosed under group liabilities.

Debentures and loan inventory of subsidiaries held outside the group should be disclosed in the consolidated statement of financial position as part of group debentures and loan inventory. They must never be disclosed as part of non-controlling interest.

Example

Assume that S Limited has €15,000 of 5% debentures, of which P Limited holds €10,000 and outsiders hold €5,000. Assume also that payables of S Limited amount to €25,000, of which €900 represents debenture interest payable, while receivables of P Limited amount to €30,000 of which €600 represents debenture interest receivable. In addition, you are informed that receivables of S Limited amount to €35,000 and payables of P Limited amount to €27,000.

Requirement   Show the balances that should appear in the consolidated statement of financial position in respect of:

(a) 6% Debentures;
(b) Receivables; and
(c) Payables.

Solution

	P Limited	S Limited	Consolidation Adjustment	Consolidated SFP
	€	€	€	€
	DR/(CR)	DR/(CR)	DR/(CR)	DR/(CR)
Invest in debentures	10,000	-	(10,000)	-
6% debentures	-	(15,000)	(10,000)	(5,000)
Payables	(27,000)	(25,000)	(600)	(51,400)
Receivables	30,000	35,000	(600)	64,400
			-	

In T a/c Form:

Investment in Debentures			
	€		€
P	10,000	Cost of control	10,000

Debentures			
	€		€
Cost of control	10,000	S	15,000
CSFP	5,000		
	15,000		15,000

Payables

	€		€
Jnl (inter-group deb. interest)	600	P	27,000
CSFP	51,400	S	25,000
	52,000		52,000

Receivables

	€		€
P	30,000	Jnl (inter-group deb. interest)	600
S	35,000	CSFP	64,400
	65,000		65,000

Cost of Control

	€		€
Investment in debentures	10,000	Debentures	10,000

Any difference (in cost of control) between the cost of the investment in debentures and value of the debentures acquired is included as part of goodwill.

Bills of Exchange

Bills receivable and bills payable between group companies must be cancelled in the same way as other inter-company balances. The cancellation process may be complicated where bills payable by one company (the accepting company) to another company within the same group (the drawing company) have been discounted by that company before the reporting date.

In such cases, the discounted bills cannot be regarded as an inter-company liability, because the payment will not be to the drawing company but to the person who discounted them. Furthermore, the amount disclosed by way of note to the accounts of the drawing company in respect of the contingent liability for bills discounted must be adjusted in the consolidated statement of financial position to exclude the contingent liability which relates to bills payable by another member of the same group.

Example

		P Limited €	S Limited €
Bills receivable:			
	from S Limited	12,000	--
	from others	30,000	6,000
		42,000	6,000
Bills payable:			
	to P Limited	--	15,000
	to others	9,000	27,000
		9,000	42,000
Note to Statement of Financial Position:			
Contingent liability for bills discounted		8,400	4,800

S Limited owes €15,000 of bills to P Limited, but P Limited has only €12,000 of bills receivable on its books. Therefore, P Limited must have discounted €3,000 worth of these bills.

The €3,000 of bills discounted by P Limited will therefore be payable by S Limited to the discounter, i.e. outside the group.

If P Limited has a contingent liability at the reporting date of €8,400 on the bills which it has discounted, only €5,400 of that is a contingent liability which arises from outside the group.

Amounts to be included in consolidated financial statements:

Bills receivable		€
P Limited (€30,000)		
S Limited (€6,000)		36,000
Bills payable		
P Limited (€9,000)		
S Limited (€27,000 + €3,000)		39,000
Note to the Consolidated Statement of Financial Position:		
Contingent liability for bills discounted		
P Limited €5,400		
S Limited €4,800		10,200

In T a/c Form:

Bills Receivable

	€		€
P	42,000	Jnl (inter-group)	12,000
S	6,000	CSFP	36,000
	48,000		48,000

Bills Payable

	€		€
JNL	12,000	P	9,000
CSFP	39,000	S	42,000
	51,000		51,000

Unrealised Profit on the Inter-group Transfer of Assets

Inventory and Unrealised Profit

Where unrealised profit arises from trading between group companies, an adjustment must be made for the unrealised profit. It must be first established in which company's books the unrealised profit has been recorded. Make the adjustment in the accounts of the selling company. If the unrealised profit has arisen as a result of P Limited selling goods to S Limited at a profit, but S Limited has not sold those goods at the year-end, the adjustment is straightforward:

DR Consolidated reserves (retained profits of P Limited)
CR Inventory

However, if the unrealised profit arose in the books of S Limited, e.g. S Limited sold goods to P Limited and P Limited still has these goods included in inventory at the year-end then allowance must be made for the non-controlling interest share in the unrealised profit:

DR Consolidated reserves (group share)
DR Non-controlling interest (non-controlling interest share)
CR Inventory

Example

At the reporting date, S Limited's inventory includes €3,200 of goods at invoice price bought from P Limited. P Limited adds $33^{1/3}$% to cost. P Limited owns 80% of S Limited.

Therefore S Limited's inventory is recorded at original cost plus $33^{1/3}$%.

The unrealised profit is $€3,200 \times \dfrac{33^{1/3}}{133^{1/3}}$

Inventory Account

		€
	Unrealised profit	800

Consolidated Reserves

	€
Unrealised profit	800

Non-current Assets (Property, Plant and Equipment) and Unrealised Profit

When one company in the group sells to another member of the group an asset which is regarded as non-current, provision must be made for any profit taken by the seller. As with the unrealised profits arising on inventory, the following should be applied:

(a) the whole of the unrealised profit should be eliminated;
(b) a part should be borne by the non-controlling interest if the unrealised profit has been included in the accounts of a subsidiary; and
(c) correct the resulting over-depreciation.

It will be remembered that, in the separate accounts of the purchasing company, depreciation will be provided on the purchase price to that company of the tangible non-current asset. In the consolidated financial statements, depreciation should be provided on the cost to the group of the non-current tangible asset. The effect of this is that, for consolidation purposes, adjustment should be made eliminating the excess depreciation.

Example

During the year P Limited (which owns 80% of the ordinary share capital of S Limited) sold to S Limited a tangible non-current asset for €30,000. The asset had been bought by P Limited on the first day of the current year for €24,000 and had thus not been depreciated by P Limited. Depreciation is provided within the group at 10% per annum on a straight-line basis. The journal adjustments would be as follows:

	€	€
DR Consolidated Reserves	6,000	
CR Tangible non-current assets		6,000

Being the elimination of unrealised profit on inter-group transfer of non-current assets.

DR   Tangible non-current assets – Accum. depreciation   600

CR   Reserves S   600

Being the correction of accumulated depreciation on assets transferred to group companies (10% x 6,000).

Example

On 1.1.X3, S Limited sold a tangible non-current asset for €100,000 to P Limited. The asset cost S Limited €50,000 on 1.1.X1. Depreciation is charged by the group at 10% per annum on a straight-line basis. P Limited owns 75% of S Limited. The current year-end is 31.12.X5.

		€
Cost to the group	1.1.X1	50,000
Depreciation	20X1	(5,000)
	20X2	(5,000)
NBV at date of transfer	1.1.X3	40,000
Value transferred	1.1.X3	100,000
Unrealised profit		60,000

DR Consolidated reserves (group share) (€60,000 x 75%)   €45,000

DR Non-controlling interest (NCI share) (€60,000 x 25%)   €15,000

CR Tangible non-current asset – cost   €60,000

Being the elimination of the unrealised tangible non-current asset profit.

An adjustment is also required to correct three years of over-depreciation. Depreciation charged by P Limited.

	€
100,000 x 10% x 3 years	30,000

Correct depreciation, i.e. based on cost to the group

	€
50,000 x 10% x 3 years	15,000
	15,000

> DR Tangible Non-current asset – Depreciation   €15,000
>
> CR Consolidated Reserves   €15,000
>
> As there has been over-depreciation charged by P, tangible non-current assets are valued too low.

Revaluation of Tangible Non-current Assets

In most cases, on acquisition of a subsidiary, the assets of the subsidiary would have been revalued for the purpose of determining the purchase price. This revaluation should be preferably recorded by the subsidiary in its own separate accounts. Failing this, the revaluation should be made as a consolidation adjustment as follows:

Dr Non-current assets
Cr Cost of control A/c (group's share)
Cr Non-controlling interest (their share)

Where a consolidation adjustment is made, depreciation should also be adjusted appropriately if the net assets revalued include any tangible non-current assets. This adjustment should be debited to the subsidiary company's reserves. The non-controlling interest should then be charged with their share of the adjustment, while the remainder should be charged against post-acquisition reserves.

Example

Assume that P Limited acquired 80% of the ordinary share capital of S Limited two years ago (31 December 20X6). The tangible non-current assets of S Limited (book value €160,000) were revalued at €180,000 at the date of acquisition. This revaluation has not been recorded in the books of S Limited. Depreciation has been provided by S Limited at the rate of 10% per annum on the reducing balanced basis since the acquisition. At the reporting date (31 December 20X8), the net book amount of S Limited's tangible non-current assets was €129,600.

Requirement   Prepare the necessary journal entries, giving effect to the revaluation and any necessary depreciation adjustment.

Solution

		€	€
1.	DR Tangible Non-current assets A/c	20,000	
	CR Cost of control A/c		16,000
	CR Non-controlling interests A/c		4,000
2.	DR Consolidated reserves A/c	3,040	
	DR Non-controlling interests A/c	760	
	CR Accumulated depreciation account		3,800

	€	€	€
Net book amount 31.12.20X6	160,000		
Valuation 31.12.20X6		180,000	
Depreciation 20X7 10%	(16,000)	(18,000)	2,000
	144,000	162,000	
Depreciation 20X8 10%	(14,400)	(16,200)	1,800
	129,600	145,800	
Extra depreciation			3,800

PROCEDURE FOR PREPARATION OF A CONSOLIDATED STATEMENT OF FINANCIAL POSITION

Having studied the basic techniques of consolidated financial statements, it might be useful to consider the following procedure/method for preparing a consolidated statement of financial position. While these procedures do not have to be completed in the order listed, they should act as a useful checklist of procedures to be considered in most questions. It is important that by practising questions you develop an approach that you are comfortable applying.

1. Establish and record the group structure.
2. Open 'T' accounts.
3. Transfer the relevant balances from the statement of financial position of the parent and the subsidiary to the 'T' accounts.
4. Put through any journal adjustments required by the question.

5. Give the non-controlling interest their share of all reserves by:

   DR Relevant reserves account
   CR Non-controlling interest

   With the non-controlling interest's percentage of the reserves (at the reporting date). Pay particular attention to the option selected for dealing with non-controlling interests at the acquisition date (either at fair value (new method) or at the non-controlling interest's proportionate share of the net identifiable assets of the entity acquired (old method)).

6. Give the non-controlling interest their share of the share capital by:

   DR Share capital
   CR Non-controlling interest

   With the share capital which was not acquired by the parent.

7. Transfer to the cost of control account the parent company's share of the subsidiary's reserves and share capital at acquisition date:

   DR Share Capital
   DR Relevant reserves account
   CR Cost of Control

8. Transfer to the cost of control account the cost of the investment in the subsidiary:

   DR Cost of control
   CR Investment

   Remember consolidated goodwill is calculated as follows: consideration paid by parent + non-controlling interest – fair value of the subsidiary's net identifiable assets. Furthermore, it is important to remember that the non-controlling interest in the above formula may be valued at its proportionate share of the subsidiary's net identifiable assets, in which case consolidated goodwill would be that relating to the parent only (old method). Alternatively, the non-controlling interest may be at its fair value (new method), in which case the consolidated goodwill represents that of both the parent and the non-controlling interest.

9. Calculate inter-company profits
   These arise most frequently in the areas of inventory and tangible non-current assets. Accounts should be opened for items in respect of which there have been inter-company profits.

   DR Retained profits
   CR Relevant asset account
   With full amount of the unrealised profit.

10. Extract balances from the accounts referred to in (2) above, inserting them into the consolidated statement of financial position.

11. Aggregate the remaining balances in the statements of financial position, inserting them into the consolidated statement of financial position.

COMPREHENSIVE EXAMPLE

On 1 January 2008 Toffer acquired the following non-current investments:

- Three million equity shares in KTE by an exchange of one share in Toffer for every two shares in KTE, plus €1.25 per acquired KTE share in cash. The market price of each Toffer share at the date of acquisition was €6, and the market price of each KTE share at the date of acquisition was €3.25; and
- Thirty per cent of the equity shares of LN at a cost of €7.50 per share in cash.

Only the cash consideration of the above investments has been recorded by Toffer. In addition, €500,000 of professional costs relating to the acquisition of KTE are included in the cost of the investment.

The summarised draft statements of financial position of the three companies at 31 December 2008 are:

	Toffer €'000	KTE €'000	LN €'000
ASSETS			
Non-current Assets			
Property, plant and equipment	18,400	10,400	18,000
Investments in KTE and LN	13,250	nil	nil
Available-for-sale investments	6,500	nil	nil
	38,150	10,400	18,000
Current Assets			
Inventory	6,900	6,200	3,600
Trade receivables	3,200	1,500	2,400
Total assets	48,250	18,100	24,000
EQUITY AND LIABILITIES			
€1 Equity shares	10,000	4,000	4,000
Retained earnings			
– at 31 December 2007	16,000	6,000	11,000
– for year ended 31 December 2008	9,250	2,900	5,000
	35,250	12,900	20,000

Non-current Liabilities			
7% Loan notes	5,000	1,000	1,000
Current Liabilities	8,000	4,200	3,000
Total equity and liabilities	48,250	18,100	24,000

Additional Information:

(i) At the date of acquisition, KTE had five years remaining of an agreement to supply goods to one of its major customers. KTE believes it is highly likely that the agreement will be renewed when it expires. The directors of Toffer estimate that the value of this customer-based contract has a fair value of €1m, an indefinite life, and has not suffered any impairment.

(ii) On 1 January 2008, Toffer sold an item of plant to KTE at its agreed fair value of €2.5m. Its carrying amount prior to the sale was €2m. The estimated remaining life of the plant at the date of sale was five years (straight-line depreciation).

(iii) During the year ended 31 December 2008, KTE sold goods to Toffer for €2.7m. KTE had marked up these goods by 50% on cost. Toffer had a third of the goods still in its inventory at 31 December 2008. There were no intra-group payables/receivables at 31 December 2008.

(iv) Toffer has a policy of valuing non-controlling interests at fair value at the date of acquisition. For this purpose, the share price of KTE at this date should be used. Impairment tests on 31 December 2008 concluded that neither consolidated goodwill nor the value of the investment in LN have been impaired.

(v) The available-for-sale investments are included in Toffer's statement of financial position (above) at their fair value on 1 January 2008, but they have a fair value of €9m at 31 December 2008.

(vi) No dividends were paid during the year by any of the companies.

Requirement Prepare the consolidated statement of financial position for Toffer as at 31 December 2008.

Solution

Tutorial Note:

• Toffer purchased 3,000,000/4,000,000 shares in KTE (i.e. 75%), paying €12.75m ((1.5m shares x €6) + (3m shares x €1.25)).

• Toffer purchased 1,200,000 shares in LN at €7.50 each = €9,000,000.

Tutorial Note: There are a number of ways of presenting the information to test the new method for calculating the non-controlling interest at the date of acquisition. As above, the subsidiary's share price just before the acquisition could be given and then used to value the non-controlling interest. It is then a matter of multiplying the share price by the number of shares held by the non-controlling interest:

e.g. 1 million x €3.25 = €3.25m (see w(ii) below).

In practice the parent is likely to have paid more than the subsidiary's pre-acquisition share price in order to gain control.

The question could simply state that the directors valued the non-controlling interest at the date of acquisition at €3.25m (for example in note (iv)).

An alternative approach would be to give in the question the value of the goodwill attributable to the non-controlling interest. In this case, the non-controlling interest's goodwill would be added to the parent's goodwill (calculated by the old method) and to the carrying amount of the non-controlling interest itself (e.g. €500,000 (see w(ii) below)).

Consolidated Statement of Financial Position of Toffer as at 31 December 2008

	€'000	€'000
ASSETS		
Non-current Assets		
PPE (€18,400 + €10,400 − €2,500 + €2,000 + €100 (w(i)))		28,400
Goodwill (w(ii))		5,000
Customer-based intangible asset		1,000
Investments:		
− Associate (w(iii))		10,500
− Other available-for-sale investments		9,000
		53,900
Current Assets		
Inventory (€6,900 + €6,200 − €300 (w(iv)))	12,800	
Trade receivables (€3,200 + €1,500)	4,700	17,500
Total assets		71,400

EQUITY AND LIABILITIES

€1 Equity shares (w(v))		11,500
Share premium (w(v))	7,500	
Retained earnings (w(vi))	30,300	37,800
		49,300
Non-controlling interests (w(vii))		3,900
		53,200
Non-current Liabilities		
7% Loan notes (€5,000 + €1,000)		6,000
Current Liabilities (€8,000 + €4,200)		12,200
Total equity and liabilities		71,400

Workings

(i) Property, plant and equipment

The transfer of the plant creates an initial unrealised profit (URP) of €500,000. This is reduced by €100,000 for each year (straight-line depreciation over five years) of depreciation in the post-acquisition period. Thus at 31 December 2008 the net unrealised profit is €400,000. This should be eliminated from Toffer's retained profits and from the carrying amount of the plant. The depreciation adjustment is made in Toffer's book as the transfer was from parent to subsidiary.

(ii) Goodwill in KTE

	€'000	€'000
Investment at cost:		
Shares issued (3,000/2 × €6)		9,000
Cash (3,000 × €1.25)		3,750
Total consideration		12,750
Equity shares of KTE	4,000	
Pre-acquisition reserves	6,000	
Customer-based contract	1,000	
	75% × 11,000	(8,250)
Parent's share of goodwill		4,500

	€'000
Fair value of non-controlling interest at date of acquisition – 1 million shares at €3.25	3,250
Non-controlling interest's share of KTE's net assets at date of acquisition (€11,000 × 25%)	(2,750)
Non-controlling interest's share of goodwill	500
Total goodwill is therefore (€4,500 + €500)	5,000

This applies the old methodology for calculating the goodwill with the non-controlling interest's goodwill calculated separately. Applying the new method of calculating goodwill gives the same total figure, but it is a little simpler:

	€'000
Consideration paid by the parent (as before)	12,750
Fair value of the non-controlling interest (as before)	3,250
	16,000
Fair value of subsidiary's net assets (based on equity as before)	(11,000)
Total goodwill	5,000

Tutorial Note   The consideration given by Toffer for the shares of KTE works out at €4.25 per share, i.e. consideration of €12.75m for 3 million shares. This is considerably higher than the market price of KTE's shares (€3.25) before the acquisition. This probably reflects the cost of gaining control of KTE. This is also why it is probably appropriate to value the non-controlling interest in KTE shares at €3.25 each, because (by definition) the non-controlling interest does not have any control. This also explains why Toffer's share of KTE's goodwill at 90% (i.e. 4,500/5,000) is much higher than its proportionate shareholding in KTE (which is 75%).

(iii) Carrying amount of LN at 31 December 2008

	€'000
Cost (4,000 x 30% x €7.50)	9,000
Share post-acquisition profit (€5,000 x 30%)	1,500
	10,500

(iv) The unrealised profit (URP) in inventory
Intra-group sales are €2.7m on which KTE made a profit of €900,000 (€2,700 x 50/150). One third of these are still in the inventory of Toffer, thus there is an unrealised profit of €300,000.

(v) Share issues

The 1.5 million shares issued by Toffer in the share exchange, at a value of €6 each, would be recorded as €1 per share as capital and €5 per share as premium, giving an increase in share capital of €1.5m and a share premium of €7.5m.

(vi) Consolidated retained earnings

	€'000
Toffer's retained earnings	25,250
Professional costs of acquisition must be expensed	(500)
KTE's post-acquisition profits (€2,900 – €300 URP) × 75%	1,950
LN's post-acquisition profits (€5,000 × 30%)	1,500
URP in plant (see (i))	(400)
Gain on available-for-sale investment (€9,000 – €6,500) (see below)	2,500
	30,300

The gain on available-for-sale investments must be recognised directly in equity.

(vii) Non-controlling interest

	€'000
Equity at 31 December 2008	12,900
Customer-based contract	1,000
URP in inventory	(300)
	13,600
The non-controlling interest's share of net identifiable assets (x 25%)	3,400
Non-controlling interest share of goodwill (w (ii))	500
	3,900

Note that subsequent to the date of acquisition, a non-controlling interest is valued at its proportionate share of the carrying value of the subsidiary's net identifiable assets (equal to its equity) plus its attributed goodwill (less any impairment). The non-controlling interest is only valued at fair value at the date of acquisition.

Tutorial Note If goodwill had been impaired by €1m, IAS 36 requires a subsidiary's goodwill impairment to be allocated between the parent and the non-controlling interest on the same basis as the subsidiary's profits and losses are allocated. Thus, of the impairment of €1m, €750,000 would be allocated to the parent (and debited to group retained earnings reducing them to €29.55m (€30,300,000 – €750,000)) and €250,000 would be allocated to the non-controlling interest, writing it down to €3.65m (€3,900,000 – €250,000). It could be argued that this requirement represents an anomaly: of the recognised goodwill (before the impairment) of €5m, only €500,000 (i.e. 10%) relates to the non-controlling interest, but it suffers 25% (its proportionate shareholding in KTE) of the goodwill impairment.

CONCLUSION

Consolidated financial statements combine the financial statements of separate legal entities controlled by a parent company into one set of financial statements for the entire group of companies. They are a representation of how the combined entities are performing as a group. The consolidated financial statements should provide a true and fair view of the financial and operating conditions of the group. In preparing consolidated financial statements, the parent company must eliminate transactions between the parent and its subsidiaries before presenting the consolidated financial statements to the public to avoid double counting and giving the reader the impression that the consolidated entity has more profits or owes more money than it actually does.

For example, let's assume that ABC acquires all of the shares of DEF. Both ABC and DEF continue as separate legal entities. ABC is the parent company and DEF is the subsidiary company. Each of these companies continues to operate their respective business and each will publish their own financial statements. However, both existing and potential investors in ABC will find it helpful to see the financial results and the financial position of the economic entity (the combination of ABC and DEF) that they control. Therefore the consolidated statement of comprehensive income of ABC reports all of the revenues that the economic entity earned from outside customers. The consolidated income statement also reports all of the expenses that were incurred outside of the economic entity. The consolidated statement of financial position of ABC will report all of the assets and liabilities of the economic entity (amounts owed and receivable between ABC and DEF are eliminated on consolidation).

QUESTIONS

Self-test Questions

1. Explain how the investment in a subsidiary is reported in the parent's own financial statements.
2. Explain the difference between pre-acquisition and post-acquisition profits of a subsidiary.
3. Explain how inter-company balances should be treated in the consolidated statement of financial position.

4. Explain how negative goodwill may arise and its accounting treatment.
5. Discuss briefly the main reasons for the preparation of consolidated financial statements.

Review Questions

(See APPENDIX ONE for Suggested Solutions to Review Questions)

Question 1

Llewellyn Limited paid €68,000 for its interest in Roberts Limited on 1 July 20X3. The following is the draft consolidation statement of financial position of Llewellyn Limited and its subsidiary Roberts Limited at 30 June 20X4.

	€	€
Assets		
Non-current assets		
Property (cost)		30,000
Plant (book value)		80,000
Goodwill		16,000
		126,000
Current assets		
Inventory		32,000
Receivables		24,000
Cash		4,000
		60,000
Total Assets		186,000
Equity and Liabilities		
Equity		
Share Capital €1		100,000
Retained earnings – Llewellyn Limited	20,000	
– Roberts (since acquisition)	12,000	32,000
Total Equity		132,000

Current Liabilities

Sundry Payables	54,000
Total Liabilities	54,000
Total Equity and Liabilities	186,000

Additional Information:

1. Llewellyn Limited acquired only 80% of the ordinary share capital of Roberts Limited, whereas it was assumed by the Assistant Accountant who drew up the draft consolidated statement of financial position that the whole of it had been acquired.
2. Inventory shown in the statement of financial position of Roberts Limited was undervalued by €1,000 at 30 June 20X3 and by €1,600 at 30 June 20X4.
3. Plant shown in the statement of financial position of Roberts Limited at 30 June 20X3 was overvalued by €2,000 (Rate of depreciation – 10% per annum).
4. Inventory held by Roberts Limited at 30 June 20X4 includes €800 transferred from Llewellyn Limited which cost the latter €600.
5. Roberts Limited has no preference capital, no reserves other than the retained profit account balance and had paid no dividends since the acquisition of the shares by Llewellyn Limited.
6. With respect to the measurement of non-controlling interests at the date of acquisition, the proportionate share method equates to the fair value method. The directors of Llewellyn Limited are confident that any goodwill arising on the acquisition of Roberts Limited has not suffered any impairment.

Requirement
(a) Present working papers in the form of ledger accounts showing the adjustments necessary to correct the Consolidated Statement of Financial Position; and
(b) Present the revised Consolidated Statement of Financial Position as at 30 June 20X4.

(Ignore taxation.)

Question 2

The following is a summary of the balances in the books of Black Limited as at 31 March 20X2:

	Black Limited	Bird Limited
	€	€
Assets		
Non-current assets		
Property, plant and equipment	190,000	190,000
Investment in Bird:		
75,000 ordinary shares	165,000	-
60,000 preference shares	60,000	-
5,000 debentures	5,000	
	420,000	190,000
Current Assets	145,500	143,400
Total Assets	565,500	333,400
Equity and Liabilities		
Equity		
Ordinary shares (€1)	300,000	100,000
7% preference shares (€1)	-	80,000
General reserve	50,000	40,000
Retained profit	98,500	44,400
	448,500	264,400
Non-current liabilities		
6% Debentures	-	20,000

Current liabilities

Trade payables		87,000	32,200
Proposed dividends:	Ordinary	30,000	10,000
	Preference	-	5,600
Debenture interest accrued		-	1,200
Total current liabilities		117,000	49,000
Total Equity and Liabilities		565,500	333,400

Additional Information

(a) Black Limited acquired the shares of Bird Limited, cum dividend on 31 March 20X1.
(b) The general reserve of Bird Limited was the same on 31 March 20X1 as on 31 March 20X2. The balance on the statement of comprehensive income of Bird Limited is made up as follows:

	€
Balance on 31 March 20X1	28,000
Net profit for the year ended 31 March 20X2	32,000
	60,000
Less provision for proposed dividends	15,600
	44,400

(c) The inventory of Bird Limited on 31 March 20X2 included €16,000 in respect of goods purchased from Black Limited. These goods had been sold by Black Limited to Bird Limited at such a price as to give Black Limited a profit of 20% on the invoice price.
(d) The balance on the statement of comprehensive income of Bird Limited on 31 March 20X1 is after providing for the preference dividend of €5,600 and a proposed ordinary dividend of €5,000, both of which were subsequently paid, but had been incorrectly credited to the statement of comprehensive income of Black Limited.
(e) No entries had been made in the books of Black Limited in respect of the debenture interest due from, or the proposed dividend of, Bird Limited for the year ended 31 March 20X2.
(f) The proposed dividends included in current liabilities at 31 May 20X2 were approved during the year ended 31 March 20X2 by the shareholders of the respective companies.
(g) With respect to the measurement of non-controlling interests at the date of acquisition, the proportionate share method equates to the fair value method. The directors of Black Limited are confident that any goodwill arising on the acquisition of Bird Limited has not suffered any impairment.

Requirement   You are required to prepare the consolidated statement of financial position of Black Limited, and its subsidiary company Bird Limited as at 31 March 20X2.

Question 3 (*Based on ICAI, P3 Summer 2003, Question 5*)

The statements of financial position of ROCK plc (ROCK) and ROLL plc (ROLL) as at 31 December 2004 are presented below.

	ROCK €'000	ROLL €'000
ASSETS		
Non-current Assets		
Property, plant and equipment	5,760	4,000
Investment in ROLL	3,330	-
Current Assets	1,260	864
	10,350	4,864
EQUITY AND LIABILITIES		
Capital and Reserves		
€0.50 ordinary shares	2,700	1,600
€1 8% preference shares	-	800
Share premium	810	160
Retained earnings	3,960	904
	7,470	3,464
Non-current Liabilities		
10% debentures 2009	1,800	800
Current Liabilities	1,080	600
	10,350	4,864

Additional Information:

1. On 1 January 2002, ROCK purchased the following shares and debentures in ROLL:

   - 2,400,000 €0.50 ordinary shares;
   - 400,000 8% €1 preference shares;
   - 10% debentures with a nominal value of €320,000.

   The nominal value of ROLL's share capital and debentures has not changed since 1 January 2002. On that date, the share premium account and the retained earnings of ROLL stood at €160,000 credit and €560,000 debit respectively. With respect to the measurement of non-controlling interests at the date of acquisition, the proportionate share method equated to the fair value method.

2. On 1 January 2002, the property, plant and equipment of ROLL had a fair value of €800,000 in excess of their book values, and a remaining useful economic life of 20 years on this date. This has not yet been reflected in the books of ROLL.
3. During the year ended 31 December 2004, ROCK sold equipment to ROLL for €1,000,000 at a profit of 25% of selling price. ROLL charges a full year's depreciation in the year of acquisition, charging €200,000 depreciation in the year ended 31 December 2004 on the basis that the equipment had a useful economic life of five years.
4. During the year ended 31 December 2004, ROLL paid an interim dividend to its preference and ordinary shareholders of €32,000 and €50,000 respectively. Dividends proposed, but not yet approved, at 31 December 2004 to ROLL's preference and ordinary shareholders amount to €32,000 and €160,000 respectively. At 31 December 2003, ROLL has accrued the debenture interest payable for the period 1 July 2003 to 31 December 2003. ROCK does not accrue dividends or interest receivable.
5. The directors of ROCK belive that the goodwill arising on the acquisition of ROLL was impaired for the first time by €333,000 during the year ended 31 December 2004.

Requirement   Prepare the consolidated statement of financial position for the ROCK Group as at 31 December 2004.

Challenging Questions

Question 1 (*Based on ICAI, P3 Autumn 1997, Question 3*)

MORN Limited, NOON Limited and NIGHT Limited are three companies involved in the production of television programmes, primarily dealing with news and current affairs. A number of the management team of MORN Limited are also key figures on the management teams of NOON Limited and NIGHT Limited, and MORN Limited has always been able to exercise a dominant influence over the policies and programming decisions of the other two companies.

On 1 January 2003, MORN Limited purchased 96,000 €1 ordinary shares in NOON Limited and 40,500 €1 ordinary shares in NIGHT Limited at a cost of €135,000 and €54,000 respectively. On the same date, NOON Limited purchased 36,000 €1 ordinary shares in NIGHT Limited at a cost of €47,250. The draft statements of financial position at 31 December 2003 of the three companies are shown below.

	MORN Limited €	NOON Limited €	NIGHT Limited €
ASSETS			
Non-current Assets			
Property, plant and equipment	214,500	90,000	50,000
Investments	189,000	47,250	-
	403,500	137,250	50,000

Current Assets			
Inventory	77,200	34,300	32,600
Receivables	189,800	158,050	143,600
Cash	11,000	8,600	4,100
	278,000	200,950	180,300
	681, 500	338,200	230,300
EQUITY & LIABILITIES			
Capital and Reserves			
Called up share capital	300,000	120,000	90,000
Retained earnings	75,000	54,000	37,500
	375,000	174,000	127,500
Non-current Liabilities	185,100	77,100	60,100
Current Liabilities	121,400	87,100	42,700
	681,500	338,200	230,300

Additional Information:

(1) On 1 January 2003, the retained earnings of NOON Limited and NIGHT Limited were €20,000 and €12,000 respectively.
(2) In arriving at the consideration for the shares in NOON Limited, property, plant and equipment was revalued at €115,000 and receivables amounting to €3,000 were deemed irrecoverable. No entry has been made in the books in respect of these valuations and there were no purchases or sales of property, plant and equipment by any of the companies during the year. The directors wish to give effect to the revaluations in the consolidated financial statements. With respect to the measurement of non-controlling interests at the date of acquisition, the proportionate share method equated to the fair value method. There is no evidence to suggest that the goodwill arising on the acquisition of NOON and NIGHT has been impaired.
(3) Property, plant and equipment represent filming equipment owned by the companies. Depreciation is to be provided at 10% per annum on a straight-line basis.

(4) During the year ended 31 December 2003, NOON Limited sold to NIGHT Limited blank films and tapes for use in programme production for €50,000 cash on delivery. NOON Limited had originally purchased the inventory for €36,000 direct from the manufacturer. At the reporting date, one half of the films and tapes still remained in inventory.

(5) Receivables of NIGHT Limited include €5,000 owed by MORN Limited.

(6) Included in the current liabilities of MORN Limited is €4,100 owed by the company to NIGHT Limited.

(7) A cheque for €900 was sent by MORN Limited on 30 December 2003 to NIGHT Limited but was not received until 2 January 2004.

Requirement Prepare the consolidated statement of financial position of MORN Limited as at 31 December 2003.

Question 2 (Based on ICAI, P3 Summer 1998, Question 4)

XTRA plc was incorporated in 1978 and makes up its accounts to 31 December each year. Its main business is the hire and retail of videos, records, compact discs and computer games. The company had traded very profitably throughout Ireland until the late 1990s when its results deteriorated dramatically as a result of fierce competition from larger retailers based in Great Britain entering the Irish market. In reaction to the falling profit margins and share price, the directors decided to try to halt the decline through a policy of acquisition and merger. The company has negotiated debt financing of up to €5m at a fixed rate of 10% per annum with Allied North West Bank should it be required.

(a) During the second half of 2003 the directors of XTRA plc and VDO plc had discussions with a view to a combination of the two companies. As a result of these negotiations it was agreed that:

- on 31 December 2003 XTRA plc should acquire 1,440,000 of the issued ordinary shares of VDO plc;
- XTRA plc should pay cash of 12 pence for each VDO plc share, plus a one for one share exchange. At the date of the offer the market price of a share in XTRA plc was €1.20 per share and the market price of a share in VDO plc was €1.15 per share. XTRA plc shares had remained relatively stable at approximately €1.20 per share during 2003, whereas VDO plc shares had ranged from €1.10 to €1.35 per share. Before the offer neither company owned any shares in the other;
- the consideration would be increased by 144,000 shares if a contingent liability in VDO plc in respect of a claim for wrongful dismissal by a former director did not crystallise.

The summarised statements of financial position at 31 December 2003 of XTRA plc and VDO plc before the proposed combination were:

	XTRA plc €m	VDO plc €m
ASSETS		
Non-current Assets		
Land	1.20	0.86
Property, plant and equipment	2.51	1.67
	3.71	2.53
Current Assets		
Inventory	0.60	0.23
Receivables	0.49	0.19
Cash in hand and at bank	0.15	0.34
	1.24	0.76
	4.95	3.29
EQUITY AND LIABILITIES		
Capital and Reserves		
€1 ordinary shares	2.00	1.50
Revaluation	0.49	-
Retained earnings	1.90	1.00
	4.39	2.50
Current Liabilities	0.56	0.79
	4.95	3.29

Additional Information

1. The fair value of the assets of VDO plc at 31 December 2003 was:

Land	€1.3m
Property, plant and equipment	€1.6m
Inventory	€0.2m
Receivables	€0.16m

2. With respect to the measurement of non-controlling interests at the date of acquisition, the proportionate share method equated to the fair value method.

Requirement
(a) Prepare the consolidated statement of financial position of XTRA plc and VDO plc.

(b) On 31 December 2003 XTRA plc acquired 90% of the ordinary shares of DAT Limited, a company involved in digital audio technology. While DAT Limited has suffered trading losses in recent years, the directors of XTRA plc are confident that, after incurring reorganisation costs of €250,000 and future trading losses of €150,000, DAT Limited will return to profit.

The purchase consideration comprised deferred consideration of €3,000,000, payable in equal instalments on 31 December 2004, 2005 and 2006. The book value of the net assets of DAT Limited was €2.2m. This included land with a book value of €800,000 but a market value of €1.1m.

XTRA plc incurred accountancy fees of €60,000 and legal fees of €40,000 in connection with the acquisition, and €40,000 in respect of time spent by directors of XTRA plc.

Requirement
(a) Calculate the goodwill to be dealt with in the consolidated financial statements of XTRA plc for the year ended 31 December 2003.
(b) Explain clearly the treatment of the deferred consideration in the statement of comprehensive income of XTRA plc for the year ended 31 December 2003 and the statement of financial position at that date.

NB   The following annuity table (extract) should be used where appropriate:

Period	10%
1	0.9090
2	0.8264
3	0.7513

Question 3 (Based on ICAI, P3 Autumn 1999, Question 5)

On 1 January 2001 HUMPTY Limited purchased 320,000 €1 ordinary shares in DUMPTY Limited. On this date the fair value of DUMPTY Limited's separable net assets differed from their book values as follows:

	Statement of financial position value at 1 January 2001	Fair value at 1 January 2001
	€'000	€'000
Property, plant and equipment	500	750
Inventory	100	125
Trade receivables	60	55

However, DUMPTY did not incorporate these fair values into its books of account. With respect to the measurement of non-controlling interests at the date of acquisition, the proportionate share method equated to the fair value method. The directors of HUMPTY believe that the goodwill arising on the acquisition of DUMPTY was impaired for the first time by €345,000 during the year ended 31 December 2003.

On 1 January 2001, the property, plant and equipment of DUMPTY Limited had a remaining useful life of five years and retained earnings stood at €150,000. During 2001 HUMPTY Limited incurred reorganisation costs of €200,000 in order to successfully incorporate DUMPTY Limited into the group. None of the property, plant and equipment of DUMPTY Limited purchased on 1 January 2001 has been sold at 31 December 2003, but the inventory purchased was sold at a profit during 2001.

During 2003 DUMPTY Limited sold goods costing €160,000 to HUMPTY Limited for €200,000. At 31 December 2003 the inventory of HUMPTY Limited includes €50,000 (at cost to HUMPTY Limited) of the goods purchased from DUMPTY Limited.

The individual company statements of financial position of HUMPTY Limited and DUMPTY Limited at 31 December 2003 are as follows:

Statement of Financial Position as at 31 December 2003

	HUMPTY Limited €'000	DUMPTY Limited €'000
ASSETS		
Non-current Assets		
Property, plant and equipment	900	700
Investment in DUMPTY Limited	1,231	-
	2,131	700
Current Assets		
Inventory	164	86
Trade receivables	196	-
Bank and cash	68	81
	428	167
	2,559	867

EQUITY AND LIABILITIES

Capital and Reserves

€1 ordinary shares	1,000	400
Retained earnings	1,217	370
	2,217	770
Non-current Liabilities	200	40
Current Liabilities	142	57
	2,559	867

Requirement

(a) Prepare the consolidated statement of financial position for HUMPTY group as at 31 December 2003.

(b) The remaining ordinary share capital of DUMPTY Limited is owned by EGG Limited, a company that is wholly owned by a director of DUMPTY Limited. During 2003 EGG Limited purchased property from DUMPTY Limited. The sale price was set by an independent property surveyor.

Discuss the implications of this transaction for the year ended 31 December 2003 with regard to IAS 24 *Related Party Disclosures*.

Question 4 (Based on ICAI, P3 Autumn 2001, Question 6)

The draft statements of financial position of NIP Limited and TUCK Limited as at 31 December 2003 are as follows:

	NIP	TUCK
	€'000	€'000
ASSETS		
Non-current Assets		
Property	5,000	2,000
Plant and equipment	3,500	2,500
	8,500	4,500

Current Assets		
Inventory	2,500	3,000
Receivables - TUCK	1,100	-
Receivables - others	400	1,000
Bills receivable from TUCK	900	-
Bank	100	100
	5,000	4,100
	13,500	8,600
EQUITY AND LIABILITIES		
Capital and Reserves		
€1 ordinary shares	1,000	1,000
Retained earnings	10,000	4,000
	11,000	5,000
Current Liabilities		
Payables	2,500	2,700
Bills payable to NIP	-	900
	2,500	3,600
	13,500	8,600

Additional Information

1. On 1 January 2003, NIP issued 900,000 €1 ordinary shares with a market value of €5 per share in return for 900,000 €1 ordinary shares in TUCK when the balance on TUCK's retained earnings was €3,000,000. On that date, the book value and fair value of net assets were the same, except that the property that had a book value of €2,200,000 was valued at €2,700,000. The revaluation has not been incorporated into the books of TUCK. Depreciation is 10% per annum on book value. The investment in TUCK has not yet been incorporated into the books of NIP. With respect to the measurement of non-controlling interests at the date of acquisition, the proportionate share method equates to the fair value method.

2. The inventory of TUCK includes items purchased from NIP for €1,250,000. NIP had made a profit of 25% on cost in respect of these items.

3. One of the products manufactured by NIP has been sold below its cost during the year ended 31 December 2003. Consequently, the directors believe that the plant and equipment used to manufacture this product have suffered a permanent diminution in value. The carrying value, at historical cost, of the plant and equipment at

31 December 2003 is €400,000 and the net realisable value is estimated to be €200,000. The anticipated net cash inflows from this product are expected to be €100,000 per annum for the next four years. (A market discount rate of 10% per annum should be used in any present value computations.)

4. During the year ended 31 December 2002, three people died using machinery manufactured by NIP. Legal proceedings were started in 2002, but NIP did not provide for potential damages at 31 December 2002 on their lawyers' advice that it was unlikely NIP would be found liable. However, by 31 December 2003, NIP's lawyers believe that, owing to developments in the case, it is probable that NIP will be found liable for damages of approximately €2,000,000.

Requirement   Prepare the consolidated statement of financial position of NIP Group as at 31 December 2003.

Present value factors:	Years	10%	Cumulative	Years	10%	Cumulative
	1	0.909	0.909	3	0.751	2.487
	2	0.827	1.736	4	0.683	3.170

CHAPTER 28

CONSOLIDATED STATEMENT OF COMPREHENSIVE INCOME

INTRODUCTION

The previous two chapters introduced the key principles associated with the preparation of consolidated financial statements, and in particular the consolidated statement of financial position. This chapter, while focusing upon the preparation of a consolidated statement of comprehensive income, develops these principles further.

COMMON ADJUSTMENTS

The following section outlines the most common adjustments which are required in preparing a consolidated statement of comprehensive income. These are:

- Inter-group sales;
- Inter-group inventory;
- Inter-group charges;
- Non-controlling interest;
- Dividends; and
- Retained profit brought forward.

This is not an exhaustive list, and care needs to be taken to identify any other potential adjustments.

Inter-Group Sales

Often companies within a group will sell goods/services to one another. When preparing group accounts it is important to remember that these in fact are not sales made by the group as they remain internal. As such exclude any inter-group revenue from the consolidated figure.

Example

A parent company has a 70% interest in a subsidiary. Items in the statements of comprehensive income of each company included the following:

	Parent €	Subsidiary €
Revenue	800,000	600,000
Cost of Sales	480,000	350,000

These figures include sales from the subsidiary to the parent company of €100,000.

Requirement   How much should be included in the consolidated statement of comprehensive income in respect of the following:

1. Revenue; and
2. Cost of Sales.

(Consider your answer before reading below.)

Solution

The sales from the subsidiary to the parent company are only internal to the group and as such should not be included in revenue in the consolidated statement of comprehensive income. Consequently, the sales have been recorded as purchases by the parent and these too need to be eliminated.

1. Revenue (€800,000 + €600,000 − €100,000) = €1,300,000
2. Cost of Sales (€480,000 + €350,000 − €100,000) = €730,000

Inter-Group Inventory

Where inter-group inventory (i.e. inventory on hand at the reporting date which has been purchased from another group company) is held by a group company at the reporting date, any profit element must be excluded. It is necessary to adjust the books of the company which made the unrealised inventory profits, i.e. the selling company.

Example

Company A is the parent company of company B, owning 80%. The year end is 31 December 2002 and consolidated accounts are to be prepared.

The following information is included:

	Company A €	Company B €
Revenue	100,000	80,000
Cost of Sales	60,000	30,000
Inventory on hand 31/12/02	50,000	30,000

Company B sold to Company A €20,000 of goods during the year, at a profit of 10%.

At 31 December 2003, Company A had remaining in inventory €8,000 of these goods.

Requirement   Prepare the adjustments required.

(Consider your answer before reading below.)

Solution

Company B is selling to A at a profit; however this profit is only realised to the group once company A sells the inventory externally. As such, any profit element which is still in inventory needs to be eliminated.

Adjustments:

1. Exclude €20,000 from Co. B's revenue and Co. A's purchases, being inter-group sales.
2. Inventory on hand at 31/12/02 includes €8,000 which was the cost from Co. B to Co. A. However the cost to the group was 8,000 x 100/110 = €7,273. Therefore the profit on the inventory is €727. This is to be eliminated from Co. B inventory holding. Increase cost of sales of Co. B by €727.

Inter Group Charges

Ensure that management charges, interest on loans, debenture interest and dividends are all cancelled out of group expenses and group incomes.

Non-controlling Interest

After 'profit after taxation', calculate the portion of profit of subsidiaries which relates to non-controlling interests (i.e. minority shareholders). The non-controlling interest in the profit of S is based on the profits after tax of S (after any adjustments required in the question).

Dividends

Dividends paid are an appropriation and therefore should be taken through reserves. Furthermore, proposed dividends cannot be accrued until approved by shareholders at the AGM (see IAS 10 *Events after the Reporting Date*). Dividends declared after the reporting date should only be recognised as liabilities at the reporting date if there is a legal obligation to receive them. Consequently, proposed dividends may need to be reversed.

With respect to dividends paid by the subsidiary (S), most of the dividends (i.e. the group's share) is paid to P and is therefore cancelled or eliminated or consolidated (a debit in S and a credit in P). The remainder of S dividend is paid to the non-controlling interest and is included in the non-controlling interest calculation referred to in the Non-controlling Interest section above.

Profit Brought Forward

The definition of this is:

- the retained profit of P at the start of the period; plus
- The group's share of the *post-acquisition* profits of the subsidiary to the start of the period.

Example

Company A acquired 80% of the ordinary shares of Company B on 1/1/2001 when the retained profits of that company were €100,000 credit. At 1/1/2002, the retained profits of the companies were:

A Limited	€800,000
B Limited	€250,000

Requirement   What are the retained profits brought forward in the consolidated statement of comprehensive income for the year ended 31/12/2002?

(Consider your answer before reading below.)

Solution

Company A Limited	€800,000
Company B Limited (80% (€250,000 – €100,000))	€120,000
	€920,000

COMPREHENSIVE EXAMPLE

Outlined below is an example of a more detailed consolidated statement of comprehensive income question Read through it carefully and slowly.

The statements of comprehensive income of Apple, Pear and Plum Limited for the year ended 31 December 2002 are shown below.

	Apple Limited €	Pear Limited €	Plum Limited €
Revenue	620,000	310,000	280,000
Less: Cost of Sales	492,000	218,000	178,000
Gross Profit	128,000	92,000	102,000
Less: Expenses			
Admin. expenses	37,200	20,000	22,000
Depreciation	10,200	7,800	6,000
Interest on loans	–	1,400	2,000
Debenture interest	–	10,000	–
Selling expenses	53,000	21,000	16,000
	100,400	60,200	46,000
Add: Sundry Income	15,100	2,600	200
Profit before tax	42,700	34,400	56,200
Income tax expense	15,100	12,000	25,000
Profit after tax	27,600	22,400	31,200

Additional Information

1. Apple Limited purchased the following shares in 1999:

   90,000 ordinary shares €1 each in Pear   (total issued: 100,000)
   180,000 ordinary shares €1 each in Plum   (total issued: 200,000)
   20,000 1% preference shares €1 each in Plum   (total issued: 100,000)

   Apple controls any operating and policy decisions in both Pear and Plum.

   The reserve balances at the dates of acquisition were:

   Pear   €1,600   DR
   Plum   €5,800   CR

2. During the year, Apple sold goods to Plum for €48,000. Of these, Plum holds goods costing Plum €2,700 at the year-end. Apple makes a 20% gross profit based on cost.

3. The retained earnings of Apple, Pear and Plum are as follows:

	Apple €	Pear €	Plum €
Profit after tax for year ended 31 December 2002	27,600	22,400	31,200
Dividends paid during year ended 31 December 2002			
- Preference	-	-	(1,000)
- Ordinary	(10,000)	(2,000)	(3,000)
Retained earnings at 1 January 2002	48,000	16,000	21,000
Retained earnings at 31 December 2002	65,600	36,400	48,200

Dividends received from subsidiaries have been included in the holding company's sundry income.

Requirement Prepare the consolidated statement of comprehensive income of Apple group for the year ended 31 December 2002.

Solution

Always begin every consolidated account question by drafting a group structure and establishing the type of interest held.

1. Group Structure

We are told that Apple Limited owns 90% of the ordinary shares in both Pear and Plum and 20% of the preference shares of Plum Limited.

	Pear Ordinary	Plum Ordinary	Preference
Group	90%	90%	20%
NCI	10%	10%	80%
	100%	100%	100%
	=> Subsidiary	=> Subsidiary	

2. Revenue (Sales)

We are told that, during the year, Apple sold goods of €48,000 to Plum. Consequently, the group (as a single entity) has sold goods to itself and has included these in both its sales and cost of sales. Any intra-group revenue therefore must be excluded from both group sales and group cost of sales, thus cancelling the transactions in the Consolidated Statement of Comprehensive Income:

	Apple €	Pear €	Plum €	Adjustment €	Consolidated €
Revenue	620,000	310,000	280,000	(48,000)	1,162,000
Cost of Sales	(492,000)	(218,000)	(178,000)	48,000	(840,000)
Gross Profit	128,000	92,000	102,000	–	322,000

Note that this adjustment has no profit effect.

3. Unrealised profit in inventory

We are told that, of the sales from Apple to Plum, €2,700 are still in Plum's inventory at the year-end. Apple makes 20% profit on cost of all sales. Consequently the group closing inventory includes a profit element on goods which the group (as a single entity) has not sold.

The unrealised profit is $$€2,700 \times \frac{20}{120} = €450$$

Closing inventory in the statement of financial position and closing inventory in cost of sales must be reduced in the books of the consolidated accounts to eliminate any unrealised profits included in inventory.

DR Cost of Sales
CR Inventory

This adjustment of €450 is made in the column of the company whose individual statement of comprehensive income includes the unrealised profit, i.e. the selling company. In this case, the goods were sold by Apple to Plum. Apple has made a 'notional' or unrealised profit from a group point of view as a result of this transaction and, consequently, it is in Apple's column that the adjustment is made.

	Apple €	Pear €	Plum €	Adjustment €	Consolidated €
Revenue	620,000	310,000	280,000	(48,000)	1,162,000
Draft Cost of Sales	(492,000)	(218,000)	(178,000)		
Inventory adjustment	(450)	-	-		
	(492,450)	(218,000)	(178,000)	48,000	(840,450)
Gross Profit	127,550	92,000	102,000	-	321,550

Note The group's gross profit has been reduced by €450. The other side of this entry is statement of financial position inventory being reduced by €450.

4. Inter-group dividends

We are told that Apple has received its share of the subsidiary dividends, i.e.

		€
Pear	90% x €2,000	1,800
Plum	Ord. 90% x €3,000	2,700
	Pref. 20% x €1,000	200
		4,700

These dividends have to be excluded from the holding company's income in the consolidated statement of comprehensive income.

	€
Sundry income per Apple Accounts	15,100
Less: dividends from subsidiaries	(4,700)
Sundry income for consolidations	10,400

	Apple	Pear	Plum	Adjustment	Consolidated
	€	€	€	€	€
Gross profit	127,550	92,000	102,000	–	321,550
Less expenses	(100,400)	(60,200)	(46,000)	–	(206,600)
Add income	10,400	2,600	200	–	13,200
Profit before tax	37,550	34,400	56,200	–	128,150
Income tax expense	(15,100)	(12,000)	(25,000)	–	52,100
Profit after tax	22,450	22,400	31,200	–	76,050

5. Non-controlling interest

It is at this stage that we recognise the fact that, although Apple has control over the activities of the companies in the group, it does *not* have legal title to 100% of the shares and consequently to all the profits. We must therefore calculate and show the amount of the 'Profit after tax' which is attributable to the non-controlling interest.

Note the additional working required in the case of preference shares being involved in the calculation.

(a) Pear: Profit after tax   €22,400
                                              x 10%
            Non-controlling interest   €2,240

(b) Plum: Profit after tax   € 31,200

	Pref. S/H	Ord. S/H
	€1,000	€30,200
	x 80%	x 10%
	€800	€3,020

Non-controlling interest €3,820

	Apple	Pear	Plum	Adjustment	Total
	€	€	€	€	€
Profit after tax	22,450	22,400	31,200		76,050
Non-controlling interest	--	(2,240)	(3,820)		(6,060)
Profit attributable to the Group	22,450	20,160	27,380		69,990

6. Dividend shuffle

Remember dividends paid are debited directly to equity. As we can see from the question, the group embarked on a policy of transferring profits from the subsidiaries to the holding company by paying dividends. We must reflect this in the consolidated retained earnings by 'shuffling' the dividend from one company to another.

Remember: 1. Subsidiary dividends only; and
            2. Group share only.

	Apple	Pear	Plum	Consolidated
	€	€	€	€
Profit attributable to the group	22,450	20,160	27,380	69,990
Pear – ordinary dividend	1,800	(1,800)	–	–
Plum – ordinary dividend	2,700	–	(2,700)	–
– preference dividend	200	–	(200)	–
	27,150	18,360	24,480	69,990

Note This must come out to be zero, i.e. it makes no difference to the total profit attributable to the group.

7. Parent company dividend

Again, remember, the parent company's dividend should be shown as a movement in retained earnings and should be subtracted after the dividend shuffle has been completed.

8. **Profit brought forward**

We are told that the reserves in the subsidiaries, when Apple purchased the shares, were:

Pear	€1,600 DR
Plum	€5,800 CR

Two points must be noted here:

1. Pre-acquisition reserves must be excluded from the consolidated accounts; and
2. Only the group share is included.

	Pear	Plum
	€	€
Reserves b/f per individual accounts	16,000	21,000
Pre-acquisition reserves	1,600	(5,800)
Post-acquisition reserves	17,600	15,200
	x 90%	x 90%
Group share only	15,840	13,680

The consolidated retained earnings can now be completed:

	Apple	Pear	Plum	Consolidated
	€	€	€	€
PATTG	22,450	20,160	27,380	69,990
Intergroup dividend	4,700	(1,800)	(2,900)	—
Parent dividend	(10,000)			(10,000)
	17,150	18,360	24,480	59,990
Reserves b/f	48,000	15,840	13,680	77,520
Reserves c/f	65,150	34,200	38,160	139,510

Your final consolidated statement of comprehensive income workings should look like this:

	Apple	Pear	Plum	Adj.	Consol.
	€	€	€	€	€
Revenue	620,000	310,000	280,000	(48,000)	1,162,000

Draft Cost of sales	492,000	218,000	178,000		
Inventory adjustment	450				
	(492,450)	(218,000)	(178,000)	(48,000)	(840,450)
Gross profit	127,550	92,000	102,000	-	321,550
less: Administration expenses	37,200	20,000	22,000	(2,000)	77,200
Depreciation	10,200	7,800	6,000		24,000
Interest on loans		1,400	2,000		3,400
Debenture Interest		10,000			10,000
Selling expenses	53,000	21,000	16,000		90,000
	(100,400)	(60,200)	(46,000)	-	(206,600)
add: Sundry income	10,400	2,600	200		13,200
Profit before tax	37,550	34,400	56,200		128,150
Income tax expense	(15,100)	(12,000)	(25,000)		(52,100)
Profit after tax	22,450	22,400	31,200		76,050
Non-controlling interest	–	(2,240)	(3,820)		(6,060)
Profit attributable to the group	22,450	20,160	27,380		69,990
Reserves b/f	48,000	15,840	13,680		77,520
Inter-group dividends	4,700	(1,800)	(2,900)		-
Dividends paid by Apple	(10,000)	–	–		(10,000)
Reserves c/f	65,150	34,200	38,160		137,510

The final solution will look as follows:

Apple Limited

Abreviated Consolidated Statement of Comprehensive Income

Year Ended 31 December 2002

	Notes	€
Revenue	(x)	1,162,000
Profit on ordinary activities before tax	(3)	128,150
Income tax expense	(x)	(52,100)
Profit on ordinary activities after tax		76,050
Non-controlling interest		(6,060)
Profit attributable to the group	(5)	69,990
Reserves brought forward		77,520
Dividends paid		(10,000)
Reserves carried forward		137,510

Notes

(3). Profit on ordinary activities is arrived at after charging:

	€
Directors' remuneration	7,000
Depreciation	24,000
Interest on loans	3,400
Debenture interest	10,000

(5). Of this amount, €29,600 is dealt with in the books of the holding company.

Alternative Workings for Apple Limited

An alternative approach to the preparation of a consolidated statement of comprehensive income is illustrated below. This approach does not use a consolidated scheme. It is important that you develop an approach that you are comfortable with.

Revenue	€	€
Apple		620,000
Pear		310,000
Plum		280,000
Inter-group		(48,000)
		1,162,000
Cost of Sales		
Apple		492,000
Pear		218,000
Plum		178,000

Inter-group	(48,000)	
Unrealised inventory profit	450	
	840,450	
Administration Expenses		
Apple	37,200	
Pear	20,000	
Plum	22,000	
	79,200	
Depreciation		
Apple	10,200	
Pear	7,800	
Plum	6,000	
	24,000	
Loan Interest		
Pear	1,400	
Plum	2,000	
	3,400	
Debenture Interest		
Pear	10,000	
Selling Expenses		
Apple	53,000	
Pear	21,000	
Plum	16,000	
	90,000	
Sundry Income		
Apple	15,100	
Less dividends received from Pear	(1,800)	
Plum (ordinary)	(2,700)	
Plum (preference)	(200)	10,400
Pear		2,600
Plum		200
		13,200
Income Tax Expense		
Apple		15,100
Pear		12,000
Plum		25,000
		52,100
Non-controlling Interest		
Pear Limited		
Profit after tax	22,400	
Add inter-group management charge	2,000	

Adjusted	24,400		
Non-controlling interest 10%			22,440
Plum Limited			
Profit after tax	31,200		
Less preference dividend	(1,000)	x 80% =	800
Ordinary profits	30,200	x 10% =	3,020
			3,820
Total non-controlling interest			6,060
Dividends Paid			
Apple only			10,000
Retained Profit Brought Forward			
Apple			48,000
Pear 90% (€16,000 + €1,600 Dr)			15,840
Plum 90% (€21,000 − €5,800)			13,680
			77,520

OTHER ADJUSTMENTS

You may be required to deal with adjustments other than those outlined above when preparing a consolidated statement of comprehensive income. These include:

- Revaluation of assets
- Acquisition of a subsidiary during the accounting period
- Opening unrealised inventory profit
- Pre-acquisition reserves
- Inter-group transfer of tangible non-current assets

Revaluation of Assets

When a holding company purchases the shares of a subsidiary, the net assets of the subsidiary must be included in the consolidated statement of financial position at their fair value at the date of acquisition. This revaluation to fair value is a consolidation adjustment only, i.e. the subsidiary does not necessarily (although it may) actually have to post the necessary revaluation journal itself. Consequently, the revaluation of the net assets to their fair values can be accounted for in either:

- the books of the subsidiary (before consolidation takes place); or
- as a consolidation adjustment.

If the revaluation is accounted for in the books of the subsidiary, then no further consolidation adjustment is required. If such a revaluation is made in the books of the subsidiary, the type of journal that may be required would be:

		€	€
DR	Land and buildings	20,000	
CR	Plant and machinery		5,000
CR	Inventory		1,000
CR	Receivables		3,000
CR	Revaluation reserve		11,000

If, however, no entries have been posted to the subsidiary's books (as is usually the case in questions), the revaluations will need to be incorporated into the consolidated financial statements. This may have an effect on the consolidated statement of comprehensive income, for example in respect of non-current assets. In this case, the depreciation charge in the subsidiary's accounts might be based on non-current assets at cost. Since these non-current assets will require a revaluation adjustment, a revised depreciation charge will have to be computed based on the re-valued amount.

Acquisition of a Subsidiary during the Accounting Period

Where a subsidiary is acquired during an accounting period, the pre-acquisition profits of that subsidiary must be excluded from the consolidated statement of comprehensive income. This effectively requires the calculation of the proportion of each item in the current year's subsidiary statement of comprehensive income that accrued before and after the date of acquisition. Only items after the date of acquisition should be included in the consolidated statement of comprehensive income.

The calculation of the pre-and post-acquisition elements are generally calculated on:

- a time-apportioned basis, e.g. revenue;
- an actual basis, e.g. exceptional items; or
- a combination of the two.

Unless the basis to be applied in the exam is stated, a time-apportioned basis will be appropriate for all items.

Example

Statement of Comprehensive Income for the Year Ended 31 December 2002

	P Limited €	S Limited €
Profit before taxation	100,000	60,000
Income tax expense	45,000	27,000
Profit after taxation	55,000	33,000

P Limited acquired 80% of S Limited on 30 April 2002.

Additional information on specific items in the newly acquired subsidiary's statement of comprehensive income is as follows:

1. Revenue and expenses
   The amount will include only the subsidiary's post-acquisition revenue and expenses (generally time-apportioned).

2. Profit before taxation
   This will include only the post acquisition results of the subsidiary (generally time-apportioned):

   $$= €60,000 \times \frac{8}{12} = €40,000.$$

3. Disclosure items relating to profit before taxation
   In relation to depreciation, auditors' remuneration and interest payable, they should be apportioned on a time basis and only the post-acquisition element should be included in the consolidated statement of comprehensive income.

4. Income tax expense
   The taxation charge will include only the subsidiary's post acquisition taxation charge (generally time-apportioned):

   $$= € 27,000 \times \frac{8}{12} = € 18,000.$$

   Prepare the consolidated statement of comprehensive income for the year ended 31 December 2002.

	P Limited €	S Limited €	Consolidated €
Profit before taxation	100,000	40,000	140,000
Income tax expense	45,000	18,000	63,000
Profit after taxation	55,000	22,000	77,000
Non-controlling interests	-	4,400	4,400
	55,000	17,600	72,600

5. Non-controlling interests
   The non-controlling interest share will be based on the (already calculated) post-acquisition profit after tax figure. Attention is brought to the fact that this

profit figure has already been time-apportioned, thus further time apportioning of the non-controlling interest figure itself would not be appropriate.

If however there is a preference dividend element in the non-controlling interest calculation, then this too must be time-apportioned before the part relating to ordinary shareholders can be calculated.

6. Subsidiary dividends
   Subsidiary dividends in the year of acquisition must be time-apportioned to ensure that only the post-acquisition element is included in the dividend shuffle.
   The remaining element, i.e. the pre-acquisition dividend, is excluded from the dividend shuffle.

7. Retained profits brought forward
   Since the subsidiary was acquired during the year, all the retained profits brought forward in relation to the subsidiary must be eliminated from the consolidated statement of comprehensive income since they are all pre-acquisition.

Opening Unrealised Inventory Profit

An adjustment may be required to reduce opening inventory where we are told that, at the beginning of the year, one company's inventory included goods purchased from another group company. In this case, the adjustment required will reduce opening inventory in cost of sales and will reduce opening reserves carried forward, by the unrealised profit element. Remember the adjustment should be made in the appropriate company's column, i.e. the company carrying the profit.

Example

The following are the statements of comprehensive income for each of the companies in PKF Group Limited for the year ended 31 December 2002.

	P Limited	K Limited	F Limited
	€	€	€
Revenue	100,000	50,000	20,000
Cost of sales	75,000	43,000	9,000
Gross profit	25,000	7,000	11,000
Administration expenses	5,000	6,000	3,000
Net profit	20,000	1,000	8,000
Balance at 1/1/02	30,000	8,500	2,500
Statement of financial position at 31/12/02	50,000	9,500	10,500

1. P Limited sold F Limited €10,000 worth of goods during the year at a mark up on cost of 25%.
2. F Limited had inventory goods purchased from P Limited:

	€
1/1/02	2,000
31/12/02	3,500

3. P Limited purchased 100% of F Limited and 80% of K Limited some years ago, when the balances of their retained profits were as follows:

	€
K Limited	2,000 Dr
F Limited	1,000 Cr

Requirement   Prepare the consolidated statement of comprehensive income workings for PKF Group Limited for the year ended 31/12/02.

(Consider your answer before reading below.)

Solution

1. Group Structure

	K Limited	F Limited
Group	80%	100%
NCI	20%	-
	100%	100%

2. Inventory adjustments
   Opening group inventory and opening group reserves are overstated by the profit element of €2,000 x 25/125 = €400.

   Closing group inventory and closing group reserves are overstated by the profit element €3,500 x 25/125 = €700.

3. Profit brought forward

	P Limited €	K Limited €	F Limited €
Reserves brought forward per individual accounts	30,000	8,500	2,500
Pre-acquisition reserves	-	2,000	(1,000)
Post-acquisition reserves	30,000	10,500	1,500
		x 80%	x 100%
Group share only	30,000	8,400	1,500
Less: Unrealised profit in opening inventory	(400)	-	-
	29,600	8,400	1,500

4. Consolidation workings

	P Limited	K Limited	F Limited	Adjustment	Consol.
	€	€	€	€	€
Revenue	100,000	50,000	20,000	(10,000)	160,000
Draft cost of sales	75,000	43,000	9,000	(10,000)	117,000
Less: Op. inventory adj.	(400)				(400)
Add: Cl. inventory adj.	700				700
Cost of sales	75,300	43,000	9,000	(10,000)	117,300
Gross profit	24,700	7,000	11,000	–	42,700
Administrative exp.	5,000	6,000	3,000	–	14,000
Net profit	19,700	1,000	8,000	–	28,700
Non-controlling interest	–	(200)	–	–	(200)
Profit att. to the Group	19,700	800	8,000	–	28,500
Reserves b/f	29,600	8,400	1,500		39,500
Reserves c/f	49,300	9,200	9,500	–	68,000

Pre-acquisition Reserves

A fundamental principle that must always be remembered in consolidated accounts is that any reserves that a subsidiary has owned prior to the acquisition of the shares by the Parent are not part of the group reserves and thus must be excluded from the reserves of the group in the consolidated accounts. Effectively, this means that the pre-acquisition reserves of a subsidiary are 'frozen' and thus any dividend made out of pre-acquisition reserves cannot be treated as a dividend to the Parent company in the consolidated accounts.

If a subsidiary does declare a dividend out of pre-acquisition reserves, then this is treated as a part-refund of the purchase consideration paid by the holding company and thus should not be reflected in the holding company's profit for the year in the consolidated account workings.

Additionally, the Parent company's reserves carried forward must also exclude any pre-acquisition reserve dividends.

Inter-group Tangible Non-current Assets (i.e. property, plant & equipment)

In Apple Limited, we learnt that where inventory has been transferred (at cost plus profit) from one group company to another, and a portion of these goods are still included in the year-end inventory of the receiving company, then the unrealised profit element on these inventory must be excluded from the consolidated accounts. Consequently, we made an adjustment to reduce the value of closing inventory included in the consolidated statement of comprehensive income and consolidated statement of financial position by the unrealised profit element. Note that this adjustment was made in the column of the company whose individual statement of comprehensive income included the unrealised profit.

Similar treatment should be applied to a situation where a group company transfers tangible non-current assets to another company at a profit. An adjustment is required to cancel any unrealised profit on such assets held at the year-end:

DR Profit on sale of non-current assets   Statement of comprehensive income   X
CR Non-current assets   Statement of financial position   X

An additional problem arises, however, in the area of tangible non-current assets, in that depreciation charges to the statement of comprehensive income would be based on the 'incorrect' inflated non-current asset value. Consequently, an additional journal is required to reduce the depreciation charge to its correct amount so that it is based on original cost to the group:

DR Accumulation depreciation   Statement of financial position   X
CR Depreciation charge   Statement of comprehensive income   X

As in the case of unrealised inventory profits, any adjustments correcting unrealised tangible non-current asset profits are made in the column of the company whose individual statement of comprehensive income included the unrealised profit, i.e. the seller of the asset.

However, any depreciation adjustment must be made in the column of the company now charging the depreciation, i.e. the buyer of the asset.

Prior to posting the correcting consolidated journals, it is vital to establish when the transfer of the tangible non-current assets took place:

- in the current period; or
- in a previous period.

If the transfer took place in the current year, then the current year's consolidated statement of comprehensive income will require adjustment with respect to:

- the profit on sale of tangible current assets;
- the depreciation charges.

If the transfer took place in a previous period, then reserves brought forward will require adjustment with respect to:

- the profit on sale of tangible non-current assets;
- the depreciation charges of previous periods since the transfer.

Additionally, in such a case note again the company column in which to make each adjustment:

- elimination of profit – seller;
- correction of depreciation – buyer.

In such a case the current year's consolidated statement of comprehensive income will require an adjustment with respect to the depreciation charge.

CONCLUSION

The preparation of a consolidated statement of comprehensive income is summarised in **Table 28.1** below. The following abbreviations are used in **Table 28.1**:

P   =   Parent
S   =   Subsidiary
IG   =   Inter-group items

Table 28.1: Pro Forma Consolidated Statement of Comprehensive Income

Item	Computation
1. Revenue	P + S minus IG
2. Cost of Sales	P + S minus IG + unrealised inventory profit
3. All expenses	P + S ± any adjustments in question such as extra or over depreciation
4. Investment Income	Only dividends received from outside the group
5. Income tax expenses	P + S
6. Non-controlling interest	S profit after taxation as adjusted. Firstly, any preference dividend is deducted and divided between P and the non-controlling interest. Secondly, the non-controlling interest in the remainder is deducted, leaving the group's share of S profit
7. Transfers to reserve	P + group's share of S
8. Retained profit brought forward	P + group's share of S post acquisition profits

Note   Remember dividends are an appropriation of profits and should be taken through reserves.

QUESTIONS

Self-test Questions

1. List and explain six of the most common adjustments typically encountered in the preparation of a consolidated statement of comprehensive income.
2. Explain how the following issues should be dealt with when preparing a consolidated statement of comprehensive income:

   (a) Revaluation of assets;
   (b) Acquisition of a subsidiary during the accounting period;
   (c) Opening unrealised inventory profit;
   (d) Pre-acquisition reserves; and
   (e) Inter-group transfer of tangible non-current assets.

Review Questions

(See APPENDIX ONE for Suggested Solutions to Review Questions.)

Question 1

X Limited owns 90% of the ordinary share capital of Y Limited. The statements of comprehensive income for X Limited and Y Limited are as follows for the year ended 31 December 2002:

	X Limited €	Y Limited €
Revenue	10,000	7,000
Cost of sales	(6,000)	(1,000)
Gross profit	4,000	6,000
Administration expenses	(500)	(600)
Depreciation	(1,000)	(1,200)
Profit before tax	2,500	4,200
Income tax expense	(400)	(100)
Profit after tax	2,100	4,100
Reserves brought forward	10,000	7,000
Reserves carried forward	12,100	11,100

Additional Information

1. X Limited purchased the shares in Y Limited on 1 January 1998, at which time Y Limited's statement of financial position contained:

		€
Revenue reserves		3,000
Tangible non-current assets	Cost	12,000
	Fair value	15,000

With respect to the measurement of non-controlling interests at the date of acquisition, the proportionate share method equated to the fair value method.

2. Tangible non-current assets are depreciated at 10% straight line. The assets in Y Limited were not re-valued to fair value at the date of acquisition by X Limited.

Requirement   Draft the consolidated statement of comprehensive income for the year ended 31 December 2002.

Question 2

CA Group Limited
Statement of Comprehensive Income for the Year Ended 31 December 2001

	C	A
	€	€
Net profit	10,000	5,000
Income tax expense	1,000	1,000
Profit after tax	9,000	4,000
Balance brought forward	15,000	6,000
Balance carried forward	24,000	10,000

Additional Information

1. C Limited purchased 60% of the ordinary share capital of A Limited on 1 January 1998 when the retained profit was a debit balance of €3,000.
2. Included in the net assets of A Limited taken over were tangible non-current assets with a book value of €12,000. At 1 January 1998, the fair value of these assets was €15,000.
3. A Limited depreciates all its tangible non-current assets on a 20% reducing balance basis, and carries all assets at cost.
4. With respect to the measurement of non-controlling interests at the date of acquisition, the proportionate share method equated to the fair value method.

Requirement   Draft the consolidated workings for the CA Group for the year ended 31 December 2001.

Question 3

The statements of comprehensive income of X Limited and Y Limited are as follows for the year ended 31 December 1998:

	X Limited	Y Limited
	€	€
Revenue	10,000	7,000
Cost of sales	(6,000)	(1,000)
Gross profit	4,000	6,000

Administration expenses	(1,000)	(500)
Distribution costs	–	(700)
Profit before tax	3,000	4,800
Income tax expense	(500)	(300)
Profit after tax	2,500	4,500

Additional Information

1. X Limited bought the following shares in Y Limited on 28 February 1998:

   - 9,000 Ordinary Shares   (issued: 10,000)
   - 1,000 10% Preference Shares   (issued: 5,000)

   With respect to the measurement of non-controlling interests at the date of acquisition, the proportionate share method equated to the fair value method.

2. The distribution costs in the statement of comprehensive income of Y Limited were incurred in November 1998.
3. During the year ended 31 December 1998, X Limited and Y Limited paid dividends of €200 and €4,500 respectively. The dividend paid by Y Limited includes the full year's dividend for preferences shares. X Limited has not yet accounted for dividends received from Y Limited.
4. Retained earnings of X Limited and Y Limited are as follows:

	X Limited	Y Limited
	€	€
Profit after tax	2,500	4,500
Retained earnings b/f	10,000	8,000
Dividends paid – year ended 31 December 1998	(200)	(4,000)
Retained earnings at 31 December 1998	12,300	8,500

Requirement   Prepare the consolidated statement of comprehensive income for the year ended 31 December 1998.

Question 4

Statement of Comprehensive Income for the Year Ended 31 December 2002

	€	€
	P Limited	S Limited
Gross profit	10,000	6,000
Administration expenses	(1,000)	(2,000)
Profit on sale of tangible non-current assets	2,000	–
Depreciation	(4,000)	(375)
Profit before tax	7,000	3,625
Income tax expense	(1,000)	(1,500)
Profit after tax	6,000	2,125

Additional Information

1. P Limited owns 75% of the equity share capital of S Limited.
2. The profit on sale of tangible non-current assets in P Limited arose as a result of a transfer of a part of its plant and machinery to S Limited on 30 June 2002.

	€
Cost to P Limited	10,000
Accumulated depreciation 30 June 2002	4,500
Net book value	5,500
Value transferred to S Limited	7,500
Profit on transfer	2,000

S Limited had no non-current assets prior to 30 June 2002 and has not acquired/disposed of any since. The group's policy is to depreciate plant at 10% on cost on a month-by-month basis. S Limited has, however, been calculating depreciation on the transferred asset at 10% of the transfer value on a month-by-month basis.

Requirement   Draft the consolidated statement of comprehensive income for the year ended 31 December 2002.

Question 5

The statements of comprehensive income of P Limited and its subsidiaries S Limited and T Limited for the year ending 31 December 20X7 are as follows:

	P Limited €	S Limited €	T Limited €
Profit before items set out hereunder	298,500	120,000	90,000
Income from quoted investment	1,200	1,500	–
Dividends receivable			
From S Limited	19,200	–	–
From T Limited	12,600	–	–
	331,500	121,500	90,000
Administrative expenses	(45,000)	(16,500)	(21,000)
Profit before tax	286,500)	105,000	69,000
Income tax expense	105,000	48,000	30,000
Profit after taxation	181,500	57,000	39,000

Additional Information

1. P Limited owns:
   (i)   80% of the ordinary shares of S Limited;
   (ii) 50% of the 6% preference shares of T Limited. The total issued amount of T Limited's 6% preference share capital is €60,000; and
   (iii) 75% of the ordinary shares of T Limited.

With respect to the measurement of non-controlling interests at the dates of acquisition, the proportionate share method equated to the fair value method.

2. At the date of acquisition of the shares by P Limited the balances of retained profits were:
   (i) S Limited €4,500 credit; and
   (ii) T Limited €1,830 debit.
3. Included in P Limited's profit is €15,000 from sale of goods to S Limited. Of these goods S Limited still has in inventory on 31 December 20X7 goods invoiced at €3,000. All goods sold by P Limited produce a profit of 25% on the selling price.
4. During the year ended 31 December 20X7, P Limited, S Limited and T Limited paid dividends of €60,000, €24,000 and €18,000 respectively.
5. Retained earnings at 31 December 20X6 were as follows:

P Limited	S Limited	T Limited
€	€	€
25,950	12,600	11,250

Requirement   Prepare the consolidated statement of comprehensive income of P Limited for the year ending 31 December 20X7 in a form suitable for publication.

Question 6

BACK plc (BACK) prepares its financial statements to 31 December each year. On 1 January 2003, BACK acquired 90% of the ordinary share capital of FRONT Limited (FRONT) at a cost of €3,808,000. The draft statements of comprehensive income of BACK and FRONT for the year ended 31 December 2003 are as follows:

	BACK	FRONT
	€'000	€'000
Revenue	90,000	7,800
Cost of sales	(60,000)	(4,900)
Gross profit	30,000	2,900
Operating expenses	(9,900)	(760)
Operating profit	20,100	2,140
Interest payable and similar charges	(160)	(40)
Interest receivable	80	20
Profit on ordinary activities before tax	20,020	2,120
Tax on profit on ordinary activities	(6,420)	(400)
Profit on ordinary activities after tax	13,600	1,720

Additional Information

1. The net assets of FRONT on 1 January 2003 were as follows:

	Carrying value	Fair value
	€'000	€'000
Property, plant and equipment	2,400	2,240
Inventory	1,200	1,040
Other net assets	640	640
	4,240	3,920

The difference between the carrying value and the fair value of property, plant and equipment is due to a revaluation of property, while the reduction in inventory relates to a change in the accounting policy for inventory in order to bring FRONT's inventory into line with those of BACK. Otherwise the accounting policies adopted by FRONT are similar to those of BACK. The required change in the closing inventory value of FRONT to ensure uniform accounting policies is a decrease of €120,000. The fair values shown above have not yet been incorporated into FRONT's financial statements.

2. Following the acquisition of shares in FRONT, the directors of BACK decided to run down certain parts of BACK's business activities. These were finally discontinued in December 2003. The combined contribution to the business of these activities in 2003 was:

	€'000
Turnover	10,000
Cost of sales	9,910
Gross profit	90
Operating expenses	(50)
Operating profit	40

3. The directors of BACK estimate that the goodwill arising on the acquisition of FRONT was impaired by €28,000 at 31 December 2003.
4. BACK and FRONT follow a policy of depreciating all fixed assets at 10% per annum on their carrying value. Depreciation is charged to cost of sales in the statement of comprehensive income.
5. FRONT purchases raw materials from BACK. During the year ended 31 December 2003, purchases of these raw materials by FRONT from BACK amounted to €10,000,000. At 31 December 2003, the inventory of FRONT included raw materials purchased from BACK at a cost of €3,000,000. BACK supplies raw materials at cost plus 25%.

Requirement   Prepare the consolidated statement of comprehensive income of BACK Group plc for the year ended 31 December 2003 in a form suitable for publication.

Challenging Questions

Question 1 (Based on ICAI, P3 Autumn 2002, Question 4)

The draft statements of comprehensive income of ARK Limited (ARK), BOAT Limited (BOAT) and CANOE Limited (CANOE) for the year ended 31 December 2003 are as follows:

	ARK €m	BOAT €m	CANOE €m
Turnover	2,100	1,260	1,680
Cost of sales	(840)	(504)	(630)
Gross profit	1,260	756	1,050
Other operating expenses	(630)	(378)	(546)
Operating profit	630	378	504
Investment income	126	–	–
Interest payable and similar charges	(252)	(126)	(168)
Profit before tax	504	252	336
Taxation	(168)	(62)	(118)
Profit after tax	336	190	218
Dividends paid	(210)	(106)	(168)
Retained profit for the year	126	84	50
Retained profit at 1 January 2003	1,050	690	195
Retained profit at 31 December 2003	1,176	774	245

Additional Information

1. On 1 January 1997, ARK purchased 160 million €1 ordinary shares in BOAT for €500 million. The net assets of BOAT at 1 January 1997 comprised:

	€m
€1 ordinary shares	200
Retained earnings	325
	525

There was no difference between the book value of BOAT's net assets and their fair value at 1 January 1997.

2. On 1 July 2003, ARK purchased 180 million €1 ordinary shares in CANOE for €458 million. The net assets of CANOE at 1 January 2003 comprised:

	€m
€1 ordinary shares	240
Retained earnings	195
	435

There was no difference between the book value of CANOE's net assets and their fair value at 1 July 2003.

3. On 1 July 2003, ARK sold its entire investment in BOAT for €950 million in cash, incurring a tax liability of €50 million in connection with the sale. ARK has not yet accounted for the effects of the sale. On 1 July 2003, the goodwill arising on the acquisition of BOAT was carried at €32 million.
4. In December 2003, ARK sold raw materials to CANOE for €30 million, making a profit of €10 million. These raw materials are included at invoice value in the inventory of CANOE at 31 December 2003.
5. It is group policy to charge all of any profit or loss arising on inter-group sales against group reserves.

Requirement   Prepare the consolidated statement of comprehensive income of ARK Group for the year ended 31 December 2003, *starting with profit before tax and ending with retained profit at 31 December 2003*, having regard to the fact that ARK does not propose to publish its own statement of comprehensive income.

Note   You may assume that transactions accrue evenly throughout the year.

Question 2 (Based on ICAI, P3 Autumn 2004, Question 1)

You are the financial accountant of WORK plc (WORK), a company that prepares its financial statements to 31 December each year. WORK has investments in two companies, REST Limited (REST) and PLAY Limited (PLAY). The statements of comprehensive income of these three companies for the year ended 31 December 2003 are as follows:

	WORK €'000	REST €'000	PLAY €'000
Revenue	75,000	64,000	14,000
Cost of sales	(37,500)	(32,000)	(7,000)
Gross profit	37,500	32,000	7,000
Other operating expenses	(20,000)	(16,000)	(3,000)
Operating profit	17,500	16,000	4,000
Investment income	2,000	–	–
Interest payable	(2,500)	(1,000)	(500)
Profit before taxation	17,000	15,000	3,500
Taxation	(4,250)	(3,500)	(875)
Profit after taxation	12,750	11,500	2,625
Dividends paid	(2,750)	–	(2,000)
Retained profit for the year	10,000	11,500	625
Retained profit at start of year	20,000	15,500	14,375
Retained profit at end of year	30,000	27,000	15,000

Additional Information

1. On 1 January 1998, WORK purchased 80% of the ordinary share capital of REST for €7,500,000. The fair value of the net assets of REST was the same as their book value on that date. The statement of financial position of REST on 1 January 1998 showed:

	€'000
€1 ordinary share capital	1,000
Retained earnings	4,000
	5,000

2. On 1 January 2003, WORK purchased 100% of the ordinary share capital of PLAY for €10,500,000. The statement of financial position of PLAY on that date showed:

	€'000		€'000
Property, plant and equipment	6,000	€1 ordinary share capital	1,625
Inventory	10,000	Retained earnings	14,375
	16,000		16,000

The fair value of the net assets of PLAY was the same as their book value on the acquisition date. Property, plant and equipment are depreciated over six years. During 2003, 50% of the inventory was sold outside the Group on normal trading terms, with the remaining inventory to be sold in 2004.

3. On 30 September 2003, WORK disposed of the whole of its investment in REST for €30,000,000. The taxation payable in connection with the disposal is €1,000,000. The effect of the disposal has not yet been incorporated into the statement of comprehensive income of WORK. The activities of REST are similar to WORK and the directors of WORK believe that the performance of the Group will not be materially affected following the disposal of REST.

4. During the year ended 31 December 2003, PLAY sold raw materials to WORK at original cost plus a mark up of 25%. At 31 December 2003, half of the raw materials sold to WORK, at a cost of €120,000, remained in WORK's inventory.

5. WORK charges PLAY a management fee of €50,000 per annum. The charge is included in revenue of WORK and the other operating expenses of PLAY.

6. There is no evidence that any goodwill arising on the acquisition of REST and PLAY has ever been impaired.

Requirement   Prepare the consolidated statement of comprehensive income of the WORK Group for the year ended 31 December 2003.

Question 3 (Based on ICAI, P3 Autumn 2005, Question 6)

MARBLE plc (MARBLE) purchased 36,000,000 of the 45,000,000 €1 ordinary shares in FALLS Limited (FALLS) on 1 April 2005 for €200,000,000. The statements of comprehensive income of both companies for the year ended 31 December 2005 are as follows:

Statement of Comprehensive Income for the Year Ended 31 December 2005

	MARBLE	FALLS
	€'000	€'000
Revenue	900,000	250,000
Cost of sales	(720,000)	(180,000)
Gross profit	180,000	70,000
Other operating expenses	(30,000)	(20,000)
Operating profit	150,000	50,000
Interest payable and similar charges	(10,000)	(4,000)
Profit on ordinary activities before taxation	140,000	46,000
Income tax expense	(35,000)	(12,000)
Profit on ordinary activities after taxation	105,000	34,000
Retained profit at start of year	210,000	80,000
Retained profit at end of year	315,000	114,000

Additional Information

1. The only fair value adjustment that is required in respect of the acquisition of FALLS relates to a building, the details of which are as follows:

	€'000
Cost	100,000
Accumulated depreciation at 1 January 2005	(8,000)
Net book value at 1 January 2005	92,000

The building, which had a useful economic life of 25 years on 1 January 2003, is in a prime commercial location and has increased dramatically in value since it was purchased by FALLS on 1 January 2003. The replacement cost of a similar building, with a similar remaining useful economic life at 1 April 2005, is €161,000,000.
2. The activities of both companies occur evenly throughout the year. In June 2005, MARBLE sold goods to FALLS for €30,000,000, and one-third of these goods remained unsold at 31 December 2005. MARBLE marks up the cost of goods sold by 25%.
3. Both MARBLE and FALLS charge depreciation on a time apportionment basis to net operating expenses. The directors of MARBLE believe that the goodwill arising on the acquisition of FALLS has been impaired by €2,910,000 at 31 December 2005.

Requirement   Prepare the consolidated statement of comprehensive income of MARBLE Group for the year ended 31 December 2005.

CHAPTER 29

ASSOCIATES

INTRODUCTION

IAS 28 *Investments in Associates* deals with accounting for investments in associates, except those held by:

- venture capital organisations; and
- mutual funds, unit trusts and similar entities including investment-linked insurance funds that upon initial recognition are designated as at fair value through profit or loss or are classified as held for trading and accounted for in accordance with IAS 39 *Financial Instruments: Recognition and Measurement*.

After having read this chapter you should:

- understand what constitutes an associate; and
- be able to account for an associate.

IMPORTANT DEFINITIONS

Associate

An entity in which the investor has significant influence and which is neither a subsidiary nor a joint venture of the investor.

Significant Influence

The power to participate in the financial and operating policy decisions of the investee but not control those policies. If an investor holds, directly or indirectly, 20% or more of the voting power of the investee, it is presumed that it has significant influence, unless it can be clearly demonstrated that this is not the case. Conversely, if less than 20%, the presumption is that the investor does not have significant influence. A majority shareholding by another investor does not preclude an investor having significant influence. Its existence is usually evidenced in one or more of the following ways:

- Representation on the board of directors;
- Participation in policy-making processes;
- Material transactions between the investor and the investee;
- Interchange of managerial personnel; or
- Provision of essential technical information.

The Equity Method

A method of accounting whereby the investment is initially recorded at cost and adjusted thereafter to reflect the investor's share of the net profit or loss of the investee/associate. The statement of comprehensive income reflects the investor's share of the results of operations of the investee. Distributions received from the investee reduce the carrying amount of the investment. Adjustments to the carrying amount may also be required arising from changes in the investee's equity that have not been included in the income statement (for example, revaluations).

The Cost Method

The investment is recorded at cost. The statement of comprehensive income reflects income only to the extent that the investor receives distributions from the investee subsequent to the date of acquisition.

ACCOUNTING FOR ASSOCIATES

Category 1

An investment in an associate, for an entity *not publishing* consolidated accounts, should be either:

(a) carried at cost;
(b) accounted for using the equity method if the equity method would be appropriate for the associate if the investor had issued consolidated accounts; or
(c) accounted for under IAS 39 as an 'available for sale financial asset'.

Basically an investor should provide the same information about its investments in associates as those entities that issue consolidated accounts.

Category 2

An investment in an associate, for an entity *publishing* consolidated accounts, should be accounted for as follows:

In the Separate Financial Statements of the Investor

Equity accounting is required in the separate financial statements of the investor even if consolidated accounts are not required, for example, because the investor has no subsidiaries. But equity accounting is not required where the investor would be exempt from preparing consolidated financial statements under IAS 27. In that circumstance, instead of equity accounting, the parent can account for the investment either:

(a) at cost;
(b) as an 'available for sale financial asset' as per IAS 39.

In the Consolidated Financial Statements of the Investor

In its consolidated financial statements, an investor should use the equity method of accounting for associates, other than in the following three exceptional circumstances:

- An investment in an associate that is acquired and held exclusively with a view to its disposal within 12 months from acquisition (i.e. in accordance with IFRS 5 *Noncurrent Assets Held for Sale and Discontinued Operations*) should be accounted for as held for trading under IAS 39. Under IAS 39, those investments are measured at fair value with fair value changes recognised in profit or loss;
- A parent that is exempted from preparing consolidated financial statements by paragraph 10 of IAS 27 may prepare separate financial statements as its primary financial statements. In those separate statements, the investment in the associate may be accounted for by the cost method or under IAS 39;
- An investor need not use the equity method and can apply IAS 39 if all of the following four conditions are met:
  - The investor is itself a wholly-owned subsidiary, or is a partially-owned subsidiary of another entity and its other owners, including those not otherwise entitled to vote, have been informed about, and do not object to, the investor not applying the equity method;
  - The investor's debt or equity instruments are not traded in a public market;
  - The investor did not file, nor is it in the process of filing, its financial statements with a securities commission or other regulatory organisation for the purpose of issuing any class of instruments in a public market; and
  - The ultimate or any intermediate parent of the investor produces consolidated financial statements available for public use that comply with IFRSs.

With the exception of the above, investments in associates must be accounted for using the equity method irrespective of whether the investor also has investments in subsidiaries or prepares group accounts. However, IAS 28 does not prescribe how the investor's share of its associate's profits should be presented in the statement of comprehensive income. The example in IAS 1 defines the share of profit of associates as the share of associate's profit attributable to equity holders of the associates, i.e. after tax and non-controlling interests in the associates. This is disclosed just before 'profit before tax'.

An investor should discontinue the use of the equity method from the date that:

(a) it ceases to have significant influence but retains either, in part or in whole, its investment. If an investor loses significant influence, it should derecognise that associate and recognise in profit or loss the difference between the sum of the proceeds received and any retained interest, and the carrying amount of the investment in the associate at the date significant influence is lost; or

(b) the use of the equity method is no longer appropriate as the associate operates under severe long-term restrictions.

From that date it accounts for the investment in accordance with IAS 39, provided the associate does not become a subsidiary or a joint venture as defined in IAS 31.

Applying the Equity Method

On acquisition any difference between the cost of acquisition and the investor's share of the fair values of the net identifiable assets is accounted for under IFRS 3. Appropriate adjustments to post-acquisition share of profits are made to account for:

(a) depreciation based on fair values; and
(b) amortisation of goodwill.

The most recent available financial statements of the associate should be used by the investor in applying the equity method and they should (usually) be drawn up to the same date as the investor. When the dates differ, the associate often prepares statements specifically for the investor to the same date but if this is impracticable then a different date may be used. However, the length of the reporting periods should be consistent from period to period. Any difference between the reporting date of the investor and its associate must not be more than three months. When different dates have to be adopted, any adjustments for significant events occurring between the date of the associate's statements and the date of the investor's financial statements must be made.

If an associate has outstanding cumulative preferred shares held by outsiders, the investor should compute its share of profits/losses after adjusting for preferred dividends whether or not declared.

If an investor's share of losses of an associate equals or exceeds its 'interest in the associate', the investor should discontinue recognising its share of further losses. The 'interest in an associate' is the carrying amount of the investment in the associate under the equity method together with any long-term interests that, in substance, form part of the investor's net investment in the associate. After the investor's interest is reduced to zero, additional losses should be recognised by a provision (liability) only to the extent that the investor has incurred legal or constructive obligations or made payments on behalf of the associate. If the associate subsequently reports profits, the investor should resume recognising its share of those profits only after its share of the profits equals the share of losses not recognised.

If an associate is accounted for using the equity method, unrealised profits and losses resulting from upstream (associate to investor) and downstream (investor to associate) transactions should be eliminated to the extent of the investor's interest in the associate. However, unrealised losses should not be eliminated to the extent that the transaction provides evidence of an impairment of the asset transferred.

Uniform accounting policies should be adopted and appropriate adjustments are made to the associate's statements but if this is not practicable that fact must be disclosed.

Statement of Financial Position

None of the individual assets and liabilities of the associate are 'consolidated' with those of the parent and subsidiaries (if there are any). Instead, under equity accounting, the investment in an associate is carried to the (consolidated) statement of financial position at a valuation.

The carrying amount of an investment in an associate in a (consolidated) statement of financial position can be arrived at by using one of two methods of calculation:

	€'000
Method 1	
Cost of investment	X
Plus	
Share of post-acquisition retained profits and reserves of Associate (to reporting date)	X
Less	
Any premium written off (because of impairment)	(X)
Carrying amount of investment	X̲
Method 2	
Group's share of net asset of Associate (at reporting date)	X
Plus	
Premium on acquisition not written off since acquistion date	X
Carrying amount of investment	X̲

It is important to remember that a premium on acquisition (goodwill) should be tested for impairment annually in accordance with IAS 36 *Impairment of Assets* and written down if there is impairment. The recoverable amount of an investment should be assessed for each individual associate unless that associate does not generate independent cash flows. In determining value in use, an entity should estimate:

(a) its share of the present value of estimated future cash flows expected to be generated by the investee as a whole, including the proceeds on ultimate disposal; or

(b) the present value of estimated future cash flows expected to arise from dividends and from ultimate disposal.

Both methods give the same result under appropriate assumptions. Any impairment loss is allocated first to goodwill in accordance with IAS 36.

Statement of Comprehensive Income

The investing group should take credit for its share of the earnings of the associate, whether or not the associate has distributed those earnings by way of dividends.

Under equity accounting the associates revenue, cost of sales, expenses etc., are not consolidated with those of the investing group. The consolidated statement of comprehensive income only includes the group's share of the associates (post–acquisition) profit after tax.

Example *(dealing with an associate in consolidated financial statements using equity accounting)*

Parent Limited purchased 90,000 ordinary shares in Apple Limited on 1 January 2003 when the retained earnings of Apple Limited were €100,000. The cost of the investment was €140,000.

Draft Statements of Financial Position as at 31 December 2004

	(Group) Parent Limited & Subsidiaries €'000	Apple Limited €'000
Assets		
Tangible non-current assets	3,260	580
Investment in Apple	140	-
Current assets	1,250	290
	4,650	870
Equity & liabilities		
Ordinary €1 shares	1,000	300
Retained earnings	2,720	400
	3,720	700
Current liabilities	930	170
Total equity & liabilities	4,650	870

Statements of Comprehensive Income for the year ended 31 December 2004

	Parent Limited & Subsidiaries €'000	Apple Limited €'000
Revenue	9,800	2,630
Cost of sales	(6,858)	(1,840)
Gross profit	2,942	790
Dividends from Apple Limited	9	-
Distribution costs	(391)	(120)
Administrative expenses	(670)	(200)
Finance costs	(410)	(120)
Profit before tax	1,480	350
Income tax expense	(440)	(110)
Profit after tax	1,040	240

Additional Information

1. The premium on acquisition (goodwill) of Apple Limited has been impaired for the first time by €5,000 during the year under review.
2. During year ended 31 December 2004, Parent Limited and Apple Limited debited €100,000 and €30,000 respectively to equity in respect of dividends paid.

Requirement Prepare the consolidated statement of comprehensive income for the year ended 31 December 2004, together with the statement of financial position as at that date, for Parent Limited.

Solution

Under equity accounting none of the assets and liabilities (net assets) of the associate are consolidated.

The associate can be dealt with by means of two journal entries:

	€'000	€'000
(1) Dr. Investment in Apple Limited	90	
Cr. Reserves		90

Being the group's share of the post-acquisition retained profits and reserves of Apple as at the reporting date (30% x (400,000 - 100,000)).

	€'000	€'000
(2) Dr. Retained profits	5	
Cr. Investment in Apple		5

Being the cumulative impairment of goodwill to the reporting date.

Tangible Non-current Assets

	€'000		€'000
Group	3,260	CSFP	3,260

Investment in Apple

	€'000		€'000
Group	140	Journal 2	5
Journal 1	90	CSFP	225
	230		230

Current Assets

	€'000		€'000
Group	1,250	CSFP	1,250

Current Liabilities

	€'000		€'000
CSFP	930	Group	930

Ordinary Shares

	€'000		€'000
CSFP	1,000	Group	1,000

Retained Earnings			
	€'000		€'000
Journal 2	5	Group	2,720
CSFP	2,805	Journal 1	90
	2,810		2,810

The individual assets and liabilities of Apple (net assets) are not included in the consolidated statement of financial position under equity accounting.

Consolidated Statement of Financial Position as at 31 December 2004

	€'000
Assets	
Tangible non-current assets	3,260
Investment in associated company (W1)	225
Current assets	1,250
	4,735
Equity and Liabilities	
Ordinary €1 shares	1,000
Retained earnings (W2)	2,805
	3,805
Current liabilities	930
Total equity & liabilities	4,735

	€'000
(W1) Investment at cost	140
Share of post-acquisition profits	90
Premium on acquisition written off	(5)
	225

The carrying amount of the investment in Apple Limited could also be calculated as follows:

	€'000
Share of net assets (€700 x 30%)	210
Premium not w/o	15
	225
Calculation of Premium	
Cost of investment	140
Acquired (30% x (€300 + €100))	120
Premium on acquisition	20
Premium	20
Written off – Impairment	5
Balance remaining	15

		€
(W2)	Parent Limited and Subsidiaries	2,720
	Apple Limited ((€400 – €100) x 30%)	90
	Impairment of goodwill	(5)
		2,805

Consolidated Statement of Comprehensive Income for the Year Ended 31 December 2004

	€'000
Revenue	9,800
Cost of sales	(6,858)
Gross profit	2,942
Distribution costs	(391)
Administrative expenses	(670)
Finance costs	(410)
Share of profit of associate [(30% x €240) – €5]	67
Net profit	1,538
Income tax expense	(440)
Profit after tax	1,098

Note   Under equity accounting the associated company's revenue, cost of sales and expenses are not consolidated with those of the group, but the group's share of A's profit after tax is included. Post-acquisition profits of the associate are included in the group's retained profits at the start of the year as long as the investment in A was brought before the start of the period under review.

Apple has declared a divident of €30,000. Parent is entitled to €9,000(€30,000 x 30%) of this and has included it as investment income in its SCI. This is not down separately in the consolidated SCI as parent includes 30% of Apple's PAIT and therefore the divident is "included" in this figure.

Disclosure

The following disclosures should be made:

(a) An appropriate listing and description of significant associates, including the proportion of ownership interest and, if different, the proportion of voting power held; and
(b) The methods used to account for such investments.

Investments in associates should be classified as non-current assets and disclosed separately in the statement of financial position. The investor's share of profits/losses should be disclosed separately in the statement of comprehensive income.

Other disclosures are:

- the fair value of investments in associates (if published);
- summarised financial information of associates, e.g. amounts of assets, liabilities, revenue and profit/loss;

- why significant influence is present if the holding is less than 20%;
- if an associate is not accounted for under equity accounting;
- the unrecognised share of losses of an associate; and
- the reporting date of the associate if different from the investor.

COMPREHENSIVE EXAMPLE

AROMA plc (AROMA) purchased 30% of THERAPY Limited (THERAPY) on 1 July 1999. At all times, AROMA participates fully in THERAPY's financial and operating policy decisions. At the date of acquisition, THERAPY's statement of financial position was as follows:

Capital and Reserves	€'000
€1 ordinary shares	1,000
Revaluation reserve	100
Revenue reserve	450
	1,550

The statements of financial position of AROMA and THERAPY as at 30 June 2003 are as follows:

	AROMA		THERAPY	
	€'000	€'000	€'000	€'000
ASSETS				
Non-current Assets				
Property, plant and equipment		4,000		3,500
Investment in THERAPY		1,000		-
		5,000		3,500
Current Assets				
Inventory	670		430	
Receivables	500		395	
Bank and cash	130	1,300	215	1,040
		6,300		4,540
EQUITY AND LIABILITIES				
Capital and Reserves				
€1 ordinary shares		2,000		1,000
Revaluation reserve		1,000		500
Revenue reserve		2,550		2,470
		5,550		3,970

Current Liabilities	750	570
	6,300	4,540

In addition, the draft statements of comprehensive income of the two companies for the year ended 30 June 2003 are as follows:

	AROMA	THERAPY
	€'000	€'000
Revenue	5,000	3,000
Cost of sales	(3,000)	(1,500)
Gross profit	2,000	1,500
Operating expenses	(750)	(440)
Trading profit	1,250	1,060
Interest	(50)	(10)
Profit before taxation	1,200	1,050
Taxation	(400)	(350)
Profit after taxation	800	700
Ordinary dividends proposed (but not approved)	(300)	(50)
Retained profit for the year	500	650

Requirement Prepare the consolidated statement of comprehensive income of AROMA Group for the year ended 30 June 2003, and statement of financial position as at that date.

Solution

Workings:

Step One
Calculate the goodwill in the investment in THERAPY.

	€'000	€'000
Cost of investment		1,000
Share capital	1,000	
Revaluation reserve	100	
Retained earnings	450	
	1,550	
	x 30%	(465)
		535

There is no evidence of impairment, therefore record at €535,000.

Step Two
Complete the top half of the statement of financial position.

	€'000
Investment in THERAPY's net assets:	
(30% x (€3,970,000 + €50,000)	1,206
Goodwill (Step 1)	535
	1,741

Step Three
Calculate statement of financial position reserves.

	€'000	€'000
Revaluation Reserve		
AROMA		1,000
THERAPY		
– at reporting date	500	
– at acquisition	(100)	
	400	
x 30%		120
		1,120
Retained Earnings		
AROMA (€2,550 + €300)		2,850
THERAPY		
– at reporting date (€2,470 + €50)	2,520	
– at acquisition	(450)	
	2,070	
x 30%		621
		3,471

Step Four
Calculate the figures to be included in the consolidated statement of comprehensive income.

	€'000
Profit after interest and tax	700
Group share 30%	210

Step Five

Prepare the statement of comprehensive income and statement of financial position.

AROMA Group
Consolidated Statement of Comprehensive Income for the Year Ended 30 June 2003

	€'000
Revenue	5,000
Cost of sales	(3,000)
Gross profit	2,000
Operating expenses	(750)
Operating profit	1,250
Interest payable	(50)
Share of profit of associate	210
Profit on ordinary activities before tax	1,410
Tax on profit on ordinary activities	(400)
Profit on ordinary activities after tax	1,010

AROMA Group
Consolidated Statement of Financial Position as at 30 June 2003

	€m	€m
ASSETS		
Non-current Assets		
Property, plant and equipment		4,000
Investments - investment in associate		1,741
		5,741
Current Assets		
Inventory	670	
Receivables	500	
Bank and cash	130	1,300
		7,041

EQUITY AND LIABILITIES	
Capital and Reserves	
Share capital	2,000
Revaluation reserve	1,120
Retained earnings	3,471
	6,591
Current Liabilities	450
	7,041

CONCLUSION

An associate is an entity in which the investor has significant influence and which is neither a subsidiary nor a joint venture of the investor. Significant influence is the power to participate in the financial and operating policy decisions of the investee, but is not control over those policies. If an investor holds, directly or indirectly, 20% or more of the voting power of the investee, it is presumed that it has significant influence unless it can be clearly demonstrated that this is not the case. In the consolidated financial statements of the investor, IAS 28 requires the use of the equity method of accounting for associates (with some exceptions). Under this method of accounting the investment is initially recorded at cost and adjusted thereafter to reflect the investor's share of the net profit or loss of the investee/associate. The statement of comprehensive income reflects the investor's share of the results of operations of the investee. While IAS 28 does not prescribe how the investor's share of its associate's profits should be presented in the statement of comprehensive income, the example in IAS 1 defines this as the share of associate's profit attributable to equity holders of the associates, i.e. after tax and minority interests in the associates. This is disclosed just before 'profit before tax'.

QUESTIONS

Self-test Questions

1. Explain the terms associate and significant influence
2. Explain the equity method of accounting and how it differs from the consolidation approach used for subsidiaries

Review Questions

(See APPENDIX ONE for Suggested Solutions to Review Questions.)

Question 1

The draft consolidated statement of comprehensive income of Parker Limited and its subsidiary companies together with the draft statement of comprehensive income of Duke Limited, for the year ended 30 September 2005, are set out below.

	Parker Limited Group €'000	Duke Limited €'000
Revenue	31,980	12,200
Gross profit	2,312	879
Dividends from Duke Limited	24	–
	2,336	879
Administrative expenses	(541)	(199)
Finance costs	(4)	–
Profit before tax	1,791	680
Income tax expense	1,108	380
Profit after tax	683	300
Non-controlling interest in subsidiaries	(41)	–
	642	300

Additional Information

1. Parker Limited acquired a 30% holding in Duke Limited on 1 October 2004.
2. The retained earnings of the Parker Limited Group and Duke Limited at 31 September 2005 are as follows:

	Parker Limited Group €'000	Duke Limited €'000
PATTG	642	300
Retained earnings at 30 September 2004	345	89
Dividends paid during year ended 30 September 2005		
- Ordinary	(100)	(80)
- Preference	(28)	–
Retained earnings at 30 September 2005	859	309

Requirement   You are required to prepare the consolidated statement of comprehensive income of Parker Limited for the year ended 30 September 2005.

Question 2

Golf Limited is a trading company, which has recently sought to diversify its interests by purchasing shares in other companies. It has been its policy to insist on appointing a director to the board of any company, so as to take an active part in the management, where its investment comprises more than 20% of the equity share capital.

The following investments have been made:

1. On 1 January 1991, 15% of the ordinary share capital of Club Limited;
2. On 1 July 1991, 30% of the ordinary share capital of Ball Limited; and
3. On 1 November 1991, 75% of the ordinary share capital of Tee Limited, and also 50,000 of the 100,000 9% preference shares of €1 each in that company. For the purposes of measuring non-controlling interests at the date of acquisition, the proportionate share method equates to the fair value method.

The draft statements of comprehensive income of the four companies for the year ended 30 June 1992 show:

	Golf Limited €	Club Limited €	Ball Limited €	Tee Limited €
Revenue	2,100,000	3,900,000	1,900,000	1,200,000
Trading profit	250,000	400,000	210,000	126,000
Dividends	46,500	–	–	–
	296,500	400,000	210,000	126,000
Income tax expense	90,000	170,000	85,000	51,000
	206,500	230,000	125,000	75,000

Additional Information

1. Included in the inventory of Tee Limited was €24,000 for goods purchased from Golf Limited, subsequent to 1 November 1991. Golf Limited realised its usual 25% gross profit, based on selling price when it sold these goods.
2. Retained earnings

	Golf Limited €	Club Limited €	Ball Limited €	Tee Limited €
Profit after tax	206,500	230,000	125,000	75,000
Retained earnings b/f	450,000	306,000	235,000	200,000
Dividends paid				
- Preference	-	(6,000)	-	(9,000)
- Ordinary	(132,000)	(100,000)	(60,000)	(32,000)
Retained earnings	524,500	430,000	300,000	234,000

3. The dividend received from Club Limited has not yet been incorporated in the draft statement of comprehensive income of Golf Limited. All other dividends have been accounted for by Golf Limited.

Requirement   Prepare the consolidated statement of comprehensive income of Golf Limited for the year ended 30 June 1992 in a form suitable for publication.

Question 3

The summarised statements of financial position of Gold Limited, Silver Limited and Bronze Limited as on 30 November 20X3 were as follows:

		Gold Limited €	Silver Limited €	Bronze Limited €
Assets				
Non-current assets				
Property, plant and equipment		100,000	70,000	50,050
Investment in Silver		100,000	–	–
Investment in Bronze		30,500	–	–
		230,500	70,000	50,050
Current assets				
Inventory		26,500	36,000	10,000
Receivables		83,750	125,000	36,300
Cash at bank		2,000	25,000	–
Cash on hand		100	–	–
Current accounts:	Gold Limited	–	–	2,500
	Silver Limited	1,000	–	–
	Bronze Limited	–	650	–
		113,350	186,650	48,800
Total Assets		343,850	256,650	98,850
Equity and Liabilities				
Equity				
Ordinary share capital (50 cents)		50,000	100,000	25,000
Share premium account		10,000	–	–
Capital reserve		61,500	59,250	5,000
Other reserves		35,000	5,000	10,000
Retained profits		26,450	45,300	15,000
Total equity		182,950	209,550	55,000
Current liabilities				
Payables		120,900	31,600	21,200
Bank overdraft		27,500	–	15,000
Taxation		10,000	15,000	7,000

Current accounts:	Gold Limited	–	500	–
	Silver Limited	–	–	650
	Bronze Limited	2,500	–	–
Total Liabilities		160,900	47,100	43,850
Total Equity and Liabilities		343,850	256,650	98,850

Additional Information

1. Shares acquired by Gold Limited in Silver Limited: 150,000 ordinary shares on 30 November 20X1 at a cost of €100,000.

   Shares acquired by Gold Limited in Bronze Limited: 20,000 ordinary shares on 30 November 20X2 at a cost of €30,500.

2. State of affairs relevant to the acquisition dates:

	Silver Limited €	Bronze Limited €
Issued share capital	100,000	25,000
Capital reserve	19,250	-
Retained profits	4,300	5,000
Contingency reserve	5,000	10,000
	128,550	40,000

3. The current account difference arises from a cheque being in transit as on 30 November 20X3.
4. All the property of Silver Limited was disposed of on 31 May 20X3 and the profit on sale credited to capital reserve.
5. One-eighth of the inventory of Silver Limited as on 30 November 20X3 has been invoiced to that company by Gold Limited at cost plus 20%.
6. With respect to the measurement of non-controlling interests at the date of acquisition, the proportionate share method equates to the fair value method. The directors of Gold Limited are confident that any goodwill arising on the acquisition of Silver Limited and Bronze Limited has not suffered any impairment.

Requirement   You are required to prepare the consolidated statement of financial position of Gold Limited and its subsidiary and associated companies on 30 November 20X3.

Challenging Questions

Question 1 (Based on ICAI, P3 Summer 2004, Question 6)

You are the accountant for COCKTAIL Group, which consists of three companies: COCKTAIL plc (COCKTAIL), UMBRELLA Limited (UMBRELLA), and CHERRY

Limited (CHERRY). The individual company statements of financial position as at 31 December 2003 are presented below.

	COCKTAIL € million	UMBRELLA € million	CHERRY € million
ASSETS			
Non-current Assets			
Property, plant and equipment	324	168	180
Investment in UMBRELLA and CHERRY	450	–	–
	774	168	180
Current Assets			
Inventory	144	108	90
Receivables	72	102	96
Current account with UMBRELLA	25	–	–
Bank and cash	288	6	6
	1,303	384	372
EQUITY AND LIABILITIES			
Capital and reserves:			
€1 ordinary shares	360	120	100
Retained earnings	822	186	212
	1,182	306	312
Current Liabilities			
Trade payables	61	33	40
Current account with COCKTAIL	–	5	–
Other payables	60	40	20
	1,303	384	372

Additional Information

1. On 1 January 1999, COCKTAIL purchased 96 million €1 ordinary shares in UMBRELLA for €330 million. The retained earnings of UMBRELLA stood at €120 million on this date and property, plant and equipment with a remaining useful life of ten years were recorded at €20 million less than their fair value. With respect to the

measurement of non-controlling interests at the date of acquisition, the proportionate share method equates to the fair value method.

2. On 1 January 2003, COCKTAIL purchased 30 million €1 ordinary shares in CHERRY for €120 million. The retained earnings of CHERRY stood at €190 million on this date. The net assets of CHERRY had a fair value that was the same as their book value.
3. During 2003 UMBRELLA sold raw materials to COCKTAIL for €2 million, making a profit of 25% on cost. COCKTAIL paid for the raw materials on delivery, and had €500,000 of these in inventory at 31 December 2003.
4. On 30 December 2003, UMBRELLA sent a cheque for €20,000,000 to COCKTAIL that was not received until 2 January 2004.
5. Dividends proposed at 31 December 2003, which are included in other payables, are as follows:

	€ million
COCKTAIL	30
UMBRELLA	20

Dividends receivable by COCKTAIL from UMBRELLA are included in receivables.

6. The directors of COCKTAIL estimate that the goodwill arising on the acquisition of UMBRELLA was impaired for the first time during the year ended 31 December 2003 by €61,000,000. It is group policy to charge a full year's depreciation in the year of acquisition.

Requirement Prepare the consolidated statement of financial position for COCKTAIL Group as at 31 December 2003.

Note
1. The answer does NOT require a consolidated statement of comprehensive income and statement of financial position in a form suitable for publication. These statements may be presented by way of a consolidation schedule.
2. Notes to the accounts are NOT required, nor is a statement indicating the amount of profit dealt with in the holding company's statement of comprehensive income.
3. All workings should be clearly shown.

Question 2 (Based on ICAI, P3 Summer 2000, Question 1)

You are the accountant for EARTH plc group, reporting directly to the Finance Director. EARTH plc group consists of three companies: EARTH plc, WIND Limited, and WATER Limited. The individual company profit and loss accounts for the year ended 31 December 2003 and statements of financial position as at that date are presented below.

Statement of Comprehensive Income for the Year Ended 31 December 2003

	EARTH plc € million	WIND Limited € million	WATER Limited € million
Revenue	460	250	300
Cost of sales	(180)	(70)	(100)
Gross profit	280	180	200
Net operating expenses	(70)	(30)	(20)
Operating profit	210	150	180
Investment income	61	-	-
Interest payable	(30)	(10)	(10)
Profit on ordinary activities before tax	241	140	170
Tax on ordinary activities	(50)	(40)	(50)
Profit on ordinary activities after tax	191	100	120
Dividends proposed	(80)	(50)	(70)
Retained profit for the year	111	50	50

Statement of Financial Position as at 31 December 2003

	EARTH plc € million	WIND Limited € million	WATER Limited € million
ASSETS			
Non-current Assets			
Property, plant and equipment	540	280	300
Investments	750	–	–
	1,290	280	300
Current Assets			
Inventory	240	180	150
Receivables	120	170	160
Bank and cash	480	10	10
	2,130	640	620

EQUITY AND LIABILITIES

Capital and Reserves

€1 ordinary shares	600	200	160
Retained earnings	1,370	310	360
	1,970	510	520
Current Liabilities	160	130	100
	2,130	640	620

Additional Information

1. On 1 January 1999 EARTH plc purchased 160 million €1 ordinary shares in WIND Limited for €550 million. The statement of comprehensive income of WIND Limited stood at €210 million on this date and property, plant and equipment with a remaining useful life of 10 years were recorded at €40 million less than their fair value. For the purposes of measuring non-controlling interests at the date of acquisition, the proportionate share method equated to the fair value method. The directors of EARTH plc estimate that the goodwill arising on the acquisition of WIND Limited was impaired for the first time during the year ended 31 December 2003 by €95 million.
2. On 1 January 2003 EARTH plc purchased 48 million €1 ordinary shares in WATER Limited for €200 million. The statement of comprehensive income of WATER Limited stood at €310 million on this date. The net assets of WATER Limited had a fair value that was the same as their book value. The goodwill arising on the acquisition of WATER Limited has not been impaired at 31 December 2003.
3. During 2003 WIND Limited sold raw materials to EARTH plc for €2 million, making a profit of 25% on cost. EARTH plc paid for the raw materials on delivery, and had €500,000 of these in inventory at 31 December 2003.
4. The profits of EARTH plc, WIND Limited, and WATER Limited accrue evenly throughout the year. It is group policy to charge a full year's depreciation in the year of acquisition. Depreciation charges are included in net operating expenses.
5. EARTH plc's investment income, which is included in receivables, represents dividends receivable from WIND Limited and WATER Limited. Dividends proposed are included in current liabilities at 31 December 2003.

Requirement
(a) Prepare the consolidated statement of comprehensive income of EARTH plc group for the year ended 31 December 2003.
(b) Prepare the consolidated statement of financial position for EARTH plc group as at 31 December 2003.

Note:
1. The answer does NOT require a consolidated statement of comprehensive income and statement of financial position in a form suitable for publication. These statements may be presented by way of a consolidation schedule.

2. Notes to the accounts are NOT required, nor is a statement indicating the amount of profit dealt with in the holding company's statement of comprehensive income.
3. All workings should be clearly shown.

Question 3 (*Based on ICAI, P3 Autumn 2001, Question 1*)

OPUS Limited (OPUS), a company which prepares its financial statements to 31 December each year, carries on business as a distributor of musical instruments. On 1 January 2003, OPUS acquired 90% of the ordinary share capital of SONATA Limited (SONATA) at a cost of €942,000. On the same day, OPUS also acquired 30% of the ordinary share capital of PRELUDE Limited (PRELUDE) at a cost of €220,000.

The draft statements of comprehensive income of OPUS, SONATA and PRELUDE for the year ended 31 December 2003 are as follows:

	OPUS	SONATA	PRELUDE
	€'000	€'000	€'000
Revenue	22,500	1,950	1,500
Cost of sales	(15,000)	(1,225)	(1,000)
Gross profit	7,500	725	500
Distribution costs	(2,200)	(175)	(90)
Administrative expenses	(275)	(15)	(10)
Operating profit	5,025	535	400
Interest payable and similar charges	(40)	(10)	(20)
Interest receivable	20	5	10
Profit on ordinary activities before tax	5,005	530	390
Tax on profit on ordinary activities	(1,605)	(100)	(80)
Profit on ordinary activities after tax	3,400	430	310
Dividends paid	(250)	–	–
Retained profit for the year	3,150	430	310

Additional Information

1. The net assets of SONATA on 1 January 2003 were as follows:

	Carrying value	Fair value
	€'000	€'000
Property, plant and equipment	600	560
Inventory	300	260
Other net assets	160	160
	1,060	980

The difference between the carrying value and the fair value of property, plant and equipment is due to a revaluation of property, while the reduction in inventory relates to a change in the accounting policy for inventory in order to bring SONATA's inventory into line with those of OPUS. Otherwise the accounting policies adopted by SONATA are similar to those of OPUS. The required change in the closing inventory of SONATA to ensure uniform accounting policies is a decrease of €30,000. The fair values shown above have not yet been incorporated into SONATA's financial statements. With respect to the measurement of non-controlling interests at the date of acquisition, the proportionate share method equates to the fair value method. The directors of OPUS believe that the goodwill arising on the acquisition of SONATA was impaired by €12,000 at 31 December 2003.

2. The fair value of the net assets of PRELUDE was the same as their book value on 1 January 2003. The statement of financial position of PRELUDE showed the following on this date:

	€'000
Share capital	200
Retained earnings	450
	650

The directors of OPUS estimate that the goodwill arising on the acquisition of PRELUDE has not been impaired at 31 December 2003.

3. Following the acquisition of shares in SONATA and PRELUDE, the directors of OPUS decided to run down certain parts of OPUS's business activities. These were finally discontinued in December 2003. The contribution to the business of these activities in 2003 was:

	€'000
Turnover	2,500
Cost of sales	2,000
Gross profit	500
Distribution costs	(290)
Administrative expenses	(200)
Operating profit	10

4. It is Group policy to charge any impairment of goodwill to cost of sales.
5. OPUS, SONATA and PRELUDE each follow a policy of depreciating all fixed assets at 10% per annum on their carrying value. Depreciation is charged to cost of sales in the statement of comprehensive income.
6. There were no inter-company sales between OPUS, SONATA and PRELUDE, and the directors of OPUS are not directors of SONATA or PRELUDE.

Requirement Assuming that SONATA is to be accounted for as a subsidiary and PRELUDE as an associate, prepare the consolidated statement of comprehensive income of OPUS Group for the year ended 31 December 2003 in a form suitable for publication.

Note

1. A statement detailing the amount of the consolidated profit dealt with in OPUS's financial statements is not required.
2. Notes to the consolidated statement of comprehensive income are not required.

CHAPTER 30

JOINT VENTURES

INTRODUCTION

IAS 31 *Interests in Joint Ventures* applies in accounting for interests in joint ventures and the reporting of joint venture assets, liabilities, income and expenses in the financial statements of venturers, regardless of the structures or forms under which the joint venture activities take place. IAS 31 does not apply to interests in jointly controlled entities held by:

- venture capital organisations; or
- mutual funds, unit trusts and similar entities including investment-linked insurance funds that upon initial recognition are designated as at fair value through profit or loss or are classified as held for trading and accounted for in accordance with IAS 39 *Financial Instruments: Recognition and Measurement*.

After having read this chapter, you should understand how to account for each of the three forms of joint ventures.

KEY DEFINITIONS

Venturer

A party to a joint venture and having joint control over that joint venture.

Joint Venture

A contractual agreement whereby two or more parties undertake an economic activity which is subject to joint control.

Joint Control

The contractually agreed sharing of control over an economic activity. Joint control may be precluded when an investee is in legal reorganisation or in bankruptcy or operates under severe long-term restrictions on its ability to transfer funds to the venturer.

Contractual Arrangement

The existence of a contract distinguishes interests involving joint control from investments in associates in which an investor has significant influence. The contract may be evidenced by way of formal contract or minutes of discussions between the venturers. It may be incorporated in the articles of the joint venture. It is usually in writing, dealing with:

(a) the activity, duration and reporting obligations of the joint venture;
(b) the appointment of the board of directors of the joint venture and voting rights of venturers;
(c) capital contributions by the venturers; and
(d) the sharing by the venturers of the output, income, expenses or results of the joint venture.

No single venturer is in a position to control unilaterally the activity but instead requires the consent of all the venturers to undertake essential decisions.

Proportionate Consolidation

A method of accounting and reporting whereby a venturer's share of each of the assets, liabilities, income and expenses of a jointly controlled entity is combined on a line-by-line basis with similar items in the venturer's financial statements or reported as separate line items.

Equity Method

Initially the investment is carried at cost and adjusted thereafter for the post-acquisition change in the venturer's share of net assets of the jointly controlled entity. The statement of comprehensive income reflects the venturer's share of results of operations of the jointly controlled entity.

FORMS OF JOINT VENTURE

IAS 31 identifies three broad types of joint venture activity:

- Jointly controlled operations;
- Jointly controlled assets; and
- Jointly controlled entities.

Each of the above forms has the common characteristic of having two or more joint venturers bound under contract and establishing joint control.

Jointly Controlled Operations

Some joint ventures involve the use of assets and other resources rather than the establishment of a corporation, partnership or other entity. Each venturer uses its own assets and incurs its own expenses and raises its own finance. The joint venture agreement usually provides a means by which revenue from the sale of the joint product and any expenses are shared among the venturers. An example might be a joint venture to manufacture, market and distribute jointly a particular product such as an aircraft. Different parts of the manufacturing process are carried out by each of the venturers and each venturer takes a share of the revenue from the sale of the aircraft but bears its own costs.

A venturer should recognise in its financial statements the following:

(a) the assets it controls and the liabilities it incurs; and
(b) the expenses it incurs and its share of the income it earns from the sale of goods or services by the joint venture.

No adjustments or other consolidated procedures are required, as the elements are already included in the separate statements of the investor. Separate accounting records may not be required for the joint venture but the venturers may prepare management accounts in order to assess the performance of the joint venture.

Jointly Controlled Assets

Some joint ventures involve joint control by the venturers over one or more assets that are dedicated for the purposes of the joint venture. Each venturer may take a share of the output and bear an agreed share of the expenses incurred. No corporation, however, is established. Many activities in oil and gas and mineral extraction involve jointly controlled assets, e.g. an oil pipeline. Another example is the joint control of property, each taking a share of the rents received and bearing a share of the expenses.

A venturer should recognise in its financial statements:

(a) its share of jointly controlled assets, classified according to their nature;
(b) any liabilities it has incurred;
(c) its share of any liabilities jointly incurred with other venturers;
(d) any income from the sale or use of the share of the output of the joint venture together with its share of any expenses incurred;
(e) any expenses incurred re its interest in the joint venture.

No adjustments or other consolidation adjustments are required as the assets, liabilities, income and expenses are already recognised in the separate financial statements of the venturer. The treatment of jointly controlled assets reflects the substance and economic reality and usually the legal form of the joint venture. Separate accounting records for the joint venture may be limited to those expenses incurred in common. Financial statements may not be prepared for the joint venture but management accounts may be needed to assess performance.

Jointly Controlled Entities

In this case a corporation is established and operates as per other legal entities except that there is a contractual arrangement between the venturers that establish joint control over the economic activity of the entity. A jointly controlled entity controls the assets of the joint venture, incurs liabilities and expenses and earns income. It may enter contracts in its own name and raise finance for itself, and each venturer is entitled to a share of the results of the jointly controlled entity. An example is when two entities combine their activities in a particular line of business by transferring relevant assets and liabilities into a jointly controlled entity or it could be a joint venture by establishing a joint entity with a foreign government.

In substance they are often similar to jointly controlled operations or jointly controlled assets. However, it does maintain its own accounting records and prepares its financial statements in the same way as other normal entities in conformity with appropriate national regulations. Each venturer usually contributes cash or other resources to the jointly controlled entity. These contributions are included in the accounting records of the venturer and recognised in its financial statements as an investment in the jointly controlled entity.

Accounting for Jointly Controlled Entities

IAS 31 allows a venturer to recognise its interest in a jointly controlled entity using either:

(a) **The benchmark treatment** – proportionate consolidation; and
(b) **The allowed alternative** – the equity method in accordance with IAS 28 *Investment in Associates*.

Proportionate Consolidation

It is essential that a venturer reflects the substance and economic reality of the arrangement. The application of proportionate consolidation means that the consolidated statement of financial position of the venturer includes its share of the assets it controls jointly and its share of the liabilities for which it is jointly responsible. The consolidated statement of comprehensive income includes the venturer's share of the income and expenses of the jointly controlled entity. Many of the procedures are similar to the consolidation procedures set out in IAS 27.

There are two different reporting formats to give effect to proportionate consolidation:

- Combine share of each of the assets, liabilities, income and expenses of the jointly controlled entity with similar items in the consolidated statements on a line-by-line basis, e.g. its share of inventory with inventory of the consolidated group; or
- Include separate line items for its share of the jointly controlled entity's assets etc., e.g. show share of a current asset of the jointly controlled entity separately as part of

current assets; show share of property of the jointly controlled entity separately as part of property etc.

Both methods are acceptable under the IAS 31 and both result in identical profits being recorded and total for each major classification of assets. However, regardless of the format selected, it is inappropriate to offset any assets or liabilities unless a legal right of set off exists and the offsetting represents the expectation as to the realisation of the asset or settlement of the liability.

Proportionate consolidation should be discontinued from the date on which the venture ceases to have joint control over a jointly controlled entity. This could happen when the venturer disposes of its interest or when external restrictions mean that it can no longer achieve its goals.

Example

(Both reporting formats)

Summarised Statements of Financial Position at 31 December 2004

	Parent Company Limited and Subsidiary €'000	Joint Venture Limited €'000
Assets		
Tangible non-current assets	300	180
Investment in joint venture	100	–
Net current assets	120	90
	520	270
Equity		
Ordinary shares	250	100
Retained profits	270	170
	520	270

Summarised Statements of Comprehensive Income

Profit before tax	180	90
Income tax expense	(50)	(30)
Profit after tax	130	60
Retained profit carried forward	190	130
Dividends	(50)	(20)
Retained profit brought forward	270	170

The Parent company acquired 50% of the ordinary shares of Joint Venture Limited when the retained profits of Joint Venture Limited were €80,000.

Workings:

Tangible Non-Current Assets

	€'000		€'000
P & S	300		
Investment in joint venture	90	CSFP	390
	390		390

Investment in Joint Venture

	€'000		€'000
		Tangible non-current assets	90
		Net current assets	45
P	100	Goodwill	10
Retained Profits	45		
	145		145

Net Current Assets

	€'000		€'000
P & S	120		
Investment in joint venture	45	CSFP	165
	165		165

Ordinary Shares

	€'000		€'000
CSFP	250	P	250
	250		250

Retained Profits

	€'000		€'000
		P & S	270
CSFP	315	Investment in joint venture	45
	315		315

Cost of Control

	€'000		€'000
Cost of investment in joint venture	100	Ordinary shares (50%)	50
		Retained earnings (50%)	40
		Goodwill (balance)	10
	100		100

Alternatively, goodwill may be calculated as follows:

	€'000
Cost of Inv. in joint venture	100
Acquired 50% (€100 + €80)	90
Goodwill	10
Post-acq profits of joint venture (€170 – €80)	90
Group's share (50%)	45

Reporting Format 1:

Consolidated Statement of Financial Position as at 31 December 2004

	€'000
Tangible non-current assets	390
Goodwill	10
Net current assets	165
	565
Ordinary shares	250
Retained profits	315
	565

Consolidated Statement of Comprehensive Income for the year ended
31 December 2004

	€'000
Profit before tax (€130 + (€70 x 50%)	165
Tax (€50 + (€30 x 50%)	65
Profit after tax	100
Retained profit carried forward (W1)	215
Retained profit brought forward	315
(W1) Retained Profit Brought Forward P & S	190
Joint venture (50% (€130 – €80)	25
	215

Reporting Format 2:

Consolidated Statement of Financial Position

	€'000	€'000
Tangible non-current assets		
Group	300	
Joint Venture	90	390
Goodwill		10
Net current assets		
Group	120	
Joint Venture	45	165
		565
Ordinary shares		250
Retained profits		315
		565

Consolidated Statement of Comprehensive Income

	€'000	€'000
Profit before tax		
Group	130	
Joint Venture	35	165
Tax Group	50	
Joint Venture	15	65
Profit before tax		100
Retained profit carried forward		215
Retained profit brought forward		315

Equity Method

As an alternative, a venturer may report its interest in a jointly controlled entity using the equity method as per IAS 28 (see Chapter 29). Those who argue that it is inappropriate to combine controlled items with jointly controlled items support the equity method. IAS 31 does not recommend the use of the equity method because proportional consolidation better reflects the substance and economic reality of a venturer's interest in a jointly controlled entity. However, the standard does permit its adoption as an alternative treatment. A venturer should discontinue the use of the equity method from the date it ceases to have joint control over or have significant influence in a jointly controlled entity.

Exceptions to Proportional Consolidation and Equity Method

Neither the proportionate consolidation nor the equity method is required in the following exceptional circumstances:

- An investment in a jointly controlled entity that is acquired and held exclusively with a view to its disposal within 12 months from acquisition should be accounted for as held for trading under IAS 39. Under IAS 39, those investments are measured at fair value with fair value changes recognised in profit or loss;
- A parent that is exempted from preparing consolidated financial statements by paragraph 10 of IAS 27 may prepare separate financial statements as its primary financial statements. In those separate statements, the investment in the jointly controlled entity may be accounted for by the cost method or under IAS 39;
- An investor in a jointly controlled entity need not use proportionate consolidation or the equity method if all of the following four conditions are met:
  - the investor is itself a wholly-owned subsidiary, or is a partially-owned subsidiary of another entity and its other owners, including those not otherwise entitled to vote, have been informed about, and do not object to, the investor not applying proportionate consolidation or the equity method,
  - the investor's debt or equity instruments are not traded in a public market,
  - the investor did not file, nor is it in the process of filing, its financial statements with a securities commission or other regulatory organisation for the purpose of issuing any class of instruments in a public market, and
  - the ultimate or any intermediate parent of the investor produces consolidated financial statements available for public use that comply with IFRSs.

OTHER ISSUES

Separate Financial Statements of a Venturer

In the separate financial statements of the venturer, its interests in the joint venture should be accounted for at cost or under IAS 39.

Transactions between a Venturer and a Joint Venture

If a venturer contributes or sells an asset to a jointly controlled entity, while the assets are retained by the joint venture, provided that the venturer has transferred the risks and rewards of ownership, it should recognise only the proportion of the gain attributable to the other venturers. The venturer should recognise the full amount of any loss incurred when it is indicative of a permanent decline in value.

The requirements for recognition of gains and losses apply equally to non-monetary contributions unless the gain or loss cannot be measured, or the other venturers contribute similar assets. Unrealised gains or losses should be eliminated against the underlying assets (proportionate consolidation) or against the investment (equity method) (see SIC 13 below). When a venturer purchases assets from a jointly controlled entity, it should not recognise its share of the gain until it resells the asset to an independent party. Losses should be recognised if they are indicative of a permanent decline in value.

SIC 13 *Jointly Controlled Entities – Non-Monetary Contributions by Venturers*

Issue

IAS 31.48 refers to both contributions and sales between a venturer and a joint venture. There is no explicit guidance on the recognition of gains and losses resulting from contributions of non-monetary assets to jointly controlled entities. Contributions to a jointly controlled entity are transfers of assets by venturers in exchange for an equity interest in the jointly controlled entity. Such contributions may take various forms and can be made simultaneously by the venturers either upon setting up the jointly controlled entity or subsequently. The consideration received by the venturer in exchange for assets contributed to the jointly controlled entity may also include cash or other consideration that does not depend on future cash flows of the jointly controlled entity. The issues are:

(a) when should the appropriate portion of gains or losses resulting from the contribution of a non-monetary asset to a jointly controlled entity in exchange for an equity interest in the jointly controlled entity be recognised by the venturer in the statement of comprehensive income?
(b) how should additional consideration be accounted for by the venturer?
(c) how should any unrealised gain or loss be presented in the consolidated statements of the venturer?

SIC 13 deals with the venturer's accounting for non monetary contributions to a jointly controlled entity in exchange for an equity interest in the jointly controlled entity that is accounted for using the equity method or proportionate consolidation.

Consensus

A venturer recognises in profit or loss for the period the portion of a gain or loss attributable to the equity interests of the other venturers except when:

- the significant risks and rewards of ownership of the contributed non-monetary asset have not been transferred to the jointly controlled entity; or
- the gain or loss cannot be measured reliably; or
- the contribution transaction lacks commercial substance.

Where any of the above applies, the gain/loss would be considered unrealised and therefore not recognised in income.

If, in addition to receiving an equity interest in the jointly controlled entity, a venturer receives monetary or non-monetary assets dissimilar to those it contributed, an

582 INTERNATIONAL FINANCIAL ACCOUNTING AND REPORTING

appropriate portion of gain/loss on the transaction should be recognised by the venturer in income.

Unrealised gains/losses on non-monetary assets contributed to jointly controlled entities should be eliminated against the underlying assets under the proportionate consolidation method or equity method. Such unrealised gains/losses should not be presented as deferred gains or losses in the venturer's consolidated statement of financial position.

DISCLOSURE

A venturer should disclose the aggregate amount of the following contingent liabilities, unless the probability of loss is remote, each separately:

(a) any contingent liabilities incurred in relation to its interest in joint ventures and its share in each contingent liability incurred jointly with other venturers;
(b) its share of contingent liabilities of the joint ventures for which it is contingently liable; and
(c) those contingent liabilities that arise because the venturer is contingently liable for the liabilities of the other venturers of a joint venture.

A venturer should disclose the aggregate amount of the following commitments re interests in joint ventures separately from other commitments:

(a) any capital commitments re joint ventures and its share in capital commitments incurred jointly with other venturers; and
(b) its share of capital commitments of the joint ventures themselves.

A venturer should disclose a listing and description of interests in significant joint ventures and the proportion of ownership interest held in jointly controlled entities. An entity that adopts line-by-line reporting for proportionate consolidation or the equity method should disclose the aggregate amounts of each of current assets, long-term assets, current liabilities, long-term liabilities, income and expenses related to interests in joint ventures.

A venturer that does not publish consolidated accounts, because it has no subsidiaries, should disclose the above information as well.

CONCLUSION

A joint venture is an entity formed between two or more parties to undertake economic activity together. The venture can be for one specific project or a continuing business relationship. A joint venture may be a limited company, a partnership or other legal structure depending on a number of considerations such as tax and tort liability. Joint ventures are often between a local and foreign company, and are often seen as a viable business alternative where companies can complement their skill sets or gain a geographic presence.

QUESTIONS

Self-test Questions

1. Explain the term joint venture.
2. Distinguish between jointly controlled operations, jointly controlled assets and jointly controlled entities.

Review Questions

Review Questions 1 and 2 deal with subsidiaries and associates and are present as revision of the consdidation principles covered in chapters 26-29. The challenging question includes a joint venture.

(See APPENDIX ONE for Suggested Solutions to Review Questions.)

Question 1   (Based on ICAI, P3 Autumn 1998, Question 2)

TRUE plc acquired 675,000 shares in FAIR Limited on 1 January 2001. The reserves of FAIR Limited at the date of acquisition comprised revenue reserve of €100,000 and capital reserve of €50,000. With respect to the measurement of non-controlling interests at the date of acquisition, the proportionate share method equated to the fair value method. The draft statements of financial position of both these companies as at 31 December 2003 are given below.

	TRUE plc		FAIR Limited	
	€	€	€	€
ASSETS				
Non-current Assets				
Property, plant and equipment		1,750,000		1,050,000
Investments – shares in Fair Limited at cost		950,000		
		2,700,000		
Current assets				
Inventory	415,000		210,000	
Receivables	510,000		240,000	
Current account with FAIR Limited	25,000		-	
Bank and cash	200,000	1,150,000	60,000	510,000
		3,850,000		1,560,000

EQUITY AND LIABILITIES

Capital and Reserves

€1 ordinary shares	2,000,000	750,000
Revenue reserve	950,000	495,000
Capital reserve	300,000	75,000
	3,250,000	1,320,000

Current Liabilities

Trade payables	450,000		185,000		
Current account with TRUE Limited	-		5,000		
Proposed dividend	150,000	600,000	50,000	240, 000	
		3,850,000		1,560,000	

In addition, the draft statements of comprehensive income of the two companies for the year ended 31 December 2003 are as follows:

	TRUE plc	FAIR Limited
	€	€
Revenue	4,050,000	990,000
Cost of sales	(2,088,000)	(558,000)
Gross profit	1,962,000	432,000
Operating expenses	(1,260,000)	(198,000)
Trading profit	702,000	234,000
Investment income	45,000	-
Profit before taxation	747,000	234,000
Taxation	(180,000)	(72,000)
Profit after taxation	567,000	162,000
Ordinary dividends paid	(255,000)	(50,000)
Ordinary dividends proposed	(150,000)	(50,000)
Retained profit for the year	162,000	62,000

Additional Information

1. TRUE plc has not yet accounted for its share of the proposed dividend by FAIR Limited.
2. On 30 December 2003 FAIR Limited sent a cheque for €20,000 to TRUE plc which was not received until 2 January 2004.
3. TRUE plc sold goods to FAIR Limited during the year at an invoice price of €225,000. The goods were invoiced at cost plus 25%. One half of these goods was still in FAIR Limited's inventory at 31 December 2003.
4. On 7 January 2004 a power failure at one of the refrigerated storage units owned by FAIR Limited destroyed inventory with a book value at the year end of €42,000. The company has negotiated a settlement of €35,000 with the insurance company.
5. On 13 January 2004 SHAKEY Limited, a customer of TRUE plc, went into receivership. There had been no movement on this customer's account since the year end, at which time SHAKEY Limited owed €30,000 to TRUE plc. Unaware of the difficulties that SHAKEY Limited was facing, no provision had been made against this account nor did any reservation of title clauses exist.
6. The directors of TRUE estimate that the goodwill arising on the acquisition of FAIR was impaired for the first time during the year ended 31 December 2003 by €84,000.

Requirement   Prepare the consolidated statement of comprehensive income of TRUE plc for the year ended 31 December 2003 and the consolidated statement of financial position as at that date.

Question 2   (Based on ICAI, P3 Summer 1999, Question 4)

Archer PLC owns a number of subsidiaries, and prepares its consolidated financial statements to 31 December each year. During 2003 ARCHER plc purchased interests in BOW Limited and ARROW Limited. Draft statements of comprehensive income for the year ended 31 December 2003 and statements of financial position as at that date for ARCHER Group (excluding BOW Limited and ARROW Limited), and for BOW Limited and ARROW Limited are presented below.

Statement of Comprehensive Income for the Year Ended 31 December 2003

	ARCHER Group €m	BOW Limited €m	ARROW Limited €m
Revenue	3,000	200	1,800
Cost of sales	(1,800)	(125)	(900)
Gross profit	1,200	75	900
Operating expenses	(500)	(25)	(260)

Operating profit	700	50	640
Interest payable	(20)	(5)	(10)
Profit before tax	680	45	630
Tax	(200)	(10)	(190)
Profit after tax	480	35	440
Dividends paid	(180)	-	(40)
Retained profit for year	300	35	400

Statement of Financial Position as at 31 December 2003

	ARCHER Group €m	BOW Limited €m	ARROW Limited €m
ASSETS			
Non-current Assets			
Property, plant and equipment	2,200	40	2,100
Investment in BOW Limited	200	-	-
Investment in ARROW Limited	800	-	-
	3,200	40	2,100
Current Assets			
Inventory	400	125	250
Receivables	300	-	240
Bank and cash	80	200	110
	3,980	365	2,700
EQUITY AND LIABILITIES			
Capital and Reserves			
€1 ordinary shares (equity)	1,200	100	600
Revaluation reserve	600	-	300
Retained earnings	1,700	235	1,500
	3,500	335	2,400
Current Liabilities	480	30	300
	3,980	365	2,700

Additional Information

1. On 1 January 2003 ARCHER plc purchased 100% of the ordinary share capital of BOW Limited. The details were as follows:

	€m
Cost of investment	200
Fair value of net assets acquired:	
– property, plant and equipment	50
– inventory	250

Property, plant and equipment are to be depreciated over five years. During 2003, 50% of the inventory was sold outside the group on normal trading terms, with the remaining inventory expected to be sold in 2004. The acquisition of BOW Limited has not yet been incorporated into the 'ARCHER Group' financial statements shown above.

2. On 1 January 2003 ARCHER plc purchased 30% of ARROW Limited. ARCHER plc contributes to ARROW plc's activities and is actively involved in ARROW Limited's financial and operating policy decisions. ARROW Limited's statement of financial position at 1 January 2003 showed:

	€m
Share capital	600
Revaluation reserve	300
Retained earnings	1,100
	2,000

The acquisition of ARROW Limited has not yet been incorporated into the 'ARCHER Group' financial statements shown above.

Requirement
(a) Explain, in the context of IAS 28 *Interests in Associates* and IAS 31 *Interests in Joint Ventures,* the difference between an associate and a joint venture.
(b) Prepare the statement of comprehensive income for the year ended 31 December 2003 and the statement of financial position as at that date for ARCHER Group.

Challenging Questions

Question 1 (Based on ICAI, P3 Summer 2006, Question 1 & 2)

You are the Finance Director of THOMPSON Group plc (THOMPSON), a group of companies that imports, blends and packs high quality tea for sale to the retail trade. THOMPSON prepares its financial statements to 31 December each year, and you have just extracted the following trial balance as at 31 December 2005 from the group's books and records:

Trial Balance as at 31 December 2005

	Note	DR €'000	CR €'000
€1 ordinary shares			1,000
Retained earnings at 31 December 2004			600
Cost of investment in ROSS Limited	1	250	
Cost of investment in DAVID Limited	2	150	
Property – cost at 31 December 2004	3	600	
Property – accumulated depreciation at 31 December 2004	4		108
Plant and equipment – cost at 31 December 2004		1,800	
Plant and equipment – accumulated depreciation at 31 December 2004	4		292
Development costs		100	
Inventory at 31 December 2004	5	260	
Trade receivables		35	
Prepayments		15	
Bank overdraft			25
Trade payables			40
Accruals			12
10% debentures	6		600
Revenue			9,500
Purchases		4,200	
Selling and distribution costs		1,750	
Administrative expenses		1,972	
Debenture interest paid		45	
Dividends paid		1,000	
		12,177	12,177

Additional Information

1. On 1 January 2005, THOMPSON purchased 60,000 €1 ordinary shares in ROSS Limited (ROSS), a company that is involved in the tea trade but whose focus is on the price of the product rather than the quality. The retained earnings of ROSS stood at €170,000 on 1 January 2005, and the net assets of ROSS had a fair value that was the same as their book value. The statement of comprehensive income of ROSS for the year ended 31 December 2005, and the statement of financial position as that date, are shown below:

Statement of Comprehensive Income for the Year Ended 31 December 2005

	€'000
Revenue	500
Cost of sales	(200)
Gross profit	300
Administrative expenses	(100)
Profit before tax	200
Income tax	(50)
Profit after tax	150

Statement of Financial Position as at 31 December 2005

	€'000
ASSETS	
Non-current Assets	
Plant and equipment	500
Current Assets	
Inventory	30
Receivables	40
Bank and cash	10
	580
EQUITY AND LIABILITIES	
Capital and Reserves	
€1 ordinary shares	200
Retained earnings	320
Current Liabilities	
Trade payables	60
	580

Only the cost of the investment in ROSS is included in THOMPSON's trial balance as at 31 December 2005. The directors of THOMPSON estimate that the goodwill arising on the acquisition of ROSS was impaired by €39,000 during the year ended 31 December 2005.

2. During the year ended 31 December 2005, THOMPSON became involved in a joint venture arrangement with GRAEME Incorporated (GRAEME) with a view to expanding their operations to other countries. THOMPSON and GRAEME each purchased 50% of the ordinary share capital in a new entity, DAVID Limited (DAVID), with each company agreeing to provide 50% of the cash and other resources required to finance DAVID. Neither THOMPSON nor GRAEME is able to control DAVID without the support of the other, and all decisions on financial and operating policy, economic performance and financial position require the consent of both THOMPSON and GRAEME. The following information is available with respect to DAVID's activities during the year ended 31 December 2005.

Statement of Comprehensive Income for the Year Ended 31 December 2005

	€'000
Revenue	300
Cost of sales	(100)
Gross profit	200
Administrative expenses	(50)
Profit before tax	150
Income tax	(30)
Profit after tax	120

Statement of Financial Position as at 31 December 2005

	€'000
ASSETS	
Non-current Assets	
Plant and equipment	290
Current Assets	
Inventory	20
Receivables	10
Bank and cash	5
	325
EQUITY AND LIABILITIES	
Capital and Reserves	
€1 ordinary shares	200
Retained earnings	120
Current Liabilities	
Trade payables	5
	325

Only the cost of the investment in DAVID is included in THOMPSON's trial balance as at 31 December 2005. The directors of THOMPSON are confident that any goodwill arising on the acquisition of DAVID has not been impaired at 31 December 2005.

3. The property shown in the trial balance was acquired a number of years ago and the estimated useful economic life was 50 years at the time of purchase. As at 31 December 2005, the property is to be revalued to €1,000,000.

4. It is group policy to provide a full year's depreciation in the year of acquisition and none in the year of disposal. All depreciation is charged to administrative expenses and is calculated as follows:

Property   – straight line over estimated useful economic life;
Plant and equipment   – 10% straight line.

5. THOMPSON's inventory at 31 December 2005 is valued by the directors at €275,000. Included in this figure is speciality tea valued at its original cost of €60,000. The replacement cost of the tea is €30,000 and its market value, based upon sales in January and February 2006, is €50,000 before selling and distribution costs of €5,000.

6. The 10% debentures were issued on 1 January 2005 and are redeemable on 31 December 2009. Interest is paid quarterly in arrears and the first payment was due on 1 April 2005.

7. In February 2006, THOMPSON received a claim from a former employee for €25,000 alleging discrimination at work and unfair dismissal in October 2005. While the directors refute the claim, they believe the courts are likely to uphold it. As the claim was received in 2006, the directors have decided not to account for it in 2005 and wait until the outcome of the case is known with certainty. The directors believe the case will not be resolved until 2007.

8. There is no trading between THOMPSON, ROSS, GRAEME and DAVID, and there was no change in the share capital of the companies during 2005.

9. THOMPSON's tax charge for 2005, which takes into account all relevant items, is €325,250.

10. It is group policy to account for associates using the equity method and for joint venture entities using either of the proportionate consolidation formats.

Requirement

(a) Prepare the consolidated statement of comprehensive income for THOMPSON for the year ended 31 December 2005 and the consolidated statement of financial position as at that date.

(b) Describe the three broad types of joint ventures identified by IAS 31 Interests in Joint Ventures;

(c) Describe how an interest in a jointly controlled entity should be accounted for in:
   (i) The separate financial statements of a venturer;
   (ii) The consolidated financial statements of a venturer.

(d) Justify the method adopted to account for DAVID in the consolidated financial statements of THOMPSON.

CHAPTER 31

FOREIGN CURRENCY TRANSACTIONS AND TRANSLATION OF FOREIGN OPERATIONS

INTRODUCTION

Carrying out business transactions in a foreign currency will have an effect on normal accountancy procedures since it is necessary to convert foreign currency payments and deposits into Euro. Holding assets and liabilities in a foreign currency will have an impact on the statement of financial position since, owing to exchange rate movements, their value might differ radically from one year to the next. When a business deals in a foreign currency it is exposed to certain risks:

- It might find that after agreeing a price for exported or imported goods the exchange rate changes before delivery. Clearly, this can work both for and against the business.
- Some countries' currencies are more volatile than others because of their inflationary or unstable economies. This makes their exchange rates more liable to extreme movements.

Of course, because exchange rates can go both up and down, a business could gamble that this will work out in their favour. However, this is extremely risky and could result in significant financial loss. It's safer to reduce the risk by using one of the forms of hedging. Hedging simply means insuring against the price of an item – in this case, currency – moving against the business in the future, e.g. forward foreign exchange contracts, opening foreign currency accounts and buying currency options. The business could also consider trading overseas in Euro – effectively transferring the foreign exchange risk to the business it is dealing with. Whether this is an appropriate solution will probably depend on the product in question and the relative bargaining strength of the two businesses.

Exchange rates can have an effect on a business's competitiveness even if it doesn't trade overseas. When a country's currency loses value against the euro, imports from that country into the eurozone become cheaper, so the business may have to respond to aggressive pricing from competitors who source from that country. Similarly, if a country's currency gains currency against sterling, eurozone exports to that country become cheaper.

IAS 21 *The Effects of Changes in Foreign Exchange Rates* prescribes how to include foreign currency transactions and foreign operations in the financial statements of an entity and how to translate financial statements into a presentation currency. IAS 21 does not apply to foreign currency derivatives and hedge accounting of foreign currency items covered by IAS 39 *Financial Instruments: Recognition and Measurement*. It also does not cover cash flows arising from transactions in a foreign currency or with the translation of cash flows of a foreign operation (see IAS 7 *Statement of Cash Flows*).

After having studied this chapter, you should understand:

- how to include foreign currency transactions and foreign operations in the financial statements of a reporting entity;
- the method of translating financial statements into a presentation currency; and
- how to account for entities reporting in the currency of a hyperinflationary economy.

IMPORTANT DEFINITIONS

Foreign Currency

A currency other than the functional currency of the entity.

Functional Currency

This is the currency of the primary economic environment in which the entity operates. An entity's functional currency reflects the underlying transactions, events and conditions that are relevant to it. In most cases the functional currency of a reporting entity is the currency of the country in which it is situated and in which it carries out most of its transactions. A reporting entity should consider certain factors when determining its functional currency including the currency:

- that mainly influences sales prices for goods and services, i.e. the currency in which prices are denominated and settled;
- of the country whose competitive forces and regulations mainly determine the sales prices of its goods and services;
- that mainly influences labour, material and other costs of providing goods/services;
- in which funds from financing activities are generated;
- in which receipts from operating activities are usually retained.

When the entity is a foreign operation the following additional factors are considered:

- Whether the activities of the foreign operation are an extension of the reporting entity;
- Whether transactions with the foreign entity are a high or low proportion of the foreign operation's activities;
- Whether cash flows of the foreign operation directly affect those of the reporting entity;
- Whether cash flows of the foreign operation are sufficient to service existing and expected debt obligations.

Where the indicators are mixed, management must exercise its judgement as to the functional currency to adopt that best reflects the underlying transactions.

Presentation Currency

The currency in which the financial statements are presented.

Exchange Rate

The ratio of exchange for two currencies.

Spot Exchange Rate

The exchange rate for immediate delivery.

Closing Rate

The spot exchange rate at the reporting date.

Exchange Difference

The difference resulting from translating one currency into another currency at different exchange rates.

Foreign Operation

A subsidiary, associate, joint venture or branch whose activities are based in a country or currency other than those of the reporting entity.

Net Investment in a Foreign Operation

The amount of the interest in the net assets of that operation. This includes long-term receivables or loans but does not include trade receivables or trade payables.

Monetary Items

Money and assets/liabilities held to be received/paid in fixed or determinable amounts. Examples include deferred tax, pensions and provisions. The feature of a non-monetary item is the absence of a right to receive a fixed or determinable amount of money (include prepayments, goodwill, intangible assets, inventory, property etc.).

FOREIGN CURRENCY TRANSACTIONS

Initial Recognition

A foreign currency transaction is a transaction denominated or requires settlement in a foreign currency including:

(a) buying or selling of goods or services whose price is denominated in a foreign currency;
(b) borrowing or lending of funds in a foreign currency; or
(c) otherwise acquires or disposes of assets denominated in a foreign currency.

A foreign currency transaction should be recorded initially by applying the spot rate at the date of the transaction. For practical reasons, an average rate for a period may be adopted unless the rate fluctuates significantly.

Reporting at Subsequent Reporting Dates

At each reporting date:

(a) monetary items should be translated at closing rate (for example, trade receivables and payables);
(b) non-monetary items measured at historic cost are translated at exchange rate at the date of the transaction (for example, tangible non-current assets and inventory);
(c) non-monetary items measured at fair value at exchange rate when value was determined.

The carrying amount is determined with other standards, e.g. IAS 2 *Inventories*, IAS 16 *Property, Plant and Equipment* and, where impairment exists, by IAS 36 *Impairment of Assets*. When the asset is non-monetary the carrying amount is determined by comparing the cost or carrying value and the NRV. The effect could be a write-down or vice versa. When several exchange rates are available, the rate to be used should be that at which future cash flows could be settled. If exchangeability is temporarily lacking, the first subsequent rate at which exchanges could be made is used.

Recognition of Exchange Differences

Exchange differences on settlement of monetary items should be expended in the period they arise with the exception of paragraph 32 differences (see below). Where a gain/loss on a non-monetary item is recognised directly in equity any exchange component of that gain/loss should be recognised directly in equity. Conversely when a gain/loss on a non-monetary item is recognised in profit or loss, any exchange component of that gain/loss should be recognised in profit or loss.

Example *(A transaction settled at the reporting date)*

Blue Limited whose year end is 31 December buys goods from a foreign company for 180,000 ricos on 31 July 2004. The transaction is settled on 31 October 2004.

Exchange Rates
31 July	€1	=	1.5	ricos
31 October	€1	=	1.6	ricos

		€	€
Dr.	Purchases	120,000	
Cr.	Trade payables		120,000
	i.e. €180,000 divided by 1.5		
Dr.	Trade payables	112,500	
Cr.	Cash		112,500
	i.e. €180,000 divided by 1.6		
Dr.	Trade payables	7,500	
Cr.	Statement of comprehensive income with exchange difference		7,500

Note: The same principles would apply to the purchase of a non-current tangible asset.

Example *(A transaction not settled at the reporting date)*

Top Limited buys goods from a foreign company for 500,000 zicos on 31 October 2004. The transaction was not settled at 31 December, the company's year end.

Rate of Exchange
31 October	€1	=	1.6 zicos
31 December	€1	=	1.75 zicos

		€	€
Dr.	Purchases	312,500	
Dr.	Trade payables		312,500
	i.e. €500,000 divided by 1.6		

At the 31 December the trade payables must be translated at the closing rate (1.75), i.e. €500,000 divided by 1.75 = €285,714

		€	€
Dr.	Trade payables	26,786	
Cr.	Statement of comprehensive income		26,786

FOREIGN CURRENCY TRANSLATION

The incorporation of a foreign operation should follow normal consolidation procedures, e.g. elimination of intercompany balances. However, an intragroup monetary asset/liability cannot be eliminated against a corresponding intragroup asset/liability without showing the results of currency fluctuations in the consolidated accounts. Such exchange differences should continue to be recognised as income/expenses or in equity, as appropriate.

IAS 27 permits the use of different reporting dates as long as no greater than three months and adjustments are made for the effects of any significant transactions between those dates. In such cases, the exchange rate to adopt is that at the reporting date of the foreign operation. The same approach should be applied to the equity method for associates and joint ventures.

Any goodwill and fair value adjustments should be treated as assets and liabilities of the foreign operation. They therefore must be expressed in the functional currency of the foreign operation and translated at the closing rate.

Presentation Currency = Functional Currency

The results and position of an entity whose functional currency is the same as the presentation currency should be translated as follows:

(a) Monetary items should be translated at closing rate;
(b) Non-monetary items measured at historic cost are translated at exchange rate at the date of the transaction;
(c) Income and expenses at the exchange rates at the dates of the transactions; and
(d) Exchange differences should be recognised as part of profit or loss.

For practical reasons an average rate may be adopted unless exchange rates were to fluctuate significantly.

Presentation Currency ≠ Functional Currency

The financial statements may be presented in any currency. If the presentation currency differs from the functional, its results and financial position need to be translated into the presentation currency. The group, in particular, needs a common currency. The results and position of an entity whose functional currency is not the currency of a hyperinflationary economy should be translated into a different presentation currency as follows:

(a) Assets and liabilities at closing rate;
(b) Income and expenses at the exchange rates at the dates of the transactions; and
(c) All exchange differences in equity as a separate component.

For practical reasons an average rate may be adopted unless exchange rates were to fluctuate significantly.

The exchange differences arise from:

(a) translating income and expenses at transaction rate and assets/liabilities at closing rate;
(b) translating opening net assets at an exchange rate different from that previously reported.

These exchange differences are not recognised as income or expenses as they have little or no direct effect on present and future cash flows from operations. If a foreign operation is not 100% owned, exchange differences should be attributable to non-controlling interests.

The results and position of an entity whose functional currency is the currency of a hyperinflationary economy should be translated as follows:

(a) All amounts at closing rate; except
(b) When amounts are being translated into the currency of a non-hyperinflationary economy, comparative amounts should be those that were presented as current year amounts in the relevant year (i.e. not adjusted for either subsequent changes in prices or exchange rates).

When the functional currency is that of a hyperinflationary economy then its financial statements should be restated under IAS 29 *Financial Reporting in Hyperinflationary Economies*. The accounts must be restated before the translation method is applied. Once it ceases to be hyperinflationary, it should use the amounts restated to the price level at the date it ceases, as the historical costs for translation into the presentation currency.

Change in Functional Currency

When there is a change in the functional currency, the translation procedures applicable to the new functional currency should be applied from the date of the change. A change should only be made if there is a change to those underlying transactions. The effect is accounted for prospectively. All items are translated using the new functional exchange rate at the date of the change. These are then treated as their historical cost. Exchange differences previously recognised in equity are not recognised as income or expenses until the disposal of the operation.

Recognition of Exchange Differences

Exchange differences on settlement of monetary items should be expended in the period they arise with the exception of paragraph 32 differences (see below). Where a gain/loss on a non-monetary item is recognised directly in equity any exchange component of that gain/loss should be recognised directly in equity. Conversely when a gain/loss on a non-monetary item is recognised in profit or loss, any exchange component of that gain/loss should be recognised in profit or loss.

Paragraph 32 states that exchange differences on a monetary item that form part of an entity's net investment in a foreign operation be recognised as income/expense in the separate financial statements of the reporting entity or foreign operation, as appropriate. They should be recorded initially in a separate component of equity and recognised in profit/loss on disposal of the net investment.

When a monetary item that forms part of an entity's net investment in a foreign operation is denominated in the functional currency of the reporting entity, an exchange difference should be recorded in equity. In addition, a monetary item that forms part of the net investment in a foreign operation may be denominated in a currency other than the functional currency. Exchange differences should be recognised in equity.

When an entity keeps its books in a currency other than its functional currency, all amounts are re-measured in the functional currency, i.e. monetary items at closing rate and non-monetary at date of transaction.

Disposal of a Foreign Operation

Any cumulative exchange differences in equity should be recognised as income or expenses when the gain or loss on disposal is recognised.

Tax Effects of All Exchange Differences

Gains and losses on foreign currency transactions may have associated tax effects and these should be accounted for under IAS 12 *Income Taxes*.

Disclosure

(All references are to the functional currency of the parent, if referring to a group.)
An entity should disclose:

(a) The amount of exchange differences included in profit or loss except those arising from IAS 39;
(b) Net exchange differences classified as a component of equity and a reconciliation at start and end of the year;
(c) When the presentation currency is different from the functional currency, that fact should be disclosed as well as disclosure of the functional currency and the reason for using a different presentation currency;
(d) When there is a change in the functional currency of either the reporting entity or a significant foreign operation, that fact and reason for the change should be disclosed;
(e) When an entity presents its financial statements in a currency different from its functional, it should describe the statements as complying with IFRSs only if they comply with all of the requirements of each applicable standard and SIC including the translation method in paragraphs 39 and 42.

Where the requirements listed in (e) are not met an entity should:

(a) clearly identify the information as supplementary;
(b) disclose the currency in which the supplementary information is displayed;

(c) disclose the entity's functional currency and method of translation used to determine the supplementary information.

FINANCIAL REPORTING IN HYPERINFLATIONARY ECONOMIES

The objective of IAS 29 *Financial Reporting in Hyperinflationary Economies* is to establish specific standards for entities reporting in the currency of a hyperinflationary economy, so that the financial information provided is meaningful.

Scope

IAS 29 applies to the primary financial statements, including consolidated, of any entity whose functional currency is the currency of a hyperinflationary economy. In a hyperinflationary economy, reporting in local currency is not useful as money loses purchasing power and therefore the accounts become misleading. IAS 29 does not establish an absolute rate. It is a matter of judgement when the standard becomes necessary but the following characteristics should be reviewed:

(a) The general population prefers to invest in non-monetary assets or in a relatively stable currency;
(b) The general population regards monetary amounts, not in terms of local currency, but in terms of a relatively stable currency;
(c) Credit sales and purchases take place at prices adjusted for the expected loss in purchasing power, even if the credit period is short;
(d) Interest rates, wages and prices are linked to a price index;
(e) The cumulative inflation rate over three years is approaching or exceeds 100%.

It is preferable that all enterprises in the same hyperinflationary economy apply the standard from the same date. It applies to the start of the reporting period in which hyperinflation is identified.

The Restatement of Financial Statements

Prices change over time due to supply and demand as well as general forces pushing up the general level of prices. In most countries, the primary statements are prepared on an historical cost basis except for the revaluation of property etc. Some enterprises, however, adopt a current cost approach using specific price increases.

In a hyperinflationary economy, financial statements must be expressed in terms of an up to date measuring unit if they are to be useful. The financial statements of an entity whose functional currency is that of a hyperinflationary economy, whether historic or current cost, must be restated in current measuring unit terms as well as corresponding figures for the previous period. The gain/loss on the net monetary position should be included within income and separately disclosed. This approach must be consistently applied from period to period. That is more important than precise accuracy.

Historical Cost Financial Statements

Statement of Financial Position

Statement of financial position amounts should be restated by applying a general price index. Monetary items are not restated, as already stated in current monetary terms; index linked bonds and loans are adjusted in accordance with the agreement. All other non-monetary assets should be restated unless already carried at NRV or market value.

Most non-monetary assets require the application of a general price index to their historic costs and accumulated depreciation from the date of acquisition to the reporting date. Inventory work in progress should be restated from the dates on which the costs of purchase and of conversion were incurred.

If detailed records of acquisition dates are not available or capable of estimation, then in rare circumstances, an independent professional assessment may form the basis for their restatement. If a general price index is not available, then an estimate should be based on movements in the exchange rate between the functional and a relatively stable foreign currency. Where non-monetary assets are revalued, these should be restated from the date of revaluation. Where non-current assets are impaired they must be reduced to their recoverable amount and inventory to NRV.

An investee that is accounted for under the equity method may report in the currency of a hyperinflationary economy. The statement of financial position and statement of comprehensive income are restated in accordance with this standard in order to calculate the investor's share of its net assets and results. If expressed in a foreign currency they are translated at closing rates.

It is not appropriate both to restate the capital expenditure financed by borrowing and to capitalise that part of the borrowing costs that compensates for inflation during the same period. It should be expensed. Also, if undue effort or cost is needed to impute interest, such assets are restated from the payment date, not the date of purchase.

On first application of the standard, owners equity must be restated by applying a general price index from the dates that different components of equity arose. Any revaluation surplus is eliminated. At the end of the first period and subsequently, all components of owners equity are restated by applying a general price index from the start of the period to date of contribution and any movements disclosed as per FRS 3.

Statement of Comprehensive Income

All items must be expressed in terms of current measuring units at the reporting date, i.e. by being restated from the dates when initially recorded by the general price index.

Gain or Loss on Net Monetary Position

Any excess of monetary assets loses purchasing power and vice versa. The gain/loss is the difference resulting from the restatement of non-monetary assets, owners equity and statement of comprehensive income items and the adjustment of index-linked assets and liabilities. The gain/loss may be estimated by applying the change in a general price index to the weighted average for the period of the difference between monetary assets and monetary liabilities. The gain or loss is included in net income. Other statement of comprehensive income items, e.g. interest, foreign exchange differences, are also associated with the monetary position. They should be presented together with the gain or loss on the net monetary position in the statement of comprehensive income.

Current Cost Financial Statements

Statement of Financial Position

Items stated at current cost are not restated, already in current measurement units.

Gain or Loss on Net Monetary Position

This is accounted for in accordance with the historic cost approach.

Taxes

Restatement may give rise to deferred tax consequences – see IAS 12.

Statement of Cash Flows

All items in the statement of cash flows are expressed in current measuring units at the reporting date.

Statement of Comprehensive Income

All amounts need to be restated from their current cost at date of transactions to the reporting date by applying a general price index.

Corresponding Figures

These are restated by applying a general price index so that comparative financial statements are presented in terms of current measuring units at the end of the reporting period.

Consolidated Financial Statements

Subsidiaries reporting in the hyperinflationary economy must be restated by applying a general price index and, if that is a foreign subsidiary, then its restated financial statements should be translated at closing rates.

Selection and Use of the General Price Index

All enterprises that report in the currency of the same economy should use the same index

Economies Ceasing to be Hyperinflationary

When an economy ceases to be hyperinflationary and an entity discontinues using this standard, it should treat the amounts expressed at the end of the previous period as the basis for its subsequent financial statements.

Disclosures

(a) The fact that the financial statements and the corresponding periods have been restated for changes in general purchasing power and are restated in terms of current measurement units at the reporting date.
(b) Whether the financial statements are based on historic cost or current cost.
(c) The identity and level of the price index at the reporting date and the movement in the index during the current and previous reporting period.

CONCLUSION

Foreign Currency Transactions

A foreign currency transaction is recorded initially in the functional currency, by applying to the foreign currency amount the spot exchange rate between the functional currency and the foreign currency at the date of the transaction. For practical reasons, a rate that approximates the actual rate at the date of the transaction is often used (e.g. an average weekly or monthly rate). Functional currency is the currency of the primary economic environment in which the entity operates.

At each reporting date:

• Foreign currency monetary items are translated using the closing rate;
• Non-monetary items that are measured in terms of historical cost in a foreign currency are translated using the exchange rate at the date of the transaction; and
• Non-monetary items that are measured at fair value in a foreign currency are translated using the exchange rates at the date when the fair value was determined.

Exchange differences arising on the settlement of monetary items or on translating monetary items at rates different from those at initial recognition are recognised in profit or loss with one exception.

Foreign Operations

- If the foreign subsidiary's activities are an extension of the parent's (same functional currency):
  - Statement of comprehensive income: actual/average rate (historic rate for non-monetary items) (dividends paid at actual rate; dividends proposed at closing rate);
  - Statement of financial position: non-monetary items at historic rate, monetary items at closing rate and shareholders' funds to balance;
  - Exchange difference: part of profit/loss for year
- If the foreign subsidiary operates in a semi-autonomous manner (translation to presentation currency):
  - Statement of comprehensive income: average rate (dividends paid at actual rate; dividends proposed at closing rate);
  - Statement of financial position: assets and liabilities at closing rate;
  - Exchange difference: taken to equity, not through the statement of comprehensive income

IAS 21 requires goodwill to be treated as an asset of the foreign operation, and goodwill and fair value adjustments should be translated at closing rates and not historic rates. IAS 21 requires that, when a foreign subsidiary is disposed of, exchange differences previously recognised in equity are 'recycled' to the statement of comprehensive income in the same period as the gain or loss arising on sale.

QUESTIONS

Self-test Questions

Question 1

IAS 21 *The Effects of Changes in Foreign Exchange Rates* defines the functional currency as the currency:

(a) in which the foreign operation measures and records its transactions.
(b) of the primary economic environment in which the entity operates.
(c) in which the financial statements are presented.
(d) of the country in which the subsidiary is located.

Question 2

According to IAS 21 *The Effects of Changes in Foreign Exchange Rates* the following statement 'the currency that affects the economic wealth of the entity' provides a definition of:

(a) functional currency.
(b) local currency.
(c) presentation currency.
(d) foreign currency.

Question 3

According to IAS 21 *The Effects of Changes in Foreign Exchange Rates* the currency in which an entity primarily generates and expends cash is considered to be the:

(a) economic currency.
(b) domestic currency.
(c) presentation currency.
(d) functional currency.

Question 4

Indicators pointing towards the local overseas currency as the functional currency include:

(i)   Parent's cash flows are directly affected on a current basis.
(ii) Cash flows are primarily in the local currency and do not affect the parent's cash flows.
(iii) Sales prices are primarily responsive to exchange rate changes in the short-term.
(iv) Production costs are determined primarily by local conditions.

(a) (i) and (iii) only;
(b) (ii) and (iv) only;
(c) (i), (iii) and (iv) only;
(d) (i), (ii) and (iv) only.

Question 5

When translating the revenue and expenses in the income statement, theoretically each item of revenue and expense should be translated using the spot exchange rate between the:

(a) functional currency and the foreign currency on the reporting date.
(b) presentation currency and the functional currency on the reporting date.
(c) functional currency and the foreign currency on the date the transaction occurred.
(d) presentation currency and the local currency on the transaction date.

Question 6

By applying the definition provided in IAS 21 *The Effects of Changes in Foreign Exchange Rates* the following items will be regarded as a monetary item:

(a) Property, plant and equipment.
(b) Land and buildings.
(c) Inventory.
(d) Accounts receivable.

Question 7

The general rule for translating liabilities denominated in a foreign currency into the functional currency is to:

(a) translate all liabilities using the current rate existing at balance date.
(b) first classify the liabilities into current and non-current.
(c) first classify the liabilities as monetary or non-monetary.
(d) translate all liabilities using the rate current on entering into the transaction.

Answers:

1 (b)
2 (a)
3 (d)
4 (b)
5 (c)
6 (d)
7 (c)

Review Questions

(See APPENDIX ONE for Suggested Solutions to Review Questions.)

Question 1

MANCO Limited has entered into the following transactions involving foreign currencies during the year ended 31 March 20X9.

1. A 20 year loan of US$ 1,000,000 was obtained from an American bank on 1 August 20X8. The proceeds of the loan were remitted when the exchange rate was US$1.75 = €1.
2. A special machine was purchased from a South American supplier, FRTZ, on 1 October 20X8 for DM55,000 when the exchange rate was DM3.15 = €1. This machine is estimated to have an effective useful life of 5 years, and the company's policy is to use the straight-line method of depreciation commencing on the date of acquisition. Payment for this machine was made in full on 15 December 20X8, when the exchange rate was DM3.00 = €1.

3. Goods for resale were purchased from a Brazilian supplier, ETIEN, on 12 February 1989, for BFr600,000 when the exchange rate was BFr68.00 = €1. This amount was still unpaid at 31 March 20X9.

The accountant at MANCO Limited, who has never before had to deal with transactions involving foreign currencies, kept the above notes but has made no entries whatsoever in the books in respect of these transactions. The relevant exchange rates at 31 March 20X9 were as follows:

US$1.80 = €1.00   DM3.20 = €1.00   BFr69.50 = €1.00

Requirement
(a) Prepare journal entries (including *cash*) to show the accountant of MANCO Limited how each of the transactions (1) to (3) above, in respect of the year ended 31 March 20X9, should be entered into the books of MANCO Limited;
(b) Show how each of the transactions (l) to (3) above would be included in the accounts of MANCO Limited for the year ended 31 March 20X9 by preparing appropriate extracts from the accounts for each transaction. (It is sufficient to indicate the amounts which should be included under the appropriate heading in the statement of financial position and statement of comprehensive income.)

Question 2

You are given the following information in relation to Quickbuck Limited:

1. Quickbuck Limited is a US subsidiary of an Irish company, Prosperous Limited.
2. You are informed that the rates of exchange between the US dollar and the Euro were as follows:

Through 20X3 and on 31 December 20X3	$3 to €1
31 December 20X4	$5 to €1
Average in 20X4	$4 to €1
Average at date of acquisition of	
Quickbuck inventory held 31 December 20X4	$4.8 to €1

3. Property, plant and equipment of Quickbuck Limited were bought in Ireland, shipped to and erected for Quickbuck Limited at a cost of €120,000.

The net book amount of property, plant and equipment of Quickbuck Limited at 31 December 20X4 was arrived at as follows:

	$
Cost	300,000
Depreciation	30,000
	270,000
Depreciation for 20X4:	30,000

4. All of the shares in Quickbuck Limited were acquired by Prosperous Limited when Quickbuck Limited was formed for €25,000.
5. When the dividends were paid from Quickbuck Limited to Prosperous Limited the rate of exchange was $4 to €1.
6. The statement of comprehensive income of Quickbuck Limited for the year ended 31 December 20X4 was as follows:

	$	$
Revenue		544,275
Opening Inventory	41,000	
Purchases	152,525	
Closing Inventory	(48,525)	145,000
Gross Profit		399,275
Depreciation	30,000	
Other expenses	271,050	301,050
Profit before Taxation		98,225
Income tax expense		24,275
Profit after Taxation		73,950
Dividends Paid	10,000	
Proposed	10,000	20,000
Profit Retained for the year		53,950

Dividends paid and proposed during the year ended 31 December 20X4 by Quickbuck Limited were as follows:

	$
Paid	10,000
Proposed	10,000

The proposed dividends were approved by shareholders of Quickbuck Limited prior to 31 December 20X4.

The Statement of Financial Position of Quickbuck Limited as at 31 December 20X4 was as follows:

Assets	$
Non-current Assets:	
Property, plant and equipment	270,000
Current Assets:	
Balance at bank	9,475
Receivables	45,500
Inventory	48,525
	103,500
Total Assets	373,500

Equity and liabilities
Equity

Ordinary Share Capital	75,000
Revenue Reserves	70,450
	145,450

Non-current liabilities:

Loan	90,000

Current liabilities:

Payables	103,775
Taxation	24,275
Dividends	10,000
	138,050
Total equity and liabilities	373,500

Requirement   You are required to translate the accounts of Quickbuck Limited into € where:

(a) Quickbuck Limited has a different functional currency than Prosperous Limited;
(b) Quickbuck Limited has the same functional currency as Prosperous Limited.

Question 3

Ray International Limited is a manufacturing company, with a wholly owned subsidiary M Distribution BV operating in the Netherlands. The draft financial statements of the parent company in €s and of the subsidiary in Dutch Guilders (DFL) for the year ended 31 December 1990 are as follows:

Statement of Comprehensive Income for the Year Ended 31 December 1990

	M Distribution BV DFL'000	RAY International Limited €'000
Revenue	12,600	10,871
Profit before taxation	1,750	2,600
Income tax expense	(210)	(1,300)
Profit for year	1,540	1,300
Balance at beginning of year	-----	480
Dividends paid during year	(500)	-----
Balance at end of year	1,040	1,780

Statements of Financial Position as at 31 December 1990

	DFL'000	€'000
Assets		
Non-current assets		
Property, plant and equipment	600	3,240
Investment in M Distribution	-	400
	600	3,640
Current Assets		
Inventory	2,020	2,390
Other	1,164	1,472
	3,184	3,862
Total assets	3,784	7,502
Equity and liabilities		
Equity		
Share capital	1,200	2,000
Retained profits	1,040	1,780
	2,240	3,780
Non-current liabilities		
Long-term loan	–	294
Current liabilities	1,544	3,428
Total equity and liabilities	3,784	7,502

Additional Information

1. M Distribution BV was incorporated and commenced trading on 1 January 1990. All property, plant and equipment was purchased on that date.
2. The relevant Dutch Guilder exchange rates are as follows:

   (a) 1 January 1990   3.0 DFL to €1
   (b) 31 December 1990   4.0 DFL to €1
   (c) Average for year   3.5 DFL to €1

3. The profit before taxation figure of the parent company includes dividend income from the subsidiary of €125,000.
4. The current assets of the parent company include a balance due from the subsidiary in respect of sales invoiced to the subsidiary in €s, of €382,000. The corresponding liability in the books of the subsidiary is recorded at 1,381,000 Dutch Guilders.
5. The revenue figure of the parent company includes sales to the subsidiary of €2,450,000. There are no inter-company profits in inventory.

Requirement   You are required to prepare the consolidated statement of comprehensive income and the consolidated statement of financial position of RAY International Limited and its subsidiary for the year ended 31 December, 1990 assuming that the functional currency of M Distribution BV is different from the functional currency of Ray International Limited.

Question 4

BELVOIR plc (BELVOIR) purchased 35,000 ordinary shares in an Australian company, PERTH Limited (PERTH), on the 30 April 2003. For the purposes of measuring non-controlling interests at the date of acquisition, the proportionate share method equated to the fair value method. The summarised statements of financial position of the two companies at 31 December 2003 are as follows:

	BELVOIR €'000	PERTH A$'000
ASSETS		
Non-current Assets		
Property, plant and equipment	50,000	150,000
Investment in PERTH	11,667	–
	61,667	150,000
Current Assets		
Inventory	75,000	200,000
Receivables	175,000	250,000
Cash	5,000	25,000
	255,000	475,000
	316,667	625,000
EQUITY AND LIABILITIES		
Capital and Reserves		
€1/A$1 ordinary shares	50,000	50,000
Capital reserve	25,000	60,000
Revenue reserve	55,000	65,000
	130,000	175,000
Provision for Liabilities and Charges	26,667	75,000
Current Liabilities	160,000	375,000
	316,667	625,000

Additional Information:

1. Included in the current liabilities of PERTH is A$75,000 in respect of proposed dividends. These were approved by the shareholders in March 2004
2. BELVOIR accounts for dividends when received.
3. The summarised statements of comprehensive income of BELVOIR and PERTH for the year ended 31 December 2003 are as follows:

	12 months to 31 December 2003	
	BELVOIR	PERTH
	€'000	A$'000
Profit before tax	35,000	70,000
Taxation	(5,000)	(20,000)
Profit after tax	30,000	50,000

4. Rates of exchange

1 January 2003	€1:A$12.5
Average for year	€1:A$14.0
30 April 2003	€1:A$13.0
31 December 2003	€1:A$15.0

Requirement   Prepare the consolidated statement of financial position of BELVOIR Group at 31 December 2003.

Question 5 (Based on ICAI, P3 Summer 2004, Question 5)

On 1 January 2000, SHINE Limited (SHINE) acquired 75% of the ordinary share capital of WISDOM Limited (WISDOM), an American company, for €36,000,000. At the date of acquisition, the book value of WISDOM's net assets, which was the same as their fair value, totalled $80,000,000. For the purposes of measuring non-controlling interests at the date of acquisition, the proportionate share method equated to the fair value method. WISDOM was to act as a selling agent for SHINE's products in the United States. SHINE accounts for dividends on a received basis, and it is Group policy to reflect any goodwill impairment within operating expenses. The summarised statements of comprehensive income for SHINE and WISDOM for the year ended 31 December 2003 are as follows:

	SHINE	WISDOM
	€'000	$'000
Revenue	460,000	24,800
Cost of sales	(238,000)	(15,400)

Gross profit	222,000	9,400
Operating expenses	(122,000)	(6,510)
Operating profit	100,000	2,890
Exceptional Item:		
- Profit on disposal of non-current assets (note1)	16,000	–
Profit before tax	116,000	2,890
Taxation	(30,000)	(930)
Profit after tax	86,000	1,960

Additional Information

1. Prior to 31 December 2003, SHINE owned a number of properties from which the company traded. On this date, SHINE sold one of the properties to BRICK Limited (BRICK) for €20,000,000. The carrying value of the property at the date of disposal was €4,000,000. On 31 December 2003, SHINE entered into a fixed rental agreement with BRICK whereby the property was leased back to SHINE under a ten-year operating lease at an annual rental of €2,500,000. The fair value of the property sold was €10,000,000, and the annual rentals for similar buildings in the area are approximately €/1,200,000.
2. The book value of WISDOM's inventory on 31 December 2002 and 31 December 2003 was $800,000 and $900,000 respectively. Inventory held at the end of 2002 and 2003 was purchased on *1 December* in each year. WISDOM does not have any non-current assets on its books.
3. The translated post-acquisition reserves of WISDOM at 31 December 2002 and 2003 were €9,900,000 and €11,100,000 respectively.
4. Exchange rates have been as follows:

	US$ = €1
1 January 2000	2.0
1 December 2002	1.6
1 January 2003	1.59
1 December 2003	1.5
31 December 2003	1.52
Average 2003	1.55

Requirement   Prepare the consolidated statement of comprehensive income for the SHINE Group for the year ended 31 December 2003.

Challenging Questions

Question 1 (Based on ICAI, P3 Summer 1997, Question 4)

The year end of STUNT Limited (STUNT) is 31 December.
(a) On 1 December 2003, STUNT purchased raw materials from DENVER Limited, its US supplier, for $84,000 with payment due on 31 January 2004. The prevailing exchange rates were as follows:

1 December 2003	€1 = $1.58
31 December 2003	€1 = $1.56
31 January 2004	€1 = $1.60
2003 average rate	€1 = $1.59

Requirement
(i)   show the value at which the invoice should be recorded in trade payables and inventory on 1 December 2003;
(ii) show the value at which the invoice should be recorded in trade payables and inventory on the 31 December 2003;
(iii) show the settlement value of the invoice;
(iv) show the accounting treatment for any exchange gain or loss arising.

(b) On 1 December 2003, STUNT sold finished goods to a Swiss company for €600,000 when the exchange rate ruling was €1 = Sf10.8. No cash was received from the Swiss company until 31 January 2004 when the exchange rate was €1 = Sf12.8. The exchange rate at 31 December 2003 was €1 = Sf9.6.

Requirement   How would the transaction be recorded at 1 December 2003, 31 December 2003 and 31 January 2004?
(c) Draft a suitable foreign currencies accounting policy note for STUNT Limited.

Question 2 (Based on ICAI, P3 Summer 1996, Question 4)

On 1 January 1986 HOME Limited purchased 80% of the shares of AWAY Limited, a company incorporated and operating in Maru, a country whose currency is Maruvian dollars (M$). The reserves of AWAY Limited amounted to M$100,000 on 1 January 1986. For the purposes of measuring non-controlling interests at the date of acquisition, the proportionate share method equated to the fair value method. Goodwill is only reduced by impairment. Impairment of €5,000 occurred during the year under review.

The statements of financial position of HOME Limited and AWAY Limited at 31 December 1995 are as follows:

	HOME Limited €'000	AWAY Limited M$'000
Assets		
Non-current assets		
Property, plant and equipment	740	815
Investment in AWAY Limited at cost	95	0
	835	815
Current assets		
Inventory	85	60
Receivables	215	80
Cash in hand and at bank	87	20
	387	160
Total assets	1,222	975
Equity and liabilities		
Equity		
Called up share capital	300	500
Reserves	615	355
	915	855
Current liabilities	307	120
Total equity and liabilities	1,222	975

Additional Information

1. The financial statements for the year ended 31 December 1995 included the following:

	HOME €'000	AWAY M$'000
Operating profit	370	297
Dividend received from AWAY Limited	9	–
Taxation charge	(160)	(77)
Dividend paid	–	(60)
Profit retained for the financial year	219	160

No other dividends were paid or proposed by either company.

2. The following exchange rates have been ascertained:

1 January 1986	M$10 = €1
31 December 1994	M$ 6 = €1
31 December 1995	M$ 5 = €1
Average rate for the year ended 31 December 1995	M$5.5 = €1

3. The functional currency of Away Limited is the M$ while the functional currency of Home Limited is the Euro.
4. Consolidated reserves at 31 December 1994 amounted to €441,000.

Requirement Prepare the consolidated statement of financial position of HOME Limited as at 31 December 1995, and a statement of movements on reserves during the year ended on that date.

Question 3 *(Based on ICAI, P3 Autumn 2000, Question 5)*

The statements of comprehensive income of TOWER Limited, KITE Limited and LINE Inc. for the year ended 31 December 2003 are shown below.

	TOWER Limited	KITE Limited	LINE Inc.
	€ million	€ million	Kd million
Revenue	850	680	1,400
Cost of sales	(340)	(260)	(840)
Gross profit	510	420	560
Net operating expenses	(355)	(290)	(240)
Operating profit	155	130	320
Investment income	45	–	–
Profit before tax	200	130	320
Tax	(60)	(40)	(100)
Profit after tax	140	90	220
Dividends paid	(100)	(60)	–
Retained profit for the year	40	30	220

Additional Information:

1. TOWER Limited purchased a 75% interest in KITE Limited on 1 January 1994 for €173 million. There was no difference between the book values and fair values of the net assets of KITE Limited at 1 January 1994, and the statement of financial position of KITE Limited at that date showed:

	€ million
Share capital (€1 ordinary shares)	100
Retained earnings	104
	204

For the purposes of measuring non-controlling interests at the date of acquisition, the proportionate share method equated to the fair value method. The directors of TOWER Limited estimate that the goodwill arising during the year ended 31 December 2003 on the acquisition of KITE Limited was impaired by €10 million.

2. LINE Inc. is situated in a foreign country and was incorporated on 1 January 2003. The company is wholly owned by TOWER Limited and acts as a foreign selling agent for TOWER Limited. There were no inter-group sales involving LINE Inc. during 2003, and the cost of sales shown in LINE Inc.'s statement of comprehensive income above is arrived at as follows:

	Kd million
Purchases (purchased evenly during the year)	1092
Closing inventory (purchased 1 December 2003)	(252)
	840

3. The currency of the foreign country is the Kid (Kd), and the exchange rates ruling during 2003 between the Pound and the Kid were as follows:

1 January 2003	Kd3:€1	31 December 2003	Kd6:€1
1 December 2003	Kd4.5:€1	Average 2003	Kd4:€1

4. KITE Limited purchases raw materials from TOWER Limited. During the year ended 31 December 2003, purchases of these raw materials by KITE Limited from TOWER Limited amounted to €100 million. At 31 December 2003 the inventory of KITE Limited included raw materials purchased from TOWER Limited at a cost of €30 million (€15 million at 31 December 2002). TOWER Limited supplies raw materials to KITE Limited at cost plus 25%.
5. It is group policy to set all of any provision for inventory profit on intra-group sales against group reserves.

Requirement   Prepare the consolidated statement of comprehensive income of TOWER Limited. for the year ended 31 December 2003.

Question 4 Based on ICAI, P3 Summer 1999, Question 3)

SUGAR plc purchased 22.5 million shares in CUBE inc. on 1 January 1995, when the retained profits of CUBE inc. were $10 million. The fair value of net assets at the date of acquisition was the same as their net book value. For the purposes of measuring non-controlling interests at the date of acquisition, the proportionate share method equated to the fair value method.

SUGAR plc and its American subsidiary, CUBE inc., sell both bottled mineral water and confectionery products in the UK and US markets respectively. There are no inter-company or inter-segment sales, and neither company has any associate undertakings. CUBE inc. carries out its day-to-day operations in US dollars and acts independently of SUGAR plc. The parent company acquired its interest in CUBE inc. as a long-term investment and, while SUGAR plc is not interested in the value of individual assets and liabilities of CUBE inc., it does control the long-term strategy of the American company.

The statements of comprehensive income for the year ended 31 December 2003 of SUGAR plc and CUBE inc., and their statements of financial position as at that date are shown below:

618 INTERNATIONAL FINANCIAL ACCOUNTING AND REPORTING

Statement of Comprehensive Income for the Year Ended 31 December 2003

	SUGAR plc		CUBE inc.	
	€'000	€'000	$'000	$'000
Revenue		160,000		125,000
Cost of sales:				
Opening inventory	35,000		30,000	
Purchases	80,000		71,000	
Closing inventory	(30,000)	(85,000)	(36,000)	(65,000)
Gross profit		75,000		60,000
Distribution costs		(25,000)		(20,000)
Administrative expenses		(20,000)		(12,000)
Operating profit		30,000		28,000
Dividend receivable		6,000		-
Interest payable		(4,000)		(3,000)
Profit before tax		32,000		25,000
Taxation		(10,000)		(8,000)
Profit after tax		22,000		17,000
Proposed dividends		(10,000)		(12,000)
Retained profit for year		12,000		5,000

Statement of Financial Position as at 31 December 2003

	SUGAR plc		CUBE inc.	
	€'000	€'000	$'000	$'000
ASSETS				
Non-current Assets:				
Property, plant and equipment	60,000		50,000	
Investments	15,000	75,000	-	50,000
Current Assets				
Inventory	25,000		40,000	
Trade receivables	28,000		35,000	
Dividends receivable	6,000		–	
Cash at bank	1,000	60,000	–	75,000
		135,000		125,000

EQUITY AND LIABILITIES

Capital and Reserves

Called up share capital (€1/$1 shares)		35,000	30,000
Retained earnings		40,000	25,000
		75,000	55,0000
Non-current Liabilities		20,000	25,000
Current Liabilities			
Trade payables	15,000		20,000
Proposed dividends	10,000		12,000
Bank loan	15,000	40,000	13,000	45,000
		135,000		125,000

Additional Information

1. Exchange rates at the relevant dates are as follows:

Date	$ to the €	Date	$ to the €
1 January 1995	2	31 December 2002	1.6
Date on which CUBE acquired:		31 December 2003	1.5
– non-current assets	1.9	Average rate 2003	1.52
– opening inventory	1.8		
– closing inventory	1.7		

2. Amounts shown as non-current liabilities by SUGAR plc and CUBE inc. represent the long-term element of the bank loan shown in current liabilities. These loans were raised by each of the companies independently and are repayable by each of the companies in their local currency.

Requirement   Prepare the consolidated statement of comprehensive income of SUGAR plc group for the year ended 31 December 2003 and the consolidated statement of financial position as at that date.

Question 5 *Based on ICAI, P3 Summer 2001, Question 4)*

The summarised statements of comprehensive income for APPLE Limited (APPLE), ORANGE Limited (ORANGE) and PEAR Inc. (PEAR) for the year ended 31 December 2003 are as follows:

	APPLE	ORANGE	PEAR
	€'000	€'000	$'000
Revenue	230,000	25,000	12,400
Cost of sales	(119,000)	(12,750)	(7,700)
Gross profit	111,000	12,250	4,700
Operating expenses	(61,000)	(9,250)	(3,255)
Profit before tax	50,000	3,000	1,445
Taxation	(15,000)	(900)	(465)
Profit after tax	35,000	2,100	980

Additional Information

1. APPLE acquired 75% of the ordinary share capital of ORANGE on 1 January 1998 for €25 million when the book value of the net assets of ORANGE was €20 million. The fair value of the net assets was the same as their book value. For the purposes of measuring non-controlling interests at the date of acquisition, the proportionate share method equated to the fair value method. The goodwill arising on the acquisition of ORANGE has not been impaired.
2. Following the acquisition of shares in ORANGE, the directors of APPLE wished to expand abroad. On 1 January 2000, APPLE acquired 75% of the ordinary share capital of PEAR, an American company, for €9 million. At the date of acquisition, the book value of PEAR's net assets, which was the same as their fair value, totalled $40 million. PEAR was to act as a selling agent for APPLE's products in the United States.
3. The book value of PEAR's inventory on 31 December 2002 and 31 December 2003 was $400,000 and $450,000 respectively. Inventory held at the end of 2002 and 2003 was purchased on 1 December in each year. PEAR does not have any non-current assets on its books.
4. The translated post-acquisition reserves of PEAR at 31 December 2002 and 2003 were €4,950,000 and €5,550,000 respectively.
5. Exchange rates have been as follows:

	US$ = €1
1 January 2000	2.0
1 December 2002	1.6

1 January 2003	1.59
1 December 2003	1.5
31 December 2003	1.52
Average 2003	1.55

6. APPLE exercises a dominant influence over the activities of both ORANGE and PEAR, and accounts for dividends on a received basis.

Requirement   Prepare the consolidated statement of comprehensive income for the APPLE Group for the year ended 31 December 2003.

Question 6 Based on ICAI, P3 Summer 2005, Questions 1 & 2)

You are an accountant with GOLD Group plc (GOLD), an Irish company involved in mining precious metals. You have responsibility for the consolidation of GOLD's financial statements, and you have just received draft financial statements for the year ended 31 December 2005 in respect of GOLD, SILVER Limited (SILVER) and COPPER Incorporated (COPPER).

Draft Statement of Comprehensive Income for the Year Ended 31 December 2005

	GOLD €'000	SILVER €'000	COPPER $'000
Revenue	600,000	105,000	33,000
Cost of sales	(360,000)	(63,000)	(20,000)
Gross profit	240,000	42,000	13,000
Net operating expenses	(120,000)	(21,000)	(6,000)
Operating profit	120,000	21,000	7,000
Income tax expense	(54,000)	(7,000)	(3,000)
Profit on ordinary activities after tax	66,000	14,000	4,000
Dividends proposed	(26,000)	–	–
Retained profits for the year	40,000	14,000	4,000
Retained profits at start of year	36,000	11,000	3,000
Retained profits at end of year	76,000	25,000	7,000

Draft Statement of Financial Position as at 31 December 2005

	GOLD €'000	SILVER €'000	COPPER $'000
ASSETS			
Non-current Assets			
Plant and machinery	130,000	30,000	10,000
Investment in SILVER	30,000	–	–
Investment in COPPER	12,000	–	–
	172,000	30,000	10,000
Current Assets			
Inventory	12,000	1,500	–
Receivables	22,500	5,000	3,000
Bank and cash	4,500	1,000	500
	39,000	7,500	3,500
Total Assets	211,000	37,500	13,500
EQUITY AND LIABILITIES			
Share Capital and Reserves			
€1 – €1 – $1 ordinary shares	12,000	5,000	1,000
Retained earnings	76,000	25,000	7,000
	88,000	30,000	8,000
Current Liabilities			
Trade payables	24,000	1,500	1,000
Taxation	73,000	6,000	4,500
Proposed dividends	26,000	–	–
	123,000	7,500	5,500
Total Equity and Liabilities	211,000	37,500	13,500

Additional Information:

1. On 1 January 2005, GOLD acquired 4,000,000 €1 ordinary shares in SILVER. On this date the book value of the net assets of SILVER approximated to their fair value. For the purposes of measuring non-controlling interests at the date of acquisition, the proportionate share method equated to the fair value method.

2. On 1 January 2003, GOLD purchased 300,000 $1 ordinary shares in COP-PER, an American company, when there was a credit balance of $2,000,000 on the revenue reserves of COPPER. On this date the book value of the net assets of COPPER approximated to their fair value. GOLD has a participating interest in COPPER, exercising significant influence over the company's operating and financial policies.

3. The directors of GOLD believe that the goodwill arising on the acquisition of SILVER and COPPER was impaired for the first time during the year ended 31 December 2005 by €1,720,000 and €312,500 respectively. Each company charges depreciation to cost of sales. COPPER purchased all items of plant and machinery on or before 1 January 2003, and none of the companies disposed of plant and machinery during the year ended 31 December 2005.

4. The rates of exchange were as follows:

1 January 2003 –	$2:€1	31 December 2005 –	$1.50:€1
1 January 2005 –	$1.80:€1	Average rate 2005	$1.60:€1

5. On 1 January 2005, GOLD entered into a finance lease in respect of excavation machinery with a cash price of €597,000. The agreement required 20 quarterly payments of €40,000 starting from 1 January 2005. None of the accounting entries in respect of this have been recorded in the company's books and records.

6. On 1 January 2005, GOLD was granted a licence to commence mining for precious metals in the mountains of Mourne. Under the terms of the mining agreement, GOLD must restore the mountains to their original state at the end of licence period in five years' time. The directors of GOLD estimate that the total cost of restoration will be €20,000,000 of which 25% will be incurred during mining and the remainder when mining ceases. GOLD's cost of capital is 10% and the risk-free rate is 4%. Mining commenced on 1 January 2005.

7. On 23 January 2006, GOLD made a one for three rights issue to existing ordinary shareholders. This involved the issue of 4,000,000 €1 ordinary shares for a consideration of €6,000,000. This is not reflected in the draft statement of comprehensive income for the year ended 31 December 2005 and draft statement of financial position as at that date shown above.

Present value factors:

Years	4%	10%
1	0.962	0.909
2	0.925	0.826
3	0.889	0.751
4	0.855	0.683
5	0.822	0.621

Requirement
(a) Prepare the consolidated statement of comprehensive income of the GOLD Group for the year ended 31 December 2005 and the consolidated statement of financial position as at that date.
(b) Prepare a memorandum addressed to the Board of GOLD explaining the rationale for the way in which the following issues were dealt with in the financial statements of GOLD for the year ended 31 December 2005:

  (i)   The method of foreign currency translation adopted for COPPER (Note 2);
  (ii) The granting of the mining licence and the associated costs (Note 6);
  (iii) The rights issue on 23 January 2006 (Note 7).

CHAPTER 32

DISPOSAL OF SUBSIDIARIES

INTRODUCTION

This chapter considers the calculation of the profit/loss on the disposal of a subsidiary under the following circumstances:

- Sale of **entire** holding in a subsidiary **at the reporting date**;
- Sale of **entire** holding in a subsidiary **during** the year;
- Sale of **part** of holding during the year;
- Sale of part of holding during the year where the remaining holding is dealt with as an associate.

After having studied this chapter, you should understand how to account for the disposal of a subsidiary under the circumstances outlined above. However, before studying this topic, it is vital that you revise how goodwill arises on acquisition and the circumstances when it should be written off (see Chapter 26).

Note All of the examples and questions in this chapter assume that for the purposes of measuring non-controlling interests at the date of acquisition, the proportionate share method equated to the fair value method.

CALCULATION OF PROFIT/LOSS ON DISPOSAL IN THE PARENT COMPANY'S ACCOUNTS

The cash received on disposal of the investment, and the profit/loss on that disposal, will be recorded in the parent company's own accounts. The profit/loss for a complete disposal is simply the difference between the sale proceeds and the carrying value of the investment. On a partial disposal, the profit/loss will be related to the shares sold by comparing the sale proceeds with the relevant proportion of the carrying value of the investment.

CALCULATION OF PROFIT/LOSS ON DISPOSAL IN THE CONSOLIDATED ACCOUNTS

Any profit/loss on disposal should be calculated as follows:

(Net Assets at date of disposal x Group share after disposal) + Sale Proceeds

less

(Net assets at date of disposal x Group share before disposal)

Note The net assets should include any goodwill which has not been written off through the statement of comprehensive Income, otherwise the profit/loss on disposal will be misstated.

Example

The following are the draft financial statements of P Limited and S Limited for the year ended 31 December 2002.

Statement of Comprehensive Income

	P Limited €	S Limited €
Profit before tax	60,000	40,000
Income tax expense	(24,000)	(16,000)
Profit after tax	36,000	24,000
Retained profit b/f	104,000	16,000
	140,000	40,000

Statement of Financial Position

Assets	P €	S €
Investment in S	75,000	–
Sundry net assets	265,000	100,000
	340,000	100,000
Equity		
Ordinary €1 shares	200,000	60,000
Reserves	140,000	40,000
	340,000	100,000

P Limited acquired 75% of the ordinary shares of S Limited on 1 January 2001 when the reserves of S Limited were € 10,000. The investment is sold for € 115,000 on 31 December 2002. Goodwill, which is accounted for in accordance with IFRS 3, suffered impairment of € 4,500 during the year ended 31 December 2001.

Requirement   Calculate the profit on disposal of the shares to be included in P Limited's own and consolidated financial statements.

Solution

		€
Profit on disposal of shares		
1.	In P Limited's own accounts:	
	Sale proceeds	115,000
	Cost of sales	(75,000)
		40,000
2.	In consolidated accounts:	
	Goodwill	
	Original value	
	€ 75,000 – 75% (€ 60,000 + € 10,000)	22,500
	Written off y/e 31/12/01 (impairment)	4,500
	Remaining	18,000
	Profit on disposal	
	Net assets of S Limited at 31/12/2002	100,000
	(€ 100,000 x 0%) + € 115,000	115,000
	Less	
	€ 100,000 x 75%	(75,000)
		40,000
	Less attributable goodwill	(18,000)
		22,000

Note S Limited is a subsidiary until 31/12/2002; therefore its results for the full year must be consolidated.

P Limited
Consolidated Statement of Comprehensive Income for the Year Ended 31
December 2002

	€
Profit on disposal of subsidiary	22,000
Operating profit	100,000
Profit before tax	122,000
Income tax expense	(40,000)
Profit after tax	82,000
Non-controlling interest (25% x €24,000)	(6,000)
Retained profit	76,000

Reserves

Retained profit for the year	76,000
Retained profit brought forward (W1)	104,000
	180,000

P Limited
Statement of Financial Position as at 31 December 2002

Assets		€
Sundry net assets	(W2)	380,000
Equity		
Ordinary € 1 shares		200,000
Reserves	(W3)	180,000
		380,000

W1

P Limited	104,000
S Limited 75% (€16,000 – €10,000)	4,500
Goodwill written off (because of impairment)	(4,500)
	104,000

W2

P Limited	265,000
Proceeds from sale of investment	115,000
	380,000

W3

P Limited	140,000
Profit on sale (per P's own accounts)	40,000
	180,000

SALE OF SHARES IN SUBSIDIARY BUT SUBSIDIARY STATUS RETAINED

When a group reduces its interest in a subsidiary undertaking, it should record any profit/ loss arising as the difference between the carrying amount of the net assets of the subsidiary attributable to the group's interest before the reduction, and the carrying amount attributable to the group's interest after the reduction together with the proceeds received.

Example

Using the example of P Limited and S Limited above except that in this instance P Limited sells a 20% holding for €34,000 on 30 September 2002. Goodwill is only written down on impairment.

Solution

		€
Profit on disposal of shares		
(i)	In the individual accounts of P Limited	
	Sale proceeds	34,000
	Less cost of sales	
	€ 75,000 x 20/75	(20,000)
		14,000
(ii)	In the consolidated accounts	
	Net assets of S at 30.9.2002	
	Capital and reserves 1/1/2002 (€60,000 + €16,000)	76,000
	Retained profit y/e 31/12/2002 X 9/12	18,000
	Net assets at 30/9/2002	94,000
	Profit on disposal	
	(€ 94,000 x 55%) + € 34,000	85,700
	Less	
	€94,000 x 75%	(70,500)
	Less	
	Attributable goodwill €18,000 x 20/75	(4,800)
		10,400

P Limited
Consolidated Statement of Comprehensive Income for the Year Ended
31 December 2002

	€
Profit on disposal of shares in subsidiary	10,400
Operating profit	100,000
Profit before tax	110,400
Income tax expense	(40,000)
Profit after tax	70,400
Non-controlling interest	
€24,000 x 25% x 9/12	(7,200)
€24,000 x 45% x 3/12	
Profit retained	63,200

Reserves
Retained profit for year	63,200
Retained profit brought forward as before	104,000
	167,200

Note S Limited is a subsidiary for the full year; therefore the full year's results are included. However, the non-controlling interest changed from 25% to 45% on 30/9/02.

Note – Goodwill:	€	€
Original value		22,500
W/o y/e 31/12/01(impairment)	4,500	
W/o on disposal	4,800	(9,300)
		13,200

P Limited
Statement of Financial Position as at 31 December 2002

Assets	
Goodwill	13,200
Sundry net assets	
(€265,000 + €34,000 + €100,000)	399,000
	412,200
Equity	
Ordinary shares	200,000
Reserves	167,200
	367,200
Non-controlling interest	
(€100,000 x 45%)	45,000
	412,200

DISPOSAL OF SHARES IN SUBSIDIARY UNDERTAKING – SUBSIDIARY TO ASSOCIATE STATUS

The calculation of the profit or loss on disposal should be made using the same formula as in the previous two examples. The results of the subsidiary should be included in the consolidated accounts until the effective date of disposal of the shares, and as an associate undertaking for the remainder of the year.

Example

Again using the example of P Limited and S Limited above. P Limited sells a 40% holding in S Limited for €68,000 on 30 September 2002. Goodwill is only reduced on impairment.

Solution

		€
Profit on disposal of shares		
(i)	In the individual accounts of P Limited:	
	Sale proceeds	68,000
	Less cost of sales	
	€75,000 x 40/75	(40,000)
	Profit	28,000
(ii)	In the consolidated accounts:	
	Net assets at 30/9/2002	
	at 1/1/02	76,000
	Retained profits to 30/9/02 (€24,000 x 9/12)	18,000
		94,000
	Profit calculation	
	(€94,000 x 35%) + €68,000	100,900
	Less	
	€94,000 x 75%	(70,500)
		30,400
	Less attributable goodwill	
	€18,000 x 40/75	(9,600)
	Profit	20,800

P Limited
Consolidated Statement of Comprehensive Income for the Year Ended
31 December 2002

	€
Profit on disposal of shares in subsidiary	20,800
Operating profit (€60,000 + (40,000 x 9/12))	90,000
	110,800
Share of profit of associate company	
(€24,000 x 3/12) x 35%	2,100
Profit before tax	112,900

Income tax expense (€24,000 + (€16,000 x 9/12))	(36,000)
Profit after tax	76,900
Non-controlling interest (€24,000 x 9/12 x 25%)	(4,500)
Retained profit	72,400
Reserves	
Retained profit for the year	72,400
Retained profit brought forward (as before)	104,000
	176,400

P Limited
Statement of Financial Position as at 31 December 2002

Assets		€
Investment in Associate company	(W1)	43,400
Sundry net assets	(W2)	333,000
		376,400
Ordinary €1 shares		200,000
Reserves		176,400
		376,400

W1	
Cost	35,000
Share of post-acquisition reserves	
(€40,000 – €10,000) x 35%	10,500
	45,500
Premium w/o (€4,500 x 35/75)	(2,100)
	43,400

W2	
Per P Limited's accounts	265,000
Proceeds from sale of shares	68,000
	333,000
Proof of reserves of P Limited	
Per P Limited's accounts	140,000
Profit on disposal of shares	28,000
Share of post-acquisition profits of associate company	10,500
Premium on acquisition written off	(2,100)
	176,400

CONCLUSION

After having studied this chapter, you should understand how to account for the disposal of a subsidiary. It is important to remember that, when an undertaking ceases to be a subsidiary undertaking the consolidated financial statements for the period should include the results of the subsidiary up to the date that it ceases to be a subsidiary. Furthermore, it is imperative that you are aware that the calculation of the profit/loss on disposal in the consolidated financial statements is different to that in the holding company's own accounts.

QUESTIONS

Review Questions

(See APPENDIX ONE for Suggested Solutions to Review Questions.)

Question 1

Smith Limited bought 80% of the share capital of Jones Limited for €324, 000 on 1 October 20X5. At that date Jones Limited's retained earnings stood at €180,000. The statement of financial position at 30 September 20X8 and the summarised statements of comprehensive income to that date are given below.

	Smith Limited	Jones Limited
	€'000	€'000
Assets		
Tangible non-current assets	360	270
Investment in Jones Limited	324	–
Net current assets	270	270
	954	540
Equity		
€1 ordinary shares	540	180
Statement of comprehensive income	414	360
	954	540
Profit before tax	153	126
Income tax expense	(45)	(36)
Retained profit	108	90
Retained profit b/f	306	270
Retained profit c/f	414	360

No entries have been made in the accounts for any of the following transactions. Assume that profits accrue evenly throughout the year and that any goodwill is accounted for in accordance with IFRS 3.

(Ignore taxation.)

Requirement   Prepare the consolidated statement of comprehensive income for the year ended 30 September 20X8, and the statement of financial position as at that date, under each of the following circumstances:

(a) Smith Limited sells its entire holding in Jones Limited for €650,000 on 30 September 20X8; and
(b) Smith Limited sells its entire holding in Jones Limited for €650,000 on 30 June 20X8.

(Assume that no goodwill is written off due to impairment.)

Challenging Questions

Using the information provided above for Review Question 1, Smith Limited.

Requirement   Prepare the consolidated statement of comprehensive income for the year ended 30 September 20X8, and the statement of financial position as at that date, under each of the following circumstances:

(a) Smith Limited sells one quarter of its holding in Jones Limited for €160,000 on 30 June 20X8; and
(b) Smith Limited sells one half of its holding in Jones Limited for €340,000 on 30 June 20X8, and the remaining holding is to be dealt with as an associate.

(Assume that no goodwill is written off due to impairment.)

CHAPTER 33

STATEMENT OF CASH FLOWS – CONSOLIDATED

INTRODUCTION

This chapter focuses upon the preparation of a consolidated statement of cash flows. The preparation of a statement of cash flows for a single entity, together with the more general issues relating to the preparation of statements of cash flow, is dealt with in Section Three, Chapter 19. After having studied this chapter you should be able to prepare a consolidated statement of cash flows in accordance with IAS 7 *Statement of Cash Flows*.

STATEMENT OF CASH FLOWS – CONSOLIDATED

A consolidated statement of cash flows should exclude internal flows of cash within the group. The cash flows of any entity which is equity accounted should only be included in the consolidated statement of cash flows to the extent of the actual cash flows between the group and entity concerned, for example, dividends received in cash and loans made or repaid. Dividends paid to the non-controlling interest should be included under the heading of 'Cash flows from financing activities'.

If subsidiaries join or leave the group during the year, then the statement of cash flows should include cash flows for the same period as that for which the group's statement of comprehensive income includes the results of the subsidiary. In respect of both acquisitions and disposals, the following details should be disclosed:

- Total purchase/disposal consideration;
- Portion of purchase/disposal consideration discharged by means of cash and cash equivalents;
- Amount of cash and cash equivalents in subsidiary disposed of; and
- Amount of assets and liabilities, other than cash and cash equivalents in the subsidiary acquired, summarised by major headings.

The amount shown in the consolidated statement of cash flows for subsidiaries purchased/disposed of is the amount paid/received net of cash and cash equivalents acquired/disposed of.

SPECIAL ISSUES WHEN PREPARING A CONSOLIDATED STATEMENT OF CASH FLOWS

In general, the principles involved in the preparation of a consolidated statement of cash flows are the same as those for an individual company. However, the following issues are peculiar to groups:

- Dealing with the non-controlling interests in subsidiaries;
- Dealing with associates and joint ventures;
- Acquisition of a subsidiary during an accounting period;
- Disposal of a subsidiary during an accounting period; and
- Dealing with foreign operations.

Dealing with Non-controlling Interests

A subsidiary gets full consolidation and therefore all its assets and liabilities are included in the consolidated statement of financial position whether or not there is a non-controlling interest. This means that cash flows for subsidiaries relating to such items as operating activities, taxation, acquisition or disposal of non-current assets are combined with those of the parent undertaking. However, certain items need special attention:

- Issue of shares for cash to non-controlling interests;
- Redemption of shares owned by non-controlling interests; and
- Dividends paid to non-controlling interests.

Cash flows relating to the first and second items would appear in the consolidated statement of cash flows under 'financing activities'. In the absence of the acquisition or disposal of a subsidiary during the period (part of which is owned by the non-controlling interests), dividends paid to non-controlling interests can be ascertained from the T account as follows:

Non-controlling Interests

	€		€
Cash (dividends paid) balance fig	X	Bal b/d (per opening CSFP)	X
Bal c/d (closing CSFP)	X	Share of PAT (per CSCI)	X
	---		---
	X		X

Dividends paid to non-controlling interests would be included under cash flows from operating activities or cash flows from financing activities in the statement of cash flows.

Dealing with Associates and Joint Ventures

Investments in Associates

If an associate is accounted for, in the consolidated accounts, using the equity method of accounting, this means that the consolidated statement of comprehensive income includes the group's share of the profit before tax of the associate plus the group share of its tax charge. Neither of these entries involves cash flow, but the group cash flow is affected by the dividends received from associates. When an investment in an associate is accounted for by using the equity method (the normal treatment), the statement of cash flows of the investor must only include cash flows between itself and the associate, e.g. dividends received from the associate, advances to or from the associate. Dividends received from associates can be calculated as follows:

Investment in Associates

	€		€
Bal B/d (from opening CSFP)	X	Dividends received from A	X
Share of associate's is profit after interest and tax	X	Balance c/d (from closing CSFP)	X
	X		X

Dividends received from associated undertakings should be included under operating cash flows.

Investments in Joint Ventures

When an interest in a jointly controlled entity (IAS 31 *Interests in Joint Ventures*) is accounted for using proportional consolidation, the reporting entity's proportionate share of the jointly controlled entity's cash flows should be included in the consolidated financial statements.

When the equity method is used, only actual cash flows from sales and purchases between the group and associate/ joint venture, and investments in and dividends from the entity should be included (NOT the share of profit included in the statement of comprehensive income). Dividends should be included in operating cash flows, where they are shown within operating profit in the statement of comprehensive income.

Acquisition of a Subsidiary during an Accounting Period

(a) The net cash flow from either the acquisition or disposal must be shown separately under investing activities.
(b) The notes to the statement of cash flows must include:
  • the total purchase or disposal consideration;
  • the portion of the consideration discharged by either cash or cash equivalents; and
  • the amount of cash and cash equivalents in the subsidiary acquired or sold.

This should be dealt with in the consolidated statement of cash flows under 'investing activities'. Any cash paid as part of the consideration would be included as a cash out flow while any balances of cash and overdrafts transferred as part of the acquisition should be offset.

Example

During the period under review P Limited acquired 80% of the ordinary shares of S Limited.

Details of the acquisition:

	€'000
Net assets acquired	
Non-current assets	500
Inventory	180
Trade receivables	140
Cash	20
Trade payables	(120)
	720
Non-controlling interest @ 20%	(144)
Goodwill	24
	600
Discharged by:	
Issue of shares	200
Cash paid	400
	600

Extract from statement of cash flows:
Investing activities
Purchase of subsidiary (€400 – €20)   (380)

Note: While P Limited paid €400,000 in cash for S Limited, the actual net cash flow is €380,000 since S Limited held cash of €20,000 at the acquisition date.

It should be noted that the non-current assets €500,000, inventory €180,000, receivables €140,000 and payables €120,000 should be excluded from changes in these items in the statement of cash flows. A note to the statement of cash flows should show a summary of the effects of the acquisition.

Disposal of a Subsidiary during an Accounting Period

When a subsidiary is disposed of during an accounting period any cash received from the sale of the investment should be shown separately under 'investing activities', with any balance of cash and overdrafts transferred as part of the sale being offset.

Example

During the accounting period Plug Plc Limited sold 80% of its holding in AMP Limited for €140,000 cash. The statement of financial position of AMP Limited at the date of disposal was:

	€'000
Tangible non-current assets	115
Inventory	55
Receivables	36
Cash	14
Payables	(60)
	160
Ordinary shares €1	50
Reserves	110
	160

Extract from consolidated statement of cash flows:

Investing Activities	€'000
Sale of subsidiary (140-14)	126

A note should be given showing a summary of the effects of the disposal as follows:

Disposal of subsidiary undertaking

Net assets disposed of	€'000
Tangible non-current assets	115
Inventory	55
Receivables	36
Cash	14
Payables	(60)
	160
Non-controlling interest @ 20%	(32)
Profit of disposal	12
	140
Satisfied by cash	140

Dealing with Foreign Operations

The Individual Company

Cash flows arising from transactions in a foreign currency should be recorded in the entity's functional currency at the exchange rate at the date of the cash flow.

Foreign Subsidiaries

The cash flows of a foreign subsidiary must be translated at the exchange rates between the functional currency and the foreign currency at the dates of the cash flows – a weighted average rate for the period can be used.

If the 'presentation' currency method is used to consolidate results, then the subsidiary's cash flows should be translated at an average rate (statement of comprehensive income). But if the average rate is used, then merely using the statement of financial position figures would not be appropriate, as the statement of cash flows would not comply with IAS 7 (some items being translated at the closing rate). Therefore the steps are:

- Prepare the statement of cash flows for each subsidiary:
- Translate each into 'Euro' using the average rate;
- Consolidate each into the consolidated statement of cash flows; and
- Foreign exchange differences on translation must be analysed into their constituent parts: non-current assets, receivables, cash, payables and non-controlling interests.

DISCLOSURE

Notes to the Cash Flow Statement (Direct and Indirect Method)

Where a group buys or sells a subsidiary, a note to the statement of cash flows should show a summary of the effects of acquisitions and disposals indicating how much of the consideration comprised cash.

In the case of a subsidiary joining or leaving a group during a year, the cash flows of the subsidiary will be included in the consolidated statement of cash flows for the same period as the group's statement of comprehensive income includes the subsidiary's results.

Where the sale or purchase of a subsidiary has a material effect on the amounts reported under the standard headings in the statement of cash flows, a note should be appended showing these effects as far as practicable.

Example

Acquisition of subsidiary
During the period the group acquired subsidiary X. The fair value of assets acquired and liabilities assumed were as follows:

	€m
Cash	40
Inventory	100
Accounts receivable	100
Property, plant and equipment	650

Trade payables	(100)
Long-term debts	(200)
Total purchase price	590
Less: Cash of X	(40)
Cash flow on acquisition net of cash acquired	550

(For other notes to the statement of cash flows, see Section Three, Chapter 19.)

QUESTIONS

Review Questions

(See APPENDIX ONE for Suggested Solutions to Review Questions.)

Question 1

Universal plc
Consolidated Statement of Financial Position as at 30 October 2004

	2004 €'000	2003 €'000
Assets		
Non-current assets		
Property, plant & equipment	2,190	1,480
Goodwill	11	–
Investment in associate	830	740
	3,031	2,220
Current assets		
Inventory	910	868
Trade receivables	650	592
Cash	15	10
	1,575	1,470
Total assets	4,606	3,690
Equity and Liabilities	1,400	1,200
Ordinary share capital	200	100
Share premium	982	766
Retained earnings	2,582	2,066
Non-controlling interest	380	230
	2,962	2,296

Non-current liabilities

10% debentures	360	280

Current liabilities

Trade payables	514	498
Bank overdraft	60	95
Corporate tax	450	328
Proposed dividends	240	180
Accruals	20	13
	1,284	1,114
Total equity and liabilities	4,606	3,690

Universal plc

Consolidated Statement of Comprehensive Income for the Year Ended 31 October 2004

	€'000	€'000
Group Operating Profit		986
Interest payable		(160)
		826
Share of profit of associate		130
		956
Taxation		(415)
Group profit after tax		541
Non-controlling interest		126
		415
Dividends		(199)
Retained profit for the year		216

Notes to the Financial Statements:

1. Group Profit before tax

	€'000
The following have been included:	
Depreciation of property, plant and equipment	167
Profit on disposal of property, plant and equipment	10

2. Property, plant and equipment

	€'000
Net Book value 1 November 2003	1,480
Additions	987
Net Book value of disposals	(110)
Depreciation charge for year	(167)
Net book value 31 October 2004	2,190

3. Called up share capital   €'000
   €1 shares fully paid
   1 November 2003   1200
   Issued for cash   200
   31 October 2004   1400

4. Reserves	Share Premium	Retained Earnings
	€'000	€'000
November 2003	100	766
Received on share issue	100	–
Profit for year	–	415
Dividends	–	(199)
31 October 2004	200	982

The dividends debited to retained earnings were approved by the shareholders prior to the reporting date.

5. Acquisition of Subsidiary: Star Limited
   Details of the acquisition are :
   Net Assets Acquired   €'000
   Property, plant and equipment   160
   Inventory   40
   Cash   20
   Payables   (50)
                                                                        170

   Goodwill   11
   Non-controlling Interest   (51)
                                                                        130

   Discharged by
   Cash   130

Requirement   Prepare the consolidated statement of cash flows of Universal plc for the year ended 31 October 2004 in accordance with IAS 7 *Statement of Cash Flows*.

Question 2 *Based on ICAI, P3 Summer 1999, Question 5)*

SWEET plc was founded in the 1970s. During the 1980s SWEET plc relied upon external acquisition to expand. For the last 7-8 years the group has focused upon internal development. However, on 1 January 2003, SWEET plc acquired 75% of the ordinary share capital of GENTLE Limited. The purchase was financed by €365 million in cash and 50 million €1 ordinary shares with a market value of €75 million. The statement of financial position of GENTLE Limited at 1 January 2003 showed:

	€m
Property, plant and equipment	420
Inventory	300
Receivables	240
Bank deposit account	19
Bank overdraft	(275)
Trade payables	(160)
Taxation	(64)
	480

The directors of SWEET estimate that the goodwill arising on the acquisition of GENTLE had been impaired by €16 million at 31 December 2003. This has been charged to 'other operating expenses' in the consolidated statement of comprehensive income for the year ended 31 December 2003.

SWEET plc
Consolidated Statement of Comprehensive Income for the Year Ended 31 December 2003

	Note	€m
Revenue		3,400
Cost of sales		(1,560)
Gross profit		1,840
Other operating expenses		(790)
Operating profit	1	1,050
Loss on disposal of property, plant and equipment	2	(26)
Interest payable	3	(190)
Profit on ordinary activities before tax		834
Tax on profit on ordinary activities	4	(290)
Profit on ordinary activities after tax		544
Non-controlling interests		(80)
Group profit		464

SWEET plc
Consolidated Statement of Financial Position as at 31 December 2003

	2003		2002	
	€m	€m	€m	€m
ASSETS				
Non-current Assets				
Property, plant and equipment (note 5)		3,280		2,960
Intangible assets		64		–
		3,344		2,960
Current Assets				
Inventory	1,220		1,280	
Receivables	1,740	2,960	1,440	2,720
		6,304		5,680
EQUITY AND LIABILITIES				
Capital and Reserves				
€1 ordinary shares		1,010		960
Reserves		1,794		1,520
		2,804		2,480
Non-controlling interests (equity)		600		496
		3,404		2,976
Non-current Liabilities				
Obligations under finance leases		1,040		960
Deferred taxation		256		184
Current Liabilities				
Bank overdraft	24		164	
Trade payables	750		680	
Taxation	190		164	
Obligations under finance leases	400		360	
Proposed dividends	240	1,604	192	1,560
		6,304		5,680

Additional Information:

1. Depreciation charged in arriving at operating profit in the consolidated statement of comprehensive income of SWEET plc for the year ended 31 December 2003 amounted to €750 million.
2. The loss on disposal of property, plant and equipment relates to the scrapping of plant and equipment during the year with a net book value of €26 million. No proceeds were received.

3. Interest payable | €m
   - on loans and overdrafts | 40
   - on finance lease rental payments | 150
   | 190

4. Taxation | €m
   - corporation tax | 245
   - deferred taxation | 45
   | 290

5. Additions to property, plant and equipment during the year include plant and equipment purchased under finance lease contracts which would have cost €480 million if purchased outright. Also, property was revalued upwards by €25 million and SWEET plc capitalised interest paid during the year of €10 million relating to the construction of a new factory.
6. During the year ended 31 December 2003, dividends of €240 million were debited to equity.

Requirement   Prepare the consolidated statement of cash flows of SWEET plc for the year ended 31 December 2003 in accordance with IAS 7 Statement of Cash Flows.

(You are not required to provide notes to the consolidated statement of cash flows.)

Challenging Questions

Question 1 (Based on ICAI, P3 Summer 1997, Question 2)

The consolidated statement of comprehensive income of VOYAGE plc for the year ended 31 December 1996 and the statement of financial position as at that date are shown below.

VOYAGE plc
Consolidated Statement of Comprehensive Income for the Year Ended
31 December 2003

	€'000
Revenue	74,364
Cost of sales	(56,680)
Gross profit	17,684
Net operating expenses	(8,906)
Operating profit	8,778

Exceptional items:
– profit on sale of property, plant and equipment	388
Interest receivable and similar income	616
Interest payable and similar charges	(447)
Profit on ordinary activities before taxation	9,335
Tax on profit on ordinary activities	(3,081)
Profit on ordinary activities after taxation	6,254
Equity non-controlling interest	(83)
Profit for financial year	6,171

VOYAGE plc

Consolidated Statement of Financial Position as at 31 December 2003

	Note	2003	2002
		€'000	€'000
ASSETS			
Non-current Assets			
Property, plant and equipment	2	24,062	19,940
Intangible assets	1	324	540
		24,386	20,480
Current Assets			
Inventory		1,939	1,771
Trade receivables		9,792	9,085
Cash in hand and at bank		3,923	3,679
		15,654	14,535
		40,040	35,015
EQUITY AND LIABILITIES			
Capital and Reserves			
Called up share capital	5	2,479	2,319
Share premium account	5	5,889	5,569
Other reserves		555	555
Retained earnings		7,040	9,379
		15,963	17,822
Non-controlling interests (equity)		483	619
		16,446	18,441

Non-current Liabilities	4	9,408	4,016
Current Liabilities	3	14,186	12,558
		40,040	35,015

Additional Information

1. Intangible fixed assets represent patents held by the company. These are amortised over the shorter of the anticipated period of profitable exploitation and the period to the expiry of the right. The company registered no new patents during 2003.

2. Property, plant and equipment

	Land & property €'000	Plant & equipment €'000	Total €'000
Cost or valuation			
At 1 January 2003	6,483	22,446	28,929
Subsidiary acquired (note 6)	1,800	3,378	5,178
Additions	–	5,611	5,611
Disposals	–	(1,092)	(1,092)
	8,283	30,343	38,626
Accumulated depreciation			
At 1 January 2003	2,582	6,407	8,989
Charge for year	820	2,232	3,052
Subsidiary acquired (note 6)	1,280	2,023	3,303
On disposal	-	(780)	(780)
	4,682	9,882	14,564
Net book value			
At 31 December 2003	3,601	20,461	24,062
At 31 December 2002	3,901	16,039	19,940

	2003	2002
	€'000	€'000

3. Current Liabilities

	2003	2002
Bank borrowings	104	-
Trade payables	8,217	7,039
Property, plant and equipment creditor	2,391	2,357
Finance lease creditor	141	202
Corporation tax	2,515	2,357
Dividends	764	592
Accruals and deferred income	54	11
	14,186	12,558

Accruals and deferred income comprise interest payable on:

	2003	2002
– Finance leases	5	6
– bank borrowings	49	5
	54	11

4. Non-current Liabilities

	2003	2002
Medium-term bank loans	3,453	-
Finance lease obligations	476	715
Deferred tax	5,479	3,301
	9,408	4,016

5. Called up share capital and share premium account

	€1 Ordinary shares €'000	Share premium €'000
At 1 January 2003	2,319	5,569
Shares issued on acquisition	160	440
Expenses connected with share issue	-	(120)
At 31 December 2003	2,479	5,889

6. Purchase of subsidiary undertaking

During 2003, VOYAGE plc purchased CHRISTY Limited, acquiring the following net assets:

	€'000
Property, plant and equipment	1,875
Inventory	456
Trade receivables	1,170
Cash at bank and in hand	42
Bank overdraft	(73)
Trade payables	(705)
Medium-term loans	(967)
Deferred taxation	(908)
	890
Consideration was satisfied by:	
Shares allotted	600
Cash	4,400
	5,000

The directors of VOYAGE plc are pleased with the positive effect CHRISTY Limited has had on turnover and operating profits.

7. During the year ended 31 December 2003, dividends of €4,400,000 were debited to equity.

Requirement   In accordance with IAS 7 *Statement of Cash Flows*, prepare each of the following for VOYAGE plc in respect of the year ended 31 December 2003:

(a) A consolidated statement of cash flows.
(b) A reconciliation of operating profit to net cash flow from operating activities.

Question 2 Based on ICAI, P3 Autumn 2000, Question 1)

A close friend became unemployed six months ago when the company she was working for was forced into liquidation due to severe cash flow problems. After months of applications and interviews, she has received two job offers, one of which is from CHOPPER plc. Before making a decision your friend wishes to obtain as much information as possible about the two companies and has asked for your assistance. She has provided you with the following information in respect to CHOPPER plc.

CHOPPER plc prepares its financial statements to 31 December each year. The company's consolidated statement of comprehensive income for the years ended 31 December 2002 and 2003, together with the consolidated statement of financial position as at those dates, are presented below.

CHOPPER PLC
Consolidated Statement of Comprehensive Income for the Year Ended
31 December 2003

	2003	2003
Continuing Operations	€ million	€ million
Turnover		
– continuing operations		
	2,100	1,850
Cost of sales	(1,670)	(1,400)
Gross profit	430	450
Other operating expenses	(150)	(95)
Operating profit		
– continuing operations	280	355
Loss on disposal of property, plant and equipment	(5)	-
Loss on disposal of discontinued operations	(10)	-
Interest payable and similar charges	(15)	(10)
Profit before tax	250	345
Tax	(80)	(85)
Profit after tax	170	260
Discontinued Operations		
Net profit for year for discontinued operations	20	25
	190	285
Non-controlling interests – equity	(38)	(57)
Group profit	152	228

CHOPPER plc
Consolidated Statement of Financial Position as at 31 December 2003

	2003	2002
	€ million	€ million
ASSETS		
Non-current Assets		
Tangible assets	780	480

Goodwill	60	100
	840	580
Current Assets		
Inventory	210	190
Trade receivables	390	250
	600	440
	1,440	1,020
EQUITY AND LIABILITIES		
Capital and Reserves		
€1 ordinary shares	100	100
Retained earnings	327	200
	427	300
Non-controlling interests	73	150
	500	450
Non-current Liabilities		
Obligations under finance leases	290	60
Deferred tax	100	50
	390	110
Current Liabilities		
Bank overdraft	12	15
Trade payables	300	275
Proposed dividend	25	20
Corporation tax	80	85
Obligations under finance leases	130	60
Accrued interest and finance charges	3	5
	550	460
	1,440	1,020

Additional Information

1. Property, plant and equipment

	€m
Cost:	
At 1 January 2003	800
Additions	620
Disposals	(370)
At 31 December 2003	1,050
Accumulated depreciation:	
At 1 January 2003	320
Charge for the year	150
On disposals	(200)
At 31 December 2003	270
Net book value:	
At 31 December 2003	780
At 31 December 2003	480

Additions during 2003 include assets purchased under finance leases that would have cost €400 million if purchased outright. None of the assets disposed of during 2003 were held under finance lease contracts.

2. On 30 June 2003 CHOPPER plc disposed of all of its 75% interest in KINGPIN Limited for €160 million in cash. KINGPIN Limited's results are classified as discontinued in the consolidated statement of comprehensive income. The loss on disposal of discontinued operations in the consolidated statement of comprehensive income is arrived at as follows:

	€m
Sale proceeds	160
Goodwill	(8)
Net assets disposed of (75% of €216 million)	(162)
	(10)

At 30 June 2003 the consolidated carrying values of the assets and liabilities of KINGPIN Limited were as follows:

ASSETS	€m	€m
Non-current Assets		
Cost	230	
Accumulated depreciation	(80)	150
Current Assets		
Trade receivables	60	
Cash at bank	56	116
		266

654 INTERNATIONAL FINANCIAL ACCOUNTING AND REPORTING

EQUITY AND LIABILITIES
Capital and Reserves

Share capital	100
Retained earnings	116
	216
Current Liabilities	
Trade payables	42
Corporation tax	8
	266

Apart from the sale of KINGPIN Limited, there were no other acquisitions or disposals of subsidiary undertakings during 2003. It is group policy to provide a full year's depreciation charge in the year of acquisition and none in the year of disposal.

3. During the year ended 31 December 2003, dividends of €25 million were debited to equity.

Requirement
(a) Prepare a consolidated statement of cash flows for the year ended 31 December 2003 for CHOPPER plc in accordance with IAS 7 *Statement of Cash Flows*.
(b) Prepare a reconciliation of operating profit to operating cash flows that clearly distinguishes between net cash flows from continuing and discontinued operations.

Question 3 (Based on ICAI, P3 Autumn 2003, Questions 1 & 2)

In recent years, TWIST plc (TWIST) has pursued an aggressive acquisition policy in order to expand its business. On 1 June 2003, TWIST purchased all of the ordinary share capital of SHOUT Limited (SHOUT), acquiring the following net assets:

	€ million
Property, plant and equipment	2,100
Inventory	950
Trade receivables	1,600
Cash at bank and in hand	10
Bank overdraft	(18)
Trade payables	(1,300)
Medium-term loans	(842)
	2,500
Consideration was satisfied by:	
Shares allotted	800
Cash	2,200
	3,000

The consolidated statement of comprehensive income of TWIST for the year ended 31 December 2003 and the statement of financial position as at that date are shown below.

TWIST plc
Consolidated Statement of Comprehensive Income for the Year Ended 31 December 2003

	€m	€m
Revenue		
– continuing operations	1,060	
– acquisitions	430	
Total turnover		1,490
Cost of sales		(1,130)
Gross profit		360
Net operating expenses		(180)
Operating profit		
– continuing operations	130	
– acquisitions	50	
Total operating profit		180
Exceptional items		
– profit on sale of property, plant and equipment in cont. ops		11
Interest receivable and similar income		21
Interest payable and similar charges		(19)
Profit on ordinary activities before taxation		193
Tax on profit on ordinary activities		(58)
Profit on ordinary activities after taxation		135
Equity non-controlling interest		(5)
Profit for financial year		130

TWIST plc
Consolidated Statement of Financial Position as at 31 December 2003

	Note	2003 € million	2002 € million
ASSETS			
Non-current Assets			
– Tangible assets	1	13,880	9,050
– Intangible assets	2	520	950
		14,400	10,000

Current Assets			
– Inventory		3,100	2,800
– Trade receivables		5,250	5,100
– Cash in hand and at bank		1,900	1,850
		10,250	9,750
		24,650	19,750

EQUITY AND LIABILITIES

Capital and Reserves			
Called up share capital	5	3,200	3,000
Share premium account	5	2,690	2,100
Other reserves		900	900
Retained earnings		3,580	3,550
		10,370	9,550
Non-controlling interests (equity)		330	1,300
		10,700	10,850
Non-current Liabilities	3	4,800	2,100
Current Liabilities	4	9,150	6,800
		24,650	19,750

Since acquisition, SHOUT has contributed €600 million to the group's net operating cash flow, paid €7 million in respect of investing activities and used €15 million for financing activities.

Additional Information

1. Property, Plant and Equipment

	€ million
Cost or valuation	
At 1 January 2003	11,200
Subsidiary acquired	3,000
Additions	4,100
Disposals	(450)
	17,850

Accumulated depreciation

At 1 January 2003	2,150
Charge for year	1,120
Subsidiary acquired	900
On disposal	(200)
	3,970

Net book value

At 31 December 2003	13,880
At 31 December 2002	9,050

2. Intangible Assets

€ million	Goodwill € million	Patents € million	Total € million
At 1 January 2003	300	650	950
Additions	500	–	500
Impairment/amortisation during the year	(300)	(630)	(930)
At 31 December 2003	500	20	520

Goodwill was impaired by €300 million during the year ended 31 December 2003. Patents are amortised over the shorter of the anticipated period of profitable exploitation and the period to the expiry of the right.

	2003 € million	2002 € million
3. Non-current Liabilities		
Medium-term bank loans	3,400	–
Finance lease obligations	1,400	2,100
	4,800	2,100

	2003 € million	2002 € million
4. Current Liabilities		
Bank borrowings	100	–
Trade payables	4,105	2,530
Fixed asset payable	2,300	1,550
Finance lease payable	145	200
Corporation tax	1,900	2,000
Dividends	570	500
Accruals and deferred income	30	20
	9,150	6,800

Accruals and deferred income comprise interest payable on:

– Finance leases	10	10
– Bank borrowings	20	10
	30	20

5. Capital and Reserves

	€1 Ordinary shares € million	Share premium € million
At 1 January 2003	3,000	2,100
Shares issued on acquisition	200	600
Expenses connected with share issue	–	(10)
At 31 December 2003	3,200	2,690

During the year ended 31 December 2003, €100 million was debited to equity in respect of dividends.

Requirement   In accordance with IAS 7 *Statement of Cash Flows*, prepare each of the following for TWIST plc in respect of the year ended 31 December 2003:

(a) A consolidated statement of cash flows;

(b) A reconciliation of operating profit to net cash flow from operating activities;

(c) Outline the disclosures that are required for the purchase of subsidiary undertakings, in accordance with IAS 7 *Statement of Cash Flows*, in respect of the acquisition of SHOUT by TWIST during the year ended 31 December 2003; and

(d) Calculate the basic earnings per share for the year ended 31 December 2003 for TWIST in accordance with IAS 33 *Earnings per Share*.

SECTION SIX

FURTHER ISSUES

CHAPTER 34

OTHER ACCOUNTING STANDARDS

INTRODUCTION

The application and integration of the principles underpinning the more common or frequently applied accounting standards are covered in previous chapters. This chapter completes the analysis of extant International Accounting Standards (IASs)/International Financial Reporting Standards (IFRSs) by examining the remaining six standards not dealt with elsewhere in the text. While these standards are interesting and relevant, they arguably have a narrow and specialised appeal. They are:

- IAS 41 *Agriculture*;
- IFRS 2 *Share-based Payment*;
- IAS 34 *Interim Financial Reporting*;
- IFRS 4 *Insurance Contracts*;
- IFRS 6 *Exploration for and Evaluation of Mineral Resources*; and
- IAS 26 *Accounting and Reporting by Retirement Benefit Plans*.

Each of these is now addressed in turn and, after you have read this chapter you should understand the basic principles underpinning each of these six accounting standards.

AGRICULTURE

IAS 41 *Agriculture* prescribes the accounting treatment, financial statement presentation, and disclosures related to agricultural activity. IAS 41 does not apply to:

- Land related to agricultural activity (IAS 16 *Property, Plant and Equipment*);
- Intangible assets related to agricultural activity (IAS 38 *Intangible Assets*); and
- The processing of agricultural produce after harvest (IAS 2 *Inventories* or another applicable Standard).

IAS 41 has been published because agriculture is very important in developing countries, as well as the developed world, in terms of GDP. The main problem in developing such a standard is the great diversity in practice in accounting that exists in agriculture. It is also very difficult to apply traditional accounting methods to agricultural activities. The contentious issues are:

(a) When and how should entities account for critical events associated with biological transformation (growth, procreation, production and degeneration) which alter the substance of biological assets;
(b) Statement of financial position classification is made difficult by the variety and characteristics of the living assets of agriculture; and
(c) The nature of management of agricultural activities means that the unit of measurement is difficult to determine.

Key Definitions

1. **Agricultural Activity** – the management by an enterprise of the biological transformation of biological assets for sale, into agricultural produce or into additional biological assets.
2. **Agricultural Produce** – the harvested product of an enterprise's biological assets
3. **Biological Asset** – A living animal or plant.
4. **Biological Transformation** – the processes of growth, degeneration, production and procreation that cause qualitative and quantitative changes in a biological asset.
5. **Group of Biological Assets** – An aggregation of similar living animals or plants.
6. **Harvest** – the detachment of produce from a biological asset or the cessation of a biological asset's life processes.

Scope

IAS 41 applies to the three elements that form part of, or result from, agricultural activity:

- Biological assets;
- Agricultural produce at the point of harvest; and
- Government grants.

Biological assets:	Agricultural produce:	Products that are the result of processing after harvest:
Sheep	Wool	Yarn, carpet
Trees in a plantation forest	Logs	Lumber
Plants	Cotton, harvested cane	Thread, clothing, sugar
Dairy cattle	Milk	Cheese
Pigs	Carcass	Sausages, cured hams
Bushes	Leaf	Tea, cured tobacco
Vines	Grapes	Wine
Fruit trees	Picked fruit	Processed fruit

Biological Assets

These are the core income producing assets of agricultural activity, held for their transformation abilities. Biological transformation leads to various different outcomes:

(a) **Asset changes** – growth (increase in quantity and/or quality); and degeneration (decrease in quantity and/or quality).
(b) **Creation of new assets** – production (separable non-living products); and procreation (separable living animals).

Asset changes are critical to the flow of future economic benefits both in and beyond the current accounting period but their relative importance depends on the purpose of the agricultural activity.

IAS 41 distinguishes between two broad categories of agricultural production:

1. **Consumable** – animals/plants harvested; and
2. **Bearer** – animals/plants that bear produce for harvest.

Biological assets are usually managed in groups of animal or plant classes with characteristics which permit sustainability in perpetuity and land often forms an integral part of the activity itself.

Recognition of Biological Assets

The recognition criteria are very similar to other assets as these may not be recognised unless the following conditions are met:

(a) the enterprise controls the asset as a result of past events;
(b) it is probable that the future economic benefits will flow to the enterprise; and
(c) the fair value or cost can be measured reliably.

Measurement of Biological Assets

IAS 41 requires that, at each reporting date, all biological assets should be measured at fair value less estimated point of sale costs. The IAS permits an alternative method of valuation if a fair value cannot be determined because market prices are not available. In that case it can be measured at cost less accumulated depreciation and impairment losses. The alternative basis is only permitted on initial recognition. Fair value has greater relevance, reliability, comparability and understandability as a measure of future economic benefits.

Determining Fair Value

The primary indicator of fair value should be net market value as this provides the best evidence of fair value when an active market exists. Markets generally differentiate between differing qualities and quantities.

Recognition

The change in the carrying amount for a group of biological assets should be allocated between:

(a) the change attributable to differences in fair value; and
(b) the physical change in biological assets held.

The total change in carrying value between the opening and closing periods thus consists of two components. IAS 41 insists that the separate disclosure of each is fundamental to appraising current period performance and future prospects. That is because they will not be reported in the same way in the financial statements. The change in carrying amount attributable to differences in fair value should be recognised in the statement of non-owner movements in equity and presented in equity under the heading of surplus/(deficit) on fair valuation of biological assets. This is the 'holding' part of the change in carrying amount. The change in carrying amount attributable to the physical change must be recognised as income or expense and described as the change in biological assets. This should enable management performance to be evaluated and thus should be included in the 'operating' part of the change in carrying amount.

In the statement of financial position the biological assets must be recorded at fair value after incorporating the consequences of all biological transformations. These assets, together with differing risk and return characteristics, should be identified clearly.

The recommended method of separating the above components is to calculate the change attributable to the differences in fair value by restating biological assets on hand at the opening statement of financial position using end of period fair values and comparing this with the closing carrying amount. There are exceptions to this approach, e.g. where production cycle is less than one year (broiler chickens, mushroom growing, cereal crops etc.). In these cases the total change in carrying amount should be reported in the statement of comprehensive income as a single item of income or expense.

Any other events giving rise to a change in biological assets of such a size, nature or incidence that their disclosure is relevant to explain the entity's performance should be included in the change in biological assets recognised as income or expense. They should be recorded as a separate item in the reconciliation required to determine the change attributable to biological transformation.

Presentation

In the statement of financial position, biological assets should be classified as a separate class of assets falling under neither current nor non-current classifications. Biological assets should also be sub-classified as follows:

(a) class of animal or plant;
(b) nature of activities (consumable or bearer); and
(c) maturity or immaturity for intended purpose.

Where activities are consumable, the maturity criterion will be attainment of harvestable specifications whereas in bearer activities it will be attainment of sufficient maturity to sustain economic harvests. In the statement of comprehensive income an analysis of income and expenses based on their nature should be presented rather than the cost of sales method. IAS 41 also requires detailed disclosures to include the measurement base used for fair value and the details of the reconciliation of the change in carrying value for the year.

Agricultural Produce

This is recognised at the point of harvest, e.g. detachment from the biological asset. It is either incapable of biological processes or such processes are dormant. Recognition ends once the produce enters trading activities or production processes within integrated agribusinesses.

Measurement and Presentation

Agricultural produce should be measured at fair value at each reporting date. The change in the carrying amount of agriculture produce held at two reporting dates should be recognised as income or expenses in the statement of comprehensive income. This will be rare as such produce is usually sold or processed within a short time.

Agricultural produce that is harvested for trading or processing activities within integrated agricultural/agricultural operations should be measured at fair value at the date of harvest and this amount is deemed cost for application of IAS 2 to consequential inventories. Agricultural produce should be classified as inventory in the statement of financial position and disclosed separately either on the face of the statement of financial position or in the notes.

Government Grants

An unconditional government grant related to a biological asset measured at fair value less estimated point of sale costs should be recognised as income when, and only when, the grant becomes receivable. If a grant requires an enterprise not to engage in agricultural activity an enterprise should only recognise the grant as income when the conditions are met. IAS 20 does not apply to such grants. However, if a biological asset is measured at cost less accumulated depreciation and impairment losses then IAS 20 does apply.

Disclosure

An enterprise should disclose the aggregate gain or loss arising during the current period on initial recognition of biological assets and agricultural produce and from the change in fair value less estimated point of sale costs of biological assets as well as a description of each group of biological assets.

If not disclosed elsewhere the following should also be disclosed:

(a) the nature of its activities involving each group of biological assets; and
(b) non-financial measures or estimates of the physical quantities of:
  (i) each group of the enterprise's biological assets at the end of the period; and
  (ii) output of agricultural produce during the period.

The methods and significant assumptions applied in determining the fair value of each group of agricultural produce at the point of harvest and each group of biological assets should be disclosed. The fair value less estimated point of sale costs of agricultural produce harvested during the period, determined at the point of harvest, should be disclosed.
  An enterprise should also disclose:

(a) the existence and carrying amounts of biological assets whose title is restricted, and the carrying amounts of biological assets pledged as security for liabilities;
(b) the amount of commitments for the development or acquisition of biological assets; and
(c) financial risk management strategies related to agricultural activity.

A reconciliation should be provided of changes in the carrying amount of biological assets between the start and the end of the current period and this should include:

(a) the gain or loss arising from changes in fair value less estimated point of sale costs;
(b) increases due to purchases;
(c) decreases due to sales;
(d) decreases due to harvest;
(e) increases resulting from business combinations;
(f) net exchange differences arising from the translation of financial statements of a foreign entity; and
(g) other changes.

Additional Disclosures for Biological Assets where Fair Value cannot be Reliably Measured

(a) Description of the biological assets;
(b) An explanation of why fair value cannot be measured reliably;
(c) If possible, the range of estimates within which fair value is highly likely to lie;
(d) The depreciation method used;
(e) The useful lives or the depreciation rates adopted; and
(f) The gross carrying amount and accumulated depreciation at start and end of the period.

If, during the current period, an enterprise measures biological assets at their cost less any accumulated depreciation and accumulated impairment losses, an enterprise should disclose any gain or loss recognised on disposal of such biological assets and the reconciliation required above should disclose amounts related to such biological assets separately. In addition, the reconciliation should include the following amounts included in net profit or loss related to those biological assets:

(a) impairment losses;
(b) reversals of impairment losses; and
(c) depreciation.

If a previously measured biological asset at cost now becomes reliably measured at fair value the following should be disclosed for those assets:

(a) description of the biological assets;
(b) explanation of why fair value has become reliably measurable; and
(c) the effect of the change.

Government Grants

The following should be disclosed:

(a) the nature and extent of government grants recognised in the financial statements;
(b) Unfulfilled conditions and other contingencies attached to the grants; and
(c) Significant decreases expected in the level of government grants.

Example

XYZ Dairy Limited
Statement of financial position as at 31 December

	20X1 €	20X0 €
ASSETS		
Non-current assets		
Dairy livestock – immature	52,060	47,730
Dairy livestock – mature	372,990	411,840
Biological assets (Note 3)	425,050	459,570
Property, plant and equipment	1,462,650	1,409,800
Total non-current assets	1,887,700	1,869,370
Current assets		
Inventories	82,950	70,650
Trade and other receivables	88,000	65,000
Cash	10,000	10,000
Total current assets	180,950	145,650
Total assets	2,068,650	2,015,020

EQUITY AND LIABILITIES

Equity

Issued capital	1,000,000	1,000,000
Accumulated profits	902,828	865,000
Total equity	1,902,828	1,865,000

Current liabilities

Trade and other payables	165,822	150,020
Total current liabilities	165,822	150,020
Total equity and liabilities	2,068,650	2,015,020

Statement of Comprehensive Income for the Year Ended 31 December 20X1

	€
Fair value of milk produced	518,240
Gains arising from changes in fair value less	
Estimated point of sale costs of dairy livestock (Note 3)	39,930
Inventories used	558,170
Staff costs	(137,523)
Depreciation expense	(127,283)
Other operating expenses	(15,250)
	(197,092)
	(477,148)
Profit from operations	81,022
Income tax expense	(43,194)
Net profit for the period	37,828

Statement of Changes in Equity for the Year Ended 31 December 20X1

	Share capital	Accumulated profits	Year ended 31 December 20X1
	€	€	€
Balance at 1 January 20X1	1,000,000	865,000	1,865,000
Net profit for the period		37,828	37,828
Balance at 31 December 20X1	1,000,000	902,828	1,902,828

Statement of Cash Flows for the Year Ended 31 December 20X1

	€
Cash flows from operating activities	
Cash receipts from sales of milk	498,027
Cash receipts from sales of livestock	97,913
Cash paid for supplies and to employees	(460,831)
Cash paid for purchases of livestock	(23,815)
	111,294
Income taxes paid	(43,194)
Net cash flow from operating activities	68,100
Cash flows from investing activities	
Purchase of property, plant and equipment	(68,100)
Net cash used in investing activities	(68,100)
Net increase in cash	0
Cash at beginning of period	10,000
Cash at end of period	10,000

Notes to the Financial Statements

1. **Operations and Principal Activities**   XYZ Dairy Limited ('the Company') is engaged in milk production for supply to various customers. At 31 December 20X1, the Company held 419 cows able to produce milk (mature assets) and 137 heifers being raised to produce milk in the future (immature assets). The Company produced 157,584kg of milk with a fair value less estimated point-of-sale costs of 518,240 (that is determined at the time of milking) in the year ended 31 December 20X1.

2. **Accounting Policies Livestock and Milk**   Livestock are measured at their fair value less estimated point-of-sale costs. The fair value of livestock is determined based on market prices of livestock of similar age, breed, and genetic merit. Milk is initially measured at its fair value less estimated point-of-sale costs at the time of milking. The fair value of milk is determined based on market prices in the local area.

3. **Biological Assets**

	€
Reconciliation of Carrying Amounts of Dairy livestock	
Carrying amount at 1 January 20X1	459,570
Increases due to purchases	26,250

Gain arising from changes in fair value less estimated point-of-sale costs attributable to physical changes	15,350
Gain arising from changes in fair value less estimated point-of-sale costs attributable to price changes	24,580
Decreases due to sales	(100,700)
Carrying amount at 31 December 20X1	425,050

4. **Financial Risk Management Strategies**   The company is exposed to financial risks arising from changes in milk prices. The Company does not anticipate that milk prices will decline significantly in the foreseeable future and, therefore, has not entered into derivative or other contracts to manage the risk of a decline in milk prices. The Company reviews its outlook for milk prices regularly in considering the need for active risk management.

Example

The following example illustrates how to separate physical change and price change. Separating the change in fair value less estimated point-of-sale costs between the portion attributable to physical changes and the portion attributable to price changes is encouraged but not required by the standard.

A herd of ten 2-year-old animals was held at 1 January 20X1. One animal aged 2.5 years was purchased on 1 July 20X1 for €108, and one animal was born on 1 July 20X1. No animals were sold or disposed of during the period. Per unit fair values less estimated point-of-sale costs were as follows:

	€
2-year-old animal at 1 January 20X1	100
Newborn animal at 1 July 20X1	70
2.5-year-old animal at 1 July 20X1	108
Newborn animal at 31 December 20X1	72
0.5-year-old animal at 31 December 20X1	80
2-year-old animal at 31 December 20X1	105
2.5-year-old animal at 31 December 20X1	111
3-year-old animal at 31 December 20X1	120

Fair value less estimated point-of-sale costs of herd at 1 January 20X1:

(10 x €100) = €1,000

Purchase on 1 July 20X1:

(1 x €108) = €108

Increase in fair value less estimated point-of-sale costs due to price change:

	€
10 x (€105 – €100)	50
1 x (€111 – €108)	3
1 x (€72 – €70)	2
	55

Increase in fair value less estimated point-of-sale costs due to physical change:

	€
10 x (€120 – €105)	150
1 x (€120 – €111)	9
1 x (€80 – €72)	8
1 x €70	70
	237

Fair value less estimated point-of-sale costs of herd at 31 December 20X1

	€
11 x €120	1,320
1 x €80	80
	1,400

SHARE-BASED PAYMENT

Entities often grant shares or share options to employees and other parties. Until IFRS 2 *Share-based* was issued, there was no IFRS on the subject. IFRS 2 prescribes the financial reporting by an entity when it undertakes a share-based payment transaction, particularly its impact in profit or loss and financial position. Transfers of an entity's equity instruments by its shareholders to suppliers are share-based payment transactions. A transaction with an employee in his/her capacity as a holder of equity of the entity is not a share-based payment transaction. Furthermore, IFRS 2 does not apply to a business combination (see IFRS 3 *Business Combinations*). Hence, equity issued in a business combination in exchange for control of the acquiree is not within the scope of IFRS 2. However, equity granted in capacity as employees (e.g. in return for continued service) are within the scope of IFRS 2.

IFRS 2 requires an entity to recognise share-based payment transactions in its financial statements. The IFRS sets out measurement principles and specific requirements for three types of share-based payment transactions:

1. Equity-settled transactions;
2. Cash-settled share-based payment transactions; and
3. Transactions in which the entity receives or acquires goods or services and the terms of the arrangement provide either the entity or the supplier a choice of whether the entity settles the transaction in cash or by issuing equity.

Equity-settled Share-based Payment Transactions

For equity-settled share-based payment transactions, the entity should measure the goods or services received, and the corresponding increase in equity, directly, at the fair value of the goods or services received, unless that fair value cannot be estimated reliably. If the entity cannot estimate reliably the fair value of the goods or services received, the entity should measure their value, and the corresponding increase in equity, indirectly, by reference to the fair value of the equity instruments granted.

For transactions with employees and others providing similar services, fair value of the services received are referred to the fair value of the equity granted, as it is not possible to estimate reliably the fair value of the services received. The fair value of equity should be measured at grant date. Typically, share options are granted to employees as part of their remuneration package. Usually, it is not possible to measure directly the services received for particular components of the employee's remuneration package. It might also not be possible to measure the fair value of the total remuneration package independently without measuring directly the fair value of equity instruments granted. As share options are sometimes granted as part of a bonus arrangement, e.g. as an incentive to the employees to remain in the entity's employ or to reward them for their efforts in improving the entity's performance. By granting shares or share options, the entity is paying additional remuneration to obtain additional benefits. Estimating the fair value of those additional benefits is likely to be difficult. Because of the difficulty of measuring directly the fair value of the services received, the entity should measure the fair value of the employee services received by reference to the fair value of the equity instruments granted.

For parties other than employees, there is a rebuttable presumption that the fair value of the goods or services received can be estimated reliably. It is measured at the date the entity obtains the goods or the counterparty renders service. In rare cases, if the entity rebuts this presumption because it cannot estimate reliably the fair value of the goods or services received, the entity should measure the goods or services received, and the corresponding increase in equity, indirectly, by reference to the fair value of the equity instruments granted, measured at the date the entity obtains the goods or the counterparty renders service.

Transactions in which Services are Received

If the equity vests immediately, the entity should presume the services rendered have been received. In this case, on grant date the entity should recognise the services received in full, with a corresponding increase in equity.

If the equity does not vest until the counterparty completes a specified period of service, the services will be received in the future, during the vesting period. The entity should account for those services as they are rendered by the counterparty during the vesting period, with a corresponding increase in equity. For example:

- if an employee is granted share options conditional upon completing three years' service, then the entity should presume that the services to be rendered by the employee as consideration for the share options will be received in the future, over that three-year vesting period; and
- if an employee is granted share options conditional upon, say, a condition being satisfied, and the length of the vesting period varies, the entity should presume that the services rendered by the employee as consideration will be received in the future, over the expected vesting period. The entity should estimate the length of the expected vesting period at grant date, based on the most likely outcome of the performance condition. If the performance condition is a market condition, the estimate of the length of the expected vesting period should be consistent with the assumptions used in estimating the fair value of the options granted, and should not be subsequently revised. If the performance condition is not a market condition, the entity should revise its estimate of the length of the vesting period, if necessary, if subsequent information indicates that the length of the vesting period differs from previous estimates.

Transactions Measured by Reference to the Fair Value of the Equity Instruments Granted

1. Determining the fair value of equity instruments granted   The fair value of equity instruments granted at the measurement date is based on market prices if available, taking into account the terms and conditions upon which those equity instruments were granted. If market prices are not available, the entity should estimate the fair value of the equity using a valuation technique to estimate what the price of those equity instruments would have been on the measurement date in an arm's length transaction between knowledgeable, willing parties. The valuation technique should be consistent with generally accepted valuation methodologies for pricing financial instruments, incorporating all factors and assumptions that knowledgeable, willing market participants would consider in setting the price. (See Appendix B below for further guidance.)

2. Treatment of vesting conditions   A grant of equity instruments might be conditional upon satisfying specified vesting conditions e.g. the employee remaining in the entity's employ for a specified period of time. There might be performance conditions that must be satisfied e.g. achieving a specified growth in profit or specified increase in the entity's share price. Vesting conditions should not be taken into account when estimating the fair value at the measurement date. Instead, vesting conditions are used to adjust the number of equity instruments included in the measurement of the transaction amount so that, ultimately, the amount recognised for goods or services received as consideration for the equity instruments granted should be based on the number of equity instruments that eventually vest. Hence, on a cumulative basis, no amount is recognised for goods or services received if the equity instruments granted do not vest because of failure to satisfy a vesting condition, e.g. the counterparty fails to complete a specified service period, or a performance condition is not satisfied.

The entity should recognise an amount for the goods/services received during the vesting period based on the best available estimate of the number of equity instruments expected to vest and should revise that estimate if subsequent information indicates that the number of equity instruments expected to vest differs from previous estimates. On vesting date, the entity should revise the estimate to equal the number of equity instruments that ultimately vested.

Market conditions, such as a target share price should be taken into account when estimating the fair value of the equity instruments granted.

3. Treatment of a reload feature A reload feature should not be taken into account when estimating the fair value. Instead, a reload option should be accounted for as a new option grant, if and when a reload option is subsequently granted.

4. After vesting date No subsequent adjustment to total equity after vesting date. The entity should not subsequently reverse the amount recognised for services received from an employee if the vested equity instruments are later forfeited or not exercised. It does not preclude the entity from recognising a transfer within equity, i.e. a transfer from one component of equity to another.

5. If the fair value of the equity instruments cannot be estimated reliably In rare cases, the entity may be unable to estimate reliably the fair value of the equity instruments granted at the measurement date. In these rare cases only, the entity should instead:

• measure the equity instruments at their intrinsic value, initially at the date the entity obtains the goods or the counterparty renders service and subsequently at each reporting date and at the date of final settlement, with any change in intrinsic value recognised in profit or loss. For a grant of share options, the share-based payment arrangement is finally settled when the options are exercised, are forfeited (e.g. upon cessation of employment) or lapse (e.g. at the end of the option's life); and
• recognise the goods or services received based on the number of equity instruments that ultimately vest or (where applicable) are ultimately exercised. To apply this requirement to share options, for example, the entity should recognise the goods or services received during the vesting period. The amount recognised for goods or services received during the vesting period should be based on the number of share options expected to vest. The entity should revise that estimate, if necessary, if subsequent information indicates that the number of share options expected to vest differs from previous estimates. On

vesting date, the entity should revise the estimate to equal the number of equity instruments that ultimately vested. After vesting date, the entity should reverse the amount recognised for goods or services received if the share options are later forfeited, or lapse at the end of the share option's life.

Modifications to the Terms and Conditions on which Equity Instruments were Granted, including Cancellations and Settlements

An entity might modify the terms and conditions on which the equity instruments were granted. For example, it might reduce the exercise price of options granted to employees (i.e. re-price the options), which increases the fair value of those options. The entity should recognise, as a minimum, the services received measured at the grant date fair value of the equity instruments granted, unless those equity instruments do not vest because of failure to satisfy a vesting condition (other than a market condition) that was specified at grant date. This applies irrespective of any modifications to the terms and conditions on which the equity instruments were granted, or a cancellation or settlement of that grant of equity instruments. In addition, the entity should recognise the effects of modifications that increase the total fair value of the share-based payment arrangement or are otherwise beneficial to the employee. (See Appendix B below for further guidance.)

If the entity cancels or settles a grant of equity instruments during the vesting period (other than a grant cancelled by forfeiture when the vesting conditions are not satisfied):

(a) the entity should account for the cancellation or settlement as an acceleration of vesting, and should therefore recognise immediately the amount that otherwise would have been recognised for services received over the remainder of the vesting period;

(b) any payment made to the employee on the cancellation or settlement of the grant should be accounted for as the repurchase of an equity interest, i.e. as a deduction from equity, except to the extent that the payment exceeds the fair value of the equity instruments granted, measured at the repurchase date. Any such excess should be recognised as an expense; and

(c) if new equity instruments are granted to the employee and, on the date when those new equity instruments are granted, the entity identifies the new equity instruments granted as replacement equity instruments for the cancelled equity instruments, the entity should account for the granting of replacement equity instruments in the same way as a modification of the original grant of equity instruments (see Appendix B below for further guidance). The incremental fair value granted is the difference between the fair value of the replacement equity instruments and the net fair value of the cancelled equity instruments, at the date the replacement equity instruments are granted. The net fair value of the cancelled equity instruments is their fair value immediately before the cancellation, less the amount of any payment made to the employee on cancellation of the equity instruments that is accounted for as a deduction from equity in accordance with (b) above. If the entity does not identify new equity instruments granted as replacement equity instruments for the cancelled equity instruments, the entity should account for those new equity instruments as a new grant of equity instruments.

If an entity repurchases vested equity instruments, the payment made to the employee should be accounted for as a deduction from equity, except to the extent that the payment exceeds the fair value of the equity instruments repurchased, measured at the re-purchase date. Any such excess should be recognised as an expense.

Cash-Settled Share-Based Payment Transactions

For cash-settled share-based payment transactions, the entity should measure the goods or services acquired and the liability incurred at the fair value of the liability. Until the liability is settled, the entity should re-measure the fair value of the liability at each reporting date and at the date of settlement, with any changes in fair value recognised in profit or loss for the period.

For example, an entity might grant share appreciation rights to employees as part of their remuneration package, whereby the employees will become entitled to a future cash payment (rather than an equity instrument), based on the increase in the entity's share price from a specified level over a specified period of time. Or an entity might grant to its employees a right to receive a future cash payment by granting to them a right to shares (including shares to be issued upon the exercise of share options) that are redeemable, either mandatorily (e.g. upon cessation of employment) or at the employee's option.

The entity should recognise the services received, and a liability to pay for those services, as the employees render service. For example, some share appreciation rights vest immediately, and the employees are therefore not required to complete a specified period of service to become entitled to the cash payment. In the absence of evidence to the contrary, the entity should presume that the services rendered by the employees in exchange for the share appreciation rights have been received. Thus, the entity should recognise immediately the services received and a liability to pay for them. If the share appreciation rights do not vest until the employees have completed a specified period of service, the entity should recognise the services received, and a liability to pay for them, as the employees render service during that period.

The liability should be measured, initially and at each reporting date, until settled at the fair value of the share appreciation rights, by applying an option pricing model, taking into account the terms and conditions on which the share appreciation rights were granted, and the extent to which the employees have rendered service to date.

Share-Based Payment Transactions with Cash Alternatives

For share-based payment transactions in which the terms of the arrangement provide either the entity or the counterparty with the choice of whether the entity settles the transaction in cash (or other assets) or by issuing equity instruments, the entity should account for that transaction, or the components of that transaction, as a cash-settled share-based payment transaction if, and to the extent that, the entity has incurred a liability to settle in cash or other assets, or as an equity-settled share-based payment transaction if, and to the extent that, no such liability has been incurred.

Share-Based Payment Transactions in which the Terms of the Arrangement Provide the Counterparty with a Choice of Settlement

If an entity has granted the counterparty the right to choose whether a share-based payment transaction is settled in cash or by issuing equity instruments, the entity has granted a compound financial instrument, which includes a debt component (i.e. the counterparty's right to demand payment in cash) and an equity component (i.e. the counterparty's right to demand settlement in equity instruments rather than in cash). For transactions with parties other than employees, in which the fair value of the goods or services received is measured directly, the entity should measure the equity component of the compound financial instrument as the difference between the fair value of the goods or services received and the fair value of the debt component, at the date when the goods or services are received.

For other transactions, including transactions with employees, the entity should measure the fair value of the compound financial instrument at the measurement date, taking into account the terms and conditions on which the rights to cash or equity instruments were granted.

The entity should account separately for the goods or services received or acquired in respect of each component of the compound financial instrument. For the debt component, the entity should recognise the goods or services acquired, and a liability to pay for those goods or services, as the counterparty supplies goods or renders service, in accordance with the requirements applying to cash-settled share-based payment transactions. For the equity component (if any), the entity should recognise the goods or services received, and an increase in equity, as the counterparty supplies goods or renders service, in accordance with the requirements applying to equity-settled share-based payment transactions.

At the date of settlement, the entity should re-measure the liability to its fair value. If the entity issues equity instruments on settlement rather than paying cash, the liability should be transferred direct to equity, as the consideration for the equity instruments issued.

If the entity pays in cash on settlement rather than issuing equity instruments, that payment should be applied to settle the liability in full. Any equity component previously recognised should remain within equity. By electing to receive cash on settlement, the counterparty forfeited the right to receive equity instruments. However, this requirement does not preclude the entity from recognising a transfer within equity, i.e. a transfer from one component of equity to another.

Share-Based Payment Transactions in which the Terms of the Arrangement Provide the Entity with a Choice of Settlement

For a share-based payment transaction in which the terms of the arrangement provide an entity with the choice of whether to settle in cash or by issuing equity instruments, the entity should determine whether it has a present obligation to settle in cash and account for the share-based payment transaction accordingly. The entity has a present obligation to settle in cash if the choice of settlement in equity instruments has no commercial substance (e.g. because the entity is legally prohibited from issuing shares), or the entity has a past practice or a stated policy of settling in cash, or generally settles in cash whenever the counterparty asks for cash settlement.

Upon settlement:

(a) if the entity elects to settle in cash, the cash payment should be accounted for as the repurchase of an equity interest, i.e. as a deduction from equity, except as noted in (c) below;

(b) if the entity elects to settle by issuing equity instruments, no further accounting is required (other than a transfer from one component of equity to another, if necessary) except as noted in (c) below; and

(c) if the entity elects the settlement alternative with the higher fair value, as at the date of settlement, the entity should recognise an additional expense for the excess value given, i.e. the difference between the cash paid and the fair value of the equity instruments that would otherwise have been issued, or the difference between the fair value of the equity instruments issued and the amount of cash that would otherwise have been paid, whichever is applicable.

Disclosures

An entity should disclose information that enables users of the financial statements to understand the nature and extent of share-based payment arrangements that existed during the period. The entity should disclose at least the following:

- a description of each type of share-based payment arrangement that existed at any time during the period, including the general terms and conditions of each arrangement, such as vesting requirements, the maximum term of options granted, and the method of settlement (e.g. whether in cash or equity). An entity with substantially similar types of share-based payment arrangements may aggregate this information, unless separate disclosure of each arrangement is necessary to enable users of the financial statements to understand the nature and extent of share-based payment arrangements that existed during the period;

- the number and weighted average exercise prices of share options for each of the following groups of options: outstanding at the beginning of the period; granted during the period; forfeited during the period; exercised during the period; expired during the period; outstanding at the end of the period; and exercisable at the end of the period;

- for share options exercised during the period, the weighted average share price at the date of exercise. If options were exercised on a regular basis throughout the period, the entity may instead disclose the weighted average share price during the period; and

- for share options outstanding at the end of the period, the range of exercise prices and weighted average remaining contractual life. If the range of exercise prices is wide, the outstanding options should be divided into ranges that are meaningful for assessing the number and timing of additional shares that may be issued and the cash that may be received upon exercise of those options.

An entity should disclose information that enables users of the financial statements to understand how the fair value of the goods or services received, or the fair value of the equity instruments granted, during the period was determined.

Appendix A: Defined Terms

1. **Cash-settled Share-based Payment Transaction** A share-based payment transaction in which the entity acquires goods or services by incurring a liability to transfer cash or other assets to the supplier of those goods or services for amounts that are based on the price (or value) of the entity's shares or other equity instruments of the entity.

2. **Employees and Others Providing Similar Services** Individuals who render personal services to the entity and either the individuals are regarded as employees for legal or tax purposes or the individuals work for the entity under its direction in the same way as individuals who are regarded as employees for legal or tax purposes, or the services rendered are similar to those rendered by employees. For example, the term encompasses all management personnel, i.e. those persons having authority and responsibility for planning, directing and controlling the activities of the entity, including non-executive directors.

3. **Equity Instrument** A contract that evidences a residual interest in the assets of an entity after deducting all of its liabilities. The Framework defines a liability as a present obligation of the entity arising from past events, the settlement of which is expected to result in an outflow from the entity of resources embodying economic benefits (i.e. an outflow of cash or other assets of the entity).

4. **Equity Instrument Granted** The right (conditional or unconditional) to an equity instrument of the entity conferred by the entity on another party, under a share-based payment arrangement.

5. **Equity-settled Share-based Payment Transaction** A share-based payment transaction in which the entity receives goods or services as consideration for equity instruments of the entity (including shares or share options).

6. **Fair Value** The amount for which an asset could be exchanged, a liability settled, or an equity instrument granted could be exchanged, between knowledgeable, willing parties in an arm's length transaction.

7. **Grant Date** The date at which the entity and another party (including an employee) agree to a share-based payment arrangement, being when the entity and the counterparty have a shared understanding of the terms and conditions of the arrangement. At grant date the entity confers on the counterparty the right to cash, other assets, or equity instruments of the entity, provided the specified vesting conditions, if any, are met. If that agreement is subject to an approval process (for example, by shareholders), grant date is the date when that approval is obtained.

8. **Intrinsic Value** The difference between the fair value of the shares to which the counterparty has the (conditional or unconditional) right to subscribe or which it has the right to receive, and the price (if any) the counterparty is (or will be) required to pay for those shares. For example, a share option with an exercise price of €15 on a share with a fair value of €20 has an intrinsic value of €5.

9. **Market Condition** A condition upon which the exercise price, vesting or exercisability of an equity instrument depends, that is related to the market price of the entity's equity instruments, such as attaining a specified share price or a specified amount of intrinsic value of a share option, or achieving a specified target that is based on the market price of the entity's equity instruments relative to an index of market prices of equity instruments of other entities.

10. **Measurement Date** The date at which the fair value of the equity instruments granted is measured for the purposes of IFRS 2. For transactions with employees and others providing similar services, the measurement date is grant date. For transactions with parties other than employees (and those providing similar services), the measurement date is the date the entity obtains the goods or the counterparty renders service.

11. **Reload Feature** A feature that provides for an automatic grant of additional share options whenever the option holder exercises previously granted options using the entity's shares, rather than cash, to satisfy the exercise price.

12. **Reload Option** A new share option granted when a share is used to satisfy the exercise price of a previous share option.

13. **Share-Based Payment Arrangement** An agreement between the entity and another party (including an employee) to enter into a share-based payment transaction, which thereby entitles the other party to receive cash or other assets of the entity for amounts that are based on the price of the entity's shares or other equity instruments of the entity, or to receive equity instruments of the entity, provided the specified vesting conditions, if any, are met.

14. **Share-Based Payment Transaction** A transaction in which the entity receives goods or services as consideration for equity instruments of the entity (including shares or share options), or acquires goods or services by incurring liabilities to the supplier of those goods or services for amounts that are based on the price of the entity's shares or other equity instruments of the entity.

15. **Share-Option** A contract that gives the holder the right, but not the obligation, to subscribe to the entity's shares at a fixed or determinable price for a specified period of time.

16. **Vest** To become an entitlement, under a share-based payment arrangement, a counterparty's right to receive cash, other assets, or equity instruments of the entity vests upon satisfaction of any specified vesting conditions.

17. **Vesting Conditions** The conditions that must be satisfied for the counterparty to become entitled to receive cash, other assets or equity instruments of the entity, under a share-based payment arrangement. Vesting conditions include service conditions, which require the other party to complete a specified period of service, and performance conditions, which require specified performance targets to be met (such as a specified increase in the entity's profit over a specified period of time).

18. **Vesting Period** The period during which all the specified vesting conditions of a share-based payment arrangement are to be satisfied.

Appendix B: Application Guidance

Shares

For shares granted to employees, the fair value of the shares should be measured at the market price of the entity's shares (or an estimated market price, if the entity's shares are not publicly traded), adjusted to take into account the terms and conditions upon which the shares were granted (except for vesting conditions that are excluded from the measurement of fair value). For example, if the employee is not entitled to receive dividends during the vesting period, this factor should be taken into account when estimating the fair value of the shares granted. Similarly, if the shares are subject to restrictions on transfer after vesting date, that factor should be taken into account, but only to the extent that the post-vesting restrictions affect the price that a knowledgeable, willing market participant would pay for that share. For example, if the shares are actively traded in a deep and liquid market, postvesting transfer restrictions may have little, if any, effect on the price that a knowledgeable, willing market participant would pay for those shares.

Share Options

For share options granted to employees, in many cases market prices are not available, because the options granted are subject to terms and conditions that do not apply to traded options. If traded options with similar terms and conditions do not exist, the fair value of the options granted should be estimated by applying an option pricing model.

The entity should consider factors that knowledgeable, willing market participants would consider in selecting the option pricing model to apply. For example, many employee options have long lives, are usually exercisable during the period between vesting date and the end of the options' life, and are often exercised early. These factors should be considered when estimating the grant date fair value of the options. For many entities, this might preclude the use of the Black-Scholes-Merton formula, which does not allow for the possibility of exercise before the end of the option's life and may not adequately reflect the effects of expected early exercise. It also does not allow for the possibility that expected volatility and other model inputs might vary over the option's life. However, for share options with relatively short contractual lives or that must be exercised within a short period of time after vesting date, the factors identified above may not apply. In these instances, the Black-Scholes-Merton formula may produce a value that is substantially the same as a more flexible option pricing model.

All option pricing models take into account, as a minimum, the following factors:

(a) the exercise price of the option;
(b) the life of the option;
(c) the current price of the underlying shares;
(d) the expected volatility of the share price;
(e) the dividends expected on the shares (if appropriate); and
(f) the risk-free interest rate for the life of the option.

Other factors that knowledgeable, willing market participants would consider in setting the price should also be taken into account. For example, a share option granted to an employee typically cannot be exercised during specified periods (e.g. during the vesting period or during periods specified by securities regulators). This factor should be taken into account if the option pricing model applied would otherwise assume that the option could be exercised at any time during its life. However, if an entity uses an option pricing model that values options that can be exercised only at the end of the options' life, no adjustment is required for the inability to exercise them during the vesting period (or other periods during the options' life) because the model assumes that the options cannot be exercised during those periods.

Similarly, another factor common to employee share options is the possibility of early exercise of the option, for example, because the option is not freely transferable, or because the employee must exercise all vested options upon cessation of employment. The effects of expected early exercise should be taken into account.

Factors that a knowledgeable, willing market participant would not consider in setting the price of a share option (or other equity instrument) should not be taken into account when estimating the fair value of share options (or other equity instruments) granted. For example, for share options granted to employees, factors that affect the value of the option from the individual employee's perspective only are not relevant to estimating the price that would be set by a knowledgeable, willing market participant.

Inputs to Option Pricing Models

In estimating the expected volatility of and dividends on the underlying shares, the objective is to approximate the expectations that would be reflected in a current market or negotiated exchange price for the option. Similarly, when estimating the effects of early exercise of employee share options, the objective is to approximate the expectations that an outside party with access to detailed information about employees' exercise behaviour would develop based on information available at the grant date. Often, there is likely to be a range of reasonable expectations about future volatility, dividends and exercise behaviour. If so, an expected value should be calculated, by weighting each amount within the range by its associated probability of occurrence.

Expectations about the future are generally based on experience, modified if the future is reasonably expected to differ from the past. In some circumstances, identifiable factors may indicate that unadjusted historical experience is a relatively poor predictor of future experience. For example, if an entity with two distinctly different lines of business disposes of the one that was significantly less risky than the other, historical volatility may not be the best information on which to base reasonable expectations for the future. In other circumstances, historical information may not be available. For example, a newly listed entity will have little, if any, historical data on the volatility of its share price. Unlisted and newly listed entities are discussed further below.

In summary, an entity should not simply base estimates of volatility, exercise behaviour and dividends on historical information without considering the extent to which the past experience is expected to be reasonably predictive of future experience.

Expected Early Exercise

Employees often exercise share options early, for a variety of reasons. For example, employee share options are typically non-transferable. This often causes employees to exercise their share options early, because that is the only way for the employees to liquidate their position. Also, employees who cease employment are usually required to exercise any vested options within a short period of time, otherwise the share options are forfeited. This factor also causes the early exercise of employee share options. Other factors causing early exercise are risk aversion and lack of wealth diversification.

The means by which the effects of expected early exercise are taken into account depends upon the type of option pricing model applied. For example, expected early exercise could be taken into account by using an estimate of the option's expected life (which, for an employee share option, is the period of time from grant date to the date on which the option is expected to be exercised) as an input into an option pricing model (e.g. the Black-Scholes-Merton formula). Alternatively, expected early exercise could be modelled in a binomial or similar option pricing model that uses contractual life as an input.

Factors to consider in estimating early exercise include the:

(a) length of the vesting period, because the share option typically cannot be exercised until the end of the vesting period. Hence, determining the valuation implications of expected early exercise is based on the assumption that the options will vest;
(b) average length of time similar options have remained outstanding in the past;
(c) price of the underlying shares. Experience may indicate that the employees tend to exercise options when the share price reaches a specified level above the exercise price;
(d) employee's level within the organisation. For example, experience might indicate that higher-level employees tend to exercise options later than lower-level employees; and
(e) expected volatility of the underlying shares. On average, employees might tend to exercise options on highly volatile shares earlier than on shares with low volatility.

The effects of early exercise could be taken into account by using an estimate of the option's expected life as an input into an option pricing model. When estimating the expected life of share options granted to a group of employees, the entity could base that estimate on an appropriately weighted average expected life for the entire employee group or on appropriately weighted average lives for subgroups of employees within the group, based on more detailed data about employees' exercise behaviour (discussed further below).

Separating an option grant into groups for employees with relatively homogeneous exercise behaviour is likely to be important. Option value is not a linear function of option term; value increases at a decreasing rate as the term lengthens. For example, if all other assumptions are equal, although a two-year option is worth more than a one-year option, it is not worth twice as much. That means that calculating estimated option value on the basis of a single weighted average life that includes widely differing individual lives would overstate the total fair value of the share options granted. Separating options granted into several groups, each of which has a relatively narrow range of lives included in its weighted average life, reduces that overstatement.

Similar considerations apply when using a binomial or similar model. For example, the experience of an entity that grants options broadly to all levels of employees might indicate that top-level executives tend to hold their options longer than middle-management employees hold theirs and that lower-level employees tend to exercise their options earlier than any other group. In addition, employees who are encouraged or required to hold a minimum amount of their employer's equity instruments, including options, might on average exercise options later than employees not subject to that provision. In those situations, separating options by groups of recipients with relatively homogeneous exercise behaviour will result in a more accurate estimate of the total fair value of the share options granted.

Expected Volatility

Expected volatility is a measure of the amount by which a price is expected to fluctuate during a period. The measure of volatility used in option pricing models is the annualised standard deviation of the continuously compounded rates of return on the share over a period of time. Volatility is typically expressed in annualised terms that are comparable regardless of the time period used in the calculation, for example, daily, weekly or monthly price observations.

The rate of return (which may be positive or negative) on a share for a period measures how much a shareholder has benefited from dividends and appreciation (or depreciation) of the share price.

The expected annualised volatility of a share is the range within which the continuously compounded annual rate of return is expected to fall approximately two-thirds of the time. For example, to say that a share with an expected continuously compounded rate of return of 12% has a volatility of 30% means that the probability that the rate of return on the share for one year will be between -18% (12% − 30%) and 42% (12% + 30%) is approximately two-thirds. If the share price is €100 at the beginning of the year and no dividends are paid, the year-end share price would be expected to be between €83.53 (€100 × $e^{-0.18}$) and €152.20 (€100 × $e^{0.42}$) approximately two-thirds of the time.

Factors to consider in estimating expected volatility include:

(a) implied volatility from traded share options on the entity's shares, or other traded instruments of the entity that include option features (such as convertible debt), if any;

(b) the historical volatility of the share price over the most recent period that is generally commensurate with the expected term of the option (taking into account the remaining contractual life of the option and the effects of expected early exercise);

(c) the length of time an entity's shares have been publicly traded. A newly listed entity might have a high historical volatility, compared with similar entities that have been listed longer. Further guidance for newly listed entities is given below;

(d) the tendency of volatility to revert to its mean, i.e. its long-term average level, and other factors indicating that expected future volatility might differ from past volatility. For example, if an entity's share price was extraordinarily volatile for some identifiable period of time because of a failed takeover bid or a major restructuring, that period could be disregarded in computing historical average annual volatility; and

(e) appropriate and regular intervals for price observations. The price observations should be consistent from period to period. For example, an entity might use the closing price for each week or the highest price for the week, but it should not use the closing price for some weeks and the highest price for other weeks. Also, the price observations should be expressed in the same currency as the exercise price.

Newly Listed Entities

An entity should consider historical volatility of the share price over the most recent period that is generally commensurate with the expected option term. If a newly listed entity does not have sufficient information on historical volatility, it should nevertheless compute historical volatility for the longest period for which trading activity is available. It could also consider the historical volatility of similar entities following a comparable period in their lives. For example, an entity that has been listed for only one year and grants options with an average expected life of five years might consider the pattern and level of historical volatility of entities in the same industry for the first six years in which the shares of those entities were publicly traded.

Unlisted Entities

An unlisted entity will not have historical information to consider when estimating expected volatility. Some factors to consider instead are set out below. In some cases, an unlisted entity that regularly issues options or shares to employees (or other parties) might have set up an internal market for its shares. The volatility of those share prices could be considered when estimating expected volatility.

Alternatively, the entity could consider the historical or implied volatility of similar listed entities, for which share price or option price information is available, to use when estimating expected volatility. This would be appropriate if the entity has based the value of its shares on the share prices of similar listed entities.

If the entity has not based its estimate of the value of its shares on the share prices of similar listed entities, and has instead used another valuation methodology to value its shares, the entity could derive an estimate of expected volatility consistent with that valuation methodology. For example, the entity might value its shares on a net asset or earnings basis. It could consider the expected volatility of those net asset values or earnings.

Expected Dividends

Whether expected dividends should be taken into account when measuring the fair value of shares or options granted depends on whether the counter-party is entitled to dividends or dividend equivalents. For example, if employees were granted options and are entitled to dividends on the underlying shares or dividend equivalents (which might be paid in cash or applied to reduce the exercise price) between grant date and exercise date, the options granted should be valued as if no dividends will be paid on the underlying shares, i.e. the input for expected dividends should be zero.

Similarly, when the grant date fair value of shares granted to employees is estimated, no adjustment is required for expected dividends if the employee is entitled to receive dividends paid during the vesting period.

Conversely, if the employees are not entitled to dividends or dividend equivalents during the vesting period (or before exercise, in the case of an option), the grant date valuation of the rights to shares or options should take expected dividends into account. That is to say, when the fair value of an option grant is estimated, expected dividends should be included in the application of an option pricing model. When the fair value of a share grant is estimated, that valuation should be reduced by the present value of dividends expected to be paid during the vesting period.

Option pricing models generally call for expected dividend yield. However, the models may be modified to use an expected dividend amount rather than a yield. An entity may use either its expected yield or its expected payments. If the entity uses the latter, it should consider its historical pattern of increases in dividends. For example, if an entity's policy has generally been to increase dividends by approximately 3% per year, its estimated option value should not assume a fixed dividend amount throughout the option's life unless there is evidence that supports that assumption.

Generally, the assumption about expected dividends should be based on publicly available information. An entity that does not pay dividends and has no plans to do so should assume an expected dividend yield of zero. However, an emerging entity with no history of paying dividends might expect to begin paying dividends during the expected lives of its employee share options. Those entities could use an average of their past dividend yield (zero) and the mean dividend yield of an appropriately comparable peer group.

Risk-free Interest Rate

Typically, the risk-free interest rate is the implied yield currently available on zero-coupon government issues of the country in whose currency the exercise price is expressed, with a remaining term equal to the expected term of the option being valued (based on the option's remaining contractual life and taking into account the effects of expected early exercise). It may be necessary to use an appropriate substitute, if no such government issues exist or circumstances indicate that the implied yield on zero-coupon government issues is not representative of the risk-free interest rate (for example, in high inflation economies). Also, an appropriate substitute should be used if market participants would typically determine the risk-free interest rate by using that substitute, rather than the implied yield of zero-coupon government issues, when estimating the fair value of an option with a life equal to the expected term of the option being valued.

Capital Structure Effects

Typically, third parties, not the entity, write traded share options. When these share options are exercised, the writer delivers shares to the option holder. Those shares are acquired from existing shareholders. Hence the exercise of traded share options has no dilutive effect.

In contrast, if share options are written by the entity, new shares are issued when those share options are exercised (either actually issued or issued in substance, if shares previously repurchased and held in treasury are used). Given that the shares will be issued at the exercise price rather than the current market price at the date of exercise, this actual or potential dilution might reduce the share price, so that the option holder does not make as large a gain on exercise as on exercising an otherwise similar traded option that does not dilute the share price. Whether this has a significant effect on the value of the share options granted depends on various factors, such as the number of new shares that will be issued on exercise of the options compared with the number of shares already issued. Also, if the market already expects that the option grant will take place, the market may have already factored the potential dilution into the share price at the date of grant.

However, the entity should consider whether the possible dilutive effect of the future exercise of the share options granted might have an impact on their estimated fair value at grant date. Option pricing models can be adapted to take into account this potential dilutive effect.

INTERIM FINANCIAL REPORTING

An interim financial report is a financial report containing either a complete set of financial statements or a set of condensed financial statements for a financial reporting period shorter than a full financial year. IAS 34 *Interim Financial Reporting* prescribes the minimum content of an interim financial report and the principles for recognition and measurement in any interim financial statements. IAS 34 does not specify which entities must publish interim financial reports, how frequently or how soon after the end of an interim period. Those are matters that are usually specified by law or regulation. However, entities that are required or choose to publish interim financial reports in accordance with IASs must apply IAS 34.

IAS 34 is not mandatory but instead strongly recommends to regulators that interim financial reporting should be a requirement for publicly traded securities. Specifically they are encouraged to:

- publish an interim report for at least the first six months of their financial year; and
- make the report available no later than 60 days after the end of the interim report.

Content of an Interim Financial Report

IAS 34 defines the minimum content of an interim report which should contain condensed financial statements together with selected explanatory notes but it should focus on new activities and events. Obviously entities can disclose the following minimum content, if they wish:

(a) Condensed statement of financial position;
(b) Condensed statement of comprehensive income;

(c) Condensed statement of all changes in equity or changes in equity other than those arising from capital transactions with owners and distributions to owners;

(d) Condensed statement of cash flows; and

(e) Selected explanatory notes.

The condensed statements should include each of the headings and subtotals that were included in its most recent annual financial statements. Additional line items should be included if their omission would make the condensed interim statements misleading.

Basic and diluted EPS should be presented on the face of a statement of comprehensive income for an interim period.

IAS 34 is not concerned with relatively minor changes from its most recent annual financial statements. However, the notes to the interim report should include the following information (unless the information is contained elsewhere in the report):

(a) A statement that the same accounting policies and methods of computation are followed in the interim statements as compared with the most recent annual statements or, if changed, a description of the nature and effect of the change;

(b) Explanatory comments about the seasonality or cyclicality of interim operations;

(c) The nature and amount of unusual items affecting assets, liabilities, incomes and expenses because of their nature, size or incidence;

(d) The nature and amount of changes in estimates of amounts reported in prior interim periods of the current financial year on changes in estimates of amounts reported in prior financial years, it those changes have a material effect in the current interim period;

(e) The issue or repurchase of equity or debt securities;

(f) Dividends paid, separately for ordinary and other shares;

(g) Segmental results for primary basis, i.e. geographical or business;

(h) Material events since the end of the interim period;

(i) Effect of business combinations during the interim report; and

(j) Changes in contingent liabilities or contingent assets since last annual reporting date.

Examples of the above include:

• Write-down of inventories to NRV and reversals;
• Acquisitions, disposals, impairments of property, plant etc. and reversals;
• Litigation settlements;
• Corrections of fundamental errors; and
• Related party transactions.

Disclosure of Compliance

If the interim report is in compliance with IAS 34, that fact should be disclosed.

Periods Covered

• A statement of financial position at the end of the current interim period, and a comparative statement of financial position as of the end of the most recent full financial year;

- Statements of comprehensive income for the current interim period and cumulatively for the current financial year to date, with comparative statements of comprehensive income for the comparable interim periods of the immediately preceding financial year;
- A statement of changes in equity cumulatively for the current financial year to date, and a comparative statement for the comparable year-to-date period of the prior year; and
- A statement of cash flows cumulatively for the current financial year to date, and a comparative statement for the comparable year-to-date period of the prior financial year.

Materiality

Materiality should be assessed in relation to the interim period financial data. It should be recognised that interim measurements rely to a greater extent on estimates than annual financial data.

Disclosure in Annual Financial Statements

If an estimate of an amount reported in an interim report is changed significantly during the final interim report, but if a separate financial report is not published for that period, the nature and amount of that change in estimate should be disclosed in a note to the annual financial statements for that financial year.

Recognition and Measurement

1. **Same Accounting Policies as Annual** – the same accounting policies should be adopted in the interim as are applied in the annual statements, except for accounting policy changes made after the date of the most recent annual financial statements that will be reflected in the next set of annual statements. The guiding principle for recognition and measurement is that an enterprise should use the same recognition and measurement principles in its interim statements as it does in its annual financial statements, e.g. a cost would not be classified as an asset in the interim report if it would not be classified as such in the annual report.
2. **Revenues Received Occasionally, Seasonally or Cyclically** – revenue which is received occasionally or seasonally should not be anticipated or deferred in interim reports. The principles of revenue recognition should be applied consistently to interim and annual reports.
3. **Costs Incurred Unevenly During the Financial Year** – these should only be anticipated or deferred if it would be appropriate to anticipate or defer the expense in the annual financial statements. It would be inappropriate to anticipate part of the cost of a major advertising campaign later in the year for which no expenses have yet been incurred.

Examples of Application of Recognition and Measurement Principles

Employer payroll taxes and insurance contributions – in some countries these are assessed on an annual basis but paid at an uneven rate during the year. It is therefore appropriate, in this situation, to adopt an estimated average annual tax rate for the year in an interim statement, not the actual tax paid. Taxes are an annual assessment but payment is uneven.

Cost of a planned major periodic overhaul – the cost of such an event must not be anticipated unless there is a legal or constructive obligation to carry out the work. A mere intention to carry out work later in the year is not sufficient justification to create a liability.

Year-end bonus – this should not be provided in the interim report unless there is a constructive obligation to pay such a bonus and it can be reliably measured.

Intangible asset – IAS 34 must follow IAS 38 *Intangible assets* and thus it would be inappropriate in an interim report to defer a cost in the expectation that it will eventually be part of a non-monetary intangible asset that has not yet been recognised.

Holiday pay – if holiday pay is an enforceable obligation on the employer, then any unpaid accumulated holiday pay may be accrued in the interim report.

Tax on income – an expense for tax should be included in the interim report and the tax rate should be the estimated average annual tax rate for the year.

Example

Assume a quarterly reporting entity expects to earn €10,000 pre-tax each quarter and operates in a tax jurisdiction with a tax rate of 20% on the first €20,000 and 30% on all additional earnings. Actual earnings match expectations. The tax reported in each quarter is as follows:

- Tax expense: €2,500; €2,500; €2,500; €2,500; Total €10,000.
- Total earnings estimate: €40,000 (€20,000 x 20%) = €4,000 + €20,000 x 30% = €6,000 i.e. €10,000 / 4 = €2,500.

Assume a quarterly reporting entity expects to earn €15,000 pre-tax in Q1 but losses of €5,000 in Q2-4. The tax rate is still 20%. The tax reported in each quarter is as follows:

- Tax expense: €3,000; (€1,000); (€1,000); (€1,000) = €Nil.

Assume year end 30 June and taxable year end 31 December. Assume pre-tax earnings €10,000 each quarter and average tax rate 30% year 1 and 40% year 2.

- Tax expense: €3,000; €3,000; €4,000; €4,000 – €14,000.

Some countries give enterprises tax credits against the tax payable based on amounts of capital expenditure on research and development. These are usually awarded on an annual basis thus it is appropriate to include anticipated tax credits within the estimated average tax rate for the year and apply it to calculate the tax on income for interim periods. However, if it relates to a one-off event it should be recognised in the interim period in which the event occurs.

Inventory valuations – should be valued in the same way as for year end accounts but it will be necessary to rely more heavily on estimates for interim reports.

Depreciation – should only be charged in the interim statement on assets that have been owned during the period but not on assets that will be acquired later in the financial year.

Foreign currency translation gains and losses – should be calculated using the same principles at the end of the year in accordance with IAS 21.

Use of Estimates

Although accounting information must be reliable and free from material error it may be necessary to sacrifice some accuracy and reliability for the sake of timeliness and cost benefits. This is particularly the case in interim reporting where estimates must be used to a greater extent in interim reporting.
Some examples are:

(a) **Inventories** – no need for full inventory count but sufficient to estimate inventory values using sales margins. Inventories based on LIFO can be estimated by taking a representative sample from each 'layer' of inventory and applying inflation indices;

(b) **Provisions** – inappropriate to bear cost of experts to advise on the appropriate amount of a provision or an expert valuer to value fixed assets at the interim date; and

(c) **Income taxes** – sufficient to apply an estimated weighted average tax rate to income earned in all jurisdictions. No need to calculate the tax rate in each country separately.

INSURANCE CONTRACTS

There is a rebuttable presumption that an insurer's financial statements will become less relevant and reliable if it introduces an accounting policy that reflects future investment margins in the measurement of insurance contracts. When an insurer changes its accounting policies for insurance liabilities, it may reclassify some or all financial assets as 'at fair value through profit or loss'.
IFRS 4 *Insurance Contracts* specifies the following:

- An entity need not account for an embedded derivative separately at fair value if the embedded derivative meets the definition of an insurance contract;

- An entity is required to unbundle (i.e. account separately for) deposit components of some insurance contracts;
- An entity may apply 'shadow accounting' (that is, account for both realised and unrealised gains or losses on assets in the same way relative to measurement of insurance liabilities); and
- Discretionary participation features contained in insurance contracts or financial instruments may be recognised separately from the guaranteed element and classified as a liability or as a separate component of equity.

IFRS 4 also specifies disclosures about:

- The amounts in the entity's financial statements that arise from insurance contracts; and
- The amount, timing and uncertainty of future cash flows from insurance contracts.

EXPLORATION FOR AND EVALUATION OF MINERAL RESOURCES

IFRS 6 *Exploration for and Evaluation of Mineral Resources* permits an entity to develop an accounting policy for exploration and evaluation assets without specifically considering the requirements of paragraphs 11 and 12 of IAS 8 *Accounting Policies, Changes in Accounting Estimates and Errors*. Thus, an entity adopting IFRS 6 may continue to use the accounting policies applied immediately before adopting the IFRS. This includes continuing to use recognition and measurement practices that are part of those accounting policies.

IFRS 6 requires entities recognising exploration and evaluation assets to perform an impairment test on those assets when facts and circumstances suggest that the carrying amount of the assets may exceed their recoverable amount. IFRS 6 varies the recognition of impairment from that in IAS 36 *Impairment of Assets* but measures the impairment in accordance with that Standard once the impairment is identified.

IFRS 6 requires disclosure of information that identifies and explains the amounts recognised in its financial statements arising from the exploration for and evaluation of mineral resources, including:

- its accounting policies for exploration and evaluation expenditures including the recognition of exploration and evaluation assets; and
- the amounts of assets, liabilities, income and expense and operating and investing cash flows arising from the exploration for and evaluation of mineral resources.

ACCOUNTING AND REPORTING BY RETIREMENT BENEFIT PLANS

IAS 26 *Accounting and Reporting by Retirement Benefit Plans* applies to the financial statements of retirement benefit plans. Retirement benefit plans are arrangements whereby an entity provides benefits for employees on or after termination of service when such benefits, or the contributions towards them, can be determined or estimated in advance of retirement from the provisions of a document or from the entity's practices.

The financial statements of a defined contribution plan contain a statement of net assets available for benefits and a description of the funding policy. The financial statements of a defined benefit plan contain either:

- a statement that shows:
  - the net assets available for benefits;
  - the actuarial present value of promised retirement benefits, distinguishing between vested and non-vested benefits; and
  - the resulting excess or deficit; or
- a statement of net assets available for benefits including either:
  - a note disclosing the actuarial present value of promised retirement benefits, distinguishing between vested and non-vested benefits; or
  - a reference to this information in an accompanying actuarial report.

The actuarial present value of promised retirement benefits is based on the benefits promised under the terms of the plan on service rendered to date using either current salary levels or projected salary levels. Retirement benefit plan investments are carried at fair value.

IAS 26 specifies disclosures in the financial statements of retirement benefit plans.

CHAPTER 35

ANALYSIS AND INTERPRETATION OF FINANCIAL INFORMATION

INTRODUCTION

Many of the previous chapters have concentrated upon how financial statements are prepared, including their features and contents. This chapter considers the significance of the figures contained in the financial statements. For example, if you were to look at the statement of financial position or statement of comprehensive income how would you decide:

- whether the company was doing well or badly?
- whether it was financially strong or financially vulnerable? and
- what would you be looking at in the figures to help you make your judgement?

This chapter addresses the following areas:

- analysis of financial statements and the use of ratios;
- categories and calculation of ratios;
- financial balance and overtrading; and
- accounting policies and the limitations of ratio analysis.

Having studied this chapter on the analysis and interpretation of financial information, you should be able to:

- calculate the main ratios and statistics commonly used in interpreting accounts; and
- produce reports analysing results over time or between activities.

ANALYSIS OF FINANCIAL STATEMENTS AND USE OF RATIOS

Ratio analysis is a tool used by entities in the analysis and interpretation of financial statements. By definition, a ratio expresses the relationship between two or more figures. On this basis, ratios are only meaningful when:

- calculated correctly;
- compared with similar ratios on an:
  - internal basis (company statistics); and
  - external basis (Industry statistics).

When comparing ratios it is important to compare 'like with like'. Therefore, any exceptional items or one-time charges need to be excluded from the calculations for comparison purposes.

Example

Company X began trading in 1994. Due to significant growth in the first 3 years, company X engaged in an aggressive acquisition policy in 1998. This led to €100,000 of one-time charges on a total net profit before tax of €50,000. Shareholders equity amounted to €1,500,000.

In this scenario, Return on Capital Employed (ROCE) before one-time charges would be 10%, whilst after would be 3.33%. When comparing 1998 ratios to past years or to industry averages, it is therefore important to compare ROCE before one-time charges as these are not standard costs.

However, notwithstanding the fact that ratios are only meaningful when compared to similar calculations, ratio analysis can be a useful tool. For example:

Internally, ratios can be used to compare:

- past performance; and
- actual results versus budgets and forecasts.

Externally, ratios may be used to compare:

- similar entities at the same stage of development; and
- entities within the same industry.

What Information does a User Require?

The various users of financial statements require information for quite different purposes. There are a large number of ratios, not all of which will be relevant to a particular situation. It is therefore important to determine the precise information needs of the user and the decisions he has to take after analysing the relevant information.

Ask yourself the questions 'What decision is being made?' and 'What information is relevant to that decision?'

Categories of Ratios

Ratios can be classified into three main groups:

- **Profitability** – this reflects the performance of company and its managers including the efficiency of asset usage;
- **Financial** – this reflects the financial structure and stability of the company; and
- **Investment** – this reflects the relationship of the number of ordinary shares and their price to the profits, dividends and assets of the company

The managers of the company are likely to be concerned about all aspects of the company and therefore may want to know about all of the key ratios in each category. Shareholders or potential investors are concerned primarily with the investment ratios although certain financial stability and profitability measures are also likely to be of interest. Creditors are most likely to be concerned about financial stability, although a bank, acting as a major source of finance, will usually also look at profitability.

Other Sources of Information

Ratio analysis on its own is not sufficient for interpreting company accounts. There are other items of information which should be looked at, such as:

- comments in the Chairman's Report and Directors' Report;
- the age and nature of the company's assets;
- current and future developments in the company's markets, at home and overseas, including recent acquisitions or disposals of a subsidiary by the company;
- any other noticeable features of the report and accounts, such as events after the reporting period, contingent liabilities, a qualified auditor's report, the company's taxation position etc; and
- any relevant government legislation.

CATEGORIES AND CALCULATION OF RATIOS

Main Categories of Ratios

Ratios can be classified or divided into many different categories. In the next six subsections, ratios will be considered under their six main headings as follows: Profitability; Liquidity; Efficiency; Growth; Investment; and Cash Flow.

Profitability

Profitability ratios need to be looked at in conjunction with liquidity (see below). Profitability ratios show the relationship between profitability and revenue. The ratios to be considered are as follows: Gross Profit on Revenue (also called gross margin); Net Profit on Revenue (also called net margin); and Contribution to Revenue.

Gross Profit on Revenue (also called Gross Margin) – This ratio is shown as a percentage and is the margin that the company makes on its sales. It indicates the efficiency of the production department as well as the pricing policy of the business. The formula is:

$$\frac{\text{Gross Profit}}{\text{Revenue}} \times 100$$

The ratio is expected to remain reasonably constant. Since the ratio consists of a small number of components, a change may be traced to changes in:

(a) *selling prices* – normally deliberate although sometimes unavoidable, for example because of increased competition;
(b) *sales mix* – often deliberate;
(c) *purchase cost* – including carriage or discounts;
(d) *production cost* – materials, labour or production overheads; and
(e) *inventory* – errors in counting, valuing or cut-off: inventory shortages.

Inter-company comparison of margins can be very useful but it is especially important to look at businesses within the same sector. For example, food retailing is able to support low margins because of the high volume of sales. A manufacturing industry would usually have higher margins.

Low margins usually suggest poor performance, inefficiency of operations and/or a poor pricing policy but may be due to expansion costs (launching a new product) or trying to increase market share. Lower margins than usual suggest scope for improvement. However, one has to take into account the type of business involved. In the supermarket trade one will find a high inventory turnover and low gross margins. By contrast, in the jewellery trade there would be low inventory turnover and high gross margins. If there are a number of products manufactured, it would be necessary to obtain different figures for the different products in order to assess individual product margins. As a rule of thumb, there is an inverse relationship between the gross profit percentage and the inventory turnover.

Above average margins are usually a sign of good management although unusually high margins may make the competition keen to join in and enjoy the 'rich pickings'.

Net Profit on Revenue (also called Net Margin) – This ratio indicates the relative efficiency of the organisation with reference to trading overheads. It is calculated after deducting all expenses but usually before interest and taxation. The formula is:

$$\frac{\text{Profit Before Interest \& Taxation}}{\text{Revenue}} \times 100$$

This ratio is affected by more factors than the gross profit margin but it is equally useful and if the company does not disclose a cost of sales it may be used on its own in lieu of the GP%.

One of the many factors affecting the trading profit margin is depreciation, which is open to considerable subjective judgement. Inter-company comparisons should be made after suitable adjustments to align accounting policies. The percentage will vary significantly from industry to industry and averages are important. A change in either the gross or net margins is a sign that a more detailed analysis should be undertaken of the possible causal factors. This might include an investigation of:

(a) Material cost to revenue;
(b) Direct labour cost to revenue;
(c) Production overheads to revenue;
(d) Administration cost to revenue; and
(e) Selling and distribution cost to revenue.

Contribution to Revenue – This reveals what sales figures must be achieved before an organisation can break even. The higher the ratio, the quicker a firm covers its fixed costs and is making profits. The formula is:

$$\frac{\text{Revenue less Variable Costs}}{\text{Revenue}}$$

A low ratio might indicate that a reduction in revenue could easily lead to a loss-making situation and hence a company would need to examine costs of sales policy quickly to prevent becoming a loss maker.

Liquidity

Liquidity is the measure of how accessible the company's cash is. The importance of liquidity to businesses cannot be overestimated. Both profitability and liquidity need to be examined individually and may often show a very weak relationship. Profitable organisations may suffer from liquidity problems that could be fatal; whilst less profitable businesses might survive or blossom because of better liquidity management. Profitability without liquidity is not enough to ensure survival.

Each of the four main liquidity ratios should now be considered in turn: Current or Working Capital Ratio; Acid Test or Quick Ratio; Receivables Ratio; and Payables Ratio.

Current Ratio (Working Capital Ratio)

$$\frac{\text{Current assets}}{\text{Current liabilities}}$$

The current ratio measures the adequacy of current assets to meet its short-term liabilities. It reflects whether the company is in a position to meet its liabilities as they fall due.

Traditionally a current ratio of 2 or higher was regarded as appropriate for most businesses to maintain creditworthiness, however, more recently a figure of 1.5 is regarded as the norm.

This ratio essentially shows the net liquid position of a company over the next 12 months. A current ratio in the region of 1.8:1 to 2:1 is generally considered acceptable.

However, it is important to note that this is only a guide and may be different from industry to industry. It is important for a company to have a relatively high current ratio as inventory is usually the biggest current asset and this may not be converted easily into cash. This is why the current ratio should always be calculated in conjunction with the acid test ratio (see below).

If a company is showing an excessive current ratio, the question may be asked, are too many liquid funds tied up in assets, indicating poor financial management. A higher figure should be regarded with suspicion as it may be due to:

(a) high levels of inventory and receivables (check working capital management ratios); or
(b) high cash levels which could be put to better use (for example by investing in non-current assets).

The current ratio should be looked at in the light of what is normal for the business. For example, supermarkets tend to have low current ratios because:

(a) there are no trade receivables; and
(b) there is usually very tight cash control as there will be considerable investment in developing new sites and improving sites.

It is also worth considering:

(a) *Availability of further finance* – for example is the overdraft at the limit? Very often this information is highly relevant but not disclosed in the accounts;
(b) *Seasonal nature of the business* – one way of doing this is to compare the interest charges in the statement of comprehensive income with the overdraft and other loans in the statement of financial position; if the interest rate appears abnormally high this is probably because the company has had higher levels of borrowings during the year;
(c) *Nature of the inventory* – as stated above where inventory is slow moving, the quick ratio probably provides a better indicator of short-term liquidity.

Acid Test or Quick ratio

$$\frac{\text{Current assets} - \text{inventory}}{\text{Current liabilities}}$$

This ratio provides an indication of the immediate liquid position of a business, i.e. by eliminating inventory from current assets it provides the acid test of whether the company has sufficient resources (receivables and cash) to settle its liabilities. The generally accepted ratio is 1:1, or perhaps a little less, depending on the type of business and the relationship with the payables. Norms for the quick ratio range from 1 to 0.7. Again, however, this is only a guide and should only be used as such. Like the current ratio it is relevant to consider the nature of the business (again supermarkets have very low quick ratios). Considerable differences will be found amongst various types of businesses. This is because of the fact that the ratio is not a precise measure of liquidity and is liable to be influenced by debt collection and credit payment periods, which will vary considerably between industries. It is important to always calculate the current ratio in conjunction with the acid test ratio. This is an effective tool to highlight any potential inventory problems. A high current ratio, but a low acid test ratio, could indicate excessive inventory holdings, which could lead to concerns of obsolescence and slow-moving inventory.

Sometimes the quick ratio is calculated on the basis of a six-week time frame (i.e., the quick assets are those which will turn into cash in six weeks; quick liabilities are those which fall due for payment within six weeks). This basis would usually include the following in quick assets:

(a) bank, cash and short term investments; and
(b) trade receivables.

Thus excluding prepayments and inventory, quick liabilities would usually include:

- bank overdraft which is usually repayable on demand;
- trade payables, tax and social security; and
- Dividends approved but still unpaid.

Corporation tax may be excluded.

When interpreting the quick ratio, care should be taken over the status of the bank overdraft. A company with a low quick ratio may actually have no problem in paying its payables if sufficient overall overdraft facilities are available.

Both the current and quick ratio may be distorted by *window dressing*; for example, if the current ratio is 1.4 and trade payables are paid just before the year end out of positive cash balances, the ratios improve as shown below:

	Before	Repayment of €400 trade payables	After
Current assets	€1,400	–€400	€1,000
Current liabilities	€1,000	–€400	€600
Current ratio	1.4		1.7

It is important to look at the limitations of the liquidity ratios:

1. They do not take into account any unutilised credit facilities, which may be available to the company in times of cash shortage. Therefore, it is useful to look for any mention of an unused draw down facility or bank overdraft limit. Whilst this does not come into the ratio calculation, it may be important for commentary purposes; and
2. They are static ratios whereas liquidity is an ever-changing area. A firm whose liquidity ratio is less than 1:1 would like to know how quickly it could reinstate itself to an acceptable position without taking drastic action. An indication of this would be revealed by the following formula:

$$\frac{\text{Current Liabilities} - \text{Liquid Assets}}{\text{Cash Flow in Normal Trading Year}} \times 365$$

In considering the liquidity ratio (and indeed the current ratio) it should also be borne in mind that these ratios should only account for short term liquidity. Therefore:

3. While a bank overdraft is legally repayable on demand, in substance it may be more in the nature of medium-term financing and could be excluded from the calculation of the liquidity ratio; and
4. Among the current assets there may be short-term investments which represent funds set aside for future capital investment in the organisation. It may be that these should not be looked upon as being applicable to the payment of current liabilities and accordingly, should perhaps be excluded from the calculation of the acid test ratio.

Receivables Ratio (alternatively called average collection period or receivables days)

$$\frac{\text{Trade Receivables}}{\text{Credit Sales (VAT inclusive)}} \times 100\%$$

$$\frac{\text{Trade Receivables}}{\text{Credit Sales (VAT inclusive)}} \times 365$$

This can be expressed as a percentage or as a number of days.

The trade receivables used may be a year-end figure or the average for the year. Where an average is used to calculate a number of days the ratio is the average number of days' credit taken by customers. Similarly, where separate credit sales figures are not available, then it may be necessary to use the total revenue figure. Whichever approach is adopted, it is important that it is applied constantly.

Where sales are seasonal in nature, it may be misleading to use the receivables figure at the accounting date. A more appropriate figure to use may be the average of the balances at the end of each month of the trading period. Where there has been a significant increase in sales towards the end of the period, the average of the opening and closing receivables balances of the trading period would reflect more accurately the substance of the situation. Otherwise, the receivables balances at the accounting date would be misleadingly high when compared to revenue.

An excessive receivables ratio is indicative of poor credit control or even a sign of over-trading. Furthermore, it may indicate that an excessive amount of money is tied up in receivables; this consideration being particularly serious in an atmosphere of high interest rates. If the receivables ratio is considered excessive, the receivables should be 'aged' in order to gain a clear picture as to the true liquidity of the receivables. The ageing process highlights the specific areas for more detailed consideration.

For cash-based businesses such as supermarkets, receivables days are unlikely to exceed 1 as there are no true credit sales. Although this may vary slightly if a significant portion of customers pay by debit or credit card as there maybe a short delay before the business receives payment. For other businesses the result should be compared with the stated credit policy. Periods of 30 days or 'at the end of the month following delivery' are common credit terms.

Increasing receivables days is usually a bad sign as it suggests lack of proper credit control. However, it may be due to:

(a) a deliberate policy to extend the stated credit period to attract more trade; and
(b) one major new customer being allowed different terms.

Falling receivables days is usually a good sign, though it could indicate that the company is suffering a cash shortage. The receivables ratio can be distorted by:

(a) using year- end figures which do not represent average receivables;
(b) debt factoring which results in very low receivables; and
(c) other credit finance agreements such as hire purchase, where there is insufficient analysis of revenue (HP receivables should be shown separately) to calculate proper ratios.

Trade Payables Ratio (alternatively called average payment period or payables days)
This ratio expresses in days the average length of credit taken by the business in settling its debts with suppliers. The formula is:

$$\frac{\text{Trade Payables}}{\text{Credit Purchases of Raw Materials (VAT inclusive)}} \times 365$$

As with the receivables ratio considered above, with a seasonal or growing business some average rather than the accounting date balances should perhaps be used. Also, due to lack of analysis, it may be necessary to use total payables and total purchases figures. An average of trade payables may also be used. Where purchases are not known, cost of sales could be used.

If the receiver's ratio is too high, it may possibly imply a potential loss of goodwill and withdrawal of credit facilities from suppliers. It might also be indicative of liquidity problems.

The ratio is always compared to previous years. Once again there are two main contrasting points:

(a) A long credit period may be good as it represents a source of free finance; or
(b) A long credit period may indicate that the company is unable to pay more quickly because of liquidity problems.

Note that if the credit period is long:

(a) The company may develop a poor reputation as a slow payer and may not be able to find new suppliers;
(b) Existing suppliers may decide to discontinue supplies; and
(c) The company may be losing out on worthwhile cash discounts.

Efficiency

Efficiency is the overall measure of the company's effective use of assets. The ratios that indicate the level of efficiency of management in utilising its assets are as follows: Return on Capital Employed; Revenue to Non-current Assets; Revenue to Net Current Assets; Inventory Turnover; and Non-current Assets to Total Assets.

Return on Capital Employed (ROCE) (Primary Ratio) The absolute figure of profit earned is not, in itself, significant since the size of the business earning that profit may vary enormously. It is significant to consider the size of the profit figure relevant to the size of the business, size being expressed in terms of the quantity of capital employed by that business.

The ratio shows how efficiently a business is using its resources and, in general, an adequate return on capital employed is why the shareholders invest in the business. ROCE is a key ratio in assessing financial achievement. It reflects the earning power of the business operations. If the return is very low, the business may be better off realising its assets and investing the proceeds in a high interest bank account! (This may sound extreme, but should be considered particularly for a small, unprofitable business with valuable assets such as freehold property.) Furthermore a low return can easily become a loss if the business suffers a downturn.

The ratio in simple form is:

$$\frac{\text{Profit}}{\text{Capital employed}} \times 100\%$$

There are a number of varying definitions of capital and of the appropriate profit to use in measuring the return. It is important to use the correct capital calculation with the relevant profit calculation. In general, the calculation is defined as above, with the following definitions:

Profit	Capital Employed
Profit before tax and interest	Gross Assets = Non-current assets and current assets
Profit before tax and interest	Net assets = Gross assets less current liabilities
Profit after tax	Shareholders' capital = Total share capital and reserves
Profit after tax and preference dividends	Shareholders' equity capital = Ordinary share capital plus reserves

Which definition is used depends on the objective of the ratio. The first two would be used where one is interested in assessing the overall profitability of the business. Profit may be before or after tax. After tax is a more accurate reflection of profits (management should seek to minimise tax) however you will know that deferred tax provisions are likely to be subjective so profit before tax may be more objective. The final two provide an indication of the return to shareholders. For example, the last one is more relevant for existing or prospective shareholders than management.

While the return on capital employed ratio is effective in revealing levels of performance, it does not provide us with an indication as to the reasons for an increase or decline in profitability. This may be indicated by a sub-division of the return on capital employed ratio into two ratios as follows: Operating Profit ÷ Revenue; and Revenue ÷ Operating Assets Employed.

A change in the return on capital employed may be the result of a change in the profit per €1 of revenue or a change in the amount of revenue achieved per €1 invested. If there has been a significant change in the assets, it may be necessary to use an average figure rather than a year-end figure. Once calculated, ROCE should be compared with:

(a) *Previous years' figures* – provided there have been no changes in accounting policies, or suitable adjustments have been made to facilitate comparison (note however that the effect of not replacing non-current assets is that their value will decrease and ROCE will increase);

(b) *Company's target ROCE* – where the company's management has determined a target return as part of its budget procedure, consistent failure by a part of the business to meet the target may make it a target for disposal;

(c) *Cost of borrowings* – if the cost of borrowing is say 10% and ROCE 7% then further borrowings will reduce EPS unless the extra money can be used in areas where the ROCE is higher than the cost of borrowings; and

(d) *Other companies in same industry* – care is required in interpretation, since there may be:
   (i) different accounting policies, e.g. research and development expenditure, inventory valuation and depreciation;
   (ii) different ages of plant, where assets are written down to low book values the ROCE will appear high; and
   (iii) leased assets which may not appear in the statement of financial position at all.

Revenue to Non-current Assets

$$\frac{\text{Revenue}}{\text{Tangible non-current assets}}$$

This ratio indicates the amount of revenue achieved for each €1 invested in non-current assets. A high ratio reveals an efficient utilisation of non-current assets. A low ratio indicates the opposite; perhaps suggesting that there is spare capacity and that consideration needs to be given to the disposal of excess assets. It is important to examine the industry, which the entity operates in as this ratio will vary significantly. In a high manufacturing industry, this ratio is particularly important and you would expect this ratio to be high, indicating effective use of the non-current assets such as plant and machinery. Conversely, in a retail organisation such as a jeweller this ratio is not so important.

It is also important to look at the depreciation history of the non-current assets involved as, in a situation where there are old assets stated at historical cost and heavily depreciated, one might have an unrealistically high ratio. Furthermore, if there are occasional valuations carried out (as opposed to regular valuations) trends will be distorted when the valuations take place.

Revenue to Net Current Assets

$$\frac{\text{Revenue}}{\text{Net current assets}}$$

This ratio reveals how effectively the working capital is being utilised. A high ratio is normally indicative of a high level of efficiency. However, it could indicate liquidity problems as a result of over-trading. To examine this scenario, one would need to look at the growth of the company and take a subjective view as to how adequately the company is coping with the growth. As with the previous ratio, this is highly dependent on the industry, since retail companies may have very low receivables and inventory levels, generating significant sales per euro of working capital.

Inventory Turnover

$$\frac{\text{Inventory}}{\text{Materials Cost of Sales}} \times 365$$

This ratio expresses in days the amount of inventory in relation to cost of sales. In extreme circumstances where one cannot obtain a cost of sales, the revenue figure is used. This should not, however, weaken any trend analysis undertaken, provided the same ratio is used consistently over the years. A low number of days indicates that management is able to turn over inventory efficiently. A high ratio may indicate poor inventory control, resulting in excessive inventories and thus an excessive investment therein and perhaps also damaged or obsolete inventories. To investigate this further, this ratio should perhaps be examined in conjunction with the current ratio and the acid test ratio. Where inventories have built up abnormally at the accounting date, then an average inventory figure should be used.

An alternative is to express this ratio as:

$$\frac{\text{Cost of Sales}}{\text{Inventory}} \times \text{times p.a.}$$

This yields a multiple expressed as, say, 10 times per annum. If format 2 is used, then simply compare turnover and inventory, though bear in mind that this is also affected by the margin achieved by the company. Sometimes an average (based on the average inventory) is calculated which has a smoothing effect but may dampen the effect of a major change in the period.

An increasing number of days (or a diminished multiple) implies that inventory is turning over less quickly. This is usually regarded as a bad sign as it may:

(a) reflect lack of demand for the goods;
(b) reflect poor inventory control, with its associated costs such as storage and insurance; and
(c) ultimately lead to inventory obsolescence and related write offs.

However, it may not necessarily be bad where:

(a) management are buying inventory in larger quantities to take advantage of trade discounts;

(b) management have increase inventory levels to avoid inventory outs; and

(c) the increase is slight and due to distortion of the ratio caused by comparing a year-end inventory figure with cost of sales for the year and that year has been one of increasing growth.

Inventory turnover ratios vary enormously with the nature of the business. For example, a fishmonger would have an inventory turnover period of 1 to 2 days, whereas a building contractor may have an inventory turnover period of 200 days. Manufacturing companies may have a inventory turnover ratio of 60 to 100 days: this period is likely to increase as the goods made become larger and more complex.

For large and complex items (for example rolling inventory or aircraft) there may be sharp fluctuations in inventory turnover according to whether delivery took place just before or just after the year end. A manufacturer should take into consideration:

(a) Reliability of suppliers – if the supplier is unreliable it is prudent to hold more raw materials; and

(b) Demand – if demand is erratic it is prudent to hold more finished goods.

Non-current Assets to Total Assets Non-current assets generate profits and in a manufacturing industry a high ratio is desirable. Before any interpretation is placed on the ratio, the following factors should be borne in mind:

(a) Investment in non-current assets depends on the nature of the business; a service industry would have much smaller non-current asset needs than a heavy manufacturing or engineering industry;

(b) The policy of the business with regard to leasing (particularly where leased assets are not accounted for under substance over form) and hiring might influence the statement of financial position movements; and

(c) Non-current assets are purchased with a view to future revenues; in the early stages of the life of a business, one might find high amounts invested in non-current assets. Therefore, it is important to always look at the stage of development of the company.

Growth

In interpreting the extent of a company's growth, the following areas would be examined:

- Revenue;
- Profit before tax;
- Non-current assets; and
- Total capital employed.

Movement in any of these areas needs to be considered in conjunction with all of the other areas. For example, an increase in revenue may explain the increase in current assets (receivables) and hence capital employed.

Investment

The following ratios are those which an actual or potential investor might use in assessing a company for investment purposes: Earnings per Share; Earnings Yield; Dividend Yield; Dividend Cover; Price Earnings Ratio; Gearing Ratio; Debt Ratio; and Interest to Earnings Ratio. Each of those ratios should now be considered in turn.

Earnings per Share – The calculation of EPS was covered in Section Four, Chapter 23. The EPS is used primarily as a measure of profitability thus an increasing EPS is seen as a good sign. The EPS is also used to calculate the price earnings ratio which is dealt with below. The limitations of EPS include

(a) In times of rising prices EPS will increase as profits increase. Thus any improvement in EPS should be viewed in the context of the effect of price level changes on the company's profits;

(b) Where there is a new share issue, the shares are included for, say, half of the year on the grounds that earnings will also increase for half of the year. However, in practice a new project does not begin generating normal returns immediately, so a new share issue is often accompanied by a decrease in EPS;

(c) EPS is dependent on an earnings figure which is a subjective measure. Some elements of that earnings figure are particularly subjective, such as the movements on provisions;

(d) EPS cannot be used as a basis of comparison between companies as the number of shares in issue in any particular company is not related to the amount of capital employed. For example, two companies may have the same amount of capital employed but one company has 100,000 €1 shares in issue and reserves of €4,900,000. Another company may have 5 million 50 cents shares in issue and reserves of €2,500,000. If earnings are the same, EPS is different;

(e) EPS is an historical figure based on historic accounts. This is a disadvantage where it is used for a forward looking figure such as the price earnings ratio. This is considered below; and

(f) The fully diluted EPS (FDEPS) is a theoretical measure of the effect of dilution on the basic EPS. There is no evidence to suggest that even the most sophisticated analysts use the FDEPS. This is because of its hypothetical nature. However, the FDEPS should serve as a warning to equity shareholders that their future earnings will be affected by diluting factors. Thus notes in the accounts relating to convertible loan stock, convertible preference shares and share options should all be analysed carefully.

Earnings Yield – This shows the return on the market price of a share. It is calculated as follows:

$$\frac{\text{Earnings per Share}}{\text{Market Price per Share}} \times 100$$

It is the reciprocal of the price earnings ratio which is discussed below in detail.

Dividend Yield – This shows the income return on an investment expressed as a percentage. It is calculated as follows:

$$\frac{\text{Gross Dividend per Share}}{\text{Market Price per Share}} \times 100$$

It allows for comparison between the return on an investment and the available return on investments in other shares, or in other forms of investment. The yield indicates the risks involved in the investment as estimated by the stock market. Where risks are said to be high, the investors will seek a high dividend yield to compensate for the risks. A low dividend yield means that the market accepts the low current return on its investment in anticipation of future expansion and profit growth. Overall, however, the yields will vary with the overall state of the stock market. Where share market prices are low, dividend yield will be high and vice versa.

Dividend Cover – This is the relationship between available profits and the dividends payable out of the profits, the dividends beings calculated on a maximum distribution basis. The *Financial Times* adjusts profits to exclude non-trading profits and losses. This ratio indicates the number of times the ordinary dividend is covered by profits attributable to the ordinary shareholders. The formula is:

$$\frac{\text{Profit after Taxation and Preference Dividend}}{\text{Ordinary Dividend}}$$

It indicates potential for increased dividends in the future, assuming that current profits are maintained. It also shows to what level profits can decline before a reduction in dividends is enforced. However, it should be noted that in anticipating future dividends, other factors, such as cash flow, capital structure and capital expenditure should be taken into account.

Note that the numerator profit figure is that which is available to the ordinary shareholders as a dividend and thus would be stated after minority interests.

Price Earnings Ratio – This is the most widely referred to stock market ratio, also commonly described as an earnings multiple. It is calculated as the 'purchase of a number of years' earnings' but it represents the market's consensus of the future prospects of that share. This is the relationship between the market price of a share and the earnings per share. The formula is:

$$\frac{\text{Market Price per Share}}{\text{Earnings per Share}}$$

The price earnings ratio shows the number of times earnings a shareholder is willing to pay in order to purchase the shares. A high price earnings ratio is indicative that the market has expectations of large growth potential for that company. Correspondingly, the lower the price earnings ratio then the lower the expected future growth. As with dividend yield, the general level of price earnings ratios on the stock market will be a reflection of the confidence of investors. Using the price earnings ratio, it is possible to compare companies, industries, and even countries. There is an average price earnings ratio published for each industry and this allows an investor to judge the market rating of his share with that of other shares in the same industry. Although two organisations may have the same earnings per share, they may have different price earnings ratios due to a difference in share prices. This difference in share prices could be the result of any of the following factors:

(a) *Investors' opinion of current earnings* – if current earnings are considered to be rising in one company and constant in another, then the former company will be more likely to have a higher share price.
(b) *Dividend policy* – the more conservative the dividend policy of a company, the more likely it is to have a lower share price, as a higher share price is needed to compensate a risky dividend policy.
(c) *Risk factor* – this varies with the different types of industries involved. This could be due to such things as the locations in which a company operates and the climate, politics, market situation.
(d) *Market in the shares* – this is particularly pertinent in Ireland; shares with a restricted market would tend to have lower share prices than shares in a more free market.
(e) *Gearing* – a company with a high gearing (see below) can expect to have a lower price earnings ratio than one with a low gearing.

Another aspect of interpreting it is that a published EPS exists for a year and therefore the P/E ratio given in a newspaper is generally based on an increasingly out-of-date EPS. To give an extreme but simple example:

Example

For the year ended 31 December 19X6, X plc had:

(i) EPS = 10 cents;
(ii) Overall market P/E ratio = 10;
(iii) P/E ratio = 20 (because market expects above average growth);
(iv) Market price at 30 April 19X7 (date of publication of previous year's accounts) = €2;
(v) During the year, X plc does even better than expected and by 29 April 19X8 the share price is up to €3, therefore giving a P/E ratio of 30 (based on EPS for year ended 31 December 19X6);
(vi) Year ended 31 December 19X7 EPS = 15 cents, announced on 30 April 19X8. This is in line with expectations so share price is unchanged and P/E ratio drops again to 20 (€3/15 cents).

Gearing

$$\frac{\text{Total Debt}}{\text{Ordinary shareholders' funds (Equity)}}$$

Note Total debt is the sum of the preference share capital, loan capital and short-term loans, and sometimes Total Capital Employed is used as the denominator.

'Gearing' is the relationship between a company's equity capital (known as residual return capital) and reserves and its fixed return capital. A company is *highly geared* if it has a substantial proportion of its capital in the form of preference shares or debentures or loan stock. A company is said to have *low gearing* if only a small proportion of its capital is in the form of preference shares, debentures or loan stock. A company financed entirely by equity shares has *no gearing*.

The importance of gearing can be illustrated by an example:

Example

Two companies, A plc and B plc, both have capital of €10,000. A plc has it all in the form of equity shares of €1 each, B plc has 5,000 €1 equity shares and €5,000 of 10% debentures. Both companies earn profits of €5,000 in year 1 and €2,000 in year 2. Tax is assumed at 35% and the dividend paid is 10 cents per share.
The capital position is therefore as follows:

	A plc €	B plc €
Shares	10,000	5,000
Debentures	–	5,000
	10,000	10,000

What is the EPS in each year?

Solution

	A plc		B plc	
	Year 1 €	Year 2 €	Year 1 €	Year 2 €
Profit before tax and debenture interest	5,000	2,000	5,000	2,000
Debenture interest	–	–	500	500
			4,500	1,500

Taxation (35%)	1,750	700	1,575	525
Earnings	3,250	1,300	2,925	975
Dividend (10%)	1,000	1,000	500	500
Retained profits	2,250	300	2,425	475
Earnings per share	32.5c	13c	58.5c	19.5c

The effects of gearing can be seen to be as follows:

(a) Debenture interest is an allowable deduction *before taxation*, whereas dividends are paid out of profits *after taxation*; company B has consistently higher retained profits than Company A.
(b) Earnings of a highly geared company are more sensitive to profit changes. This is shown by the following table:

	A plc	B plc
Change in profit before interest and taxation	-60%	-60%
Change in earnings	-60%	-66 $^2/_3$ %

The reason for the fluctuation is obviously the element of debenture interest which must be paid regardless of profit level.

This more than proportionate change in earnings is important in relation to the share price of the companies. Many investors value their shares by applying a multiple (known as the P/E ratio) to the earnings per share. Applying a multiple of *say* 10 to the EPS disclosed above would indicate share valuations as follows:

	A plc		B plc	
Year	1	2	1	2
Share price	€3.25	€1.30	€5.85	€1.95

Thus the share price of a highly geared company will often be more volatile than a company with only a small amount of gearing.

Not all companies are suitable for a highly geared structure. A company must have two fundamental characteristics if it is to use gearing successfully. These are as follows:

1. Relatively stable profits Debenture interest must be paid whether or not profits are earned. A company with erratic profits may have insufficient funds in a bad year with which to pay debenture interest. Thus would result in the appointment of a receiver and possibly the liquidation of the company.

2. Suitable assets for security Most issues of loan capital are secured on some or all of the company's assets which must be suitable for the purpose. A company with most of its capital invested in fast depreciating assets or inventory subject to rapid changes in demand and price would not be suitable for high gearing.

The classic examples of companies which are suited to high gearing are those in property investment and the hotel/leisure services industry. These companies generally enjoy relatively stable profits and have assets which are highly suitable for charging. Note that, nonetheless, these are industries that could be described as cyclical.

Companies not suited to high gearing would include those in the extractive industries and high-tech industries where constant changes occur. These companies could experience erratic profits and would generally have inadequate assets to pledge as security.

Debt Ratio The debt ratio or gearing ratio appropriate to a particular business depends on the stability in value and realisability of the assets concerned. It may be calculated simply as:

$$\frac{\text{Total Debt}}{\text{Total Assets}}$$

Other methods commonly used for expressing gearing include:

(i) Debt/equity ratio, calculated by taking:

$$\frac{\text{Loans + redeemable preference share capital}}{\text{Ordinary share capital + reserves + non-controlling interests}}$$

This is more sensitive than:

(ii) Percentage of capital employed represented by borrowings

$$\frac{\text{Loans + redeemable preference share capital}}{\text{Total capital}}$$

Where total capital is loans, redeemable preference share capital, ordinary share capital and non-controlling interests.

Interest to Earnings Ratio (Interest Cover) – the formula is as follows:

$$\frac{\text{Profit before Interest \& Taxation}}{\text{Loan Interest Paid and Payable}}$$

This formula gives an indication of the amount of coverage of the fixed interest requirements. It indicates the margin a company has available in the event of a downturn in earnings before it is unable to cover its fixed interest requirements.

Cash Flow

The preparation of a statement of cash flows is covered in Chapter 19 and Chapter 33 (IAS 7 *Statement of Cash Flows*). It is, therefore, only necessary at this point to consider what information this statement offers to the analyst.

The statement enables us to see what the management has done with the cash coming in under its control. The general principles one is looking for are:

(a) Long-term acquisitions should be covered by long-term funds;

(b) Conversely, long-term funds raised (share issues, loans) should be used for productive purposes (e.g. non-current assets, acquisition) and not allowed to lie about as excessive working capital; and

(c) Working capital level should be maintained, and some increase in working capital is necessary as inflation or growth necessitates increases in inventory holding and receivables financing.

Two useful ratios are:

Trading Cash Flow Ratio: $\dfrac{\text{Funds generated by operating activities}}{\text{Inventory}}$

This ratio highlights the ability of the company to generate sufficient funds from trading to cover its working capital requirements, payment of tax, dividends and loan service costs, without recourse to other inflows.

Net Cash Flow Ratio $\dfrac{\text{Net Cash inflow/outflow before financing}}{\text{Revenue}}$

This ratio highlights the ability of the company to generate sufficient funds to meet any loan repayments and to finance future developments.

Bear in mind that a published statement of cash flows covers a whole year and may not reveal the critical points of cash shortage which may arise during the year, particularly for a company engaged in a seasonal trade. It is, therefore, appropriate for companies to prepare cash forecasts showing the movements of cash over shorter periods, perhaps months or even weeks.

FINANCIAL BALANCE AND OVERTRADING

Financial Balance

'Financial balance' is the balance between the various forms of available finance relative to the requirements of the business. A business must have a *sufficient level of long-term capital* to finance its long-term investment in non-current assets. Part of the investment in current assets would also be financed by relatively permanent capital with the balance being provided by trade credit and other short-term borrowings. Any expansion in activity will normally require a broadening of the long-term capital base, without which 'overtrading' may develop (see below).

Suitability of finance is also a key factor. A permanent expansion of a company's activities should not be financed by temporary, short-term borrowings. A short-term increase in activity such as the 'January sales' in a retail trading company could ideally be financed by overdraft.

A major addition to non-current assets such as the construction of a new factory would not normally be financed on a long-term basis by overdraft. It might be found, however, that the expenditure was temporarily financed by short-term loans until construction was completed, when the overdraft would be 'funded' by a long-term borrowing secured on the completed building.

Overtrading

Overtrading arises where a company expands its turnover fairly rapidly without securing additional long-term capital adequate for its needs. The symptoms of overtrading are:

- inventory increasing, possibly more than proportionately to sales;
- receivables increasing, possibly more than proportionately to sales;
- cash and liquid assets declining at a fairly alarming rate; and
- payables increasing rapidly.

The above symptoms simply imply that the company has expanded without giving proper thought to the necessity to expand its capital base. It has consequently continued to rely on its payables and probably its bank overdraft to provide the additional finance required. It will reach a stage where payables will withhold further supplies and bankers will refuse to honour further cheques until borrowings are reduced. The problem is that borrowings cannot be reduced until sales revenue is earned, which in turn cannot be achieved until production is completed, which in turn is dependent upon materials being available and wages paid. Overall result – deadlock and rapid financial collapse!

This is a particularly difficult stage for any small to medium company. They have reached a stage in their life when conventional creditor and overdraft facilities are being stretched to the maximum, but they are probably too small to manage floatation. In many cases, by proper planning, the company can arrange fixed-term loan funding from the bank rather than relying exclusively on overdraft finance.

ACCOUNTING POLICIES AND THE LIMITATIONS OF RATIO ANALYSIS

The Effect of Choice of Accounting Policies

Where accounting standards allow alternative treatment of items in the accounts, then the accounting policy note should declare which policy has been chosen (IAS 8). It should then be applied consistently.

Changing accounting policies can have a radical effect on the results of a company. A change in accounting policy is treated as a prior period adjustment. The problem with this situation is that the directors may be able to manipulate the results of a company through changes of accounting policy.

The effect of such a change is very short-term. Most analysts and sophisticated users will discount its effect immediately except to the extent that it will affect any dividend (because of the effect on distributable profits).

Limitations of Ratio Analysis

(a) Unless ratios are calculated in a uniform manner, from uniform data, comparisons can be very misleading.

(b) The accounting periods covered by the financial statements may not reflect represent-ative financial positions. It must be remembered that a balance sheet is a statement of position. It indicates the state of affairs at a particular point in time. Abnormal accounting date figures will distort any ratios produced. Additionally, any 'window dressing' techniques will distort the statement of financial position. In such circum-stances, a statement of financial position drawn up a short period before or after the accounting date might reveal a much different situation, particularly in the current area of the statement of financial position. Therefore, it is important to always look at events prior to and after the reporting date and, if necessary, use average figures to compute the ratios.

Many businesses produce accounts to a date on which there are relatively low amounts of trading activity. Retail organisations often have an end of February accounting date (after the peak pre-Christmas trading and the January sales). As a result the items on a statement of financial position are not representative of the items throughout the accounting period.

(c) Financial statements themselves have limitations as they contain arbitrary estimates and figures which are based on personal decisions.

(d) The application of accounting policies in the preparation of financial statements must be understood when attempting to interpret financial ratios. Ratios are only compara-ble when the figures used therein are computed in the same manner from year to year or from firm to firm. Therefore any changes in accounting policies by firms that are being compared will render the ratios incomparable.

(e) The earning power of a business may well be affected by factors which are not reflected in the financial statements. Thus, these do not necessarily represent a complete pic-ture of a business but only a collection of those parts which can be translated into money terms, e.g. the size of the order book is normally ignored in financial state-ments. Ratios are only a guide and should be used in conjunction with a subjective viewpoint:

- What are the future plans of the company?
- What is the life cycle of the product?
- What customer profile does the company have?
- What is the market share the company occupies?
- Is the business a high risk type or in a relatively stable industry?

(f) Ratios must not be used as the sole test of efficiency. Concentration on ratios may inhibit the incentive to grow and expand, to the detriment of the long-term interests of the company. Favourable trends in ratios may not be examined any further. However, this may well be a short-sighted view, and the current performance may be at the expense of long-term strategic performance. All movements in ratios need to be examined and all underlying reasons explained.

(g) A few simple ratios do not provide an automatic means of running a company. Business problems usually involve complex patterns which cannot be solved solely by the use of ratios. Ratios do not provide control; they merely indicate where controls are flawed and highlight areas for improvement. Therefore, it is important to analysis ratios carefully as it is only by investigation that the weak controls are identified.

Ratio analysis is susceptible to the same underlying weaknesses and economic factors as accounts themselves. For example, in times of high inflation, capital employed may be understated and cost of sales may be understated, resulting in overstated profits. Thus, one would be relating overstated profits to understated capital employed. The result could be a significant overstatement of return. On this basis, it is important to comment on any economic factors affecting the entity and highlight the impact they have on the ratios.

CONCLUSION

While a popular choice, students often do not score well on questions dealing with the analysis and interpretation of financial information. As a poor examination technique is a common issue, it may be helpful to approach such examination questions in the following manner:

1. Read the question and identify from what viewpoint you are reporting, i.e. investor, purchaser etc;
2. Compute a ratio schedule with 2-3 main ratios for each section for each year;
3. Address the ratios and link any trends, i.e. low inventory turnover with low acid test ratio;
4. Write the commentary, considering the format and include a limitations caveat; and
5. Include any assumptions that you may have made.

Common mistakes in such questions include:

(i) too much time devoted to the calculations and too many ratios calculated;
(ii) insufficient commentary as a result of time wasted on calculations;
(iii) irrelevant ratios calculated and used;
(iv) not reading question properly to identify the interested party, i.e. bank manager, company management, investor;

(v)   calculations and commentary mixed – calculations should be kept in supporting schedules/appendices;

(vi) the report merely restates the data rather than drawing conclusions from the ratios; and

(vii) failure to deliver on the requirements of the question, e.g. if asked for memorandum, do not write a letter etc.

QUESTIONS

Self-test Questions

1. When is ratio analysis used?
2. What are the limitations of ratio analysis?
3. Name the main categories of ratio analysis.
4. How do you treat one-time charges in ratio analysis?
5. Who are the primary users of ratio analysis?

Review Questions

(See APPENDIX ONE for Suggested Solutions to Review Questions)

Question 1

DUL Limited is a small manufacturing company which commenced trading in 1976. The Managing Director, Mr Evans, is of the opinion that the company is performing extremely well in a period of high inflation and recession. However, the company's bankers are concerned at the high level of overdraft, and Mr Evans has engaged you, as Management Consultant, to report upon the company's performance.

The following information is made available to you:

Summarised Statements of Comprehensive Income for the Years Ended 30 June

	2000 €'000	2001 €'000	2002 €'000
Revenue	100	140	196
Profit before interest	11	13	14
Interest	5	7	9
Profit before tax	6	6	5
Income tax expense	2	2	3
Retained profits	4	4	2

Summarised Statements of Financial Position as at 30 June

	2000 €'000	2001 €'000	2002 €'000
Assets			
Non-current assets	40	56	78
Current assets			
Inventories	20	28	39
Receivables	20	28	43
	40	56	82
Total assets	80	112	160
Equity and Liabilities			
Equity			
Share capital	15	15	15
Revenue reserves	10	14	16
	25	29	31
Non-current liabilities			
Deferred taxation	3	5	8
Current liabilities			
Payables	10	28	57
Bank overdraft	42	50	64
	52	78	121
Total equity and liabilities	80	112	160

Requirement   You are required, on the basis of the information supplied, to prepare a report to the Managing Director of DUL Limited, commenting upon the performance and financial position of the company.

Question 2

You are the Management Accountant of Fry plc. Laurie plc is a competitor in the same industry and it has been operating for two years. Summaries of Laurie plc's statements of comprehensive income and statements of financial position for the previous three years are given below.

Summarised Statements of Comprehensive Income for the Years Ended 31 December

	19X0 €M	19X1 €M	19X2 €M
Revenue	840	981	913
Cost of sales	(554)	(645)	(590)
Gross profit	286	336	323
Selling, distribution and administration expenses	(186)	(214)	(219)
Profit before interest	100	122	104

Interest	(6)	(15)	(19)
Profit on ordinary activities before taxation	94	107	85
Income tax expense	(45)	(52)	(45)
Profit on ordinary activities after taxation	49	55	40

Summarised Statements of Financial Position as at 31 December

	19X0 €M	19X1 €M	19X2 €M
Assets			
Non-current assets			
Tangible assets at net book value	176	206	216
Intangible assets	36	40	48
	212	246	264
Current assets			
Inventories	237	303	294
Receivables	105	141	160
Bank	52	58	52
	394	502	506
Total Assets	606	748	770
Equity and Liabilities			
Equity			
Ordinary share capital	100	100	100
Retained profits	299	330	346
	399	430	446
Non-current liabilities			
Long-term loans	74	138	138
Current liabilities			
Trade payables	53	75	75
Other payables	80	105	111
	133	180	186
Total Equity and Liabilities	606	748	770

During each of the years ended 31 December 19x0, 19x1, and 19x2, €24m was debited to equity in respect of dividends paid.

You may assume that the index of retail prices has remained constant between 19X0 and 19X2.

Requirement   Write a report to the Finance Director of Fry plc which analyses the performance of Laurie plc and showing any calculations in an appendix to this report.

Question 3

Limetree Limited was founded by Cindy and Eugene Lemmon in 1985. The company manufactures and distributes luxury soft furnishings to the retail trade in Ireland. In common with many start-ups, the company encountered some financial difficulty in the early years. However, with the support of its bank it has managed to grow and prosper. Its revenue and profitability levels have increased each year since 1988, helped by the demand for new houses.

The company prepares its accounts to 30 June each year. Operating results and statements of financial position to 30 June 1992 and 1993 are shown in Appendix 1. The year to 30 June 1993 was the first year since start-up that the company experienced a fall in demand, caused by the slump in demand for houses during the year.

The company's bank manager has been receiving the monthly accounts since December 1992, when the overdraft limit of €400,000 was breached. He has asked to see the year's accounts to 30 June 1993 by the end of July in order to assess the overall financial position of the company.

You are given the following financial indicators for companies operating in the same industry as Limetree:

- Operating gearing   7.5
- Debt/Equity   65%
- Return on Equity   14%
- Dividend Cover   2
- Interest Cover   3

Requirement

(a) Calculate in respect of Limetree the same indicators as are set out above for the industry for the years to 30 June 1992 and 1993.

(b) Using the results of your answer at (a), and from a review of the information available in Appendix I:

(i) Identify matters that may be of concern to the bank manager, giving reasons for your answer;

(ii) Outline the points you would make to the bank manager in support of the company's financial performance and position.

APPENDIX 1
Limetree Limited
Summarised Operating Results

	30 June 1993 €'000	30 June 1992 €'000
Revenue	7,640	8,000
Cost of sales		
Materials	(1,240)	(1,380)
Labour	(2,530)	(2,550)
Overheads	(990)	(950)
	(4,760)	(4,880)
Gross Profit	2,880	3,120
Selling and Distribution	(685)	(640)
Administration	(1,880)	(1,910)
Operating Profit	315	570
Interest	(134)	(94)
Profit before tax	181	476
Income tax expense @ 40%	(72)	(190)
Profit after tax	109	286

Limetree Limited
Statement of Financial Position

	30 June 1993 €'000	30 June 1992 €'000
Assets		
Non-Current Assets	969	843
Current Assets		
Inventories	1,010	824
Receivables	1,210	1,180
	2,220	2,004
Total Assets	3,189	2,847
Equity and Liabilities		
Equity		
Share capital & premium	350	300
Retained earnings	749	650
	1,099	950
Non-Current Liabilities		
Long-term loan from bank	500	500

Current Liabilities		
Payables	1,064	847
Taxation	72	190
Bank overdraft	454	360
	1,590	1,397
Total Equity and Liabilities	3,189	2,847

During the years ended 30 June 1992 and 1993, €60,000 and €10,000 respectively was debited to equity in respect of dividends paid.

Question 4

You are given the following summarised financial statements of Holly plc which is a competitor of your company.

Summarised Statements of Comprehensive Income for the Years Ended 31 December

	1992 €m	1993 €m	1994 €m	1995 €m
Revenue	35,100	39,000	41,700	42,900
Cost of sales	(22,800)	(25,800)	(28,200)	(30,300)
Gross profit	12,300	13,200	13,500	12,600
Distribution costs	1,800	2,100	2,400	3,000
Administration costs	5,400	5,700	6,900	5,700
	(7,200)	(7,800)	(9,300)	(8,700)
Operating profit	5,100	5,400	4,200	3,900
Interest	(150)	(600)	(1,200)	1,500
Profit before taxation	4,950	4,800	3,000	2,400
Income tax expense	(750)	(150)	(300)	(450)
Profit after taxation	4,200	4,650	2,700	1,950

Summarised Statements of Financial Position as at 31 December

	1992 €m	1993 €m	1994 €m	1995 €m
Assets				
Non-Current Assets	6,672	8,586	8,268	
Current assets				
Inventories	4,800	5,400	5,100	4,500
Receivables	6,300	7,800	9,000	9,600
Bank	204	–	–	–
	11,304	13,200	14,100	14,100
Total Assets	15,900	19,872	22,686	22,368

Equity and Liabilities

Equity

Ordinary share capital	6,900	6,900	6,900	6,900
General reserve	2,910	2,910	2,910	2,910
Retained profits	1,320	2,070	2,370	2,820
	11,130	11,880	12,180	12,630
Non-current Liabilities				
Loans	–	1,500	3,000	3,300
Current Liabilities				
Trade payables	2,160	2,400	2,220	2,106
Other payables	2,610	2,190	2,010	1,584
Bank overdraft	–	1,902	3,276	2,748
	4,770	6,492	7,506	6,438
Total Equity and Liabilities	15,900	19,872	22,686	22,368

During the years ended 31 December 1992, 1993, 1994 and 1995, €3,600m, €3,900m, €2,400m and €1,500m was debited to equity in respect of dividends paid.

Requirement   You are required to prepare a report for the board of Directors of your company interpreting the financial statements of Holly plc from 1992 to 1995 including an analysis of its profitability and financial position.

Question 5

The details given below are a summary of the statements of financial position of six public companies engaged in different industries.

	A	B	C	D	E	F
Assets						
Land and other buildings	10	2	26	24	57	5
Other non-current assets	17	1	34	–	13	73
Inventories and work in progress	44	–	22	55	16	1
Trade receivables	6	77	15	4	1	13
Other receivables	11	–	–	8	2	5
Cash and investments	12	20	3	9	11	3
	100	100	100	100	100	100
Equity and Liabilities						
Capital and reserves	37	5	62	58	55	50
Non-current Liabilities	12	5	4	13	6	25
Current Liabilities						
Trade payables	32	85	34	14	24	6
Other payables	16	5	–	14	15	11
Bank overdraft	3	–	–	1	–	8
	100	100	100	100	100	100

The activities of each company are as follows:

1. Operator of a chain of retail supermarkets;
2. Sea ferry operator;
3. Property investor and house builder. Apart from supplying managers, including site management, for the house building side of its operations this company completely subcontracts all building work;
4. A vertically integrated company in the food industry, which owns farms, flour mills, bakeries and retail outlets;
5. Commercial bank with a network of branches; and
6. Contractor in the civil engineering industry.

Note   No Company employs off-balance sheet finance such as leasing.

Requirement

(a) State which of the above activities relate to which set of statement of financial position details giving a brief summary of your reasoning in each case. (No marks will be awarded for matching where no explanation is given.)
(b) What do you consider to be the major limitations of ratio analysis as a means of interpreting accounting information?

Question 6

Egg Limited Accountant, Mr Montague, has assembled the following data from the company's last five sets of historical cost accounts.

	19X5	19X4	19X3	19X2	19X1
Net profit margin:					
$\dfrac{\text{Profit before tax and interest}}{\text{Revenue}}$	5.6%	5.4%	4.9%	5.1%	5.3%
Return on capital employed:					
$\dfrac{\text{Profit before tax and interest}}{\text{Total assets less current liabilities}}$	12.1%	13.4%	11.8%	14.2%	14.4%
Interest cover:					
$\dfrac{\text{Profit before interest and tax}}{\text{Interest}}$	2.4	5.2	5.5	6.0	2.9
Dividend cover:					
$\dfrac{\text{Earnings}}{\text{Ordinary dividend}}$	2.3	2.1	1.8	2.0	2.7
Gearing:					
$\dfrac{\text{Debt}}{\text{Equity}}$	60.7%	57.2%	44.5%	12.8%	34.6%

$\dfrac{\text{Debt}}{\text{Equity} + \text{minority interests}}$	56.3%	54.0%	41.9%	11.1%	32.4%

Quick ratio:

$\dfrac{\text{Current assets less inventory}}{\text{Current liabilities}}$	68.6%	68.2%	72.5%	109.4%	90.2%

Current ratio:

$\dfrac{\text{Current assets}}{\text{Current liabilities}}$	141.8%	141.5%	147.2%	189.1%	180.6%

Asset turnover:

$\dfrac{\text{Revenue}}{\text{Total assets less current liabilities}}$	2.2	2.5	2.4	2.8	2.7

Working capital turnover:

$\dfrac{\text{Revenue}}{\text{Working capital}}$	7.8	7.2	6.3	6.7	5.5

Earnings per share:	Pretax	18.44c	15.75c	12.15c	14.35c	16.67c
	Net	11.96c	10.08c	8.12c	8.41c	10.79c
Ordinary dividend per share		5.2c	4.8c	4.5c	4.2c	4.0c
Net assets per share		94.7c	90.2c	86.2c	86.3c	81.8c

Requirement   You are required to prepare a report for Mr Montague on the company's financial state and progress over the period based on the information in the report, and commenting on its possible limitations if there have been price changes in the period.

Challenging Questions

Question 1 (Based on ICAI, P3 Summer 1996, Question 3)

The statement of comprehensive income of HOTPOT plc for the year ended 31 December 1995, and statement of financial position as at that date, is as follows:

Summarised Statement of Comprehensive Income for the Year Ended 31 December 1995

	Notes	€'000
Revenue		4,020
Cost of sales	(1)	(2,110)
Gross profit		1,910
Distribution costs		(320)
Administrative expenses	(1)	(500)
Operating profit		1,090
Interest paid		(300)
Income tax expense		(360)
Net profit after taxation		430

Balance Sheet as at 31 December

	Notes	1995 €'000	1994 €'000
Assets			
Non-current assets			
Tangible assets	(2)	9,470	7,420
Current assets			
Inventory		850	750
Receivables		2,275	1,980
Cash in hand and at bank		175	580
		3,300	3,310
Total Assets		12,770	10,730
Equity and Liabilities			
Equity			
Called up share capital (€1 ordinary shares)	(4)	1,200	1,000
Share premium account		535	660
Retained profits		3,380	3,150
		5,115	4,810
Non-current liabilities	(5)	4000	2,000
		9,115	6,810
Current liabilities	(3)	3,655	3,920
Total Equity and Liabilities		12,770	10,730

Additional Information

(1) Cost of sales includes wages and salaries of €480,000. Administrative expenses include wages and salaries of €348,000 and bad debts of €62,000.

	1995 €'000	1995 €'000	1994 €'000	1994 €'000
(2) Tangible non-current assets				
Land and buildings at cost		4,840		3,070
Less: Accumulated depreciation		660		510
		4,180		2,560
Plant, machinery and equipment at cost	15,140		14,510	
Less: Accumulated depreciation	9,850	5,290	9,650	4,860
		9,470		7,420

During the year, plant which had originally cost €1,460,000, and on which accumulated depreciation of €712,000 had been provided, was sold for €700,000.

(3) Current liabilities

	1995	1994
	€'000	€'000
Bank overdraft	2,000	1,300
Payables	1,214	1,382
Taxation	320	1,150
PAYE & PRSI/NIC	41	28
Dividends	80	60
	3,655	3,920

(4) The company made a rights issue of 1 for 20 at €1.50 per share payable in full on the 1 January 1995. On 1 April 1995, a bonus issue of 1 for 7 was made.

(5) On 1 January 1995, the company issued a further €2,000,000 mortgage debentures. Interest was paid on all debentures on 30 June and 31 December, 1995.

(6) During the year ended 31 December 1995, €200,000 was debited to equity in respect of dividends paid.

Requirement   Using only the common information provided above:

(a) Calculate for HOTPOT plc for 1994 and 1995:
   (i) The current ratio and the acid test ratio; and
   (ii) TWO alternative gearing ratios.

(b) Explain the significance of the gearing ratio in analysing the accounts of a business, and set out your reasons for selecting the methods of calculation you have used in (a) above;

(c) Draft a brief report for the management of HOTPOT plc commenting on the liquidity and gearing of the company at 31 December, 1995, as compared with the previous year.

Question 2 (Based on ICAI, P3 Summer 1995, Question 1)

The following draft accounts have been prepared for DOLAN plc for the year ended 31 December 1994:

Summarised Statements of Comprehensive Income for the Years Ended 31 December

	1994		1993	
	€'000	€'000	€'000	€'000
Revenue		24,350		23,100
Purchases	16,100		16,000	
Inventory movement	350	16,450	(400)	15,600
Gross profit		7,900		7,500
Depreciation	100		85	
Other operating expenses	6,400		6,365	
Interest payable	300	6,800	250	6,700

Net profit before tax	1,100	800
Income tax expense	(300)	(200)
Net profit after tax	800	600
Dividends	(500)	(400)
	300	200

Balance Sheet as at 31 December

	1994 €'000	1993 €'000
Assets		
Non-current assets	5,750	4,300
Inventories	3,150	3,500
Trade receivables	3,600	3,200
Bank	650	–
	13,150	11,000
Equity and Liabilities		
Share capital	4,000	4,000
Revaluation reserve	1,000	–
Retained earnings	680	380
10% debentures	3,000	2,500
Bank overdraft	–	450
Trade payables	3,600	3,000
Taxation	370	270
Dividends	500	400
Total equity and liabilities	13,150	11,000

During the years ended 31 December 1993 and 1994, €400,000 and €500,000 was debited to equity in respect of dividends paid.

Requirement   Prepare a *brief* report for the Board of DOLAN plc on the performance of the company during 1994 as compared with the previous year. You should include in your report a schedule of appropriate ratios.

Question 3 (Based on ICAI, P3 Summer 1992, Question 2)

SWIZZLE Limited produces a range of alcoholic and soft drinks and also owns a number of public houses and inns. The company's latest published accounts have been summarised as follows:

Summarised Statements of Comprehensive Income for the Years Ended 31 December

	1991	1990
	€'000	€'000
Revenue	10,800	8,600
Operating profit	1,405	1,032
Income from other non-current asset investments	43	31
Interest payable and similar charges	(470)	(260)
Profit on ordinary activities before taxation	978	803
Income tax expense	(298)	(203)
Profit for the year	680	600

Statements of Financial Position as at 31 December

	1991	1990
	€'000	€'000
Assets		
Non-current assets		
Tangible assets	14,180	8,120
Investments	480	350
	14,660	8,470
Current assets	1,970	1,650
Total Assets	16,630	10,120
Equity and Liabilities		
Equity		
Ordinary Share Capital €1	1,200	800
Share premium	510	300
Revaluation reserve	3,500	–
Retained profits	4,970	4,540
	10,180	5,640
Non-current liabilities	4,220	2,360
Current liabilities	2,230	2,120
Total Equity and Liabilities	16,630	10,120

The notes to the accounts state that the company revalued its non-industrial properties on 31 December 1991. It is company policy not to provide depreciation on these properties, but to maintain them out of revenue expenditure to a standard which ensures that their estimated aggregate realisable value exceeds their net book amounts. During year ended 31 December 1990 and 1991, €200,000 and €250,000 was debited to equity in respect of dividends paid.

Requirement   Prepare a report for the Managing Director of SWIZZLE Limited on the financial performance of the company during 1991. Insofar as the information provided permits, your report should include appropriate ratios and be presented under the following main headings:

(a) Profitability;
(b) Assets utilisation;
(c) Solvency; and
(d) Gearing.

CHAPTER 36

ACCOUNTING FOR PARTNERSHIPS

INTRODUCTION

This chapter deals with accounting for partnerships. In the previous chapters, the terminology used in the revised IAS 1 *Presentation of Financial Statements* was adopted, not least because the focus was on the application of accounting standards in a corporate context. For example, the terms 'income statement' and 'balance sheet' were replaced by 'statement of comprehensive income' and 'statement of financial position' respectively. However, given the nature of partnerships, it is considered more appropriate to revert to using 'income statement' and 'balance sheet' in this chapter. After having read this chapter, you should:

- be aware of the key aspects of the Partnership Act 1890;
- understand the basic accounting principles with respect to partnerships;
- be able to account for simple partnership changes, partnership changes requiring adjustments to asset values, the dissolution of a partnership, amalgamations and the conversion of a partnership to a limited company

Each of these areas is now addressed in turn.

PARTNERSHIP ACT 1890

The Partnership Act 1890 defines a partnership as 'the relation which exists between persons carrying on business in common with a view of profit'. The main substance of a partnership is that each partner is an agent of all the others for the purpose of the business. Each partner is therefore bound by the acts of the other partners and each partner can be sued in his own name for the whole or any partnership debts.

Every partnership is set up by an agreement between the partners, either orally or in writing. If the agreement between the partners is silent on any matter affecting relationship between the partners, then the relevant provisions of the Partnership Act of 1980 apply.

The main section of the Partnership Act 1890 which is relevant from an accounting point of view is Section 24 which states among other things that:

(a) No interest is paid on capital of the partners;
(b) No remuneration is paid to partners for acting in the business;
(c) Profits and losses are to be shared equally between partners; and
(d) Interest at the rate of 5% per annum is paid on loans made by partners to the partnership in excess if their agreed capitals.

It should be emphasised that the above rules only apply in the absence of a different agreement between the partners. The partnership agreement will cover such items as those mentioned above, in addition to setting out other rights and duties of partners which are important to the satisfactory running of the partnership.

BASIC PRINCIPLES

Before looking at the basic rules which are particular to partnership accounts, it should be emphasised that the basic book keeping and accounting procedures adopted in relation to companies apply equally to partnerships. The differences arise in dealing with the ownership of the partnership and the accounting for that partnership.

The Conventional Methods of Dividing Profit and Maintaining Equity between Partners

A partnership agreement, which need not necessarily be in written form, will govern the relationships between the partners. Important matters to be covered include:

(a) name of firm, the type of business, and duration;
(b) capital to be introduced by partners;
(c) distribution of profits between partners;
(d) drawings by partners;
(e) arrangements for dissolution, or on the death or retirement of partners;
(f) settling of disputes; and
(g) preparation and audit of accounts.

The division of profit stated in the partnership agreement may be quite complex in order to reflect the expected differing efforts and contributions of the partners. For example, some or all of the partners may be entitled to a salary to reflect the differing management involvement in the business. Interest on capital may be provided to reflect the differing amounts of capital contributed. The profit shares may differ to reflect seniority or greater skills.

It is important to appreciate, however, that all of the above examples are means of dividing the profits of the partnership and are not expenses of the business. A partnership salary is merely a device for calculating the division of profit; it is not a salary in the normal meaning of the term.

Accounting Distinctions between Partnerships and Sole Traders

The accounting techniques developed for sole traders are generally applicable to partnerships, but there are certain important differences

Item	Sole trader's books	Partnership's books
Capital introduced	Capital account	Partners' fixed capital accounts
Drawings and share of the profit	Capital account	Partners' current accounts
Division of profits	Not applicable – one proprietor only	Appropriation account

Capital Accounts

At the commencement of the partnership an agreement will have to be reached as to the amount of capital to be introduced. This could be in the form of cash or other assets. Whatever the form of assets introduced and debited to asset accounts, it is normal to make the credit entry to fixed capital accounts. These are so called because they are not then used to record drawings or shares of profits but only major changes in the relations between partners. In particular, fixed capital accounts are used to deal with:

(a) capital introduced or withdrawn by new or retiring partners; and
(b) revaluation adjustments.

The balances on fixed capital accounts do not necessarily bear any relation to the division of profits. However, to compensate partners who provide a larger share of the capital, it is common for notional interest on capital accounts to be paid to partners. This is dealt with through the appropriation account.

Current Accounts

These are used to deal with the regular transactions between the partners and the firm, i.e. matters other than those sufficiently fundamental to be dealt with through the capital accounts. Most commonly these are:

(a) share of profits, interest on capital and partners' salaries usually computed annually; and
(b) monthly drawings against the annual share of profit.

Recording the Partners' Shares of Profit/ Losses and their Drawings in the Ledger Accounts and Balance Sheet Presentation

Example 1

Nab and Crag commenced business in partnership on 1 January 20X6, contributing as fixed capital €5,000 and €10,000 cash respectively. All profits and losses are shared equally. The profit for the year ended 31 December 20X6 amounted to €10,000. Drawings for Nab and Crag amounted to €3,000 and €4,000 respectively.

You are required to prepare the capital and current accounts and balance sheet extracts.

Partners' capital accounts

		Nab €	Crag €			Nab €	Crag €
				20X6			
				1 Jan	Cash	5,000	10,000

Partners' current accounts

		€	€			€	€
20X6				20X6			
1 Dec	Drawings	3,000	4,000	31 Dec	Share of profits	5,000	5,000
	Balance c/d	2,000	1,000				
		5,000	5,000			5,000	5,000
				20X6			
				1 Jan	Balance b/d	2,000	1,000

The above accounts are presented in a columnar format. This is quite common in a partnership set of books as each partner will have similar transactions during the year. A columnar format allows two (or more) separate accounts to be shown using the same narrative. It is important to remember though that each partner's account is separate from the other partner(s).

Balance sheet at 31 December 20X6 (extract)

	Current accounts €	€	Capital accounts €
Partners' account:			
Nab	5,000	2,000	7,000
Crag	10,000	1,000	11,000
	15,000	3,000	18,000

Note that the current account balances of €2,000 and €1,000 will be credited in the following year with profit shares and debited with drawings.

One of the main differences between the capital section of the balance sheet of a sole trader and a partnership is that the partnership balance sheet will often only give the closing balances whereas the sole trader's movements in capital are shown.

The main reason for the difference is simply one of space. Movements in the capital and current accounts for a few partners cannot be easily accommodated on the face of the balance sheet.

Example 2

The information is the same as in Example 1, except that Nab's drawings are €5,300. The current accounts now become:

Partners' current accounts

		Nab €	Crag €			Nab €	Crag €
20X6				20X6			
	Drawings	5,300	4,000		Share of profits	5,000	5,000
31 Dec	Balance c/d		1,000	31 Dec	Balance c/d	300	
		5,300	5,000			5,300	5,000
20X7				20X7			
1 Jan	Balance b/d	300		1 Jan	Balance b/d		1,000

Note that Nab's current account is overdrawn. How do we present this in the balance sheet?

Balance sheet at 31 December 20X6 (extract)

	Capital accounts €	Current accounts €	€
Partners' accounts:			
Nab	5,000	(300)	4,700
Crag	10,000	1,000	11,000
	15,000	700	15,700

Appropriation Account

The appropriation account is a ledger account dealing with the allocation of net profit between the partners. In practice it is often included as the final part of the income statement.

An important point is that all allocations of profit to partners in their capacity as partners, and during the time they actually are partners, are made through the appropriation account. This applies even though such allocations may be described as partners' salaries, interest on capital or a share of profits.

Example 3

Pike and Scar are in partnership and have the following profit-sharing arrangements:

(a) Interest on capital is to be provided at a rate of 8% pa;
(b) Pike and Scar are to receive salaries of €6,000 and €8,000 pa respectively;
(c) The balance of profit or loss is to be divided between Pike and Scar in the ratio 3: 2.

Net profit for the year amounts to €20,000 and capital account balances are Pike €12,000 and Scar €9,000.

You are required to prepare:

(a) a statement showing the allocation of profit between the partners; and
(b) relevant entries in the income statement and appropriation account.

Solution

(a) Allocation of net profit of €20,000

	Pike €	Scar €	Total €
Interest on capital	960	720	1,680
Salaries	6,000	8,000	14,000
Balance of profits (€20,000 – €15,680) in ratio 3:2	(3/5) 2,592	(2/5) 1,728	4,320
Totals	9,552	10,448	20,000

Note that this is only a calculation of the allocation of profit and not part of the double entry book keeping system, merely providing the figures for the appropriation account.

Extract from income statement and appropriation account for the year ended

	€	€
Sales		X
Cost of sales		X
Gross profit		X
Expenses		X
Net profit		20,000

Allocated to:

Pike	9,552	
Scar	10,448	20,000

The income statement appropriation account is closed by transferring the profit shares to the credit of the partners' current accounts. The double entry is therefore:

Debit	Credit	With
Income statement appropriation account	Pike's current account	€9,552
Income statement appropriation account	Scar's current account	€10,448

For the purposes of examinations (and in practice) parts (a) and (b) above can be amalgamated as follows:

Extract from income statement and appropriation account for the year ended

	€
Sales	X
Cost of sales	X
Gross profit	X
Expenses	X
Net profit for year	20,000

Appropriation statement

	Pike	Scar	Total
	€	€	€
Interest on capital	960	720	1,680
Salaries	6,000	8,000	14,000
Balance of profits (€20,000 – €15,680) in ratio 3: 2	2,592 (3/5)	1,728 (2/5)	4,320
Totals	9,552	10,448	20,000

The debits actually being made are as before (€9,552 and €1 0,448).

Example 4

The facts are the same as for Example 3, except that net profit is now only €3,680. You are required to show the allocation of profit between the partners.

Allocation of net profit of €3,680

	Pike	Scar	Total
	€	€	€
Interest on capital	960	720	1,680
Salaries	6,000	8,000	14,000
Balance of loss €3,680 – €15,680			
= (€12,000) to be shared in ratio 3:2	(7,200)	(4,800)	(12,000)
Totals	(240)	3,920	3,680

The double entry in this case is:

Debit	Credit	With
Income statement appropriation account	Scar's current account	€3,920
Pike's current account	Income statement appropriation account	€240

The relevant part of the income statement would show:

	€	€
Net profit		3,680
Allocated to:		
Scar	3,920	
Pike	(240)	
		3,680

One point which regularly causes difficulties is the partners' salaries. The key is to remember at the outset that a partner's salary is an appropriation of profit, whereas a salary paid to an employee is an expense.

Accordingly a salary to which a partner is entitled is included as part of the appropriation statement. Questions sometimes state that a partner has withdrawn his salary. In this case

(a) Include the salary in the appropriation statement as usual; and
(b) Quite separately treat the withdrawal of the salary as drawings.

Debit	Credit	With
Partners' current account	Bank	Amount withdrawn

Guaranteed Minimum Profit Share

In certain partnership agreements a partner may be guaranteed a minimum share of profits. The appropriation of profit would proceed in the normal way. If the result is that the partner has less than this minimum, the deficit will be made good by the other partners (normally in profit-sharing ratio).

Example 5

Tessa, Laura and Jane are in partnership and have the following profit-sharing arrangements:

(a) Tessa and Laura are to receive salaries of €20,000 and €30,000 respectively;
(b) the balance of profit or loss is to be divided Tessa 1, Laura 2, and Jane 3; and
(c) Tessa is guaranteed a minimum profit share of €25,000.

The net profit for the year is €68,000.

You are required to show the appropriation account for the year.

Appropriation Account

	Tessa €	Laura €	Jane €	Total €
Net profit				68,000
Salaries	20,000	30,000	–	(50,000)
				18,000
Balance of profits (1:2:3)	3,000	6,000	9,000	(18,000)
	23,000	36,000	9,000	
Adjustment	2,000			
Laura 2/5 x 2,000		(800)		
Jane 3/5 x 2,000			(1,200)	
Total	25,000	35,200	7,800	68,000

Interest on Drawings

Occasionally there is a provision in a partnership agreement for a notional interest charge on the drawings by each partner. The interest charges are merely a negative profit share – they are a means by which total profits are allocated between the partners. The reason for an interest on drawings provision is that those partners who draw out more cash than their colleagues in the early part of an accounting period should suffer a cost.

Example 6

Dick and Dastardly are in partnership. The capital and current accounts as at 1 January 20X7 shows:

	€ Capital	€ Current
Dick	50,000	2,500
Dastardly	20,000	3,000

The partnership agreement provides for the following:

(a) profits and losses are shared between Dick and Dastardly in percentages 60 and 40;
(b) interest on capital at 10% per annum is allowed; and
(c) interest on drawings is charged at 12% per annum.

Drawings for the year to 31 December 20X7 are:

	Dick €	Dastardly €
1 February 20X7	5,000	2,000
30 September 20X7	2,000	5,000

The profit for the year is €20,000.

You are required to prepare the appropriation account and the current accounts for the year ended 31 December 20X7.

Solution

Appropriation account for the year ended 31 December 20X7

	Dick €	Dastardly €	€
Profit for the year			20,000
Add: Interest on drawings (see working)	(610)	(370)	980
			20,980
Less: Interest on capital:			
50,000 x 10%	5,000		
20,000 x 10%		2,000	(7,000)
Balance in profit-sharing ratio:			13,980
13,980 x 60%	8,388		
13,980 x 40%		5,592	(13,980)
Total allocation	12,778	7,222	20,000

Current accounts

		Dick €	Dastardly €			Dick €	Dastardly €
20X7:				**20X7:**			
1 Feb	Drawing	5,000	2,000		Balance b/d	2,500	3,000
30 Sep	Drawing	2,000	5,000	31 Dec	Share of		
	Balance c/d	8,278	3,222		profits	12,778	7,222
		15,278	10,222			15,278	10,222

Working

		Dick €	Dastardly €
Interest on drawings:			
1 February 20X7	5,000 x 12% x 11/12	550	
	2,000 x 12% x 11/12		220
30 September 20X7	2,000 x 12% x 3/12	60	
	5,000 x 12% x 3/12		150
		610	370

Example 7

You should now be in a position to follow through from the trial balance stage a full example of partnership accounts.

You are provided with the following information regarding the partnership of Dacre, Hutton and Tod. The trial balance at 31 December 20X6 is as follows:

	Dr €	Cr €
Sales		50,000
Inventory at 1 January 20X6	6,000	
Purchases	29,250	
Carriage inwards	250	
Carriage outwards	400	

Payables		4,000
Cash at bank	3,900	
Current accounts:		
Dacre		900
Hutton		750
Tod		1,350
Capital accounts:		
Dacre		4,000
Hutton		5,000
Tod		6,000
Drawings:		
Dacre	2,000	
Hutton	3,000	
Tod	5,000	
Sundry expenses	2,800	
Receivables	13,000	
Shop fittings:		
Cost	8,000	
Accumulated depreciation		1,600
	73,600	73,600

Additional information:

(a) Closing inventory is valued for accounts purposes at €5,500;
(b) Depreciation of €800 is to be provided on the shop fittings; and
(c) The profit-sharing arrangements are as follows:
   (i) Interest on capital is to be provided at a rate of 1 0% per annum;
   (ii) Dacre and Tod are to receive salaries of €3,000 and €4,000 per annum respectively; and
   (iii) The balance of profit or loss is to be divided between Dacre, Hutton and Tod in the ratio of 3: 8: 4.

You are required to prepare final accounts together with current accounts of the partners.

Solution

Dacre, Hutton and Tod
Income statement for the year ended 31 December 20X6

	€	€
Sales		50,000
Opening inventory	6,000	
Purchases	29,250	
Carriage inwards	250	
	35,500	
Less: Closing inventory	5,500	30,000
Gross profit		20,000
Sundry expenses	2,800	
Carriage outwards	400	
Depreciation	800	4,000
Net profit		16,000
Allocated to:		
Dacre	4,900	
Hutton	4,500	
Tod	6,600	
	16,000	

Balance sheet as at 31 December 20X6

	Cost	Acc depn	
	€	€	€
Non-current Assets			
Shop fittings	8,000	2,400	5,600
Current Assets			
Inventory		5,500	
Receivables		13,000	
Cash		3,900	22,400
			28,000

Partners' accounts

	Capital accounts	Current accounts	Total
	€	€	€
Dacre	4,000	3,800	7,800
Hutton	5,000	2,250	7,250
Tod	6,000	2,950	8,950
	15,000	9,000	24,000
Current Liabilities			
Payables			4,000
			28,000

Partners' current accounts

		Dare	Hutton	Tod			Dare	Hutton	Tod
		€	€	€			€	€	€
20X6					20X6				
	Drawing	2,000	3,000	5,000	1 Jan	Bal b/d	900	750	1,350
31 Dec	Bal c/d	3,800	2,250	2,950		IS app	4,900	4,500	6,600
		5,800	5,250	7,950			5,800	5,250	7,950
					20X7				
					1 Jan	Bal b/d	3,800	2,250	2,950

Workings:

The adjustments for inventory and depreciation should by now be familiar.

The new development is that, having calculated the profit for the period, it has to be appropriated between Dacre, Hutton and Tod. To calculate their respective shares an appropriation statement is used.

	Dacre	Hutton	Tod	Total
	€	€	€	€
Interest on capital	400	500	600	1,500
Salaries	3,000	–	4,000	7,000
Balance of profit (€16,000 – €8,500) in ratio 3:8:4	1,500	4,000	2,000	7,500
	4,900	4,500	6,600	16,000

This gives us the figures for the double entry:

Dr   Income statement appropriation
Cr   Partners' current accounts

BASIC PARTNERSHIP CHANGES

Partnership changes may occur in three quite different situations:

(a) when a partner leaves, dies or retires;
(b) when a new partner enters the partnership; and
(c) when existing partners change their profit-sharing arrangements.

From the accounting viewpoint there are two aspects:

(a) dividing profits between old and new partners when the change occurs during the course of the financial period; and
(b) the problem of valuing partnership assets, especially goodwill, at the time of the change (see below).

Division of Profits in a Partnership Change

There will be many occasions when a partnership change does not take place at a convenient date (such as the accounting year end!).

For the purpose of dividing profits equitably between the partners concerned, it is necessary to apportion (or allocate) profits between those arising before the change, and those arising afterwards.

In most cases where the trade is not of a seasonal nature, sales occur at an even rate during the year. It will then be reasonable to apportion sales on a time basis. Having apportioned the profit between the different parts of the year, it is then allocated between the partners according to their arrangements for sharing profits during those periods. This is demonstrated below.

Example 8

Gavel and Kirk are in partnership, sharing profits in the ratio 3: 2, after Gavel has received a salary of €2,000 per annum. The accounting year-end of the partnership is 31 December. On 30 June 20X6, Blea is admitted to the partnership. The new profit-sharing arrangements provide for Gavel's salary of €2,000 per annum to be maintained, and for Blea to receive a salary of €3,000 per annum. The balance is to be shared between Gavel, Kirk and Blea in the ratio 2: 2: 1.

The net profit for the year to 31 December 20X6 is €22,000.

You are required to show the transfer to the partners' current accounts for the year ended 31 December 20X6.

Assuming that the net profit of €22,000 accrues evenly over the year, it may be apportioned on a time basis as follows:

	€
1 January 20X6 to 30 June 20X6 6/12 x €22,000	11,000
1 July 20X6 to 31 December 20X6 6/12 x €22,000	11,000
	22,000

The net profit relating to each six-month period is allocated according to the profit-sharing arrangements operating during that period.

Statement of allocation of profit

	Gavel €	Kirk €	Blea €	Total €
Six months to 30 June 20X6				
Salary:				
Gavel 6/12 x €2,000	1,000	–	–	1,000
Balance of profit (€11,000-€1,000) in ratio 3:2	6,000	4,000	–	10,000
	7,000	4,000	–	11,000

Six months to 31 December 20X6

	Gavel €	Kirk €	Blea €	Total €
Salary:				
Gavel 6/12 x €2,000	1,000	–	–	1,000
Blea 6/12 x €3,000	–	–	1,500	1,500
Balance of profit (€11,000-€2,500) in ratio 2:2:1	3,400	3,400	1,700	8,500
	4,400	3,400	3,200	11,000
Totals – 12 months	11,400	7,400	3,200	22,000

Remember that the salaries are expressed at an annual rate! Interest on capital percentages are also expressed at an annual rate so a similar problem of time apportionment could apply elsewhere.

Partners' current accounts - Extract

Gavel €	Kirk €	Blea €		Gavel €	Kirk €	Blea €
			Income statement			
			Appropriation:			
			To 30 June	7,000	4,000	–
			To 31 Dec 20X6	4,400	3,400	3,200

Apportionment of Profit - Some Complications

Unless otherwise instructed, it is acceptable to apportion profits on a time basis. Occasionally the question may specify some alternative basis.

Example 9

Assume that in the previous example the net profit of €22,000 was arrived at as follows:

	€	€
Sales (€96,000 in six months to 30 June 20X6)		160,000
Cost of sales		(118,000)
Gross profit		42,000
Selling and distribution expenses	5,500	
Administrative expenses	12,500	
Financial expenses	2,000	
		20,000
Net profit		22,000

You are required to show the apportionment of profit between the two parts of the year. Assume that gross profit and selling expenses are to be apportioned on a turnover basis and all other items on a time basis. The allocation of profit between the partners is not required.

	€
Turnover:	
Six months to 30 June 20X6	96,000
Six months to 31 December 20X6	64,000
	160,000

The ratio of turnover is therefore 96:64 or 3:2.

	Six months to 30 June 20X6		Six months to 31 December 20X6		Total	
	€	€	€	€	€	€
Gross profit (3:2)		25,200		16,800		42,000
Selling expenses (3:2)	3,300		2,200		5,500	
Administrative expenses (1:1)	6,250		6,250		12,500	
Financial expenses (1:1)	1,000		1,000		2,000	
		10,550		9,450		20,000
Net profit		14,650		7,350		22,000

The apportionment of net profit is therefore:

	€
Six months to 30 June 20X6	14,650
Six months to 31 December 20X6	7,350
	22,000

As can be seen, in a seasonal business, where sales fluctuate greatly from month to month, the apportionment of a net profit on a time basis may give a misleading picture.

Partnership Changes Involving No Adjustments to Asset Values – Recording Introductions and Withdrawals of Capital in the Ledger Accounts

For the sake of clarity two unrealistic assumptions will be made, namely that at the date of partnership changes:

(a) All tangible assets (e.g., inventory, non-current assets) are stated in the accounts at their current value; and
(b) Goodwill is ignored.

These unrealistic assumptions will be removed (see below), but first two possible causes of a change in the partnership will be considered – the retirement of an existing partner and the admission of a new partner.

Retirement of an Existing Partner

When a partner retires it is important first of all to ensure that his current account is credited with his share of profits and debited with his drawings up to the date of retirement. The balances on his current and capital accounts are then transferred to a loan account and becomes a liability of the business. The manner and timing of the payment of this liability are likely to be regulated by the partnership agreement. In practice the amount will probably be paid in instalments, with allowance for interest on the unpaid balance. Since the former partner is no longer a partner of the business, the interest cannot be regarded as an appropriation of profit and must be regarded as an expense of the partnership (in the same way as interest on a bank overdraft).

Example 10

Birk, How and Stile have been in partnership for many years. Birk retired from the partnership on 1 July. At 30 June the summarised balance sheet showed the following position:

			€
Sundry assets			27,296

Partners' accounts	Capital accounts	Current accounts	Total
	€	€	€
Birk	12,000	1,735	13,735
How	8,000	2,064	10,064
Stile	3,000	497	3,497
	23,000	4,296	27,296

It is assumed that the current account balances reflect profit shares and drawings up to 30 June. At that date the balances on Birk's capital and current accounts should be transferred to a loan account and regarded as a liability of the partnership. A balance sheet at 1 July would then appear:

			€
Sundry assets			27,296

Partners' accounts	Capital accounts	Current accounts	
	€	€	€
How	8,000	2,064	10,064
Stile	3,000	497	3,497
	11,000	2,561	13,561
Loan account – Birk			13,735
			27,296

Birk is now a creditor of the partnership as he is no longer a partner.

Admission of a New Partner

A new partner will often be required to bring in cash as a contribution to the fixed capital of the partnership. This cash is therefore credited to the partner's capital account.

Facts as in the previous example. Tarn is admitted to the partnership on 3 July. He brings in cash of €2,500 as his fixed capital. The partners' current accounts would not be affected, but the capital accounts would appear as follows:

Example 11

Partners' capital accounts

	Birk €	How €	Stile €	Tarn €		Birk €	How €	Stile €	Tarn €
2 July:					1 July:				
Loan account	12,000	–	–	–	Balance b/d	12,000	8,000	3,000	–
					3 July:				
					Cash	–	–	–	2,500

A summarised balance sheet at 3 July would then show the following position:

	€
Sundry assets (€27,296 + 2,500)	29,796

Partners' accounts	Capital accounts €	Current accounts €	Total €
How	8,000	2,064	10,064
Stile	3,000	497	3,497
Tarn	2,500	–	2,500
	13,500	2,561	16,061
Loan account – Birk			13,735
			29,796

If Tarn had contributed his capital share in the form of an asset other than cash, for example a car valued at €2,500, the double entry would have been:

Debit	Credit	With
Motor car account	Tarn's capital account	€2,500

The only effect on the balance sheet would then be the make-up of the sundry assets figure of €16,061 as between non-current and current assets.

PARTNERSHIP CHANGES REQUIRING ADJUSTMENTS TO ASSET VALUES

Introduction

Two unrealistic assumptions have been made so far:

(a) No notice was taken of any difference between the current value of individual tangible assets and the amount at which they were stated in the books of account. On a change in partnership-sharing arrangements, such account must be taken as partners are entitled to share capital profits in the same ratio as they share revenue profits. Thus, just as we time-apportion profits between periods before and after the change, so we need to take account of capital gains or losses at the date of change. This topic is explored further below; and

(b) Goodwill was ignored. Its nature and measurement is dealt with later.

Why a Revaluation is Required on a Partnership Change

Any change in a partnership (and remember a change can be an admission of a new partner, the retirement of an old partner or a change in profit-sharing ratios) affects partners' rights to profits and assets. The entitlement to a one-third share in profits means an entitlement to a one-third share in the assets which exist in the partnership as well.

To the extent that the current worth of the assets is different from their book value, a profit or loss will have accrued on the asset from the date of acquisition of the asset to the date of the partnership change. This profit or loss will need to be allocated to each partner in the old profit-sharing ratio as the partnership change triggers off new profit-sharing ratios. The gain/loss is computed by re-valuing the net assets at the date of change.

Adjustments in Respect of Tangible Assets

Wherever there is a change in profit-sharing arrangements, a partnership will take account of changes in the value of its tangible assets. In this instance use will be made of a revaluation account to calculate the overall gain or loss on the revaluation; this will then be shared between the old partners in their old profit-sharing ratios. The initial bookkeeping entries are as follows:

Debit	Credit	With
Assets	Revaluation	Increases in assets values
Revaluation	Assets	Decreases in assets values
Liabilities	Revaluation	Decreases in liability values
Revaluation	Liabilities	Increases in liability values

At this stage the balance on the revaluation account will represent the surplus or deficiency on the revaluation, which will be shared between the old parties in their old profit-sharing ratios, via:

Debit	*Credit*	*With*
Revaluation or Partner's capital accounts	Partners' capital accounts Revaluation	Surplus on revaluation Deficit on revaluation

Example 12

Trooper, Tremlett and Arkle are in partnership, sharing profits in the ratio 4: 3: 3. As at 1 January 20X6 Randall is to be admitted to the partnership, thereafter profits are to be shared equally. Randall is to introduce capital of €30,000.

The partnership's balance sheet as at 31 December 20X5 shows the following:

	€	€
Non-current assets:		
Property		70,000
Plant and machinery		30,000
Fixtures and fittings		25,000
		125,000
Current assets:		
Inventory	35,000	
Receivables	28,000	
Bank	17,000	80,000
		205,000

	Capital €	Revenue €	Total €
Partners' accounts:			
Trooper	50,000	2,000	52,000
Tremlett	53,750	4,000	57,750
Arkle	65,000	3,000	68,000
	168,750	9,000	177,750
Current liabilities:			27,250
Payables			205,000

For the purposes of the revaluation the assets of the partnership are to be re-valued as follows:

	€
Property	80,000
Plant and machinery	27,500
Fixtures and fittings	32,100
Inventory	36,350
Receivables	27,750

You are required to show the:

(a) revaluation account;
(b) partners' capital accounts; and
(c) balance sheet of the partnership as at 1 January 20X6.

Solution

(a)

Revaluation

	€	€		€
Plant and machinery		2,500	Property	10,000
Receivables		250	Fixtures	7,100
Profit on realisation:			Inventory	1,350
Trooper(4)	6,280			
Tremlett	4,710			
Arkle	4,710			
		15,700		
		18,450		18,450

(b)

Partners' capital accounts

	Trooper	Tremlett	Arkle	Randall		Trooper	Tremlett	Arkle	Randall
	€	€	€	€		€	€	€	€
Balance c/d	56,280	58,460	69,710	30,000	Balance b/d	50,000	53,750	65,000	
					Revaln	6,280	4,710	4,710	
					Bank				30,000
	56,280	58,460	69,710	30,000		56,280	58460	69,710	30,000

(c)

Trooper, Tremlett, Arkle and Randell
Balance Sheet as at 1 January 20X6

	€	€
Non-current assets:		
Property		80,000
Plant and machinery		27,500
Fixtures and fittings		32,100
		139,600
Current assets:		
Inventory	36,350	
Receivables	27,750	
Bank	47,000	111,100
		250,700

	Capital	Current	Total
	€	€	€
Partners' accounts:			
Trooper	56,280	2,000	58,280
Tremlett	58,460	4,000	62,460
Arkle	69,710	3,000	72,710
Randall	30,000	–	30,000
	214,450	9,000	223,450
Current liabilities:			
Payables			27,250
			250,700

Note that the capital accounts were adjusted for the change in asset values as it is a capital transaction. In particular the revaluation does not create realised profits (i.e. they are not in the form of cash) and thus partners cannot increase their drawings out of their current accounts.

Goodwill

Measurement of Goodwill

As has previously been suggested, there can be no precise valuation of goodwill, which has to be essentially the result of an exercise of judgement of the worth of the business as a whole by the parties involved.

In examination questions the examiner will either tell you the valuation to be placed on the goodwill, or give sufficient information to enable you to calculate the figure. The most likely possibilities are as follows:

(a) Goodwill is valued at €12,000;
(b) X introduces €3,000 in payment for his share of one quarter of the goodwill. If a quarter share is valued at €3,000, then the total value for goodwill is €12,000;
(c) Goodwill is to be valued at three times last year's profit of €4,000. Three times last year's profit is €12,000, giving the total value for goodwill; and
(d) The business is worth €200,000 and the fair value of the tangible net assets is €160,000. Goodwill is therefore €40,000.

Adjustments in Respect of Goodwill

There are two main situations as regards goodwill:

(a) the partners wish to include goodwill as an asset in their balance sheet, which is the least likely situation in practice; or
(b) the partners do not wish to include goodwill as an asset in their balance sheet but the effect of goodwill needs to be reflected in their capital accounts.

Goodwill included as an Asset in the Balance Sheet

In this situation use can be made of the revaluation account in the normal fashion:

Debit	Credit	With
Goodwill	Revaluation	Increase in the value of goodwill
Revaluation	Goodwill	Decrease in the value of goodwill

If goodwill has not previously been incorporated in the books, the entry is:

Debit	Credit	With
Goodwill	Revaluation	The agreed value of goodwill

Example 13

Laid, Back and Gower are in partnership sharing profits 5:3:2. As at 1 January 20X7 Gooch is to be admitted to the partnership; thereafter profits are to be shared equally. Gooch is to introduce capital of €40,000, of which €10,000 represents a payment for his share of the goodwill, which is subsequently to be disclosed in the books.

The partnership's balance sheet as at 31 December 20X6 shows the following:

	€	€
Non-current assets:		
Property		42,500
Plant and machinery		16,750
Fixtures and fittings		12,800
		72,050
Current assets:		
Inventory	15,800	
Receivables	29,471	
Bank	18,623	63,894
		135,944
Partners' capital accounts:		
Laid		61,237
Back		18,476
Gower		31,518
		111,231
Current liabilities:		
Payables		24,713
		135,944

For the purposes of the revaluation the assets of the partnership are to be revalued as follows:

	€
Property	75,000
Plant and machinery	21,250
Fixtures and fittings	11,000

You are required to show:

(a) the revaluation account;
(b) the partners' capital accounts; and
(c) the balance sheet of the partnership as at 1 January 20X7.

Solution

(a)

	€	€		€
Fixtures and fittings		1,800	Property	32,500
Profit on revaluation:			Plant and machinery	4,500
Laid (5)	37,600		Goodwill	40,000
Back (3)	22,560			
Gower (2)	15,040			
		75,200		
		77,000		77,000

If Gooch is introducing €10,000 for his share of the goodwill (one quarter thereof), the total value of goodwill must be €40,000.

(b)

Partners' capital accounts

	Laid	Back	Gower	Gooch		Laid	Back	Back	Gooch
	€	€	€	€		€	€	€	€
Bal. c/d	98,837	41,036	46,558	40,000	Bal. b/d	61,237	18,476	31,518	
					Bank				40,000
					Revaluation	37,600	22,560	15,040	
	98,837	41,036	46,558	40,000		98,837	41,036	46,558	40,000

(c)

Laid, Black, Gower and Gooch
Balance sheet as at 1 January 20X7

	€	€
Non-current assets:		
Goodwill		40,000
Property		75,000
Plant and machinery		21,250
Fixtures and fittings		11,000
		147,250
Current assets:		
Inventory	15,800	
Receivables	29,471	
Bank	58,623	103,894
		251,144
Partners' capital accounts:		
Laid	98,837	
Back	41,036	
Gower	46,558	
Gooch	40,000	226,431
Less: Current liabilities		
Payables		24,713
		251,144

Goodwill is the only Asset that Requires Revaluation

Quite often, it is only goodwill which requires to be revalued. The book value of the tangible assets may be fairly close to their market value and thus the time and expense involved in making valuations is too much compared to the benefits.

If only goodwill is being revalued, the revaluation account need not be used. The revaluation increase (or decrease) can be transferred from the goodwill account to the partner's capital accounts.

Example 14

The Faldo, Woosnam partnership is to admit Newcomer into the partnership as at 1 July 20X6. Faldo and Woosnam currently share profits 3:1 after annual salaries of €100,000 each.

As from 1 July 20X6 the profit sharing ratio will be Faldo 3, Woosnam 2, Newcomer 2, after annual salaries of €120,000 each.

The partnership balance sheet as at 30 June 20X6 shows:

	€
Assets:	45,000

Partners' account:	Capital €	Current €	Total €
Faldo	20,000	8,000	28,000
Woosnam	12,000	5,000	17,000
	32,000	13,000	45,000

Goodwill which does not currently appear on the balance sheet is estimated to be worth €280,000, Newcomer is to pay €90,000 capital into the business. Goodwill is to remain as an asset in the books.

You are required to show the partnership balance sheet as at 1 July 20X6 after the admission of Newcomer.

Solution

Faldo, Woosnam and Newcomer
Balance sheet as at 1 July 20X6

	€
Goodwill	280,000
Other assets (€45,000 + €90,000)	135,000
	415,000

Partners' accounts	Capital €	Current €	Total €
Faldo	230,000	8,000	238,000
Woosnam	82,000	5,000	87,000
Newcomer	90,000	–	90,000
	402,000	13,000	415,000

Workings

Goodwill

	€	€
Valuation to capital accounts	280,000	

Capital accounts

	Faldo	Woosnam	Newcomer		Faldo	Woosnam	Newcomer
	€	€	€		€	€	€
Balance c/d	230,000	82,000	90,000	Balance b/d	20,000	12,000	
				Goodwill 3:1	210,000	70,000	
				Cash			90,000
	230,000	82,000	90,000		230,000	82,000	90,000

Goodwill not included as an Asset in the Balance Sheet

In many cases goodwill will not be shown on the balance sheet after a partnership change despite the fact that a new partner, for example, has paid for a share.

There are a number of reasons why partnerships do not wish to record goodwill in the balance sheet:

Subjective nature of valuation – the value attached to goodwill on a partnership change is either a matter of negotiation between the partners or derived from a formula in the partnership agreement. It only represents a value attached to the asset at the time of the change. In changing business conditions in the future its value may be very different.

Taxation – for capital gains tax purposes it is generally disadvantageous to record partnership goodwill as an asset.

Amortisation (depreciation) – if goodwill is recorded as an asset should it not be depreciated like any other non-current asset?

Some would say yes and some no. The argument is, however, avoided if goodwill is not shown in the first place.

This will not change the need to make entries; the old partners by allowing another person into partnership are sharing their business with him. They are thus selling some of the past goodwill to him and this fact needs to be recorded in the capital accounts.

The approach to be adopted in this instance is to open up temporarily an account for goodwill, using the following journal entries

Debit	Credit	With
Goodwill New partner's capital accounts	Old partners' capital accounts Goodwill	Their share of the goodwill (using old profit-sharing ratio) Their share of the goodwill (using new profit-sharing ratio)

In simple terms this can be described as:

(a) Write up goodwill in the old profit-sharing ratios (OPSR); and
(b) Write it down in the new profit-sharing ratios (NPSR).

Example 15

Francis, Robson and Hateley are in partnership sharing profits 7:2:1. As at 1 January 20X8 Harford is to be admitted to the partnership; thereafter profits are to be shared 3:3:3:1. Harford is to introduce capital of €50,000, of which €12,000 represents a payment for his share of the goodwill, not to be disclosed in the books.

An extract from the partnership balance sheet as at 31 December 20X7 shows the following:

	€
Capital accounts:	
Francis	36,761
Robson	27,304
Hateley	29,287
	93,352

Assuming that there are no other re-valuations necessary to other assets you are required to show:

(a) partners' capital accounts; and
(b) goodwill account.

Solution

(a)

Partners' capital account

	Francis €	Robson €	Hateley €	Harford €		Francis €	Robson €	Hateley €	Harford €
Gwill	36,000	36,000	36,000	12,000	Bal. b/d	36,761	7,304	29,287	
					Bank				50,000
Bal. c/d	84,761	15,304	5,287	38,000	Gwill	84,000	24,000	12,000	
	120,761	51,304	41,287	50,000		120,761	51,304	41,287	50,000

(b)

Goodwill

	€		€
Francis (7)	84,000	Francis (3)	36,000
Robson (2)	24,000	Robson (3)	36,000
Hateley (1)	12,000	Hateley (3)	36,000
		Harford (1)	12,000
	120,000		120,000

If Harford is introducing €12,000 for his share of the goodwill (one-tenth thereof) the total value of goodwill must be €120,000.

Conclusion

Goodwill invariably appears as a complication in questions involving partnerships. The key is to follow the requirements of the question.

Confusion often arises in the case of goodwill not shown in the books in the sense that it appears most unfair that Harford, in the previous example, for instance, pays in €50,000 on admission to the partnership and yet ends up with only €38,000 on his capital account. However, the point to remember is that the balance sheet does not include goodwill.

If goodwill were subsequently to be included in the books, say on 2 January 20X8, Harford's capital account would be credited with his share of the goodwill (l/10 x €120,000 = €12,000).

Similarly, if the partnership were dissolved, Harford would be entitled to a one-tenth share in the profit on the disposal of the partnership, which would include the valuation placed on the goodwill.

In any event the key is to follow the requirement in the question, which is likely to treat the partners fairly.

DISSOLUTION OF PARTNERSHIP

Objective of Dissolution

The objective of dissolution is to dispose of the partnership assets, pay off the liabilities and distribute the balance to the partners according to their entitlements.

The amount each partner receives is the balance on his or her capital account plus his or her share of the profit arising on the disposal of the assets (or minus any share of loss). If the final result is that a partner's account is in deficit, he or she has to pay the money in to allow the other partners to draw out their full entitlement.

Reasons for Dissolution

Possible reasons for dissolution include:

(a) death or retirement of a partner;
(b) disagreement among the partners;
(c) continuing trading losses; and
(d) completion of the purpose for which the partnership was formed.

Whatever the reason, the accounting treatment is the same.

The Realisation Account

The first bookkeeping step in dealing with dissolution is to open a realisation account, sometimes called a dissolution account. All the assets balances except cash in hand and cash at bank are transferred in to the debit of the realisation account. The proceeds of sale of these assets will be credited to the realisation account, the balance on which will then be the profit or loss on the dissolution, subject to some minor items.

The assets could be sold separately or as a single going concern unit. In either case the proceeds are credited to the realisation account.

Dealing with Liabilities

The liabilities of the partnership have to be paid – credit cash and debit the liability accounts.

It may be that liabilities are paid off for a little more or less than the book amounts, perhaps because of cash discounts or negotiated settlements. Any such difference is debited or credited to the realisation account as representing the loss or profit arising on the final settlement of the liabilities.

Expenses of Dissolution

The expenses of dissolution are simply debited to the realisation account when paid.

Assets Taken Over by the Partners

It may be that partners agree to takeover certain partnership assets at dissolution. To record this we simply credit the realisation account and debit the capital account of the partner concerned.

Partners' Accounts

Partners may have both capital accounts and current accounts. The distinction between them ceases to have any meaning on dissolution and current account balances should be transferred to the capital accounts.

Sale of Business as a Going Concern – Goodwill

If the business is sold as a going concern, this means that a single sum is received for all or most of the assets. The value of unrecorded goodwill may be an element in the total consideration, but there is no need to record this specially. The total consideration is credited to the realisation account (debit cash) and the value attributed to the goodwill merely added to the profit on the sale and is thus automatically credited to the partners in their profit-sharing ratios.

Sale of Business as a Going Concern – Liabilities Taken Over

A purchaser of the business may agree to take over all or some of the partnership's liabilities. The easiest way to deal with this is to credit the liabilities taken over to the realisation account, so that the profit or loss arising on the sale in the realisation account is the difference between the consideration and the *net assets* taken over.

Final Settlement with the Partners

When all the entries described above have been recorded, there will remain only the partners' capital accounts and the cash at bank. It only remains to draw cheques to pay the partners the balances due to them. Any partner with a debit balance on his or her capital account will pay in cash to clear the balance.

It could happen that the dissolution is spread over a long period so that payments on account are made to the partners as the sale of the assets proceeds.

Example 16

Here is a comprehensive example covering nearly all the procedures described above.

A, B and C share profits 4:3:3. They agree to dissolve their partnership at the end of the financial year, when the balance sheet appeared as follows:

	€	€
Non-current assets, at cost less depreciation:		
Freehold		40,000
Plant and machinery		15,000
Motor vehicles (three cars)		16,000
		71,000
Current assets:		
Inventory	50,000	
Receivables	25,000	
Cash	15,000	
		90,000
		161,000

Partners' account:

	A €	B €	C €	Total €
Capital	40,000	30,000	20,000	90,000
Current	15,000	10,000	5,000	30,000
	55,000	40,000	25,000	120,000
Current liabilities				21,000
Loan account – D				20,000
				161,000

The following are sold for cash:

	€
Freehold	80,000
Plant and machinery	13,000
Inventory	43,000
	136,000

The payables are settled for €20,000.
C takes over the receivables at an agreed value of €22,000.
A takes over D's loan at its book value.
A, B and C take over the cars at the following valuations:

A	€6,000
B	€8,000
C	€4,000

Realisation expenses are €2,000.
Prepare the ledger accounts to show the closing of the partnership records.

Solution

Numbers in brackets refer to sequence of entries.

Realisation account

	€		€
Book value of assets:		Sale or disposal proceeds:	
Realisation expenses		(i) Cash – sold	
To partners – profit on realisation in PSR		(ii) Partners' accounts – assets taken over	
(1) Freehold account	40,000	(2) Cash – sale proceeds	136,000
(1) Plant and machinery account	15,000	(4) Discount received on payables	1,000

	€		€
(1) Motor vehicles account	16,000	Partners' accounts – assets taken over:	
(1) Inventory account	50,000	(5) C receivables	22,000
(1) Receivables account	25,000	(5) A motor car	6,000
(7) Cash – realisation expenses	2,000	(5) B motor car	8,000
Partners' accounts – profit on		(5) C motor car	4,000
A 40% €11,600			
B 30% €8,700			
C 30% €8,700	29,000		
	177,000		177,000

Partners' accounts

	A €	B €	C €		A €	B €	C €
(5) Receivables taken over			22,000	Balances b/d:			
(5) Motor cars taken over	6,000	8,000	4,000	Capital accounts	40,000	30,000	20,000
(8) Cash to settle	80,600	40,700	7,700	Current accounts	15,000	10,000	5,000
				(6) D's loan account	20,000		
				Realisation Account: Profit	11,600	8,700	8,700
	86,600	48,700	33,700		86,600	48,700	33,700

Payables' account

	€		€
(3) Cash	20,000	Balance b/d	21,000
(4) Realisation account discount received on settlement	1,000		
	21,000		21,000

D's loan account

	€		€
(6) Cash	20,000	Balance b/d	20,000

	€		€
Cash account			
Balance b/d	15,000	(3) Payables	20,000
Sale proceeds to realisation account:		(7) Realisation expenses	2,000
		Partners' accounts to settle	
(2) Freehold	80,000	(8)A	80,600
(2) Plant/machinery	13,000	(8)B	40,700
(2) Inventory	43,000	(8)C	7,700
	136,000		129,000
	151,000		151,000

AMALGAMATIONS

Procedure

Step 1 – Each trader/partner will record the capital profit or loss accruing to him at the date of the merger. Values will be placed on the tangible net assets and goodwill of each trader's/partner's business and these values can be incorporated into the trader's/partner's books by use of a revaluation account. The entries will be similar to the revaluation of assets on a partnership change. The balancing figure in the revaluation account will be transferred to the trader's capital account.

Step 2 – Any assets not being taken over by the new partnership are removed from the trader's/partner's books by transferring the book value of the assets to the debit of the trader's/partner's capital account.

Step 3 – The separate books can now be merged at the agreed values. The new partnership assets will be the sum of the assets of the two sole trader's/partner's and each person's capital account will be their opening balance of capital in the new partnership. If goodwill is not to appear as an asset in the balance sheet, the combined amount needs to be written off against each partner's capital account in a new profit-sharing ratio.

Example 17

A agrees to amalgamate with C to form X & Co.
The balance sheets of the two businesses at the date of the merger were as follows:

	A €	C €
Non-current assets:		
Freehold property	10,000	
Plant and machinery	4,000	7,000
Motor vehicle	3,000	
	17,000	7,000
Current assets:		
Inventory	4,000	3,000
Receivables	2,000	1,000
Cash at bank	2,000	4,000
	25,000	15,000
Capital accounts:		
A	18,000	
C		9,000
Loan from F	2,000	
Trade payables	5,000	6,000
	25,000	15,000

X & Co was to take over all the assets and liabilities of the two businesses except:

(a) F's loan, for which A agreed to take over responsibility; and
(b) A was to take over the car

The following were the agreed values placed on the assets of the old businesses.

	A €	C €
Goodwill	9,000	3,000
Freehold property	14,000	–
Plant and machinery	3,000	6,000
Inventory	4,000	2,000
Receivables	2,000	1,000

Trade payables were taken over at their book value.

Profit sharing in the new firm is 3:1 between A and C.

Goodwill was not to appear in the new firm's balance sheet.

You are required to prepare the:

(a) balance sheet of X & Co immediately following the amalgamation; and
(b) closing entries in the books of A and C to record the revaluation and the entries in their capital accounts.

Solution

(a) X & Co – Balance sheet after merger

	€	€
Non-current assets:		
Freehold property		14,000
Plant and machinery (3,000 + 6,000)		9,000
		23,000
Current assets:		
Inventory (4,000 + 2,000)	6,000	
Receivables (2,000 + 1,000)	3,000	
Cash (2,000 + 4,000)	6,000	15,000
		38,000
Capital accounts:		
A		20,000
B		7,000
		27,000
Current liabilities:		
Trade payables (5,000 + 6,000)		11,000
		38,000

Example 18

P and Q are in partnership in a similar business to R and S. It is agreed that the two partnerships should amalgamate into one firm called Letters. The profit-sharing ratios are as follows:

	P	Q	R	S
Old Firms	3	2	3	2
New Firm	8	5	4	3

At the date of amalgamation, the balance sheets of the two firms were as follows:

	PQ €	RS €			PQ €	RS €
Assets	39,000	33,000	Capital	P	20,000	
Bank	1,000	2,000		Q	15,000	
				R		16,000
				S		12,000
			Liabilities		5,000	7,000
	40,000	35,000			40,000	35,000

The agreement to amalgamate provides that the assets of PQ be valued at €45,000 and the assets of RS be valued at €29,000. Payables are to be taken over at net book value.

The capital of Letters is to be €66,000 and is to be contributed by the partners in their new profit sharing ratio.

Close the books of PQ and RS and prepare the opening balance sheet of Letters.

Solution

	Total	P	Q	R	S
New Profit sharing ratio	20	8	5	4	3
Capital to be contributed	€66,000	€26,400	€16,500	€13,200	€9,900

Realisation accounts

	PQ €	RS €			PQ €	PQ €	RS €	RS €
Assets	39,000	33,000	Payables			5,000		7,000
Profit on Realisation			Assets to					
P: 3/5 €3,600			Letters	45,000			29,000	
Q: 2/5 €2,400		6,000	Less:					
			Payables	5,000	40,000		7,000	22,000
			Loss on Realisation					
			R: 3/5				2,400	
			S: 2/5				1,600	4,000
	45,000	33,000			45,000			33,000

Bank accounts

	PQ €	RS €			PQ €	RS €
Balance	1,000	2,000	Capital Account	Q	900	
Capital Account P	2,800			R		400
				S		500
			Letters		2,900	1,100
	3,800	2,000			3,800	2,000

Capital accounts

	P €	Q €	R €	S €		P €	Q €	R €	S €
Loss on Realisation			2,400	1,600	Balance	20,000	15,000	16,000	12,000
Balance to Letters	26,400	16,500	13,200	9,900	Profit on Realisation	3,600	2,400		
Bank		900	400	500	Bank	2,800			
	26,400	17,400	16,000	12,000		26,400	17,400	16,000	12,000

Letters

	PQ €	RS €			PQ €	RS €
Assets (net)	40,000	22,000	Capital Account	P	26,400	
Bank	2,900	1,100		Q	16,500	
				R		13,200
				S		9,900
	42,900	23,100			42,900	23,100

Letters – balance sheet

	€		€
Assets	74,000	Capital Account P €26,400	
Bank	4,000	Q €16,500	
		R €13,200	
		S € 9,900	66,000
		Liabilities	12,000
	78,000		78,000

CONVERSION TO A LIMITED COMPANY

Sometimes the assets and liabilities of a partnership are transferred to a limited company in exchange for shares and the partnership is dissolved. There are basically two stages involved in this process:

(a) Closing the partnership books; and
(b) Setting up the purchasing company's books.

Closing the Partnership Books

1. Transfer all assets (except cash) and liabilities to the realisation account at book value;
2. Clear the Current accounts to the Capital accounts;
3. The purchase consideration to be paid by the company should be credited to the realisation account and debited to a 'personal account' opened for the purchasing company;
4. Close off the realisation account transferring any balance to the Partners' accounts in their profit sharing ratio;
5. Close off the Purchasing Company's personal account by crediting it with shares, debentures or cash as appropriate; and
6. Close off the partners' accounts by debiting them with shares, debentures or cash in agreed proportions.

The Purchasing Company's Books

1. Record the acquisition by using a 'Purchase of Business Account';
2. In the Purchase of Business Account:
    *   Credit it with the assets taken over, debiting the individual ledger accounts;
    *   Debit it with the liabilities taken over, crediting the individual ledger accounts;
    *   Debit it with the purchase consideration, creating the appropriate accounts; and
    *   Any difference between the purchase consideration paid and the value of the assets acquired will be treated either as goodwill or a capital reserve.

Example 19

Macbeth and Hamlet are in partnership selling draughty castles, sharing profits in the ratio 3:2. Their draft balance sheet at 31 December 20X8 is as follows:

	Cost €	Depreciation €	Net €
Non-current assets			
Freehold premises	30,000		30,000
Fixtures and fittings	5,000	4,000	1,000
Motor vehicles	4,000	1,000	3,000
	39,000	5,000	34,000
Current assets			
Sundry receivables			20,000
Cash at bank			600
			54,600
Partnership accounts			
Capital accounts			
Macbeth			20,000
Hamlet			2,500
			22,500
Current accounts			
Macbeth			3,000
Hamlet			500
			26,000
Non-current liabilities			
Loan – Macbeth			16,000
Current liabilities			
Sundry payables			12,600
			54,600

Lear Limited is incorporated for the purpose of taking over the business. It is to acquire the freehold premises at a valuation of €40,000 and the other assets (with the exception of cash and motor vehicles) at book value. These values are to be introduced into Lear Limited's books. The current liabilities are also taken over by the new company.

The purchase consideration of €60,000 is to be settled by 20,000 ordinary €1 shares in Lear Limited and cash of €30,000, obtained by a bank overdraft. Hamlet is to take over both cars at a valuation of €2,500 and the partners have agreed to divide the shares in their profit-sharing ratio. Macbeth's loan is to be repaid in cash by the partnership.

Show the ledger account transactions necessary to record the above in the partnership.

Solution

(1)

Realisation A/C

	€		€
Premise s	30,000	Motor vehicles	2,500
F &F	1,000	Payables	12,600
MV	3,000	Loan	16,000
Receivables	20,000	Purchase consideration	
Loan (bank)	16,000	(Lear Limited)	60,000
Partners:			
Hamlet	8,440		
Macbeth	12,660		
	91,100		91,100

(2)

Capital accounts

	Macbeth	Hamlet		Macbeth	Hamlet
	€	€		€	€
Cars		2,500	Balance b/d	20,000	2,500
Lear – Shares	18,000	12,000	Current A/c	3,000	500
Bank	17,660		Realisation A/c	12,660	8,440
			Bank		3,060
	35,660	14,500		35,660	14,500

(3)

Lear Limited A/c

	€		€
Realisation account	60,000	Partners' Account: (Shares)	
		Macbeth	18,000
		Hamlet	12,000
			30,000
		Bank	30,000
	60,000		60,000

(4)

Cash A/C

	€		€
Balance b/d	600	Loan	16,000
Lear	30,000	Macbeth	17,660
Hamlet	3,060		
	33,660		33,660

(5) Lear Limited

Purchase of Business A/C

	€		€
Payables	12,600	Premises	40,000
Purchase Consideration:		Fixtures & fittings	1,000
Share capital	20,000	Receivables	20,000
Share premium	10,000		
Bank	30,000	∴ Goodwill	11,600
	72,600		72,600

Example 20

A, B and C are in partnership sharing profits and losses 5/8, 2/8 and 1/8. They decide to form a limited company, ABC Limited, and transfer the net assets, other than cash thereto. The balance sheet of the partnership at the date of transfer was as follows:

	€				€
Assets	35,000	Capital Account:	A	€12,000	
Bank	5,000		B	€10,000	
			C	€8,000	30,000
		Payables			10,000
	40,000				40,000

The assets (excluding bank) are being taken over at a valuation of €50,000, payables at net book value. The purchase consideration is €45,000 made up of 160,000 ordinary shares of 25 cents each, to be divided amongst the partners A: 1/2, B 1/4, C: 1/4 and €5,000 10% debentures to be divided in profit-sharing ratio.

Close the books of the partnership and show the opening balance sheet of ABC Limited.

Solution

The first step is to prepare the realisation account transferring the book value of the assets into the account and, if any liabilities are being taken over, the book value of the liabilities as a credit into the account. The purchase consideration is then credited into the account and debited to an account with the new company (ABC Limited) and the difference is the profit or loss on realisation. In this example there is a profit of €20,000 which is divided between the partners in their profit-sharing ratio. See below.

Realisation Account

		€			€
Assets		35,000	Payables		10,000
Profit on realisation:			ABC Limited - Net assets		45,000
Capital A/c A 5/8	€12,500				
B 2/8	€5,000				
C 1/8	€2,500				
	20,000				
	55,000				55,000

The next step is to set out the capital accounts of the partners in columnar form as set out below:

Capital Accounts

	A €	B €	C €		A €	B €	C €
Ordinary shares in ABC Limited	20,000	10,000	10,000	Balances	12,000	10,000	8,000
				Profit on realisation	12,500	5,000	2,500
Debentures in ABC Limited	3,125	1,250	625	Bank Account			125
Bank account	1,375	3,750					
	24,500	15,000	10,625		24,500	15,000	10,625

The capital accounts have opening balances of €12,000, €10,000 and €8,000 respectively. The profit on realisation is credited to their accounts from the realisation account. Their accounts are debited with the purchase consideration which is in the form of:

 (i) 160,000 ordinary shares of 25 cents each; and
(ii) €5,000 10% debentures.

The credits are to the accounts with the new company (ABC Limited.).

   The ordinary shares are to be divided amongst the partners as agreed in the ratios of A:1/2, B:1/4, C:1/4 therefore the 160,000 shares at 25 cents each, i.e. €40,000 will be divided as follows:

A   €20,000 (80,000 shares);
B   €10,000 (40,000 shares)
C   €10,000 (40,000 shares)

On the other hand the debentures are to be divided as agreed in their profit-sharing ratio so they will be divided as follows:

A   (5/8)   €3,125
B   (2/8)   €1,250
C   (1/8)   €625

The balance remaining in the bank account is then distributed to the partners to pay off the remaining balance in their capital accounts. In the solution to this question it is assumed that C has sufficient funds to pay off the debit balance of €125 which arises on his account. If not, that balance would be borne by the other partners on the basis of their last agreed capitals.

Bank Account

	€			€
Balance	5,000	Capital Account	A	1,375
Capital Account C	125		B	3,750
	5,125			5,125

ABC Limited

	€		€
Realisation Account	45,000	Capital Account – Shares	40,000
		Debentures	5,000
	45,000		45,000

New Company: ABC Limited

In addition to closing down the books of the partnership it is necessary to set up an opening balance sheet of the new company. This balance sheet will include the ordinary shares and debentures issued by the company which are offset by the assets less liabilities taken over. The balance sheet of ABC Limited in this example will be as follows:

Balance Sheet

	€		€
Assets	50,000	Ordinary shares	40,000
Goodwill (see note 3)	5,000	10% debentures	5,000
		Payables	10,000
	55,000		55,000

Notes

1. 160,000 shares of 25 cents each were issued, thus the ordinary share capital will be €40,000.
2. €5,000 of 10% debentures were also issued.
3. The assets taken over are brought in to the new balance sheet at the valuation when taken over, i.e. €50,000 and the liabilities, in this case payables, at €10,000. This means that there are net assets taken over of €40,000 which cost the company €45,000 and therefore the company has paid for goodwill in the amount of €5,000 which must also be included in the opening balance sheet to balance it.

Example 21

Apple, Pear, Banana and Grape are in partnership sharing profits and losses 7:4:2:2. At 31 December 1986 they decide to form a limited company called Fruit Limited. At that date the Balance Sheet of the Partnership was as follows:

	€			€
Goodwill	30,000	Capital Account	Apple	80,000
Property	70,000		Pear	30,000
Plant	23,600		Banana	19,000
Motor Vehicles	12,900		Grape	17,000
				146,000
Inventory	32,300	Loan Account -	Apple	9,000
Receivables	30,300	Payables		31,700
		Bank overdraft		12,400
	199,100			199,100

The company is to take over all assets and liabilities except the bank overdraft and Apple's loan which is to be settled by the other partners in their profit-sharing ratio. The costs of conversion, which amounted to €3,200, are to be paid by the partnership.

The payables are to be taken over at a discount of €1,900 and the assets at the following valuations.

	€
Goodwill	Nil
Property	85,000
Plant	22,000
Motor Vehicles	10,700
Inventory	27,600
Receivables	29,100

The purchase consideration is €140,000, made up of 125,000 ordinary shares of €1 each (€65,000 of which are payable to Apple, the balance to be divided among the other partners in their profit sharing ratio) and €10,000 in cash.

You are required to close the books of the partnership, and prepare the opening Balance Sheet of Fruit Limited, assuming all the above transactions have taken place.

Solution

Realisation Account

	€			€
Assets at NBV	199,100	Payables		31,700
Bank - Cost of Conversion	3,200	Fruit Limited - Purchase		
		consideration		140,000
		Loss on realisation		
		Apple	7/15	14,280	
		Pear	4/15	8,160	
		Banana	2/15	4,080	
		Grape	2/15	4,080	30,600
	202,300			202,300

Loan Account - Apple

			€		€
Capital Account	Pear	4/8	4,500	Balance	9,000
	Banana	2/8	2,250		
	Grape	2/8	2,250		
			9,000		9,000

Bank Account

		€		€
Fruit Limited		10,000	Balance	12,400
Capital Account	Apple	1,880	Cost of conversion	3,200
	Pear	4,860	Capital Account Banana	1,570
	Grape	430		
		17,170		17,170

Capital Accounts

	Apple €	Pear €	Banana €	Grape €		Apple €	Pear €	Banana €	Grape €
Loss on					Balance	80,000	30,000	19,000	17,000
Realisation	14,280	8,160	4,080	4,080	Loan Apple		4,500	2,250	2,250
Fruit - Ord.					Bank	1,880	4,860	–	430
Shares	65,000	30,000	15,000	15,000					
Share									
Premium	2,600	1,200	600	600					
Bank			1,570						
	81,880	39,360	21,250	19,680		81,880	39,360	21,250	19,680

Example

Fruit Limited

	€			€	€	€
Purchase consideration	140,000	Ordinary Shares:				
		Apple				65,000
		Pear	4/8	30,000		
		Banana	2/8	15,000		
		Grape	2/8	15,000	60,000	125,000
		Share Premium:				
		Apple	65/125		2,600	
		Pear	30/125		1,200	
		Banana	15/125		600	
		Grape	15/125		600	5,000
		Cash				10,000
	140,000					140,000

Fruit Limited
Balance Sheet - 1 January 1986

	€		€
Property	85,000	Ordinary shares o f €1 each	125,000
Plant	22,000	Share Premium	5,000
Motor Vehicles	10,700	Capital reserve (see note)	4,600
Inventory	27,600		134,600
Receivables	29,100	Payables	29,800
		Bank overdraft	10,000
	174,400		174,400

This is to be divided amongst the partners in the ratio of the shares issued.

Capital Reserve

		€	€
Asset Valuations:			
	Property	85,000	
	Plant	22,000	
	Motor Vehicles	10,700	
	Inventory	27,600	
	Receivables	29,100	
		174,400	
Less:	Payables	29,800	144,600
Purchase consideration			140,000
Capital Reserve			4,600

Capital reserve is effectively the opposite of goodwill.

CONCLUSION

Having studied this chapter on Partnership Accounts you should ensure that you understand the following key points:

- The initial capital put into the business by each partner is shown by means of a capital account for each partner.
- Each partner also has a current account.
- The net profit of the partnership is appropriated by the partners according to some previously agreed ratio.
- Partners may be charged interest on their drawings and may receive interest on capital. If a partner makes a loan to the business, he will receive interest on it in the normal way.
- On admission or retirement of a partner, one partnership ends and another begins. The goodwill of the old partnership must be valued and attributed to the old partners in the old profit-sharing ratio, as should any profit or loss on revaluation of assets. If goodwill (or revaluation profits and losses) are not to be retained in the books, they must be attributed to the new partners in the new profit-sharing ratio (debit capital accounts for goodwill and revaluation surplus, credit for revaluation deficit).
- The conversion of a partnership business to a limited company effectively involves the dissolution of the partnership. The assets are transferred to the company in exchange for an issue of shares and loan stock.

QUESTIONS

Self-test Questions

1. What is a Partnership?
2. What is the difference between a partner's capital account and a partner's current account?
3. How is profit shared between partners?
4. What are the entries required to introduce goodwill into a partnership and subsequently to eliminate it?
5. If tangible assets are revalued on admission of a partner, how is the profit or loss on revaluation treated?
6. What does a realisation account act as?
7. What is the entry for the purchase consideration from a company for the partnership assets?
8. Where does the balance on the realisation account go?
9. In the company's books, where does the balance on the vendor account go?

Review Questions

(See APPENDIX ONE for Suggested Solutions to Review Questions.)

Question 1 *(Based on ICAI, P2 Summer 1997)*

Murphy, Noonan and MacIntyre are in partnership sharing profits and losses in the ratio
4:3:1. The following balance sheet was available for the partnership for the year ended 31
December 1995:

	€'000	€'000
Non-current assets		
Premises		150,000
Fixtures and fittings		65,000
Motor vehicles		40,000
		255,000
Current assets		
Inventory	20,000	
Receivables	15,000	
Bank	25,000	
		60,000
		315,000
Capital accounts		
Murphy	120,000	
Noonan	90,000	
MacIntyre	40,000	250,000
Current accounts		
Murphy	7,500	
Noonan	4,200	
MacIntyre	3,300	15,000
Loan from MacIntyre		10,000
Current liabilities		
Payables		40,000
		315,000

The following additional information is available:

(1) On 31 December 1995, MacIntyre decided to retire from the partnership, and on
1 January 1996, Riordan was admitted to the partnership. It was agreed that the new
profit sharing ratio would be Murphy, Noonan, Riordan 5:4:1.
(2) On 31 December 1995, some of the assets and liabilities of the partnership were revalued as follows:

	€'000
Premises	200
Fixtures and fittings	40
Inventory	15

All other assets and liabilities remained at their existing book values.

(3) It was agreed that Riordan would introduce €40,000 into the partnership, this amount to include €6,000 in respect of Riordan's share of goodwill. A goodwill account is not to be maintained permanently in the accounts of the partnership.

(4) On MacIntyre's retirement, it was agreed that he should take his car at its net book value in part payment of all that is owed to him by the partnership, excluding his loan. In relation to his loan of €10,000, MacIntyre agreed to an immediate repayment of half this amount, with the balance remaining as a loan to the partnership.

(5) Profits for the year ended 31 December 1996 were €28,000.

(6) Cash drawings in the year ended 31 December 1996 were as follows:

	€
Murphy	4,000
Noonan	2,000
Riordan	1,000

(7) Following a major disagreement between the partners on 31 December 1996, it was decided that the partnership should be dissolved. The firm paid its payables in full, paid realisation expenses of €2,000, and repaid MacIntyre's loan of €5,000. The assets of the firm realised €270,000.

(8) The balance sheet extract for the partnership (before dissolution) at 31 December 1996 was as follows:

	€'000
Premises	200
Fixtures and fittings	40
Motor vehicles	35
Inventory	23
Receivables	35
Bank	4.7
Payables	(40)
Loan from MacIntyre	(5)
	292.7

Requirement

(a) Prepare the revaluation account at 31 December 1995.

(b) Prepare the realisation account on the dissolution of the partnership.

(c) Prepare the partners' capital and current accounts to reflect all of the above transactions.

Question 2 *(Based on ICAI, P2 Summer 1996)*

North, South and East have been in partnership for many years sharing profits in the ratio 5:3:2. On 1 January, 1995, they formed a company, Direction Limited, to take over the assets and liabilities of the partnership at that date. The following information is available:

(1) The balance sheet of the partnership as at 31 December, 1994, is as follows:

		€'000
Non-current assets		85
Inventory		15
Trade receivables		35
Bank		5
		140
Capital accounts		
North		40
South		35
East		20
Current accounts		
North		8
South		4
East		3
Payables		30
		140

(2) The agreement to take over the net assets of the partnership provides that the non-current assets would be taken over at a value of €130,000 and receivables at €30,000. All other assets and liabilities are to be taken over at book value.

(3) The company is to issue €1 ordinary shares to the partners in proportion to the final balances remaining on their capital accounts (after the transfer of current account balances) at 31 December 1994.

(4) The company was incorporated on 1 January 1995.

(5) It is agreed that the three partners should become directors of the company and should each receive directors' fees of €2,000 per annum.

(6) Direction Limited prepared the following trial balance at 31 December 1995:

	€'000	€'000
Non-current assets	230	
Receivables	60	
Inventory	25	
Bank	20	
Payables	–	40
Share capital and reserves	–	295
	335	335

Requirement

(a) Close the books of the partnership.
(b) Prepare the balance sheet of Direction Limited for the year ended 31 December 1995.

Question 3 (Based on ICAI, P2 Summer 1999)

Redcar, Pontefract and Haydock are in partnership sharing profits 5:3:2. The year end of the partnership is 31 December. On 31 December 1998, Haydock retires from the partnership. The summarised balance sheet of the partnership at that date is as follows:

Redcar, Pontefract & Haydock
Balance Sheet as at 31 December 1998

	€'000	€'000
Non-current assets		120
Current assets	50	
Bank	10	
		60
		180
Capital accounts		
Redcar	80	
Pontefract	40	
Haydock	20	140
Current liabilities		40
		180

The following additional information is available:

1. On the same date that Haydock retired, it was agreed that Ludlow would be admitted as a partner. Ludlow would introduce €50,000 into the partnership; this amount was to include €5,000 in respect of his share of goodwill. A goodwill account is *not* to be maintained in the books of the partnership.
2. The new profit-sharing ratio would be: Redcar : Pontefract : Ludlow 6:3:1.
3. At 31 December 1998, non-current assets were valued at €160,000 and current assets were valued at €45,000. The balance owing to Haydock on his retirement should be transferred to a loan account.

Requirement Assuming that the assets of the partnership are to be taken over at their revalued amounts, show:

(a) the revaluation account;
(b) the partners' capital account; and
(c) the amended balance sheet of the partnership to reflect the above changes.

Question 4 *(Based on ICAI, P2 Summer 2000)*

BECKHAM and ADAMS are in partnership sharing profits in the ratio of 5:3. NOO-NAN and NORTON are in partnership in a similar business sharing profits in the ratio of 5:4. It is decided that the two partnerships should amalgamate to form one firm A B & N.

The following information is available:

(1) The profit-sharing ratios in the new firm will be as follows:
    BECKHAM: ADAMS: NOONAN: NORTON – 10:7:8:5
(2) The balance sheets of the two firms at the date of the amalgamation were as follows:

	BECKHAM & ADAMS	NOONAN and NORTON
	€'000	€'000
Non-current assets	50	30
Current Assets		
Inventory	10	12
Receivables	20	13
Bank	15	5
	95	60
Capital Accounts		
Beckham	50	
Adams	25	
Noonan		35
Norton		15
Current Liabilities		
Payables	15	10
Taxation payable	5	—
	95	60

(3) Under the terms of the amalgamation, the following was agreed:
    (i) The non-current assets of BECKHAM and ADAMS would be valued at €70,000 while the non-current assets of NOONAN and NORTON would be valued at €20,000.
    (ii) The inventory of BECKHAM and ADAMS would be valued at €7,000 while the inventory of NOONAN and NORTON would be valued at €10,000.
    (iii) All other assets and all liabilities to be taken over at their book values.
(4) The capital of A B & N is to be contributed by the partners in their profit-sharing ratios and is to amount in total to €130,000.

Requirement

(a) Close the books of the partnerships of BECKHAM and ADAMS, and NOONAN and NORTON by preparing the following accounts:
  (i) The partners' capital account;
  (ii) The realisation account;
  (iii) The bank account.
(b) Prepare the opening balance sheet of A B & N.

Question 5 *(Based on ICAI, P2 Autumn 2000)*

Rod, Hook and Bait are in partnership sharing profits in the ratio 6: 4: 2. The balance sheet of the partnership as at 31 December 1998 was as follows:

	€'000	€'000
Non-current assets		2,000
Current assets		
Inventory	300	
Receivables	900	
Bank	100	
		1,300
		3,300
Capital accounts		
Rod		1,300
Hook		800
Bait		400
		2,500
Current liabilities		
Payables	600	
Accruals	200	
		800
		3,300

The following additional information is available:
(1) On 31 December 1998, Hook retired from the partnership. On the same date Line was admitted as a partner. It was agreed that Line should introduce €400,000 into the partnership, this amount to include €40,000 in respect of his share of goodwill. (A goodwill account is not to be maintained in the books of the partnership.) The new profit-sharing ratio will be Rod: Bait: Line 7:3:2. The balance owing to Hook on his retirement is to be transferred to a loan account.
(2) On 1 July 1999, the business was sold to FISH Limited. Under the terms of the sale agreement, the non-current assets were to be taken over at a value of €2,500,000, and inventory at €240,000. All other assets and liabilities were to be taken over at book value.

(3) FISH Limited issued €1 ordinary shares to the partners in proportion to the final balances on their capital accounts at 30 June 1999. The profit available for appropriation for the six-month period ended 30 June 1999 was €100,000.

(4) FISH Limited was incorporated and commenced trading on 1 July 1999.

Requirement

(a) Prepare the partners' capital accounts at 31 December 1998 to reflect the retirement of Hook and the entry of Line to the partnership.

(b) Close the books of the partnership by preparing the following accounts:
    (i) Realisation account
    (ii) Partners' capital accounts

(Ignore depreciation.)

Challenging Questions

Question 1 *(Based on ICAI, P2 Autumn 2000)*

Pop, Fizz and Bottle are in partnership as a soft drink distributor sharing profits in the ratio 5:3:2. The summarised balance sheet of the partnership as at 31 December 2000 is as follows:

Summarised Balance Sheet as at 31 December 2000

	€'000	€'000
Non-current assets		120
Current assets		
Inventory	32	
Receivables	68	
Cash at bank.	125	
		225
		345
Capital accounts		
Pop	160	
Fizz	140	
Bottle	20	
		320
Current liabilities		
Payables	25	
		345

The following additional information is available:

(1) It was decided that the partnership would convert into a limited company trading as BUBBLES Limited on 1 April 2001.
(2) On conversion, the non-current assets were valued at €170,000 and the partners decided that book debts were overstated as their customer X Limited had been declared bankrupt, whilst owing €8,000 to the partnership. Discussions with the receiver indicated they were only expecting to receive 25 cents for every €1 outstanding by X Limited to the partnership. 5% of the remaining general debt was also deemed to be non-collectible and, accordingly, it was agreed to provide for this amount before the book debts were transferred.
(3) Pop, Fizz and Bottle will be directors in the newly formed company, each receiving a salary of €10,000 per annum.
(4) The partners' final capital accounts will not be repaid to them. These will be converted into loan accounts in the limited company.
(5) The issued share capital of the company will be 200,000 €1 ordinary shares. The partners have agreed that, on incorporation, they will allocate their shareholding in the same proportion as their old profit sharing ratio. These shares will be purchased through the directors' loan accounts.
(6) The profits of the partnership for the last three months of trading ended 31 March 2001 (before adjusting for the bad debt provision) were €65,000 and it is assumed that these profits were all received in cash during the period. Profits are allocated to partners after charging interest on opening capital of 20% per annum, as agreed in the partnership agreement.

Requirement

(a) Close the books of the partnership by preparing the following accounts:

  (i)   Realisation account
  (ii) Partners' capital accounts as at 31 March 2001.

(b) Prepare the opening balance sheet for BUBBLES Limited as at 1 April 2001.

Question 2 (Based on ICAI, P2 Autumn 2001)

Law and Order are partners in a solicitors' partnership sharing profits in the ratio 3:2. The year end of the partnership is 31 December. The summarised balance sheet of the partnership as at 31 December 1999 is as follows:

Law and Order – Balance Sheet as at 31 December 1999

	€'000	€'000
Non-current Assets		
Property	30	
Office equipment	20	
		50
Current assets	18	
Cash at bank	17	
		35
		85
Capital accounts		
Law	40	
Order	20	
		60
Current liabilities		25
		85

The following additional information is available:

1. On 1 July 2000 Law retired and on that date a new partner, Judge, was admitted. The new profit sharing ratio is to be 1:1.
2. Set out below are relevant extracts from the partnership agreement:
   (i) On the retirement of a partner the assets of the partnership must be revalued and the partners' capital accounts adjusted accordingly; and
   (ii) Profits are allocated in the partners' profit-sharing ratio after interest on capital and salaries have been deducted. Interest on capital of 10% per annum for Law and 5% per annum for Order is calculated on the partners' opening capital accounts. Judge is not entitled to interest on capital.

   Agreed partner salaries per annum are as follows:

	€
Law	17,000
Order	30,000
Judge	21,000

   (iii) Partners are entitled to drawings of €1,000 per month, which will be credited to their capital account. This provision also applies to new partners.
3. On 1 July 2000 Judge paid €10,000 into the practice in respect of goodwill. No goodwill account is to be maintained in the accounts.
4. On 1 July 2000, the property held by the partnership was valued at €55,000. The book value of all the remaining assets and liabilities (except for the bank balance) remained the same.
5. On his retirement Law's capital account will be converted into a loan account.
6. Net profits of the partnership for the year ended 31 December 2000 were €112,000. Assume that all profits have been earned evenly during the year and have been received in cash at bank.

Requirement Prepare each of the following:

(a) Income statement appropriation account for the year ended 31 December 2000.

(b) Partners' capital accounts as at 31 December 2000.

(c) Balance sheet of the partnership as at 31 December 2000.

Question 3 *(Based on ICAI, P2 Summer 2002)*

Shamrock, Thistle and Leek are a partnership, sharing profits in the ratio 5:3:2 respectively, and are involved in the design of Gaelic theme pubs. STOUT Limited ('STOUT') has decided to purchase the business at the end of its financial year (31 December 2001). The balance sheet of the partnership as at that date is as follows:

	€	€
Non-current Assets (net of depreciation)		
Land & buildings		260,000
Plant & equipment		40,000
Motor vehicles (see Note (i))		32,000
		332,000
Current Assets		
Inventory (at cost)	61,000	
Receivables	130,000	
Cash at bank and in hand	2,500	
		193,500
		525,500
Capital Accounts		
Shamrock		140,000
Thistle		80,000
Leek		77,000
		297,000
Non-current liabilities (see Note (ii))		59,500
Building loan	67,000	
Other liabilities (see Note (i))	102,500	
		169,500
		525,500

Notes to the accounts:

(i) Other liabilities comprise:

	€
Trade payables	48,000
Accrued expenses	12,500
VAT & PAYE	23,000
Bank loans:	
Car 1	8,000
Car 2	11,000
	102,500

The net book values in respect of the above cars financed by way of bank loans are €18,000 for Car 1 and €14,000 for Car 2 respectively. There are no other motor vehicles in the business.

(ii) Long-term liabilities are made up as follows:
Bank Loans:
Car 1   €16,000
Car 2   €8,000
Building Loan €35,000

The following additional details are also available:

1. Shamrock is to keep his car (Car 1) personally, and also pay off the bank loan thereon personally. (This asset and corresponding liability are not to be taken over by STOUT.)
2. All other non-current assets and the bank loan liabilities in respect of Car 2 only are being taken over by STOUT at an agreed price of €450,000.
3. Of the inventory, it has been agreed that 20% is actually worthless. Apart from this, STOUT is purchasing the remainder at cost less 5%.
4. Receivables, less a general provision of 7.5%, are to be taken over by STOUT.
5. Trade payables and accrued expenses are to be taken over by STOUT at a value of €55,000.
6. As well as the VAT and PAYE balances disclosed in the accounts, which STOUT Limited will pay in full, the auditors of STOUT have discovered an additional VAT liability of €16,000. They intend to disclose this to the authorities, and interest and penalties of 12% will accrue in respect of this additional liability. It has been agreed that the partners will pay for 50% of this additional VAT liability and 80% of penalties.
7. The building loan liability is not being taken over by STOUT. Instead, this loan should be allocated to the partners in proportion to their profit-sharing ratio.
8. Legal costs relating to the sale of the partnership amount to €15,000 and are to be paid by the partners.

Requirement Prepare a realisation account and the partners' capital accounts to show the closure of the partnership books.

Question 4 *(Based on ICAI, P2 Autumn 2002)*

Jones, Hopkins and Lewis are in partnership sharing profits in the following ratio:

Jones	40%
Hopkins	30%
Lewis	30%

Interest on capital is charged on the opening capital accounts of Jones and Lewis at 3% and 5% respectively. Hopkins receives an annual salary of €15,000. The financial year end of the partnership is 31 December each year.

On 1 July 2001 Clarke was introduced as a fourth partner in the business. The revised profit-sharing ratios are as follows.

Jones	30%
Hopkins	20%
Lewis	20%
Clarke	30%

The new partner (Clarke) is to receive an annual salary of €5,000 – interest on capital and salaries in respect of the other partners is to remain unchanged.

The following is the draft trial balance of the partnership as at 31 December 2001:

	€	€
Sales		275,000
Opening inventory	60,000	
Purchases	125,000	
Motor expenses	15,000	
Salaries	30,000	
Telephone	6,000	
Heat & light	5,000	
General expenses	1,000	
Property – cost	50,000	
Property – additions	20,000	
Property - accumulated depreciation		6,000
Equipment – cost	75,000	
Equipment – accumulated depreciation		36,600
Motor cars – cost	100,000	
Motor cars – accumulated depreciation		56,250
Trade receivables	15,000	

Cash at bank	6,500	
Cash on hand	200	
Bank overdraft		16,000
Loan account		15,000
Trade payables		23,000
Opening capital		
– Jones		120,150
– Hopkins		94,000
– Lewis		93,000
Drawings		
– Jones	80,000	
– Hopkins	70,000	
– Lewis	70,000	
– Clarke	6,300	
	735,000	735,000

On the advice of the partners, the following adjustments have to be made to the above draft trial balance:

1. Inventory

An inventory-take was conducted at the year end. Inventory was valued at €82,000 based on cost. However, 15% of this inventory has a net realisable value of only €6,000. A further €8,000 of the total inventory is considered obsolete and should be written off.

2. Non-current Assets

No depreciation for the year ended 31 December 2001 has been included in the draft trial balance. Depreciation should be provided for as follows:

Property	4% per annum on a straight-line basis;
Equipment	20% per annum on a reducing-balance basis; and
Motor cars	25% per annum on a reducing-balance basis.

3. Receivables

A specific bad debt of €1,200 is to be provided for. General bad debts should be provided for, based on 1.5% of all remaining receivables.

4. Accruals

Year-end accruals have *not* been included in the draft trial balance. Accruals are to be provided as follows:

Accountancy   €1,500   Heat & light   €500   Telephone   €300

5. Capital Grant

At the year end a capital grant of €12,000 was receivable in respect of the year's property additions. This is to be released to the income statement in line with depreciation. No entries have been included in the draft trial balance in respect of this capital grant.

6. Goodwill

At the time of Clarke's admission to the partnership goodwill was valued at €15,000. No goodwill account is to be maintained in the accounts.

7. Assume that the profits or losses accrue evenly over the course of the year.
8. No revaluation of non-current assets was required at any time during the year.

Requirement   In order to account for the admission of Clarke to the partnership and, in light of the above adjustments, draft each of the following:

(a) The income statement for the year ended 31 December 2001.
(b) The balance sheet as at 31 December 2001.
(c) The partners' individual capital accounts as at 31 December 2001.

Question 5 *(Based on ICAI, P2 Summer 2003)*

Bob, Chris and David are in partnership sharing profits in the following ratios:

    Bob   60%
    Chris 30%
    David 10%

On 31 December 2002 David retires from the partnership. The summarised balance sheet of the partnership as at that date is as follows:

Summarised Balance Sheet as at 31 December 2002

	€'000	€'000
Non-current Assets		
Property	230	
Office equipment	85	
Motor vehicles	64	379
Current Assets	55	
Cash at bank	18	
		73
		452
Capital accounts		
Bob		168
Chris		140
David		120

	428
Current Liabilities	24
	452

The following additional information is available:

(1) On 31 December 2002 Alan is admitted as a partner. Alan is to introduce cash of €60,000 into the partnership, including €5,000 for his share of the goodwill. A goodwill account is not to be maintained in the books of the partnership. The partners have also agreed that Alan can also introduce his own car into the partnership. The car has a value of €15,000.

(2) After the change in partners, the new profit sharing ratio is to be as follows:

Alan	10%
Bob	50%
Chris	40%

(3) On 31 December 2002, the property was valued at €500,000. This revaluation is to be reflected in the accounts.

(4) On leaving the partnership, David took his company car and computer. It was agreed that David could take these assets at their respective net book values. The assets were both purchased on 1 January 1999 for €30,000 and had been depreciated at 20% on a straight-line basis.

(5) On retirement, any balance remaining on David's capital account will be converted into a loan.

Requirement   Prepare each of the following:

(a) The partner's amended capital accounts as at 31 December 2002; and
(b) The amended balance sheet for the new partnership as at 31 December 2002.

APPENDIX ONE

REVIEW QUESTIONS: SUGGESTED SOLUTIONS

CHAPTER 1

REVIEW QUESTIONS – SUGGESTED SOLUTIONS

Question 1

(a) *The Corporate Report* identified seven 'user groups' who are potential users of financial reports. These are as follows:

(i) The *equity investor group* comprises both existing holders of equity interest in the business entity (e.g. ordinary shareholders in a limited company) and investors who might be interested in investing in the equity of business;

(ii) The *loan creditor group* includes both long-term loan creditors of the business (e.g. debenture holders) and short-term creditors (e.g. banks providing an overdraft facility);

(iii) The *employee group* includes both existing and prospective employees of the business, and possibly also it's past employees (if they receive a pension from the business);

(iv) The *analyst adviser group* includes financial analysts and journalists, economists, trade unions, stockbrokers and credit-rating agencies. Members of this group use published accounts for their own research purposes or to provide analysis and advice for other groups such as investors, employees and the general public;

(v) The *business contact group* includes customers, trade creditors and suppliers of the business and, in a different sense, competitors, and also those interested in a business merger or takeover;

(vi) *Government departments* (both local and national) may have a varying interest in published accounts (e.g. tax authorities have a different interest from departments concerned with promoting or regulating trade and commerce); and

(vii) *The public* includes taxpayers, rate-payers, political parties, consumer groups, environment protection societies and local pressure groups etc.

(b) The needs of each user of financial accounts will vary according to the group or groups to which the user belongs.

    (i) Equity investors need information to help them reach share trading decisions, such as whether to buy or sell certain shares and whether or not to subscribe to a new share issue. Information might also be required to help them make voting decisions at general meetings. They need to make judgements about future share prices and future dividends. To help them, information about the past results of the business, the current situation and forecast future prospects are required.

    (ii) Long-term loan creditors are interested in similar issues to those described in (i) above. For listed securities, investors want information to assist them in trading decisions. They are also concerned about the security of their loan, and information about the efficiency of management may be helpful, as well as about the economic stability and vulnerability of the borrower. If debenture trust deeds or articles of association restrict the borrowing capacity of the borrower, the long-term loan creditors may use published accounts to check that the terms of the deed or articles are being adhered to.

    (iii) Short-term loan creditors (such as banks) are concerned with the short-term liquidity of the borrower and its ability to meet its debt payments when they fall due. Information about the liquidity of the borrower will affect the loan debenture of this group.

    (iv) The employee group requires information to help make an assessment about the security and prospects of employment, and to help in reaching a judgement about the level of wages or salaries which they might justifiably expect to receive. Other information needs concern the ability of the business to continue paying wages, conditions (health and safety etc.) at work, the contributions made by employees to the business, training and career prospects.

    (v) The analyst-adviser group acts as an agency for members of other user groups, and its information needs will therefore be the same as those of the user groups it advises. For example, stockholders need information similar to the requirements of equity investors and loan investors, whereas trade unions need information which is of interest to employees. Analysts and advisers will probably be capable of a more sophisticated analysis of information, and might therefore require more detailed information.

    (vi) The business contact group's information needs are variable. Regular suppliers need to know about the long-term supply requirements and financial viability of the business; and trade creditors want to know about its ability to pay its debts on time and without default. Customers are concerned about the continuing supply of goods from the business (including prices, quality and conditions of sale). Competitors attempt to make comparisons between the results of the reporting entity and their own performance. Those concerns interested in a merger or takeover will have the same information needs as the equity investor group.

    (vii) The government as a debtor or creditor of a business may have the same information needs as members of the business contact group. As tax collectors, the government will demand tax returns from a business and may also be concerned about the ability of the business to pay additional levies from, say, a new tax. The central government may want returns in order to analyse the national balance of payments, gross national product and other such indicators of national economic performance.

(viii) In general, government departments and agencies need information to assess the likely effect of government policies in achieving the government's political or economic aims.

(ix) Members of the public require information to help them assess the effect of the business entity on the community as a whole. *The Corporate Report* noted that 'members of the community may wish to know about the role of economic entities as employers, cash flows, profitability and efficiency of enterprises, contributions to political organisations, pressure groups and charities, their impact on the balance of trade, transactions with home and overseas governments, compliance with law and voluntary actions and expenditure affecting society or the environment. Corporate reports cannot satisfy all the imaginable information needs to the public'.

(c) The purpose of financial statements is to present information to people who wish to know something of the performance and situation of the reporting business entity. Accountancy is largely an information system for management, owners of the business and others.

The government clearly considers that not only existing shareholders but also other users of accounts are entitled to information about certain business entities and, to this end, there have been a variety of enactments about the amount of accounting information to be published. In particular, the company legislation specifies minimum information which companies must publish and file, for public inspection, with the registrar. The government's assessment of user needs therefore influences financial reporting.

While individual business entities might decide voluntarily to provide extra information to users of accounts, it would appear that, in practice, information disclosure is kept to the minimum required by law or an accounting standard.

In theory, the needs of different user groups should be ascertained and the way in which they use financial information to reach decisions should be analysed. Financial statements can then be prepared which help them to make their decisions. If necessary users should also be educated to understand properly what the accounting information is telling them.

The Corporate Report considered the needs of various user groups, and came to the conclusion that, although some 'missing' information needs could be met by additional disclosures in existing financial statements (e.g. in notes to the accounts), there was also a need for additional financial statements (such as a value-added statement, an employment report, a statement of money exchanges with government, a statement of future prospects etc.). The discussion paper recommended that financial statements should be consciously moulded and developed to meet the needs of users for decision-making.

The paper also acknowledged, however, that some users' needs are more important than the needs of others. For example, the information needs of the public are too broad to be accommodated and no concessions should be made to the needs of business competitors. It would seem reasonable to presume that the most important user groups are equity investors (existing or potential owners of the business) and employees, together with loan creditors and trade creditors.

The claim of shareholders (as owners of the business) to the greatest amount of information is perhaps acknowledged by the company legislation which allows small and medium-sized companies to file modified accounts, although full accounts must be presented to shareholders.

The information needs of employees are not yet well catered for by financial statements, although some companies publish employment and/or employee reports voluntarily. Company legislation also calls for more disclosure of employment information than hitherto. Company legislation has also called for disclosure of information which may assist loan or creditor groups in making lending decisions to a company (e.g. information about guarantees and financial commitments, contingent liabilities etc.).

Published financial information is rarely adapted to suit the needs of the analyst-adviser group for more sophisticated information, although some businesses might agree voluntarily to supply economists or statisticians etc. with confidential information for their work.

It has also been suggested that financial statements should be simplified to help users who do not properly understand accounting information. Most notably, some companies simplify their results and present them in an employee report, to give their employees some useful understanding of the financial situation of their business. This type of report is voluntary and very few businesses provide them.

In summary, it may be concluded that the information needs of some users are more prominent than the needs of others. These needs are considered by government legislation, regulations in accounting standards and on a voluntary basis by individual business entities. To a certain extent, each of these attempts to ensure that a fixed minimum amount of information is provided to help user groups reach decisions concerning the reporting business entity, although more concern has been shown so far for company accounts than for the accounts of unincorporated entities.

Question 2

Investment decisions are largely based on financial information and analysis. Financial reports, which are prepared for shareholders, potential shareholders and other uses, are, however, based on principles and rules that vary from country to country. This makes comparability and transparency of financial information very difficult. Some multinationals may have to prepare reports on activities on several bases for use in different countries and this can create an unnecessary financial burden and can damage the credibility of financial reports.

The increasing levels of cross-border financing transactions and securities trading have highlighted the need for financial information to be based on a single set of rules and principles. An internationally accepted accounting framework is also beneficial to developing countries that cannot bear the cost of establishing a national standard-setting body.

Question 3

A conceptual framework provides guidance on the broad principles of financial reporting. It highlights how items should be recorded and, on how they should be measured and presented. The setting of broad principles could assist in the development of accounting standards, ensuring that the principles are followed consistently as standards and rules are developed.

A conceptual framework can provide guidance on how similar items are treated. By providing definitions and criteria that can be used in deciding the recognition and measurement of items, conceptual frameworks can act as a point of reference for those setting standards, those preparing and those using financial information.

The existence of a conceptual framework can remove the need to address the underlying issues over and over again. Where underlying principles have been established and the accounting standards are based on these principles, there is no need to deal with them fully in each of the standards. This will save the standard-setters time in developing standards and will again ensure consistent treatment of items.

Where a technical issue is raised but is not specifically addressed in an accounting standard, a conceptual framework can help provide guidance on how such items should be treated. Where a short-term technical solution is provided by the standard-setters, the existence of a conceptual framework will ensure that the treatment is consistent with the broad set of agreed principles.

Chapter 2

REVIEW QUESTIONS – SUGGESTED SOLUTIONS

Question 1

V Limited
Statement of Comprehensive Income for the Year Ended 30 September 20X1

Notes		€'000	€'000
	Revenue		430
	Cost of sales		(188)
	Gross profit		242
	Distribution costs	(25)	
	Administrative expenses	(21)	(46)
1.	Profit from operations		196
	Income from investments		12
	Finance cost		(14)
	Profit before tax		194
2.	Income tax expense		(50)
	Profit for the year		144

V Limited
Statement of financial position as at 30 September 20X1

Notes		€'000	€'000
	ASSETS		
	Non-current assets		
4.	Tangible assets		498
	Investments		100
			598

Current Assets		
Inventory	13	
Receivables	23	
Bank	157	193
		791

EQUITY AND LIABILITIES

Capital and reserves		
Issued capital	100	
Retained earnings	415	515
Non-current Liabilities		
Loan notes	140	
Deferred tax	45	
Deferred Income	24	209
Current Liabilities		
Trade Payables	7	
Taxation	57	
Deferred Income	3	67
		791

(Note "5." appears beside Deferred tax)

Notes

1. Profit from operations

Profit from operations is arrived at after charging:	€'000
Depreciation	32
Staff costs	74

2. Taxation (statement of comprehensive income)

	€'000
Taxation estimated for this year	57
Under provision for previous year	10
Decrease in deferred tax provision	(17)
Charge to statement of comprehensive income	50

3. Dividends proposed
   A final dividend of €50,000 is proposed for the year.

4. Tangible non-current assets

	Land & Buildings	Plant	Total
Cost	€'000	€'000	€'000
At 1 October 20X0	450	210	660
Additions	0	70	70
At 30 September 20X1	450	280	730
Depreciation			
At 1 October 20X0	40	160	200
Charge for year	4	28	32
At 30 September 20X1	44	188	232
Carrying amount at 30 September 20X1	406	92	498
Carrying amount at 1 October 20X0	410	50	460

5. Deferred Taxation

	€'000
Opening balance	62
Decrease in provision	(17)
	45

6. Statement of Changes in Equity (extract)

Retained Earnings	€'000
Profit for the year	144
Dividends paid (€48,000 + €72,000)	120
Retained profit for the year	24
Retained earnings at 30 September 20X0	391
Retained earnings at 30 September 20X1	415

Workings:

1. Analysis of expenses

	Cost of Sales	Distribution Costs	Administrative Expenses
	€'000	€'000	€'000
Opening inventory	10		
Purchases	102		
Advertising		15	
Administration salaries			14
Manufacturing wages	60		
Audit fee			7
Bad debts		10	
Government grant	(3)		
Depreciation:			
Building	4		
Plant	28		
Closing inventory	(13)		
	188	25	21

2. Taxation

	DR €'000		CR €'000
Balance brought down	10	SCI under provision	10
		SCI charge for the year	57
Balance c/d	57		
	67		67
		Balance b/d	57

Question 2

(a)

Rose Limited
Statement of Changes in Equity for the Year Ended 31 December 2008

	Share Capital €	Share Premium €	Revaluation Reserve €	Retained Earnings €	Total Equity €
At 31 December 2007	300,000	50,000	80,000	1,280,000	1,710,000
Change in accounting policy	-	-	-	(35,000)	(35,000)
Restated balance	300,000	50,000	80,000	1,245,000	1,675,000
Changes in Equity for 2008					
Dividends	-		-	(25,000)	(25,000)
Total comprehensive income*	-	-	70,000	100,000	170,000
Bonus issue of share capital	30,000	(30,000)	-	-	-
Rights issue	30,000	15,000	-	-	45,000
Total Changes in Equity in 2008	60,000	(15,000)	70,000	75,000	190,000
At 31 December 2008	360,000	35,000	150,000	1,320,000	1,865,000

*Total Comprehensive Income	€
Profit for the year	120,000
Gain on revaluation of property	70,000
Valuation gain on available for sale investments	10,000
Valuation gain on available for sale investments transferred to statement of comprehensive income on sale	(30,000)
	170,000

CHAPTER 3

REVIEW QUESTIONS – SUGGESTED SOLUTIONS

Question 1

(a) The advantages of harmonising accounting standards

The users and preparers of financial statements should benefit from having one accounting language. For example:

- **Investors** – both individual and corporate, would be able to compare the financial results of different companies internationally as well as nationally in making investment decisions. There is a growing amount of investment across borders and differences in accounting practices inhibit cross-border analysis. Harmonisation of accounting practices would therefore be of benefit to such analysts;
- **Global/international companies** – management control would be improved because harmonisation would aid internal communication of financial information, and the consolidation of foreign subsidiaries and associated companies would be easier. In addition, in today's global capital and trading markets, the appraisal of foreign companies for takeovers and mergers would be more straightforward and, by making the accounts more easily understood by foreign investors, companies would have better access to foreign investor funds. The reporting requirements of overseas inventory exchanges would be similar and a reduction in audit costs might be achieved;
- **Governments of developing countries** – would save time and money if they could adopt international standards and, if these were used internally, they could attempt to control the activities of foreign multinational companies in their own country. This would make it more difficult for companies to 'hide' behind different foreign accounting practices;
- **International accounting firms** – accounting and auditing would be much easier if similar accounting practices existed throughout the world;
- **Tax authorities** – it would be easier to calculate the tax liability of investors, including multinationals who receive income from overseas sources.

(b) The reasons why harmonisation has not yet been achieved
    The main factors are:

- **Different user groups** – there is no consensus on who the relevant user groups are and their respective importance. In the USA, investor and creditor groups are given prominence, while in Europe employees enjoy a higher profile;
- **Different purposes of financial reporting** – in some countries the purpose is solely for tax assessment, while in others it is for investor decision-making;
- **Different legal systems** – these prevent the development of certain accounting practices and restrict the options available;
- **Nationalism** – this has resulted in an unwillingness to accept another country's standards;
- **Different needs** – developing countries are behind in the standard-setting process and they need to develop the basic standards and principles already in place in most developed countries;
- **Cultural differences** – have resulted in objectives for accounting systems differing from country to country; and
- **Lack of strong accountancy bodies** – many countries do not have a strong independent accountancy profession to press for better standards and greater harmonisation.

Chapter 4

REVIEW QUESTIONS – SUGGESTED SOLUTIONS

Question 1

Issue 1 The amounts cannot be off-set. Although a legal right of off-set exists and the two companies intend to settle net, the amounts cannot be settled net as they are due on different dates. This is specifically prohibited by IFRS 7 *Financial Instruments: Disclosures* (previously IAS 32 *Financial Instruments: Disclosure and Presentation*).

Issue 2 MASTERTICKETS should recognise €500 as revenue. The agency acts purely as an agent for the promoter and therefore its revenue arises from the rendering of services, i.e. earning commission by selling tickets. The ownership of the €4,500 belongs to the promoter.

Issue 3 LAGAN makes its money by promoting a service – the website – that brings together buyers and sellers of products. LAGAN is neither a buyer nor a seller and takes no risks related to the products. It earns a fee for making a market (through the website). LAGAN should only recognise revenue of €40,000.

Issue 4 The upfront fee should be spread over the service period, i.e. the customer is not buying 'activation', but is buying a mobile phone service. Therefore the upfront fee should be matched with the cost of providing the service over the life of the contract.

Issue 5

	€'000
(a) Total profit/loss	
Contract price	15,000
Costs to date	(9,250)
Estimated to complete	(4,000)
Estimated contract profit/loss	1,750

(b) Attributable profit/loss*		
Stage of completion	11/17 = 64.7%	
Costs certified/Estimated total costs	€8,500/€13,250 = 64.2%	
Turnover	€9,500/€15,000 = 63.3%	
Cash received	€9,000/€15,000 = 60%	
Therefore attributable profit/loss	Take say (63%)	1,103

(c) Revenue	
Costs certified to date**	8,500
Attributable profit	1,103
	9,603

(d) Inventory – LT contract balance	
Costs to date	9,250
Cost of sales	(8,500)
	750

(e) Receivable	
Revenue recognised	9,603
Received	(9,000)
	603

Note:

* The calculation of attributable profit/loss is subjective and alternative assumptions maybe equally valid.

** Costs certified to date are taken as cost of sales since this represents the 'cost' of the contract value completed. Then as stated in the question this figure is adjusted by attributable profit to arrive at contract revenue.

CHAPTER 5

REVIEW QUESTIONS – SUGGESTED SOLUTIONS

Question 1

RIGHT: not an investment property as used and occupied by HELIX. Depreciate in accordance with IAS 16 *Property, Plant and Equipment.*

LEFT: not an investment property as let to, and occupied by, another group company. Depreciate in accordance with IAS 16 *Property, Plant and Equipment.*

UP: an investment property under IAS 40 *Investment Property* as, per IAS 28 *Investments in Associates*, an associate company is not a group company. No depreciation to be charged.

DOWN: an investment property under IAS 40 *Investment Property.* Depreciate over 12 years.

CHAPTER 6

REVIEW QUESTIONS – SUGGESTED SOLUTIONS

Question 1

MEMORANDUM

Date:
To:
From:
Subject:

Review Point 1

The company uses the properties and therefore they are not 'investment properties' under IAS 40 *Investment Property*. IAS 16 *Property, Plant and Equipment* does not allow companies to take a selective approach to the valuation of non-current assets within the same class. Therefore, if WELLER wishes to move to market value, both properties will have to be shown at market value. Also following revaluation, depreciation should be based upon the revalued amount. The revaluation loss on the Derry property should be taken to the statement of comprehensive income along with the depreciation charge.

The revaluation gain on the Cork property will be credited to the equity/revaluation reserve (and shown under 'other comprehensive income' in the statement of comprehensive income), i.e. it is not included in arriving at the profit/loss for the year.

Review Point 2

Previously IAS 23 *Borrowing Costs* allowed companies to choose whether or not to capitalise the €600,000 loan interest. However, in accordance with the revised IAS 23 (effective for accounting periods beginning on or after 1 January 2009 – see Chapter 7), WELLER must capitalise qualifying borrowing costs.

For:

- Greater comparability between the cost of purchased non-current assets and the cost of self-constructed non-current assets; and
- Better matching of income and expenditure since depreciation will include the capitalised interest.

Against:

- Too arbitrary and therefore reduces the comparability of financial statements.

In many cases, borrowing will not be as specific as in this case. It is more likely to form part of the company's general financing. Although it is still possible to capitalise a percentage of the borrowing cost, determining the amount will be much more difficult. IAS 23 suggests using a capitalisation rate based upon a weighted average of the rates applicable to general borrowing. But this will be a very judgmental process.

Review Point 3

Rental payments during a fitting-out period should not be capitalised as, under IAS 16 *Property, Plant and Equipment,* such payments are not costs that are directly attributable to bringing the fixtures and fittings into their intended use, nor are they finance costs.

IAS 17 *Leases* requires rentals under operating leases to be charged on a straight-line basis over the lease term and therefore it is not possible to defer the payments and spread them over the period when the property is in use.

Review Point 4

Reasons	*Problems*
1. Different management intentions with respect to operational lives, intended use and renewal policy.	1. Appraisal of company financial performance and reported profit.
2. Use of estimates with respect to residual values and lives based upon management views, intentions, past experience and foresight.	2. Lack of consistency between companies.
3. Application of accounting concepts (prudence).	3. Results in different profit/loss on disposal being reported.
4. Maintenance and repair policies.	

Review point 5

The primary justification for non-depreciation of freehold land is that land does not wear out in the same way as all other assets and therefore does not have a finite life span. Also the usefulness of land does not erode with age. Generally, the value of land will rise through time and land requires little or no maintenance.

CHAPTER 7

REVIEW QUESTIONS – SUGGESTED SOLUTIONS

Question 1

The revised IAS 23 *Borrowing Costs* (effective for accounting periods beginning on or after 1 January 2009) states that qualifying borrowing costs *must be* capitalised. Therefore, based upon the information provided, ROBINSON will be required to capitalise €600,000 loan interest.

As all companies are now required to capitalise qualifying borrowing costs, this should result in:

- Greater comparability between the cost of purchased non-current assets and the cost of self-constructed non-current assets;
- Better matching of income and expenditure since depreciation will include the capitalised interest.

In many cases, borrowing will not be as specific as in this case. It is more likely to form part of the company's general financing. Although it is still possible to capitalise a percentage of the borrowing cost, determining the amount will be much more difficult. IAS 23 suggests using a capitalisation rate based upon a weighted average of the rates applicable to general borrowing. But this will be a very judgmental process.

CHAPTER 8

REVIEW QUESTIONS – SUGGESTED SOLUTIONS

Question 1

(a) Definition

A lease is classified as a finance lease if it transfers substantially all the risks and rewards incidental to ownership.

An operating lease is a lease other than a finance lease.

(b) Accounting Treatment

Finance Lease   A finance lease should be recorded in the statement of financial position of a lessee as an asset and as an obligation to pay future rentals. At the inception of the lease the sum to be recorded both as an asset and as a liability should be the fair value of the asset or the present value of the minimum lease payments if lower.

Rentals payable should be apportioned between the finance charge and a reduction of the outstanding obligation for future amounts payable. The total finance charge under a finance lease should be allocated to accounting periods during the lease term so as to produce a constant periodic rate of charge on the remaining balance of the obligation for each accounting period, or a reasonable approximation thereto.

The depreciation policy for depreciable leased assets should be consistent with that for depreciable assets that are owned. If there is no reasonable certainty that the lessee will obtain ownership by the end of the lease term, the asset should be fully depreciated over the shorter of the lease term and its useful life.

Operating Lease   The rental under an operating lease should be recognised as an expense in the statement of comprehensive income on a straight-line basis over the lease term, even if the payments are not made on such a basis.

(c) Disclosure Requirements

Disclosure should be made of the policies adopted for accounting for operating leases and finance leases.

Finance Lease The gross amounts of assets which are held under finance leases together with the related accumulated depreciation should be disclosed by each major class of asset.

The total depreciation allocated for the period in respect of assets held under finance leases should be disclosed by each major class of asset.

The amounts of obligations related to finance leases (net of finance charges allocated to future periods) should be disclosed separately under non-current liabilities and current liabilities in the statement of financial position.

The net obligations under finance leases should be analysed as follows in the notes to the accounts: payable next year; payable in 2 to 5 years; and payable after 5 years.

The aggregate finance charges allocated for the period in respect of finance leases should be disclosed.

Operating Lease   The total of operating lease rentals charged as an expense in the statement of comprehensive income should be disclosed.

The notes to the financial statement must disclose the minimum lease payments for the following periods: not later than one year; later than one year but not later than five years; and later than five years.

Question 2

Statement of comprehensive income: depreciation €16,000 (€64,000 ÷ 4) plus interest €6,400 = decrease profit by €22,400.

Non-current Assets: Cost €64,000 less depreciation €16,000 = increase non-current assets by €48,000.

Liabilities: €80,000 − €20,000 = €60,000 less interest suspense €9,600 = increase liabilities by €50,400.

Opening Bal.	Rental	Capital	Interest	Closing Bal.
€	€	€	€	€
64,000	20,000	13,600	6,400[1]	50,400

[1] When the rental payment is in arrears, the interest is calculated on the opening balance.

Question 3

(a) Effect on projected profits

	200X	200Y	200Z
	€	€	€
Depreciation charge	12,500	25,000	25,000
Finance charge (interest (W3))	7,823	13,393	8,549
Effect on profit before tax	20,323	38,393	33,549

Note: Depreciation for non-current assets held under finance leases must be consistent with that for similar assets which are owned. If there is no reasonable certainty that the lessee will obtain ownership at the end of the lease, the asset should be depreciated over the shorter of the lease term or the life of the asset (IAS 17.27). Given the machine has an estimated useful life of six years and the secondary lease period is at €1 per annum, it is considered appropriate to depreciate the machine over six years (rather than four being the shorter of the lease term).

(b) Statement of financial position (Extracts)

	31 May 200X	31 May 200Y	31 May 200Z
	€	€	€
Non-current Assets			
Leased machinery	150,000	150,000	150,000
Accumulated depreciation	(12,500)	(37,500)	(62,500)
Net book value	137,500	112,500	87,500
Non-current liabilities			
Obligations under finance leases	74,266	39,716	–
	74,266	39,716	–
Current liabilities			
Obligations under finance leases	30,044	34,550	39,716
Accruals and deferred income	7,823	5,570	2,995
	37,867	40,120	42,711

Note: The lease commences on 30 November 200W and the first accounting period ends 31 May 200X. Therefore, the first period includes the lease for 6 months only.

W1 Calculation of Finance Charges
Total lease payments ignoring secondary period

			€
Minimum lease payments	4 x €45,690	=	182,760
Less fair value of asset			(150,000)
Implicit finance charge			32,760

Note: We are told that the interest rate implicit in the lease is 15%. Therefore, we can spread the finance charges over the life of lease as set out in W3.

	€
W2 Opening Capital Amount	
Asset value	150,000
– Payment in advance	45,690
Opening amount	104,310

W3 Spreading the Finance Charge

Period	Opening Capital Balance €	Lease payment on 30/11 €	Interest* €	Date Interest Paid €	Capital Repaid €	Closing Capital Balance €	Total Annual Interest €
30/11/0W – 31/5/0X	104,310^	–	7,823	30.11.00	–	104,310	7,823
31/5/0X – 30/11/0X	104,310	45,690	7,823	30.11.00	30,044	74,266 31.5.01	N/A
30/11/0X –31/5/0Y	74,266	–	5,570	30.11.01	–	74,266	13,393
31/5/0Y – 30/11/0Y	74,266	45,690	5,570	30.11.01	34,550	39,716 31.5.02	N/A
30/11/0Y – 31/5/0Z	39,716	–	2,979	30.11.02	–	39,716	8,549
31/5/0Z – 30/11/0Z	39,716	45,690	2,979	30.11.02	39,732	(16)	2,979

*Interest is calculated at 15% on the outstanding capital balance for each half-year period.

	€
^Fair value	150,000
Less 1st payment in advance (deemed to be capital)	45,690
	104,310

Note The first payment is in advance and is deemed to be all capital. Therefore, as the payment in the year to 31/5/0X was deemed to be a 'capital' advance, an accrual of €7,823 must be made in respect of the finance charge for this year in accordance with the matching concept.

It is arguably equally valid to assume that the first payment (in advance) includes the repayment of both interest and capital. Although there would still be an interest expense in the statement of comprehensive income for the year ended 31/5/0X, there would be no interest accrual in the statement of financial position at the end of the period. This assumption would therefore result in a different CL/NCL split.

Question 4

(a) Operating Lease
Annual charge to statement of comprehensive income is €2,500 x 4 = €10,000, i.e. the amount payable for the year.

(b) (i) Sum of Digits Approach

		€
Finance Charge Computation		
Total payments 2,500 x 12		30,000
Cost of Asset		25,000
Finance Charge		5,000

No. of payments (excluding advance payment) = 11

Sum of Digits = $\frac{11}{12}$ (11 + 1) = 66

Period		€		€	
1.	11/66 x	5,000	=	833	}
2.	10/66 x	5,000	=	757	}2,878
3.	9/66 x	5,000	=	682	}
4.	8/66 x	5,000	=	606	}
5.	7/66 x	5,000	=	530	}
6.	6/66 x	5,000	=	455	}
7.	5/66 x	5,000	=	379	}1,667
8.	4/66 x	5,000	=	303	}
9.	3/66 x	5,000	=	227	}
10.	2/66 x	5,000	=	152	}455
11.	1/66 x	5,000	=	76	}
				5,000	

Year	Finance Charge €	Depreciation €	Total Charge €
1.	2,878	4,167	7,045
2.	1,667	4,167	5,834
3.	455	4,167	4,622
4.	–	4,167	4,167
5.	–	4,166	4,167
6.	–	4,166	4,167

Note: Leased assets are depreciated over the shorter of the lease term or its useful life when it is not reasonably certain that ownership will transfer to the lessee.

The lease term is the period for which the lessee has contracted to lease the asset *and* any further terms which the lessee has the option to continue to lease the asset, with or without further payment, which option it is reasonably certain at the inception of the lease that the lessee will exercise.

(b) (ii) Actuarial Approach

Net cost to lessor	€
Cost of asset	25,000
Advance lease payments	2,500
	22,500

Calculation of implicit rate of interest

$$\text{PV Factor} = \frac{\text{Net Cost}}{\text{Payments}} = \frac{22,500}{2,500} = 9$$

Interest rate equating a factor of 9 over 11 payments is 3.5%.
Division of rentals between finance charge element and capital element:

Period	Capital Sum at Start	Rental	Capital Sum during Period	Finance Charge	Capital Repayments	Capital Sum at End
	€	€	€	€	€	€
1.	25,000	2,500	22,500			22,500
				787	1,713	
2.	22,500	2,500	20,787			20,787
				728	1,772	
3.	20,787	2,500	19,015			19,015
				666	1,834	
4.	19,015	2,500	17,181			17,181
				601	1,899	
5.	17,181	2,500	15,282			15,282
				535	1,965	
6.	15,282	2,500	13,317			13,317
				466	2,034	
7.	13,317	2,500	11,283			11,283
				395	2,105	
8.	11,283	2,500	9,178			9,178
				321	2,179	
9.	9,178	2,500	6,999			6,999
				245	2,255	
10.	6,999	2,500	4,744			4,744
				166	2,334	
11.	4,744	2,500	2,410			2,410
				84	2,416	
12.	2,410	2,500		6		

Charge to statement of comprehensive income:

Year	Finance Charge €	Depreciation €	Total €
1.	2,782	4,167	6,949
2.	1,717	4,167	5,884
3.	501	4,167	4,668
4.		4,167	4,167
5.		4,166	4,167
6.		4,166	4,167

(c) Statement of financial position (Extracts)   €
Non-current assets
Assets purchased under finance lease
Cost   25,000
Accumulated Depreciation   4,167
                                            20,833

Non-current Liabilities
Leasehold obligations   9,178

Current Liabilities

Finance charges accrued   601
Leasehold obligations   8,003

CHAPTER 9

REVIEW QUESTIONS – SUGGESTED SOLUTIONS

Question 1

Mr Denis Lyons	Barrett Wiltshire & Co.
Managing Director	Chartered Accountants
Sea Pharmaceuticals plc	10 High Street
Clonshaugh Industrial Estate	Kilkenny
Coolock	
Dublin	

14 June 200X

Dear Mr Lyons,

Further to our recent conversation, I wish to outline the suggested accounting treatment appropriate for your research and development expenditure and the related capital grants receivable.

Research and Development

My understanding is that your project is to discover and develop a treatment drug for seal viruses. To determine the appropriate accounting treatment, we must refer to the guidance set out in IAS 38 *Intangible Assets*. The provisions of IAS 38 as applied to the facts of your case would suggest the following:

1. The cost of initial investigative work into seal viruses should be expensed to the statement of comprehensive income as incurred, as it falls into the category of research.
2. The cost of development work (i.e. the application of research findings to the development of sea vaccines) should be:
    (a) expensed to statement of comprehensive income as incurred, if it does not satisfy the conditions for recognition as an intangible asset; or

(b) capitalised as an intangible asset in the statement of financial position if the following five conditions are satisfied:
  (i) Technical feasibility of completing the intangible asset;
  (ii) Intention by the entity to complete the asset and use or sell it;
  (iii) The ability of the entity to use or sell the asset;
  (vi) The likelihood of the asset generating probable future economic benefits, e.g. existence of a market for the output of the asset; and
  (v) The ability to measure the expenditure attributable to the asset.

Government Grants

The general rule, as outlined in IAS 20 *Accounting for Government Grants and Disclosure of Government Assistance* for the treatment of government grants, is that they should be accounted for in a manner consistent with the related expenditure. The portion of the grants attributable to the original investigative work should be credited to the statement of comprehensive income when received. If the development costs qualify for capitalisation as an intangible asset under the provisions of IAS 38 above, then the related grants can be treated on a similar basis, i.e. the entire grant relating to the development costs can be credited to a deferred income account and amortised to the statement of comprehensive income over the period in which revenues are expected to be generated.

I trust that the above has addressed the main issues relevant to your case. If I can be of any further assistance, please call.

Yours faithfully,

Question 2

Profit for the year ended 31 December 200Y would be €300,000, i.e. the €100,000 written off the intangible asset balance during 200Y would have been written off in previous years.

CHAPTER 10

REVIEW QUESTIONS – SUGGESTED SOLUTIONS

Question 1

Allocation of Impairment Loss:

	Goodwill €m	Property €m	Machinery €m	Motor Vehicles €m	Other €m
Carrying amount	20	60	40	20	20
Impairment loss €60m	20	-	20	10	10
Revised carrying value	Nil	60	20	10	10

Explanation:

(a) The loss is firstly allocated to the goodwill, i.e. €20m.
(b) No impairment can be allocated to the property because its fair value less cost to sell is greater than its carrying amount.
(c) The remainder of the loss, i.e. €40m, is apportioned between the remaining assets pro rata to their carrying amounts: 40:20:20
    Machinery   €40m x 40/80 = €20m
    Motor vehicles   €40m x 20/80 = €10m
    Other assets   €40m x 20/80 = €10m

Question 2

1. Present value of future cash flows:

	Domestic			**Commercial**		
	Cash flow	Pv – 10%	NPV	Cash flow	Pv – 12%	NPV
	€		€	€		€
2009	1,200	0.909	1,090.8	1,200	0.893	1,071.6
2010	900	0.826	743.4	1,300	0.797	1,036.1
2011	2,700	0.751	2,027.7	1,600	0.712	1,139.2
2012	1,500	0.683	1,024.5	1,500	0.636	954
2013	1,600	0.620	992	900	0.567	510.3
2014	1,800	0.564	1,015.2	1,800	0.507	912.6
			6,893.6			5,623.8

2. Recoverable amount – higher of NPV & NRV:

	€	€
NPV	6,893.6	5,623.8
NRV	7,500	4,200
	Therefore NRV €7,500	Therefore NPV €5,623.8

3. Impairment loss – lower of carrying value and recoverable amount:

	€	€
CV	7,200	9,300
RA	7,500	5,623.8
Impairment	-	3,676.2

4. Allocated over the Commercial IGU

	n/a	Revised Carrying Value	
		€	€
		3,676.2	–
	Goodwill	(1,200)	–
	Other IA	(300)	–
		2,176.2	
PPE [6,400 – (6400/7,800 x 2.176.2)]			4,614.4
Inventory [1,400 – (1,400/7,800 x 2,176.2)]			1,009.4
			5,623.8

Note

Impairment Loss for a CGU An impairment loss should be recognised only if its recoverable amount is less than its carrying amount. Where the impairment loss cannot be identified as relating to a specific asset, it should be apportioned within the CGU to reduce the *most subjective values first*, as follows:

(a) First against goodwill to its implied value (it could be argued that after reducing goodwill, the impairment loss should next be allocated against 'other intangible assets' on the basis that these are the next 'most subjective values'. Much will depend on the nature of these assets and the decision may often be a matter of judgement. Hence, in this solution, the impairment loss has been allocated against 'other intangibles' in full before applying (b) below.);

(b) Then to other assets on a pro rata basis based on the carrying amount of each asset in the unit.

These are treated as impairment losses on individual assets. In allocating the loss an asset should not be reduced below the higher of:

(i)   its net selling price (if determinable);
(ii) its value in use (if determinable); and
(iii) zero.

The amount of the loss that would otherwise have been allocated to the asset shall be allocated to the other assets on a pro rata basis.

If the recoverable amount of each individual asset in a CGU cannot be estimated without undue cost or effort IAS 36 requires an arbitrary allocation between assets of the CGU other than goodwill.

If the recoverable amount of an individual asset cannot be determined:

(a) An impairment loss is recognised for the asset if its carrying value is greater than the higher of its net selling price and the results of the procedures described above;

(b) No impairment loss is recognised if the related CGU is not impaired even if its net selling price is less than its carrying amount.

CHAPTER 11

REVIEW QUESTIONS – SUGGESTED SOLUTIONS

Question 1

Memorandum

Date: dd/mm/yy
To: J. Jones, Group Chief Accountant
From: B. Williams, Accounting Consultant
Subject: Valuation of Subsidiary Company's Inventory

General

Before considering the particular circumstance relating to each subsidiary, IAS 27 *Separate and Consolidated Financial Statements* requires that all companies in a group should prepare their financial statements using uniform accounting policies for like transactions and other events in similar circumstances. IAS 2 *Inventories* states that inventories should be valued at the lower of cost and net realisable value.

Screws Limited

It is considered that the use of selling price less 20% as a basis of valuing inventories in a manufacturing company is not satisfactory in the light of IAS 2 *Inventories* as it is considered unlikely that such a method could give a reasonable approximation to actual cost.

The finished goods should be valued at the lower of cost or net realisable value. Cost should be taken as that expenditure which has been incurred in the normal course of business in bringing the goods to their present location and condition and should include, in addition to the cost of purchase, such costs of conversion as are appropriate to that location and condition.

The cost of conversion would comprise of:

(a) costs specifically attributable to the units of production;
(b) production overheads (based on the normal level of activity); and
(c) other overheads, if any, incurred in bringing the goods to their present location and condition.

Brackets Limited

Note: When answering this part of the question, it has been assumed that the last consignment consisted of 200 tons or more. If the last consignment did not consist of 200 tons, then the cost of the brass would be determined by using the cost of the latest 200 tons purchased, i.e. on a FIFO basis.

	Cost per ton at 31 December
	€
Brass purchase cost	500.00
Conversion Cost (€ 20,000/700)	171.43
	671.43

	Net realisable value per ton
	€
Market price	520.00
Less: selling costs (€30,000/700)	(42.86)
	477.14

Consequently, the inventory held at the year-end should be valued at €477.14 per tonne.

Frames Limited

IAS 21 *The Effects of Changes in Foreign Exchange Rates* states that a foreign currency transaction should be recorded by the reporting entity on initial recognition in the functional currency by applying the spot exchange rate between the functional currency and the foreign currency at the date of the transaction. The date of the transaction is defined as the date on which the transaction first qualifies for recognition under IFRS. Consequently, the inventory should be valued at the rate prevailing on 15 November. The exchange fluctuation between the date of purchase (15 November) and the date of payment (10 December) should be treated as an exchange loss in inventory in the current year's statement of comprehensive income. Year-end inventories should, therefore, be valued at 95% of €100,000, i.e. €95,000.

Concrete Blocks

IAS 2 states that costs of conversion of inventories include costs directly related to the units of production such as direct labour. They also include a systematic allocation of fixed and variable production overheads that are incurred in converting materials into finished goods. The allocation of fixed production overheads is based in the normal capacity of the production facilities. It would seem that the use of the term 'based on normal level of activity' suggests that fixed overheads should be included in the valuation of inventory. It would appear, therefore, that in order to comply with the standard, it would be necessary to continue to include fixed factory overheads.

Question 2

(a) A retailer with:

- A large range of low price commodities;
- A strong management information system; and
- Reasonably consistent margins throughout the accounting period.

Examples: Superquinn, HMV

Examples of enterprises where such a method would NOT be appropriate would be:

- Hi-Fi shop (individual items can be easily valued at actual cost);
- An enterprise with weak information systems, i.e. details of departmental or product margins may be unavailable; and
- Manufacturing enterprise.

(b) No prior-period adjustment should be made. The company's accounting policy should be to value inventory at the lower of cost or Net Realisable Value (NRV). The previous calculations of measuring actual costs and the new calculations measuring selling price less an estimated profit margin are both *methods* to value inventory at cost. The change described is therefore a change in method not a change in accounting policy. Consequently, no prior-period adjustment is required.

(c) Factors to be considered include:
   (i) Are departmental or product gross-margin analyses sufficient?
        It would be inappropriate for Superquinn (for example) to use a blanket 10% gross margin for the 'food department' when meats and dairy products would presumably be sold at quite different gross margins.
  (ii) Is VAT properly deducted from the total selling prices?
 (iii) How are the estimated profit margins calculated? The margins must include all costs of purchase (as defined in IAS 2) but exclude all other costs, e.g. administration costs. (Costs of conversion would be irrelevant because if such costs were incurred, say by a manufacturing company, this method would be appropriate.)
  (iv) How do the estimated profit margins compare with actual profit margins?
   (v) How are 'special promotions' or 'sale prices' listed at the year end (which would result in a lower sales price for certain goods) treated?

REVIEW QUESTIONS – SUGGESTED SOLUTIONS

Question 1

Adjustments to draft accounts:

	DR €	CR €
Cost of sales (€270,000 + €103.500) (Note 1)	373,500	
Work in progress (Note 2)		173,500
Provision for loss on contract		200,000

Note 1:	€'000	€'000
Contact Price		3,000
Costs to date	1,420	
Estimated cost to completion	1,350	
Estimated total cost		(2,770)
Estimated total profit on completion		230
Additional costs		(500)
Expected loss		(270)
Anticipated profit included originally in the accounts		
€230,000 x 45%		103.5
Adjustment needed – reduce profits by		373.5

Note 2:		
Work in progress – Contract Account		
Costs to date		1,420.0
Transfer to cost of sales (€2,770,000 x 45%)		(1,246.5)
Balance		173.50

Question 2

The following four accounts can be used:

1. Work in Progress;
2. Revenue;
3. Trade Receivables; and
4. Receivables – Amounts Recoverable On Contracts (AROC).

A cost of sales account may also be used.

Y/e 31 July 20x8

The decision when to take credit for attributable profit is often subjective. At 31 July 20X8 the contract was 30% complete. While profit could often be taken at this point, none is taken in this instance so as to illustrate how this is accounted for. However, the contract is expected to be profitable overall, so it is appropriate to show as turnover a proportion of the total contract value which will produce a zero profit – IAS 11 states that revenue can be recognised to the extent of contract costs incurred which are expected to be recoverable.

Cost of Sales = 30% × €750,000 = €225,000
Therefore revenue = €225,000

Work in Progress				Revenue			
	€'000		€'000		€'000		€'000
						Rec	
Bank	230	Cost of Sales	225	SCI	225	AROC	225
		Balance c/d	5				
	230		230				

Receivables – Trade				Receivables – Amts recoverable on Contracts			
	€'000		€'000		€'000		€'000
		Bank	250	Revenue	225	Trade rec.	270
Amounts Recoverable	270	Bal c/d	20	Balance c/d	45		
	270		270		270		270

Y/e 31 July 20X9

	€'000	€'000
Estimated Total Profit (€1,000,000 – €780,000) =		220
Attributable Profit = €220,000 x 65%		143
Cost of Sales = €780,000 x 65% =	507	
Less Amount y/e 31/7/X8	(225)	
	282	

Revenue = €143,000 + €282,000 = €425,000

Work in Progress

	€'000		€'000
Balance b/d	5	Cost of Sales	282
Bank	290	Balance c/d	13
	295		295

Revenue

	€'000		€'000
SCI	425	Rec AROC	425

Receivables – Trade

	€'000		€'000
Balance c/d Amounts	20	Bank	250
Recoverable	410	Balance c/d	180
	430		430

Receivables – Amts recoverable on Contracts

	€'000		€'000
Revenue	425	Balance B/d	45
Balance c/d	30	Trade rec.	410
	455		455

Y/e 31 July 20Y0

	€'000	€'000
Estimated Total Profit		280
Attributable Profit (€280,000 x 100%)	280	
Less taken in previous periods	143	137
Cost of Sales (€820,000 x 100%)	820	
Less Amounts w/o in previous periods (€ 225,000 + €282,000)	(507)	
This period	313	

Revenue = Cost of Sales + Attributable Profit = €313,000 + €137,000 = € 450,000

Work in Progress

	€'000		€'000
Balance b/d	13	Cost of Sales	313
Bank	300		
	313		313

Revenue

	€'000		€'000
SCI	450	Receivables AROC	450

Receivables – Trade

	€'000		€'000
Balance c/d Amounts	180	Bank	600
Recoverable	420		
	270		270

Receivables – Amts recoverable on Contracts

	€'000		€'000
Revenue	450	Balance B/d	30
		Trade rec.	420
	450		450

Extracts from Financial Statements for Year Ended 31 July 20X9

Statement of Comprehensive Income		€'000
Revenue		425
Cost of Sales		282
Gross Profit		143

Statement of Financial Position		
Inventory – Long-term Contract Balances	(W1)	Nil
Trade Receivables		180
Current liabilities		
Payments on Account	(W2)	17

W1	Long-term Contract Balances	
	Cost to date	520
	Transferred to Cost of Sales	507
		13
	Excess payments on account	(13)
		Nil

W2	Receivables – Amounts Recoverable on Contracts	
	Recorded as Revenue	650
	Less: progress billings invoiced	680
	Excess payments on account	30
	Deducted from long-term contract balances	(13)
	Treated as current liability	17

Notes to Financial Statement for Year Ended 31 July 20X9

Construction Contract	€'000
Contract revenue recognised as revenue in the period	425
Contract costs incurred and recognised profits to date (520 + 143)	663
Advances received	500

Gross amount due to customer

Cost incurred to date	520
Recognised profit	143
Recognised losses	–
Progress billings	(680)
	(17)

Question 3

Total Profit/Loss	Contract 20D	Contract 21D	Contract 22D
	€	€	€
Contract Price	500,000	300,000	400,000
Direct costs to date	180,000	150,000	120,000
Indirect costs to date	27,000	22,500	18,000
Direct costs to complete	220,000	160,000	330,000
Indirect costs to complete	33,000	24,000	49,500
	460,000	356,500	517,500
Total Profit (Loss)	40,000	(56,500)	(117,500)
Attributable Profit			

Contract 20D

$40,000 \times \dfrac{207}{460} =$ 18,000

Foreseeable Loss		(56,500)	(117,500)

Profit-making Contract

Statement of Comprehensive Income	Contract 20D
Attributable profit	18,000
Cost of sales	207,000
Revenue	225,000

Statement of Financial Position

(i) Amounts Recoverable on Contracts

Revenue	225,000
Progress billings invoiced	220,000
	5,000

(ii) Trade Receivables

Progress billings invoiced	220,000
Progress billings received	200,000
	20,000

(iii) Work in progress

Costs incurred to date	207,000
Cost of sales	207,000
	–

Note: Contract 20D is 45% complete at 30/6/Y0 so it is assumed that there is reasonable certainty as to the outcome.

Loss-making Contracts
Statement of comprehensive income

$$€$$

(i) Contract 21D

Revenue 300,000 x $\dfrac{172,500}{356,500}$	145,161
Cost of sales	(172,500)
Provision for foreseeable losses (balancing figure)	(29,161)
Gross loss	(56,500)

(ii) Contract 22D

Revenue 400,000 x $\dfrac{138,000}{517,500}$	106,667
Cost of sales	(138,000)
Provision for foreseeable losses (balancing figure)	(86,167)
Gross loss	(117,500)

Statement of Financial Position

	Contract 21D	Contract 22D
	€	€
(i) Amounts Recoverable on Contracts		
Revenue	145,161	106,667
Progress billings invoiced	100,000	70,000
	45,161	36,667
(ii) Trade Receivables		
Progress billings invoiced	100,000	70,000
Progress billings received	100,000	40,000
	–	30,000
(iii) Long-term contracts		
Costs incurred to date	172,500	138,000
Less: Cost of sales to date	(201,661)	(224,167)
Provision for foreseeable losses	(29,161)	(86,167)

Summary

Statement of comprehensive income (Extracts)

	€
Revenue (W1)	476,828
Cost of sales (W2)	(632,828)
Gross Loss	(156,000)

Statement of Financial Position (Extracts)

Current Assets

	€
Amounts recoverable on contracts (W3)	86,828
Trade Receivables (W4)	50,000

Current Liabilities

Provision for loss-making contracts	115,328

(W1)	€	(W3)	€
20D	225,000	20D	5,000
21D	145,161	21D	45,161
22D	106,667	22D	36,667
	476,828		86,828

REVIEW QUESTIONS – SUGGESTED SOLUTIONS – CHAPTER 12   841

(W2)	€	(W4)	€
20D	207,000		
21D	172,500	20D	20,000
Prov. for loss	29,161	22D	30,000
22D	138,000		
Prov. for loss	86,167		
	632,828		50,000

CHAPTER 13

REVIEW QUESTIONS – SUGGESTED SOLUTIONS

Question 1

(a)

		€	€
Capital allowances (Note 1):			
Capital allowances		4,750,000	
Depreciation charged		(3,250,000)	
Net originating differences			1,500,000
Tax loss (Note 2):	DT asset offset against DT liability.		(250,000)
Royalties (Note 4):	SCI charge less than amount allowable for tax, therefore provision needed.		50,000
			1,300,000
SCI charge:	@25%		325,000
SFP:	O/balance		250,000
	SCI charge		325,000
	C/balance		575,000

(b)

(i) **Asset revaluations** – IAS 16 *Property, Plant and Equipment* favours the use of the 'cost' model, although the valuation model is permitted. IAS 16 requires residual values to be reviewed at each reporting date. IAS 16 takes the same approach to asset revaluations as to the capitalisation of interest, i.e. neither required nor forbidden but, if adopted, then it must be applied consistently. All assets of a particular class must be revalued, but not necessarily all classes of asset. A class of asset is defined as a category of non-current asset having a similar nature, function or use in the business of the company.

Where a policy of revaluation is adopted, IAS 16 does not require an 'expert valuer' to conduct the valuations and valuations need only be conducted 'regularly'.

IAS 16 requires increases in an asset's residual value, based on current prices, to reduce the ongoing depreciation charge. If the residual value equals or exceeds the asset's carrying value, the depreciation charge is reduced to zero.

Revaluation losses may be reported differently. Under IAS 16, revaluation decreases are only charged to the statement of comprehensive income to the extent that they exceed previous surpluses.

(ii) **IAS 12** *Income Taxes* – The timing difference prior to revaluation is €200,000 (€800,000 – €600,000). The tax payable (€50,000) is an unavoidable tax liability. If the asset is retained, future tax allowances will be €1,200,000 and future depreciation will be €1,400,000. The tax payable on net reversing timing differences is €50,000. If the property is sold, then the tax written down value is €1,200,000 and €1,400,000 for accounts purposes. Therefore the unavoidable tax liability on the reversing timing difference is €50,000.

Under IAS 12 revaluing the property to €1,800,000 will create an unavoidable incremental tax liability as deferred tax is required on all revaluation gains (rather than only when there is an agreement to sell a revalued asset). IAS 12 requires deferred tax to be provided on temporary differences rather than timing differences.

(iii) **Discounting** – IAS 12 does not allow deferred tax assets and liabilities to be discounted.

CHAPTER 14

REVIEW QUESTIONS – SUGGESTED SOLUTIONS

Question 1

(a) **At 31 December 20X9** – There is a present obligation as a result of a past obligating event. The obligating event is the giving of the guarantee, which gives rise to a legal obligation. However, at 31 December 20X9 no transfer of economic benefits is probable in settlement of the obligation.

No provision is recognised. The guarantee is disclosed as a contingent liability unless the probability of any transfer is regarded as remote.

(b) **At 31 December 20Y0** – As above, there is a present obligation as a result of a past obligating event, namely the giving of the guarantee.

At 31 December 20Y0 it is probable that a transfer of economic events will be required to settle the obligation. A provision is therefore recognised for the best estimate of the obligation.

Question 2

King Limited *cannot avoid* the cost of repairing or replacing all items of product that manifest manufacturing defects in respect of which warranties are given before the date of the statement of financial position, and a provision for the cost of this should therefore be made.

King Limited is obliged to repair or replace items that fail within the entire warranty period. Therefore, in respect *of this year's sales,* the obligation provided for at the date of the statement of financial position should be the cost of making good items for which defects have been notified but not yet processed, *plus* an estimate of costs in respect of the other items sold for which there is sufficient evidence that manufacturing defects will manifest themselves during their remaining periods of warranty cover.

Question 3

(a) **At 31 December 200W** – On the basis of the evidence available when the financial statements were approved, there is no obligation as a result of past events. No provision is recognised. The matter is disclosed as a contingent liability unless the probability of any transfer is regarded as remote.

(b) **At 31 December 200X** – On the basis of the evidence available, there is a present obligation. A transfer of economic benefits in settlement is probable.

A provision is recognised for the best estimate of the amount needed to settle the present obligation.

Question 4

Memorandum

Date:
To:
From
Subject:

Issue 1: Under IAS 37 *Provisions, Contingent Liabilities and Contingent Assets*, a present obligation exists as a result of gaining the licence. There is the probable transfer of economic benefits and the amount of outflow can be reasonably estimated. Therefore it is necessary to create a provision for the full amount and capitalise the obligation as it meets the definition of an asset since it provides future economic benefits. Basing a provision on projected output is no longer allowed. The €120,000,000 should be provided for now, taking account of the time value of money. The funds can be set aside and reinvested at the risk-free rate.

6 years @ 4%:   Present value = 0.790 x €120,000,000 = €94,800,000

Therefore discount = €25,200,000.

At 1/1/03:

Dr	Non-current assets	€94,800,000	
Cr	Provisions		€94,800,000

Depreciation each year: (€94,800,000 ÷ 6 years)

Dr	SCI	€15,800,000	
Cr	Non-current assets		€15,800,000

Unwinding the discount:

Year	Opening Balance	Finance Cost @ 4%	Closing Balance
	€	€	€
2003	94,800,000	3,792,000	98,592,000
2004	98,592,000	3,943,680	102,535,680
2005	102,535,680	4,101,427	106,637,107
2006	106,637,107	4,265,484	110,902,591
2007	110,902,591	4,436,104	115,338,695
2008	115,338,695	4,613,548	119,952,243
		25,152,243	(Rounding €47,757)

The interest charge becomes progressively higher as it reflects the compounding of earnings of funds set aside earlier. The interest may be classified as exceptional if material.

Issue 2: The depreciation policy appears reasonable so long as the estimate of UEL of 12 years is appropriate and the aircraft will have no residual value. But it is also necessary to consider industry practice.

With respect to the overhaul provision, there is no 'present obligation' to carry out the overhaul since it could be avoided by selling the jet when three years have elapsed. Therefore, no provision can be recognised. The depreciation takes account of future incidence of maintenance.

However, it might be possible to divide the asset into 'different component parts' with different lives and depreciate each accordingly. But need to consider whether each 'part' is separately distinguishable.

Issue 3: IAS 38 *Intangible Assets* states that expenditure recognised as an expense in previous year should NOT be reinstated.

Issue 4: IAS 37 *Provisions, Contingent Liabilities and Contingent Assets* deals with recoveries from third parties. RUÁ is liable for 100% to the customer and therefore must provide for the full amount.

If RUÁ is virtually certain that COLUMBUS will honour their 50% and reimburse €2,500,000, the amount due may be shown as an asset.

Issue 5: The work was completed during the year ended 31 December 2003 and therefore it is relevant to the financial statements for the year ended 31 December 2003. The non-recoverable legal fees of €25,000 should be provided for.

As a successful outcome is put at 75%, it is reasonable to treat the claim as a contingent liability and disclose by way of note, explaining the background to the claim and the expectations for a successful outcome.

Issue 6: Assuming the bills were discounted with recourse and therefore there is a risk that, if the bills are dishonoured, RUÁ will have to settle the liability. Under IAS 37 *Provisions, Contingent Liabilities and Contingent Assets*, the contingent liability of €4,000,000 should be disclosed in the notes to the financial statements.

CHAPTER 15

REVIEW QUESTIONS – SUGGESTED SOLUTIONS

Question 1

(a) This is an adjusting event, and an adjustment should be made to the accounts in respect of the €20,000 owing at the date of the statement of financial position, putting through a charge in the statement of comprehensive income and writing off the debt in the statement of financial position. No adjustment should be made in respect of the further €10,000 arising after the date of the statement of financial position, as this is a non-adjusting event. However, if €10,000 is material in the context of the company's accounts, then a note should be attached to the financial statements stating that further debts incurred in respect of Cronser Limited after the date of the statement of financial position of €10,000 are unlikely to be recoverable.

(b) This is an adjusting event as it relates to the writing-off of the debt prior to the date of the statement of financial position, part of which is now recoverable. It is therefore appropriate to bring in a credit to the statement of comprehensive income in respect of the recoverable part of the debt and to include it as an asset in the statement of financial position. However, the company should be very sure that the dividend is receivable before treating it as an adjusting event.

(c) This is a non-adjusting event as the fire occurred after the date of the statement of financial position. However, as the amount of the inventory lost is most likely material to the company, it will be necessary to disclose the item in a note to the accounts.

Question 2

IAS 10 *Events after the Reporting Period* deals with the treatment of 'those events, both favourable and unfavourable, which occur between the date of the statement of financial position and the date on which the financial statements were approved by the board of directors'. A distinction is then made between events after the end of the reporting period, which are:

(i) adjusting events that provide additional evidence of conditions that existed at the date of the statement of financial position and have a material effect on the amounts included in the accounts (e.g. receipt of money from a debtor who had been regarded as a bad debt);

(ii) non-adjusting events that create new conditions, which did not exist at the date of the statement of financial position (e.g. a new issue of shares).

IAS 10 requires that:

(i) financial statements should be prepared on the basis of conditions which existed at the date of the statement of financial position;

(ii) if there is an adjusting event after the end of the reporting period which materially affects the view of conditions existing at the date of the statement of financial position the amounts to be included in the financial statements should be amended to reflect the event;

(iii) If there is a non-adjusting event after the end of the reporting period which is of such material significance that not to report it would prevent users of the financial statements from reaching a proper understanding of the financial position, it should be disclosed by way of note to the accounts. The note should describe the nature of the event and an estimate of its financial effect (or a statement that it is not practicable to make such an estimate);

(iv) The financial statements should also disclose the date on which they were authorised for issue by the board of directors. This is a necessary requirement so those users can establish the duration of the period after the date of the statement of financial position.

The treatment of the events arising in the case of Fabricators Limited would be as follows:

(a) The fall in value of the investment in Patchup Limited has arisen over the previous year and that company's financial accounts for the year to 28 February 20X1 provide additional evidence of conditions that existed at the date of the statement of financial position. The loss of €50,000 is material in terms of the trading profit figure and, as an adjusting event, should be reflected in the financial statements of Fabricators Limited.

(b) The destruction of inventory by a fire on 30 April (one month after the date of the statement of financial position) must be considered to be a non-adjusting event (i.e. 'a new condition which did not exist at the date of the statement of financial position'). Since the loss is material, being €250,000, it should be disclosed by way of a note to the accounts. The note should describe the nature of the event and an estimate of its financial effect. Non-reporting of this event would prevent users of the financial statements from reaching a proper understanding of the financial position.

(c) The confirmation by the customer that no remedial work was required on the plant supplied and that no further liability would arise means that an overprovision has been made in the accounts to 31 March. Since this condition 'existed at the date of the statement of financial position' this event is an adjusting event and the provision of €60,000 should be written back in the year-end accounts.

CHAPTER 16

REVIEW QUESTIONS – SUGGESTED SOLUTIONS

Question 1

dd/mm/yy
The Directors
Electronic Manufacturers Limited
Dublin

Dear Sirs,

Accounting Treatment of Government Grants

The grants which have been approved for the new production facilities fall into two distinct classes:

1. The grant for training costs – revenue-based grant; and
2. The grant for plant – capital-based grant.

These grants are treated differently for accounting purposes. IAS 20 provides that:

(a) Revenue-based grants are to be credited to revenue in the period in which the related revenue expenditure has been incurred and, where actual amounts are not known precisely, appropriate estimates must be made; and
(b) Capital-based grants are to be credited to revenue over the life of the appropriate tangible non-current assets by either:
  (i) reducing the costs of the assets by the full amount of the grants; or
  (ii) treating the amount of the grant as deferred credit, a portion of which is transferred to revenue annually. Where this method is used the amount of the deferred credit should, if material, be shown separately in the statement of financial position and separate from the shareholders' funds.

Where there is a contingent liability to repay any grant received, this must be disclosed by way of a note to the accounts.

As far as the company is concerned, I recommend that the following accounting policies be adopted:

- **Training grants** – these grants be credited to revenue as they accrue due; and
- **Grants on plant** – these grants be treated as deferred credits and disclosed in the statement of financial position under the heading 'Government Grants' and allocated to the statement of comprehensive income over the life of the individual items of plant at the same rates as depreciation is charged.

I consider that the foregoing treatment of grants on plant is the most suitable as it will enable more accurate management information to be compiled on such matters as the rate of return on capital employed, comparative costs with existing plant, and control over the actual ordering and installation costs of the plant. As grants can vary depending on government action, more reliable statistics can be compiled for future use.

Either accounting treatment of the capital-based grant will result in the same net profit figure because, while the depreciation charge in method (b)(i) will be lower than that in method (b)(ii), a compensatory amount will be transferred from the deferred credit account 'Government Grants' to credit the statement the comprehensive income in method (b)(ii).

In the financial statements the following notes should be included:

Accounting Policies

1. Grants:

Grants receivable on additions to tangible non-current assets are credited to the Government Grants Account and are allocated to the statement of comprehensive income over the estimated effective lives of the assets concerned. Revenue-based grants are credited directly to the statement of comprehensive income in the year in which they become due.

2. Government Grants:

	€
Balance at start of year	X
Receivable for year	X
Released to statement of comprehensive income	(X)
Balance at end of year	X

3. Contingent Liabilities:

Under various agreements between the company and the Industrial Development Authority, the company has received grants amounting to €_____. There exists a contingent liability to repay in whole or in part the grants received if certain circumstances set out in the agreements occur before receipt of the final instalment of the grants or within ten years thereafter.

Question 2

Depreciation per year:

$$\frac{\text{Cost less residual value}}{\text{Useful Life}} \quad = \quad \frac{\text{€25,000} - \text{€1,000}}{4} \quad = \quad \text{€6,000 p.a.}$$

Amortisation of capital grant:

$$\frac{\text{Amount received}}{\text{Useful Life}} \quad = \quad \frac{\text{€6,000}}{4} \quad = \quad \text{€1,500 p.a.}$$

Depreciation is charged to the statement of comprehensive income based on the gross cost less any residual value of the plant. On the assumption that this cost is apportioned over the 4 years' useful life by means of the straight-line method of depreciation, the annual depreciation charge will be €6,000.

Capital grants on fixed assets are amortised to the statement of comprehensive income over the useful life of the related assets in the same ratio as the related depreciation is written off. This means that there will be a credit of €1,500 to the statement of comprehensive income each year.

The amount of the grant, €6,000, will be credited to a deferred income account (e.g. Capital Grants Received) and each year an amount of €1,500 will be debited thereto and credited to the statement of comprehensive income. The €1,500 will be shown separately in the statement of comprehensive income and not deducted from the depreciation. It will be described as capital grants released. The balance on the Capital Grants Received account will be shown separately in the statement of financial position under its own heading 'Deferred Income'; it will not be shown as part of the shareholders' funds.

The grant of €500 for wages will be credited to the statement of comprehensive income in the year in which the expenditure to which it relates is incurred, i.e. the year 20X0–X1.

The purchase price €25,000 of the plant and equipment will be shown in the statement of financial position as an addition to the previous year's gross cost of fixed assets (plant and machinery). The depreciation charge will be added to the total depreciation brought forward from the previous year.

There should be a note to the statement of financial position indicating the conditions precedent to the repayment of any of the grants, if applicable.

The accounting policy followed by the company in respect of grants should also be disclosed.

CHAPTER 17

REVIEW QUESTIONS – SUGGESTED SOLUTIONS

Question 1

The asset in the statement of financial position will be:

	€m
The fair value of the plan assets	130
The present value of the defined benefit obligation	(105)
Cumulative unrecognised actuarial losses	4
	29

The cumulative unrecognised actuarial losses, plus the present value of refunds from the plan and reductions in future contributions, amount to €27 million (€4 million + €23 million). Therefore, the asset is restricted to this figure. The amount written off the asset should go to the statement of comprehensive income.

Question 2

There are three possible treatments:

1. The company could recognise the portion of the net actuarial gain or loss in excess of 10% of the greater of the defined benefit obligation or the fair value of the plan assets at the beginning of the year.

   The unrecognised actuarial gain at the beginning of the year was €4 million. The limit of the corridor is 10% of €30 million (i.e. €3 million) as the fair value of the assets is greater than the value of the obligation. The difference is €1 million which, divided by 10 years, is €100,000 to be recognised in profit or loss. The accounting for the corridor approach takes no account of actuarial gains and losses arising in the year – instead it considers the state of the plan at the previous year end.

2. The actuarial gains and losses can be recognised in full in the statement of recognised income and expense. Accordingly, the €5 million gain will be recognised in the statement. This gain cannot be recycled through the statement of comprehensive income and should be added to retained earnings.

3. Any other systematic method that results in a faster recognition of actuarial gains and losses in the statement of comprehensive income can be used. So, all the actuarial gain of €5 million can be recognised in the statement of comprehensive income, but this is extremely rare in practice.

Question 3

It is assumed that 10% (6 ÷ €60 million) of the previously unrecognised actuarial gains relate to the obligation eliminated.

Statement of financial position after curtailment:

	Obligation before curtailment €m	Gain on curtailment €m	Obligation after curtailment €m
Net present value of obligation	60	(6)	54
Fair value of plan assets	(48)	–	(48)
	12	(6)	6
Unrecognised actuarial gains	4	(0.4)	3.6
Net liability	16	(6.4)	9.6

CHAPTER 18

REVIEW QUESTIONS – SUGGESTED SOLUTIONS

Question 1

(a) Define profits available for distribution

Available profits are defined as:

- Accumulated realised profits less accumulated realised losses;
- The total of the net assets must be equal or more than the aggregate of the called-up share capital plus undistributable reserves.

Undistributable reserves include:

- Share premium account;
- Capital redemption reserve;
- Excess of accumulated unrealised profits over accumulated unrealised losses;
- Any reserve that the company is prohibited from distributing.

Disclosure requirement:

There are no statutory requirements for companies to distinguish in their accounts between distributable and non-distributable reserves, although it might become necessary to make some disclosure in order to give a true and fair view.

In the group accounts, there is a presumption that the holding company could arrange for the profits dealt with in the accounts of the subsidiary companies to be passed up to the holding company and be available for distribution to the shareholders of the holding company.

(b)

(i) Research and development activities

Only distributions to be made out of the company's net realised profits are permitted. In determining net realised profits, any amount shown in respect of development costs, which is included as an asset in the statement of financial position, is to be treated as a realised loss unless the directors consider that there are special circumstances that justify a decision not to treat the development costs as a realised loss. If the directors decide that there is justification, the accounts must explain the circumstances that are being relied on. In general, if development costs are carried forward in accordance with the provisions of IAS 38, this will normally provide the directors with appropriate justification.

(ii) Net deficit on revaluation reserve

The diminution in the value of the non-current assets will reduce the distributable reserves of Prosperous because the company is a public company and, consequently, any distribution must not reduce its net assets to less than its share capital and undistributable reserves.

(iii) Excess depreciation

When a company has revalued a non-current asset to show an unrealised profit, it will be required to charge depreciation on the revalued amount in the statement of comprehensive income. However, when determining the distributable profits, the excess depreciation is added back to the realised profit disclosed in the statement of comprehensive income on the grounds that it is a part realisation of the revaluation surplus. It will be appropriate, therefore, to make a transfer annually from undistributable to distributable reserves, i.e. from the revaluation reserve to the profit and loss account.

Question 2

Hay plc: €900,000 ((€200,000) + €200,000 + €600,000 + €300,000)

Bee plc: €520,000 (€100,000 + (€200,000) + €600,000 + €20,000*)
* = Depreciation adjustment

	€
Depreciation based on revalued figure	50,000
Depreciation based on historical figure	30,000
Difference	20,000

Sea Limited: €100,000 ((€200,000) + €300,000). Since Sea Limited is a private company, the unrealised profit (the revaluation reserve) is ignored.

Question 3

This question tests both the legal definition of distributable profits and the application of this knowledge to both written and numerical situations.

(a) The general rule is that distributable profits consist of accumulated realised profits less accumulated realised losses. Realised profits and losses are determined by reference to generally accepted accounting principles at the time the accounts are prepared. There is a further restriction for public limited companies that may not make a distribution unless the net assets immediately after the distribution are not less than the total share capital plus undistributable reserves.

(b)

(i) A provision for bad debts would be realised since it is generally accepted accounting practice to make such provisions in accordance with the accounting concept of prudence and the underlying assumptions set out in the *Framework* document.
(ii) The dividend receivable from a subsidiary would be regarded as realised since by convention it is generally accepted accounting practice to accrue for such dividends even though they may not yet have been approved at the annual general meeting of the subsidiary.
(iii) Any surplus arising from a revaluation of an asset would be regarded as unrealised. It will only be realised when that asset is sold.

(c)

(i) The accumulated realised profits less accumulated realised losses is the profit and loss account balance of €200,000.
(ii) The accumulated realised profits less accumulated losses are €200,000. However there is a further restriction in the case of public limited companies as follows:

Share Capital and Undistributable Reserves	
Issued Share Capital	€200
Share Premium Account	€175
Capital Redemption Reserve	€125
General Reserve	€100
Distributable profits is net assets of €625 less	€600 = €25

It would make no difference to the public company whether the deficit on the revaluation reserve arose on the revaluation of all assets or just an individual asset.

However, if Global Sports is a private company and revaluation was the result of an individual asset being revalued, then this must be treated as a realised loss and the distributable reserves would therefore be:

Retained Earnings	€200
Revaluation Reserve – Realised Loss	€175
Distributable Profit	€ 25

CHAPTER 19

REVIEW QUESTIONS – SUGGESTED SOLUTIONS

Question 1

Statement of Cash Flows for the Year Ended 31 December 200X

	€'000	€'000
Net cash flows from operating activities		
Operating profit	350	
Depreciation charge	90	
Loss on sale of tangible non-current assets	13	
Profit on sale of non-current asset investments	(5)	
Increase in inventories	(48)	
Increase in receivables	(75)	
Increase in payables	8	
Cash generated from operating activities	333	
Interest received	25	
Interest paid	(75)	
Dividends paid	(80)	
Tax paid	(130)	
Net cash flows from operating activities		73
Cash flows from investing activities		
Payments to acquire tangible non-current assets	(201)	
Payments to acquire intangible non-current assets	(50)	

Receipts from sales of tangible non-current assets	32	
Receipts from sale of non-current asset investments	30	
Net cash flows from investing activities		(189)
Cash flows from financing activities		
Issue of share capital	60	
Long-term loan	120	
Net cash flows from financing		(180)
Increase in cash and cash equivalents (Note)		64
Cash and cash equivalents at 1/1/200X (Note)		(97)
Cash and cash equivalents at 31/12/200X (Note)		33

Notes to the Statement of cash flows:

1. Analysis of the Balances of Cash and Cash Equivalents as shown in the Statement of Financial Position

	200X €'000	200W €'000	Change in Year €'000
Cash in hand	2	1	1
Short-term investments	50	–	50
Bank overdraft	(85)	(98)	13
	(33)	(97)	64

Workings:

Wk 1 Tangible Assets

	€'000		€'000
Balance b/d	595	Disposals	85
Revaluation reserve	9		
Therefore additions	201	Balance c/d	720
	805		805

Wk 2 Depreciation

	€'000		€'000
Disposal	40	Balance b/d	290
Balance c/d	340	Inc. start	90
	380		380

Wk 3

Disposal a/c

	€'000		€'000
Tangible assets	85	Depreciation	40
		Cash	32
		Inc. stat	13
	85		85

Wk 4

Taxation

	€'000		€'000
Cash	130	Balance b/d	110
Balance c/d	120	Inc. stat	140
	250		250

Wk 5

Dividends

	€'000		€'000
Cash	80	Balance b/d	80
Balance c/d	100	Equity	100
	180		180

Workings for Direct Method:

Wk 6

Purchases	€'000
Cost of sales	1,814
Closing stock	(150)
Opening stock	102
Purchases	1,862

Wk 7

Trade Payables

	€'000		€'000
Cash	1,859	Balance b/d	119
Balance c/d (€127 - €5)	122	Inc. Stat.	1,862
	1,981		1,981

860 INTERNATIONAL FINANCIAL ACCOUNTING AND REPORTING

Wk 8		Receivables	
	€'000		€'000
Balance b/d	315	Cash	2,478
IS (Revenue)	2,553	Balance c/d	390
	2,868		2,868

Direct Method – Cash generated from Operating Activities

	€'000
Cash received from customers	2,478
Cash paid to suppliers for goods and services*	(2,060)
Cash paid to and on behalf of employees (see question, note (e))	(85)
Cash generated from operating	333

	€'000
*Trade payables	1,859
Distribution	125
Administrative	264
Depreciation	(90)
Wages	(90)
Net loss on disposals	(8)
	2,060

Question 2

(a) Statement of cash flows for Year Ended 31 December 2003

	€'000	€'000
Operating activities		
Net cash flows from operating activities (See part (b))		1,574
Investing activities		
Receipts from sales of property, plant and equipment (Working 4)	350	
Payments to acquire property, plant and equipment (Working 5)	(2,571)	
Net cash flows from investing activities		(2,221)
Financing activities		
Capital element of finance leases (Working 6)	(151)	

Issue of shares, including premium	300	
Share issue expenses	(50)	
Medium-term bank loans (Working 7)	1,726	
Net cash inflow from financing		1,825
Increase in cash and cash equivalents during the year*		1,178
Cash and cash equivalents at start of year		1,840
Cash and cash equivalents at end of year		3,018

* *Proof:*

Movement bank and cash	1,230	
Movement overdraft	(52)	
	1,178	

(b) Reconciliation of operating profit to net cash flows from operating activities

	€'000
Operating profit	4,389
Amortisation of patents (W8)	108
Depreciation	1,526
Increase in inventory (W9)	(1,194)
Increase in trade receivables (W10)	(1,464)
Increase in trade payables (W11)	588
	3,953
Interest received	308
Interest paid (W1)	(203)
Tax paid (W3)	(370)
Dividends paid (W2)	(2,114)
	1,574

Workings:

1. Interest paid	€'000
Balance at beginning of year	6
Statement of comprehensive income	224
Balance at end of year	(27)
Paid during the year	203

2. Dividends paid

Balance at beginning of year	296
Statement of comprehensive income	2,200
Balance at end of year	(382)
Paid during the year	2,114

3. Tax paid

Balance at beginning of year (€1,178 + €1,650)	2,828
Statement of comprehensive income	1,540
	4,368
Balance at end of year (€1,258 + €2,740)	(3,998)
Paid during the year	370

4. Cash from sale of non-current assets

Per statement of comprehensive income	194
NBV of assets disposed (€546 – €390)	156
Cash received	350

5. Purchase of property, plant and equipment

Balance at end of year (NBV)	10,877
Net book value of disposals	156
Depreciation charge	1,526
Increase in fixed asset payable (€1,196 – €1,178)	(18)
	12,541
Balance at start of year (NBV)	(9,970)
Cash paid	2,571

6. Capital element of finance leases

Balance at beginning of year (€101 + €358)	459
Balance at end of year (€70 + €238)	(308)
	151

7. Medium-term loans

Balance at end of year	1,726
Balance at beginning of year	–
	1,726

8. Amortisation of patents

Balance at beginning of year	270
Balance at end of year	(162)
Amortised during the year	108

9. Increase in inventory

Balance at end of year	2,080
Balance at beginning of year	(886)
Increase in inventory	1,194

10. Increase in trade receivables

Balance at end of year	6,006
Balance at beginning of year	(4,542)
Increase in trade receivables	1,464

11. Increase in trade payables

Balance at end of year	4,108
Balance at beginning of year	(3,520)
Increase in trade payables	588

CHAPTER 20

REVIEW QUESTIONS – SUGGESTED SOLUTIONS

Question 1

Issue 1 – Sale of division

(a) Per IFRS 5 *Non-current Assets Held for Sale and Discontinued Operations*, this should be classified as relating to 'discontinued operations' since it represents withdrawal from the market (as indicated by different customer base) and changing the nature and focus of operations which is consistent with company's long-term plans. Discontinued operations may be disclosed at the foot of the statement of comprehensive income or, alternatively, profit from discontinued operations can be analysed in a separate column on the face of the statement of comprehensive income. This former treatment has been adopted resulting in a €500,000 profit for discontinued operations being disclosed at the foot of the company's statement of comprehensive income.

(b) 'Extraordinary items' have been banned and it is a decision for the company to highlight/separately disclose 'exceptional' items. IAS 1 *Presentation of Financial Statements* makes no reference to 'super exceptional" items. The €1,000,000 profit could be included in 'administrative expenses'.

Issue 2 – Closure of retail outlets

APF Limited is not clearly demonstrably committed to the termination and therefore the operation is not discontinued under IFRS 5 *Non-current Assets Held for Sale and Discontinued Operations*. No provision should be made for the expected trading loss of €800,000. The assets are stated at their recoverable amount, therefore no adjustment is required.

CHAPTER 21

REVIEW QUESTIONS – SUGGESTED SOLUTIONS

Question 1

If Keano Limited had always adopted the new policy, the following additional amounts would have been written off to the Statement of Comprehensive Income:

	€'000	€'000
2001	(400 – 100)	300
2002	(600 – 250)	350
2003	(300 – 325)	(25)
		625

This is the total prior-period adjustment in the 2004 financial statements, i.e. the total cumulative adjustment up to the end of the previous period as if the new policy had been previously used.

Note:

This amount should be analysed between:

(a) the amount affecting the previous year, i.e. 2003 – €25,000 credit; and
(b) the amount affecting the retained profits at the start of the previous year, i.e. 1 January 2003 €650,000 debit.

Statement of Retained Earnings

	2004			2003
	€'000	€'000	€'000	€'000
Retained profit for the year		1,820		1,605 (1580 + 25)
Retained Earnings Brought Forward				
As previously reported	4,440		2,860	

Prior-period adjustment	(625)	(650)
As restated	3,815	2,210
Retained Earnings Carried Forward	5,635	3,815

Accounting Entry in 2004

	€'000	€'000
DR Retained Earnings	625	
CR Development Expenditure		625

Note:

If Keano Limited (in the 2004 financial statements) had decided that the expenditure on the projects on hand should not be deferred to future periods because management were of the opinion that it may not be recovered (prudence) – this would not be a change in an accounting policy.

Question 2

The total prior period adjustment in the cumulative error up to 31 May 2004.

	€
31 May 2004	80,000
31 May 2003	60,000
	140,000
less attributable tax 40%	(56,000)
	84,000

Analyse the total into:

(a) The amount affecting the immediate past year, i.e. 31 May 2005   = €48,000
(b) The amount affecting the retained profit up to 31 May 2003   = €36,000

Revised Statements of Comprehensive Income:

	2005	2004
	€	€
Profit before tax	710,000	560,000
Income tax expenses	(284,000)	(224,000)
Profit after tax	426,000	336,000

Statement of Retained Profit:

	2005	2004
	€	€
Retained profit for the year	326,000	236,000
Retained profit brought forward		
As previously reported	1,174,000	890,000
Prior-period adjustment	(84,000)	(36,000)
As restated	1,090,000	854,000
Retained profit carried forward	1,416,000	1,090,000

CHAPTER 22

REVIEW QUESTIONS – SUGGESTED SOLUTIONS

Question	Answer
1.	(c)
2.	(b)
3.	(c)
4.	(a)
5.	(b)
6.	Yes – (a), (b), (c) & (d); No – (e), (f) & (g)
7.	(b)
8.	(a)
9.	(c)
10.	(a)
11.	(a) (iii) & (v); (b) (ii); (c) (iv); (d) (i)
12.	(c)
13.	(b)
14.	(b)
15.	(c)
16.	(a)

CHAPTER 23

REVIEW QUESTIONS – SUGGESTED SOLUTIONS

Question 1

(a)

	Earnings
	€
Profit before tax	2,323,000
Less Taxation	(1,058,000)
Profit after tax	1,265,000
Less: preference dividends	(276,000)
Earnings	989,000
Earnings per share	989,000
	4,140,000
	= 23.9 cent

(b)

Shares in issue at 31 December 20X4 = 4,140,000 + 4,140,000/4 = 5,175,000

EPS	€989,000
	5,175,000
	= 19.1 cent

(c)

The first step is to calculate the theoretical ex-rights price. Consider the holder of 5 shares.

	No.	€
Before rights issue	5 @ 1.80	9.00
Rights issue	1 @ 1.20	1.20
After rights issue	6	10.20

The theoretical ex-rights price is therefore €10.20/6 = €1.70

The number of shares in issue before the rights issue must be multiplied by the fraction:

Market price on last day of quotation cum rights	= €1.80
Theoretical ex-rights price	€1.70

Number of shares in issue during the year:

	Proportion of year	Shares in issue	Fraction	Total
1.1.X4 – 1.10.X4	9/12 x	4,140,000	x 1.8/1.7	3,287,647
	3/12 x	4,968,000		1,242,000
				4,529,647

$$\text{EPS} = \frac{€989,000}{4,529,647} = 21.8 \text{ cent}$$

(d)

The maximum number of shares into which the loan stock could be converted is 90% x 1,150,000 = 1,035,000. The calculation of fully diluted EPS should be based on the assumption that such a conversion actually took place on 1 January 20X4. Shares in issue during the year would then have numbered (4,140,000 + 1,035,000) = 5,175,000 and revised earnings would be as follows.

	€	€
Earnings from (a) above		989,000
Interest saved by conversion	115,000	
Less attributable taxation	(57,500)	57,500
		1,046,500

$$\text{EPS} = \frac{1,046,500}{5,175,000} = 20.2 \text{ cent}$$

Question 2

1. Basic EPS

	20X1	20X0
	€'000	€'000
Profit after tax	500	400
14% Non Cumulative Pref. Div. Paid		(20)
10% Cumulative Pref. Div. Proposed	(30)	(30)
14% Non-cumulative Pref. Div. Proposed	(60)	(40)
	410	310

Earnings	€410,000	€310,000
Ordinary Shares	100,000	100,000
Basic EPS =	410 cent	310 cent

2. Issue at Full Market Price

The denominator should be weighted in accordance with the portion of the year in which the additional shares were in issue.

	20X1	20X0
Earnings (€)	410,000	310,000
Ordinary Shares	100,000 + (5,000 x 9/12)	100,000
Basic EPS	= 395 cent	= 310 cent

Note: Earno Limited should not be compared with Plum plc above. It has been assumed in Earno that the additional cash generated by the share has been a factor in increasing earnings from €310,000 in 20X0 to €410,000 in the current year.

3. Capitalisation Issue

	20X1	20X0
Earnings	€410,000	€310,000
Ordinary Shares	100,000 + 20,000	100,000
Basic EPS	342 cent	310 cent

As shares have been issued without any cash being generated, it is necessary to adjust the 20X0 EPS figure so as to preserve comparability.

$$€3.1 \times \frac{100,000}{120,000} = €2.58$$

	20X1	20X0
Correct Basic EPS	342c	258c

4. Share Exchange

EPS = €410,000

100,000 + (10,000 x 8/12) = 384 cent

The reason that the additional 10,000 shares are taken in for 8 months only is that any earnings of the subsidiary prior to 30 April would be pre-acquisition and, as such, should be excluded from group earnings. It has been assumed that the subsidiary's earnings have been a factor in increasing earnings since 20X0.

5. Rights issue for less than full market price
    We could regard this issue as being partly a bonus issue and partly an issue at full market price. The bonus portion is then treated as in (3) above:

(a) The bonus shares being deemed in issue from 1 January 20X1; and
(b) The 20X0 EPS figure being reduced as in (3) above.

Calculation of Theoretical Ex-Rights price:

i.e. the price to which the share should fall after the rights issue

100,000 @ €4 =	400,000
20,000 @ €2 =	40,000
120,000	€440,000

Theoretical ex-rights price = $\frac{€440,000}{€120,000}$ = €3.67

	20X1	20X0
Earnings	€410,000	€310,000
Ordinary Shares	(100,000 x 6/12 x €4) + (120,000 x 6/12) / €3.67	100,000
Basic EPS	358 cent	310 cent

It is necessary, however, to adjust the EPS ratio of 20X0, as shares have been issued during 20X1 for which the full market price was not obtained.

	20X1	20X0
Basic EPS	358 cent	3.10 x (3.67/4) = 284 cent

6. Fully Diluted Earnings Per Share

(a) Another class of equity ranking for dividend in the future:

	20X1
Earnings	€410,000
Ordinary Shares	100,000 + 10,000
FDEPS	= 373 cent

(b) Convertible Securities

Earnings per basic EPS	€410,000
Interest saved if €5,000 of 10% debentures are converted into ordinary shares on 31 March 20X1 (5,000 x 10% x 9/12 x 50%)	187
	€410,187

	20X1
Earnings	410,187
Number of shares	100,000 + (5,000 x 30/100 x 9/12)
FDEPS	= 406 cent

The DEPS is not calculated for 20X0 as the same assumptions did not apply.

CHAPTER 24

REVIEW QUESTIONS – SUGGESTED SOLUTIONS

Question	Answer
1.	4
2.	2
3.	2
4.	2
5.	3
6.	(iii)
7.	1
8.	(iv)
9.	1
10.	(i)
11.	(i)

CHAPTER 25

REVIEW QUESTIONS – SUGGESTED SOLUTIONS

Question 1

(a)		€'000
Total proceeds		30,000
Issue costs		(300)
		29,700
Total payments	
– dividends €30,000 x 0.04 x 5 years		(6,000)
– redemption 30,000 x €1.35		(40,500)
		(16,800)

Finance cost	O/bal	FC (10%)	Paid	C/bal
	€'000	€'000	€'000	€'000
2004	29,700	2,970	(1,200)	31,470
2005	31,470	3,147	(1,200)	33,417
2006	33,417	3,342	(1,200)	35,559
2007	35,559	3,556	(1,200)	37,915
2008	37,915	3,792	(41,700)	-
			(Rounding €7)	

(b)

Statement of financial position as at 31 December 2008 €'000

Capital and Reserves

€1 ordinary shares 300,000

Redeemable preference shares	-
Capital redemption reserve	30,000
Share premium account	77,000
Retained earnings (€182,500 – €30,000)	152,500
	559,500

Question 2

		€
Proceeds	9m x €0.95	8,550,000
Issue costs		(76,400)
Net proceeds		8,473,600

O/bal	Amount borrowed €	Interest @ 10% €	Paid (6%) €	C/bal €
2008	8,473,600	847,360	(540,000)	8,780,960
2009	8,780,960	878,096	(540,000)	9,119,056
2010	9,119,056	911,906	(540,000)	9,490,962
2011	9,490,962	949,096	(10,440,000)	Nil*

*€58 rounding difference

Example:

2008	DR	SCI – finance costs	€847,360	
		CR Bank		€540,000
		CR Debentures		€307,360

CHAPTER 26

REVIEW QUESTIONS – SUGGESTED SOLUTIONS

Question 1

As the recoverable amount of the CGU as a whole is €450, some of this must relate to the (unrecognised) goodwill of the NCI. Therefore, IAS 36 requires a notional adjustment for the goodwill of the NCI, before being compared to the recoverable amount of €450.

	Goodwill	Net assets	Total
	€	€	€
Carrying amount – Parent	160	500	660
Notional adjustment – NCI	40	-	40
	200	500	700
Recoverable amount			(450)
Impairment loss			250

If the goodwill of Parent is €160 and this represents 80%, then the goodwill attributable to the NCI is €40 (€160 x 20%/80%). This impairment loss is first allocated to €200 goodwill of €200 (eliminating it) and the remaining €50 (€250 – €200) to the identifiable net assets, leaving a carrying amount of €450 (€500 – €50), which is now equal to the recoverable amount of the CGU.

REVIEW QUESTIONS – SUGGESTED SOLUTIONS

Question 1

(a)

	€	€
1. Cost of Investment in Roberts		68,000
Goodwill		(16,000)
		52,000

2. Therefore 100% of Roberts' capital and reserves at acquisition date = €52,000
3. Plant @ acquisition over-valued by 2,000

	€	€
Dr Cost of Control 80%	1,600	
Dr Non-controlling interest 20%	400	
Cr Plant		2,000
4. Dr CSCI	200	
Cr Inventory		200

Being unrealised profit included in Roberts' inventory purchased for Llewellyn

In the draft consolidated statement of financial position 100% of post acquisition profits of Roberts = €12,000, and 20% of this must be transferred to non-controlling interest.

Cost of Control

	€		€
Cost	68,000	Capital and Reserves	52,000
		Goodwill c/d	16,000
	68,000		68,000
Balance b/d	16,000	Journal 2	800
Journal 1	10,400		
Journal 3	1,600	Balance c/d	27,200
	28,000		28,000

Consolidated Reserves

	€		€
Journal 4	200	Balance b/f	32,000
Journal 5	2,400	Journal 2	480
Balance c/d	30,040	Journal 3	160
	32,640		32,640

Non-controlling Interest

	€			€
JNL 3	400	JNL	1	10,400
			2	320
Bal c/d	12,760		3	40
			5	2,400
	13,160			13,160

Journal Adjustments:

	DR	CR
	€	€

1. Dr Cost of Control   10,400
    Cr Non-controlling interest   10,400
    Being transfer of 20% of Roberts Capital and Reserves at acquisition date to non-controlling interest.

2. Dr Inventory   1,600
       (a) Cr Cost of Control   800
       (b) Cr Consolidated Reserves   480
       (c) Cr Non-controlling Interest   320

    (a) 80% x €1,000 (Pre-acq.)
    (b) 80% x (€1,600 – €1,000) (Post-acq.)
    (c) 20% x 1,600

    Being adjustment to opening and closing inventory to correct Assistant Accountant's assumption that Llewellyn had acquired 100% of Roberts.

3. (a) Dr Cost of Control(Pre-acq.)   1,600
         Dr Non-controlling Interest   400
         Cr Plant   2,000
    (b) Dr Depreciation Provision   200
         Cr Consolidated Reserves (Post-acq.)   160
         Cr Non-controlling Interest   40

    Being adjustment to plant to reflect over valuation and correct acquisition percentage.

4. Dr Consolidated Reserves   200
      Cr Inventory   200

   Being unrealised profit included in Roberts' inventory purchased from hlewellyn

5. Dr Consolidated Reserves   2,400
      Cr Non-controlling Interest   2,400

   Being NCI's share of post acquisition profits (20%) incorrectly credited to Llewellyn by Assistant Accountant.

Being transfer of 20% of the post-acquisition profits of Roberts Limited to non-controlling interest.

(b)

Revised Consolidated SFP as at 30 June 20X4

	€		€
Property	30,000	Ordinary Shares	100,000
Plant at book value	78,200		
		Retained profits	30,040
Goodwill	27,200		
		Non-controlling interest	12,760
		Payables	54,000
Inventory	33,400		
Receivables	24,000		
Cash	4,000		
	196,800		196,800

Question 2

Black Limited
Consolidated Statement of Financial Position as at 31 March 20X2

Assets	€
Non-current Assets	
Property, plant and equipment	380,000
Goodwill	31,050
	411,050
Current Assets	285,700
Total Assets	696,750
Equity and Liabilities	
Equity	
Ordinary share capital	300,000
General reserve	50,000

Retained profits	111,650
	461,650
Non-controlling interest	66,100
	527,750
Non-current Liabilities 6% Debentures	15,000
Current Liabilities	
Trade payables	119,200
Proposed dividends	33,900
Debenture interest accrued	900
	154,000
Total Equity and Liabilities	696,750

Correcting Entries in Books:

	€	€
(i) Incorrect credit of dividends received out of pre-acquisition profits to SCI of BLACK Limited		
Retained Profits	7,950	
Cost of Control Account		7,950
(ii) Correction of the incorrect pre-acquisition reserve calculation		
Cost of Investment	7,950	
Statement of comprehensive income		7,950
(iii) Credit of debenture interest receivable by Black Limited from Bird Limited		
Debenture interest receivable	300	
Retained Profits		300
(iv) Reversal of dividends payable by Bird Limited from Black Limited		
Dividends Payable	15,600	
Statement of comprehensive income		15,600
(v) Correction of unrealised inventory profit		
Statement of comprehensive income	3,200	
Inventory (€16,000 x 20%)		3,200

Group Structure:

	Bird	
	Ord.	Pref.
Group	75%	75%
Non-controlling interest	25%	25%
	100%	100%

Cost of Control Account

	€		€
Cost of investment: Ord	165,000	OSC	75,000
Pref	60,000	PSC	60,000
Pre-acquisition Dividend	7,950	Retained Profits	28,950
		General Reserve	30,000
		Pre-acquisition Dividend	7,950
		Goodwill	31,050
	232,950		232,950

Tutorial Notes to Cost of Control Account:

1. A dividend has been declared out of Bird Limited's pre-acquisition profits. The group share of the dividend is as follows:

$$
\begin{array}{lr}
& € \\
\text{Ordinary} \quad 5,600 \times 75\% = & 4,200 \\
\text{Preference} \ 5,000 \times 75\% = & \underline{3,750} \\
& \underline{7,950}
\end{array}
$$

The cost of investment has been reduced as this is effectively a refund of Black Limited's purchase consideration (see journal (ii) above). Black Limited has incorrectly recognised this amount as income in a previous statement of comprehensive income. Thus, group reserves must also be reduced by €7,950.

2. Note that the profit figure used to calculate group share of pre-acquisition profits is that before the dividend has been deducted.

Profit after dividend at 31/3/X1	€28,000
Add back pre-acquisition dividend	€10,600
	€38,600

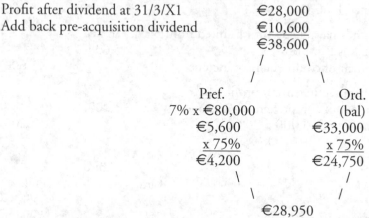

3. Note that the profit figure above used to calculate the pre-acquisition reserves was that before the pre-acquisition dividends. This is not strictly correct because, by their very nature, pre-acquisition dividends reduce the level of reserves that existed at the date of acquisition. Consequently, this is corrected by crediting back some of the already frozen reserves to the consolidated reserves account and debiting the cost of control (see journal (i) above). The amount of the correction is the group share of the pre-acquisition dividend.

Non-controlling interest Account

	€		€
		OSC	25,000
Other payables	3,900	PSC	20,000
Balance carried down	66,100	SCI	15,000
		General Reserve	10,000
	70,000		70,000

Tutorial Notes to Non-controlling Interest Account:

1. Note that the profit before the deduction of the current year dividend has been used to calculate the non-controlling interest share of reserves.

Reserves before dividend   60,000

```
                    /            \
                   /              \
              Pref                  Ord.
         7% x 80,000                (bal)
            5,600                   54,400
           x 25%                    x 25%
            1,400                    13,600
                 \                  /
                  \                /
                      15,000
```

The non-controlling interest share of the dividends for the year is as follows:

			€
Ordinary	10,000 x 25%	=	2,500
Preference	5,600 x 25%	=	1,400
			3,900

This amount is to be re-classified as 'other payables'.

2. Debentures and debenture interest must not be posted to the non-controlling interest account.

Consolidated Reserves

	€		€
		Balance b/d — Black	98,500
		— Bird	44,400
Cost of Control Account	28,950		
Non-controlling interest	15,000	Pre-acquisition dividend (i)	7,950
Inventory Adjustment	3,200	Debenture interest due	300
		Dividend proposed	15,600
Pre-acquisition dividend (ii)	7,950		
Balance carried down	111,650		
	166,750		166,750

Tutorial Note on Consolidated Reserves:

1. The reserves of Black Limited above incorrectly include a dividend made by Bird out of pre-acquisition reserves, of €7,950. Such a dividend should be treated as a refund of capital not as income and thus the group reserves have been reduced by €7,950.
2. The dividends proposed by Bird Limited are reversed. No adjustment to reverse them out of Black is required as they were not recognised as receivable in the books of Black Limited.
3. Debenture interest payable by Bird Limited has not been recognised in the books of Black Limited. The group share of this interest, i.e. €1,200 x 25%, has been credited to group reserves.

General Reserves

	€			€
Cost of Control	15,000	Balance b/d	– Black	50,000
Non-controlling interest	5,000		– Bird	20,000
Balance carried down	50,000			
	70,000			70,000

Black Limited.
Alternative Presentation of Workings
Journal Adjustments

	€	€
1. DR Retained Profits Black	3,200	
CR Inventory		3,200
Being unrealised inventory profit		
2. DR Retained Profits Black	7,950	
CR Investment in Bird		7,950
Being dividends from pre-acquisition profits		
3. DR Debenture Interest Receivable	300	
CR Retained Profits Black		300
Being debenture interest receivable		
4. DR Dividends receivable	11,700	
CR Retained Profits Black		11,700
Being dividends receivable from Bird		

i.e.   Pref. €5,600 x 75%   =   4,200
            Ord. €10,000 x 75%   =   7,500

	€	€
5. DR Debenture Int. Accrued	300	
CR Debenture Int. Receivable		300
Being cancellation of inter-group balance		

6. DR Proposed dividends   11,700
    CR Dividends Receivable   11,700
    Being cancellation of inter-group balance

Property Plant & Equipment

	€		€
Black	190,000	CSFP	380,000
Bird	190,000		
	380,000		380,000

Inv. In Bird

	€		€
Ordinary shares	165,000	Journal 2	7,950
Preference shares	60,000	Cost of Control	222,050
Debentures	5,000		
	230,000		230,000

Current Assets

	€		€
Black	145,500	Journal 1	3,200
Bird	143,400	CSFP	285,700
	288,900		288,900

Ord. Shares

	€		€
Cost of Control	75,000	Black	300,000
Non-controlling interest	25,000	Bird	100,000
CSFP	300,000		400,000
	400,000		400,000

Pref. Shares

	€		€
Cost of Control	60,000	Black	-
Non-controlling interest	20,000	Bird	80,000
	80,000		80,000

General Reserve

	€		€
Cost of Control	30,000	Black	50,000
(75% x €40,000)		Bird	40,000
Non-controlling Interest	10,000		
(25% x €40,000)			
CSFP	50,000		
	90,000		90,000

Retained Profit

	€		€
Journal 1 Black	3,200	Black	98,500
Journal 2 Black	7,950	Bird	44,400
Cost of Control	21,000	Journal 3 Black	300
(75% x €28,000)		Journal 4 Black	11,700
Non-controlling interest	11,100		
(25% x €44,400)			
CSFP	111,650		
	154,900		154,900

Trade Payables

	€		€
CSFP	119,200	Black	87,000
		Bird	32,200
	119,200		119,200

Proposed Dividends

	€		€
Journal 6	11,700	Black	30,000
CSFP Black	30,000	Bird Ord	10,000
NCI	3,900	Pref	5,600
	45,600		45,600

Debentures Int. Accrued

	€		€
Journal 5	300	Bird	1,200
CSFP	900		
	1,200		1,200

Debentures Int. Receivable

	€		€
Journal 3	300	Journal 5	300

Dividends Receivable

	€		€
Journal 4	11,700	Journal 6	11,700

Cost of Control

	€		€
Inv. in Bird	222,050	Ord. Shares	75,000
		Pref. Shares	60,000
		Debs.	5,000
		Gen. Reserve	30,000
		Retained Profit	21,000
		Goodwill – CSFP	31,050
	222,050		222,050

Non-controlling Interest

	€		€
CSFP	66,100	Ord. Shares	25,000
		Pref. Shares	20,000
		Gen. Reserve	10,000
		Retained Profit	11,100
	66,100		66,100

Question 3

ROCK Group
Consolidated Statement of Financial Position as at 31 December 2004

	ROCK	ROLL	Adjustments	Consol.
	€'000	€'000	€'000	€'000
ASSETS				
Non-current Assets				
Property, plant and equipment	5,760	4,000	W1 600, W2 (120) W3 50, W3 (250), W6 200	10,240
Goodwill			W1 1,110, W7 (333)	777
Investment in ROLL	3,330	-	W1 (3,330)	-
Current Assets	1,260	864		2,124
				13,141
EQUITY AND LIABILITIES				
Capital and Reserves				
€0.50 ordinary shares	2,700	1,600	W1 (1,200), W6 (400)	2,700
8% €1 preference share capital	-	800	W1 (400), W6 (400)	-
Share premium	810	160	W1 (120), W6 (40)	810
Retained earnings	3,960	904	W1 420, W2 (90), W3 50, W3 (250), W4 192, W5 16, W6 (274), W7 (333)	4,595
				8,105

Non-controlling interests	-	-	W2 (30), W6 400, W6 400, W6 200, W6 40, W6 274	1,284
	7,470	3,464		9,389
Non-current Liabilities				
10% debentures	1,800	800	W1 (320)	2,280
Current Liabilities	1,080	600	W4 (192), W5 (16)	1,472
				13,141

Workings:

1. Cost of control

€0.5 ordinary shares	2,400,000/3,200,000	= 75% (MI = 25%)
€1 preference shares	400,000/800,000	= 50% (MI = 50%)

	€'000	€'000
Cost of investment		3,330
NCI:		
Ordinary shares 800,000 x €0.5		400
Preference shares 400,000 x €1		400
10% debentures ((Total €800,000) less acquired by Rock €320,000)		480
Share premium €160,000 x 25%		40
RE €560,000 DR x 25%		(140)
Fair value €800,000 x 25%		200
		4,710
Ordinary shares 3,200,000 x €1	1,600	
Preference shares 800,000 x €1	800	
10% debentures	800	
Share premium	160	
RE	(560)	

Fair value	800	(3,600)
Goodwill		1,110
Impairment – year ended 31/12/04		(333)
		777

2. Fair value adjustment

PPE of ROLL to be increased by €800,000 less additional depreciation:
€800,000/20 years = €40,000 pa x 3 years = €120,000
(Group 75% = €90,000; MI 25% = €30,000)

3. Intercompany sale of PPE

		€'000
Cost to ROLL		1,000,000
Profit @ 25%		(250,000)

Therefore reduce PPE and group reserves by €250,000 less depreciation.

Depreciation charged	€1,000,000/5	200,000
Revised depreciation	€750,000/5	150,000
Excess depreciation		50,000

4. Proposed dividends

Assume no legal liability at 31/12/04 to pay both the preference and ordinary proposed dividends (IAS 10). Therefore, proposed dividends should be reversed.

DR	Current liabilities	€192,000
CR	Retained earnings	€192,000

5. Debenture interest due to ROCK

€320,000 x 10% x 6/12 = €16,000
Remove amounts due to ROCK from ROLL's Current Liabilities and increase group retained earnings. ROCK does not accrue interest receivable.

6. Non-controlling interests

		€'000
Ordinary share	€1,600,000 x 25%	400
Preference shares	€800,000 x 50%	400
Fair value adjustment	€800,000 x 25%	200
Fair value adjustment (depn) (NCI share)	See W2	(30)
Share premium	€160,000 x 25%	40
Retained earnings	(€904,000 + €192,000) x 25%	274
		1,284

7. Group reserves

		€'000
ROCK		3,960
ROLL	(€904,000 + €192,000)	1,096
		5,056
Pre-acquisition (W1)		420
Goodwill impairment (W1)		(333)
Additional depreciation (W2)		(90)
Intercompany FA sale (W3)		(250)
Depreciation (W3)		50
Debenture interest (W5)		16
NCI (W6)		(274)
		4,595

REVIEW QUESTIONS – SUGGESTED SOLUTIONS

Question 1

	X Limited	Y Limited	Consolidated
	€	€	€
Revenue	10,000	7,000	17,000
Cost of sales	(6,000)	(1,000)	(7,000)
Gross profit	4,000	6,000	10,000
Administration expenses	(500)	(600)	(1,100)
Depreciation (W3)	(1,000)	(1,500)	(2,500)
Profit before tax	2,500	3,900	6,400
Income Tax Expense	(400)	(100)	(500)
Profit after tax	2,100	3,800	5,900
Non-controlling interest (W4)	--	(380)	(380)
PATTG	2,100	3,420	5,520
Reserves brought forward (W5)	10,000	2,520	12,520
Reserves carried forward	12,100	5,940	18,040

Workings

1. Group structure

	Y Limited
Group	90%
Non-controlling interest	10%
	100%

2. Tangible non-current assets
   Tangible non-current assets included in Y Limited statement of financial position are understated:

=>	DR	Tangible non-current assets	€3,000
	CR	Revaluation reserve	€3,000

This journal is a statement of financial position entry and thus does not affect the solution's statement of comprehensive income.

3. Depreciation

Depreciation charges included in Y Limited statement of comprehensive income are based on cost. For consolidation purposes, this must be amended to ensure that the depreciation charge is based on the re-valued amount:

		Depreciation on		
		Cost	Fair value	Difference
		€	€	€
Year ended:	1998	1,200	1,500	300
	1999	1,200	1,500	300
	2000	1,200	1,500	300
	2001	1,200	1,500	300
	2002	1,200	1,500	300
		6,000	7,500	1,500

Depreciation in Y Limited is thus understated in:

	€
• the current year (2002)	300
• prior years since acquisition (1998 – 2001)	1,200
	1,500

This requires two adjustments:

(a) Increase the current year charge in Y Limited by €300:

DR	Depreciation (SCI)	€300	
CR	Accumulation depreciation (SFP)		€300

(b) Increase prior year's charge in Y Limited by €1,200:

DR	Revenue reserves	€1,200	
CR	Accumulation depreciation (SFP)		€1,200

4. Non-controlling interest

	€
Y Limited – Profit after Tax (as adjusted by extra depreciation for current year)	3,800
	x 10%
Non-controlling interest	380

5. Reserves brought forward

	€ Y Limited
Reserves b/fwd per individual accounts	7,000
Pre-acquisition reserves	(3,000)
Post-acquisition reserves	4,000
Depreciation adjustment (W3)	(1,200)
Post-acquisition reserves (as adjusted)	2,800
	x 90%
Group share only	2,520

Key points:

- The current year's depreciation adjustment is made in the subsidiary statement of comprehensive income column;
- The accumulated depreciation adjustment is made to subsidiary reserves prior to calculating the group share only; and
- In this way, only 90% of the relevant adjustment is included in the consolidated statement of comprehensive income.

Question 2

1. Group structure:

	Group	60%
	NCI	40%
		100%
		=> Subsidiary

2. Tangible non-current assets

	Based on book value €	Based on fair value €	SCI diff. €
1 January 1998	12,000	15,000	
Depreciation	(2,400)	(3,000)	600
31 December 1998	9,600	12,000	
Depreciation	(1,920)	(2,400)	480
31 December 1999	7,680	9,600	
Depreciation	(1,536)	(1,920)	384
31 December 2000	6,144	7,680	
Depreciation	(1,229)	(1,536)	307
31 December 2001	4,915	6,144	

=> Reserves of A Limited for consolidation purposes at 31 December 2000 are overstated by:

		€
Depreciation	1998	600
	1999	480
	2000	384
		1,464

Profit for the year is overstated for 2001 by €307.

3. Calculation of reserves brought forward

	C €	A €
Per individual accounts	15,000	6,000
Pre-acquisition reserves		3,000
Post-acquisition reserves	15,000	9,000
Depreciation adjustment		(1,464)
	15,000	7,536
		x 60%
Group share only	15,000	4,522

4. Consolidated statement of comprehensive income workings

	C	A	Adjustment	Consolidated
	€	€		€
Net profit (draft)	10,000	5,000		15,000
Depreciation adjustment		(307)		(307)
Net profit	10,000	4,693		14,693
Income tax expense	1,000	1,000		(2,000)
Profit after tax	9,000	3,693		12,693
Non-controlling interest (40%)	--	(1,477)		(1,477)
Profit attributable to the group	9,000	2,216		11,216
Balance brought forward	15,000	4,522		19,522
Balance carried forward	24,000	6,738		30,738

Question 3

	X Limited	Y Limited (10 months)	Consolidated
	€	€	€
Revenue	10,000	5,833	15,833
Cost of sales	(6,000)	(833)	(6,833)
Gross profit	4,000	5,000	9,000
Administration expenses	(1,000)	(417)	(1,417)
Distribution costs	-	(700)	(700)
Profit before tax	3,000	3,883	6,883
Income tax expense	(500)	(250)	750)
Profit after tax	2,500	3,633	6,133
Non-controlling interest (W3)	--	(656)	(656)
PATTG	2,500	2,977	5,477

Workings:

1. Group Structure

	Y Limited	
	Ord	Pref
Group	90%	20%
NCI	10%	80%
	100	100

2. Acquisition during the year

Time-apportion all items in Y Limited by 10/12, except the distribution costs, which arose entirely after 28 February 1998.

3. Non-controlling interest

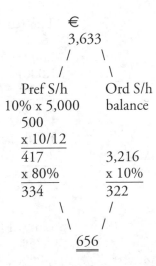

Y Limited – Profit after tax

€
3,633

Pref S/h
10% x 5,000
500
x 10/12
417
x 80%
334

Ord S/h
balance

3,216
x 10%
322

656

Note that where there is a preference dividend element in the non-controlling interest calculation, then this too must be time-apportioned before the part related to the ordinary shareholders can be calculated.

4. Subsidiary dividends

These must be time-apportioned, with only the post-acquisition element being included in the dividend shuffle in the calculation of consolidated retained earnings.

		Total	Post-acquisition		Group Share
		€	€		€
Y Limited:	Preference dividends	500 x 10/12	417	x 20%	83
	Ordinary dividends	3,500 x 10/12	2,917	x 90%	2,625
		4,000	3,334		2,708

5. Consolidated retained earnings

	X Limited	Y Limited	Group
	€	€	€
PATTG	2,500	2,977	5,477
Retained earnings b/f	10,000	-	10,000
Subsidiary dividends (W4)	2,708	(2,708)	-
X Limited Dividends paid	(200)	-	(200)
Retained earnings c/f	15,008	269	15,277

Note Y Limited had no post-acquisition reserves at 1 January 1998.

Question 4

	P Limited €	S Limited €	Consolidated €
Gross profit	10,000	6,000	16,000
Administration expenses	(1,000)	(2,000)	(3,000)
Depreciation	(4,000)	(500)	(4,500)
Profit before tax	5,000	3,500	8,500
Income tax expense	(1,500)	(1,000)	(2,500)
Profit after tax	3,500	2,500	6,000
Non-controlling interest (W4)	--	(625)	(625)
PATTG	3,500	1,875	5,375

1. Group Structure

	S Limited
Group	75%
Non-controlling interest	25%
	100% => Subsidiary

2. Unrealised tangible non-current asset profit   €   €
   Cancel the unrealised non-current asset profit
   DR Profit on sale of non-current asset P Limited   2,000
   CR Tangible non-current assets   2,000

3. Correct depreciation charge   €

   Charged by S Limited (€7,500 x 10% x 6/12)   375
   Current charge in accordance with group policy
   (€10,000 x 10% x 6/12)   500
                                                        125

   DR Depreciation charge – SCI – S Limited   125
   CR Accumulated depreciation SFP   125

4. Non-controlling interest
   Profit after tax S Limited (after depreciation adjustment) 2,500
                                                           x 25%
   Non-controlling interest   625

Note

(i) The adjustment correcting the unrealised profit is made in P Limited as this is the company whose statement of comprehensive income included the unrealised profit, i.e. the selling company.

(ii) The adjustment correcting the depreciation is made in S Limited as this is the company where individual statement of comprehensive income included the incorrect depreciation charge, i.e. the buying company.

Question 5

P Limited
Consolidated Statement of Comprehensive Income for the Year Ended 31 December 20X7

		20X7 €	20X6 €
Operating profit		425,250	
Investment income	(X)	2,700	
Profit before tax	(2)	427,950	
Income tax expense	(X)	(183,000)	
Profit after taxation		244,950	
Non-controlling interest		(22,050)	
Profit attributable to the Group	(4)	222,900	

Notes to the Statement of comprehensive income (extracts):

2. Profit before tax
   This amount has been arrived at after charging

	€
Directors remuneration	21,750
Depreciation	55,500

4. Profit attributable to the Group
Of this amount €181,500 has been dealt with in the books of the Parent company.

6. Retained earnings

	€
Profit for year ended 31 December 20X7	222,900
Balance b/f	42,240
Dividends paid during year ended 31 December 20X7	(60,000)
Balance c/f	205,140

Consolidated Statement of Comprehensive Income Workings

	P €	S €	T €	Consol. €
Profit before below items	298,500	120,000	90,000	
Inventory profit	(750)			
Administration expenses	(45,000)	(16,500)	(21,000)	
Operating profit	252,750	103,500	69,000	425,250
Investment income	1,200	1,500	-	2,700
Profit before tax	253,950	105,000	69,000	427,950
Income tax expense	(105,000)	(48,000)	(30,000)	(183,000)
Profit after tax	148,950	57,000	39,000	244,950
Non-controlling interest	-	(11,400)	(10,650)	22,050
	148,950	45,600	28,350	222,900

Retained Earnings

PATTG	148,950	45,600	28,350	222,900
Dividend – S Limited	19,200	(19,200)		
– T Limited	12,600	-	(12,600)	-
P Limited	(60,000)	-	-	(60,000)
Retained profit for year	120,750	26,400	15,750	162,900
Balance B/Fwd	25,950	6,480	9,810	42,240
Balance C/Fwd	146,700	32,880	25,560	205,140

1. Group structure

	S		T	
		Ord.		Pref.
Group	80%	75%		50%
Non-controlling interest	20%	25%		50%
	100%	100%		100%

2. Unrealised inventory profit

	€
Inter-co inventory held (selling price)	3,000
	x 25%
Unrealised profit	750

3. Non-controlling interest

S Limited   € 57,000 x 20%   = €11,400

T Limited   € 39,000
                   /   \

PSC	OSC
6% x €60,000	(bal)
= €3,600	€35,400
x50%	x25%
€1,800	€8,850
\ € 10,650 /	

4. Reconciliation of dividends from subsidiaries
   S Limited   € 24,000 x 80% = €19,200

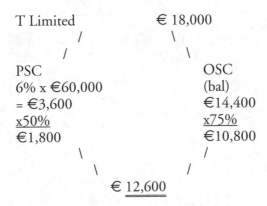

T Limited   € 18,000

PSC   OSC
6% x €60,000   (bal)
= €3,600   €14,400
x50%   x75%
€1,800   €10,800

€ 12,600

5. Calculation of Reserves b/f

	S1 €	T1 €
Per individual accounts	12,600	11,250
Pre-acquisition	(4,500)	1,830
Post-acquisition	8,100	13,080
	x80%	x75%
Group share of post-acquisition	6,480	9,810

Alternative approach to workings:

	€	€
P	286,500	
Less dividends from S & T	(31,800)	
Dividends from quoted investment	(1,200)	253,500
S (€121,500 – €16,500)	105,000	
Less dividends from quoted investment	1,500	103,500
T (€90,000 – €21,000)		69,000
Unrealised inventory profit €3,000 x 25%		(750)
		425,250

Investment Income

P	1,200	
S	1,500	2,700

Note: these are dividends received from outside the group.

Income tax expense

P	105,000
S	48,000
T	30,000
	183,000

Non-controlling interest   €

S

Profit after tax	€57,000 x 20%	11,400

T   €

Profit after tax	39,000		
Less pref div	€3,600 x 50% =	1,800	
Ordinary profits	€35,400 x 25% =	8,850	10,650
			22,050

Note The unrealised inventory profit affects the profits of the selling company, i.e. P. Therefore, in this case it does not have a bearing on the calculation of non-controlling interest.

Retained profits B/f

P		25,950
S	80% (€12,600 – €4,500)	6,480
T	75% (€11,250 + €1,830)	9,810
		42,240

Question 6

BACK Group plc
Consolidated Statement of Comprehensive Income for the Year Ended 31 December 2003

€'000

Continuing Operations:

Revenue (€87,800 – Disc. €10,000)	77,800
Cost of Sales (€55,472 – €9,910)	(45,562)
Gross Profit	32,238

Operating Expenses (€10,660 – €50)	(10,610)
Operating Profit	21,628
Interest Payable and Similar Charges	(200)
Interest receivable	100
Profit before Tax	21,528
Taxation	(6,820)
Profit after Tax	14,708
Non-controlling interests	(173.6)
Profit from continuing operations	14,534.4

Discontinued Operations:

Profit from discontinued operations	40
	14,574.4

Workings:

	BACK €'000	FRONT €'000	Adjustments DR €'000	Adjustments CR €'000	FINAL €'000
Revenue	90,000	7,800	(W5a) 10,000		87,800
				(W5a) 10,000	
			(W1) 28	(W3) 40	
Cost of Sales	(60,000)	(4,900)	(W5b) 600	(W2) 16	(55,472)
Gross Profit	30,000	2,900	10,628	10,056	32,328
Operating Exp.	(9,900)	(760)		-	(10,660)
Oper. Profit	20,100	2,140	10,628	10,056	21,668
Interest Pay.	(160)	(40)			(200)
Interest Rec.	80	20			100
PBT	20,020	2,120	10,678	10,056	21,568

Tax	(6,420)	(400)			(6,820)
PAT	13,600	1,720	10,678	10,056	14,748
NCI (W6)	-	-	173.6	-	(173.6)
Profit for Year	13,600	1,720	10,801.6	10,056	14,574.40

Workings:

1. FRONT – Goodwill (90% = Subsidiary)

	€
a) Purchase consideration	3,808,000
NA acquired (90% x €3,920,000)	(3,528,000)
Goodwill	280,000

Impaired by €28,000 during the year (Cost of sales)

b) FRONT – retained profits at 1/1/03 are all pre-acquisition.

2. FRONT – Depreciation adjustment on revaluation

	€
Downward revaluation – €160,000 x 10% (Credit Cost of sales)	16,000

3. FRONT – Inventory adjustment due to accounting policy change

	€
Opening inventory down	160,000
Closing inventory down	120,000
Net effect – Credit Cost of sales	40,000

4. Rundown of BACK's activities

   – meets definition of 'discontinued' under IFRS 5 and therefore show separately in statement of comprehensive income.
   – if rundown costs are considered 'exceptional', therefore disclose separately within normal statutory heading.

5. Intercompany transactions

   a) Reduce the sales of BACK and cost of sales of FRONT by €10,000,000
   b) Inventory profit – €3,000,000 x 25/125 = €600,000

Note: Sales are from BACK to FRONT therefore profit deducted from BACK only.

6. NCI

	€000
FRONT:PAT	1,720
Depriciation adjustment (W2)	16
	1,736
x 10%	173.6

CHAPTER 29

REVIEW QUESTIONS – SUGGESTED SOLUTIONS

Question 1

Parker Group
Consolidated Statement of Comprehensive Income for the Year Ended 30 September 2005

	€'000
Turnover	31,980
Group profit (Note 1)	1,767
Share of profits of associate	90
Profit before taxation	1,857
Taxation	1,108
Profit after taxation	749
Profit attributable to non-controlling interests in subsidiaries	(41)
Profit attributable to the company	708

	Parker Limited Group		Duke Limited
Group profit	€ '000		€'000
Trading profits	2,312		879
Admin expenses	(541)		(199)
Finance cost	(4)		0
	1,767		680
		x 30%	204
Tax – associate (Duke 380 x 30%)			(114)
			90

Group revenue reserve at beginning of year per draft accounts	345

Note No revenue reserved for Duke Limited can be included at 1 October, 2004, as the investment by the group in that company was made during the year under review.

	€'000
Revenue Reserve at End of Year	
Profit for year ended 30 September 2005	708
Revenue reserve b/f	345
Ordinary dividends paid year ended 30 September 2005	(100)
Preference dividends paid year ended 30 September 2005	(28)
	925

Note Duke Limited is accounted for using the equity method.

Question 2

Golf Limited
Consolidated Statement of Comprehensive Income for the Year Ended 30 June 1992

	€
Revenue	2,876,000
Group Profit	343,000
Share of profit of associate	37,500
Profit before taxation	380,500
Income tax expense	124,000
Profit after taxation	256,500
Profit attributable to non-controlling interests	14,000
Profit attributable to the company (Note 1)	242,500

Note 1: Profit attributable to the company
  Of this profit €212,000 is dealt with in the accounts of the parent company.
  (Note to students: €169,000 + €6,000 (Inventory Profit) + €37,000 = €212,000)

Note 2: Revenue reserves at end of year
  This amount is dealt with in the accounts of:

	€
– the parent company	524,000
– the subsidiary company	17,000
– the associated company	19,500
	560,500

Note IAS 28 *Investments in Associates* does not prescribe how the investors share of its associates profit should be presented in the statement of comprehensive income. The example in IAS 1 defines the share of profit of associates as the share of associates' profit attributable to equity holders of the associates, i.e. after tax and non-controlling interests in the associates. This is disclosed just before 'profit before tax'.

Group Structure:

	Club Ord.	Ball Ord.	Tee Ord.	Pref.
Group	15%	30%	75%	50%
Non-controlling interest	85%	70%	25%	50%
	100%	100%	100%	100%

Note

(a)   Club is a trade investment and is thus accounted for only to the extent of dividends receivable. Note (2) to the question indicates that Golf has not yet accounted for the dividend received from Club. Hence, the following adjustment is required in Golf's books

DR	Bank	€15,000
CR	Statement of comprehensive income	€15,000

(b)   Ball is an associated company to be accounted for under the provisions of IAS 28.

Consolidated Statement of Comprehensive Income Workings:

	Golf €	Tee (2/3) €	Ball €	Adj. €	Total €
Revenue	2,100,000	800,000		(24,000)	2,876,000
Draft Profit	250,000	84,000			
Dividend from Club	15,000				
Inventory adjustment	(6,000)				
Group Profit	259,000	84,000			343,000
Associated company profit			37,500		37,500
Profit before tax					380,500
Taxation	(90,000)	(34,000)			(124,000)
Profit after tax	169,000	50,000	37,500		256,500
Non-controlling interest		14,000			14,000
PATTC	169,000	36,000	37,500		242,500
Retained Earnings:					
PATTC	169,000	36,000	37,500		242,500
Tee – Ordinary	16,000	(16,000)	---		----
– Preference	3,000	(3,000)			
Ball – Ordinary	18,000			(18,000)	
	206,000	17,000		19,500	242,500
Golf – Ordinary	(132,000)				(132,000)
Retained profit for year	74,000	17,000		19,500	110,500
Balance brought forward	450,000	-		-	450,000
Balance carried forward	524,000	17,000		19,500	560,500

Notes to workings:

1. €24,000 intra-group sales to be eliminated
2. Tee acquired on 1/11/91 – thus 2/3 of results to be taken in
3. Non-controlling interest

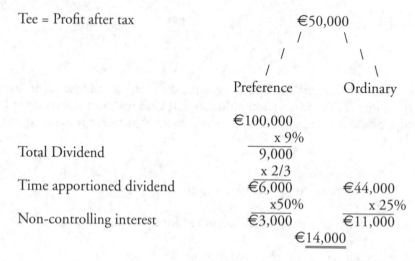

	Preference	Ordinary
	€100,000	
	x 9%	
Total Dividend	9,000	
	x 2/3	
Time apportioned dividend	€6,000	€44,000
	x50%	x 25%
Non-controlling interest	€3,000	€11,000
	€14,000	

4. Dividend shuffle

Tee:

	Ordinary	Preference
	€	€
Total dividend	32,000	9,000
	x 2/3	x 2/3
Post-acquisition dividends	21,333	6,000
	x75%	x50%
Group Share only	16,000	3,000

Ball: Ordinary dividend €60,000 x 30% = €18,000

Note to students Dividends should be apportioned on a time basis, thus 1/3 of dividends are pre-acquisition.

Alternative approach to consolidated statement of comprehensive income workings:

Group Profit

	€
Golf:	250,000
Tee x 8 months (€126,000 x 2/3)	84,000
Unrealised inventory profit (€24,000 x 25%)	(6,000)
Dividends from Club (Note)	15,000
	343,000

The dividend from Club must be included as it is from a company outside the group.

Share of Profit of Associate

	€
Ball PBT €210,000 x 30%	63,000
Taxation €85,000 x 30%	(25,500)
	37,500

Income tax expenses

	€	€
Group: Golf	90,000	
Tee (8 months) €51,000 x 2/3	34,000	124,000

Non-controlling interest

	€	€
Tee		
Profit after tax consolidated		
(i.e. 8 months) 2/3 x €75,000 =	50,000	
Less pref div. (€9,000 x 2/3)	6,000 x 50% =	3,000
Ordinary profits	44,000 x 25% =	11,000
		14,000

Retained Profit B/f

Both the subsidiary (Tee) and the associate Ball were bought during the year under review. Therefore, they cannot be included in the group retained profit b/f as there were no post-acquisition profits in those companies at 1 July 2001.

Golf only   €450,000

Question 3

Gold Limited

Consolidated Balance as at 30 November 20X3

Assets	€
Non-current assets	
Property, plant and equipment	170,000
Goodwill	3,587
Investment in associate (see Note 1)	36,500
	210,087
Current Assets	
Inventory	61,750
Receivables	208,750
Bank and cash	27,600
Current account with associate	650
	298,750
Total Assets	508,837
Equity and Liabilities	
Equity	
Ordinary share capital	50,000
Share premium	10,000
Capital reserve	93,500
Other reserves	35,000
Retained earnings	60,450
	248,950
Non-controlling interest	52,387
	301,337
Current Liabilities	
Payables	152,500
Bank overdraft	27,500
Taxation	25,000
Current account with associate	2,500
	207,500
Total Equity and Liabilities	508,837

Journal Adjustments

		€	€
1.	DR Cash	500	
	CR Current account with Silver		500

Being cash in transit at reporting date (adjusted in the accounts of the parent).

		€	€
2.	DR Retained profits Gold	750	
	CR Inventory		750

Being unrealised profit on inventory ($€36,000 \times 1/8 \times 1/6$)

		€	€
3.	DR Inventory in Bronze	6,000	
	CR Cap res ($€5,000 \times 40\%$)		2,000
	CR Ret. Profits ($€10,000 \times 40\%$)		4,000

Cost of Control Account

	€		€
Investment in Silver Limited	100,000	Ordinary Share Capital	75,000
		Capital Reserve	14,438
		Revenue Reserve	3,225
		Contingency Reserve	3,750
		Goodwill	3,587
	100,000		100,000

Alternatively:

		€
Cost of investment		100,000
Non-controlling Interest at Acquisition:	€	
Ordinary shares	100,000	
Capital reserves	19,250	
Revenue reserve	4,300	
Contingency reserve	5,000	
	128,550	
	x 25%	32,137
Net assets acquired		(128,550)
Goodwill		3,587

Capital Reserve Account

	€		€
Cost of Control (19,250 x 3/4)	14,438	Gold Limited	61,500
NCI (€59,250 x 1/4)	14,812	Silver Limited	59,250
Consolidated SFP	93,500	Investment in Associated	
		Company	2,000
	122,750		122,750

Retained Profits

	€		€
Cost of Control (€4,300 x 3/4)	3,225	Gold Limited	26,450
NCI (€45,300 x 1/4)	11,325	Silver Limited	45,300
Journal 2	750	Investment in Associated	
Consolidated SFP	60,450	Company	4,000
	75,750		75,750

Other Reserves

	€		€
Cost of Control (€5,000 x 3/4)	3,750	Gold Limited	35,000
NCI (€5,000 x 1/4)	1,250	Silver Limited	5,000
Consolidated SFP	35,000		
	40,000		40,000

Non-controlling Interests

	€		€
Consolidated SFP	52,387	Ordinary Share Capital	25,000
		Capital Reserve	14,812
		Revenue Reserve	11,325
		Contingency Reserve	1,250
	52,387		52,387

Investment In Associated Company Account

	€		€
Cost of Investment	30,500	Consolidated SFP	36,500
Revenue Reserve – Associate (€15,000 – €5,000) x 40%	4,000		
Capital Reserve – Associate (€5,000 x 40%)	2,000		
	36,500		36,500

C/A with Silver

	€		€
Gold	1,000	Journal 1	500
		Contra	500
	1,000		1,000

C/A with Bronze

	€		€
CSFP	2,500	Gold	2,500
	2,500		2,500

C/A with Gold

	€		€
Contra	500	Silver	500
	500		500

C/A with Bronze

	€		€
Silver	650	CSFP	650
	650		650

The current account balances between Gold and Bronze, and Silver and Bronze will be transferred to the consolidated statement of financial position as they are not inter-group.

Inventory

	€		€
Gold	26,500	Journal 2	750
Silver	36,000	CSFP	61,750
	62,500		62,500

Cash

	€		€
Gold	100		
Journal 1	500	CSFP	600
	600		600

Workings:

1. Group structure

	Silver	Bronze
Group	75%	40%
NCI	25%	60%
	100%	100%

2. Group Share of Net Assets of Bronze:
   40% x €55,000 = €22,000

3. Premium on Acquisition:
   €30,500 − (40% x €40,000) = €14,500

	€
Note 1: Investment in Associated Company	
Groups Share of Net Assets	22,000
Premium on Acquisition	14,500
	36,500

Note 2: Treatment of Associated Company
The associated company is stated at cost plus the group's share of retained post-acquisition profits/reserves.

	€
Thus, for example, for revenue reserves	
Balance at acquisition	5,000
Balance at 30.11.X3	15,000
Post-acquisition retained profits	10,000
Group share (x 40%)	4,000

Entry required is:

DR	Investment in associated company	€4,000
CR	Consolidated revenue reserves	€4,000

CHAPTER 30

REVIEW QUESTIONS – SUGGESTED SOLUTIONS

Question 1

True plc
Consolidated Statement of Comprehensive Income for the Year Ended 31 December 2003

	€
Revenue (W5)	4,815,000
Cost of sales (W5)	(2,443,500)
Gross profit (W5)	2,371,500
Operating expenses (W5)	(1,572,000)
Profit on ordinary activities before taxation	799,500
Taxation (W5)	(252,000)
Profit on ordinary activities after taxation	547,500
Non-controlling interests (W7)	(16,200)
	531,300

True plc
Consolidated Statement of Financial Position as at 31 December 2003

	€	€
ASSETS		
Non-current Assets		
Property, plant and equipment		2,800,000
Goodwill		56,000
		2,856,000
Current Assets		
Inventory (W4)	602,500	
Receivables	720,000	
Bank and cash (incl. €20k in transit)	280,000	1,602,500
		4,458,500

EQUITY AND LIABILITIES

Capital and Reserves

€1 ordinary shares	2,000,000
Revenue reserve (W2)	1,364,000
Capital reserve (W3)	322,500
	3,686,500
Minority interest	137,000
	3,823,500

Current Liabilities

Trade payables	635,000
	4,458,500

Workings:

1. Balance sheet consolidation schedule

(i) Dividends declared after the reporting date should not be recognised as liabilities unless there is a legal obligation to receive them (IAS 10 *Events after the Reporting Date*). There is no entitlement to ordinary dividends until they are approved at the AGM by the shareholders, and therefore the proposed dividends should be reversed.

DR	Current liabilities	200,000	
CR	Revenue reserves		200,000

The adjusted balance on TRUE and FAIR's revenue reserve at 31 December 2003 is €1,100,000 and €545,000 respectively.

Furthermore, dividends paid should be debited directly to equity (IAS 32, paragraph 35).

(ii) The inter-company accounts differ by €20,000, being cash in transit from FAIR Limited to TRUE plc. This will appear as a current asset in the consolidated statement of financial position.

(iii) Minority interest (at reporting date)

		€
Share capital	(10% x €750,000)	75,000
Revenue reserve (10% x €545,000)		54,500
Capital reserve	(10% x €75,000)	7,500
		137,000

(iv) Goodwill

	€		€
Cost of investment			950,000
NCI:			
Share capital	750,000		
Revenue reserves	100,000		
Capital reserves	50,000		
	900,000	x 10%	90,000
NA acquired			(900,000)
Goodwill (W2)			140,000

The goodwill was impaired by €84,000 during the year ended 31 December 2003 and therefore the statement of financial position value at 31 December 2003 is €56,000.

2. Revenue reserve

	€
TRUE plc	1,100,000
Share of FAIR Limited's post-acquisition reserves	
(€545,000 – 100,000) x 90%	400,500
	1,500,500
Goodwill impairment (W1 (iv))	(84,000)
less unrealised profit in inventory (W4)	(22,500)
less bad debt provision (incl. in TRUE op. expenses (Per qu., note 5))	(30,000)
	1,364,000

3. Capital reserve

	€
TRUE plc	300,000
Share of FAIR Limited's post-acquisition reserves	
(€75,000 – 50,000) x 90%	22,500
	322,500

4. Unrealised profit in inventory

25/125 x 225,000 x 50% = €22,500

Therefore eliminate in full against the group revenue reserves as TRUE plc originally recorded the profit.

5. Consolidation schedule

	TRUE €	FAIR €	Adjusted €	Consolidated €
Revenue	4,050,000	990,000	(225,000)	4,815,000
Cost of sales	(2,088,000)	(558,000)	(202,500)	(2,443,500)
Gross profit	1,962,000	432,000	(W4) (22,500)	2,371,500
Op. exp.	(W8) (1,290,000)	(198,000)	(W1iv) (84,000)	(1,572,000)
Taxation	(180,000)	(72,000)		(252,000)

6. Dividends received by TRUE plc from FAIR Limited,

   i.e. paid dividends only since TRUE had not yet accounted for the proposed dividend

   90% x €50,000 = €45,000.

   Therefore all investment income recorded in TRUE plc's SCI is intra-group.

7. Minority interest based on profit after tax of FAIR Limited is €16,200 (162,000 x 10%).

8. Power failure   = non-adjusting event after the reporting period.
   Bad debt   = provision required.

Question 2

Associates
IAS 28 *Investment in Associates* applies when accounting for investments in associates.

Key Definitions

Associate – An entity in which the investor has significant influence and which is neither a subsidiary nor a joint venture of the investor.
Significant influence – The power to participate in the financial and operating policy decisions of the investee but is not control over those policies.
The equity method – A method of accounting whereby the investment is initially recorded at cost and adjusted thereafter for the post acquisition change in the investor's share of net assets of the investee. The statement of comprehensive income reflects the investor's share of the results of operations of the investee.

The cost method – The investment is recorded at cost. The statement of comprehensive income reflects income only to the extent that the investor receives distributions from the investee subsequent to the date of acquisition.

Significant influence – If an investor holds, directly or indirectly, 20% or more of the voting power of the investee, it is presumed that it has significant influence, unless it can be clearly demonstrated that this is not the case. Conversely, if less than 20%, the presumption is that the investor does not have significant influence. A majority shareholder by another investor does not preclude an investor having significant influence. Its existence is usually evidenced in one or more of the following ways:

- Representation on the board of directors;
- Participation in policy-making processes;
- Material transactions between the investor and the investee;
- Interchange of managerial personnel; or
- Provision of essential technical information.

Consolidated Financial Statements   In consolidated financial statements, IAS 28 requires the use of the equity method of accounting for associates. All investments in associates must be accounted for using the equity method, irrespective of whether the investor also has investments in subsidiaries or prepares group accounts. IAS 28 does not prescribe how the investor's share of its associate's profits should be presented in the statement of comprehensive income. The example in IAS 1 defines the share of profit of associates as the share of associate's profit attributable to equity holders of the associates, i.e. after tax and minority interests in the associates. This is disclosed just before 'profit before tax'.

Separate Financial Statements of the Investor   An investment in an associate, for an entity publishing consolidated accounts, should be either:

- carried at cost;
- accounted for using the equity method as per IAS 28; or
- accounted for as an 'available for sale financial asset' as per IAS 39.

An investment in an associate, for an entity not publishing consolidated accounts, should be either:

(a) carried at cost;
(b) accounted for using the equity method if the equity method would be appropriate for the associate if the investor had issued consolidated accounts; or
(c) accounted for under IAS 39 as an 'available for sale financial asset'.

Basically an investor should provide the same information about its investments in associates as those entities that issue consolidated accounts.

Disclosure: The following disclosures should be made:

- An appropriate listing and description of significant associates, including the proportion of ownership interest and, if different, the proportion of voting power held; and
- The methods used to account for such investments.

Investments in associates should be classified as long-term assets and disclosed separately in the statement of financial position. The investor's share of profits/losses should be disclosed separately in the statement of comprehensive income.

Joint Ventures: IAS 31 Interests in Joint Ventures applies in accounting for interests in joint ventures and the reporting of joint venture assets, liabilities, income and expenses in the financial statements of venturers, regardless of the structures or forms under which the joint venture activities take place.

Key Definitions

Joint venture – a contractual agreement whereby two or more parties undertake an economic activity which is subject to joint control.
Joint control – the contractually agreed sharing of control over an economic activity.
Venture – a party to a joint venture and having joint control over that joint venture.
Proportionate consolidation – A method of accounting and reporting whereby a venturer's share of each of the assets, liabilities, income and expenses of a jointly controlled entity is combined on a line-by-line basis with similar items in the venturer's financial statements or reported as separate line items.

Forms of Joint Venture: IAS 31 identifies three broad types of joint venture activity:

- jointly controlled operations;
- jointly controlled assets; and
- jointly controlled entities.

They all have the common characteristics of having two or more joint venturers bound under contract and establishing joint control.

Financial Statements of a Venturer

Proportionate consolidation: A venturer recognises its interest in a jointly controlled entity using either proportionate consolidation or the equity method in accordance with IAS 28. Proportional consolidation is the preferred method under IAS 31, with equity accounting a permitted alternative. It is essential that a venturer reflects the substance and economic reality of the arrangement. The application of proportionate consolidation means that the consolidated statement of financial position of the venturer includes its share of the assets it controls jointly and its share of the liabilities for which it is jointly responsible. The consolidated statement of comprehensive income includes the venturer's share of the income and expenses of the jointly controlled entity. Many of the procedures are similar to consolidation procedures set out in IAS 27.

There are different reporting formats to give effect to proportionate consolidation:

- Combine the share of each of the assets, liabilities, income and expenses of the jointly controlled entity with similar items in the consolidated statements on a line-by-line basis, e.g. its share of inventory with inventory of the consolidated group;
- Include as separate line items its share of the jointly controlled entity's assets etc.

Both methods are acceptable; however, regardless of format, it is inappropriate to offset any assets or liabilities unless a legal right of set off exists and the offsetting represents the expectation as to the realisation of the asset or settlement of the liability. Proportionate consolidation should be discontinued from the date on which it ceases to have joint control over a jointly controlled entity. This could happen when the venturer disposes of its interest or when external restrictions mean that it can no longer achieve its goals.

Equity method: As an alternative, a venturer should report its interest in a jointly controlled entity using the equity method as per IAS 28. Those who argue that it is inappropriate to combine controlled items with jointly controlled items support the equity method. The standard does not recommend the use of the equity method because proportional consolidation better reflects the substance and economic reality of a venturer's interest in a jointly controlled entity. However, the standard does permit its adoption as an alternative treatment. A venturer should discontinue the use of the equity method from the date it ceases to have joint control over or have significant influence in a jointly controlled entity.

Disclosure: A venturer should disclose the aggregate amount of the following contingent liabilities, unless the probability of loss is remote, each separately:

- any contingent liabilities incurred in relation to its interest in joint ventures and its share in each contingent liability incurred jointly with other venturers;
- its share of contingent liabilities of the joint ventures for which it is contingently liable; and
- those contingent liabilities that arise because the venturer is contingently liable for the liabilities of the other venturers of a joint venture.

A venturer should disclose the aggregate amount of the following commitments re interests in joint ventures separately from other commitments:

- any capital commitments re joint ventures and its share in capital commitments incurred jointly with other venturers; and
- its share of capital commitments of the joint ventures themselves.

A venturer should disclose a listing and description of interests in significant joint ventures and the proportion of ownership interest held in jointly controlled entities. An entity that adopts line-by-line reporting for proportionate consolidation or the equity method should disclose the aggregate amounts of each of current assets, long-term assets, current liabilities, long-term liabilities, income and expenses related to interests in joint ventures. A venturer that does not publish consolidated accounts, because it has no subsidiaries, should disclose the above information as well.

(b)

ARCHER Group
Consolidated Statement of Comprehensive Income for the Year Ended 31 December 2003

	€m	€m
Revenue (3,000 + 200)		3,200
Cost of sales (1,800 + 125)		(1,925)
Gross profit (1,200 + 75)		1,275
Operating expenses (500 + 25 – 100 (W1))		(425)
Operating profit		850
Interest payable (20 + 5)		(25)
Share of profit of associate (W2e)		132
Profit on ordinary activities before tax		957
Tax on profit on ordinary activities – group (200 + 10)		(210)
Profit on ordinary activities after tax		747

ARCHER Group
Consolidated Statement of Financial Position as at 31 December 2003

	€m	€m
ASSETS		
Non-current Assets		
Property, plant and equipment (2,200 + 40)		2,240
Investments - investment in associate (ARROW Limited)		920
		3,160
Current Assets		
Inventory (400 + 125)	525	
Receivables (300)	300	
Bank and cash (80 + 200 + 12)	292	1,117
		4,277

EQUITY AND LIABILITIES
Capital and Reserves
Share capital   1,200
Revaluation reserve   600
RE (1,700 + negative goodwill 100 (W1) + sub. 35 +
assoc. 120 (W2d) + divs. 12)

    1,967
    3,767

Current Liabilities (480 + 30)   510
    4,277

Workings:

1. Acquisition of BOW Limited (Note 1)

There is negative goodwill of €100m arising on the acquisition of BOW. In accordance with IFRS 3 Business Combinations, this should be recognised in the statement of comprehensive income.

2. Purchase of ARROW Limited. (30%)

a) Goodwill   €m   €m
   Cost of investment   800
   Share capital   600
   Revaluation reserve   300
   Retained earnings   1,100
    2,000
    @ 30%   600
   Goodwill   200

No evidence of impairment therefore carried at €200m.

b) Investment in associate   €m
   30% x €2,400   720
   Unamortised goodwill   200
    920

c) Revaluation reserve   €m
   ARROW Limited   @ 31/12/03   300
      @ acquisition date   (300)
    nil

d) SCI account   €m

    ARROW Limited   @ 31/12/03   1,500

                     @ acquisition date   1,100

                                   400

                   @ 30%   120

e) Share of operating profits in associate   €m

    Operating profit – €640m x 30%   192

    Interest payable – €10m x 30%   (3)

    Tax on profits – €190m x 30%   (57)

IAS 28 does not prescribe how the investor's share of its associate's profits should be presented in the statement of comprehensive income. The example in IAS 1 defines the share of profit of associates as the share of associate's profit attributable to equity shareholders of the associates, i.e. after taxation and minority interests. This is disclosed just before profit before tax.

3. Answer assumes that depreciation has already been charged in BOW Limited's accounts,

    i.e.   Fv @ 1/1/03   = €50 / 5 = €10m

             Bv @ 31/12/03   = €40m

4. Dividends paid are debited directly to equity.

CHAPTER 31

REVIEW QUESTIONS – SUGGESTED SOLUTIONS

Question 1

(A) JOURNAL ENTRIES

(i) TRANSACTION 1

		€	€
J.1	Dr Cash 571,429		
	Cr Loan Account	571,429	
	Being a loan of US$lm received at $1.75 = €1		571,429
J.2	Dr Loan Account	15,873	
	Cr Statement of comprehensive income		15,873
	Being retranslation of US$ loan at closing exchange rate of $1.80 = €1		

TRANSACTION 2

		€	€
J.3	Dr Property, plant and equipment	17,460	
	Cr Trade Payables – Frtz		17,460
	Being purchase of assets of DM55,000 at DM 3.15= €1		
J.4	Dr Statement of comprehensive income	1,746	
	Cr Accumulated depreciation		1,746
	Being depreciation of non-current asset for half year at 20%		
J.5	Dr Trade payables – Frtz	17,460	
	Dr Statement of Comprehensive Income	873	
	Cr Cash		18,333
	Being settlement of non-current asset Purchase at DM 3.0 = €1		

TRANSACTION 3

J.6   Dr Purchases   8,824
      Cr Trade payables – Etien   8,824
      Being purchase of goods for re-sale at BFr 68.00 = €1

      Dr Trade payables – Etien   191
      Cr Statement of comprehensive income   191
      Being gain on retranslation on BFR 600,000 at BFr 69.50 = €1

      Include these items in closing inventory (if any still held at 31 March 20X9) at the
      exchange rate of BFr 68.00 = €1

(ii) EXTRACTS FROM ACCOUNTS

TRANSACTION 1
SFP: Current liabilities:
                US Bank Loan (571,429 –15,873)   €555,556

      SCI: Exchange Gain   €15,873
                (included in Profit on Ordinary
                Activities before taxation)

TRANSACTION 2
SFP: Non-current Assets
                Cost
                Property, plant and equipment   €17,460

                Accumulated Depreciation
                Property, plant and equipment   €1,746

      SCI: Included in Profit on Ordinary Activities
                before taxation
                Depreciation   €1,746
                Exchange Loss   €873

TRANSACTION 3
SFP: Current laibilities:
                Trade Payables – (8,824 – 191)   €8,633

      SCI: Included in Profit on Ordinary activities
                Exchange gain   €191

Question 2

(A) PRESENTATION CURRENCY
1. Translate Opening Net Assets

	$	Rate	€
Ordinary Share Capital	75,000	3	25,000
Reserves	16,500		5,500 *(bal)
	91,500	3	30,500

* Proof of opening Reserves:

(1) At opening rate	16,500 ⁓ 3		5,500
plus			
(2) Ordinary Share Capital at			
opening rate	75,000 ⁓ 3	25,000	
Ordinary Share Capital at			
acquisition rate	75,000 ⁓ 3	(25,000)	-
			5,500

2. Translate retained earnings for year

	$	Rate	€
Profit after Tax	73,950	4	18,488
Dividends Paid	(10,000)	4	(2,500)
Dividends Proposed	(10,000)	5	(2,000)
Retained Profit	53,950		13,988

Full statement of comprehensive income has not been reproduced here, as all items before profit after tax are translated at the average rate. Full statement of comprehensive income would be expected in an examination.

3. Calculate Translation Adjustment

		€	€
(1) Net Asset Difference			
Opening Net Assets ⁓ Closing Rate			
Opening Net Assets ⁓ Opening Rate			
91,500 ⁓ 5	=	18,300	
91,500 ⁓ 3	=	(30,500)	
			(12,200)
(2) Average Rate Difference			
Retained Profit ⁓ Closing Rate			
per SCI			
53,950 ⁓ 5	=	10,790	
per SCI.	=	(13,988)	(3,198)
Total Exchange Loss			(15,398)

4. Prepare Movement on Reserves

Balance at 1.4.x 4	(W.1)	5,500
Retained Profit	(W.2)	13,988
Exchange Losses	(W.3)	(15,398)
Balance at 31.12.X4		4,090

5. Translate Statement of Financial Position

	$	Rate	€
Ordinary Share Capital	75,000	3	25,000
Reserves	70,450		4,090
	145,450		29,090
Loan	90,000	5	18,000
	235,450		47,090
Total Net Assets	235,450	5	47,090

(Full statement of financial position would be required in an examination)

(B) FUNCTIONAL CURRENCY METHOD

1. Translate Opening Statement of Financial Position

	$	Rate	€
Ordinary Share Capital	75,000	3	25,000
Reserves	16,500		25,500
	91,500		50,500
Property, plant & equip.	300,000	2.5	120,000
Inventory	41,000	3	13,667
Monetary Liabilities	*(249,500)	3	(83,167)
	91,500		50,500

2. Translate Statement of Financial Position

	$	Rate	€
Property, plant & equip.	270,000	2.5	108,000
Current Assets – Bank	9,475	5	1,895
– Receivables	45,500	5	9,100
– Inventory	48,525	4.8	10,109
Current Liabilities – Payables	(103,775)	5	(20,755)
– Taxation	(24,275)	5	(4,855)
– Dividends	(10,000)	5	(2,000)
	235,450		101,494
Ordinary Share Capital	75,000	3	25,000
Reserves	70,450		58,494
	145,450		83,494
Loan	90,000	5	18,000
	235,450		101,494

3. Translate Statement of Comprehensive Income

	$	Rate	€
Revenue	544,275	4	136,069
Opening Inventory	41,000	3	13,667
Purchases	152,525	4	38,131
Closing Inventory	(48,525)	4.8	(10,109)
	145,000		41,689
Gross Profit	399,275		94,380
Depreciation	(30,000)	2.5	(12,000)
Other Expenses	(271,050)	4	(67,762)
Exchange Gain/(Loss) (Bal)	-		28,945
Profit before Tax	98,225		43,563
Income tax expense	24,275	4	6,069
Profit after Tax	73,950		37,494

Note The difference between opening and closing net assets of Quickbuck Limited is the retained profit for the year in Euros:

	€
Closing net assets	83,494
Opening net assets	50,500
	32,994

The exchange difference, i.e. €28,945, is the balancing figure in the translated statement of comprehensive income.

Question 3

Ray International Limited and Subsidiary
Consolidated Statement of Comprehensive Income for the Year Ended 31 December 1990

	€'000
Revenue	12,021
Profit before tax	2,933
Income tax expense	(1,360)
Profit for year	1,573
Revenue reserves at start of year	480
Foreign currency translation reserve movement	(150)*
Revenue reserves at end of year	1,903

* Opening net investment of 1,200 Dfl

At opening rate of 3 Dfl to €	=	400
At closing rate of 4 Dfl to €	=	300
		(100)

Profits for year of 1,393 Dfl

At average rate of 3.5 Dfl	=	398
At closing rate of 4 Dfl	=	348
		(50)
		(150)

Ray International Limited and Subsidiary
Consolidated Statement of Financial Position as at 31 December 1990

	€'000
Assets	
Non-current assets	3,390
Current assets	
Inventory	2,895
Other	1,381
	4,276
Total assets	7,666
Equity and liabilities	
Equity	
Share capital	2,000
Retained profit	1,903
	3,903
Non-current liabilities	
Long-term loan	294
Current liabilities	3,469
Total equity and liabilities	7,666

Workings:

Statements of Comprehensive Income and Retained Earnings for Year

	M Distribution BV Dfl '000	Rate	MD. BV €'000	Ray Inter'l Limited €'000	Adj.	Consolidated
Revenue	12,600	3.5	3,600	10,871	(2,450) a	12,021
Profit before tax	1,603 b	3.5	458	2,600	(125)	2,933
Income tax expense	(210)	3.5	(60)	(1,300)	-	(1,360)
Profit for year	1,393	3.5	398	1,300	(125)	1,573
Dividend	(500)	Actual	(125)	-	125 c	-
	893		273	1,300		1,573
Exchange Loss			(150)			(150)
Balance at beginning of year	-		-	480	-	480
Balance at end of year	893	4	123	1,780	-	1,903

Statements of Financial Position

	M BV	Rate	€'000	M €'000	Ray Inter'l	Adj.	Consol.
Non-current assets	600	4		150	3,240		3,390
Investment					400	(400)	
Current assets							
Inventory	2,020	4	505		2,390		2,895
Other	1,164		291		1,472	(382) d	1,381
	3,184		796		3,862		4,276
Current Liabilities	1,691b	4	423		3,428	(382)	(3,469)
	1,493		373		434		807
Total net assets	2,093			523	4,074	(400)	4,197
Share capital	1,200	actual		400	2,000	(400)	2,000
Retained profits	893			123	1,780		1,903
	2,093			523	3,780	(400)	3,903
Loan	-			-	294	-	294
	2,093			523	4,074	(400)	4,197

Adjustments:

(a) Elimination of intercompany sales
(b) Translation of intercompany balance at year end in books of MI Distribution BV:

	Dfl
Receivable in Ray's books	
= €382,000 @ year end rate =	1,528,000
Payable in MI's books	1,381,000
Difference on exchange	147,000
Profit before taxation	1,750,000
Currency adjustment	147,000
	1,603,000
Current liabilities	1,544,000
Currency adjustment	147,000
	1,691,000

(c) Elimination of intercompany dividend €125,000
(d) Elimination of intercompany account €382,000

Alternative T A/c Workings

Property Plant and Equipment

	€		€
R	3,240	CSFP	3,390
M	150		
	3,390		3,390

Investment in M

	€		€
R	400	Cost of Control	400
	400		400

Inventory

	€		€
R	2,390	CSFP	2,895
M	505		
	2,895		2,895

Other

	€		€
R	1,472	Inter company debt	382
M	291	CSFP	1381
	1,763		1,763

Current Liabilities

	€		€
Inter company debt	382	R	3,428
CSFP	3,469	M	423
	3,851		3,851

Capital and reserves

	€		€
Cost of Control (100% x 400) M	400	R Capital	2,000
		Reserves	1,780
CSFP Capital	2000		
Reserves	1,903	M Capital	400
		Pre-acquisition reserves	-
		Post-acquisition reserves	123
	4,303		4,303

Loan

	€		€
CSFP	294	R	294
	294		294

Cost of Control

	€		€
Inv	400	Cap & reserves	400
	400		400

Question 4

BELVOIR plc
Consolidated Statement of Financial Position as at 31 December 2003

	BELVOIR €'000	PERTH A$	PERTH €'000	Adjustments €'000	Consol. €'000
ASSETS					
Non-current Assets					
Tangible assets	50,000	150,000	10,000		60,000
Investment in PERTH	11,667	-	-	(11,667)	-
	61,667	150,000	10,000		60,000
Current Assets					
Inventory	75,000	200,000	13,333		88,333
Receivables	175,000	250,000	16,667		191,667
Cash	5,000	25,000	1,667		6,667
	255,000	475,000	31,667		286,667
	316,667	625,000	41,667		346,667
EQUITY AND LIABILITIES					
Capital and Reserves					
Ordinary shares	50,000	50,000	3,333	(3,333)	50,000
Capital reserves	25,000	60,000	4,000	(4,000)	25,000
Currency reserve	-	-	-		(W6) (1,555)
Revenue reserve	55,000	65,000	4,334		(W3) 56,555
	130,000	175,000	11,667		130,000
Non-controlling interests					(W2) 5,000
					135,000
Non-current Liabilities					
Provisions	26,667	75,000	5,000		31,667

Current Liabilities

Payables	160,000	375,000	25,000 (W4) (5,000)		180,000
	316,667	625,000	41,667		346,667

Workings:

1. Cost of control

	DR €'000	CR €'000
Investment in PERTH	11,667	
NCI:		
Shares (50,000/13 x 30%)	1,154	
Capital reserve (60,000/13 x 30%)	1,384	
Revenue reserve at 1/4/03*	2,461	
Shares (50,000/13)		3,846
Capital reserve (60,000/13)		4,615
Revenue reserve at 1/4/03**		8,205
	16,666	16,666

Therefore goodwill is €nil.

*	Profit for year	A$50,000
	Time % (4/12)	A$16,667
	Reserves at 1/1/03	A$90,000
	(65k+75k–50k)	A$106,667 x 0.3 / 13

**	Profit for year	A$50,000
	Time % (4/12)	A$16,667
	Reserves at 1/1/03	A$90,000
	(65k+75k–50k)	A$106,667 / 13

2. Non-controlling interest

	DR €'000	CR €'000
Ordinary shares (15,000/15)		1,000
Capital reserve (60,000/15@30%)		1,200
Closing revenue reserve ((65,000 + 75,000)/15@30%)		2,800
Balance	5,000	
	5,000	5,000

3. Consolidated revenue reserve
    CR

	DR €'000	€'000
BELVOIR		55,000
PERTH ((65,000 + 75,000)/15)		9,333
Non-controlling interest account	2,800	
Cost of control (W1)	5,744	
Currency difference on opening reserves (W5)		766
Balance	56,555	
	65,099	65,099

4. Proposed dividend – PERTH
    CR

	DR €'000	€'000
Should be reversed:		
DR Current liabilities (A$75,000/15)	5,000	
CR Revenue reserves		5,000

5. Currency difference

		€'000
A$106,667 @ 70% = 74,667/13	=	5,744
A$106,667 @ 70% = 74,667/15	=	4,978
		766

6. Currency reserve

PERTH share of NA at 30/4/03	A$'000	Xrate	€'000
Revenue reserves	74,667	13	5,744
Capital reserves	42,000	13	3,231
Share capital	35,000	13	2,692
	151,667		11,667
30/4/03 NA at 31/12/03 rate	151,667	15	10,112
			1,555

Question 5

SHINE Group
Consolidated Statement of Comprehensive Income for the Year Ended 31 December 2003

	SHINE €'000	WISDOM €'000 (W3)	FINAL €'000
Revenue	460,000	16,000	476,000
Cost of sales	(238,000)	(9,900)	(247,900)
Gross profit	222,000	6,100	228,100
Operating expenses	* (116,000)	** (4,300)	(120,300)
Profit before tax	106,000	1,800	107,800
Taxation	(30,000)	(600)	(30,600)
Profit after tax	76,000	1,200	77,200
Non-controlling interests (25%)	-	(300)	(300)
Retained profit for the year	76,000	900	76,900

* Including profit on disposal of €6,000,000
** Including exchange difference (W3)

Workings:

1. Sale and leaseback

Where a sale and leaseback transaction results in an operating lease, the property should be treated as if sold and the lease accounted for under IAS 17 *Leases*. If the sale is at fair value, the profit on disposal should be recognised immediately.

However this sale and leaseback is at greater than fair value, and therefore profit of €6m (€10m – €4m) should be recognised immediately. The balance of sales value over fair value should be deferred and amortised over the shorter of the lease term and period to next rental review,

i.e. €20m – €10m = €10m / 10 years = €1m.

Given the sales value is greater than fair value, the annual rental of €2.5m is likely to have been adjusted for excess price paid for property. Therefore, the substance of transaction is essentially a sale or a loan and part of the annual rental is effectively a financing cost

(€2.5m – €1.2m = €1.3m). The excess over fair value (€10m) should be treated as a loan and €1.3m represents loan repayment (interest and capital).

As the sale and operating lease took place at the end of the year, only the profit on disposal of €6m needs to be adjusted for in the 2003 financial statements.

2. Purchase of WISDOM on 1 January 2000

	€'000
Purchase consideration	36,000
NCI – Fair value of net assets (€40m x 25%)	10,000
Fair value of net assets	(40,000)
	6,000

There is no evidence of impairment, therefore no adjustment required.

3. Translation of WISDOM

	$'000	ER*	€'000
Turnover	24,800	1.55	16,000
Opening inventory	800	1.6	500
Purchases (bal)	15,500	1.55	10,000
Closing inventory	(900)	1.5	(600)
Cost of sales	15,400		9,900
Gross profit	9,400		6,100
Operating expenses	(6,510)	1.55	(4,200)
Profit before tax	2,890		1,900
Taxation	(930)	1.55	(600)
Profit after tax	1,960		1,300
Exchange difference (bal)			(100)
Profit for the year (W4)			1,200

* WISDOM is a selling agent, therefore use average rate for statement of comprehensive income, except for opening inventory and closing inventory (no depreciation).

4. Exchange difference

	€'000
Post-acquisition reserve at 31/12/2003	11,100
Post-acquisition reserve at 31/12/2002	9,900
Profit for 2003	1,200

CHAPTER 32

REVIEW QUESTIONS – SUGGESTED SOLUTIONS

Question 1

(a) Consolidated Statement of Financial Position as at 30 September 20X8

	€'000
Assets	
Tangible non-current assets	360
Net current assets (€270 + €650)	920
	1,280

Equity	
€1 ordinary shares	540
Retained earnings (W3)	740
	1,280

Consolidated Statement of Comprehensive Income for the year ended 30 September 20X8

	€'000
Profit on disposal of subsidiary (W1)	182
Profit before tax (€153 + €126)	279
Income tax expense (€45 + €36)	(81)
	380
Non-controlling interest (20% x €90)	(18)
Profit attributable to members of Smith Limited	362
Retained profit brought forward (W2)	378
Retained profit carried forward	740

Workings:

1   Profit on disposal in Jones Limited

	€'000
Sales proceeds	650
Cost	(324)
Profit in Smith Limited	326

Calculation of group profit on disposal:				€
Net assets at date of disposal x	Group holding after disposal	+ Sale proceeds		
€540	x	0%	+ €650 =	650
Less				
Net assets at date of disposal x	Group holding before disposal			
€540	x	€80%		(432)
less				
Attributable Goodwill				(36)
				182

	€'000
Note: goodwill	
Cost of investment	324
Acquired 80% x (€180 + €180)	288
	36

2 Retained profit brought forward

	€'000
Smith	306
Jones: 80% x (€270 – €180)	72
	378

3 Retained Profit carried forward

	€'000
Smith	414
Profit on disposal (W1)	326
	740

(b) Net assets at 30/6/X8

At 1/10/X7	450.0
Retained profit to 30/6/X8 (€90 x 9/12)	67.5
	517.5

Consolidated Statement of Financial Position as at 30 September 20X8

	€'000
Assets	
Non-current assets	360
Net current assets (€270 + €650)	920
	1,280
Equity	
Ordinary shares	540
Retained profits (W3)	740
	1280

Consolidated Statement of Comprehensive Income for the year ended 30 September 20X8

Note: Jones Limited is a subsidiary for 9 months.

	€'000
Profit before tax (€153 + (9/12 x €126))	247.5
Profit on sale of subsidiary	200.0
Tax €45 + (€36 x 9/12))	(72.0)
Profit after tax	375.5
Non-controlling interest	
(20% x €90 x 9/12)	13.5
Profit attributable to members of Smith Limited	362.0
Retained profit brought forward as before	378.0
Retained profit carried forward (W3)	740.0

Workings:

1. Profit on disposal in Smith Limited

	€'000
Sale proceeds	650
Cost	(324)
Profit in Smith Limited	326

Calculation of group profit on disposal:					€
Net assets at date of disposal x Group holding after disposal			+ Sale proceeds		
€517.5	x 0%		+ €650	=	650
Less					
Net assets at date of disposal x Group holding before disposal					
€517.5	x 80%				(414)
Less					
Attributable Goodwill					(36)
					200

2. Retained profit brought forward

	€'000
Smith	306
Jones: 80% x (€270 – €180)	72
	378

3. Retained profit carried forward

	€'000
Smith	414
Profit on disposal (W1)	326
	740

REVIEW QUESTIONS – SUGGESTED SOLUTIONS

Question 1

Universal PLC
Cash Flow Statement for the year ended 31 October 2004

	€'000	€'000
Net cash flow from operating activities		
Operating profit		986
Depreciation		167
Profits on sale of tangible non-current assets		(10)
Increase in inventory		(2)
Increase in trade receivables		(58)
Decrease in trade payables & accruals		(27)
Cash generated from operations		1,056
Interest paid		(160)
Dividends paid by Universal plc		(139)
Dividends paid to non-controlling interest		(27)
Dividends received from associate		40
Tax paid		(293)
Net cash flow from operating activities		477
Cash flows from investing activities		
Payments to require tangible non-current assets	(827)	
Receipts from sale of tangible non-current assets	120	
Purchase of subsidiary company (€130 – €20)	(110)	
Net cash flow from investing activities		(817)
Cash flows from financing activities		
Issue of share capital at a premium	300	
Issue of debentures	80	
Net cash flow from financing		380
Increase in cash and cash equivalents		40
Cash and cash equivalents at 1 November 2003		(85)
Cash and cash equivalents at 31 October 2004		(45)

Workings:

W1		Investment in Associate	
	€'000		€'000
Bal b/d	740	Share of Tax	80
Share of profit	210	therefore cash (dividend)	40
		Bal c/d	830
	950		950

W2	Inventory
	€'000
At 31 October 2004	910
At 1 November 2003	868
Increase	42
Less acquired with new subsidiary Star Limited	(40)
change	2

W3		Non-controlling Interest	
	€'000		€'000
Therefore cash dividend	27	Bal b/d	230
Bal c/d	380	SCI	126
		Acquisition during Year (Star Limited)	51
	407		407

W4	€'000
Additions during year	987
Less acquired with Star Limited	160
Per statement of cash flows	827

W5		Taxation	
	€'000		€'000
Therefore cash	293	Bal b/d	328
Bal c/d	450	SCI	415
	743		743

W6		Dividends paid by U	
	€'000		€'000
Cash	139	Balance b/d	180
Balance c/d	240	Equity	199
	379		379

Question 2

SWEET plc
Consolidated Cash Flow Statement for the Year Ended 31 December 2003

	Working	€m	€m
Net cash flows from operating activities	2		1,378
Cash flows from investing activities			
Purchase of PPE	5	(161)	
Sale of PPE		-	
Purchase of GENTLE		(365)	
Net o/d of GENTLE (€275k – €19k)		(256)	(782)
Cash flows from financing activities			
Dividends paid to non-controlling interests	3	(96)	
Capital element of finance lease repaid	6	(360)	(456)
Increase in cash and cash equivalents			140
Cash and cash equivalents at 1 January 2003			(164)
Cash and cash equivalents at 31 December 2003 (o/d)			(24)

Workings:

1. Goodwill	€m
NA acquired (75% x €480m)	360
Paid (€365m + €75m)	(440)
	80

Impairment	€16m

2. Operating cash flows	€m
Net profit before tax and interest	1,050
Goodwill impairment	16
Depreciation	750
Inventory (€1,280 – (€1,220 – €300)	360
Receivables (€1,440 – (€1,740 – €240)	(60)
Payables (€680 – (€750 – €160)	(90)
	2,026

Interest paid (incl. interest capitalised)	(50)
Interest element of lease (N3)	(150)
Tax (W4)	(256)
Equity dividends paid (PY bal.)	(192)
	1,378

3. Non-controlling interests — €m
Opening balance	496
GENTLE – % NA (25% x €480)	120
Statement of comprehensive income	80
Closing balance	(600)
	96

4. Taxation — €m
Opening balance (€164m + €184m)	348
GENTLE liabilities	64
Statement of comprehensive income	290
Closing balance (€190m + €256m)	(446)
Paid	256

5. PPE — €m
Opening balance	2,960
Revaluation	25
GENTLE Limited	420
Depreciation	(750)
Loss on disposal	(26)
Closing balance	(3,280)
Inc. PPE	651
Finance lease PPE	(480)
Interest capitalised	(10)
Cash paid	161

6. Finance leases (capital) — €m
Opening balance (€360 + €960)	1,320
New during year	480
Closing balance (€400 + €1,040)	(1,440)
Cash paid	360

7. Reserves — €m
Opening balance	1,520
SCI (€464m - €240m)	224
Revaluation	25
Share premium	25
	1,794

CHAPTER 35

REVIEW QUESTIONS – SUGGESTED SOLUTIONS

Question 1

Belfast
31 July 1992

Mr Evans
Managing Director
DUL Limited
Belfast

Dear Mr Evans

Report on the performance of DUL Limited

As requested, I have examined the accounts of DUL Limited for each of the three years ended 30 June 2002, together with the statements of financial position as at 30 June 2000, 2001 and 2002.

My examination indicated that the company is 'overtrading', i.e. it has expanded its business to a level which is inconsistent with the amount of permanent funding and working capital available. In so doing the company now is in the position where, unless immediate remedial action is taken, it is in danger of 'going under'.

Before I list the characteristics of overtrading which I noted in your company, I will set out some symptoms which are generally regarded as characteristic of 'overtrading':

1. Undue dependence on other people's money, e.g. bank borrowings and trade payables;
2. High debt/equity ratio with the majority of borrowing being short-term;
3. Tight liquidity;
4. Low working capital to revenue for the type of business;
5. Growth in net profit not keeping pace with revenue;
6. Not operating within the normal credit terms for the type of business; and
7. Over-optimism in the investment in non-current assets, especially where this is financed by payables money.

The more of the foregoing characteristics that are evidenced, the more critical is the financial condition of the company. It must be pointed out, however, that adverse trends in ratios are indicative rather than absolute figures since many companies have survived when their ratios were out of line with normal expectancies. Generally speaking, once an adverse and sharp change in direction takes place it can become almost irreversible if left unchecked for long.

While I have calculated a number of ratios based upon the figures in your accounts (see my comments below), I wish to advise you that I need access to more detailed information in order to make particular rather than generalised comments. These ratios would seem to indicate as follows:

(a) Revenue. The company is growing substantially in terms of the monetary value of sales, a compound growth of 40% per annum has been achieved, and the investment in Non-Current Assets has also increased at the same rate. This is not unusual for a new company, especially a small company, although it would be unrealistic to expect this growth to continue, a tailing off is probable.

(b) Profit margins are inexorably falling. The key margin of profit before interest and tax has fallen from 11% in 2000 to 9.29% in 2001 and 7.14% in 2002. This trend is indicative of sales being made without reference to their profitability with possibly a market share target in view.

(c) Interest charges have continually increased, reflecting the higher bank overdraft, and the 'cover' in terms of profit before interest is falling. In 2002 the increase in interest resulted in a fall in profit after interest in comparison with each of the preceding years. This is a very dangerous trend.

(d) Debt to equity (shareholders' funds) ratio. The ratio of debt (borrowings) to equity has increased from a base of 168% in 2000 to a high of 206% in 2002 and, as you have told me, the bank is very concerned at its size. One of the contributory causes of this is the insufficient profits being earned in order to build up the equity base.

(e) Liquidity and working capital. The working capital is the difference between the current assets and current liabilities and provides the buffer within which a business finances the peaks in its cash cycle of production, revenue, receivables less trade credit received. The working capital is also a measure of the equity interest in the current assets as distinguished from the non-current assets. The smaller the relation of working capital becomes to revenue the lower is the tolerance point to fluctuations in the business. In DUL Limited there is a negative working capital which is worsening every year and this, combined with the increasing size of the bank overdraft, is extremely dangerous.

(f) Relationship between profits and revenue. If the growth in sales in not matched by profits retained in the business, the company will become more dependent on borrowings to finance the net assets required to support the revenue. The eventual outcome will be lower profits as margins become reduced through inability to meet interest charges. The revenue growth of DUL Limited has not been matched by a corresponding growth in profits before interest due to a fall in profit margins: the resulting effects of this situation as outlined are clearly evident in the company. It would seem that the company has concentrated on revenue growth or market share without consideration of profitability; alternatively, management information and/or internal controls may be weak.

(g) Credit from suppliers. The taking of extended credit from suppliers affects credit rating, eventually resulting in difficulty in obtaining credit and suppliers; it may even result in cash with order terms of supply. Eventually, profitability will suffer as productivity becomes disrupted. If a major supplier becomes disaffected, the company would be left very exposed. There may be a connection between the taking of extended credit from suppliers and the continual rise in the bank overdraft, endeavouring to allay the bank's concern through the expediency of not paying suppliers.

Conclusion

The company appears to have been undercapitalised from its inception and this defect has been compounded by the subsequent lack of profitability. To ensure the survival of the company it is essential that an immediate investigation is made into the profitability of each product line with the cutting out of unprofitable or least profitable lines, disposal of any resulting surplus non-current assets, a corresponding reduction in inventories and receivables, a reduction in overheads and an increase in productivity. An immediate look at your own credit control procedures is necessary since receivables have increased in 2002 to 80 days from a previous period of 73 days. As a corollary to this, it is necessary to gain the confidence of your bankers and I suggest that you see your bankers (before they ask you to see them) and place your proposals before them and get their support. The only alternative is the injection of substantial fresh capital.

If you require any additional information or assistance in the investigation I suggested, I will be glad to help.

Yours sincerely,

A. Wiseman

Question 2

To	Finance Director
From	Management Accountant
Subject	Performance of Laurie plc 19X0 to 19X2

As requested please find below my analysis of the company's performance based upon information provided.

1. Profitability
The gross profit margin has remained relatively static over the three-year period, although it has risen by approximately 1% in 19X2. ROCE, while improving very slightly in 19X1 to 21.5% has dropped dramatically in 19X2 to 17.8%. The net profit margin has also fallen in 19X2, in spite of the improvement in the gross profit margin. This marks a rise in expenses, which suggests that they are not being well controlled. The utilisation of assets compared to the revenue generated has also declined reflecting the drop in trading activity between 19X1 and 19X2.

2. Trading levels

It is apparent that there was a dramatic increase in trading activity between 19X0 and 19X1, but then a significant fall in 19X2. Revenue rose by 17% in 19X1 but fell by 7% in 19X2. The reason for this fluctuation is unclear. It may be the effect of some kind of on-off event, or it may be the effect of a change in product mix. Whatever the reason, it appears that improved credit terms granted to customers (receivables payment period up from 46 to 64 days) has not stopped the drop in revenue.

3. Working capital

Both the current ratio and quick ratio demonstrate an adequate working capital situation, although the quick ratio has shown a slight decline. There has been an increased investment over the period in inventories and receivables, which has been only partly financed by longer payment periods to payables and a rise in other payables mainly between 19X0 and 19X1.

4. Capital Structure

The level of gearing of the company increased when a further €64m was raised in long-term loans in 19X1 to add to the €74m already in the statement of financial position. Although this does not seem to be a particularly high level of gearing, the debt/equity ratio did rise from 18.5% to 32.0% in 19X1. The interest charge has risen to €19m from €6m in 19X0. The 19X1 charge was €15m, suggesting that either the interest rate on the loan is flexible, or that the full interest charge was not incurred in 19X1. The new long-term loan appears to have funded the expansion in both non-current and current assets.

Question 3

(a) Calculation of Relevant Indicators

(i) Operating Gearing = Contribution / Profit before interest and tax
1992: 3,120/570 = 5.5
1993: 2,880/315 = 9.1
Industry = 7.5

(ii) Debt/ Equity
1992: (500 + 360o/d)/(300 + 650) = 90.5%
1993: (500 + 454o/d)/(350 + 749) = 86.8%
Industry = 65%

(iii) Return on Equity
1992: 286/950 = 30%
1993: 109/1,099 = 9.9%
Industry = 14%

(iv) Dividend Cover
1992: 286/60 = 4.8
1993: 109/10 = 10.9
Industry = 2

(v) Interest Cover
1992: 570 / 94 = 6.1
1993: 315 / 134 = 2.4
Industry = 3

(b) The bank manager may be concerned at the company's financial performance and position for the following reasons:

   (i) The level of financial gearing is high by industry standards. The bank has an exposure of €954,000. Not all of this is secured

   (ii) The high level of operating gearing in 1993 is a worrying feature from the bank's point of view because it suggests that the level of business risk is high. The combination of high business risk and financial risk may not be satisfactory from the view point of a provider of finance.

   (iii) The interest cover has fallen significantly, caused by the fall in profits, increased overdraft and possibly higher interest rates during the year. The company's ability to repay borrowing may be questioned if this trend continues.

   (iv) The operating result discloses a fall in revenue but no overall fall in costs. This suggests, and is confirmed by the measure of operating gearing, that the fixed-cost base of the company is high. Further falls in revenue could therefore result in a corresponding drop in profit levels.

   (v) The bank manager may also seek explanations for the increase in inventory and receivable days despite the fall in revenue. While the increase was financed by taking more credit from suppliers, it would be a matter of concern if this source of credit was withdrawn and the company was forced to ask the bank for increased finance solely due to inefficient management of working capital

(c) The following points in support of the company would be made:

   (i) This is the first year in many that has seen a fall in demand for the company's products. As this is related to the demand for houses, it is possible that the fall in revenue was for reasons outside the control of management, e.g. interest rate/housing crisis. In the event, turnover fell only by 4.5%. The resolution of the interest rate/housing crisis could well result in a resumption of the company's growth.

   (ii) The dividend for 1993 has been sharply reduced. This illustrates that the equity holders are willing to 'share the pain'.

   (iii) The equity holders also invested €50,000 during the year, thereby contributing to a resolution of the cash crisis mid-year.

   (iv) While the company's debt/equity is higher than the industry average, it has fallen by 4% since 1992. In addition, the interest cover is only marginally lower than the industry average.

   (v) While a relatively high proportion of the company's costs are fixed, this is also true for the industry. Given the performance in 1992, where the company's operating gearing was 5.5 compared to the industry's 7.5, it is apparent that the company's difficulties are sales related, and not necessarily purely cost related.

(vi) The company is backed by non-current assets of almost €1 million, which should be of comfort to the bank. This represents an increase of €126,000 since 1992.

(vii) The company has been responsive to the Bank Manager's request for information, e.g. monthly accounts since December.

Question 4

From: Financial Director
To: Board of Directors
Date: 31 October 1996
Subject: Profitability and financial position of HOLLY from 1992 to 1995

(a) Purpose
The purpose of this report is to provide an assessment of the trading performance, operational efficiency and financial position of HOLLY for the four years ended 31 December 1995. This analysis is based on the published accounts for this period.

(b) Growth

	1993	1994	1995
Increase in revenue	11%	7%	3%
Increase in non-current assets	45%	29%	-4%
Increase in net assets	7%	3%	4%

From the above it can be seen that, while non-current assets increased significantly over the period, there was little real growth in either net assets or revenue. This suggests that the increase in non-current assets has not produced corresponding increases in revenue and has been financed at least partly by additional loans.

(c) Profitability

	1992	1993	1994	1995
Gross margin	35%	34%	32%	29%
Net margin	14%	12%	7%	6%
Distribution costs/revenue	5%	5%	6%	7%
Administration costs/revenue	15%	15%	17%	13%
Return on capital employed	44%	36%	20%	15%
Return on equity	38%	39%	22%	15%
Dividend payout ratio	86%	84%	89%	77%

Each of the above indicators of profitability shows a declining trend which should be a cause for concern. The reduction in gross margin from 35% in 1992 to 29% in 1995 could be due to a changed sales mix which could be satisfactory if the total revenue were increasing; since it is not, it indicates an increasing inability to pass on higher costs of raw materials and production costs in prices.

This trend is compounded by the steeper fall in the net margin. The reason for this is the marked increase in the ratio of distribution costs to revenue and (apart from 1995, which may have been untypical) no reduction in the ratio of administration costs/revenue. Either these costs are somewhat out of control or the expansion in revenue has not been adequate to deliver economies of scale in these departments.

The above trends are reflected in the sharp fall in ROCE and the almost equally significant fall in the return on shareholders' equity. Unless this trend is arrested HOLLY will have considerable difficulty in the future in attracting or replacing its financing.

In spite of declining profitability the payout ratio remains very high, and suggests that inadequate funds are being retained to finance growth.

(d) Operating efficiency/working capital management

	1992	1993	1994	1995
Revenue/non-current assets	7.6	5.8	4.9	5.2
Inventories/revenue – days	50	51	45	38
Receivables/revenue – days	66	73	79	82
Trade payables/cost of sales – days	35	34	29	25

Revenue generated has fallen markedly over the period. The improvement in 1995 reflects lower non-current assets rather than a relative increase in revenue. Even allowing for the time lag between investment and increased sales, this suggests that the asset base is not being worked hard enough.

Inventory turnover is, however, improving which indicates that active inventory management is being undertaken. Receivables, on the other hand, have increased by a quarter in relation to revenue. Whether the current level is acceptable can only be judged by comparing the amount of credit given with the industry norm, which may also have increased over the period. The amount of credit taken from suppliers is lower in 1992 than it was in 1995 and this seems inconsistent with the receivables position. It is possible, however, that purchases and sales are made in different markets which have experienced different trends, and comparison with the industry norm is necessary.

(e) Financial condition

	1992	1993	1994	1995
Current ratio	2.4	2.0	1.9	2.2
Acid test	1.4	1.2	1.2	1.5
Gearing	-	11%	20%	21%
Total debt/equity ratio	43%	67%	86%	77%
Interest cover (times)	34	9	3.5	2.6

The short-term liquidity position appears satisfactory compared to the generally accepted norms of two for the current ratio and one for the acid test ratio. At present, however, the company does not have any cash and is operating on the overdraft. This means that continued liquidity depends on the ability to turn receivables into cash quickly; clearly this has been a problem in the past as the average credit period granted has increased. The ability of HOLLY to pay its debts as they become due could be critically affected by the solvency or liquidity of a major customer.

The gearing ratio has increased to a level which is not unreasonably high, but the ratio of debt to equity has increased considerably as new long-term loans have been taken on, the overdraft increased (although the overdraft has fallen in the last year under consideration) and only a small proportion of profits retained. Accordingly the interest cover has fallen to 2.6 times which may be considered dangerously low. HOLLY is unlikely to be able to take on any more interest-bearing debt and consideration should probably be given to a further injection of equity capital.

In summary, HOLLY has gone through a period of stagnant profitability with falling rates of growth in revenue. This has adversely affected the statement of financial position as long-term debt, and a substantial overdraft has been taken on to finance an expansion of non-current assets and some working capital problems. Some improvements in the working capital problem have been seen in the last year (a fall in inventory levels and in the overdraft level), however, an improvement in the receivables collection rate is necessary to ease the liquidity problem further.

Question 5

Tutorial note: Although some of the six statements of financial position have similarities in their asset structures, there are a few features that stand out and make identification easy. Once the obvious matches have been ticked off, a process of elimination leads gradually to a complete solution.

(a) Company 5, the bank, should be easy to identify. Most of a bank's assets and liabilities are monetary: loans and advances (receivables) and customer deposits (payables). Other assets and liabilities are small in comparison. This picture fits in with statement of financial position B.

   Company 1, the retail supermarket chain, would be expected to have a high level of investment in shop premises (land and buildings). Inventories would also account for a significant proportion of assets. Most sales are on cash terms, so receivables are negligible while cash levels should be relatively high. This picture fits in with statement of financial position E.

   The main assets of a sea ferry operator are the ferries themselves 'other non-current assets' in the statements of financial position given in the question. . Each ferry owned would be a very major purchase and one would expect to see a significant amount of long-term external finance. This picture fits in with statement of financial position F.

   Company 3 is engaged in two activities: property investment (high level of inventories) and house building (high level of investment in land). This picture fits in well with statement of financial position D.

   The remaining two companies (the vertically integrated company in the food industry and the civil engineering contractor) might each be expected to have a fairly broad spectrum of assets. However, there are two features indicating that the contractor is represented by statement of financial position A.

   (i) Statement of financial position A shows that the company's major asset is inventories and work in progress.
   (ii) Statement of financial position C shows a big investment in land and buildings, as would be expected of a company owning farms, flour mills, bakeries and retail outlets.

Summary

Statement of financial position	Company
A	6. Civil engineering contractor
B	5. Commercial bank
C	4. Company in food industry
D	3. Property investor/house builder
E	1. Retail supermarket chain
F	2. Sea ferry operator

(b) Limitations of Ratio Analysis

Accounts are not wholly comparable with each other in spite of adherence to IASs because there are sometimes several permissible methods of accounting and IASs do not always cover all areas on which a company needs to have an accounting policy. For example, different companies may apply different criteria to decide whether a contract should be accounted for as a long or a short-term contract in accordance with IAS 11. Additionally, points of detail in applying IASs will differ; each company will have a different estimate of the economic lives of its non-current assets and so will depreciate them at different rates and on different bases.

Ratio analysis applied to historical cost accounts takes no account of inflation or current costs, especially as there is no requirement to revalue appreciating assets yearly. ROCE, for example, will appear to be higher for a company whose asset base is stated at historical cost and/or is fully depreciated than for a company whose assets are new and/or revalued and which makes the same profits. Ratio analysis is therefore of limited value in predicting future performance or in showing the rate of return in real terms.

Because the statement of financial position is stated as at a particular day, ratios derived from that day's figures may not reflect the company's usual circumstances. For example, it is common practice to run inventories down before the reporting date to minimise the disruption caused by a full inventory-take and to reduce inventories and payables, thus improving the company's apparent liquidity. In this case, calculating the current ratio and inventory and payables turnover periods from year-end figures will not produce meaningful results.

Ratios such as ROCE which produce measures expressed in percentage terms can be misleading because they necessarily take no account of absolute values. Thus, an investor told that company A's ROCE is 20% may think that it is a better investment vehicle than company B whose ROCE is only 15%. However, if told that company A has total net assets employed of €100,000 whereas company B has €5 million, then he may feel differently.

Question 6

Tutorial note: This is a straightforward question on interpretation of accounts which provides you with all the ratios you need. You should, as with all interpretation questions, spend some time thinking about the ratios before you start writing. Mark what you think are the significant trends shown in the question and make brief notes which will serve as an answer plan. Then proceed to discuss each area, using sensible headings to break your report up, and including a brief introduction and conclusion.

To: E Montague, Company Accountant
From: A Student

Date: 28 February 19X6

Introduction

This report discusses the trends shown in the five year summary prepared by you from the published accounts for the five years ended 31 December 19X5. It also considers how price changes over that period may have limited the usefulness of the historical cost data provided.

Profitability

The net profit margin has remained fairly constant, although it dropped in 19X3. Asset revenue has decreased over the five years, pulling back a little in 19X4. Return on capital, the primary ratio produced by combining these two secondary ratios, has therefore decreased over the period but was at its lowest in 19X3.

These findings seem to indicate that assets are not being used efficiently and that this has caused the decrease in return on assets. Inflation may be responsible for increases in revenue which would mask even worse decreases in efficiency.

Interest and dividend cover

Interest cover improved markedly between 19X1 and 19X2, falling back a little in 19X3 and 19X4 but now only a little above the 19X1 level, indicating increases in debt and/or interest rates. Dividend cover, however, after dropping below 19X1 levels for three years, has now recovered some lost ground. In both cases cover was adequate, even at the lowest points; however, since there has been a substantial increase in gearing, interest cover ought to be watched carefully. Profits may be available to cover interest and dividends but this must be matched by good cash flow.

Debt to equity

Debt equity fell in 19X2 but has steadily increased until in 19X5 it was almost double its 19X1 level. Minority interests appear to have remained a relatively insignificant element in the group's funding. It is more likely that debt has increased than that equity has decreased (for example, because of the purchase or redemption of own shares). Interest cover has fallen in line with this increase in borrowing as a proportion of long-term capital. It would be interesting to know why dividend cover is constant. It is possible that dividends have been cut in real terms?

Liquidity

Both the current and quick ratios have declined over the period, although in 19X2 they both improved. However, they have been fairly constant between 19X3 and 19X5 and are quite high, although comments on the adequacy of these ratios are of very limited utility in the absence of information about the company's activities and industry averages.

The reduction may have been planned to reduce the costs involved in maintaining high levels of inventory and allowing generous credit to customers. From the differential between the quick and current ratios it would seem that inventory is a significant asset here. However, current liabilities must not be allowed to increase to the extent that current assets (and especially liquid assets) are insufficient to cover them, as this can lead to a liquidity crisis. Worsening liquidity ratios can be an indicator of overtrading but this most often arises when expansion is funded from short-term borrowings, whereas here new long-term capital in the form of debt appears to have been found.

Because working capital has fallen in size, it is now being used more efficiently, generating more sales from a reduced base. It would seem likely, given the slight fall in asset turnover, that non-current asset turnover has worsened considerably and that the improvement in working capital turnover has compensated for this in calculating total asset turnover. It may be that long-term borrowings have financed capital expenditure which has not yet affected operations. (An increase in the amount of non-current assets would decrease non-current asset turnover if revenue did not increase correspondingly.)

Investors' ratios

Earnings, dividends and net assets per share have all increased over the period. There has, therefore, been no need to increase dividends regardless of fluctuations in earnings.
The increase in net assets per share seems to indicate either that retained profits and borrowings have been used to increase non-current asset expenditure or (less likely) that assets have been revalued each year.

Inflation

Historical cost accounts do not show the effect on the group's operating capacity of rising prices over the period. The modest increases in EPS and dividend do not suggest that profit has increased sufficiently to compensate for more than a very low level of inflation. It is also possible that the value of assets is understated, so that ROCE and asset turnover measures are all understated. The underlying trends in real terms may be very much worse than those shown in historical cost terms.

Conclusion

The group would appear, from this superficial analysis, to be a steady performer but not expanding fast. This may be an advantage in times of recession and debt and is probably not so high as to cause liquidity problems nor have shareholders come to expect a high payout ratio. However, inflation may be eroding its profits. The possible recent expansion of non-current assets may help it to grow in future, as will its improved working capital management.

REVIEW QUESTIONS – SUGGESTED SOLUTIONS

Question 1

REVALUATION ACCOUNT

		€			€
(a) 31.12.95	To Fixtures & Fittings a/c	25,000	31.12.95	By Premises a/c	50,000
	Inventory a/c	5,000			
	Capital a/cs				
	Murphy –1/2	10,000			
	Noonan – 3/8	7,500			
	MacIntyre – 1/8	2,500			
		50,000			50,000

REALISATION ACCOUNT

		€			€
(b) 31.12.96	To Transfer – Asset Accounts (Wk 4)	333,000	31.12.96	By Bank Sale of Assets	270,000
	Bank – Realisation Expenses	2,000		Capital a/cs Less Divisible	
				Murphy 1/2	32,500
				Noonan – 4/10	26,000
				Riordan – 1/10	6,500
		335,000			335,000

Workings:

1. MacIntyre Car

Since there is no indication as to the net book value of MacIntyre's car, it is assumed that a fair value might be €5,000, being the total NBV of all the cars divided in profit ratio (MacIntyre 1/8). The quality of each partner's car would probably reflect each partner's share in the firm.

2. Goodwill
Valuation:
Riordan paid €6,000 for 1/10 share

	∴ value = 6,000 x 10	= €60,000

Old Goodwill Divisible

Murphy	4/8 x 60,000	= €30,000
Noonan	3/8 x 60,000	= €22,500
MacIntyre	1/8 x 60,000	= €7,500

New Goodwill Divisible

Murphy	5/10 x 60,000	= €30,000
Noonan	4/10 x 60,000	= €24,000
Riordan	1/10 x 60,000	= €6,000

3. Profits for 1996 Divisible

Total Profit		€28,000
Murphy	5/10	€14,000
Noonan	4/10	€11,200
Riordan	1/10	€2,800

4. Assets Transferred to Realisation Account

	€
Premises	200
Fixtures	40
Motor Vehicles	35
Inventory	23
Receivables	35
	333

5. Memorandum Bank Account

	DR €	CR €
Balance 31.12.96	4,700	
Proceeds of Realisation of Assets	270,000	
Payment of Loan to MacIntyre		5,000
Payment of Payables		40,000
Payment of Expenses		2,000
Payment of Capital a/c Balances		
Murphy		115,000
Noonan		83,400
Riordan		29,300
	274,700	274,700

Question 2

JOURNALS

		DR €'000	CR €'000
Jan 1	Realisation Account	140	
Jan 1	To Non-current Assets Account		85
	Inventory Account		15
	Receivables Account		35
	Bank		5

Transfer of balances on Asset Accounts to Realisation Account

Jan 1	Payables' Account	30	
	To Realisation Account		30

Transfer of balance on Payables' Accounts

Jan 1	Direction Limited	150	
	To Realisation Account		150

Agreed value of assets less liabilities taken over

Jan 1	Realisation Account	40	
	To Partners' Capital Accounts		
	North		20
	South		12
	East		8

Profit on takeover of assets less liabilities by Direction Limited, divided in profit ratios.

Jan 1	Partners' Capital Accounts		
	North	68	
	South	51	
	East	31	
	To Direction Limited		150

Allocation of Ordinary Shares to partners in proportion to the balances on Capital Accounts

Jan 1	Partners' Current Accounts		
	North	8	
	South	4	
	East	3	

To Partners' Capital Accounts

North	8
South	4
East	3

Transfer of Partners' Current Accounts Balances to Partners' Capital Accounts

PARTNERS' ACCOUNTS
– CAPITAL

1995		€'000 North	€'000 South	€'000 East
Jan 1	by Balance	40	35	20
'	Transfer Current Accounts	8	4	3
'	Realisation Account	20	12	8
		68	51	31
Jan 1	to Direction Limited	68	51	31
		68	51	31

– CURRENT

1995		North	South	East
Jan 1	by Balances	8	4	3
Jan 1	to Transfer to Capital Accounts	8	4	3

REALISATION ACCOUNT

1995		€'000	1995		€'000
Jan 1	to Asset Accounts	140	Jan 1	by Direction Limited	150
			'	Payables	30
	'Profit on Realisation Divisible				
	North ½ 20				
	South 3/10 12				
	East 2/10 8				
		180			180

DIRECTION LIMITED

1995		€'000	1995		€'000
Jan 1	to Realisation Account	150	Jan 1	by Partners' Capital Accounts	
				North	68
				South	51
				East	31
		150			150

DIRECTION LIMITED
BALANCE SHEET AS AT 31 DECEMBER 1995

NON-CURRENT ASSETS	€	€
At 1 January 1995	130,000	
Additions during year	100,000	230,000
CURRENT ASSETS		
Inventory	25,000	
Receivables	60,000	
Bank	20,000	
		105,000
		335,000
REPRESENTED BY		
Issued Share Capital		
150,000 €1 ordinary shares, fully paid		150,000
Retained earnings		145,000
		295,000
CURRENT LIABILITIES		
Payables falling due within 1 year		40,000
		335,000

Workings

1. Retained Profit for year to 31 December 1995

Share Capital and Reserves	295
Less: Issued Share Capital	(150)
Retained Profit for year	145

2. Division of Profit on Realisation
   The profit on realisation (40K) is divisible in the ratio
   in which the partners share profit via
   North ½ (20K), South 3/10 (12K) and East 2/10 (8K)

3. Increase in non-current assets

The book value of non-current assets at 31 December 1995 was	230
The valuation at 1 January 1995 was	130
Therefore additions during year were	100

4. Net Assets at Takeover Valuation

Non-current assets	130
Inventory	15
Receivables	30
Bank	5
	180
Less: Payables	30
Satisfied by issue of 150,000	150
Ordinary shares of €1 each	

Question 3

(i)

Revaluation Account

	€'000		€'000
Current assets	5	Non-current assets	40
		Goodwill *	50
Revaluation surplus:			
Redcar	42.5		
Pontefract	25.5		
Haydock	17		
	90		90

*Goodwill €5,000 = 1/10 share thus total goodwill €50,000

Capital Accounts

	Redcar €'000	Pontefract €'000	Haydock €'000	Ludlow €'000
Opening balance	80	40	20	-
Revaluation surplus	42.5	25.5	17	
Capital introduced				50
Transfer to loan account			(37)	
Closing balance	122.5	65.5	0	50

Balance sheet of partnership to reflect changes:

	€'000
Goodwill	50
Non-current assets	160
Current assets	45
Bank (10k + 50k)	60
	315
Capital Accounts	
Redcar	122.5
Pontefract	65.5
Ludlow	50
Loan due to Haydock	37
	275
Current liabilities	40
	315

(ii)

Capital Accounts

	Redcar €'000	Pontefract €'000	Haydock €'000	Ludlow €'000
Opening balance	80	40	20	-
Revaluation surplus*	42.5	25.5	17	
Revaluation surplus**	(46.4)	(30.9)	-	(7.7)
Capital introduced				50
Transfer to loan account			(37)	
Closing balance	76.1	34.6	0	42.3

*Surplus credited to old partners in old profit-sharing ratios.
** Surplus debited to new partners in new profit-sharing ratio 6:4:1

(iii)
Balance sheet of partnership to reflect changes:

	€'000
Non-current assets	120
Current assets	50
Bank (10k + 50k)	60
	230
Capital Accounts	
Redcar	76.1
Pontefract	34.6
Ludlow	42.3
Loan due to Haydock	37
Current liabilities	40
	230

Question 4

(i) Close the books of the partnerships

Realisation Account

	B&A €'000	N&N €'000		B&A €'000	N&N €'000
Non-current assets	50.0	30.0	Liabilities	20.0	10.0
Inventory	10.0	12.0	Non-current assets	70.0	20.0
Receivables	20.0	13.0	Inventory	7.0	10.0
Payables	20.0	10.0	Receivables	20.0	13.0
Profit on realisation			Loss on realisation		
Beckam	10.6		Noonan		6.7
Adams	6.4		Norton		5.3
	117.0	65.0		117.0	65.0

Bank Account

	B&A €'000	N&N €'000		B&A €'000	N&N €'000
Bal b/d	15.0	5.0	Capital Beckham	17.3	
			Capital Adams	1.1	
Capital Noonan		6.4			
Capital Norton		12.0			
Bal c/d	3.4		Bal c/d		23.4
	18.4	23.4		18.4	23.4

(ii)

Partnership Balance Sheet

	€'000
Non-current assets (70 + 20)	90.0
Current Assets	
Inventory (7 + 10)	17.0
Receivables (20 + 13)	33.0
Bank (23.4 - 3.4)	20.0
	160.0
Capital a/c's	
Beckham	43.3
Adams	30.3
Norton	34.7
Noonan	21.7
Current liabilities (20 + 10)	30.0
	160.0

Question 5

(i) Partners' Capital Accounts

	Rod €'000	Hook €'000	Bait €'000	Line €'000		Rod €'000	Hook €'000	Bait €'000	Line €'000
Goodwill	140	-	60	40	Bal b/d	1,300	800	400	-
Loan To Hook		880			Capital				400
					Goodwill*	120	80	40	
Bal c/d	1,280	-	380	360					
	1,420	880	440	400		1,420	880	440	400

* Goodwill 2/12 = 40,000, therefore total value = 240,000

(ii) (1) Realisation Account

	€'000		€'000
Non-current assets	2,000	Non-current assets	2,500
Inventory	300	Inventory	240
Profit on Realisation			
Rod (7/12)	257		
Bait (3/12)	110		
Line (2/12)	73		
	2,740		2,740

(ii) (2) Partners' Capital Accounts

	Rod €'000	Hook €'000	Bait €'000	Line €'000		Rod €'000	Hook €'000	Bait €'000	Line €'000
					Bal b/d	1,280	-	380	360
					Profit	58	-	25	17
Bal c/d	1,338	-	405	377					
	1,338	-	405	377		1,338	-	405	377

Partner's Capital Account 01/07/99

	Rod €'000	Hook €'000	Bait €'000	Line €'000		Rod €'000	Hook €'000	Bait €'000	Line €'000
					Bal b/d	1,338	-	405	377
					Realisation	257	-	110	73
Bal c/d	1,595	-	515	450					
	1,595	-	515	450		1,595	-	515	450

INDEX